D0322822
30125

ML

A Companion to Econometric Analysis of Panel Data

A Companion to Econometric Analysis of Panel Data

by

Badi H. Baltagi

WILEY
A John Wiley and Sons, Ltd., Publication

Copyright © 2009 John Wiley & Sons Ltd, The Atrium, Southern Gate, Chichester,
West Sussex PO19 8SQ, England

Telephone (+44) 1243 779777

Email (for orders and customer service enquiries): cs-books@wiley.com
Visit our Home Page on www.wiley.com

All Rights Reserved. No part of this publication may be reproduced, stored in a retrieval system or transmitted in any form or by any means, electronic, mechanical, photocopying, recording, scanning or otherwise, except under the terms of the Copyright, Designs and Patents Act 1988 or under the terms of a licence issued by the Copyright Licensing Agency Ltd, Saffrom House, 6-10 Kirby Street, London EC1N 8TS, UK, without the permission in writing of the Publisher. Requests to the Publisher should be addressed to the Permissions Department, John Wiley & Sons Ltd, The Atrium, Southern Gate, Chichester, West Sussex PO19 8SQ, England, or emailed to permreq@wiley.com, or faxed to (+44) 1243 770620.

Designations used by companies to distinguish their products are often claimed as trademarks. All brand names and product names used in this book are trade names, service marks, trademarks or registered trademarks of their respective owners. The Publisher is not associated with any product or vendor mentioned in this book.

This publication is designed to provide accurate and authoritative information in regard to the subject matter covered. It is sold on the understanding that the Publisher is not engaged in rendering professional services. If professional advice or other expert assistance is required, the services of a competent professional should be sought.

Other Wiley Editorial Offices

John Wiley & Sons Inc., 111 River Street, Hoboken, NJ 07030, USA

Jossey-Bass, 989 Market Street, San Francisco, CA 94103-1741, USA

Wiley-VCH Verlag GmbH, Boschstr. 12, D-69469 Weinheim, Germany

John Wiley & Sons Australia Ltd, 42 McDougall Street, Milton, Queensland 4064, Australia

John Wiley & Sons (Asia) Pte Ltd, 2 Clementi Loop #02-01, Jin Xing Distripark, Singapore 129809

John Wiley & Sons Canada Ltd, 6045 Freemont Blvd, Mississauga, Ontario, L5R 4J3, Canada

Wiley also publishes its books in a variety of electronic formats. Some content that appears in print may not be available in electronic books.

UNIVERSITY OF STRATHCLYDE
23 MAR 2011
UNIVERSITY LIBRARY

Library of Congress Cataloging-in-Publication Data

Baltagi, Badi H. (Badi Hani)
A companion to Econometric analysis of panel data / by Badi H. Baltagi.
p. cm.
"This book is intended as a companion to Econometric analysis of panel data by Baltagi (2008)"–Preface.
Includes bibliographical references and index.
ISBN 978-0-470-74403-1 (pbk.)
1. Econometrics. 2. Panel analysis. I. Baltagi, Badi H. (Badi Hani) Econometric analysis of panel data. II. Title.
HB139.B347 2008
330.01′5195–dc22

2008049825

British Library Cataloguing in Publication Data

A catalogue record for this book is available from the British Library

ISBN 978-0-470-74403-1 (PB)

Typeset in 10/12pt Times by Laserwords Private Limited, Chennai, India

D
330.0182
BAL

Contents

Preface

This book is intended as a companion to *Econometric Analysis of Panel Data* (Baltagi, 2008). It is aimed at advanced undergraduate and graduate econometrics courses studying panel data. The prerequisites include a good background in mathematical statistics and econometrics. A knowledge of matrix algebra is necessary for this topic; see Abadir and Magnus (2005).

Panel data econometrics has been increasingly popular among both micro- and macro-econometricians, as evidenced by the plethora of panel data applications in economics, finance, marketing, agricultural economics, business, political science, sociology and other social sciences. The increased availability of panel data from household surveys has been hailed as one of the most important developments in applied social research in the last 30 years. Several econometrics textbooks have been written on this subject, including Arellano (2003), Baltagi (2008), Hsiao (2003) and Wooldridge (2002). The purpose of this book is to add value to the existing textbooks on panel data by solving exercises in a logical and pedagogical manner, helping the reader understand, learn and teach panel data. These exercises are based upon those in Baltagi (2008) and are complementary to that text, even though they are standalone material, and readers can learn the basic material as they go through these exercises. Not all topics in panel data are covered, and readers will have to refer to the advanced texts to learn more. Topics not covered in this book include duration models and hazard functions, sample selection, semi- and non-parametric methods in panels, random coefficients and Bayesian panel models. For an introduction to Bayesian econometric methods, see Koop *et al.* (2007).

This book starts by providing some background material on partitioned regressions and the Frisch–Waugh–Lovell theorem, showing the reader some applications of this material that are useful in practice. Then it goes through the basic material on fixed and random effects models in one-way and two-way error components models, following the same outline as in Baltagi (2008). Basic estimation, hypothesis tests and prediction are covered in Chapters 2–4. This includes maximum likelihood estimation, testing for poolability of the data, testing for the significance of individual and time effects, as well as Hausman's test for correlated effects. Chapters 5–12 provide extensions of panel data techniques to serial correlation, spatial correlation, heteroskedasticity, seemingly unrelated regressions, simultaneous equations, dynamic panel models, incomplete panels, measurement error, count panels, rotating panels, limited dependent variables, and nonstationary panels. The book also provides some empirical illustrations and examples using Stata and EViews that the reader can replicate. The *data sets* are provided on the Wiley web site (http://www.wileyeurope.com/college/baltagi).

In writing this set of exercises and their solutions, I have benefited from teaching panel data courses at Syracuse University, Texas A&M University, University of California-San Diego, University of Arizona, University of Cincinnati, Seoul National University, University of Innsbruck, University of Leicester, University of Paris II, Universitat Pompeu Fabra, Barcelona Graduate School of Economics, University of Coimbra, Universidad del Rosario, Tor Vergata University, University of Rome La Spienza, University of Mannheim, University of Munich, University of Vienna and the Institute for Advanced Studies, as well as at the International Monetary Fund, Inter-American Development Bank, Netherlands Network of Economics (NAKE), German Institute for Economic Research (DIW), European Central Bank, Banco de Portugal and Centro Interuniversitario de Econometria (CIDE).

I would like to thank my students and co-authors and the colleagues who have had a direct and indirect influence on the contents of this book, who are too numerous to list.

Syracuse, New York

1

Partitioned Regression and the Frisch–Waugh–Lovell Theorem

This chapter introduces the reader to important background material on the partitioned regression model. This should serve as a refresher for some matrix algebra results on the partitioned regression model as well as an introduction to the associated Frisch–Waugh–Lovell (FWL) theorem. The latter is shown to be a useful tool for proving key results for the fixed effects model in Chapter 2 as well as artificial regressions used in testing panel data models such as the Hausman test in Chapter 4.

Consider the partitioned regression given by

$$y = X\beta + u = X_1\beta_1 + X_2\beta_2 + u \tag{1.1}$$

where y is a column vector of dimension $(n \times 1)$ and X is a matrix of dimension $(n \times k)$. Also, $X = [X_1, X_2]$ with X_1 and X_2 of dimension $(n \times k_1)$ and $(n \times k_2)$, respectively. One may be interested in the least squares estimates of β_2 corresponding to X_2, but one has to control for the presence of X_1 which may include seasonal dummy variables or a time trend; see Frisch and Waugh (1933) and Lovell (1963). For example, in a time-series setting, including the time trend in the multiple regression is equivalent to detrending each variable first, by residualing out the effect of time, and then running the regression on these residuals. Davidson and MacKinnon (1993) denote this result more formally as the FWL theorem.

The ordinary least squares (OLS) normal equations from (1.1) are given by:

$$\begin{bmatrix} X_1'X_1 & X_1'X_2 \\ X_2'X_1 & X_2'X_2 \end{bmatrix} \begin{bmatrix} \widehat{\beta}_{1,\text{OLS}} \\ \widehat{\beta}_{2,\text{OLS}} \end{bmatrix} = \begin{bmatrix} X_1'y \\ X_2'y \end{bmatrix} \tag{1.2}$$

Exercise 1.1 *(Partitioned regression).* Show that the solution to (1.2) yields

$$\widehat{\beta}_{2,\text{OLS}} = (X_2'\overline{P}_{X_1}X_2)^{-1}X_2'\overline{P}_{X_1}y \tag{1.3}$$

where $P_{X_1} = X_1(X_1'X_1)^{-1}X_1'$ is the projection matrix on X_1, and $\overline{P}_{X_1} = I_n - P_{X_1}$.

Solution

Write (1.2) as two equations:

$$(X_1'X_1)\widehat{\beta}_{1,\text{OLS}} + (X_1'X_2)\widehat{\beta}_{2,\text{OLS}} = X_1'y$$
$$(X_2'X_1)\widehat{\beta}_{1,\text{OLS}} + (X_2'X_2)\widehat{\beta}_{2,\text{OLS}} = X_2'y$$

Solving for $\widehat{\beta}_{1,\mathrm{OLS}}$ in terms of $\widehat{\beta}_{2,\mathrm{OLS}}$ by multiplying the first equation by $(X_1'X_1)^{-1}$, we get

$$\widehat{\beta}_{1,\mathrm{OLS}} = (X_1'X_1)^{-1}X_1'y - (X_1'X_1)^{-1}X'X_1'X_2\widehat{\beta}_{2,\mathrm{OLS}} = (X_1'X_1)^{-1}X_1'(y - X_2\widehat{\beta}_{2,\mathrm{OLS}})$$

Substituting $\widehat{\beta}_{1,\mathrm{OLS}}$ in the second equation, we get

$$X_2'X_1(X_1'X_1)^{-1}X_1'y - X_2'P_{X_1}X_2\widehat{\beta}_{2,\mathrm{OLS}} + (X_2'X_2)\widehat{\beta}_{2,\mathrm{OLS}} = X_2'y$$

Collecting terms, we get $(X_2'\overline{P}_{X_1}X_2)\widehat{\beta}_{2,\mathrm{OLS}} = X_2'\overline{P}_{X_1}y$. Hence, $\widehat{\beta}_{2,\mathrm{OLS}} = (X_2'\overline{P}_{X_1}X_2)^{-1}$ $X_2'\overline{P}_{X_1}y$ as given in (1.3). $\overline{P}_{X_1}$ is the orthogonal projection matrix of X_1 and $\overline{P}_{X_1}X_2$ generates the least squares residuals of each column of X_2 regressed on all the variables in X_1. In fact, if we write $\widetilde{X}_2 = \overline{P}_{X_1}X_2$ and $\widetilde{y} = \overline{P}_{X_1}y$, then

$$\widehat{\beta}_{2,\mathrm{OLS}} = (\widetilde{X}_2'\widetilde{X}_2)^{-1}\widetilde{X}_2'\widetilde{y} \tag{1.4}$$

using the fact that $\overline{P}_{X_1}$ is idempotent. For a review of idempotent matrices, see Abadir and Magnus (2005, p.231). This implies that $\widehat{\beta}_{2,\mathrm{OLS}}$ can be obtained from the regression of $\widetilde{y}$ on $\widetilde{X}_2$. In words, the residuals from regressing y on X_1 are in turn regressed upon the residuals from each column of X_2 regressed on all the variables in X_1. If we premultiply (1.1) by $\overline{P}_{X_1}$ and use the fact that $\overline{P}_{X_1}X_1 = 0$, we get

$$\overline{P}_{X_1}y = \overline{P}_{X_1}X_2\beta_2 + \overline{P}_{X_1}u \tag{1.5}$$

Exercise 1.2 *(The Frisch–Waugh–Lovell theorem).* Prove that:
(a) the least squares *estimates* of β_2 from equations (1.1) and (1.5) are numerically identical;
(b) the least squares *residuals* from equations (1.1) and (1.5) are identical.

Solution

(a) Using the fact that $\overline{P}_{X_1}$ is idempotent, it immediately follows that OLS on (1.5) yields $\widehat{\beta}_{2,\mathrm{OLS}}$ as given by (1.3). Alternatively, one can start from (1.1) and use the result that

$$y = P_Xy + \overline{P}_Xy = X\widehat{\beta}_{\mathrm{OLS}} + \overline{P}_Xy = X_1\widehat{\beta}_{1,\mathrm{OLS}} + X_2\widehat{\beta}_{2,\mathrm{OLS}} + \overline{P}_Xy \tag{1.6}$$

where $P_X = X(X'X)^{-1}X'$ and $\overline{P}_X = I_n - P_X$. Premultiplying (1.6) by $X_2'\overline{P}_{X_1}$ and using the fact that $\overline{P}_{X_1}X_1 = 0$, one gets

$$X_2'\overline{P}_{X_1}y = X_2'\overline{P}_{X_1}X_2\widehat{\beta}_{2,\mathrm{OLS}} + X_2'\overline{P}_{X_1}\overline{P}_Xy \tag{1.7}$$

But $P_{X_1}P_X = P_{X_1}$. Hence, $\overline{P}_{X_1}\overline{P}_X = \overline{P}_X$. Using this fact along with $\overline{P}_XX = \overline{P}_X[X_1, X_2] = 0$, the last term of (1.7) drops out yielding the result that $\widehat{\beta}_{2,\mathrm{OLS}}$ from (1.7) is identical to the expression in (1.3). Note that no partitioned inversion was used in this proof. This proves part (a) of the FWL theorem. To learn more about partitioned and projection matrices, see Chapter 5 of Abadir and Magnus (2005).

(b) Premultiplying (1.6) by $\overline{P}_{X_1}$ and using the fact that $\overline{P}_{X_1}\overline{P}_X = \overline{P}_X$, one gets

$$\overline{P}_{X_1} y = \overline{P}_{X_1} X_2 \widehat{\beta}_{2,\text{OLS}} + \overline{P}_X y \tag{1.8}$$

Note that $\widehat{\beta}_{2,\text{OLS}}$ was shown to be numerically identical to the least squares estimate obtained from (1.5). Hence, the first term on the right-hand side of (1.8) must be the fitted values from equation (1.5). Since the dependent variables are the same in equations (1.8) and (1.5), $\overline{P}_X y$ in equation (1.8) must be the least squares residuals from regression (1.5). But $\overline{P}_X y$ is the least squares residuals from regression (1.1). Hence, the least squares residuals from regressions (1.1) and (1.5) are numerically identical. This proves part (b) of the FWL theorem. Several applications of the FWL theorem will be given in this book.

Exercise 1.3 *(Residualing the constant).* Show that if X_1 is the vector of ones indicating the presence of a constant in the regression, then regression (1.8) is equivalent to running $(y_i - \overline{y})$ on the set of variables in X_2 expressed as deviations from their respective sample means.

Solution

In this case, $X = [\iota_n, X_2]$ where ι_n is a vector of ones of dimension n. $P_{X_1} = \iota_n(\iota_n'\iota_n)^{-1}\iota_n' = \iota_n\iota_n'/n = J_n/n$, where $J_n = \iota_n\iota_n'$ is a matrix of ones of dimension n. But $J_n y = \sum_{i=1}^n y_i$ and $J_n y/n = \overline{y}$. Hence, $\overline{P}_{X_1} = I_n - P_{X_1} = I_n - J_n/n$ and $\overline{P}_{X_1} y = (I_n - J_n/n)y$ has a typical element $(y_i - \overline{y})$. From the FWL theorem, $\widehat{\beta}_{2,\text{OLS}}$ can be obtained from the regression of $(y_i - \overline{y})$ on the set of variables in X_2 expressed as deviations from their respective means, i.e., $\overline{P}_{X_1} X_2 = (I_n - J_n/n)X_2$. From the solution of Exercise 1.1, we get

$$\begin{aligned}\widehat{\beta}_{1,\text{OLS}} &= (X_1'X_1)^{-1}X_1'(y - X_2\widehat{\beta}_{2,\text{OLS}}) = (\iota_n'\iota_n)^{-1}\iota_n'(y - X_2\widehat{\beta}_{2,\text{OLS}}) \\ &= \frac{\iota_n'}{n}(y - X_2\widehat{\beta}_{2,\text{OLS}}) = \overline{y} - \overline{X}_2'\widehat{\beta}_{2,\text{OLS}}\end{aligned}$$

where $\overline{X}_2' = \iota_n' X_2/n$ is the vector of sample means of the independent variables in X_2.

Exercise 1.4 *(Adding a dummy variable for the ith observation).* Show that including a dummy variable for the ith observation in the regression is equivalent to omitting that observation from the regression. Let $y = X\beta + D_i\gamma + u$, where y is $n \times 1$, X is $n \times k$ and D_i is a dummy variable that takes the value 1 for the ith observation and 0 otherwise. Using the FWL theorem, prove that the least squares estimates of β and γ from this regression are $\widehat{\beta}_{\text{OLS}} = (X^{*\prime}X^*)^{-1}X^{*\prime}y^*$ and $\widehat{\gamma}_{\text{OLS}} = y_i - x_i'\widehat{\beta}_{\text{OLS}}$, where X^* denotes the X matrix without the ith observation, y^* is the y vector without the ith observation and (y_i, x_i') denotes the ith observation on the dependent and independent variables. Note that $\widehat{\gamma}_{\text{OLS}}$ is the forecasted OLS residual for the ith observation obtained from the regression of y^* on X^*, the regression which excludes the ith observation.

Solution

The dummy variable for the ith observation is an $n \times 1$ vector $D_i = (0, 0, \ldots, 1, 0, \ldots, 0)'$ of zeros except for the ith element which takes the value 1. In this case,

$P_{D_i} = D_i(D_i'D_i)^{-1}D_i' = D_iD_i'$ which is a matrix of zeros except for the ith diagonal element which takes the value 1. Hence, $I_n - P_{D_i}$ is an identity matrix except for the ith diagonal element which takes the value zero. Therefore, $(I_n - P_{D_i})y$ returns the vector y except for the ith element which is zero. Using the FWL theorem, the OLS regression

$$y = X\beta + D_i\gamma + u$$

yields the same estimates as $(I_n - P_{D_i})y = (I_n - P_{D_i})X\beta + (I_n - P_{D_i})u$ which can be rewritten as $\widetilde{y} = \widetilde{X}\beta + \widetilde{u}$ with $\widetilde{y} = (I_n - P_{D_i})y$, $\widetilde{X} = (I_n - P_{D_i})X$. The OLS normal equations yield $(\widetilde{X}'\widetilde{X})\widehat{\beta}_{\text{OLS}} = \widetilde{X}'\widetilde{y}$ and the ith OLS normal equation can be ignored since it gives $0'\widehat{\beta}_{\text{OLS}} = 0$. Ignoring the ith observation equation yields $(X^{*\prime}X^*)\widehat{\beta}_{\text{OLS}} = X^{*\prime}y^*$, where X^* is the matrix X without the ith observation and y^* is the vector y without the ith observation. The FWL theorem also states that the residuals from $\widetilde{y}$ on $\widetilde{X}$ are the same as those from y on X and D_i. For the ith observation, $\widetilde{y}_i = 0$ and $\widetilde{x}_i = 0$. Hence the ith residual must be zero. This also means that the ith residual in the original regression with the dummy variable D_i is zero, i.e., $y_i - x_i'\widehat{\beta}_{\text{OLS}} - \widehat{\gamma}_{\text{OLS}} = 0$. Rearranging terms, we get $\widehat{\gamma}_{\text{OLS}} = y_i - x_i'\widehat{\beta}_{\text{OLS}}$. In other words, $\widehat{\gamma}_{\text{OLS}}$ is the forecasted OLS residual for the ith observation from the regression of y^* on X^*. The ith observation was excluded from the estimation of $\widehat{\beta}_{\text{OLS}}$ by the inclusion of the dummy variable D_i.

The results of Exercise 1.4 can be generalized to including dummy variables for several observations. In fact, Salkever (1976) suggested a simple way of using dummy variables to compute forecasts and their standard errors. The basic idea is to augment the usual regression in (1.1) with a matrix of observation-specific dummies, i.e., a dummy variable for each period where we want to forecast:

$$\begin{bmatrix} y \\ y_o \end{bmatrix} = \begin{bmatrix} X & 0 \\ X_o & I_{T_o} \end{bmatrix} \begin{bmatrix} \beta \\ \gamma \end{bmatrix} + \begin{bmatrix} u \\ u_o \end{bmatrix} \tag{1.9}$$

or

$$y^* = X^*\delta + u^* \tag{1.10}$$

where $\delta' = (\beta', \gamma')$. X^* has in its second part a matrix of dummy variables, one for each of the T_o periods for which we are forecasting.

Exercise 1.5 *(Computing forecasts and forecast standard errors)*

(a) Show that OLS on (1.9) yields $\widehat{\delta}' = (\widehat{\beta}', \widehat{\gamma}')$, where $\widehat{\beta} = (X'X)^{-1}X'y$, $\widehat{\gamma} = y_o - \widehat{y}_o$, and $\widehat{y}_o = X_o\widehat{\beta}$. In other words, OLS on (1.9) yields the OLS estimate of β without the T_o observations, and the coefficients of the T_o dummies, i.e., $\widehat{\gamma}$, are the forecast errors.

(b) Show that the first n residuals are the usual OLS residuals $e = y - X\widehat{\beta}$ based on the first n observations, whereas the next T_o residuals are all zero. Conclude that the mean square error of the regression in (1.10), s^{*2}, is the same as s^2 from the regression of y on X.

(c) Show that the variance–covariance matrix of $\widehat{\delta}$ is given by

$$s^2(X^{*\prime}X^*)^{-1} = s^2\begin{bmatrix}(X'X)^{-1} & \\ & [I_{T_o} + X_o(X'X)^{-1}X_o']\end{bmatrix} \tag{1.11}$$

where the off-diagonal elements are of no interest. This means that the regression package gives the estimated variance of $\widehat{\beta}$ and the estimated variance of the forecast error in one stroke.

(d) Show that if the forecasts rather than the forecast errors are needed, one can replace y_o by zero, and I_{T_o} by $-I_{T_o}$ in (1.9). The resulting estimate of γ will be $\widehat{y}_o = X_o\widehat{\beta}$, as required. The variance of this forecast will be the same as that given in (1.11).

Solution

(a) From (1.9) one gets

$$X^{*\prime}X^* = \begin{bmatrix}X' & X_o' \\ 0 & I_{T_o}\end{bmatrix}\begin{bmatrix}X & 0 \\ X_o & I_{T_o}\end{bmatrix} = \begin{bmatrix}X'X + X_o'X_o & X_o' \\ X_o & I_{T_o}\end{bmatrix}$$

and

$$X^{*\prime}y^* = \begin{bmatrix}X'y + X_o'y_o \\ y_o\end{bmatrix}$$

The OLS normal equations yield

$$X^{*\prime}X^*\begin{bmatrix}\widehat{\beta}_{\text{OLS}} \\ \widehat{\gamma}_{\text{OLS}}\end{bmatrix} = X^{*\prime}y^*$$

or $(X'X)\widehat{\beta}_{\text{OLS}} + (X_o'X_o)\widehat{\beta}_{\text{OLS}} + X_o'\widehat{\gamma}_{\text{OLS}} = X'y + X_o'y_o$ and $X_o\widehat{\beta}_{\text{OLS}} + \widehat{\gamma}_{\text{OLS}} = y_o$. From the second equation, it is obvious that $\widehat{\gamma}_{\text{OLS}} = y_o - X_o\widehat{\beta}_{\text{OLS}}$. Substituting this in the first equation yields

$$(X'X)\widehat{\beta}_{\text{OLS}} + (X_o'X_o)\widehat{\beta}_{\text{OLS}} + X_o'y_o - X_o'X_o\widehat{\beta}_{\text{OLS}} = X'y + X_o'y_o$$

which upon cancellation gives $\widehat{\beta}_{\text{OLS}} = (X'X)^{-1}X'y$. Alternatively, one could apply the FWL theorem using $X_1 = \begin{bmatrix}X \\ X_o\end{bmatrix}$ and $X_2 = \begin{bmatrix}0 \\ I_{T_o}\end{bmatrix}$. In this case, $X_2'X_2 = I_{T_o}$ and

$$P_{X_2} = X_2(X_2'X_2)^{-1}X_2' = X_2X_2' = \begin{bmatrix}0 & 0 \\ 0 & I_{T_o}\end{bmatrix}$$

This means that

$$\overline{P}_{X_2} = I_{n+T_o} - P_{X_2} = \begin{bmatrix}I_n & 0 \\ 0 & 0\end{bmatrix}$$

Premultiplying (1.9) by $\overline{P}_{X_2}$ is equivalent to omitting the last T_o observations. The resulting regression is that of y on X, which yields $\widehat{\beta}_{\text{OLS}} = (X'X)^{-1}X'y$ as obtained above.

(b) Premultiplying (1.9) by $\overline{P}_{X_2}$, the last T_o observations yield zero residuals because the observations on both the dependent and independent variables are zero. For this to be true in the original regression, we must have $y_o - X_o\widehat{\beta}_{\text{OLS}} - \widehat{\gamma}_{\text{OLS}} = 0$. This means that $\widehat{\gamma}_{\text{OLS}} = y_o - X_o\widehat{\beta}_{\text{OLS}}$ as required. The OLS residuals of (1.9) yield the usual least squares residuals

$$e_{\text{OLS}} = y - X\widehat{\beta}_{\text{OLS}}$$

for the first n observations and zero residuals for the next T_o observations. This means that $e^{*\prime} = (e'_{\text{OLS}}, 0')$ and $e^{*\prime}e^* = e'_{\text{OLS}}e_{\text{OLS}}$ with the same residual sum of squares. The number of observations in (1.9) are $n + T_o$ and the number of parameters estimated is $k + T_o$. Hence, the new degrees of freedom in (1.9) are $(n + T_o) - (k + T_o) = (n - k) =$ the degrees of freedom in the regression of y on X. Hence, $s^{*2} = e^{*\prime}e^*/(n - k) = e'_{\text{OLS}}e_{\text{OLS}}/(n - k) = s^2$.

(c) Using partitioned inverse formulas on $(X^{*\prime}X^*)$ one gets

$$(X^{*\prime}X^*)^{-1} = \begin{bmatrix} (X'X)^{-1} & -(X'X)^{-1}X'_o \\ -X_o(X'X)^{-1} & I_{T_o} + X_o(X'X)^{-1}X'_o \end{bmatrix}$$

Hence, $s^{*2}(X^{*\prime}X^*)^{-1} = s^2(X^{*\prime}X^*)^{-1}$ and is given by (1.11).

(d) If we replace y_o by 0 and I_{T_o} by $-I_{T_o}$ in (1.9), we get

$$\begin{bmatrix} y \\ 0 \end{bmatrix} = \begin{bmatrix} X & 0 \\ X_o & -I_{T_o} \end{bmatrix}\begin{bmatrix} \beta \\ \gamma \end{bmatrix} + \begin{bmatrix} u \\ u_o \end{bmatrix}$$

or $y^* = X^*\delta + u^*$. Now

$$X^{*\prime}X^* = \begin{bmatrix} X' & X'_o \\ 0 & -I_{T_o} \end{bmatrix}\begin{bmatrix} X & 0 \\ X_o & -I_{T_o} \end{bmatrix} = \begin{bmatrix} X'X + X'_oX_o & -X'_o \\ -X_o & I_{T_o} \end{bmatrix}$$

and $X^{*\prime}y^* = \begin{bmatrix} X'y \\ 0 \end{bmatrix}$. The OLS normal equations yield

$$(X'X)\widehat{\beta}_{\text{OLS}} + (X'_oX_o)\widehat{\beta}_{\text{OLS}} - X'_o\widehat{\gamma}_{\text{OLS}} = X'y$$

and

$$-X_o\widehat{\beta}_{\text{OLS}} + \widehat{\gamma}_{\text{OLS}} = 0$$

From the second equation, it immediately follows that $\widehat{\gamma}_{\text{OLS}} = X_o\widehat{\beta}_{\text{OLS}} = \widehat{y}_o$, the forecast of the T_o observations using the estimates from the first n observations. Substituting this in the first equation yields

$$(X'X)\widehat{\beta}_{\text{OLS}} + (X'_oX_o)\widehat{\beta}_{\text{OLS}} - X'_oX_o\widehat{\beta}_{\text{OLS}} = X'y$$

which gives $\widehat{\beta}_{\text{OLS}} = (X'X)^{-1}X'y$. Alternatively, one could apply the FWL theorem using $X_1 = \begin{bmatrix} X \\ X_o \end{bmatrix}$ and $X_2 = \begin{bmatrix} 0 \\ -I_{T_o} \end{bmatrix}$. In this case, $X_2'X_2 = I_{T_o}$ and $P_{X_2} = X_2X_2' = \begin{bmatrix} 0 & 0 \\ 0 & -I_{T_o} \end{bmatrix}$ as before. This means that $\overline{P}_{X_2} = I_{n+T_o} - P_{X_2} = \begin{bmatrix} I_n & 0 \\ 0 & 0 \end{bmatrix}$.

As in part (a), premultiplying by $\overline{P}_{X_2}$ omits the last T_o observations and yields $\widehat{\beta}_{\text{OLS}}$ based on the regression of y on X from the first n observations only. The last T_o observations yield zero residuals because the dependent and independent variables for these T_o observations have zero values. For this to be true in the original regression, it must be true that $0 - X_o\widehat{\beta}_{\text{OLS}} + \widehat{\gamma}_{\text{OLS}} = 0$, which yields $\widehat{\gamma}_{\text{OLS}} = X_o\widehat{\beta}_{\text{OLS}} = \widehat{y}_o$ as expected. The residuals are still $(e'_{\text{OLS}}, 0')$ and $s^{*2} = s^2$ for the same reasons given above. Also, using partitioned inverse, one gets

$$(X^{*\prime}X^*)^{-1} = \begin{bmatrix} (X'X)^{-1} & (X'X)^{-1}X_o' \\ X_o(X'X)^{-1} & I_{T_o} + X_o(X'X)^{-1}X_o' \end{bmatrix}$$

Hence, $s^{*2}(X^{*\prime}X^*)^{-1} = s^2(X^{*\prime}X^*)^{-1}$ and the diagonal elements are as given in (1.11).

2

The One-way Error Component Model

2.1 THE ONE-WAY FIXED EFFECTS MODEL

Consider the panel data regression model

$$y_{it} = \alpha + X'_{it}\beta + u_{it}, \quad i = 1, \ldots, N, \quad t = 1, \ldots, T \tag{2.1}$$

where i denotes the cross-section dimension, t denotes the time-series dimension, α is a scalar, β is $K \times 1$ and X_{it} is the itth observation on K explanatory variables. Most panel data applications utilize a one-way error component model for the disturbances, with

$$u_{it} = \mu_i + \nu_{it} \tag{2.2}$$

where μ_i denotes the *unobservable* individual-specific effect and ν_{it} denotes the remainder disturbance. For example, in an earnings equation in labor economics, y_{it} will measure earnings of the head of the household, whereas X_{it} may contain variables such as experience, education, union membership, sex, and race. Note that μ_i is time-invariant and accounts for any individual-specific effect that is not included in the regression. In this case we could think of it as the individual's unobserved ability. The remainder disturbance ν_{it} varies with individuals and time and can be thought of as the usual disturbance in the regression. In vector form (2.1) can be written as

$$y = \alpha\iota_{NT} + X\beta + u = Z\delta + u \tag{2.3}$$

where y is $NT \times 1$, X is $NT \times K$, $Z = [\iota_{NT}, X]$, $\delta' = (\alpha', \beta')$ and ι_{NT} is a vector of ones of dimension NT. Also, (2.2) can be written as

$$u = Z_\mu \mu + \nu \tag{2.4}$$

where $u' = (u_{11}, \ldots, u_{1T}, u_{21}, \ldots, u_{2T}, \ldots, u_{N1}, \ldots, u_{NT})$, $\mu' = (\mu_1, \ldots, \mu_N)$, and

$$\nu' = (\nu_{11}, \ldots, \nu_{1T}, \ldots, \nu_{N1}, \ldots, \nu_{NT}),$$

with the observations stacked such that the slower index is over individuals and the faster index is over time. $Z_\mu = I_N \otimes \iota_T$ where I_N is an identity matrix of dimension N, ι_T is a vector of ones of dimension T and $\otimes$ denotes Kronecker product. See Abadir and Magnus (2005, p.273) for a good review of Kronecker product. Z_μ is a selector matrix of ones and zeros, or simply the matrix of individual dummies.

Under the *fixed effects* model, the μ_i are assumed to be fixed parameters to be estimated and the remainder disturbances stochastic with ν_{it} independent and identically distributed

$\text{IID}(0, \sigma_\nu^2)$. The X_{it} are assumed independent of the ν_{it} for all i and t. One can substitute the disturbances given by (2.4) into (2.3) to get

$$y = \alpha \iota_{NT} + X\beta + Z_\mu \mu + \nu = Z\delta + Z_\mu \mu + \nu \tag{2.5}$$

and then perform ordinary least squares (OLS) on (2.5) to get estimates of α, β and μ. This is called least squares dummy variables (LSDV). Note that Z is $NT \times (K+1)$ and Z_μ, the matrix of individual dummies, is $NT \times N$. In practice, one of the dummy variables is removed to avoid the dummy variable trap. If N is large, (2.5) will include too many individual dummies, and the matrix to be inverted by OLS is large and of dimension $N + K$.

Exercise 2.1 *(One-way fixed effects regression).* This is based on Problem 2.1 in Baltagi (2008).

(a) Show that the projection matrix on Z_μ is the averaging matrix over time for each individual; call it P.
(b) Let $Q = I_{NT} - P$. Show that P and Q are symmetric and idempotent matrices, that are orthogonal to each other and sum to the identity matrix.
(c) Using the Frisch–Waugh–Lovell theorem, show that the LSDV estimator from (2.5) can be obtained as a *within regression* by premultiplying the model by Q and performing OLS on the resulting transformed model:

$$Qy = QX\beta + Q\nu \tag{2.6}$$

Solution

(a) Note that $Z'_\mu Z_\mu = TI_N$, and $Z_\mu Z'_\mu = I_N \otimes J_T$, where J_T is a matrix of ones of dimension T. Hence, $P = Z_\mu(Z'_\mu Z_\mu)^{-1}Z'_\mu$, the projection matrix on Z_μ reduces to $I_N \otimes \bar{J}_T$ where $\bar{J}_T = J_T/T$. P is a matrix which averages the observation across time for each individual. The typical element of Py is $\bar{y}_{i.} = \sum_{t=1}^{T} y_{it}/T$ repeated T times for each individual.
(b) Let $Q = I_{NT} - P$. This is the orthogonal projection matrix on Z_μ which yields the residuals from the regression of any variable on Z_μ. The typical element of Qy is $(y_{it} - \bar{y}_{i.})$ which obtains the deviations from individual means. Because P and Q are projection matrices, they are (i) symmetric and idempotent, i.e., $P' = P$ and $P^2 = P$. This means that the $\text{rank}(P) = \text{tr}(P) = N$ and $\text{rank}(Q) = \text{tr}(Q) = N(T-1)$. This uses the result that the rank of an idempotent matrix is equal to its trace; see Abadir and Magnus (2005, p.231). Also, (ii) P and Q are orthogonal, i.e. $PQ = 0$, since $PQ = P(I_{NT} - P) = P - P^2 = P - P = 0$, and (iii) they sum to the identity matrix $P + Q = I_{NT}$. In fact, any two of these properties imply the third; see Graybill (1961, Theorem 1.68).
(c) Using the FWL theorem, OLS on (2.5) yields the same estimates of β and the same residuals as OLS on (2.6). This uses the fact that P is the projection matrix on Z_μ and $Q = I_{NT} - P$. Also, the fact that $QZ_\mu = Q\iota_{NT} = 0$, since $PZ_\mu = Z_\mu$. Note that the Q matrix wipes out the individual effects. Also, $QZ = [0, QX]$ since $Q\iota_{NT} = 0$. This is a regression of $\widetilde{y} = Qy$ with typical element $(y_{it} - \bar{y}_{i.})$ on $\widetilde{X} = QX$ with typical element $(X_{it,k} - \bar{X}_{i.,k})$ for the kth regressor, $k = 1, 2, \ldots, K$. This involves the inversion

of a $(K \times K)$ matrix rather than $(N+K) \times (N+K)$ as in (2.5). The resulting OLS estimator is

$$\widetilde{\beta} = \left(X'QX\right)^{-1} X'Qy \tag{2.7}$$

with $\mathrm{var}(\widetilde{\beta}) = \sigma_\nu^2(X'QX)^{-1} = \sigma_\nu^2(\widetilde{X}'\widetilde{X})^{-1}$, since $E(Q\nu) = 0$ and $\mathrm{var}(Q\nu) = Q\,\mathrm{var}(\nu)Q' = \sigma_\nu^2 Q$ using the fact that $\nu \sim (0, \sigma_\nu^2 I_{NT})$.

Exercise 2.2 *(OLS and GLS for fixed effects).* This is based on Problem 2.2 in Baltagi (2008).

(a) Show that (2.6) satisfies the necessary and sufficient condition for OLS to be equivalent to GLS (see Baltagi, 1989b).
(b) Using the generalized inverse, show that OLS or GLS on (2.6) yields $\widetilde{\beta}$, the within estimator given in (2.7).

Solution

(a) For the general linear model $y = X\beta + u$ with $E(uu') = \Omega$, a necessary and sufficient condition for OLS to be equivalent to GLS is given by $X'\Omega^{-1}\overline{P}_X = 0$, where $\overline{P}_X = I - P_X$ and $P_X = X(X'X)^{-1}X'$ (see Baltagi, 1989b). For (2.6), this condition can be written as

$$(X'Q)(Q/\sigma_\nu^2)\overline{P}_{QX} = 0$$

Using the fact that Q is idempotent, the left-hand side can be written as $(X'Q)\overline{P}_{QX}/\sigma_\nu^2$ which is clearly 0, since $\overline{P}_{QX}$ is the orthogonal projection of QX.

One can also use Zyskind's (1967) condition for OLS to be equivalent to GLS given by $P_X\Omega = \Omega P_X$. For equation (2.6), this condition can be written as $P_{QX}(\sigma_\nu^2 Q) = (\sigma_\nu^2 Q)P_{QX}$. But $P_{QX} = QX(X'QX)^{-1}X'Q$. Hence, $P_{QX}Q = P_{QX}$ and $QP_{QX} = P_{QX}$ and the condition is met.

(b) Alternatively, we can verify that OLS and GLS yield the same estimates. Note that $Q = I_{NT} - P$, where $P = I_N \otimes \overline{J}_T$ is idempotent and is therefore its own generalized inverse. The variance–covariance matrix of the disturbance $\widetilde{\nu} = Q\nu$ in (2.6) is $E(\widetilde{\nu}\widetilde{\nu}') = E(Q\nu\nu'Q) = \sigma_\nu^2 Q$ with generalized inverse Q/σ_ν^2. To learn more about the generalized inverse, see Abadir and Magnus (2005, p.295). OLS on (2.6) yields

$$\widehat{\beta} = (X'QQX)^{-1}X'QQy = (X'QX)^{-1}X'Qy$$

which is $\widetilde{\beta}$ given by (2.7). Also, GLS on (2.6) using the generalized inverse yields

$$\widehat{\beta} = (X'QQQX)^{-1}X'QQQy = (X'QX)^{-1}X'Qy = \widetilde{\beta}$$

For large labour or consumer panels, where N is very large, regressions like (2.5) may not be feasible, since one is including $N-1$ dummies in the regression. This fixed effects (FE) least squares, also known as LSDV, suffers from a large loss of degrees of freedom. We are estimating $N-1$ extra parameters, and too many dummies may aggravate the problem of multicollinearity among the regressors. In addition, this FE estimator cannot estimate the effect of any time-invariant variable such as sex, race, religion, schooling or union participation. These time-invariant variables are wiped out by the Q transformation. Alternatively, one can see that these time-invariant variables are spanned by the individual dummies in (2.5) and therefore any regression package attempting (2.5) will fail, signaling perfect multicollinearity. If (2.5) is the true model, LSDV is the best linear unbiased estimator (BLUE) as long as ν_{it} is the standard classical disturbance with mean 0 and variance–covariance matrix $\sigma_\nu^2 I_{NT}$. Note that as $T \to \infty$, the FE estimator is consistent. However, if T is fixed and $N \to \infty$, as is typical in short labor panels, then only the FE estimator of β is consistent; the FE estimators of the individual effects $\alpha + \mu_i$ are not consistent since the number of these parameters increases as N increases. This is the incidental parameter problem discussed by Neyman and Scott (1948) and reviewed more recently by Lancaster (2000). Note that when the true model is FE as in (2.5), OLS on (2.1) yields biased and inconsistent estimates of the regression parameters. This is an omission variables bias due to the fact that OLS deletes the individual dummies when in fact they are relevant.

Exercise 2.3 *(Testing for fixed effects).* Show that the test statistic for the joint significance of the dummies, i.e., $H_0 : \mu_1 = \mu_2 = \cdots = \mu_{N-1} = 0$, is a simple Chow (1960) test:

$$F_0 = \frac{(\text{RRSS} - \text{URSS}/N - 1)}{\text{URSS}/(NT - N - K)} \overset{H_0}{\sim} F_{N-1,N(T-1)-K} \tag{2.8}$$

where RRSS is the restricted residual sums of squares obtained from OLS on the pooled model (2.3) ignoring the fixed effects, and the unrestricted residual sums of squares (URSS) is obtained from the LSDV regression given by (2.5).

Solution

This is a standard application of the F-test for the joint significance of $N - 1$ dummy variables in regression (2.5). If N is large, one cannot perform regression (2.5). Using the FWL theorem, *URSS* is obtained from (2.6) using the fact that the residuals from (2.5) are the same as those from (2.6). However, one has to be careful with the degrees of freedom. The degrees of freedom in regression (2.6) are $NT - K$ since the intercept and the dummies are not included. This is misleading, since the proper degrees of freedom in regression (2.5) are $N(T - 1) - K$. This also means that the s^2 of the within regression in (2.5) as obtained from a typical regression package divides the residual sums of squares by $NT - K$ which is improper. The proper s^2, say s^{*2} from the LSDV regression in (2.5), would divide the same residual sums of squares by $N(T - 1) - K$. Therefore, one has to adjust the variances obtained from the within regression (2.6) by multiplying the variance–covariance matrix by s^{*2}/s^2 or simply by multiplying by $[NT - K]/[N(T - 1) - K]$.

2.2 THE ONE-WAY RANDOM EFFECTS MODEL

There are too many parameters in the FE model and the loss of degrees of freedom can be avoided if the μ_i can be assumed random. In this case $\mu_i \sim \text{IID}(0, \sigma_\mu^2)$, $\nu_{it} \sim \text{IID}(0, \sigma_\nu^2)$, and the μ_i are independent of the ν_{it}. In addition, the X_{it} are independent of the μ_i and ν_{it}, for all i and t.

Exercise 2.4 *(Variance–covariance matrix of the one-way random effects model)*

(a) Show that the random effects (RE) model yields homoskedastic variances, with $\text{var}(u_{it}) = \sigma_\mu^2 + \sigma_\nu^2$ for all i and t, and an equicorrelated block-diagonal covariance matrix which exhibits serial correlation over time only between the disturbances of the same individual.

(b) Using (2.4), show that the variance–covariance matrix of u is given by

$$\Omega = E(uu') = \sigma_\mu^2(I_N \otimes J_T) + \sigma_\nu^2(I_N \otimes I_T)$$

(c) Derive Ω^{-1}, $\Omega^{-1/2}$ and, in general, $\Omega^r = (\sigma_1^2)^r P + (\sigma_\nu^2)^r Q$, where r is an arbitrary scalar.

Solution

(a) From (2.2) $u_{js} = \mu_j + \nu_{js}$, and $\text{cov}(u_{it}, u_{js}) = E(\mu_i\mu_j) + E(\nu_{it}\nu_{js})$, using the fact that the expected value of the cross-products is zero, since μ_i and ν_{it} are independent. In fact, $E(\mu_i\nu_{js}) = E(\mu_j\nu_{it}) = 0$ for all $i, j = 1, 2, \ldots, N$; and $s, t = 1, 2, \ldots, T$. Hence,

$$\begin{aligned} \text{cov}(u_{it}, u_{js}) &= \sigma_\mu^2 + \sigma_\nu^2 && \text{for } i = j, t = s \\ &= \sigma_\mu^2 && \text{for } i = j, t \neq s \end{aligned}$$

and zero otherwise. This also means that the correlation coefficient between u_{it} and u_{js} is

$$\begin{aligned} \rho = \text{correl}(u_{it}, u_{js}) &= 1 && \text{for } i = j, t = s \\ &= \sigma_\mu^2/(\sigma_\mu^2 + \sigma_\nu^2) && \text{for } i = j, t \neq s \end{aligned}$$

and zero otherwise.

(b) From (2.4)

$$\begin{aligned} \Omega = E(uu') &= Z_\mu E(\mu\mu')Z_\mu' + E(\nu\nu') \\ &= \sigma_\mu^2(I_N \otimes J_T) + \sigma_\nu^2(I_N \otimes I_T) \end{aligned} \tag{2.9}$$

using the assumptions $E(\mu'\nu) = 0$, $E(\mu\mu') = \sigma_\mu^2 I_N$ and $E(\nu\nu') = \sigma_\nu^2 I_{NT}$.

(c) We now use a simple trick described by Wansbeek and Kapteyn (1982). Replace J_T by $T\bar{J}_T$, and I_T by $E_T + \bar{J}_T$, where E_T is by definition $I_T - \bar{J}_T$. In this case,

$$\Omega = T\sigma_\mu^2(I_N \otimes \bar{J}_T) + \sigma_\nu^2(I_N \otimes E_T) + \sigma_\nu^2(I_N \otimes \bar{J}_T)$$

Collecting like terms with the same matrices, we get

$$\Omega = (T\sigma_\mu^2 + \sigma_\nu^2)(I_N \otimes \bar{J}_T) + \sigma_\nu^2(I_N \otimes E_T) = \sigma_1^2 P + \sigma_\nu^2 Q \tag{2.10}$$

where $\sigma_1^2 = T\sigma_\mu^2 + \sigma_\nu^2$. This is the spectral decomposition representation of Ω, with σ_1^2 being the first unique characteristic root of Ω of multiplicity N and σ_ν^2 is the second unique characteristic root of Ω of multiplicity $N(T-1)$. From Exercise 2.1, we know that P and Q are symmetric, idempotent, orthogonal to each other and sum to the identity matrix. Hence,

$$\Omega^{-1} = \frac{1}{\sigma_1^2}P + \frac{1}{\sigma_\nu^2}Q \tag{2.11}$$

and

$$\Omega^{-1/2} = \frac{1}{\sigma_1}P + \frac{1}{\sigma_\nu}Q \tag{2.12}$$

and, in general, $\Omega^r = (\sigma_1^2)^r P + (\sigma_\nu^2)^r Q$ where r is an arbitrary scalar. In fact,

$$\Omega\Omega^{-1} = (\sigma_1^2 P + \sigma_\nu^2 Q)\left(\frac{1}{\sigma_1^2}P + \frac{1}{\sigma_\nu^2}Q\right) = P + Q = I_{NT}$$

since $P^2 = P$, $Q^2 = Q$ and $PQ = 0$. Similarly,

$$\Omega^{-\frac{1}{2}}\Omega^{-\frac{1}{2}} = \left(\frac{1}{\sigma_1}P + \frac{1}{\sigma_\nu}Q\right)\left(\frac{1}{\sigma_1}P + \frac{1}{\sigma_\nu}Q\right) = \frac{1}{\sigma_1^2}P^2 + \frac{1}{\sigma_\nu^2}Q^2$$
$$= \frac{1}{\sigma_1^2}P + \frac{1}{\sigma_\nu^2}Q = \Omega^{-1}$$

Exercise 2.5 *(Fuller and Battese (1973) transformation for the one-way random effects model).* This is based on Problem 2.4 in Baltagi (2008). Show that GLS on the RE model is equivalent to the regression of y^* on X^* and a constant, where $y^* = \sigma_\nu\Omega^{-1/2}y$ has a typical element $y_{it} - \theta\overline{y}_{i.}$ with $\theta = 1 - \sigma_\nu/\sigma_1$ and X^* is similarly defined.

Solution

GLS on (2.1) is equivalent to OLS after premultiplying (2.1) by $\sigma_\nu\Omega^{-1/2} = Q + (\sigma_\nu/\sigma_1)P$ derived in Exercise 2.4. Hence,

$$y^* = \sigma_\nu\Omega^{-\frac{1}{2}}y = Qy + (\sigma_\nu/\sigma_1)Py = y - Py + (\sigma_\nu/\sigma_1)Py = y - (1 - (\sigma_\nu/\sigma_1))Py$$
$$= y - \theta Py$$

where $\theta = 1 - (\sigma_\nu/\sigma_1)$. Recall that the typical element of Py is $\overline{y}_{i.}$. Therefore, the typical element of y^* is $y_{it}^* = y_{it} - \theta\overline{y}_{i.}$. Now we can obtain GLS as a weighted least squares of y^* on X^* and a constant.

The best quadratic unbiased (BQU) estimators of the variance components arise naturally from the spectral decomposition of Ω. In fact, $Pu \sim (0, \sigma_1^2 P)$, $Qu \sim (0, \sigma_\nu^2 Q)$ and

$$\widehat{\sigma}_1^2 = \frac{u'Pu}{\text{tr}(P)} = T\sum_{i=1}^{N}\overline{u}_{i.}^2/N \tag{2.13}$$

and

$$\widehat{\sigma}_\nu^2 = \frac{u'Qu}{\text{tr}(Q)} = \frac{\sum_{i=1}^{N}\sum_{t=1}^{T}(u_{it} - \overline{u}_{i.})^2}{N(T-1)} \quad (2.14)$$

provide the BQU estimators of σ_1^2 and σ_ν^2, respectively (see Balestra, 1973).

Exercise 2.6 *(Unbiased estimates of the variance components: the one-way model).* This is based on Problem 2.5 in Baltagi (2008). Show that $\widehat{\sigma}_1^2$ and $\widehat{\sigma}_\nu^2$ are unbiased estimators of σ_1^2 and σ_ν^2, respectively.

Solution

$E(u'Pu) = E(\text{tr}(uu'P)) = \text{tr}(E(uu')P) = \text{tr}(\Omega P)$. But, from (2.10), $\Omega P = \sigma_1^2 P$ since $PQ = 0$. Hence,

$$E(\widehat{\sigma}_1^2) = \frac{E(u'Pu)}{\text{tr}(P)} = \frac{\text{tr}(\sigma_1^2 P)}{\text{tr}(P)} = \sigma_1^2$$

Similarly, $E(u'Qu) = \text{tr}(\Omega Q) = \text{tr}(\sigma_\nu^2 Q)$ where the last equality follows the fact that $\Omega Q = \sigma_\nu^2 Q$ since $PQ = 0$. Hence,

$$E(\widehat{\sigma}_\nu^2) = \frac{E(u'Qu)}{\text{tr}(Q)} = \frac{\text{tr}(\sigma_\nu^2 Q)}{\text{tr}(Q)} = \sigma_\nu^2$$

The true disturbances are not known and therefore (2.13) and (2.14) are not feasible. Wallace and Hussain (1969) suggest substituting OLS residual $\widehat{u}_{\text{OLS}}$ instead of the true u. Amemiya (1971) shows that these estimators of the variance components have a different asymptotic distribution from that knowing the true disturbances. He suggests using FE residuals instead of the OLS residuals. In this case $\widetilde{u} = y - \widetilde{\alpha}\iota_{NT} - X\widetilde{\beta}$ where $\widetilde{\alpha} = \overline{y}_{..} - \overline{X}'_{..}\widetilde{\beta}$ and $\overline{X}'_{..}$ is a $1 \times K$ vector of averages of all regressors. Substituting these $\widetilde{u}$ for u in (2.13) and (2.14), we get the Amemiya-type estimators of the variance components. Swamy and Arora (1972) suggest running two regressions to get estimates of the variance components from the corresponding mean square errors of these regressions. The first regression is the within regression, given in (2.6), which yields the following s^2 corrected for the proper degrees of freedom:

$$\widehat{\widehat{\sigma}}_\nu^2 = [y'Qy - y'QX(X'QX)^{-1}X'Qy]/[N(T-1) - K] \quad (2.15)$$

The second regression is the *between regression* which runs the regression of averages across time, i.e.,

$$\overline{y}_{i.} = \alpha + \overline{X}'_{i.}\beta + \overline{u}_{i.} \qquad \text{for } i = 1, \ldots, N \quad (2.16)$$

This is equivalent to premultiplying the model in (2.5) by P and running OLS. The only caution is that the latter regression has NT observations because it repeats the averages

T times for each individual, while the cross-section regression in (2.16) is based on N observations. To remedy this, one can run the cross-section regression

$$\sqrt{T}\bar{y}_{i.} = \alpha\sqrt{T} + \sqrt{T}\bar{X}'_{i.}\beta + \sqrt{T}\bar{u}_{i.} \quad \text{for } i = 1, \dots, N \tag{2.17}$$

where $\text{var}(\sqrt{T}\bar{u}_{i.}) = \sigma_1^2$. This regression will yield an s^2 given by

$$\widehat{\widehat{\sigma}}_1^2 = (y'Py - y'PZ(Z'PZ)^{-1}Z'Py)/(N - K - 1) \tag{2.18}$$

Exercise 2.7 *(Feasible unbiased estimates of the variance components: the one-way model).* This is based on Problem 2.6 in Baltagi (2008).

(a) Show that $\widehat{\widehat{\sigma}}_\nu^2$ is unbiased for σ_ν^2.
(b) Show that $\widehat{\widehat{\sigma}}_1^2$ is unbiased for σ_1^2.

Solution

(a) $\widehat{\widehat{\sigma}}_\nu^2$ is the s^2 from the regression given by (2.6) corrected for the proper degrees of freedom. In fact,

$$\widehat{\widehat{\sigma}}_\nu^2 = y'Q[I_{NT} - P_{QX}]Qy/[N(T-1) - K]$$

where $P_{QX} = QX(X'QX)^{-1}X'Q$. Substituting Qy from (2.6) into $\widehat{\widehat{\sigma}}_\nu^2$, one gets

$$\widehat{\widehat{\sigma}}_\nu^2 = \nu'Q[I_{NT} - P_{QX}]Q\nu/[N(T-1) - K]$$

with $Q\nu \sim (0, \sigma_\nu^2 Q)$. Therefore,

$$\begin{aligned} E[\nu'Q[I_{NT} - P_{QX}]Q\nu] &= E[\text{tr}\{Q\nu\nu'Q[I_{NT} - P_{QX}]\}] \\ &= \sigma_\nu^2 \text{tr}\{Q - QP_{QX}\} = \sigma_\nu^2\{N(T-1) - \text{tr}(P_{QX})\} \end{aligned}$$

where the last equality follows from the fact that $QP_{QX} = P_{QX}$. Also,

$$\text{tr}(P_{QX}) = \text{tr}(X'QX)(X'QX)^{-1} = \text{tr}(I_K) = K.$$

Hence, $E(\widehat{\widehat{\sigma}}_\nu^2) = \sigma_\nu^2$.

(b) $\widehat{\widehat{\sigma}}_1^2$ is the s^2 from the regression given by $Py = PZ\delta + Pu$ corrected for the proper degrees of freedom. In fact,

$$\widehat{\widehat{\sigma}}_1^2 = y'P[I_{NT} - P_{PZ}]Py/(N - K - 1)$$

where $P_{PZ} = PZ(Z'PZ)^{-1}Z'P$. Substituting Py into $\widehat{\widehat{\sigma}}_1^2$, one gets

$$\widehat{\widehat{\sigma}}_1^2 = u'P[I_{NT} - P_{PZ}]Pu/(N - K - 1)$$

with $Pu \sim (0, \sigma_1^2 P)$. Therefore,

$$E(u'P[I_{NT} - P_{PZ}]Pu) = E[\text{tr}\{Puu'P(I_{NT} - P_{PZ})\}] = \sigma_1^2 \text{tr}\{P - PP_{PZ}\}$$
$$= \sigma_1^2\{N - \text{tr}(P_{PZ})\}$$

where the last equality follows from the fact that $PP_{PZ} = P_{PZ}$. Also,

$$\text{tr}(P_{PZ}) = \text{tr}(Z'PZ)(Z'PZ)^{-1} = \text{tr}(I_{K+1}) = K + 1$$

Hence, $E(\widehat{\widehat{\sigma}}_1^2) = \sigma_1^2$.

Note that stacking the following two transformed regressions we just performed yields

$$\begin{pmatrix} Qy \\ Py \end{pmatrix} = \begin{pmatrix} QZ \\ PZ \end{pmatrix} \delta + \begin{pmatrix} Qu \\ Pu \end{pmatrix} \tag{2.19}$$

and the transformed error has mean 0 and variance–covariance matrix given by

$$\begin{pmatrix} \sigma_\nu^2 Q & 0 \\ 0 & \sigma_1^2 P \end{pmatrix}$$

EViews computes the Wallace and Hussain (1969), Amemiya (1971) and Swamy and Arora (1972) estimators as options under the random effects panel data procedure. These are illustrated in the next empirical exercise.

2.2.1 Empirical Example 1

Baltagi and Griffin (1983) considered the following gasoline demand equation:

$$\ln \frac{\text{Gas}}{\text{Car}} = \alpha + \beta_1 \ln \frac{Y}{N} + \beta_2 \ln \frac{P_{\text{MG}}}{P_{\text{GDP}}} + \beta_3 \ln \frac{\text{Car}}{N} + u$$

where Gas/Car is motor gasoline consumption per auto, Y/N is real per capita income, $P_{\text{MG}}/P_{\text{GDP}}$ is real motor gasoline price and Car/N denotes the stock of cars per capita. This panel consists of annual observations across 18 OECD countries, covering the period 1960–78. The data for this example are given as Gasoline.dat on the Wiley web site. It is Example 2 in Baltagi (2008, p.26).

Exercise 2.8 *(Gasoline demand in the OECD)*

(a) Obtain the OLS and FE estimators of this gasoline demand equation.
(b) Using EViews, compute the Wallace and Hussain (1969), Amemiya (1971) and Swamy and Arora (1972) feasible GLS estimators of the RE model. Compare the different estimates of the price and income elasticities of gasoline. This is based on Problem 2.12 in Baltagi (2008).

Table 2.1 Gasoline Demand Data. OLS Results

Dependent Variable: GAS
Method: Panel Least Squares

Sample: 1960 1978
Cross-sections included: 18
Total panel (balanced) observations: 342

Variable	Coefficient	Std. Error	t-Statistic	Prob.
C	2.391326	0.116934	20.45017	0.0000
INC	0.889962	0.035806	24.85523	0.0000
PMG	−0.891798	0.030315	−29.41796	0.0000
CAR	−0.763373	0.018608	−41.02325	0.0000

R-squared	0.854935	Mean dependent var	4.296242
Adjusted R-squared	0.853648	S.D. dependent var	0.548907
S.E. of regression	0.209990	Akaike info criterion	−0.271888
Sum squared resid	14.90436	Schwarz criterion	−0.227037
Log likelihood	50.49289	F-statistic	663.9993
Durbin-Watson stat	0.137461	Prob.(F-statistic)	0.000000

Solution

(a) The EViews output for the OLS estimator, along with the corresponding summary statistics, is shown in Table 2.1, while that for the FE estimator with country effects is given in Table 2.2.

(b) The EViews output for the Wallace and Hussain (1969) feasible GLS estimator is given in Table 2.3, while that for the Amemiya (1971) feasible GLS estimator is given in Table 2.4. Note that EViews designates the Amemiya (1971) procedure as Wansbeek and Kapteyn (1989) since the latter paper generalizes the Amemiya method to deal with unbalanced or incomplete panels (see Chapter 9). The EViews output for the Swamy and Arora (1972) feasible GLS estimator is given in Table 2.5.

The price elasticity of gasoline is much higher for OLS (−0.89) as compared with FE (−0.32) or the feasible GLS estimators (−0.45, −0.37, and −0.42, respectively). The income elasticity of gasoline is much higher for OLS (0.89) as compared with FE (0.66) or the feasible GLS estimators (0.55, 0.60, and 0.55, respectively).

Table 2.2 Gasoline Demand Data. Fixed Effects Results

Dependent Variable: GAS
Method: Panel Least Squares

Sample: 1960 1978
Cross-sections included: 18
Total panel (balanced) observations: 342

Variable	Coefficient	Std. Error	t-Statistic	Prob.
C	2.402670	0.225309	10.66387	0.0000
INC	0.662250	0.073386	9.024191	0.0000
PMG	−0.321702	0.044099	−7.294964	0.0000
CAR	−0.640483	0.029679	−21.58045	0.0000

Effects Specification

Cross-section fixed (dummy variables)

R-squared	0.973366	Mean dependent var	4.296242
Adjusted R-squared	0.971706	S.D. dependent var	0.548907
S.E. of regression	0.092330	Akaike info criterion	−1.867450
Sum squared resid	2.736491	Schwarz criterion	−1.631979
Log likelihood	340.3340	F-statistic	586.5556
Durbin-Watson stat	0.326578	Prob.(F-statistic)	0.000000

Table 2.3 Gasoline Demand Data. Wallace and Hussain Estimator

Dependent Variable: GAS
Method: Panel EGLS (Cross-section random effects)

Sample: 1960 1978
Cross-sections included: 18
Total panel (balanced) observations: 342
Wallace and Hussain estimator of component variances

Variable	Coefficient	Std. Error	t-Statistic	Prob.
C	1.938318	0.201817	9.604333	0.0000
INC	0.545202	0.065555	8.316682	0.0000
PMG	−0.447490	0.045763	−9.778438	0.0000
CAR	−0.605086	0.028838	−20.98191	0.0000

Effects Specification

Cross-section random S.D./Rho	0.196715	0.7508
Idiosyncratic random S.D./Rho	0.113320	0.2492

Weighted Statistics

R-squared	0.826568	Mean dependent var	0.562884
Adjusted R-squared	0.825029	S.D. dependent var	0.233119
S.E. of regression	0.097513	Sum squared resid	3.213953
F-statistic	536.9632	Durbin-Watson stat	0.299781
Prob.(F-statistic)	0.000000		

Unweighted Statistics

R-squared	0.750484	Mean dependent var	4.296242
Sum squared resid	25.63603	Durbin-Watson stat	0.037583

Table 2.4 Gasoline Demand Data. Amemiya/Wansbeek and Kapteyn Estimator

Dependent Variable: GAS
Method: Panel EGLS (Cross-section random effects)

Sample: 1960 1978
Cross-sections included: 18
Total panel (balanced) observations: 342
Wansbeek and Kapteyn estimator of component variances

Variable	Coefficient	Std. Error	t-Statistic	Prob.
C	2.188322	0.216372	10.11372	0.0000
INC	0.601969	0.065876	9.137941	0.0000
PMG	−0.365500	0.041620	−8.781832	0.0000
CAR	−0.620725	0.027356	−22.69053	0.0000

Effects Specification

Cross-section random S.D./Rho	0.343826	0.9327
Idiosyncratic random S.D./Rho	0.092330	0.0673

Weighted Statistics

R-squared	0.835065	Mean dependent var	0.264177
Adjusted R-squared	0.833602	S.D.dependent var	0.225791
S.E. of regression	0.092104	Sum squared resid	2.867329
F-statistic	570.4327	Durbin-Watson stat	0.315210
Prob.(F-statistic)	0.000000		

Unweighted Statistics

R-squared	0.670228	Mean dependent var	4.296242
Sum squared resid	33.88179	Durbin-Watson stat	0.026675

Table 2.5 Gasoline Demand Data. Swamy and Arora Estimator

Dependent Variable: GAS
Method: Panel EGLS (Cross-section random effects)

Sample: 1960 1978
Cross-sections included: 18
Total panel (balanced) observations: 342
Swamy and Arora estimator of component variances

Variable	Coefficient	Std. Error	t-Statistic	Prob.
C	1.996698	0.178235	11.20260	0.0000
INC	0.554986	0.057174	9.706890	0.0000
PMG	−0.420389	0.038657	−10.87482	0.0000
CAR	−0.606840	0.024672	−24.59636	0.0000

Effects Specification

Cross-section random S.D./Rho	0.195545	0.8177
Idiosyncratic random S.D./Rho	0.092330	0.1823

Weighted Statistics

R-squared	0.829310	Mean dependent var	0.462676
Adjusted R-squared	0.827795	S.D. dependent var	0.230099
S.E. of regression	0.095485	Sum squared resid	3.081707
F-statistic	547.3996	Durbin-Watson stat	0.304481
Prob.(F-statistic)	0.000000		

Unweighted Statistics

R-squared	0.730918	Mean dependent var	4.296242
Sum squared resid	27.64625	Durbin-Watson stat	0.033940

Exercise 2.9 *(System estimation of the one-way model: OLS versus GLS).* This is based on Problem 2.7 in Baltagi (2008).

(a) Show that OLS on this system of $2NT$ observations given in (2.19) yields OLS on the pooled model (2.3).
(b) Also, show that GLS on this system of $2NT$ observations given in (2.19) yields GLS on the pooled model (2.3).

Solution

(a) OLS on (2.19) yields

$$\begin{aligned}\widehat{\delta}_{\text{OLS}} &= \left[(Z'Q, Z'P)\begin{pmatrix}QZ\\PZ\end{pmatrix}\right]^{-1}(Z'Q, Z'P)\begin{pmatrix}Qy\\Py\end{pmatrix}\\ &= (Z'QZ + Z'PZ)^{-1}(Z'Qy + Z'Py)\\ &= (Z'(Q+P)Z)^{-1}Z'(Q+P)y = (Z'Z)^{-1}Z'y\end{aligned}$$

since $Q + P = I_{NT}$.

(b) GLS on (2.19) yields

$$\begin{aligned}\widehat{\delta}_{\text{GLS}} = &\left((Z'Q, Z'P)\begin{bmatrix}\sigma_\nu^2 Q & 0\\ 0 & \sigma_1^2 P\end{bmatrix}^{-1}\begin{pmatrix}QZ\\PZ\end{pmatrix}\right)^{-1}\\ &(Z'Q, Z'P)\begin{bmatrix}\sigma_\nu^2 Q & 0\\ 0 & \sigma_1^2 P\end{bmatrix}^{-1}\begin{pmatrix}Qy\\Py\end{pmatrix}\end{aligned}$$

Using the generalized inverse

$$\begin{bmatrix}\sigma_\nu^2 Q & 0\\ 0 & \sigma_1^2 P\end{bmatrix}^{-1} = \begin{bmatrix}Q/\sigma_\nu^2 & 0\\ 0 & P/\sigma_1^2\end{bmatrix}$$

one gets

$$\begin{aligned}\widehat{\delta}_{\text{GLS}} &= [(Z'QZ)/\sigma_\nu^2 + (Z'PZ)/\sigma_1^2]^{-1}[(Z'Qy)/\sigma_\nu^2 + (Z'Py)/\sigma_1^2]\\ &= (Z'\Omega^{-1}Z)^{-1}Z'\Omega^{-1}y\end{aligned}$$

where Ω^{-1} is given by (2.11).

Alternatively, one could get rid of the constant α by running the following stacked regressions:

$$\begin{pmatrix}Qy\\(P-\overline{J}_{NT})y\end{pmatrix} = \begin{pmatrix}QX\\(P-\overline{J}_{NT})X\end{pmatrix}\beta + \begin{pmatrix}Qu\\(P-\overline{J}_{NT})u\end{pmatrix} \tag{2.20}$$

This follows from the fact that $Q\iota_{NT} = 0$ and $(P - \overline{J}_{NT})\iota_{NT} = 0$. The transformed error has zero mean and variance–covariance matrix

$$\begin{pmatrix}\sigma_\nu^2 Q & 0\\ 0 & \sigma_1^2(P-\overline{J}_{NT})\end{pmatrix}$$

Exercise 2.10 *(GLS is a matrix weighted average of between and within)*

(a) Show that OLS on the system of $2NT$ observations in (2.20) yields OLS on the pooled model (2.3).
(b) Show that GLS on (2.20) yields GLS on (2.3).
(c) Show that $\widehat{\beta}_{\text{GLS}}$ is a matrix weighted average of $\widetilde{\beta}_{\text{Within}}$ and $\widehat{\beta}_{\text{Between}}$.
(d) What happens to the GLS estimator if $\sigma_\mu^2 = 0$? or if $T \to \infty$?

Solution

(a) OLS on (2.20) yields

$$\begin{aligned}\widehat{\beta}_{\text{OLS}} &= [X'QX + X'(P - \overline{J}_{NT})X]^{-1}[X'Qy + X'(P - \overline{J}_{NT})y]\\ &= [X'(I_{NT} - \overline{J}_{NT})X]^{-1}X'(I_{NT} - \overline{J}_{NT})y\end{aligned}$$

(b) GLS on (2.20) yields

$$\begin{aligned}\widehat{\beta}_{\text{GLS}} &= [(X'QX/\sigma_\nu^2) + X'(P - \overline{J}_{NT})X/\sigma_1^2]^{-1}\\ &\quad\times[(X'Qy/\sigma_\nu^2) + X'(P - \overline{J}_{NT})y/\sigma_1^2]\\ &= [W_{XX} + \phi^2 B_{XX}]^{-1}[W_{Xy} + \phi^2 B_{Xy}] \qquad (2.21)\end{aligned}$$

with $\text{var}(\widehat{\beta}_{\text{GLS}}) = \sigma_\nu^2[W_{XX} + \phi^2 B_{XX}]^{-1}$. Note that $W_{XX} = X'QX$, $B_{XX} = X'(P - \overline{J}_{NT})X$ and $\phi^2 = \sigma_\nu^2/\sigma_1^2$.

(c) The within estimator of β is $\widetilde{\beta}_{\text{Within}} = W_{XX}^{-1}W_{Xy}$ and the between estimator of β is $\widehat{\beta}_{\text{Between}} = B_{XX}^{-1}B_{Xy}$. $\widehat{\beta}_{\text{GLS}}$ is a matrix weighted average of $\widetilde{\beta}_{\text{Within}}$ and $\widehat{\beta}_{\text{Between}}$ weighting each estimate by the inverse of its corresponding variance. In fact,

$$\widehat{\beta}_{\text{GLS}} = W_1\widetilde{\beta}_{\text{Within}} + W_2\widehat{\beta}_{\text{Between}} \qquad (2.22)$$

where

$$W_1 = [W_{XX} + \phi^2 B_{XX}]^{-1}W_{XX}$$

and

$$W_2 = [W_{XX} + \phi^2 B_{XX}]^{-1}(\phi^2 B_{XX}) = I - W_1$$

This was demonstrated by Maddala (1971).

(d) If $\sigma_\mu^2 = 0$ then $\phi^2 = 1$ and $\widehat{\beta}_{\text{GLS}}$ reduces to $\widehat{\beta}_{\text{OLS}}$. If $T \to \infty$, then $\phi^2 \to 0$ and $\widehat{\beta}_{\text{GLS}}$ tends to $\widetilde{\beta}_{\text{Within}}$. Note that the within estimator ignores the between variation, and the between estimator ignores the within variation. The OLS estimator gives equal weight to the between and within variations. Only GLS weights them by the inverse of their corresponding variance.

Exercise 2.11 *(Efficiency of GLS compared to within and between estimators).* This is based on Problem 2.8 in Baltagi (2008).

(a) Show that $\text{var}(\widetilde{\beta}_{\text{Within}}) - \text{var}(\widehat{\beta}_{\text{GLS}})$ is a positive semi-definite matrix.
(b) Show that $\text{var}(\widehat{\beta}_{\text{Between}}) - \text{var}(\widehat{\beta}_{\text{GLS}})$ is a positive semi-definite matrix.

Solution

(a) From (2.21) we have

$$\text{var}(\widehat{\beta}_{\text{GLS}}) = \sigma_\nu^2[W_{XX} + \phi^2 B_{XX}]^{-1}$$

where $W_{XX} = X'QX$, $B_{XX} = X'(P - \overline{J}_{NT})X$ and $\phi^2 = \sigma_\nu^2/\sigma_1^2$. The within estimator is given by (2.7) with $\text{var}(\widetilde{\beta}_{\text{Within}}) = \sigma_\nu^2 W_{XX}^{-1}$. Hence,

$$(\text{var}(\widehat{\beta}_{\text{GLS}}))^{-1} - (\text{var}(\widetilde{\beta}_{\text{Within}}))^{-1} = \frac{1}{\sigma_\nu^2}[W_{XX} + \phi^2 B_{XX}] - \frac{1}{\sigma_\nu^2} W_{XX} = \phi^2 B_{XX}/\sigma_\nu^2$$

which is positive semi-definite. Hence, $\text{var}(\widetilde{\beta}_{\text{Within}}) - \text{var}(\widehat{\beta}_{\text{GLS}})$ is positive semi-definite. This last result uses the well-known fact that if $A^{-1} - B^{-1}$ is positive semi-definite, then $B - A$ is positive semi-definite. However, as $T \to \infty$ for any fixed $N, \phi^2 \to 0$ and both $\widehat{\beta}_{\text{GLS}}$ and $\widetilde{\beta}_{\text{Within}}$ have the same asymptotic variance.

(b) Similarly,

$$(\text{var}(\widehat{\beta}_{\text{GLS}}))^{-1} - (\text{var}(\widehat{\beta}_{\text{Between}}))^{-1} = \frac{1}{\sigma_\nu^2}[W_{XX} + \phi^2 B_{XX}] - \frac{1}{\sigma_1^2} B_{XX} = W_{XX}/\sigma_\nu^2$$

which is positive semi-definite. Hence, $\text{var}(\widehat{\beta}_{\text{Between}}) - \text{var}(\widehat{\beta}_{\text{GLS}})$ is positive semi-definite.

2.2.2 Maximum Likelihood Estimation

Under normality of the disturbances, one can write the likelihood function as

$$L(\alpha, \beta, \phi^2, \sigma_\nu^2) = \text{constant} - \frac{NT}{2}\log\sigma_\nu^2 + \frac{N}{2}\log\phi^2 - \frac{1}{2\sigma_\nu^2}u'\Sigma^{-1}u \tag{2.23}$$

where $\Omega = \sigma_\nu^2\Sigma$, $\phi^2 = \sigma_\nu^2/\sigma_1^2$ and $\Sigma = Q + \phi^{-2}P$ from (2.10). This uses the fact that $|\Omega| =$ product of its characteristic roots $= (\sigma_\nu^2)^{N(T-1)}(\sigma_1^2)^N = (\sigma_\nu^2)^{NT}(\phi^2)^{-N}$. Note that there is a one-to-one correspondence between ϕ^2 and σ_μ^2. In fact, $0 \leqslant \sigma_\mu^2 < \infty$ translates into $0 < \phi^2 \leqslant 1$. Breusch (1987) concentrates the likelihood with respect to α and σ_ν^2. In this case, $\widehat{\alpha}_{mle} = \bar{y}_{..} - \overline{X}'_{..}\widehat{\beta}_{mle}$ and $\widehat{\sigma}^2_{\nu,mle} = (1/NT)\widehat{u}'\widehat{\Sigma}^{-1}\widehat{u}$ where $\widehat{u}$ and $\widehat{\Sigma}$ are based on maximum likelihood estimates of β, ϕ^2 and α. Let $d = y - X\widehat{\beta}_{mle}$; then $\widehat{\alpha}_{mle} = (1/NT)\iota'_{NT}d$ and $\widehat{u} = d - \iota_{NT}\widehat{\alpha}_{mle} = d - \overline{J}_{NT}d$. This implies that $\widehat{\sigma}^2_{\nu,mle}$ can be rewritten as

$$\widehat{\sigma}^2_{\nu,mle} = d'[Q + \phi^2(P - \overline{J}_{NT})]d/NT \tag{2.24}$$

and the concentrated likelihood becomes

$$L_C(\beta, \phi^2) = \text{constant} - \frac{NT}{2}\log\{d'[Q + \phi^2(P - \overline{J}_{NT})]d\} + \frac{N}{2}\log\phi^2 \tag{2.25}$$

Exercise 2.12 *(Maximum likelihood estimation of the random effects model).* This is based on Problem 2.9 in Baltagi (2008).

(a) Maximize (2.25) over ϕ^2, given β, and show that

$$\widehat{\phi}^2 = \frac{d'Qd}{(T-1)d'(P-\overline{J}_{NT})d} = \frac{\sum\sum(d_{it}-\overline{d}_{i.})^2}{T(T-1)\sum(\overline{d}_{i.}-\overline{d}_{..})^2} \tag{2.26}$$

(b) Maximize (2.25) over β, given ϕ^2, and show that

$$\widehat{\beta}_{mle} = [X'(Q+\phi^2(P-\overline{J}_{NT}))X]^{-1}X'[Q+\phi^2(P-\overline{J}_{NT})]y \tag{2.27}$$

Solution

(a) Differentiating (2.25) with respect to ϕ^2 yields

$$\frac{\partial L_C}{\partial\phi^2} = -\frac{NT}{2}\cdot\frac{d'(P-\overline{J}_{NT})d}{d'[Q+\phi^2(P-\overline{J}_{NT})]d} + \frac{N}{2}\cdot\frac{1}{\phi^2}$$

Setting $\partial L_C/\partial\phi^2 = 0$, we get $Td'(P-\overline{J}_{NT})d\phi^2 = d'Qd + \phi^2 d'(P-\overline{J}_{NT})d$. Solving for ϕ^2, we get $\widehat{\phi}^2(T-1)d'(P-\overline{J}_{NT})d = d'Qd$ which yields (2.26).

(b) Differentiating (2.25) with respect to β yields

$$\frac{\partial L_C}{\partial\beta} = -\frac{NT}{2}\cdot\frac{1}{d'[Q+\phi^2(P-\overline{J}_{NT})]d}\cdot\frac{\partial}{\partial\beta}d'[Q+\phi^2(P-\overline{J}_{NT})]d$$

Setting $\partial L_C/\partial\beta = 0$ is equivalent to solving

$$\frac{\partial d'[Q+\phi^2(P-\overline{J}_{NT})]d}{\partial\beta} = 0$$

Using the fact that $d = y - X\beta$, this yields

$$-2X'[Q+\phi^2(P-\overline{J}_{NT})](y-X\widehat{\beta}) = 0$$

Solving for $\widehat{\beta}$, we get

$$X'[Q+\phi^2(P-\overline{J}_{NT})]X\widehat{\beta} = X'[Q+\phi^2(P-\overline{J}_{NT})]y$$

which yields (2.27).

One can iterate between β and ϕ^2 until convergence. Breusch (1987) shows that provided $T>1$, any ith iteration β, call it β_i, gives $0<\phi^2_{i+1}<\infty$ in the $(i+1)$th iteration. More importantly, Breusch (1987) shows that these ϕ^2_i have a remarkable property of forming a *monotonic* sequence. In fact, starting from the within estimator of β, for $\phi^2 = 0$, the next ϕ^2 is finite and positive and starts a monotonically *increasing* sequence of ϕ^2. Similarly, starting from the between estimator of β, for $\phi^2 \to \infty$ the next ϕ^2 is finite and positive and starts a monotonically *decreasing* sequence of ϕ^2. Hence, to guard against the possibility of a local maximum, Breusch (1987) suggests starting with $\widetilde{\beta}_{\text{Within}}$ and $\widehat{\beta}_{\text{Between}}$ and iterating. If these two sequences converge to the same maximum, then this is the global maximum. If one starts with $\widehat{\beta}_{\text{OLS}}$ for $\phi^2 = 1$, and the next iteration obtains a larger ϕ^2, then we have a local maximum at the boundary $\phi^2 = 1$.

Exercise 2.13 *(Prediction in the one-way random effects model).* This is based on Problem 2.10 in Baltagi (2008). Suppose we want to predict S periods ahead for the ith individual. For the GLS model, knowing the variance–covariance structure of the disturbances, Goldberger (1962) showed that the best linear unbiased predictor (BLUP) of $y_{i,T+S}$ is

$$\widehat{y}_{i,T+S} = Z'_{i,T+S}\widehat{\delta}_{\text{GLS}} + w'\Omega^{-1}\widehat{u}_{\text{GLS}} \quad \text{for } s \geqslant 1 \tag{2.28}$$

where $\widehat{u}_{\text{GLS}} = y - Z\widehat{\delta}_{\text{GLS}}$ and $w = E(u_{i,T+S}u)$. Show that for the one-way error component model given in (2.1) and (2.2) the BLUP for $y_{i,T+S}$ corrects the GLS prediction by a fraction of the mean of the GLS residuals corresponding to that ith individual.

Solution

Note that for period $T + S$,

$$u_{i,T+S} = \mu_i + \nu_{i,T+S} \tag{2.29}$$

From (2.2) and (2.29), $E(u_{i,T+S}u_{jt}) = \sigma_\mu^2$, for $i = j$, and zero otherwise. The only correlation over time occurs because of the presence of the same individual across the panel. The ν_{it} are not correlated for different time periods. In vector form,

$$w = E(u_{i,T+S}u) = \sigma_\mu^2(0, \ldots, 0, \ldots, 1, \ldots, 1, \ldots, 0, \ldots, 0)'$$

where there are T ones for the ith individual. This can be rewritten as $w = \sigma_\mu^2(l_i \otimes \iota_T)$ where l_i is the ith column of I_N, i.e., l_i is a vector that has 1 in the ith position and zero elsewhere. In this case

$$w'\Omega^{-1} = \sigma_\mu^2(l_i' \otimes \iota_T')\left[\frac{1}{\sigma_1^2}P + \frac{1}{\sigma_\nu^2}Q\right] = \frac{\sigma_\mu^2}{\sigma_1^2}(l_i' \otimes \iota_T') \tag{2.30}$$

since $(l_i' \otimes \iota_T')P = (l_i' \otimes \iota_T')$ and $(l_i' \otimes \iota_T')Q = 0$. Using (2.30), the typical element of $w'\Omega^{-1}\widehat{u}_{\text{GLS}}$ becomes $((T\sigma_\mu^2/\sigma_1^2)\overline{\widehat{u}}_{i.,\text{GLS}})$ where $\overline{\widehat{u}}_{i.,\text{GLS}} = \sum_{t=1}^{T}\widehat{u}_{it,\text{GLS}}/T$. This predictor was considered by Taub (1979).

2.2.3 Empirical Example 2

Cornwell and Rupert (1988) consider a returns to schooling example based on a panel of 595 individuals observed over the period 1976–82 and drawn from the Panel Study of Income Dynamics. A description of the data is given in Cornwell and Rupert (1988) and is available as a Stata data set named cornrup.dta. In particular, log wage is regressed on years of education (ED), weeks worked (WKS), years of full-time work experience (EXP), occupation (OCC = 1, if the individual is in a blue-collar occupation), residence (SOUTH = 1, SMSA = 1, if the individual resides in the South, or in a standard metropolitan statistical area), industry (IND = 1, if the individual works in a manufacturing industry), marital status (MS = 1, if the individual is married), sex and race (FEM = 1, BLK = 1, if the individual is female or black), union coverage (UNION = 1, if the individual's wage is set by a union contract) and time dummies to capture productivity and price level effects.

Exercise 2.14 *(Mincer wage equation)*

(a) Obtain the OLS, FE, GLS, between and maximum likelihood estimators of this earnings equation.
(b) Compare the different estimates of the returns to schooling.
(c) Compute the F-statistic for the significance of the fixed individual effects described in Exercise 2.3.

Solution

(a) The Stata output for the various estimators is shown in Tables 2.6–2.10.
(b) The OLS estimator indicates that an additional year of schooling produces a 5.7% wage gain. The within transformation eliminates the individual effects and all the time-invariant variables including ED. The between estimator indicates that an additional year of schooling produces a 5.1% wage gain. This is compared to 10% for GLS and 13.6% for maximum likelihood.

Table 2.6 Mincer Wage Equation. OLS Results

```
**********OLS results*************************************************************
. reg lwage wks south smsa ms exp exp2 occ ind union fem blk ed

      Source |       SS       df       MS              Number of obs =    4165
-------------+------------------------------           F(12,  4152)  =  259.54
       Model |  380.139227    12  31.6782689           Prob > F      =  0.0000
    Residual |  506.765675  4152   .12205339           R-squared     =  0.4286
-------------+------------------------------           Adj R-squared =  0.4270
       Total |  886.904902  4164  .212993492           Root MSE      =  .34936
             |
-------------+----------------------------------------------------------------
       lwage |      Coef.   Std. Err.      t    P>|t|     [95% Conf. Interval]
-------------+----------------------------------------------------------------
         wks |   .0042161   .0010814     3.90   0.000      .002096    .0063361
       south |  -.0556374   .0125271    -4.44   0.000    -.0801972   -.0310775
        smsa |   .1516671   .0120687    12.57   0.000      .128006    .1753282
          ms |   .0484485   .0205687     2.36   0.019     .0081229    .0887741
         exp |   .0401046   .0021592    18.57   0.000     .0358715    .0443378
        exp2 |  -.0006734   .0000474   -14.19   0.000    -.0007664   -.0005804
         occ |  -.1400093   .0146567    -9.55   0.000    -.1687443   -.1112744
         ind |   .0467886   .0117935     3.97   0.000     .0236671    .0699102
       union |   .0926267   .0127995     7.24   0.000     .0675329    .1177206
         fem |  -.3677852   .0250971   -14.65   0.000    -.4169889   -.3185816
         blk |  -.1669376   .0220422    -7.57   0.000    -.2101521   -.1237231
          ed |   .0567042   .0026128    21.70   0.000     .0515817    .0618267
       _cons |   5.251124   .0712868    73.66   0.000     5.111363    5.390884
------------------------------------------------------------------------------
```

Table 2.7 Mincer Wage Equation. Fixed Effects Results

```
***************fixed effects estimates ****************************************
. xtreg lwage wks south smsa ms exp exp2 occ ind union,fe

Fixed-effects (within) regression               Number of obs      =      4165
Group variable (i): id                          Number of groups   =       595

R-sq:  within  = 0.6581                         Obs per group: min =         7
       between = 0.0261                                        avg =       7.0
       overall = 0.0461                                        max =         7

                                                F(9,3561)          =    761.75
corr(u_i, Xb)  = -0.9100                        Prob > F           =    0.0000

------------------------------------------------------------------------------
       lwage |      Coef.   Std. Err.       t    P>|t|     [95% Conf. Interval]
-------------+----------------------------------------------------------------
         wks |   .0008359   .0005997     1.39   0.163    -.0003398    .0020117
       south |  -.0018612   .0342993    -0.05   0.957    -.0691094     .065387
        smsa |  -.0424691   .0194284    -2.19   0.029     -.080561   -.0043773
          ms |  -.0297259   .0189836    -1.57   0.117    -.0669456    .0074939
         exp |   .1132083    .002471    45.81   0.000     .1083635    .1180531
        exp2 |  -.0004184   .0000546    -7.66   0.000    -.0005254   -.0003113
         occ |  -.0214765   .0137837    -1.56   0.119    -.0485012    .0055482
         ind |   .0192101   .0154463     1.24   0.214    -.0110744    .0494946
       union |   .0327849   .0149229     2.20   0.028     .0035266    .0620431
       _cons |   4.648767    .046022   101.01   0.000     4.558535    4.738999
-------------+----------------------------------------------------------------
     sigma_u |  1.0338102
     sigma_e |  .15199444
         rho |  .97884144   (fraction of variance due to u_i)
------------------------------------------------------------------------------
F test that all u_i=0:     F(594, 3561) =    38.25           Prob > F = 0.0000
```

Table 2.8 Mincer Wage Equation. Random Effects Results

```
*******************random effects estimates ********************************
. xtreg lwage wks south smsa ms exp exp2 occ ind union fem blk ed, re theta

Random-effects GLS regression                   Number of obs      =      4165
Group variable (i): id                          Number of groups   =       595

R-sq:  within  = 0.6124                         Obs per group: min =         7
       between = 0.2539                                        avg =       7.0
       overall = 0.2512                                        max =         7

Random effects u_i ~ Gaussian                   Wald chi2(12)      =   2654.74
corr(u_i, X)       = 0 (assumed)                Prob > chi2        =    0.0000
theta              = .78633141

------------------------------------------------------------------------------
       lwage |      Coef.   Std. Err.       z    P>|z|     [95% Conf. Interval]
-------------+----------------------------------------------------------------
         wks |   .0010347   .0007734     1.34   0.181    -.0004811    .0025505
       south |  -.0166176   .0265265    -0.63   0.531    -.0686086    .0353734
        smsa |  -.0138231   .0199927    -0.69   0.489    -.0530081    .0253619
          ms |  -.0746283   .0230052    -3.24   0.001    -.1197178   -.0295389
         exp |   .0820544   .0028478    28.81   0.000     .0764729    .0876359
        exp2 |  -.0008084   .0000628   -12.87   0.000    -.0009316   -.0006853
         occ |  -.0500664   .0166469    -3.01   0.003    -.0826937    -.017439
         ind |   .0037441   .0172618     0.22   0.828    -.0300883    .0375766
       union |   .0632232     .01707     3.70   0.000     .0297666    .0966798
         fem |  -.3392101   .0513033    -6.61   0.000    -.4397628   -.2386575
         blk |  -.2102803   .0579888    -3.63   0.000    -.3239363   -.0966243
          ed |   .0996585   .0057475    17.34   0.000     .0883937    .1109234
       _cons |    4.26367   .0977162    43.63   0.000      4.07215     4.45519
-------------+----------------------------------------------------------------
     sigma_u |  .26265814
     sigma_e |  .15199444
         rho |  .74913774   (fraction of variance due to u_i)
------------------------------------------------------------------------------
```

Table 2.9 Mincer Wage Equation. Between Results

```
. xtreg  lwage wks south smsa ms exp exp2 occ ind union fem blk ed, be

Between regression (regression on group means)  Number of obs      =      4165
Group variable: id                              Number of groups   =       595

R-sq:  within  = 0.0763                         Obs per group: min =         7
       between = 0.5443                                        avg =       7.0
       overall = 0.4173                                        max =         7

                                                F(12,582)          =     57.93
sd(u_i + avg(e_i.))=  .2688673                  Prob > F           =    0.0000

------------------------------------------------------------------------------
       lwage |      Coef.   Std. Err.      t    P>|t|     [95% Conf. Interval]
-------------+----------------------------------------------------------------
         wks |   .0091891   .0036044     2.55   0.011     .0021099    .0162683
       south |  -.0570535   .0259678    -2.20   0.028    -.1080556   -.0060515
        smsa |   .1757753   .0257568     6.82   0.000     .1251877    .2263629
          ms |   .1147817   .0476975     2.41   0.016     .0211015    .2084618
         exp |   .0319011   .0047769     6.68   0.000     .0225191    .0412831
        exp2 |  -.0005656   .0001049    -5.39   0.000    -.0007716   -.0003597
         occ |  -.1676197   .0338167    -4.96   0.000    -.2340373   -.1012022
         ind |   .0579175   .0255412     2.27   0.024     .0077534    .1080817
       union |   .1090687   .0292318     3.73   0.000     .0516559    .1664814
         fem |  -.3170612   .0547253    -5.79   0.000    -.4245443   -.2095781
         blk |  -.1578043   .0450119    -3.51   0.000    -.2462098   -.0693988
          ed |    .051436   .0055546     9.26   0.000     .0405265    .0623454
       _cons |   5.121431   .2042494    25.07   0.000     4.720275    5.522587
------------------------------------------------------------------------------
```

(c) The F-statistic for the significance of the individual effects is given at the bottom of the fixed effects regression as $F(594, 3561) = 38.25$ with a p-value of 0.0000 showing significance of the individual effects.

Table 2.10 Mincer Wage Equation. Maximum Likelihood Estimates

```
. xtreg  lwage wks south smsa ms exp exp2 occ ind union fem blk ed, mle

Random-effects ML regression                    Number of obs      =      4165
Group variable: id                              Number of groups   =       595

Random effects u_i ~ Gaussian                   Obs per group: min =         7
                                                               avg =       7.0
                                                               max =         7

                                                LR chi2(12)        =   2856.48
Log likelihood  =  307.87331                    Prob > chi2        =    0.0000

------------------------------------------------------------------------------
       lwage |      Coef.   Std. Err.      z    P>|z|     [95% Conf. Interval]
-------------+----------------------------------------------------------------
         wks |   .0008401   .0006039     1.39   0.164    -.0003435    .0020237
       south |   .0057702   .0315859     0.18   0.855    -.0561369    .0676774
        smsa |  -.0474777    .018957    -2.50   0.012    -.0846327   -.0103227
          ms |  -.0413826   .0189917    -2.18   0.029    -.0786056   -.0041596
         exp |   .1072079   .0024832    43.17   0.000      .102341    .1120748
        exp2 |  -.0005146   .0000545    -9.44   0.000    -.0006214   -.0004077
         occ |  -.0251183   .0137761    -1.82   0.068    -.0521189    .0018822
         ind |   .0137957   .0152879     0.90   0.367    -.0161681    .0437595
       union |   .0387287   .0148103     2.61   0.009      .009701    .0677565
         fem |  -.1756221   .1130883    -1.55   0.120    -.3972711     .046027
         blk |  -.2612074   .1374601    -1.90   0.057    -.5306244    .0082095
          ed |   .1356154   .0126737    10.70   0.000     .1107754    .1604554
       _cons |   3.126217   .1775977    17.60   0.000     2.778132    3.474302
-------------+----------------------------------------------------------------
    /sigma_u |   .8394941   .0276607                      .7869936    .8954969
    /sigma_e |   .1533452   .0018566                      .1497493    .1570276
         rho |   .9677113   .0022638                      .9630158    .9719034
------------------------------------------------------------------------------
Likelihood-ratio test of sigma_u=0: chibar2(01)= 3662.25 Prob>=chibar2 = 0.000
```

Exercise 2.15 *(Bounds for s^2 in a one-way random effects model).* This is based on Problem 2.14 in Baltagi (2008). For the random one-way error component model given in (2.1) and (2.2), consider the OLS estimator of $\text{var}(u_{it}) = \sigma^2$, which is given by $s^2 = \widehat{u}'_{\text{OLS}}\widehat{u}_{\text{OLS}}/(n-K')$, where $n = NT$ and $K' = K+1$.

(a) Show that $E(s^2) = \sigma^2 + \sigma_\mu^2[K' - \text{tr}(I_N \otimes J_T)P_x]/(n-K')$.

(b) Consider the inequalities given by Kiviet and Krämer (1992) which state that

$$0 \leqslant \text{mean of } (n-K') \text{ smallest roots of } \Omega \leqslant E(s^2)$$
$$\leqslant \text{mean of } (n-K') \text{ largest roots of } \Omega \leqslant \text{tr}(\Omega)/(n-K')$$

where $\Omega = E(uu')$. Show that for the one-way error component model, these bounds are

$$0 \leqslant \sigma_\nu^2 + (n-TK')\sigma_\mu^2/(n-K') \leqslant E(s^2) \leqslant \sigma_\nu^2 + n\sigma_\mu^2/(n-K')$$
$$\leqslant n\sigma^2/(n-K')$$

As $n \to \infty$, both bounds tend to σ^2, and s^2 is asymptotically unbiased, irrespective of the particular evolution of X.

Solution

(a) This solution is based on Baltagi and Krämer (1994). From (2.3), one gets $\widehat{\delta}_{\text{OLS}} = (Z'Z)^{-1}Z'y$ and $\widehat{u}_{\text{OLS}} = y - Z\widehat{\delta}_{\text{OLS}} = \overline{P}_Z u$, where $\overline{P}_Z = I_{NT} - P_Z$ with $P_Z = Z(Z'Z)^{-1}Z'$. Also, $E(s^2) = E[\widehat{u}'\widehat{u}/(NT - K')] = E[u'\overline{P}_Z u/(NT - K')] = \text{tr}(\Omega\overline{P}_Z)/(NT - K')$ which, from (2.9), reduces to

$$E(s^2) = \sigma_\nu^2 + \sigma_\mu^2(NT - \text{tr}(I_N \otimes J_T)P_Z)/(NT - K')$$

since $\text{tr}(I_{NT}) = \text{tr}(I_N \otimes J_T) = NT$ and $\text{tr}(P_Z) = K'$. By adding and subtracting σ_μ^2, one gets

$$E(s^2) = \sigma^2 + \sigma_\mu^2[K' - \text{tr}(I_N \otimes J_T)P_Z]/(NT - K')$$

where $\sigma^2 = E(u_{it}^2) = \sigma_\mu^2 + \sigma_\nu^2$ for all i and t.

(b) Nerlove (1971) derived the characteristic roots and vectors of Ω given in (2.9). These characteristic roots turn out to be σ_ν^2 with multiplicity $N(T-1)$ and $(T\sigma_\mu^2 + \sigma_\nu^2)$ with multiplicity N. Therefore, the smallest $(n - K')$ characteristic roots are made up of the $(n - N)\sigma_\nu^2$s and $N - K'$ of the $(T\sigma_\mu^2 + \sigma_\nu^2)$s. This implies that the mean of the $n - K'$ smallest characteristic roots of $\Omega = [(n - N)\sigma_\nu^2 + (N - K')(T\sigma_\mu^2 + \sigma_\nu^2)]/(n - K')$. Similarly, the largest $n - K'$ characteristic roots are made up of the $N(T\sigma_\mu^2 + \sigma_\nu^2)$s and $n - N - K'$ of the σ_ν^2s. This implies that the mean of the $n - K'$ largest characteristic roots of $\Omega = [N(T\sigma_\mu^2 + \sigma_\nu^2) + (n - N - K')\sigma_\nu^2]/(n - K')$. Using the Kiviet and Krämer (1992) inequalities, one gets

$$0 \leqslant \sigma_\nu^2 + (n - TK')\sigma_\mu^2/(n - K') \leqslant E(s^2) \leqslant \sigma_\nu^2 + n\sigma_\mu^2/(n - K') \leqslant n\sigma^2/(n - K')$$

As $n \to \infty$, both bounds tend to σ^2, and s^2 is asymptotically unbiased, irrespective of the particular evolution of X.

Exercise 2.16 *(Heteroskedastic fixed effects models).* This is based on Baltagi (1996) and is also Problem 2.17 in Baltagi (2008). Consider the fixed effects model

$$y_{it} = \alpha_i + u_{it}, \quad i = 1, 2, \ldots, N, \quad t = 1, 2, \ldots, T_i \tag{2.31}$$

where y_{it} denotes output in industry i at time t and α_i denotes the industry fixed effect. The disturbances u_{it} are assumed to be independent with heteroskedastic variances σ_i^2. Note that the data are unbalanced with different numbers of observations for each industry.

(a) Show that OLS and GLS estimates of α_i are identical.
(b) Let $\sigma^2 = \sum_{i=1}^N T_i\sigma_i^2/n$ be the average disturbance variance where $n = \sum_{i=1}^N T_i$. Show that the GLS estimator of σ^2 is unbiased, whereas the OLS estimator of σ^2 is biased. Also show that this bias disappears if the data are balanced or the variances are homoskedastic.

(c) Define $\lambda_i^2 = \sigma_i^2/\sigma^2$ for $i = 1, 2\ldots, N$. Show that for $\alpha' = (\alpha_1, \alpha_2, \ldots, \alpha_N)$,

$$\begin{aligned} &E[\text{estimated var}(\widehat{\alpha}_{\text{OLS}}) - \text{true var}(\widehat{\alpha}_{\text{OLS}})] \\ &= \sigma^2[(n - \textstyle\sum_{i=1}^{N} \lambda_i^2)/(n - N)] \, \text{diag}(1/T_i) - \sigma^2 \, \text{diag}(\lambda_i^2/T_i) \end{aligned} \tag{2.32}$$

This problem shows that if there are no regressors in the unbalanced panel data model, fixed effects with heteroskedastic disturbances can be estimated by OLS rather than GLS. However, one has to correct the standard errors computed by the OLS regression.

Solution

(a) The model can be written in matrix form as

$$y = X\alpha + \nu \tag{2.33}$$

where $y' = (y_{11}, \ldots, y_{1T_1}, \ldots, y_{N1}, \ldots, y_{NT_N})$, $X = \text{diag}(\iota_{T_i})$ with ι_{T_i} denoting a vector of ones of dimension T_i, $\alpha' = (\alpha_1, \ldots, \alpha_N)$ and $\nu' = (\nu_{11}, \ldots, \nu_{1T_1}, \ldots, \nu_{N1}, \ldots, \nu_{NT_N})$. Therefore,

$$\widehat{\alpha}_{\text{OLS}} = (X'X)^{-1}X'y = \text{diag}(\iota'_{T_i}/T_i)y = (\bar{y}_{1.}, \ldots, \bar{y}_{N.})' \tag{2.34}$$

where $\bar{y}_{i.} = \sum_{t=1}^{T_i} y_{it}/T_i$ for $i = 1, 2, \ldots, N$. Similarly, using the fact that $\text{var}(\nu) = \Sigma_\nu = \text{diag}(\sigma_i^2 I_{T_i})$, where I_{T_i} denotes an identity matrix of dimension T_i, one gets

$$\begin{aligned} \widehat{\alpha}_{\text{GLS}} &= [X' \, \text{diag}(I_{T_i}/\sigma_i^2)X]^{-1}[X' \, \text{diag}(I_{T_i}/\sigma_i^2)y] \\ &= \text{diag}(\sigma_i^2/T_i) \, \text{diag}(\iota'_{T_i}/\sigma_i^2)y = \text{diag}(\iota'_{T_i}/T_i)y = (\bar{y}_{1.}, \ldots, \bar{y}_{N.})' \end{aligned} \tag{2.35}$$

The Zyskind (1967) necessary and sufficient condition for OLS to be equivalent to GLS is that $P_X\Sigma_\nu = \Sigma_\nu P_X$, where $P_X = X(X'X)^{-1}X'$. In this case, $P_X = \text{diag}(J_{T_i}/T_i)$, where $J_{T_i} = \iota_{T_i}\iota'_{T_i}$. Hence,

$$\begin{aligned} P_X\Sigma_\nu &= \left[\text{diag}(\sigma_i^2 I_{T_i})\right]\left[\text{diag}(J_{T_i}/T_i)\right] = \text{diag}\left[\sigma_i^2(J_{T_i}/T_i)\right] \\ &= \left[\text{diag}(J_{T_i}/T_i)\right]\left[\text{diag}(\sigma_i^2 I_{T_i})\right] = \Sigma_\nu P_X \end{aligned} \tag{2.36}$$

(b) Note that $\Sigma_\nu = \sigma^2\Omega$ where $\Omega = \text{diag}(\lambda_i^2 I_{T_i})$. By defining σ^2 as an average variance of the disturbances, we have $\sigma^2 = \text{tr}(\Sigma_\nu)/n$. This also means that $\text{tr}(\Omega) = \sum_{i=1}^{N} \lambda_i^2 T_i = n$, which can also be verified using the fact that $\sigma_i^2 = \sigma^2\lambda_i^2$. The OLS estimator of σ^2 is given by $s^2 = e'e/(n - N)$, where e denotes the least squares residuals. This can be rewritten as $s^2 = y'Qy/(n - N)$, where

$$Q = I_n - X(X'X)^{-1}X' = \text{diag}(E_{T_i}) \tag{2.37}$$

with $E_{T_i} = I_{T_i} - \bar{J}_{T_i}$ and $\bar{J}_{T_i} = \iota_{T_i}\iota'_{T_i}/T_i$. Therefore $s^2 = \nu' Q\nu/(n - N)$ since $Qy = Q\nu$ from (2.33) using the fact that $QX = 0$. But

$$E(\nu' Q\nu) = \text{tr}\,(\Sigma_\nu Q) = \sigma^2\ \text{tr}(\Omega Q) = \sigma^2\ \text{tr}[\text{diag}(\lambda_i^2 E_{T_i})] \qquad (2.38)$$
$$= \sigma^2 \sum_{i=1}^{N} \lambda_i^2 (T_i - 1) = \sigma^2 \left(n - \sum_{i=1}^{N} \lambda_i^2\right)$$

Hence, $E(s^2) = \sigma^2(n - \sum_{i=1}^{N} \lambda_i^2)/(n - N)$, which in general is not equal to σ^2. If the data are balanced, so that $T_i = T$ for all $i = 1, 2, \ldots, N$, then $\sum_{i=1}^{N} \lambda_i^2 = N$ and $E(s^2) = \sigma^2$. Of course, this will also be true when the variances are homoskedastic, i.e., $\lambda_i^2 = 1$ for $i = 1, 2, \ldots, N$.

Similarly, the GLS estimator of σ^2 is given by $s_*^2 = e'_{\text{GLS}}\Omega^{-1}e_{\text{GLS}}/(n - N)$, where e_{GLS} denotes the GLS residuals. But GLS is identical to OLS and

$$s_*^2 = e'\Omega^{-1}e/(n - N) = y' Q\Omega^{-1} Qy/(n - N) = \nu' Q\Omega^{-1} Q\nu/(n - N) \qquad (2.39)$$

with $E(\nu' Q\Omega^{-1} Q\nu) = \sigma^2\text{tr}(\Omega Q\Omega^{-1} Q) = \sigma^2\text{tr}[\text{diag}(\lambda_i^2 E_{T_i})\ \text{diag}(E_{T_i}/\lambda_i^2)] = \sigma^2\text{tr}[\text{diag}(E_{T_i})] = \sigma^2(n - N)$. Hence, $E(s_*^2) = \sigma^2$.

(c) The *true* $\text{var}(\widehat{\alpha}_{\text{OLS}}) = (X'X)^{-1}(X'\Sigma_\nu X)(X'X)^{-1} = \sigma^2\text{diag}(1/T_i)\text{diag}(T_i\lambda_i^2)\ \text{diag}(1/T_i) = \sigma^2\text{diag}(\lambda_i^2/T_i)$. This is equal to $\text{var}(\widehat{\alpha}_{\text{GLS}}) = (X'\Sigma_\nu^{-1}X)^{-1}$ as it should be. However, the regression packages compute *estimated* $\text{var}(\widehat{\alpha}_{\text{OLS}}) = s^2(X'X)^{-1} = s^2\ \text{diag}(1/T_i)$. The resulting bias is therefore

$$E[\textit{estimated}\ \text{var}(\widehat{\alpha}_{\text{OLS}}) - \textit{true}\ \text{var}(\widehat{\alpha}_{\text{OLS}})] = \sigma^2 \left[\left(n - \sum_{i=1}^{N} \lambda_i^2\right)/(n - N)\right] \text{diag}(1/T_i)$$
$$-\sigma^2\ \text{diag}(\lambda_i^2/T_i)$$

This bias will be zero under homoskedasticity, i.e., for $\lambda_i^2 = 1$ for all $i = 1, 2, \ldots, N$. For the balanced case where $T_i = T$ for all $i = 1, 2, \ldots, N$, this bias reduces to $\sigma^2\ \text{diag}[(1 - \lambda_i^2)/T]$. Since $E(s^2) = \sigma^2$ for the balanced data case, the latter bias is totally due to using the wrong formula for $\text{var}(\widehat{\alpha}_{\text{OLS}})$. This is known as the direct bias. See also Kleiber (1997).

3

The Two-way Error Component Model

Wallace and Hussain (1969) considered the regression model given by (2.1), but with two-way error component disturbances:

$$u_{it} = \mu_i + \lambda_t + \nu_{it}, \qquad i = 1, \ldots, N, \qquad t = 1, \ldots, T \tag{3.1}$$

where μ_i denotes the unobservable individual effect, λ_t denotes the unobservable time effect and ν_{it} is the remainder stochastic disturbance term. Note that λ_t is individual-invariant and accounts for any time-specific effect that is not included in the regression. For example, it could account for strike year effects that disrupt production; oil embargo effects that disrupt the supply of oil and affect its price; Surgeon General reports on the ill-effects of smoking, or government laws restricting smoking in public places, all of which could affect consumption behavior. In vector form, (3.1) can be written as

$$u = Z_\mu \mu + Z_\lambda \lambda + \nu \tag{3.2}$$

where Z_μ, μ and ν were defined earlier in Chapter 2. We continue to stack the observations such that the slower index is over individuals and the faster index is over time. In this case, $Z_\lambda = \iota_N \otimes I_T$ where I_T is an identity matrix of dimension T, and ι_N is a vector of ones of dimension N. $\lambda' = (\lambda_1, \ldots, \lambda_T)$ is the vector of time effects. Z_λ, is a selector matrix of ones and zeros that pick up the time effects, or simply the matrix of time dummies.

3.1 THE TWO-WAY FIXED EFFECTS MODEL

If the μ_i and λ_t are assumed to be fixed parameters to be estimated and the remainder disturbances stochastic with $\nu_{it} \sim \text{IID}(0, \sigma_\nu^2)$, then (3.1) represents a two-way fixed effects error component model. The X_{it} are assumed independent of the ν_{it} for all i and t. One can substitute the disturbances given by (3.2) into (2.3) to get

$$y = \alpha \iota_{NT} + X\beta + Z_\mu \mu + Z_\lambda \lambda + \nu = Z\delta + Z_\mu \mu + Z_\lambda \lambda + \nu$$

and then perform LSDV to get estimates of α, β, μ and λ. Note that Z is $NT \times (K+1)$; Z_μ, the matrix of individual dummies, is $NT \times N$; and Z_λ, the matrix of time dummies, is $NT \times T$. If N or T is large, there will be too many dummy variables in the regression, $(N-1)+(T-1)$ of them, and this causes an enormous loss in degrees of freedom. In addition, this attenuates the problem of multicollinearity among the regressors. Rather than invert a large $(N+T+K-1)$ matrix, Exercise 3.1 shows that one can obtain the two-way fixed effects estimates of β by performing the following within transformation given by Wallace and Hussain (1969):

$$Q_\Delta = E_N \otimes E_T = I_N \otimes I_T - I_N \otimes \bar{J}_T - \bar{J}_N \otimes I_T + \bar{J}_N \otimes \bar{J}_T \tag{3.3}$$

This transformation 'sweeps' the μ_i and λ_t effects. In fact, $\widetilde{y} = Q_\Delta y$ has a typical element $\widetilde{y}_{it} = (y_{it} - \overline{y}_{i.} - \overline{y}_{.t} + \overline{y}_{..})$ where $\overline{y}_{..} = \sum_{i=1}^{N}\sum_{t=1}^{T} y_{it}/NT$, and one would perform the regression of $\widetilde{y} = Q_\Delta y$ on $\widetilde{X} = Q_\Delta X$ to get the within estimator $\widetilde{\beta} = (X'Q_\Delta X)^{-1}X'Q_\Delta y$.

Exercise 3.1 *(Two-way fixed effects regression).* This is based on Problem 3.1 in Baltagi (2008).

(a) Show that the projection matrix on Z_λ is the averaging matrix over individuals for each time period, call it P_{Z_λ}.

(b) Consider the panel regression model (2.3), with two-way error component disturbances defined in (3.2). Use the Frisch–Waugh–Lovell theorem described in Chapter 1 to prove that the within estimator is given by $\widetilde{\beta} = (X'Q_\Delta X)^{-1}X'Q_\Delta y$ with Q_Δ defined in (3.3). Hint: Use the result that if $\Delta = [X_1, X_2]$ then $P_\Delta = P_{X_1} + P_{[Q_{X_1}X_2]}$.

(c) *Within two-way is equivalent to two withins one-way*. This is based on Baltagi (1998). Show that the within two-way estimator of β can be obtained by applying two within (one-way) transformations. The first is the within transformation ignoring the time effects followed by the within transformation ignoring the individual effects. Show that the order of these two within (one-way) transformations is unimportant. Give an intuitive explanation for this result. See Li (1999).

Solution

(a) Note that $Z_\lambda' Z_\lambda = NI_T$ and $Z_\lambda Z_\lambda' = J_N \otimes I_T$, where J_N is a matrix of ones of dimension N. Hence, the projection on Z_λ is $P_{Z_\lambda} = Z_\lambda(Z_\lambda' Z_\lambda)^{-1}Z_\lambda' = \overline{J}_N \otimes I_T$, where $\overline{J}_N = J_N/N$. P_{Z_λ} is a matrix which averages the observation across individuals for each time period. The typical element of $P_{Z_\lambda}y$ is $\overline{y}_{.t} = \sum_{i=1}^{N} y_{it}/N$.

(b) This is a concise derivation of the Wallace and Hussain (1969) within transformation which was derived by 'trial, error and generalization'. Here $\Delta = [Z_\mu, Z_\lambda]$, where $Z_\mu = I_N \otimes \iota_T$ and $Z_\lambda = \iota_N \otimes I_T$. Using the hint, one gets

$$P_\Delta = P_{Z_\mu} + P_{[Q_{[Z_\mu]}Z_\lambda]} = P + P_{QZ_\lambda} = P + QZ_\lambda(Z_\lambda' QZ_\lambda)^{-1}Z_\lambda' Q$$

where $P = I_N \otimes \overline{J}_T$ and $Q = I_N \otimes E_T$. Using the fact that $QZ_\lambda = \iota_N \otimes E_T$, $Z_\lambda' QZ_\lambda = NE_T$, $(Z_\lambda' QZ_\lambda)^{-} = N^{-1}E_T$, one gets $P_{QZ_\lambda} = \overline{J}_N \otimes E_T$. Hence

$$P_\Delta = P + \overline{J}_N \otimes E_T$$

which means that

$$\begin{aligned} Q_\Delta &= I_{NT} - P_\Delta = Q - \overline{J}_N \otimes E_T \\ &= I_N \otimes E_T - \overline{J}_N \otimes E_T \\ &= E_N \otimes E_T \end{aligned}$$

as required. Note that the order does not matter, i.e., one could have orthogonalized on Z_λ. In fact,

$$P_\Delta = P_{Z_\lambda} + P_{[Q[Z_\lambda]Z_\mu]}$$

where $P_{Z_\lambda} = \bar{J}_N \otimes I_T$ and $Q_{Z_\lambda} = E_N \otimes I_T$. Using the fact that

$$Q_{[Z_\lambda]}Z_\mu = (E_N \otimes \iota_T)$$

$$Z'_\mu Q_{[Z_\lambda]}Z_\mu = TE_N, \qquad (Z'_\mu Q_{[Z_\lambda]}Z_\mu)^- = \frac{1}{T}E_N$$

one gets

$$P_{[Q[Z_\lambda]Z_\mu]} = E_N \otimes \bar{J}_T.$$

Hence,

$$P_\Delta = \bar{J}_N \otimes I_T + E_N \otimes \bar{J}_T$$

which means that

$$Q_\Delta = I_{NT} - P_\Delta = E_N \otimes I_T - E_N \otimes \bar{J}_T = E_N \otimes E_T$$

as required.

(c) The within one-way transformation ignoring the time effect is given by

$$Q_\mu = I_N \otimes E_T = I_N \otimes I_T - I_N \otimes \bar{J}_T$$

This transformation subtracts the individual means from each variable. The within one-way tranformation ignoring the individual effect is given by

$$Q_\lambda = E_N \otimes I_T = I_N \otimes I_T - \bar{J}_N \otimes I_T$$

This transformation subtacts the time means from each variable. The resulting regression, after the preceding two within one-way tranformations, is given by

$$Q_\lambda Q_\mu y = Q_\lambda Q_\mu X\beta + Q_\lambda Q_\mu \nu$$

The OLS estimator of β for the preceding regression, $\widetilde{\beta}$, is given by $\widetilde{\beta} = (X'Q'_\mu Q'_\lambda Q_\lambda Q_\mu X)^{-1}X'Q'_\mu Q'_\lambda Q_\lambda Q_\mu y$. By noting that $Q'_\mu = Q_\mu$, $Q'_\lambda = Q_\lambda$, and $Q_\lambda Q_\mu = (E_N \otimes I_T)(I_N \otimes E_T) = E_N \otimes E_T = Q_\Delta$, we have $\widetilde{\beta} = (X'Q_\Delta X)^{-1}X'Q_\Delta y = \widetilde{\beta}_W$; i.e., the within two-way transformation is equivalent to two within one-way transformations. Note that the order of these two within one-way tranformations is unimportant:

$$Q_\mu Q_\lambda = (I_N \otimes E_T)(E_N \otimes I_T) = E_N \otimes E_T = Q_\lambda Q_\mu$$

The typical element in the resulting regression after the within two-way tranformation is

$$(y_{it} - \bar{y}_{i.} - \bar{y}_{.t} + \bar{y}_{..}) = (X_{it} - \bar{X}_{i.} - \bar{X}_{.t} + \bar{X}_{..})'\beta + (\nu_{it} - \bar{\nu}_{i.} - \bar{\nu}_{.t} + \bar{\nu}_{..})$$

where $\bar{y}_{i.}$, $\bar{y}_{.t}$, and $\bar{y}_{..}$ denote the average over time, the average over individuals and the overall average, respectively. This follows from the fact that the transformation $I_N \otimes \bar{J}_T$ yields the average over time for each individual, the transformation $\bar{J}_N \otimes I_T$ yields the average over individuals for each time period and the transformation $\bar{J}_N \otimes \bar{J}_T$ yields the overall average. Now consider the two within one-way transformations. For the first one-way transformation given by Q_μ, the typical element in the resulting regression is

$$(y_{it} - \bar{y}_{i.}) = (X_{it} - \bar{X}_{i.})'\beta + (\nu_{it} - \bar{\nu}_{i.})$$

After applying the second within one-way transformation Q_λ to the preceding regression, the typical element of the resulting regression becomes

$$(y_{it} - \bar{y}_{i.} - \bar{y}_{.t} + \bar{y}_{..}) = (X_{it} - \bar{X}_{i.} - \bar{X}_{.t} + \bar{X}_{..})'\beta + (\nu_{it} - \bar{\nu}_{i.} - \bar{\nu}_{.t} + \bar{\nu}_{..})$$

which is the same as the typical element for the two-way within transformation.
Computational warning: As in the one-way model, s^2 from the regression obtained by premultiplying by Q_Δ has to be adjusted for loss of degrees of freedom. In this case, one divides by $(N-1)(T-1)-K$ and multiplies by $(NT-K)$ to get the proper degrees of freedom to compute the variance–covariance matrix of the within estimator.

3.2 THE TWO-WAY RANDOM EFFECTS MODEL

If $\mu_i \sim \text{IID}(0, \sigma_\mu^2)$, $\lambda_t \sim \text{IID}(0, \sigma_\lambda^2)$ and $\nu_{it} \sim \text{IID}(0, \sigma_\nu^2)$ independent of each other, then this is the two-way *random* effects model. In addition, X_{it} is independent of μ_i, λ_t and ν_{it} for all i and t.

Exercise 3.2 *(Variance–covariance matrix of the two-way random effects model).* This is based on Problem 3.3 in Baltagi (2008).

(a) Show that the random effects model yields homoskedastic variances, with $\text{var}(u_{it}) = \sigma_\mu^2 + \sigma_\lambda^2 + \sigma_\nu^2$ for all i and t, and $\text{cov}(u_{it}, u_{js}) = \sigma_\mu^2$, when $i = j$ and $s \neq t$; also $\text{cov}(u_{it}, u_{js}) = \sigma_\lambda^2$ when $s = t$ and $i \neq j$, and zero otherwise.
(b) Using (3.2), show that the variance–covariance matrix of u is given by

$$\Omega = E(uu') = \sigma_\mu^2(I_N \otimes J_T) + \sigma_\lambda^2(J_N \otimes I_T) + \sigma_\nu^2(I_N \otimes I_T)$$

(c) Derive Ω^{-1}, $\Omega^{-1/2}$ and, in general, Ω^r, where r is an arbitrary scalar.

Solution

(a) From (3.1), $u_{js} = \mu_j + \lambda_s + \nu_{js}$ and $\text{cov}(u_{it}, u_{js}) = E(\mu_i\mu_j) + E(\lambda_t\lambda_s) + E(\nu_{it}\nu_{js})$, using the fact that the expected value of the cross-products is zero, since μ_i, λ_t and ν_{it}

are independent of each other for all $i, j = 1, 2, \ldots N$; and $s, t = 1, 2, \ldots, T$. Hence, the disturbances are homoskedastic with $\text{var}(u_{it}) = \sigma_\mu^2 + \sigma_\lambda^2 + \sigma_\nu^2$ for all i and t,

$$\begin{aligned} \text{cov}(u_{it}, u_{js}) &= \sigma_\mu^2 \quad i = j, t \neq s \\ &= \sigma_\lambda^2 \quad i \neq j, t = s \end{aligned} \tag{3.4}$$

and zero otherwise. This means that the correlation coefficient

$$\begin{aligned} \text{correl}(u_{it}, u_{js}) &= \sigma_\mu^2/(\sigma_\mu^2 + \sigma_\lambda^2 + \sigma_\nu^2) \quad & i = j, t \neq s \\ &= \sigma_\lambda^2/(\sigma_\mu^2 + \sigma_\lambda^2 + \sigma_\nu^2) \quad & i \neq j, t = s \\ &= 1 & i = j, t = s \\ &= 0 & i \neq j, t \neq s \end{aligned} \tag{3.5}$$

(b) From (3.2), one can compute the variance–covariance matrix

$$\begin{aligned} \Omega = E(uu') &= Z_\mu E(\mu\mu')Z_\mu' + Z_\lambda E(\lambda\lambda')Z_\lambda' + \sigma_\nu^2 I_{NT} \\ &= \sigma_\mu^2(I_N \otimes J_T) + \sigma_\lambda^2(J_N \otimes I_T) + \sigma_\nu^2(I_N \otimes I_T) \end{aligned} \tag{3.6}$$

using the assumptions $E(\mu'\nu) = 0$, $E(\mu'\lambda) = 0$, $E(\lambda'\nu) = 0$, $E(\mu\mu') = \sigma_\mu^2 I_N$, $E(\lambda\lambda') = \sigma_\lambda^2 I_T$, and $E(\nu\nu') = \sigma_\nu^2 I_{NT}$.

(c) Using the Wansbeek and Kapteyn (1982) trick, we replace J_N by $N\bar{J}_N$, I_N by $E_N + \bar{J}_N$, J_T by $T\bar{J}_T$ and I_T by $E_T + \bar{J}_T$, and collect terms with the same matrices. This gives

$$\Omega = \sum_{i=1}^{4} \lambda_i Q_i \tag{3.7}$$

where $\lambda_1 = \sigma_\nu^2$, $\lambda_2 = T\sigma_\mu^2 + \sigma_\nu^2$, $\lambda_3 = N\sigma_\lambda^2 + \sigma_\nu^2$ and $\lambda_4 = T\sigma_\mu^2 + N\sigma_\lambda^2 + \sigma_\nu^2$. Correspondingly, $Q_1 = E_N \otimes E_T$, $Q_2 = E_N \otimes \bar{J}_T$, $Q_3 = \bar{J}_N \otimes E_T$ and $Q_4 = \bar{J}_N \otimes \bar{J}_T$. The λ_i are the distinct characteristic roots of Ω and the Q_i are the corresponding matrices of eigenprojectors. λ_1 is of multiplicity $(N-1)(T-1)$, λ_2 is of multiplicity $N-1$, λ_3 is of multiplicity $T-1$, and λ_4 is of multiplicity 1. Each Q_i is symmetric and idempotent ($Q_i^2 = Q_i$) with its rank equal to its trace. Moreover, the Q_i are pairwise orthogonal ($Q_i Q_j = 0$ for $i \neq j$) and sum to the identity matrix $\left(\sum_{i=1}^4 Q_i = I_{NT}\right)$. The advantages of this spectral decomposition are that

$$\Omega^r = \sum_{i=1}^{4} \lambda_i^r Q_i \tag{3.8}$$

where r is an arbitrary scalar. In fact, $\Omega\Omega^{-1} = \left(\sum_{i=1}^4 \lambda_i Q_i\right)\left(\sum_{i=1}^4 (1/\lambda_i) Q_i\right) = \sum_{i=1}^4 Q_i^2 = \sum_{i=1}^4 Q_i = I_{NT}$. Similarly, $\Omega^{-1/2} = \sum_{i=1}^4 (1/\lambda_i^{1/2}) Q_i$ with

$$\Omega^{-1/2}\Omega^{-1/2} = \sum_{i=1}^{4} (1/\lambda_i) Q_i^2 = \sum_{i=1}^{4} 1/\lambda_i Q_i = \Omega^{-1}$$

Exercise 3.3 *(Fuller and Battese (1973) transformation for the two-way random effects model).* This is based on Problem 3.3 in Baltagi (2008). Show that GLS on the two-way random effects model is equivalent to the regression of y^* on X^* and a constant, where $y^* = \sigma_\nu \Omega^{-1/2} y$ has a typical element given by

$$y^*_{it} = y_{it} - \theta_1 \bar{y}_{i.} - \theta_2 \bar{y}_{.t} + \theta_3 \bar{y}_{..} \tag{3.9}$$

where $\theta_1 = 1 - (\sigma_\nu/\lambda_2^{1/2})$, $\theta_2 = 1 - (\sigma_\nu/\lambda_3^{1/2})$ and $\theta_3 = \theta_1 + \theta_2 + (\sigma_\nu/\lambda_4^{1/2}) - 1$.

Solution

Fuller and Battese (1973) suggested premultiplying the regression equation by

$$\sigma_\nu \Omega^{-1/2} = \sum_{i=1}^{4} (\sigma_\nu/\lambda_i^{1/2}) Q_i \tag{3.10}$$

and performing OLS on the resulting transformed regression y^* on Z^*, where $y^* = \sigma_\nu \Omega^{-1/2} y$ and $Z^* = \sigma_\nu \Omega^{-1/2} Z$. Using (3.8), one gets

$$\begin{aligned} y^* = \sigma_\nu \Omega^{-1/2} y &= \sum_{i=1}^{4} \left(\sigma_\nu/\lambda_i^{1/2}\right) Q_i y \\ &= \left(y_{it} - \bar{y}_{i.} - \bar{y}_{.t} + \bar{y}_{..}\right) + \left(\sigma_\nu/\lambda_2^{1/2}\right)\left(\bar{y}_{i.} - \bar{y}_{..}\right) + \left(\sigma_\nu/\lambda_3^{1/2}\right)\left(\bar{y}_{.t} - \bar{y}_{..}\right) + \left(\sigma_\nu/\lambda_4^{1/2}\right)\bar{y}_{..} \\ &= y_{it} - \theta_1 \bar{y}_{i.} - \theta_2 \bar{y}_{.t} + \theta_3 \bar{y}_{..} \end{aligned}$$

with θ_1, θ_2 and θ_3 defined below (3.9).

The BQU estimators of the variance components arise naturally from the fact that $Q_i u \sim (0, \lambda_i Q_i)$. Hence,

$$\widehat{\lambda}_i = u' Q_i u / \text{tr}(Q_i) \tag{3.11}$$

is the BQU estimator of λ_i for $i = 1, 2, 3$ (see Balestra, 1973). These ANOVA estimators are minimum variance unbiased under normality of the disturbances (see Graybill, 1961).

Exercise 3.4 *(Unbiased estimates of the variance components: the two-way model).* Show that $\widehat{\lambda}_i$ is unbiased for λ_i for $i = 1, 2, 3$.

Solution

$$E(u' Q_i u) = E(\text{tr}(uu' Q_i)) = \text{tr}(E(uu') Q_i) = \text{tr}(\Omega Q_i)$$

From (3.7), $\Omega Q_i = \lambda_i Q_i$ since $Q_i Q_j = 0$ for $i \neq j$. Hence, from (3.11), $E(\widehat{\lambda}_i) = E(u' Q_i u)/\text{tr}(Q_i) = \text{tr}(\Omega Q_i)/\text{tr}(Q_i) = \text{tr}(\lambda_i Q_i)/\text{tr}(Q_i) = \lambda_i$ for $i = 1, 2, 3$.

As in the one-way error component model, the true disturbances are not known and therefore (3.11) is not feasible. Wallace and Hussain (1969) suggest substituting OLS residual $\widehat{u}_{\text{OLS}}$ instead of the true u. Amemiya (1971) shows that these estimators of the variance components have a different asymptotic distribution from that knowing the true disturbances. He suggests using fixed effects residuals instead of the OLS residuals. In this case $\widetilde{u} = y - \widetilde{\alpha}\iota_{NT} - X\widetilde{\beta}$, where $\widetilde{\alpha} = \overline{y}_{..} - \overline{X}'_{..}\widetilde{\beta}$ and $\overline{X}'_{..}$ is a $1 \times K$ vector of averages of all regressors. Substituting these $\widetilde{u}$ for u in (3.11), we get the Amemiya-type estimators of the variance components. Swamy and Arora (1972) suggest running three least squares regressions and estimating the variance components from the corresponding mean square errors of these regressions. The first regression corresponds to the within regression which transforms the original model by $Q_1 = E_N \otimes E_T$. This yields the following estimate of σ_ν^2:

$$\widehat{\widehat{\lambda}}_1 = \widehat{\widehat{\sigma}}_\nu^2 = [y'Q_1y - y'Q_1X(X'Q_1X)^{-1}X'Q_1y]/[(N-1)(T-1) - K] \tag{3.12}$$

The second regression is the between individuals regression which transforms the original model by $Q_2 = E_N \otimes \overline{J}_T$. This is equivalent to the regression of $(\overline{y}_{i.} - \overline{y}_{..})$ on $(\overline{X}_{i.} - \overline{X}_{..})$ and yields the following estimate of $\lambda_2 = T\sigma_\mu^2 + \sigma_\nu^2$:

$$\widehat{\widehat{\lambda}}_2 = [y'Q_2y - y'Q_2X(X'Q_2X)^{-1}X'Q_2y]/[(N-1) - K] \tag{3.13}$$

from which one obtains $\widehat{\widehat{\sigma}}_\mu^2 = (\widehat{\widehat{\lambda}}_2 - \widehat{\widehat{\sigma}}_\nu^2)/T$. The third regression is the between time-periods regression which transforms the original model by $Q_3 = \overline{J}_N \otimes E_T$. This is equivalent to the regression of $(\overline{y}_{.t} - \overline{y}_{..})$ on $(\overline{X}_{.t} - \overline{X}_{..})$ and yields the following estimate of $\lambda_3 = N\sigma_\lambda^2 + \sigma_\nu^2$:

$$\widehat{\widehat{\lambda}}_3 = [y'Q_3y - y'Q_3X(X'Q_3X)^{-1}X'Q_3y]/[(T-1) - K] \tag{3.14}$$

from which one obtains $\widehat{\widehat{\sigma}}_\lambda^2 = (\widehat{\widehat{\lambda}}_3 - \widehat{\widehat{\sigma}}_\nu^2)/N$.

Exercise 3.5 *(Feasible unbiased estimates of the variance components: the two-way model).* This is based on Problem 3.5 in Baltagi (2008). Show that $\widehat{\widehat{\lambda}}_i$ is unbiased for λ_i for $i = 1, 2, 3$.

Solution

$\widehat{\widehat{\lambda}}_i$ is the s^2 from the regression given by premultiplying (2.3) by Q_i adjusted for the proper degrees of freedom. In fact,

$$\widehat{\widehat{\lambda}}_i = y'Q_i[I_{NT} - P_{Q_iX}]Q_iy/[\text{tr}(Q_i) - K]$$

since $Q_i\iota_{NT} = 0$ and $P_{Q_iZ} = P_{Q_iX}$ for $i = 1, 2, 3$. Substituting $Q_iy = Q_iX\beta + Q_iu$ into $\widehat{\widehat{\lambda}}_i$ gives

$$\widehat{\widehat{\lambda}}_i = u'Q_i[I_{NT} - P_{Q_iX}]Q_iu/[\text{tr}(Q_i) - K]$$

with $Q_i u \sim (0, \lambda_i Q_i)$. Therefore,

$$E[u'Q_i(I_{NT} - P_{Q_iX})Q_iu] = E[\text{tr}\{Q_iu'uQ_i(I_{NT} - P_{Q_iX})\}]$$
$$= \lambda_i \ \text{tr}(Q_i - Q_iP_{Q_iX}) = \lambda_i[\text{tr}(Q_i) - K]$$

where the last equality follows from the fact that $Q_iP_{Q_iX} = P_{Q_iX}$. Also

$$\text{tr}(P_{Q_iX}) = \text{tr}(X'Q_iX)(X'Q_iX)^{-1} = \text{tr}(I_K) = K.$$

Hence, $E(\widehat{\widehat{\lambda}}_i) = \lambda_i$.

Stacking the three transformed regressions just performed yields

$$\begin{pmatrix} Q_1y \\ Q_2y \\ Q_3y \end{pmatrix} = \begin{pmatrix} Q_1X \\ Q_2X \\ Q_3X \end{pmatrix} \beta + \begin{pmatrix} Q_1u \\ Q_2u \\ Q_3u \end{pmatrix} \tag{3.15}$$

since $Q_i\iota_{NT} = 0$ for $i = 1, 2, 3$, and the transformed error has mean 0 and variance–covariance matrix given by $\text{diag}[\lambda_i Q_i]$ with $i = 1, 2, 3$.

Exercise 3.6 *(System estimation of the two-way model: OLS versus GLS).* This is based on Problem 3.4 in Baltagi (2008).

(a) Perform OLS on the system of equations of $3NT$ observations given in (3.15) and show that the resulting estimator of β is the same OLS estimator of β using (2.3).
(b) Perform GLS on the system of equations (3.15) and show that $\widehat{\beta}_{\text{GLS}}$ is the same GLS estimator of β using (2.3).
(c) Show that $\widehat{\beta}_{\text{GLS}}$ is a matrix weighted average of three estimators: the between time-periods estimator, the between individuals estimator, and the within estimator of β.
(d) What happens to the GLS estimator if $\sigma_\mu^2 = \sigma_\lambda^2 = 0$? or if T and $N \to \infty$?

Solution

(a) OLS on (3.15) yields

$$\widehat{\beta}_{\text{OLS}} = [X'(Q_1 + Q_2 + Q_3)X]^{-1}[X'(Q_1 + Q_2 + Q_3)y]$$

but

$$\sum_{i=1}^{4} Q_i = I_{NT}$$

therefore,

$$(Q_1 + Q_2 + Q_3) = I_{NT} - Q_4 = (I_{NT} - \overline{J}_{NT}).$$

Substituting this in $\widehat{\beta}_{\text{OLS}}$ gives the required result:

$$\widehat{\beta}_{\text{OLS}} = (X'(I_{NT} - \overline{J}_{NT})X)^{-1}X'(I_{NT} - \overline{J}_{NT})y$$

(b) GLS on (3.15) yields

$$\widehat{\beta}_{\mathrm{GLS}} = \left[(X'Q_1, X'Q_2, X'Q_3) \begin{bmatrix} \lambda_1 Q_1 & 0 & 0 \\ 0 & \lambda_2 Q_2 & 0 \\ 0 & 0 & \lambda_3 Q_3 \end{bmatrix}^{-1} \begin{pmatrix} Q_1 X \\ Q_2 X \\ Q_3 X \end{pmatrix} \right]^{-1}$$

$$\times \left[(X'Q_1, X'Q_2, X'Q_3) \begin{bmatrix} \lambda_1 Q_1 & 0 & 0 \\ 0 & \lambda_2 Q_2 & 0 \\ 0 & 0 & \lambda_3 Q_3 \end{bmatrix}^{-1} \begin{pmatrix} Q_1 y \\ Q_2 y \\ Q_3 y \end{pmatrix} \right]$$

Using the generalized inverse

$$(\mathrm{diag}[\lambda_i Q_i])^{-1} = \mathrm{diag}[Q_i/\lambda_i]$$

one gets

$$\widehat{\beta}_{\mathrm{GLS}} = \left(\sum_{i=1}^{3} (X'Q_i X)/\lambda_i \right)^{-1} \left(\sum_{i=1}^{3} (X'Q_i y)/\lambda_i \right)$$

which is the GLS estimator of β from (2.3).

(c) $\widehat{\beta}_{\mathrm{GLS}}$ can be rewritten as

$$\begin{aligned} \widehat{\beta}_{\mathrm{GLS}} &= [(X'Q_1X)/\sigma_\nu^2 + (X'Q_2X)/\lambda_2 + (X'Q_3X)/\lambda_3]^{-1} \\ &\quad \times [(X'Q_1y)/\sigma_\nu^2 + (X'Q_2y)/\lambda_2 + (X'Q_3y)/\lambda_3] \\ &= [W_{XX} + \phi_2^2 B_{XX} + \phi_3^2 C_{XX}]^{-1}[W_{Xy} + \phi_2^2 B_{Xy} + \phi_3^2 C_{Xy}] \end{aligned} \tag{3.16}$$

with $\mathrm{var}(\widehat{\beta}_{\mathrm{GLS}}) = \sigma_\nu^2[W_{XX} + \phi_2^2 B_{XX} + \phi_3^2 C_{XX}]^{-1}$. Note that $W_{XX} = X'Q_1X$, $B_{XX} = X'Q_2X$ and $C_{XX} = X'Q_3X$ with $\phi_2^2 = \sigma_\nu^2/\lambda_2$, $\phi_3^2 = \sigma_\nu^2/\lambda_3$. Also, the within estimator of β is $\widetilde{\beta}_W = W_{XX}^{-1}W_{Xy}$, the between individuals estimator of β is $\widehat{\beta}_B = B_{XX}^{-1}B_{Xy}$ and the between time-periods estimator of β is $\widehat{\beta}_C = C_{XX}^{-1}C_{Xy}$. This shows that $\widehat{\beta}_{\mathrm{GLS}}$ is a matrix-weighted average of $\widetilde{\beta}_W$, $\widehat{\beta}_B$ and $\widehat{\beta}_C$. In fact,

$$\widehat{\beta}_{\mathrm{GLS}} = W_1\widetilde{\beta}_W + W_2\widehat{\beta}_B + W_3\widehat{\beta}_C \tag{3.17}$$

where

$$\begin{aligned} W_1 &= [W_{XX} + \phi_2^2 B_{XX} + \phi_3^2 C_{XX}]^{-1} W_{XX} \\ W_2 &= [W_{XX} + \phi_2^2 B_{XX} + \phi_3^2 C_{XX}]^{-1}(\phi_2^2 B_{XX}) \\ W_3 &= [W_{XX} + \phi_2^2 B_{XX} + \phi_3^2 C_{XX}]^{-1}(\phi_3^2 C_{XX}) \end{aligned}$$

This was demonstrated by Maddala (1971).

(d) Note that (i) if $\sigma_\mu^2 = \sigma_\lambda^2 = 0$, then $\phi_2^2 = \phi_3^2 = 1$ and $\widehat{\beta}_{\mathrm{GLS}}$ reduces to $\widehat{\beta}_{\mathrm{OLS}}$, and (ii) if T and $N \to \infty$, then ϕ_2^2 and $\phi_3^2 \to 0$ and $\widehat{\beta}_{\mathrm{GLS}}$ tends to $\widetilde{\beta}_{\mathrm{W}}$.

Exercise 3.7 *(Prediction in the two-way random effects model).* This is based on Problem 3.7 in Baltagi (2008). What is the best linear unbiased predictor of $y_{i,T+S}$ for the ith individual, S periods ahead for the two-way error component regression model?

Solution

From (3.1), for period $T + S$,

$$u_{i,T+S} = \mu_i + \lambda_{T+S} + \nu_{i,T+S} \tag{3.18}$$

and

$$\begin{aligned} E(u_{i,T+S}u_{jt}) &= \sigma_\mu^2 \quad \text{for } i = j \\ &= 0 \quad \text{for } i \neq j \end{aligned} \tag{3.19}$$

for $t = 1, 2, \ldots, T$ and $S > 0$. The only correlation over time occurs because of the presence of the same individual across the panel. The λ_t and ν_{it} are not correlated for different time periods. In vector form,

$$w = E(u_{i,T+S}u) = \sigma_\mu^2(l_i \otimes \iota_T)$$

just like the one-way error component model (see Exercise 2.13), where l_i is the ith column of I_N. However, Ω^{-1} is given by (3.8), and

$$w'\Omega^{-1} = \sigma_\mu^2(l_i' \otimes \iota_T')\left[\sum_{i=1}^{4}\frac{1}{\lambda_i}Q_i\right] \tag{3.20}$$

Using the fact that

$$\begin{aligned} (l_i' \otimes \iota_T')Q_1 &= (l_i' \otimes \iota_T')(E_N \otimes E_T) = 0 \\ (l_i' \otimes \iota_T')Q_3 &= (l_i' \otimes \iota_T')(\bar{J}_N \otimes E_T) = 0, \text{ since } \iota_T'E_T = 0 \\ (l_i' \otimes \iota_T')Q_4 &= (l_i' \otimes \iota_T')(\bar{J}_N \otimes \bar{J}_T) = (\iota_N' \otimes \iota_T')/N = \iota_{NT}'/N \\ (l_i' \otimes \iota_T')Q_2 &= (l_i' \otimes \iota_T')(E_N \otimes \bar{J}_T) = (l_i' \otimes \iota_T') - \iota_{NT}'/N \end{aligned} \tag{3.21}$$

one gets

$$w'\Omega^{-1} = \frac{\sigma_\mu^2}{\lambda_2}[(l_i' \otimes \iota_T') - \iota_{NT}'/N] + \frac{\sigma_\mu^2}{\lambda_4}(\iota_{NT}'/N) \tag{3.22}$$

Therefore, the typical element of $w'\Omega^{-1}\widehat{u}_{\text{GLS}}$ where $\widehat{u}_{\text{GLS}} = y - Z\widehat{\delta}_{\text{GLS}}$ is

$$\frac{T\sigma_\mu^2}{T\sigma_\mu^2 + \sigma_\nu^2}(\bar{\widehat{u}}_{i.,\text{GLS}} - \bar{\widehat{u}}_{..,\text{GLS}}) + \frac{T\sigma_\mu^2}{T\sigma_\mu^2 + N\sigma_\lambda^2 + \sigma_\nu^2}\bar{\widehat{u}}_{..,\text{GLS}} \tag{3.23}$$

or

$$\frac{T\sigma_\mu^2}{T\sigma_\mu^2+\sigma_\nu^2}\bar{\widehat{u}}_{i.,\text{GLS}}+T\sigma_\mu^2\left[\frac{1}{\lambda_4}-\frac{1}{\lambda_2}\right]\bar{\widehat{u}}_{..,\text{GLS}}$$

where $\bar{\widehat{u}}_{i.,\text{GLS}}=\sum_{t=1}^{T}\widehat{u}_{it,\text{GLS}}/T$ and $\bar{\widehat{u}}_{..,\text{GLS}}=\sum_{i=1}^{N}\sum_{t=1}^{T}\widehat{u}_{it,\text{GLS}}/NT$. See Baltagi (1988a) and Koning (1989). In general, $\bar{\widehat{u}}_{..,\text{GLS}}$ is not necessarily zero. The GLS normal equations are $Z'\Omega^{-1}\widehat{u}_{\text{GLS}}=0$. However, if Z contains a constant, then $\iota_{NT}'\Omega^{-1}\widehat{u}_{\text{GLS}}=0$. Using the expression for Ω^{-1} in (3.8), one gets $\iota_{NT}'\Omega^{-1}=\sum_{i=1}^{4}\frac{1}{\lambda_i}\iota_{NT}'Q_i=\frac{1}{\lambda_4}\iota_{NT}'$ since $\iota_{NT}'Q_i=0$ for $i=1,2,3$. This is clear from the definitions of the Q_i given below (3.7). Hence, $\iota_{NT}'\Omega^{-1}\widehat{u}_{\text{GLS}}=\frac{1}{\lambda_4}\iota_{NT}'\widehat{u}_{\text{GLS}}=\frac{1}{\lambda_4}\sum_{i=1}^{N}\sum_{t=1}^{T}\widehat{u}_{it,\text{GLS}}=0$ which means that $\bar{\widehat{u}}_{..,\text{GLS}}=0$. Therefore, for the two-way model, if there is a constant in the model, the BLUP for $y_{i,T+S}$ corrects the GLS prediction by a fraction of the mean of the GLS residuals corresponding to that ith individual

$$\widehat{y}_{i,T+S}=Z_{i,T+S}'\widehat{\delta}_{\text{GLS}}+\left(\frac{T\sigma_\mu^2}{T\sigma_\mu^2+\sigma_\nu^2}\right)\bar{\widehat{u}}_{i.,\text{GLS}} \tag{3.24}$$

This looks exactly like the BLUP for the one-way model but with a different GLS estimator based on a different Ω. If there is no constant in the model, the last term in (3.24) should be replaced by (3.23).

Exercise 3.8 *(Variance component estimation under misspecification).* This is based on Baltagi and Li (1991c) and is also Problem 3.12 in Baltagi (2008). This problem investigates the consequences of under- or overspecifying the error component model on the variance component estimates. Since the one-way and two-way error component models are popular in economics, we focus on the following two cases:

(1) *Underspecification*: In this case, the true model is two-way, given by (3.1), while the estimated model is one-way, given by (2.2), with $\mu_i\sim\text{IID}(0,\sigma_\mu^2)$, $\lambda_t\sim\text{IID}(0,\sigma_\lambda^2)$, $\nu_{it}\sim\text{IID}(0,\sigma_\nu^2)$ independent of each other and among themselves.
   - (a) Knowing the true disturbances (u_{it}), show that the BQU estimator of σ_ν^2 for the misspecified one-way model is biased upwards, while that of σ_μ^2 remains unbiased.
   - (b) Show that if the u_{it} are replaced by the one-way LSDV residuals, the variance component estimate of σ_ν^2 given in part (a) is inconsistent, while that of σ_μ^2 is consistent.

(2) *Overspecification*: In this case, the true model is one-way, given by (2.2), while the estimated model is two-way, given by (3.1).
   - (c) Knowing the true disturbances (u_{it}), show that the BQU estimators of σ_μ^2, σ_λ^2 and σ_ν^2 for the misspecified two-way model remain unbiased.
   - (d) Show that if the u_{it} are replaced by the two-way (LSDV) residuals, the variance components estimates given in part (c) remain consistent.

Solution

This is based on Baltagi and Li (1992a).

(a) The BQU estimators of the variance components for the one-way model are given by (2.13):

$$\widehat{\sigma}_\nu^2 = \frac{u'(I_N \otimes E_T)u}{N(T-1)} \tag{3.25}$$

$$\widehat{\sigma}_1^2 = \frac{u'(I_N \otimes \overline{J}_T)u}{N} \tag{3.26}$$

where $\sigma_1^2 = T\sigma_\mu^2 + \sigma_\nu^2$ and $u' = (u_{11}, \ldots, u_{1T}, \ldots, u_{N1}, \ldots, u_{NT})$ is the vector of known disturbances. I_N is an identity matrix of dimension N, $\overline{J}_T = J_T/T$ where J_T is a matrix of ones of dimension T and $E_T = I_T - \overline{J}_T$. For the two-way model, Ω is given by (3.6),

$$\Omega = \sigma_\nu^2 I_{NT} + \sigma_\mu^2(I_N \otimes J_T) + \sigma_\lambda^2(J_N \otimes I_T)$$

Using the fact that E_T and $\overline{J}_T$ are idempotent and $\overline{J}_T E_T = 0$, one gets

$$\begin{aligned} E(\widehat{\sigma}_\nu^2) &= \text{tr}[\Omega(I_N \otimes E_T)/N(T-1)] \\ &= \frac{1}{N(T-1)}\text{tr}[\sigma_\nu^2(I_N \otimes E_T) + \sigma_\lambda^2(J_N \otimes E_T)] = \sigma_\nu^2 + \sigma_\lambda^2 \end{aligned}$$

which is biased upwards by σ_λ^2. Similarly,

$$E(\widehat{\sigma}_1^2) = \text{tr}[\Omega(I_N \otimes \overline{J}_T)/N] = \sigma_\nu^2 + T\sigma_\mu^2 + \sigma_\lambda^2$$

which is also biased upwards by σ_λ^2. Now, $\widehat{\sigma}_\mu^2 = (\widehat{\sigma}_1^2 - \widehat{\sigma}_\nu^2)/T$. Taking expected values and substituting $E(\widehat{\sigma}_1^2)$ and $E(\widehat{\sigma}_\nu^2)$, we get $E(\widehat{\sigma}_\mu^2) = \sigma_\mu^2$.

(b) For the regression model $y = X\beta + u$, where X is $NT \times K$, the one-way LSDV residuals are given by $\widetilde{u} = y - X\widetilde{\beta}$, where $\widetilde{\beta} = (X'QX)^{-1}X'Qy$ with $Q = I_N \otimes E_T$. This can also be written as $\widetilde{u} = Mu$, where $M = I - X(X'QX)^{-1}X'Q$. In this case, substituting $\widetilde{u}$ in (3.25), we get

$$\widetilde{\sigma}_\nu^2 = \frac{\widetilde{u}'Q\widetilde{u}}{N(T-1)} = \frac{u'MQMu}{N(T-1)} = \frac{u'Qu}{N(T-1)} - \frac{u'QX(X'QX)^{-1}X'Qu}{N(T-1)}$$

Using the fact that $Q\Omega Q = Q\Omega = \sigma_\nu^2 Q + N\sigma_\lambda^2(\overline{J}_N \otimes E_T)$ and plim$[X'QX/NT]$, plim$[X'X/NT]$ are finite positive definite as N and T both $\to \infty$, we get

$$\text{plim}\frac{u'Qu}{N(T-1)} = \lim \frac{\text{tr}(Q\Omega)}{N(T-1)} = \sigma_\nu^2 + \sigma_\lambda^2$$

and

$$\text{plim}\frac{u'QX(X'QX)^{-1}X'Qu}{N(T-1)} = \lim \frac{\text{tr}(X'Q\Omega QX)(X'QX)^{-1}}{N(T-1)}$$

$$= \lim \frac{\sigma_\nu^2 K}{N(T-1)} + \lim \frac{\sigma_\lambda^2}{(T-1)} \text{ tr}\left[\frac{X'(\overline{J}_N \otimes E_T)X}{NT}\right]\left[\frac{X'QX}{NT}\right]^{-1} = 0$$

Hence,

$$\text{plim}\widetilde{\sigma}_\nu^2 = \sigma_\nu^2 + \sigma_\lambda^2$$

Similarly, substituting $\widetilde{u}$ in (3.26), we get

$$\widetilde{\sigma}_\mu^2 = \frac{\widetilde{u}'(I_N \otimes \overline{J}_T)\widetilde{u}}{NT} - \frac{\widetilde{\sigma}_\nu^2}{T}$$

Therefore,

$$\text{plim } \widetilde{\sigma}_\mu^2 = \text{plim}\frac{u'M'(I_N \otimes \overline{J}_T)Mu}{NT} = \lim \frac{\text{tr}[M\Omega M'(I_N \otimes \overline{J}_T)]}{NT}$$

Using the fact that $Q\Omega(I_N \otimes \overline{J}_T) = 0$, one gets

$$\text{plim } \widetilde{\sigma}_\mu^2 = \lim \frac{\text{tr}[\Omega(I_N \otimes \overline{J}_T)]}{NT} + \lim \frac{\text{tr}[X'Q\Omega QX(X'QX)^{-1}X'(I_N \otimes \overline{J}_T)X(X'QX)^{-1}]}{NT}$$

$$= \sigma_\mu^2$$

(c) The BQU estimators for the two-way model are given by (3.11):

$$\widehat{\sigma}_\nu^2 = \frac{u'(E_N \otimes E_T)u}{(N-1)(T-1)} \tag{3.27}$$

$$\widehat{\sigma}_1^2 = \frac{u'(E_N \otimes \overline{J}_T)u}{(N-1)} \tag{3.28}$$

and

$$\widehat{\sigma}_2^2 = \frac{u'(\overline{J}_N \otimes E_T)u}{(T-1)} \tag{3.29}$$

where $\sigma_1^2 = T\sigma_\mu^2 + \sigma_\nu^2$ and $\sigma_2^2 = N\sigma_\lambda^2 + \sigma_\nu^2$. The variance–covariance matrix for the one-way model is given by (2.9),

$$\Omega = E(uu') = \sigma_\nu^2 I_{NT} + \sigma_\mu^2(I_N \otimes J_T)$$

Therefore,

$$E(\widehat{\sigma}_\nu^2) = \text{tr}[\Omega(E_N \otimes E_T)]/(N-1)(T-1) = \sigma_\nu^2$$

Similarly,

$$E(\widehat{\sigma}_1^2) = \text{tr}[\Omega(E_N \otimes \overline{J}_T)]/(N-1) = T\sigma_\mu^2 + \sigma_\nu^2 = \sigma_1^2$$

and

$$E(\widehat{\sigma}_2^2) = \text{tr}[\Omega(\overline{J}_N \otimes E_T)]/(T-1) = \sigma_\nu^2$$

Now $\widehat{\sigma}_\mu^2 = (\widehat{\sigma}_1^2 - \widehat{\sigma}_\nu^2)/T$. Taking expected values and substituting $E(\widehat{\sigma}_1^2)$ and $E(\widehat{\sigma}_\nu^2)$ gives $E(\widehat{\sigma}_\mu^2) = \sigma_\mu^2$. Similarly, $\widehat{\sigma}_\lambda^2 = (\widehat{\sigma}_2^2 - \widehat{\sigma}_\nu^2)/N$. Taking expected values and substituting $E(\widehat{\sigma}_2^2)$ and $E(\widehat{\sigma}_\nu^2)$, we get $E(\widehat{\sigma}_\lambda^2) = 0$. Hence, $\widehat{\sigma}_\mu^2$, $\widehat{\sigma}_\lambda^2$ and $\widehat{\sigma}_\nu^2$ remain unbiased for an overspecified model.

(d) The two-way LSDV residuals are given by $\widetilde{u} = Mu$ where $M = I - X(X'QX)^{-1}X'Q$ with $Q = E_N \otimes E_T$. In this case, substituting $\widetilde{u}$ in (3.27) and taking plim give

$$\text{plim}\ \widetilde{\sigma}_\nu^2 = \text{plim}\ \widetilde{u}'(E_N \otimes E_T)\widetilde{u}/(N-1)(T-1) = \lim\ \text{tr}[\Omega M'QM/(N-1)(T-1)]$$

Using the fact that $Q\Omega Q = \Omega Q = \sigma_\nu^2 Q$, we get

$$\text{plim}\ \widetilde{\sigma}_\nu^2 = \lim \frac{\text{tr}(\Omega Q)}{(N-1)(T-1)} - \lim \sigma_\nu^2 \frac{\text{tr}(X'QX)(X'QX)^{-1}}{(N-1)(T-1)} = \sigma_\nu^2$$

Similarly, substituting $\widetilde{u}$ in (3.28), we get

$$\widetilde{\sigma}_\mu^2 = \frac{1}{T}\left[\frac{\widetilde{u}'\overline{A}\widetilde{u}}{N-1}\right] - \frac{\widetilde{\sigma}_\nu^2}{T}$$

where $\overline{A} = E_N \otimes \overline{J}_T$. Hence,

$$\text{plim}\ \widetilde{\sigma}_\mu^2 = \text{plim} \frac{u'M'\overline{A}Mu}{T(N-1)}$$

Using the fact that $\Omega\overline{A} = \sigma_\nu^2\overline{A} + \sigma_\mu^2 E_N \otimes J_T$ and $Q\overline{A} = 0$, we get

$$\text{plim}\ \widetilde{\sigma}_\mu^2 = \lim \frac{\text{tr}(\Omega\overline{A})}{(N-1)T} + \lim \frac{\text{tr}(X'Q\Omega QX)(X'QX)^{-1}(X'\overline{A}X)(X'QX)^{-1}}{(N-1)T}$$
$$= \sigma_\mu^2$$

Finally, substituting $\widetilde{u}$ in (3.29), we get

$$\widetilde{\sigma}_\lambda^2 = \frac{\widetilde{u}'\overline{B}\widetilde{u}}{N(T-1)} - \frac{\widetilde{\sigma}_\nu^2}{N}$$

where

$$\overline{B} = \overline{J}_N \otimes E_T$$

Hence,

$$\text{plim } \widetilde{\sigma}_\lambda^2 = \text{plim } \frac{u'M\overline{B}Mu}{N(T-1)}$$

Using the fact that $\overline{B}\Omega = \sigma_\nu^2 \overline{B}$ and $\overline{B}Q = 0$, we get

$$\text{plim } \widetilde{\sigma}_\lambda^2 = \lim \text{tr} \frac{(\overline{B}\Omega)}{N(T-1)} + \lim \text{ tr} \frac{(X'Q\Omega QX)(X'QX)^{-1}(X'\overline{B}X)(X'QX)^{-1}}{N(T-1)} = 0$$

Hence, all estimators of the variance components are consistent for the overspecified model.

Exercise 3.9 *(Bounds for s^2, in a two-way random effects model).* This is based on Problem 3.13 in Baltagi (2008). For the random two-way error component model described by (2.1) and (3.1), consider the OLS estimator of $\text{var}(u_{it}) = \sigma^2$, which is given by $s^2 = \widehat{u}'_{\text{OLS}}\widehat{u}_{\text{OLS}}/(n-K')$, where $n = NT$ and $K' = K+1$.

(a) Show that

$$E(s^2) = \sigma^2 - \sigma_\mu^2[\text{tr}(I_N \otimes J_T)P_x - K']/(n-K') \tag{3.30}$$
$$-\sigma_\lambda^2[\text{tr}(J_N \otimes I_T)P_x - K']/(n-K')$$

(b) Consider the inequalities given by Kiviet and Krämer (1992) which are reproduced in Exercise 2.15, part (b). Show that for the two-way error component model, these bounds are given by the following two cases:
(1) For $T\sigma_\mu^2 < N\sigma_\lambda^2$,

$$0 \leqslant \sigma_\nu^2 + \sigma_\mu^2(n-T)/(n-K') + \sigma_\lambda^2(n-NK')/(n-K') \leqslant E(s^2)$$
$$\leqslant \sigma_\nu^2 + \sigma_\mu^2[n/(n-K')] + \sigma_\lambda^2[n/(n-K')] \leqslant \sigma^2[n/(n-K')]$$

(2) For $T\sigma_\mu^2 > N\sigma_\lambda^2$,

$$0 \leqslant \sigma_\nu^2 + \sigma_\mu^2(n-TK')/(n-K') + \sigma_\lambda^2(n-N)/(n-K') \leqslant E(s^2)$$
$$\leqslant \sigma_\nu^2 + \sigma_\mu^2[n/(n-K')] + \sigma_\lambda^2[n/(n-K')] \leqslant \sigma^2[n/(n-K')]$$

In either case, as $n \to \infty$, both bounds tend to σ^2 and s^2 is asymptotically unbiased, irrespective of the particular evolution of X.

Solution

(a) This solution is based on Baltagi and Krämer (1994). Using the same approach in the solution to Exercise 2.15, we get $E(s^2) = \text{tr}(\Omega \overline{P}_Z)/(NT - K')$.

Using (3.4), it is easy to show that

$$\text{tr}(\Omega \overline{P}_Z) = \sigma_\mu^2 \,\text{tr}(I_N \otimes J_T)\overline{P}_Z + \sigma_\lambda^2 \,\text{tr}(J_N \otimes I_T)\overline{P}_Z + \sigma_\nu^2 \,\text{tr}(\overline{P}_Z)$$

This reduces to

$$\text{tr}(\Omega \overline{P}_Z) = \sigma_\nu^2(n - K') + \sigma_\mu^2(n - \text{tr}(I_N \otimes J_T)P_Z) + \sigma_\lambda^2[n - \text{tr}(J_N \otimes I_T)P_Z]$$

Since $\text{tr}(\overline{P}_Z) = n - K'$, $\text{tr}(I_N \otimes J_T) = \text{tr}(J_N \otimes I_T) = n$. Adding and subtracting $K'\sigma_\mu^2 + K'\sigma_\lambda^2$ and dividing by $(n - K')$ gives the required result

$$E(s^2) = \sigma^2 - \sigma_\mu^2[\text{tr}(I_N \otimes J_T)P_Z - K']/(n - K')$$
$$-\sigma_\lambda^2[\text{tr}(J_N \otimes I_T)P_Z - K']/(n - K')$$

where $\sigma^2 = E(u_{it}^2) = \sigma_\mu^2 + \sigma_\lambda^2 + \sigma_\nu^2$ for all i and t.

(b) Nerlove (1971) showed that the characteristic roots and vectors of Ω are given by σ_ν^2 with multiplicity $(N-1)(T-1)$; $T\sigma_\mu^2 + \sigma_\nu^2$ with multiplicity $N - 1$; $N\sigma_\lambda^2 + \sigma_\nu^2$ with multiplicity $T - 1$; and $T\sigma_\mu^2 + N\sigma_\lambda^2 + \sigma_\nu^2$ with multiplicity 1. Therefore, if $T\sigma_\mu^2 < N\sigma_\lambda^2$, then the smallest $(n - K')$ characteristic roots are made up of the $(NT - N - T + 1)\sigma_\nu^2$s, the $(N-1)(T\sigma_\mu^2 + \sigma_\nu^2)$s and $(T - K')(N\sigma_\mu^2 + \sigma_\nu^2)$s. These average to $\sigma_\nu^2 + \sigma_\mu^2(n - T)/(n - K') + \sigma_\lambda^2(n - NK')/(n - K')$. Similarly, the largest $(n - K')$ characteristic roots are made up of one $(T\sigma_\mu^2 + N\sigma_\lambda^2 + \sigma_\nu^2)$, $(T-1)(N\sigma_\lambda^2 + \sigma_\nu^2)$s, $(N-1)(T\sigma_\mu^2 + \sigma_\nu^2)$s and $[(N-1)(T-1) - K']\sigma_\nu^2$s. These average to $\sigma_\nu^2 + \sigma_\mu^2[n/(n - K')] + \sigma_\lambda^2[n/(n - K')]$. These are the required bounds for the Kiviet and Krämer (1992) inequalities. If $T\sigma_\mu^2 > N\sigma_\lambda^2$, then the ordering of the characteristic roots changes, but the analysis is still the same and will lead to the same upper bound but a different lower bound. As $n \to \infty$, all bounds tend to σ^2, and s^2 is asymptotically unbiased.

Exercise 3.10 *(Nested effects).* This is based on Baltagi (1993) and is also Problem 3.14 in Baltagi (2008). In many economic applications, the data may contain nested groupings. For example, data on firms may be grouped by industry, data on states by region, and data on individuals by profession. In this case, one can control for unobserved industry and firm effects using a nested error component model. Consider the regression equation

$$y_{ijt} = x'_{ijt}\beta + u_{ijt}, \quad \text{for } i = 1, \ldots, M, \quad j = 1, \ldots, N, \quad t = 1, 2, \ldots, T \tag{3.31}$$

where y_{ijt} could denote the output of the jth firm in the ith industry for the tth time period. x_{ijt} denotes a vector of k inputs, and the disturbance is given by

$$u_{ijt} = \mu_i + \nu_{ij} + \varepsilon_{ijt} \tag{3.32}$$

where $\mu_i \sim \text{IID}(0, \sigma_\mu^2)$, $\nu_{ij} \sim \text{IID}(0, \sigma_\nu^2)$, and $\varepsilon_{ijt} \sim \text{IID}(0, \sigma_\varepsilon^2)$, independent of each other and among themselves. This assumes that there are M industries with N firms in each industry observed over T periods.

(a) Derive $\Omega = E(uu')$ and obtain $\Omega^{-1}$and $\Omega^{-1/2}$.
(b) Show that $y^* = \sigma_\varepsilon \Omega^{-1/2} y$ has a typical element

$$y_{ijt}^* = (y_{ijt} - \theta_1 \bar{y}_{ij.} + \theta_2 \bar{y}_{i..})$$

where $\theta_1 = 1 - (\sigma_\varepsilon/\sigma_1)$ with $\sigma_1^2 = (T\sigma_\nu^2 + \sigma_\varepsilon^2)$; $\theta_2 = (\sigma_\varepsilon/\sigma_2) - (\sigma_\varepsilon/\sigma_1)$ with $\sigma_2^2 = (NT\sigma_\mu^2 + T\sigma_\nu^2 + \sigma_\varepsilon^2)$; $\bar{y}_{ij.} = \sum_{t=1}^T y_{ijt}/T$; and $\bar{y}_{i..} = \sum_{j=1}^N \sum_{t=1}^T y_{ijt}/NT$. See Xiong (1995).

Solution

(a) If we arrange the data in vector form such that i is the slowest running index, followed by j with t being the fastest running index, then

$$u' = (u_{111}, u_{112}, \ldots, u_{11T}, u_{121}, u_{122}, \ldots, u_{12T}, \ldots, u_{1N1}, \ldots,$$
$$u_{1NT}, \ldots, u_{MN1}, \ldots, u_{MNT})$$

and the model in vector form is given by

$$y = X\beta + u$$

with

$$u = (I_M \otimes \iota_N \otimes \iota_T)\mu + (I_M \otimes I_N \otimes \iota_T)\nu + (I_M \otimes I_N \otimes I_T)\varepsilon \tag{3.33}$$

where $\mu' = (\mu_1, \ldots, \mu_M)$, $\nu' = (\nu_{11}, \nu_{12}, \ldots, \nu_{1N}, \ldots, \nu_{M1}, \nu_{M2}, \ldots, \nu_{MN})$, and ε, y and X follow the same ordering as u. Of course x'_{ijt} is the ijtth row of X. I_M denotes an identity matrix of dimension M and ι_T denotes a vector of ones of dimension T. In this case

$$\Omega = E(uu') = \sigma_\mu^2(I_M \otimes J_N \otimes J_T) + \sigma_\nu^2(I_M \otimes I_N \otimes J_T) + \sigma_\varepsilon^2(I_M \otimes I_N \otimes I_T) \tag{3.34}$$

since $\mu \sim (0, \sigma_\mu^2 I_M)$, $\nu \sim (0, \sigma_\nu^2 I_{MN})$ and $\varepsilon \sim (0, \sigma_\varepsilon^2 I_{MNT})$. $J_N = \iota_N \iota_N'$ is a matrix of ones of dimension N. Defining $\bar{J}_N = J_N/N$ and $E_N = I_N - \bar{J}_N$, both of which are idempotent matrices that sum to I_N, one can use the Wansbeek and Kapteyn (1982) trick to obtain the spectral decomposition of Ω. In essence, one replaces J_N by $N\bar{J}_N$ and I_N by $E_N + \bar{J}_N$ to get

$$\Omega = NT\sigma_\mu^2(I_N \otimes \bar{J}_N \otimes \bar{J}_T) + T\sigma_\nu^2(I_M \otimes (E_N + \bar{J}_N) \otimes \bar{J}_T) + \sigma_\varepsilon^2(I_M \otimes (E_N + \bar{J}_N)$$
$$\otimes (E_T + \bar{J}_T))$$

Collecting like terms gives the spectral decomposition of Ω,

$$\Omega = (NT\sigma_\mu^2 + T\sigma_\nu^2 + \sigma_\varepsilon^2)(I_M \otimes \overline{J}_N \otimes \overline{J}_T) + (T\sigma_\nu^2 + \sigma_\varepsilon^2)(I_M \otimes E_N \otimes \overline{J}_T)$$
$$+\sigma_\varepsilon^2(I_M \otimes I_N \otimes E_T)$$

In this case

$$\Omega^{-1} = (NT\sigma_\mu^2 + T\sigma_\nu^2 + \sigma_\varepsilon^2)^{-1}(I_M \otimes \overline{J}_N \otimes \overline{J}_T) + (T\sigma_\nu^2 + \sigma_\varepsilon^2)^{-1}(I_M \otimes E_N \otimes \overline{J}_T)$$
$$+(\sigma_\varepsilon^2)^{-1}(I_M \otimes I_N \otimes E_T)$$

and

$$\Omega^{-1/2} = (NT\sigma_\mu^2 + T\sigma_\nu^2 + \sigma_\varepsilon^2)^{-1/2}(I_M \otimes \overline{J}_N \otimes \overline{J}_T) + (T\sigma_\nu^2 + \sigma_\varepsilon^2)^{-1/2}$$
$$(I_M \otimes E_N \otimes \overline{J}_T) + (\sigma_\varepsilon^2)^{-1/2}(I_M \otimes I_N \otimes E_T)$$

(b) Multiplying by σ_ε and collecting terms gives

$$\sigma_\varepsilon\Omega^{-1/2} = I_{MNT} - (1 - \sigma_\varepsilon/\sigma_1)(I_M \otimes I_N \otimes \overline{J}_T) + ((\sigma_\varepsilon/\sigma_1) + (\sigma_\varepsilon/\sigma_2))$$
$$(I_M \otimes \overline{J}_N \otimes \overline{J}_T)$$

Therefore, $y^* = \sigma_\varepsilon\Omega^{-1/2}y$ has typical element

$$y_{ijt}^* = (y_{ijt} - \theta_1\overline{y}_{ij.} + \theta_2\overline{y}_{i..})$$

as described in the text of the problem.

Exercise 3.11 *(Three-way error component model).* This is based on Problem 3.15 in Baltagi (2008), based in turn on Baltagi (1987). Ghosh (1976) considered the three-way error component model

$$u_{itq} = \mu_i + \lambda_t + \eta_q + \nu_{itq} \tag{3.35}$$

where $i = 1, \ldots, N$, $T = 1, \ldots, T$, and $q = 1, \ldots, M$. Ghosh (1976) argued that in international or interregional studies, there might be two rather than one cross-sectional components; for example, i might denote countries and q might be regions within each country. These four *independent* components are assumed to be random with $\mu_i \sim \text{IID}(0, \sigma_\mu^2)$, $\lambda_t \sim \text{IID}(0, \sigma_\lambda^2)$, $\eta_q \sim \text{IID}(0, \sigma_\eta^2)$, and $\nu_{itq} \sim \text{IID}(0, \sigma_\nu^2)$. Ghosh ordered the observations such that the fastest index is q, while the slowest index is t, so that

$$u' = (u_{111}, \ldots, u_{11M}, u_{121}, \ldots, u_{12M}, \ldots, u_{1N1}, \ldots,$$
$$u_{1NM}, \ldots, u_{T11}, \ldots, u_{T1M}, \ldots, u_{TN1}, \ldots, u_{TNM})$$

(a) Show that the error has mean zero and variance–covariance matrix

$$\Omega = E(uu') = \sigma_\nu^2(I_T \otimes I_N \otimes I_M) + \sigma_\lambda^2(I_T \otimes J_N \otimes J_M) \\ +\sigma_\mu^2(J_T \otimes I_N \otimes J_M) + \sigma_\eta^2(J_T \otimes J_N \otimes I_M) \quad (3.36)$$

(b) Using the Wansbeek and Kapteyn (1982) trick, show that $\Omega = \sum_{j=1}^{5} \xi_j V_j$, where $\xi_1 = \sigma_\nu^2$, $\xi_2 = NM\sigma_\lambda^2 + \sigma_\nu^2$, $\xi_3 = TM\sigma_\mu^2 + \sigma_\nu^2$, $\xi_4 = NT\sigma_\eta^2 + \sigma_\nu^2$ and $\xi_5 = NM\sigma_\lambda^2 + TM\sigma_\mu^2 + NT\sigma_\eta^2 + \sigma_\nu^2$. Also

$$\begin{aligned} V_1 &= I_T \otimes I_N \otimes I_M - I_T \otimes \bar{J}_N \otimes \bar{J}_M - \bar{J}_T \otimes I_N \otimes \bar{J}_M \\ &\quad -\bar{J}_T \otimes \bar{J}_N \otimes I_M + 2\bar{J}_T \otimes \bar{J}_N \otimes \bar{J}_M \\ V_2 &= E_T \otimes \bar{J}_N \otimes \bar{J}_M, \quad \text{where } E_T = I_T - \bar{J}_T \\ V_3 &= \bar{J}_T \otimes E_N \otimes \bar{J}_M \\ V_4 &= \bar{J}_T \otimes \bar{J}_N \otimes E_M \\ V_5 &= \bar{J}_T \otimes \bar{J}_N \otimes \bar{J}_M \end{aligned} \quad (3.37)$$

are all symmetric, idempotent and sum to the identity matrix.

(c) Conclude that $\Omega^{-1} = \sum_{j=1}^{5}(1/\xi_j)V_j$ and $\sigma_\nu\Omega^{-1/2} = \sum_{j=1}^{5}(\sigma_\nu/\sqrt{\xi_j})V_j$ with the typical element of $\sigma_\nu\Omega^{-1/2}y$ being

$$y_{tiq} - \theta_1\bar{y}_{t..} - \theta_2\bar{y}_{.i.} - \theta_3\bar{y}_{..q} - \theta_4\bar{y}_{...}$$

where the dot indicates a sum over that index and a bar means an average. Here, $\theta_j = 1 - \sigma_\nu/\sqrt{\xi_{j+1}}$ for $j = 1, 2, 3$ while $\theta_4 = \theta_1 + \theta_2 + \theta_3 - 1 + (\sigma_\nu/\sqrt{\xi_5})$.

(d) Show that the BQU estimator of ξ_j is given by $u'V_ju/\text{tr}(V_j)$ for $j = 1, 2, 3, 4$. Show that BQU estimators of $\sigma_\nu^2, \sigma_\mu^2, \sigma_\eta^2$ and σ_λ^2 can be obtained using the one-to-one correspondence between the ξ_j and σ^2s.

Davis (2002) gives an elegant generalization to the multi-way unbalanced error component model.

Solution

(a) The disturbances can be written in vector form as

$$u = (\iota_T \otimes I_N \otimes \iota_M)\mu + (I_T \otimes \iota_N \otimes \iota_M)\lambda + (\iota_T \otimes \iota_N \otimes I_M)\eta \\ +(I_T \otimes I_N \otimes I_M)\nu$$

where $\mu' = (\mu_1, \ldots, \mu_N)$, $\lambda' = (\lambda_1, \ldots, \lambda_T)$, $\eta' = (\eta_1, \ldots, \eta_M)$, and

$$\nu' = (\nu_{111}, \ldots, \nu_{11M}, \nu_{121}, \ldots, \nu_{12M}, \ldots, \nu_{1N1}, \ldots, \\ \nu_{1NM}, \ldots, \nu_{T11}, \ldots, \nu_{T1M}, \ldots, \nu_{TN1}, \ldots, \nu_{TNM})$$

all independent of each other and among themselves with zero means and variances in $\sigma_\mu^2 I_N$, $\sigma_\lambda^2 I_T$, $\sigma_\eta^2 I_M$ and $\sigma_\nu^2 I_{TNM}$, respectively. In this case

$$\begin{aligned}\Omega = E(uu') &= (\iota_T \otimes I_N \otimes \iota_M)E(\mu\mu')(\iota_T' \otimes I_N \otimes \iota_M')\\ &+(I_T \otimes \iota_N \otimes \iota_M)E(\lambda\lambda')(I_T \otimes \iota_N' \otimes \iota_M')\\ &+(\iota_T \otimes \iota_N \otimes I_M)E(\eta\eta')(\iota_T' \otimes \iota_N' \otimes I_M) + E(\nu\nu')\\ &= \sigma_\mu^2(J_T \otimes I_N \otimes J_M) + \sigma_\lambda^2(I_T \otimes J_N \otimes J_M) + \sigma_\eta^2(J_T \otimes J_N \otimes I_M)\\ &+\sigma_\nu^2(I_T \otimes I_N \otimes I_M)\end{aligned}$$

(b) Using the Wansbeek and Kapteyn (1982) trick, we replace J_s by $s\bar{J}_s$, where $\bar{J}_s = J_s/s$. Also replace I_s by $E_s + \bar{J}_s$, where $E_s = I_s - \bar{J}_s$ for $s = T, N$ and M. We get

$$\begin{aligned}\Omega &= MT\sigma_\mu^2(\bar{J}_T \otimes (E_N + \bar{J}_N) \otimes \bar{J}_M) + NM\sigma_\lambda^2((E_T + \bar{J}_T) \otimes \bar{J}_N \otimes \bar{J}_M)\\ &+TN\sigma_\eta^2(\bar{J}_T \otimes \bar{J}_N \otimes (E_M + \bar{J}_M)) + \sigma_\nu^2((E_T + \bar{J}_T) \otimes (E_N + \bar{J}_N) \otimes (E_M + \bar{J}_M))\end{aligned}$$

Collecting like terms,

$$\begin{aligned}\Omega &= (MT\sigma_\mu^2 + \sigma_\nu^2)(\bar{J}_T \otimes E_N \otimes \bar{J}_M) + (NM\sigma_\lambda^2 + \sigma_\nu^2)(E_T \otimes \bar{J}_N \otimes \bar{J}_M)\\ &+(TN\sigma_\eta^2 + \sigma_\nu^2)(\bar{J}_T \otimes \bar{J}_N \otimes E_M)\\ &+\sigma_\nu^2[(E_T \otimes E_N \otimes E_M) + (E_T \otimes E_N \otimes \bar{J}_M) + (E_T \otimes \bar{J}_N \otimes E_M)\\ &+(\bar{J}_T \otimes E_N \otimes E_M)] + (MT\sigma_\mu^2 + NM\sigma_\lambda^2 + TN\sigma_\eta^2 + \sigma_\nu^2)(\bar{J}_T \otimes \bar{J}_N \otimes \bar{J}_M)\\ &= \sum_{j=1}^{5} \xi_j V_j\end{aligned}$$

Only V_1 needs an explanation. This is the fourth term corresponding to σ_ν^2. By adding the first two terms and expanding the third term in that expression, we get $E_T \otimes E_N \otimes I_M + E_T \otimes \bar{J}_N \otimes I_M - E_T \otimes \bar{J}_N \otimes \bar{J}_M + \bar{J}_T \otimes E_N \otimes E_M$. Adding the first two terms and replacing E_s by $I_s + \bar{J}_s$ for $s = T, N$ and M yields

$$\begin{aligned}&I_T \otimes I_N \otimes I_M - \bar{J}_T \otimes I_N \otimes I_M - I_T \otimes \bar{J}_N \otimes \bar{J}_M + \bar{J}_T \otimes \bar{J}_N \otimes \bar{J}_M\\ &+\bar{J}_T \otimes I_N \otimes I_M - \bar{J}_T \otimes I_N \otimes \bar{J}_M - \bar{J}_T \otimes \bar{J}_N \otimes I_M + \bar{J}_T \otimes \bar{J}_N \otimes \bar{J}_M\end{aligned}$$

Canceling the second and fifth terms and combining the fourth and eighth terms yields V_1.

(c) Note that all the V_j are made up of $\bar{J}_s$ and E_s, so they are all symmetric and idempotent. In fact, these V_j are pairwise orthogonal to each other as $E_s\bar{J}_s = 0$ and they sum to the identity matrix. Hence, Ω^{-1} and $\Omega^{-1/2}$ are as given with $\sigma_\nu\Omega^{-1/2} = \sum_{j=1}^{5}(\sigma_\nu/\sqrt{\xi_j})V_j$. Therefore,

$$\sigma_\nu\Omega^{-1/2}y = V_1 y + (\sigma_\nu/\xi_2)V_2 y + (\sigma_\nu/\xi_3)V_3 y + (\sigma_\nu/\xi_4)V_4 y + (\sigma_\nu/\xi_5)V_5 y$$

Replacing E_s by $\overline{J}_s + I_s$ for $s = N, T$ and M and collecting like terms, we get

$$\sigma_\nu \Omega^{-1/2} y = y - \theta_1 (I_T \otimes \overline{J}_N \otimes \overline{J}_M) y - \theta_2 (\overline{J}_T \otimes I_N \otimes \overline{J}_M) y$$
$$-\theta_3 (\overline{J}_T \otimes \overline{J}_N \otimes I_M) y - \theta_4 (\overline{J}_T \otimes \overline{J}_N \otimes \overline{J}_M) y$$

where θ_j is as defined for $j = 1, 2, 3, 4$. Hence, the typical element of $\sigma \Omega^{-1/2} y$ is given by

$$y_{tiq} - \theta_1 \overline{y}_{t..} - \theta_2 \overline{y}_{.i.} - \theta_3 \overline{y}_{..q} - \theta_4 \overline{y}_{...}$$

as required.

(d) Given the spectral decomposition of Ω, the BQU estimates of the corresponding characteristic roots ξ_j are given by $u'V_j u/\text{tr}(V_j)$ for $j = 1, 2, 3, 4$, and ξ_5 has no unbiased estimator (see Balestra, 1973). The BQU estimates of $\sigma_\nu^2, \sigma_\mu^2, \sigma_\eta^2$ and σ_λ^2 can be obtained from the one-to-one correspondence between the ξ_j and the σ^2s described in part (b) of the problem. Feasible estimates of the variance components can be obtained by replacing the true disturbances by OLS residuals as in Wallace and Hussain (1969) or fixed effects residuals as in Amemiya (1971).

Exercise 3.12 *(A mixed error component model).* This is based on Baltagi and Krämer (1995) and is also Problem 3.16 in Baltagi (2008). Consider the panel data regression equation with a two-way mixed error component model described by (3.1) where the individual-specific effects are assumed to be random, with $\mu_i \sim (0, \sigma_\mu^2)$ and $\nu_{it} \sim (0, \sigma_\nu^2)$ independent of each other and among themselves. The time-specific effects, i.e., the λ_t, are assumed to be fixed parameters to be estimated. In vector form, this can be written as

$$y = X\beta + Z_\lambda \lambda + w \tag{3.38}$$

where $Z_\lambda = \iota_N \otimes I_T$, and

$$w = Z_\mu \mu + \nu \tag{3.39}$$

with $Z_\mu = I_N \otimes \iota_T$. Applying the FWL theorem yields

$$Q_\lambda y = Q_\lambda X\beta + Q_\lambda w \tag{3.40}$$

where $Q_\lambda = E_N \otimes I_T$ with $E_N = I_N - \overline{J}_N$ and $\overline{J}_N = \iota_N \iota_N'/N$. This is the familiar within time-effects transformation, with the typical element of $Q_\lambda y$ being $y_{it} - \overline{y}_{.t}$ and $\overline{y}_{.t} = \sum_{i=1}^N y_{it}/N$. Let $\Omega = E(ww')$; this is the familiar one-way error component variance–covariance matrix given in (2.8).

(a) Show that GLS estimator of β obtained from (3.38) by premultiplying by $\Omega^{-1/2}$ first and then applying the FWL theorem yields the same estimator as GLS on (3.40) using the generalized inverse of $Q_\lambda \Omega Q_\lambda$. This is a special case of a more general result proved by Fiebig *et al.* (1996).

(b) Show that pseudo-GLS on (3.40) using Ω rather than $Q_\lambda \Omega Q_\lambda$ for the variance of the disturbances yields the same estimator of β as found in part (a). In general, pseudo-GLS may not be the same as GLS, but Fiebig *et al.* (1996) provided a necessary and sufficient condition for this equivalence that is easy to check in this case. In fact, this amounts to checking whether $X'Q_\lambda \Omega^{-1} Z_\lambda = 0$.

For computational purposes, these results imply that one can perform the within time-effects transformation to wipe out the matrix of time dummies and then do the usual Fuller and Battese (1973) transformation without worrying about the loss in efficiency of not using the proper variance–covariance matrix of the transformed disturbances.

Solution

This is based on Xiong (1996a).

(a) From (2.9) and (2.10) one can deduce that $\Omega = E(ww') = \sigma_\nu^2 Q_\mu + \sigma_1^2 P_\mu$, where $P_\mu = I_N \otimes \overline{J}_T$, $Q_\mu = I_{NT} - P_\mu = I_N \otimes E_T$ and $\sigma_1^2 = T\sigma_\mu^2 + \sigma_\nu^2$. Also, $\Omega^{-1/2} = Q_\mu/\sigma_\nu + P_\mu/\sigma_1$ (see (2.12)). Premultiplying the regression model (3.38) by $\Omega^{-1/2}$ and using the Frisch–Waugh theorem yields

$$\widehat{\beta}_{\text{GLS}} = (X'\Omega^{-1/2} M \Omega^{-1/2} X)^{-1} X'\Omega^{-1/2} M \Omega^{-1/2} y \tag{3.41}$$

where $M = I_{NT} - \Omega^{-1/2} Z_\lambda (Z_\lambda' \Omega^{-1} Z_\lambda)^{-1} Z_\lambda' \Omega^{-1/2}$. Now

$$\Omega^{-1/2} Z_\lambda = (\iota_N \otimes E_T)/\sigma_\nu + (\iota_N \otimes \overline{J}_T)/\sigma_1 \tag{3.42}$$

and $Z_\lambda' \Omega^{-1} Z_\lambda = N(E_T/\sigma_\nu^2 + \overline{J}_T/\sigma_1^2)$ with $(Z_\lambda' \Omega^{-1} Z_\lambda)^{-1} = (\sigma_\nu^2 E_T + \sigma_1^2 \overline{J}_T)/N$. Therefore, it can easily be verified that

$$\begin{aligned} \Omega^{-1/2} M \Omega^{-1/2} &= \Omega^{-1} - \Omega^{-1} Z_\lambda (Z_\lambda' \Omega^{-1} Z_\lambda)^{-1} Z_\lambda' \Omega^{-1} \\ &= (E_N \otimes E_T)/\sigma_\nu^2 + (E_N \otimes \overline{J}_T)/\sigma_1^2 \end{aligned} \tag{3.43}$$

Substituting (3.43) in (3.41) yields $\widehat{\beta}_{\text{GLS}}$. We have to show that this is equivalent to performing GLS on (3.40), i.e.,

$$\widehat{\beta}_2 = (X'Q_\lambda (Q_\lambda \Omega Q_\lambda)^- Q_\lambda X)^{-1} X'Q_\lambda (Q_\lambda \Omega Q_\lambda)^- Q_\lambda y \tag{3.44}$$

Now

$$Q_\lambda \Omega Q_\lambda = \sigma_\nu^2 Q_\lambda Q_\mu Q_\lambda + \sigma_1^2 Q_\lambda P_\mu Q_\lambda = \sigma_\nu^2 (E_N \otimes E_T) + \sigma_1^2 (E_N \otimes \overline{J}_T)$$

and the Moore–Penrose generalized inverse can be easily verified to be

$$(Q_\lambda \Omega Q_\lambda)^- = (E_N \otimes E_T)/\sigma_\nu^2 + (E_N \otimes \overline{J}_T)/\sigma_1^2 \tag{3.45}$$

Hence,

$$Q_\lambda (Q_\lambda \Omega Q_\lambda)^- Q_\lambda = (E_N \otimes E_T)/\sigma_\nu^2 + (E_N \otimes \overline{J}_T)/\sigma_1^2 \tag{3.46}$$

Substituting (3.46) in (3.44) yields $\widehat{\beta}_2 = \widehat{\beta}_{\text{GLS}}$.

(b) Now GLS on (3.40) using Ω rather than $Q_\lambda \Omega Q_\lambda$ yields the pseudo-GLS estimator

$$\widetilde{\beta} = (X'Q_\lambda \Omega^{-1} Q_\lambda X)^{-1} X' Q_\lambda \Omega^{-1} Q_\lambda y \tag{3.47}$$

It is simple to show that

$$Q_\lambda \Omega^{-1} Q_\lambda = Q_\lambda Q_\mu Q_\lambda/\sigma_\nu^2 + Q_\lambda P_\mu Q_\lambda/\sigma_1^2 = (E_N \otimes E_T)/\sigma_\nu^2 + (E_N \otimes \overline{J}_T)/\sigma_1^2$$

which is the same expression in (3.43) and (3.46). Hence, $\widetilde{\beta} = \widehat{\beta}_2 = \widehat{\beta}_{\text{GLS}}$. Note that the necessary and sufficient condition derived in Fiebig *et al.* (1996) for the equality of $\widetilde{\beta} = \widehat{\beta}_{\text{GLS}}$ can be verified as follows:

$$\begin{aligned} X'Q_\lambda \Omega^{-1} Z_\lambda &= X'(Q_\lambda Q_\mu Z_\lambda/\sigma_\nu^2 + Q_\lambda P_\mu Z_\lambda/\sigma_1^2) \\ &= X'(E_N \iota_N \otimes E_T/\sigma_\nu^2 + E_N \iota_N \otimes \overline{J}_T/\sigma_1^2) = 0 \end{aligned}$$

since $E_N \iota_N = 0$.

3.2.1 Empirical Example

Munnell (1990) considered the following Cobb–Douglas production function relationship investigating the productivity of public capital in private production:

$$\ln Y = \alpha + \beta_1 \ln K_1 + \beta_3 \ln K_2 + \beta_3 \ln L + \beta_4 \text{ Unemp} + u \tag{3.48}$$

where Y is gross state product, and K_1 is public capital, which includes highways and streets, water and sewer facilities and other public buildings and structures. K_2 is the private capital stock based on the Bureau of Economic Analysis national stock estimates, L is labor input measured as employment in non-agricultural payrolls. Unemp is the state unemployment rate included to capture business cycle effects. This panel consists of annual observations for 48 contiguous states over the period 1970–86. This data set was provided by Munnell (1990) and is provided on the Wiley web site. It is Example 3 in Baltagi (2008, p.28).

Exercise 3.13 *(Productivity of public capital in private production).* This is based on Problem 3.10 in Baltagi (2008).

(a) Obtain the OLS and FE estimates of the Cobb–Douglas production function given in (3.48), allowing for a two-way error component model as described in (3.1).
(b) Using EViews, compute the Wallace and Hussain (1969), Amemiya (1971) and Swamy and Arora (1972) feasible GLS estimators of the RE model, and compare the different estimates of the public capital coefficient.
(c) Compute the F-statistic for testing that the state and time dummy variables are jointly significant, the F-statistic for testing that the state and dummy variables are jointly significant, conditional on the presence of the time dummies, and the F-statistic for testing that the time dummies are jointly significant conditional on the presence of the state dummies. These are simple F tests obtained from fixed effects regressions, and are computed using EViews by clicking on the 'Redundant Fixed Effects Tests' option.

(d) Obtain the mixed effects estimates allowing the time effects to be fixed and the state effects to be random. This can be done easily in EViews.

Solution

(a) The EViews output for the OLS estimator is given in Table 3.1, while that for the two-way FE estimator is given in Table 3.2.

Table 3.1 Public Capital Productivity Data. OLS Results

Dependent Variable: LNY
Method: Panel Least Squares

Sample: 1970 1986
Periods included: 17
Cross-sections included: 48
Total panel (balanced) observations: 816

	Coefficient	Std. Error	t-Statistic	Prob.
C	1.643302	0.057587	28.53588	0.0000
LNK1	0.155007	0.017154	9.036311	0.0000
LNK2	0.309190	0.010272	30.10036	0.0000
LNL	0.593935	0.013747	43.20329	0.0000
U	−0.006733	0.001416	−4.753682	0.0000

R-squared	0.992593	Mean dependent var	10.50885
Adjusted R-squared	0.992557	S.D. dependent var	1.021132
S.E. of regression	0.088096	Akaike info criterion	−2.014663
Sum squared resid	6.294143	Schwarz criterion	−1.985837
Log likelihood	826.9824	Hannan-Quinn criter.	−2.003600
F-statistic	27171.71	Durbin-Watson stat	0.079269
Prob.(F-statistic)	0.000000		

Table 3.2 Public Capital Productivity Data. Two-way FE Results

Dependent Variable: LNY
Method: Panel Least Squares

Sample: 1970 1986
Cross-sections included: 48
Total panel (balanced) observations: 816

Variable	Coefficient	Std. Error	t-Statistic	Prob.
C	3.677420	0.263380	13.96242	0.0000
LNK1	−0.030173	0.026937	−1.120162	0.2630
LNK2	0.168832	0.027656	6.104605	0.0000
LNL	0.769303	0.028142	27.33659	0.0000
U	−0.004221	0.001139	−3.706443	0.0002

Effects Specification

Cross-section fixed (dummy variables)
Period fixed (dummy variables)

R-squared	0.998965	Mean dependent var	10.50885
Adjusted R-squared	0.998872	S.D. dependent var	1.021132
S.E.of regression	0.034289	Akaike info criterion	−3.828338
Sum squared resid	0.879443	Schwarz criterion	−3.436303
Log likelihood	1629.962	F-statistic	10776.83
Durbin-Watson stat	0.333512	Prob.(F-statistic)	0.000000

(b) Tables 3.3, 3.4, and 3.5, respectively, show the Wallace and Hussain (1969), Amemiya (1971), and Swamy and Arora (1972) two-way random effects estimators. With the exception of OLS, the estimates of the public capital coefficient are insignificant in this production function. In fact, the OLS estimate of β_1, the coefficient of $\ln K_1$, is 0.155 with a t-statistic of 9.04. In contrast, the FE two-way estimate of β_1 is -0.03 with a t-statistic of 1.12. The RE or feasible GLS estimator of β_1 using the Swamy and Arora (1972) option is 0.018 with a t-statistic of 0.77. This means that except for the OLS results, we cannot reject that public capital is unproductive in this production function.

Table 3.3 Public Capital Productivity Data. Two-way Wallace and Hussain Estimator

Dependent Variable: LNY
Method: Panel EGLS (Two-way random effects)

Sample: 1970 1986
Cross-sections included: 48
Total panel (balanced) observations: 816
Wallace and Hussain estimator of component variances

Variable	Coefficient	Std. Error	t-Statistic	Prob.
C	2.391982	0.138328	17.29215	0.0000
LNK1	0.025618	0.023363	1.096516	0.2732
LNK2	0.257807	0.021280	12.11516	0.0000
LNL	0.741795	0.023711	31.28496	0.0000
U	−0.004546	0.001058	−4.296918	0.0000

Effects Specification

Cross-section random S.D./Rho	0.082440	0.8163
Period random S.D./Rho	0.015946	0.0305
Idiosyncratic random S.D./Rho	0.035715	0.1532

Weighted Statistics

R-squared	0.929145	Mean dependent var	1.044902
Adjusted R-squared	0.928796	S.D. dependent var	0.131598
S.E. of regression	0.035116	Sum squared resid	1.000057
F-statistic	2658.734	Durbin-Watson stat	0.337792
Prob.(F-statistic)	0.000000		

Unweighted Statistics

R-squared	0.991016	Mean dependent var	10.50885
Sum squared resid	7.634595	Durbin-Watson stat	0.059616

Table 3.4 Public Capital Productivity Data. Two-way Amemiya/Wansbeek and Kapteyn Estimator

Dependent Variable: LNY
Method: Panel EGLS (Two-way random effects)

Sample: 1970 1986
Cross-sections included: 48
Total panel (balanced) observations: 816
Wansbeek and Kapteyn estimator of component variances

Variable	Coefficient	Std. Error	t-Statistic	Prob.
C	2.852064	0.185016	15.41526	0.0000
LNK1	0.002211	0.024690	0.089565	0.9287
LNK2	0.216667	0.024380	8.886971	0.0000
LNL	0.770048	0.025840	29.80026	0.0000
U	−0.003981	0.001080	−3.687160	0.0002
		Effects Specification		
Cross-section random S.D./Rho			0.153895	0.9273
Period random S.D./Rho			0.026080	0.0266
Idiosyncratic random S.D./Rho			0.034289	0.0460
		Weighted Statistics		
R-squared	0.858257	Mean dependent var		0.545434
Adjusted R-squared	0.857558	S.D. dependent var		0.089592
S.E. of regression	0.033813	Sum squared resid		0.927252
F-statistic	1227.659	Durbin-Watson stat		0.337468
Prob.(F-statistic)	0.000000			
		Unweighted Statistics		
R-squared	0.988198	Mean dependent var		10.50885
Sum squared resid	10.02906	Durbin-Watson stat		0.043918

Table 3.5 Public Capital Productivity Data. Two-way Swamy and Arora Estimator

Dependent Variable: LNY
Method: Panel EGLS (Two-way random effects)

Sample: 1970 1986
Cross-sections included: 48
Total panel (balanced) observations: 816
Swamy and Arora estimator of component variances

Variable	Coefficient	Std. Error	t-Statistic	Prob.
C	2.363478	0.138905	17.01501	0.0000
LNK1	0.017855	0.023321	0.765620	0.4441
LNK2	0.265592	0.020982	12.65785	0.0000
LNL	0.744896	0.024114	30.89004	0.0000
U	−0.004576	0.001018	−4.495262	0.0000

Effects Specification

Cross-section random S.D./Rho	0.082790	0.8434
Period random S.D./Rho	0.009839	0.0119
Idiosyncratic random S.D./Rho	0.034289	0.1447

Weighted Statistics

R-squared	0.932116	Mean dependent var	1.030197
Adjusted R-squared	0.931781	S.D. dependent var	0.135616
S.E. of regression	0.035421	Sum squared resid	1.017518
F-statistic	2783.974	Durbin-Watson stat	0.348386
Prob.(F-statistic)	0.000000		

Unweighted Statistics

R-squared	0.991114	Mean dependent var	10.50885
Sum squared resid	7.551630	Durbin-Watson stat	0.060565

(c) The redundant fixed effects tests (Table 3.6) show that both state and time dummies are significant in this Cobb–Douglas production function and ought to be included. EViews gives the F-statistic along with the corresponding likelihood ratio test below it. It also gives the backup restricted regressions which are not shown here to save space.

Table 3.6 Public Capital Productivity Data. Redundant Fixed Effects

Redundant Fixed Effects Tests

Test cross-section and period fixed effects

Effects Test	Statistic	d.f.	Prob.
Cross-section F	93.801842	(47,748)	0.0000
Cross-section Chi-square	1575.407574	47	0.0000
Period F	12.319268	(16,748)	0.0000
Period Chi-square	190.859574	16	0.0000
Cross-Section/Period F	73.101795	(63,748)	0.0000
Cross-Section/Period Chi-square	1605.958679	63	0.0000

(d) The mixed effects estimates, allowing the time effects to be fixed and the state effects to be random, show that the public capital coefficient estimate is again insignificant (0.031 with a t-statistic of 1.32); see Table 3.7. The F-statistic for the significance of the fixed period effects is 10.31 and is distributed as $F(16, 795)$ under the null of no period fixed effects. This rejects the null. Note that the restricted regression in this case is a one-way model with state random effects.

Table 3.7 Public Capital Productivity Data. Mixed Effects Results

Dependent Variable: LNY
Method: Panel EGLS (Cross-section random effects)
Mixed model (fixed period, random cross-section)
Sample: 1970 1986
Periods included: 17
Cross-sections included: 48
Total panel (balanced) observations: 816
Swamy and Arora estimator of component variances

	Coefficient	Std. Error	t-Statistic	Prob.
C	2.485743	0.142920	17.39255	0.0000
LNK1	0.031111	0.023567	1.320125	0.1872
LNK2	0.242728	0.022160	10.95348	0.0000
LNL	0.743566	0.023536	31.59220	0.0000
U	−0.004555	0.001102	−4.133710	0.0000

Effects Specification

	S.D.	Rho
Cross-section random	0.082790	0.8536
Period fixed (dummy variables)		
Idiosyncratic random	0.034289	0.1464

Weighted Statistics

R-squared	0.964320	Mean depend ent var	10.50885
Adjusted R-squared	0.963423	S.D. dependent var	0.182825
S.E. of regression	0.034966	Sum squared resid	0.971970
F-statistic	1074.324	Durbin-Watson stat	0.328953
Prob.(F-statistic)	0.000000		

4

Test of Hypotheses Using Panel Data

4.1 TESTS FOR POOLABILITY OF THE DATA

The question of whether to pool the data or not naturally arises with panel data. The restricted model is the pooled model given by (2.3) representing a behavioral equation with the same parameters over time and across regions. The unrestricted model, however, is the same behavioral equation but with different parameters, say across countries:

$$y_i = Z_i\delta_i + u_i, \qquad i = 1, 2, \ldots, N \tag{4.1}$$

where $y_i' = (y_{i1}, \ldots, y_{iT})$, $Z_i = [\iota_T, X_i]$, and X_i is $(T \times K)$. δ_i' is $1 \times (K+1)$ and u_i is $T \times 1$. The important thing to notice is that δ_i is different for every country equation. Here, T is assumed to be large and N is fixed. We want to test the hypothesis $H_0\colon \delta_i = \delta$ for all $i = 1, 2, \ldots, N$, so that under H_0 we can write the restricted model given in (4.1) as

$$y = Z\delta + u \tag{4.2}$$

where $Z' = (Z_1', Z_2', \ldots, Z_N')$ and $u' = (u_1', u_2', \ldots, u_N')$. The unrestricted model can also be written as

$$y = \begin{pmatrix} Z_1 & 0 & \ldots & 0 \\ 0 & Z_2 & \ldots & 0 \\ \vdots & & \ddots & \vdots \\ 0 & 0 & \ldots & Z_N \end{pmatrix} \begin{pmatrix} \delta_1 \\ \delta_2 \\ \vdots \\ \delta_N \end{pmatrix} + u = Z^*\delta^* + u \tag{4.3}$$

where $\delta^{*\prime} = (\delta_1', \delta_2', \ldots, \delta_N')$ and $Z = Z^*I^*$ with $I^* = (\iota_N \otimes I_{K'})$, an $NK' \times K'$ matrix, with $K' = K + 1$. Hence the variables in Z are all linear combinations of the variables in Z^*.

Exercise 4.1 *(Chow (1960) test).* This is based on Problem 4.1 in Baltagi (2008).

(a) Assuming that $u \sim N(0, \sigma^2 I_{NT})$, show that the restricted residual sum of squares (RRSS) under the null hypothesis $H_0\colon \delta_i = \delta$ for all i, is the pooled OLS residual sum of squares.
(b) Show that the unrestricted residual sum of squares (URSS) is the sum of N residual sum of squares performed on each country regression separately.
(c) Let the restricted residuals be denoted by $e = My$, where $M = (I_{NT} - Z(Z'Z)^{-1}Z')$. Also, let the unrestricted residuals be denoted by $e^* = M^*y$, where $M^* = I_{NT} - Z^*(Z^{*\prime}Z^*)^{-1}Z^{*\prime}$. Show that $MM^* = M^*$.
(d) Show that $e'e - e^{*\prime}e^*$ is independent of $e^{*\prime}e^*$.

(e) Show that $(e'e - e^{*\prime}e^*)/\sigma^2$ is distributed as $\chi^2_{(N-1)K'}$ and $e^{*\prime}e^*/\sigma^2$ is distributed as $\chi^2_{N(T-K')}$.

(f) Conclude that the Chow test for H_0 is distributed as an $F((N-1)K', N(T-K'))$.

Solution

(a) Under the null hypothesis H_0, the restricted maximum likelihood estimator for δ in (4.2) is pooled OLS,

$$\widehat{\delta}_{\mathrm{OLS}} = \widehat{\delta}_{mle} = (Z'Z)^{-1}Z'y \tag{4.4}$$

and therefore

$$y = Z\widehat{\delta}_{\mathrm{OLS}} + e \tag{4.5}$$

implying that the pooled OLS residuals satisfy

$$e = (I_{NT} - Z(Z'Z)^{-1}Z')y = My = M(Z\delta + u) = Mu$$

since $MZ = 0$. Hence, the RRSS is $e'e$.

(b) Similarly, under the assumption that $u \sim N(0, \sigma^2 I_{NT})$, the maximum likelihood estimator for each δ_i is given by

$$\widehat{\delta}_{i,\mathrm{OLS}} = \widehat{\delta}_{i,mle} = (Z_i'Z_i)^{-1}Z_i'y_i \tag{4.6}$$

and therefore

$$y_i = Z_i\widehat{\delta}_{i,\mathrm{OLS}} + e_i \tag{4.7}$$

implying that $e_i = (I_T - Z_i(Z_i'Z_i)^{-1}Z_i')y_i = M_iy_i = M_i(Z_i\delta_i + u_i) = M_iu_i$ since $M_iZ_i = 0$, and this is true for $i = 1, 2, \ldots, N$. In fact, the maximum likelihood estimator of the unrestricted model given in (4.3) yields OLS on that model, $\widehat{\delta}^* = (Z^{*\prime}Z^*)^{-1}Z^{*\prime}y$, and therefore $y = Z^*\widehat{\delta}^* + e^*$ with $e^* = M^*y = M^*u$. But $Z^{*\prime}Z^*$ is block diagonal, and so is the projection matrix $Z^*(Z^{*\prime}Z^*)^{-1}Z^{*\prime}$. In fact,

$$M^* = I_{NT} - Z^*(Z^{*\prime}Z^*)^{-1}Z^{*\prime} = \begin{pmatrix} M_1 & 0 & \ldots & 0 \\ 0 & M_2 & \ldots & 0 \\ \vdots & & \ddots & \vdots \\ 0 & 0 & \ldots & M_N \end{pmatrix}$$

is block diagonal, which means that $e^{*\prime}e^* = y'M^*y = \Sigma_{i=1}^N y_i'M_iy_i = \Sigma_{i=1}^N e_i'e_i$. This proves that the URSS is the sum of N residual sums of squares performed on each country separately.

(c) $M = I_{NT} - Z(Z'Z)^{-1}Z'$ and $M^* = I_{NT} - Z^*(Z^{*\prime}Z^*)^{-1}Z^{*\prime}$ are projection matrices and therefore are symmetric and idempotent. From (4.3), it is clear that $Z = Z^*I^*$

with $I^* = (\iota_N \otimes I_{K'})$, ι_N being a vector of ones of dimension N and $K' = K + 1$. We have

$$MM^* = I_{NT} - Z(Z'Z)^{-1}Z' - Z^*(Z^{*\prime}Z^*)^{-1}Z^{*\prime} + Z(Z'Z)^{-1}Z'Z^*(Z^{*\prime}Z^*)^{-1}Z^{*\prime}$$

Substituting $Z = Z^*I^*$, the last term reduces to

$$Z(Z'Z)^{-1}Z'Z^*(Z^{*\prime}Z^*)^{-1}Z^{*\prime} = Z(Z'Z)^{-1}I^{*\prime}Z^{*\prime}Z^*(Z^{*\prime}Z^*)^{-1}Z^{*\prime} = Z(Z'Z)^{-1}Z'$$

Hence,

$$MM^* = I_{NT} - Z^*(Z^{*\prime}Z^*)^{-1}Z^{*\prime} = M^*$$

(d) Now $e'e - e^{*\prime}e^* = u'(M - M^*)u$ and $e^{*\prime}e^* = u'M^*u$. Under the assumption that $u \sim N(0, \sigma^2 I_{NT})$, these two quadratic forms in u are independent since $(M - M^*)M^* = 0$.
(e) $u'(M - M^*)u/\sigma^2$ and $u'M^*u/\sigma^2$ are distributed as χ^2 since $(M - M^*)$ and M^* are idempotent and $u \sim N(0, \sigma^2 I_{NT})$. The degrees of freedom are $\mathrm{tr}(M - M^*)$ and $\mathrm{tr}(M^*)$, respectively. This yields $NT - K' - N(T - K') = (N - 1)K'$ and $N(T - K')$, respectively.
(f) Dividing the quadratic forms by their respective degrees of freedom, and taking their ratio leads to the test statistic

$$F_{obs} = \frac{(e'e - e^{*\prime}e^*)/(\mathrm{tr}(M) - \mathrm{tr}(M^*))}{e^{*\prime}e^*/\mathrm{tr}(M^*)} = \frac{(e'e - e_1'e_1 - e_2'e_2 - \ldots - e_N'e_N)/(N-1)K'}{(e_1'e_1 + e_2'e_2 + \cdots + e_N'e_N)/N(T - K')} \tag{4.8}$$

This is the standard Chow (1960) test extended from two regressions to the case of N regressions. Under H_0, F_{obs} is distributed as $F((N-1)K', N(T - K'))$. See also Fisher (1970) for an elegant proof of this result.

Next, we generalize this Chow test for poolability to the case where $u \sim N(0, \sigma^2\Sigma)$, in which Σ is a known positive definite matrix.

Exercise 4.2 *(Roy (1957) and Zellner (1962) test).* This is based on Problem 4.2 in Baltagi (2008).

(a) Assuming that $u \sim N(0, \sigma^2\Sigma)$, show that the RRSS under the null hypothesis $H_0: \delta_i = \delta$ for all i is the pooled OLS residual sum of squares on the restricted model given in (4.2) after premultiplying it by $\Sigma^{-1/2}$.
(b) Show that the URSS can be obtained from OLS on (4.3) after premultiplying it by $\Sigma^{-1/2}$.
(c) Show that the test for the null hypothesis $H_0: \delta_i = \delta$ for all i can be obtained as a simple Chow test for H_0 after premultiplying the restricted and unrestricted models in (4.2) and (4.3) by $\Sigma^{-1/2}$.
(d) Show that the resulting test statistic derived in (c) can be computed as

$$\dot{F}_{obs} = \frac{y'[\Sigma^{-1}(Z^*(Z^{*\prime}\Sigma^{-1}Z^*)^{-1}Z^{*\prime} - Z(Z'\Sigma^{-1}Z)^{-1}Z')\Sigma^{-1}]y/(N-1)K'}{(y'\Sigma^{-1}y - y'\Sigma^{-1}Z^*(Z^{*\prime}\Sigma^{-1}Z^*)^{-1}Z^{*\prime}\Sigma^{-1}y)/N(T - K')} \tag{4.9}$$

Solution

(a) Given Σ, we premultiply the restricted model given in (4.2) by $\Sigma^{-1/2}$ and we call $\Sigma^{-1/2}y = \dot{y}$, $\Sigma^{-1/2}Z = \dot{Z}$ and $\Sigma^{-1/2}u = \dot{u}$. Hence,

$$\dot{y} = \dot{Z}\delta + \dot{u} \tag{4.10}$$

with $E(\dot{u}\dot{u}') = \Sigma^{-1/2}E(uu')\Sigma^{-1/2'} = \sigma^2 I_{NT}$. Under the null hypothesis H_0, the restricted maximum likelihood estimator for δ in (4.10) is pooled OLS of $\dot{y}$ on $\dot{Z}$ yielding $\widehat{\dot{\delta}}_{\text{OLS}} = (\dot{Z}'\dot{Z})^{-1}\dot{Z}'\dot{y}$ and the restricted residuals $\dot{e} = \dot{y} - \dot{Z}\widehat{\dot{\delta}}_{\text{OLS}} = \dot{M}\dot{y} = \dot{M}\dot{u}$, where $\dot{M} = I_{NT} - \dot{Z}(\dot{Z}'\dot{Z})^{-1}\dot{Z}'$, since $\dot{M}\dot{Z} = 0$. Hence, the RRSS is $\dot{e}'\dot{e}$.

(b) Similarly, we premultiply the unrestricted model given in (4.3) by $\Sigma^{-1/2}$ and we call $\Sigma^{-1/2}Z^* = \dot{Z}^*$. Therefore,

$$\dot{y} = \dot{Z}^*\delta^* + \dot{u} \tag{4.11}$$

with $E(\dot{u}\dot{u}') = \sigma^2 I_{NT}$. The maximum likelihood estimator of the unrestricted model given in (4.3) can be obtained from OLS on (4.11), i.e., $\widehat{\dot{\delta}}^*_{\text{OLS}} = (\dot{Z}^{*\prime}\dot{Z}^*)^{-1}\dot{Z}^{*\prime}\dot{y}$, with the unrestricted residuals $\dot{e}^* = \dot{y} - \dot{Z}^*\widehat{\dot{\delta}}^*_{\text{OLS}} = \dot{M}^*\dot{y} = \dot{M}^*\dot{u}$, where $\dot{M}^* = I_{NT} - \dot{Z}^*(\dot{Z}^{*\prime}\dot{Z}^*)^{-1}\dot{Z}^{*\prime}$, since $\dot{M}^*\dot{Z}^* = 0$. Hence, the URSS is $\dot{e}^{*\prime}\dot{e}^*$.

(c) Now we can test $H_0: \delta_i = \delta$ for every $i = 1, 2, \ldots, N$ by using the Chow statistic derived in Exercise 4.1 only applied to the transformed models (4.10) and (4.11) since $\dot{u}_{.} \sim N(0, \sigma^2 I_{NT})$. Note that $\dot{Z} = \Sigma^{-1/2}Z$ and $\dot{Z}^* = \Sigma^{-1/2}Z^*$. Using $Z = Z^*I^*$and premultiplying both sides by $\Sigma^{-1/2}$ yields $\dot{Z} = \dot{Z}^*I^*$. Both $\dot{M}$ and $\dot{M}^*$ are projection matrices that are symmetric and idempotent, and satisfy $\dot{M}\dot{M}^* = \dot{M}^*$. The proof is the same as that of $MM^* = M^*$ given in Exercise 4.1 with $\dot{Z}$ replacing Z and $\dot{Z}^*$ replacing Z^*. Using the same proofs as in Exercise 4.1, we obtain the following test statistic for H_0:

$$\dot{F}_{obs} = \frac{(\dot{e}'\dot{e} - \dot{e}^{*\prime}\dot{e}^*)/(\text{tr}(\dot{M}) - \text{tr}(\dot{M}^*))}{\dot{e}^{*\prime}\dot{e}^*/\text{tr}(\dot{M}^*)} \sim F((N-1)K', N(T-K')) \tag{4.12}$$

(d) Using the fact that $\dot{M}$ and $\dot{M}^*$ are symmetric and idempotent, we can rewrite (4.12) as

$$\dot{F}_{obs} = \frac{(\dot{y}'\dot{M}\dot{y} - \dot{y}'\dot{M}^*\dot{y})/(N-1)K'}{\dot{y}'\dot{M}^*\dot{y}/N(T-K')} \tag{4.13}$$

$$= \frac{(y'\Sigma^{-1/2}\dot{M}\Sigma^{-1/2}y - y'\Sigma^{-1/2}\dot{M}^*\Sigma^{-1/2}y)/(N-1)K'}{y'\Sigma^{-1/2}\dot{M}^*\Sigma^{-1/2}y/N(T-K')} \tag{4.14}$$

But

$$\dot{M} = I_{NT} - \Sigma^{-1/2}Z(Z'\Sigma^{-1}Z)^{-1}Z'\Sigma^{-1/2'}$$

and

$$\dot{M}^* = I_{NT} - \Sigma^{-1/2}Z^*(Z^{*\prime}\Sigma^{-1}Z^*)^{-1}Z^{*\prime}\Sigma^{-1/2'}$$

so that

$$\Sigma^{-1/2}\dot{M}\Sigma^{-1/2} = \Sigma^{-1} - \Sigma^{-1}Z(Z'\Sigma^{-1}Z)^{-1}Z'\Sigma^{-1}$$

and

$$\Sigma^{-1/2}\dot{M}^{*}\Sigma^{-1/2} = \Sigma^{-1} - \Sigma^{-1}Z^{*}(Z^{*\prime}\Sigma^{-1}Z^{*})^{-1}Z^{*\prime}\Sigma^{-1}$$

Substituting these terms in (4.14) we get the required result in (4.9). This test is a special application of a general test for linear restrictions described in Roy (1957) and used by Zellner (1962) to test for aggregation bias in a set of seemingly unrelated regressions.

4.2 TESTS FOR INDIVIDUAL AND TIME EFFECTS

For the random two-way error component model given in (3.1), Breusch and Pagan (1980) derived a Lagrange multiplier (LM) test to test $H_0 : \sigma_\mu^2 = \sigma_\lambda^2 = 0$. The loglikelihood function under normality of the disturbances is given by

$$L(\delta, \theta) = \text{constant} - \frac{1}{2}\log|\Omega| - \frac{1}{2}u'\Omega^{-1}u \tag{4.15}$$

where $\theta' = (\sigma_\mu^2, \sigma_\lambda^2, \sigma_\nu^2)$ and Ω is given by (3.6) as

$$\Omega = \sigma_\mu^2(I_N \otimes J_T) + \sigma_\lambda^2(J_N \otimes I_T) + \sigma_\nu^2 I_{NT} \tag{4.16}$$

The information matrix is block-diagonal between θ and δ. Since H_0 involves only θ, the part of the information matrix due to δ is ignored.

Exercise 4.3 *(Breusch and Pagan (1980) Lagrange multiplier test).* This is based on Problem 4.5 in Baltagi (2008).

(a) Compute the score $D(\widetilde{\theta}) = (\partial L/\partial\theta)|_{\widetilde{\theta}_{mle}}$, the first derivative of the likelihood with respect to θ, evaluated at the restricted maximum likelihood estimate of θ under H_0, which is denoted by $\widetilde{\theta}_{mle}$.
(b) Compute the information matrix for this model, denoted by

$$J(\theta) = E\left[-\frac{\partial^2 L}{\partial\theta\partial\theta'}\right] = [J_{rs}], \quad r, s = 1, 2, 3$$

(c) Obtain the Breusch and Pagan (1980) LM statistic given by $\text{LM} = \widetilde{D}'\widetilde{J}^{-1}\widetilde{D}$. Show that it is the sum of two LM statistics. The first one tests $H_0^a : \sigma_\mu^2 = 0$, and the second tests $H_0^b : \sigma_\lambda^2 = 0$.

Solution

(a) Hartley and Rao (1967) or Hemmerle and Hartley (1973) give a useful general formula to obtain $D(\theta)$:

$$\partial L/\partial\theta_r = -\frac{1}{2}\text{tr}[\Omega^{-1}(\partial\Omega/\partial\theta_r)] + \frac{1}{2}[u'\Omega^{-1}(\partial\Omega/\partial\theta_r)\Omega^{-1}u] \tag{4.17}$$

for $r = 1, 2, 3$. Also, from (4.16), $(\partial\Omega/\partial\theta_r) = (I_N \otimes J_T)$ for $r = 1$, $(J_N \otimes I_T)$ for $r = 2$, and I_{NT} for $r = 3$. The restricted maximum likelihood estimator of Ω under H_0 is $\widetilde{\Omega} = \widetilde{\sigma}_\nu^2 I_{NT}$, where $\widetilde{\sigma}_\nu^2 = \widetilde{u}'\widetilde{u}/NT$ and $\widetilde{u}$ are the OLS residuals. Using $\text{tr}(I_N \otimes J_T) = \text{tr}(J_N \otimes I_T) = \text{tr}(I_{NT}) = NT$ gives

$$D(\widetilde{\theta}) = \begin{bmatrix} -\frac{1}{2}\text{tr}[(I_N \otimes J_T)/\widetilde{\sigma}_\nu^2] + \frac{1}{2}[\widetilde{u}'(I_N \otimes J_T)\widetilde{u}/\widetilde{\sigma}_\nu^4] \\ -\frac{1}{2}\text{tr}[(J_N \otimes I_T)/\widetilde{\sigma}_\nu^2] + \frac{1}{2}[\widetilde{u}'(J_N \otimes I_T)\widetilde{u}/\widetilde{\sigma}_\nu^4] \\ -\frac{1}{2}\text{tr}[I_{NT}/\widetilde{\sigma}_\nu^2] + \frac{1}{2}[\widetilde{u}'\widetilde{u}/\widetilde{\sigma}_\nu^4] \end{bmatrix}$$

$$= \frac{-NT}{2\widetilde{\sigma}_\nu^2}\begin{bmatrix} 1 - \dfrac{\widetilde{u}'(I_N \otimes J_T)\widetilde{u}}{\widetilde{u}'\widetilde{u}} \\ 1 - \dfrac{\widetilde{u}'(J_N \otimes I_T)\widetilde{u}}{\widetilde{u}'\widetilde{u}} \\ 0 \end{bmatrix} \tag{4.18}$$

(b) For the information matrix, we use a result due to Harville (1977):

$$J_{rs} = E[-\partial^2 L/\partial\theta_r\partial\theta_s] = \frac{1}{2}\text{tr}[\Omega^{-1}(\partial\Omega/\partial\theta_r)\Omega^{-1}(\partial\Omega/\partial\theta_s)] \tag{4.19}$$

Using $\widetilde{\Omega}^{-1} = (1/\widetilde{\sigma}_\nu^2)I_{NT}$, $\text{tr}[(I_N \otimes J_T)(J_N \otimes I_T)] = \text{tr}(J_{NT}) = NT$, $\text{tr}(I_N \otimes J_T)^2 = NT^2$ and $\text{tr}(J_N \otimes I_T)^2 = N^2T$ yields

$$\widetilde{J} = \frac{1}{2\widetilde{\sigma}_\nu^4}\begin{bmatrix} \text{tr}(I_N \otimes J_T)^2 & \text{tr}(J_{NT}) & \text{tr}(I_N \otimes J_T) \\ \text{tr}(J_{NT}) & \text{tr}(J_N \otimes I_T)^2 & \text{tr}(J_N \otimes I_T) \\ \text{tr}(I_N \otimes J_T) & \text{tr}(J_N \otimes I_T) & \text{tr}(I_{NT}) \end{bmatrix} = \frac{NT}{2\widetilde{\sigma}_\nu^4}\begin{bmatrix} T & 1 & 1 \\ 1 & N & 1 \\ 1 & 1 & 1 \end{bmatrix} \tag{4.20}$$

with

$$\widetilde{J}^{-1} = \frac{2\widetilde{\sigma}_\nu^4}{NT(N-1)(T-1)}\begin{bmatrix} (N-1) & 0 & (1-N) \\ 0 & (T-1) & (1-T) \\ (1-N) & (1-T) & (NT-1) \end{bmatrix} \tag{4.21}$$

(c) Therefore the Breusch–Pagan LM test is given by

$$\begin{aligned} \text{LM} &= \widetilde{D}'\widetilde{J}^{-1}\widetilde{D} \\ &= \frac{NT}{2(N-1)(T-1)}\left[(N-1)\left[1 - \frac{\widetilde{u}'(I_N \otimes J_T)\widetilde{u}}{\widetilde{u}'\widetilde{u}}\right]^2 \right. \\ &\quad \left. + (T-1)\left[1 - \frac{\widetilde{u}'(J_N \otimes I_T)\widetilde{u}}{\widetilde{u}'\widetilde{u}}\right]^2\right] \\ &= \text{LM}_1 + \text{LM}_2 \end{aligned} \tag{4.22}$$

where

$$\text{LM}_1 = \frac{NT}{2(T-1)}\left[1 - \frac{\widetilde{u}'(I_N \otimes J_T)\widetilde{u}}{\widetilde{u}'\widetilde{u}}\right]^2 \tag{4.23}$$

and

$$\text{LM}_2 = \frac{NT}{2(N-1)}\left[1 - \frac{\widetilde{u}'(J_N \otimes I_T)\widetilde{u}}{\widetilde{u}'\widetilde{u}}\right]^2 \tag{4.24}$$

Under H_0, LM is asymptotically distributed as a χ_2^2. This LM test requires only OLS residuals and is easy to compute. This may explain its popularity. In addition, if one wants to test $H_0^a : \sigma_\mu^2 = 0$, following the derivation given above, one gets LM_1 which is asymptotically distributed under H_0^a as χ_1^2. Similarly, if one wants to test H_0^b ; $\sigma_\lambda^2 = 0$, by symmetry, one gets LM_2 which is asymptotically distributed as χ_1^2 under H_0^b.

One problem with the Breusch–Pagan test is that it assumes that the alternative hypothesis is two-sided when we know that the variance components are non-negative. This means that the alternative hypotheses should be one-sided. Honda (1985) suggests a *uniformly most powerful* test for $H_0^a : \sigma_\mu^2 = 0$ which is based upon

$$\text{HO} \equiv A = \sqrt{\frac{NT}{2(T-1)}}\left[\frac{\widetilde{u}'(I_N \otimes J_T)\widetilde{u}}{\widetilde{u}'\widetilde{u}} - 1\right] \overset{H_0^a}{\rightarrow} N(0,1) \tag{4.25}$$

Note that the square of this $N(0, 1)$ statistic is the Breusch and Pagan (1980) LM_1 test statistic given in (4.23). Honda (1985) finds that this test statistic is robust to non-normality. Moulton and Randolph (1989) showed that the asymptotic $N(0, 1)$ approximation for this one-sided LM statistic can be poor even in large samples. This occurs when the number of regressors is large or the intra-class correlation of some of the regressors is high. They suggest an alternative standardized Lagrange multiplier (SLM) test whose asymptotic critical values are generally closer to the exact critical values than those of the LM test. This SLM test statistic centers and scales the one-sided LM statistic so that its mean is zero and its variance is one:

$$\text{SLM} = \frac{\text{HO} - E(\text{HO})}{\sqrt{\text{var}(\text{HO})}} = \frac{d - E(d)}{\sqrt{\text{var}(d)}} \tag{4.26}$$

where $d = \widetilde{u}'D\widetilde{u}/\widetilde{u}'\widetilde{u}$ and $D = (I_N \otimes J_T)$. Using the results on moments of quadratic forms in regression residuals (see Evans and King, 1985), we get

$$E(d) = \text{tr}(D\overline{P}_Z)/p \tag{4.27}$$

and

$$\text{var}(d) = 2\{p\ \text{tr}(D\overline{P}_Z)^2 - [\text{tr}(D\overline{P}_Z)]^2\}/p^2(p+2) \tag{4.28}$$

where $p = n - (K+1)$ and $\overline{P}_Z = I_n - Z(Z'Z)^{-1}Z'$. Under the null hypothesis H_0^a, SLM has an asymptotic $N(0, 1)$ distribution.

Similarly, for $H_0^b: \sigma_\lambda^2 = 0$, the one-sided Honda-type LM test statistic is

$$B = \sqrt{\frac{NT}{2(N-1)}}\left[\frac{\widetilde{u}'(J_N \otimes I_T)\widetilde{u}}{\widetilde{u}'\widetilde{u}} - 1\right] \tag{4.29}$$

which is asymptotically distributed as $N(0, 1)$ under H_0^b. Note that the square of this statistic is the corresponding two-sided LM test given by LM_2 in (4.24). This can be standardized as in (4.26) with $D = (J_N \otimes I_T)$.

Exercise 4.4 *(Locally mean most powerful one-sided test).* This is based on Problem 4.6 in Baltagi (2008). For $H_0^c: \sigma_\mu^2 = \sigma_\lambda^2 = 0$, the two-sided LM test, given by Breusch and Pagan (1980), is $A^2 + B^2 \sim \chi_2^2$. King and Wu (1997) suggest a locally mean most powerful (LMMP) one-sided test which for H_0^c is given by

$$KW = \widetilde{S}^+/(\iota_2'(g^{11})^{-1}\iota_2)^{1/2}$$

where ι_2 is a vector of ones of dimension 2. The numerator of this test statistic is obtained from the sum of the scores

$$\widetilde{S}^+ = \sum_{i=1}^{2}(\partial L/\partial\theta_i)_{\widetilde{\theta}'=(0,0,\widetilde{\sigma}_\nu^2)}$$

where $(\partial L/\partial\theta_i)_{\widetilde{\theta}=(0,0,\widetilde{\sigma}_\nu^2)}$ is given by (4.18) and $\widetilde{\sigma}_\nu^2 = \widetilde{u}'\widetilde{u}/NT$ with $\widetilde{u}$ denoting the OLS residuals. g^{11} gives the corresponding elements of the inverse of the information matrix given by (4.21). Show that the King and Wu statistic for H_0^c is given by

$$KW = \frac{\sqrt{T-1}}{\sqrt{N+T-2}}A + \frac{\sqrt{N-1}}{\sqrt{N+T-2}}B \tag{4.30}$$

where A and B were defined in (4.25) and (4.29).

Solution

Substituting (4.18) into $\widetilde{S}^+$ gives

$$\widetilde{S}^+ = \frac{NT}{2\widetilde{\sigma}_\nu^2}\left[\frac{\widetilde{u}'(I_N \otimes J_T)\widetilde{u}}{\widetilde{u}'\widetilde{u}} + \frac{\widetilde{u}'(J_N \otimes I_T)\widetilde{u}}{\widetilde{u}'\widetilde{u}} - 2\right]$$

The denominator of the KW statistic is obtained by substituting g^{11} given in (4.21), i.e.,

$$\begin{aligned}(\iota_2'(g^{11})^{-1}\iota_2)^{1/2} &= \left\{\frac{NT(N-1)(T-1)}{2\widetilde{\sigma}_\nu^4}(1, 1)\begin{bmatrix}\frac{1}{(N-1)} & 0 \\ 0 & \frac{1}{(T-1)}\end{bmatrix}\begin{pmatrix}1\\1\end{pmatrix}\right\}^{1/2} \\ &= \left\{\frac{NT(N-1)(T-1)}{2\widetilde{\sigma}_\nu^4}\left(\frac{1}{N-1} + \frac{1}{T-1}\right)\right\}^{1/2} \\ &= \left\{\frac{NT(N+T-2)}{2\widetilde{\sigma}_\nu^4}\right\}^{1/2}\end{aligned}$$

Dividing $\widetilde{S}^+$ by $(\iota_2'(g^{11})^{-1}\iota_2)^{1/2}$ leads to

$$KW = \frac{\sqrt{NT}}{\sqrt{2}\sqrt{N+T-2}}\left[\frac{\widetilde{u}'(I_N \otimes J_T)\widetilde{u}}{\widetilde{u}'\widetilde{u}} + \frac{\widetilde{u}'(J_N \otimes I_T)\widetilde{u}}{\widetilde{u}'\widetilde{u}} - 2\right]$$

which is the required expression in (4.30). This is distributed as $N(0, 1)$ under H_0^c. This test statistic was derived by Baltagi *et al.* (1992).

Following the Moulton and Randolph (1989) standardization of the LM test for the one-way error component model, Honda (1991) suggested a standardization of his 'handy' one-sided test for the two-way error component model.

Exercise 4.5 *(Standardized Honda (1985) test).* This is based on Problem 4.7, part (a), in Baltagi (2008). Honda (1985) does not derive a uniformly most powerful one-sided test for H_0^c, but he suggests a 'handy' one-sided test given by

$$\text{HO} = (A + B)/\sqrt{2} \tag{4.31}$$

where A is defined in (4.25) and B is defined in (4.29). This is distributed as $N(0, 1)$ under H_0^c. Show that standardized Honda test statistic can be obtained from (4.26) with $d = \widetilde{u}'D\widetilde{u}/\widetilde{u}'\widetilde{u}$, and

$$D = \frac{1}{2}\sqrt{\frac{NT}{(T-1)}}(I_N \otimes J_T) + \frac{1}{2}\sqrt{\frac{NT}{(N-1)}}(J_N \otimes I_T) \tag{4.32}$$

Solution

For $H_0^c : \sigma_\mu^2 = \sigma_\lambda^2 = 0$, Honda's (1991) handy one-sided test is given by (4.31). Note that the (-1) terms in both A and B cancel out when we subtract the expectations of this test statistic. Hence, the standardized HO test can be based upon the standardization of

$$\frac{1}{2}\sqrt{\frac{NT}{(T-1)}}\left[\frac{\widetilde{u}'(I_N \otimes J_T)\widetilde{u}}{\widetilde{u}'\widetilde{u}}\right] + \frac{1}{2}\sqrt{\frac{NT}{(N-1)}}\left[\frac{\widetilde{u}'(J_N \otimes I_T)\widetilde{u}}{\widetilde{u}'\widetilde{u}}\right]$$

ignoring the (-1) terms. This can be rewritten as

$$\frac{\widetilde{u}'\left[\frac{1}{2}\sqrt{\frac{NT}{(T-1)}}(I_N \otimes J_T) + \frac{1}{2}\sqrt{\frac{NT}{(N-1)}}(J_N \otimes I_T)\right]\widetilde{u}}{\widetilde{u}'\widetilde{u}}$$

or, equivalently, as $d = \widetilde{u}'D\widetilde{u}/\widetilde{u}'\widetilde{u}$ with D defined by (4.32) as required. Hence, the standardized HO test for H_0^c is given by (4.26) with D defined by (4.32).

Exercise 4.6 *(Standardized King and Wu (1997) test).* This is based on Problem 4.7, part (b), in Baltagi (2008). Show that the standardized KW test can be obtained from (4.26), with $d = \widetilde{u}'D\widetilde{u}/\widetilde{u}'\widetilde{u}$ and

$$D = \frac{\sqrt{NT}}{\sqrt{2}\sqrt{N+T-2}}[(I_N \otimes J_T) + (J_N \otimes I_T)] \tag{4.33}$$

Solution

The King and Wu (1997) test for H_0^c is given by

$$KW = \frac{\sqrt{T-1}}{\sqrt{N+T-2}}A + \frac{\sqrt{N-1}}{\sqrt{N+T-2}}B$$

with A and B defined in (4.25) and (4.29), respectively. Again, the (-1) terms in both A and B cancel out when we subtract the expectation of this test statistic. Hence, the standardized KW test can be based upon the standardization of

$$\sqrt{\frac{NT(T-1)}{2(T-1)(N+T-2)}}\left[\frac{\widetilde{u}'(I_N \otimes J_T)\widetilde{u}}{\widetilde{u}'\widetilde{u}}\right] + \sqrt{\frac{NT(N-1)}{2(N-1)(N+T-2)}}\left[\frac{\widetilde{u}'(J_N \otimes I_T)\widetilde{u}}{\widetilde{u}'\widetilde{u}}\right]$$

ignoring the (-1) terms. This can be rewritten as

$$\frac{\sqrt{\frac{NT}{2(N+T-2)}}\widetilde{u}'[(I_N \otimes J_T) + (J_N \otimes I_T)]\widetilde{u}}{\widetilde{u}'\widetilde{u}}$$

or equivalently as $d = \widetilde{u}'D\widetilde{u}/\widetilde{u}'\widetilde{u}$ with D defined by (4.33). Hence, the standardized KW test for H_0^c is given by (4.26) with D defined by (4.33). With this new D matrix, $E(d)$ and var(d) can be computed using (4.27) and (4.28). Under $H_0^c : \sigma_\mu^2 = \sigma_\lambda^2 = 0$, these SLM statistics are asymptotically $N(0, 1)$ and their asymptotic critical values should be closer to the exact critical values than those of the corresponding unstandardized tests.

When one uses HO given in (4.25) to test $H_0^a : \sigma_\mu^2 = 0$ one implicitly assumes that the time-specific effects do not exist. This may lead to incorrect decisions especially when the variance of the time effects (assumed to be zero) is large. To overcome this problem, Baltagi *et al.* (1992) suggest testing the individual effects assuming that the time-specific effects are present (i.e. assuming $\sigma_\lambda^2 > 0$).

Exercise 4.7 *(Conditional Lagrange multiplier test: random individual effects).* Show that the LM test for testing $H_0^d : \sigma_\mu^2 = 0$ (assuming $\sigma_\lambda^2 > 0$) is given by

$$\text{LM}_\mu = \frac{\sqrt{2}\widetilde{\sigma}_2^2\widetilde{\sigma}_\nu^2}{\sqrt{T(T-1)[\widetilde{\sigma}_\nu^4 + (N-1)\widetilde{\sigma}_2^4]}}\widetilde{D}_\mu \tag{4.34}$$

where

$$\widetilde{D}_\mu = \frac{T}{2}\left\{\frac{1}{\widetilde{\sigma}_2^2}\left[\frac{\widetilde{u}'(\bar{J}_N \otimes \bar{J}_T)\widetilde{u}}{\widetilde{\sigma}_2^2} - 1\right] + \frac{(N-1)}{\widetilde{\sigma}_\nu^2}\left[\frac{\widetilde{u}'(E_N \otimes \bar{J}_T)\widetilde{u}}{(N-1)\widetilde{\sigma}_\nu^2} - 1\right]\right\} \tag{4.35}$$

with $\widetilde{\sigma}_2^2 = \widetilde{u}'(\overline{J}_N \otimes I_T)\widetilde{u}/T$ and $\widetilde{\sigma}_\nu^2 = \widetilde{u}'(E_N \otimes I_T)\widetilde{u}/T(N-1)$. The estimated disturbances $\widetilde{u}$ denote the one-way GLS residuals using the maximum likelihood estimates $\widetilde{\sigma}_\nu^2$ and $\widetilde{\sigma}_2^2$. LM_μ is asymptotically distributed as $N(0,1)$ under H_0^d.

Solution

This derivation follows the same steps described in the solution to Exercise 4.3. In fact, the unrestricted loglikelihood function $L(\delta, \theta)$ under normality is given by (4.15), where $\theta' = (\sigma_\mu^2, \sigma_\lambda^2, \sigma_\nu^2)$ and Ω is given by (4.16). Also, $\partial L/\partial\theta_r$ is given by (4.17) and $\partial\Omega/\partial\theta_r$ is given below that equation for $r = 1, 2, 3$. Under $H_0^d : \sigma_\mu^2 = 0$ (assuming $\sigma_\lambda^2 > 0$)

$$\Omega^{-1} = \frac{1}{\sigma_2^2}(\overline{J}_N \otimes I_T) + \frac{1}{\sigma_\nu^2}(E_N \otimes I_T)$$

where $\sigma_2^2 = N\sigma_\lambda^2 + \sigma_\nu^2$ and $\overline{J}_N = J_N/N$. The restricted maximum likelihood estimator of σ_ν^2 is $\widetilde{\sigma}_\nu^2 = \widetilde{u}'(E_N \otimes I_T)\widetilde{u}/T(N-1)$ and that of σ_2^2 is $\widetilde{\sigma}_2^2 = \widetilde{u}'(\overline{J}_N \otimes I_T)\widetilde{u}/T$. These are the solutions to $D_\nu = \partial L/\partial\sigma_\nu^2 = 0$ and $D_\lambda = \partial L/\partial\sigma_\lambda^2 = 0$. $\widetilde{u}$ is the one-way GLS residuals using the restricted maximum likelihood estimates $\widetilde{\sigma}_\nu^2$ and $\widetilde{\sigma}_2^2$. In fact, from (4.17),

$$D_\mu = \partial L/\partial\sigma_\mu^2 = -\frac{1}{2}\,\text{tr}[\Omega^{-1}(I_N \otimes J_T)] + \frac{1}{2}[u'\Omega^{-1}(I_N \otimes J_T)\Omega^{-1}u]$$

Under the null hypothesis H_0^d this yields

$$\widetilde{D}_\mu = \frac{T}{2}\left\{\frac{1}{\widetilde{\sigma}_2^2}\left[\frac{\widetilde{u}'(\overline{J}_N \otimes \overline{J}_T)\widetilde{u}}{\widetilde{\sigma}_2^2} - 1\right] + \frac{(N-1)}{\widetilde{\sigma}_\nu^2}\left[\frac{\widetilde{u}'(E_N \otimes \overline{J}_T)\widetilde{u}}{(N-1)\widetilde{\sigma}_\nu^2} - 1\right]\right\}$$

which is the term given in (4.35). Similarly,

$$\widetilde{D}_\nu = -\frac{1}{2\widetilde{\sigma}_2^2}\,\text{tr}(\overline{J}_N \otimes I_T) - \frac{1}{2\widetilde{\sigma}_\nu^2}\,\text{tr}(E_N \otimes I_T) + \frac{1}{2\widetilde{\sigma}_2^4}\widetilde{u}'(\overline{J}_N \otimes I_T)\widetilde{u} + \frac{1}{2\widetilde{\sigma}_\nu^4}\widetilde{u}'(E_N \otimes I_T)\widetilde{u}$$

$$\widetilde{D}_\lambda = -\frac{1}{2\widetilde{\sigma}_2^2}\,\text{tr}(J_N \otimes I_T) + \frac{1}{2\widetilde{\sigma}_2^4}\widetilde{u}'(J_N \otimes I_T)\widetilde{u}$$

The last two score equations when set equal to zero yield estimates of σ_ν^2 and σ_2^2. Using (4.19), Ω^{-1} under H_0^d and $\partial\Omega/\partial\theta_r$ for $r = 1, 2, 3$, we get the information matrix. For example,

$$J_{11} = E[-\partial^2 L/\partial\theta_1^2] = \frac{1}{2}\,\text{tr}[\Omega^{-1}(I_N \otimes J_T)]^2$$

with

$$\widetilde{J}_{11} = \frac{1}{2}\,\text{tr}\left[\frac{1}{\widetilde{\sigma}_2^2}(\overline{J}_N \otimes J_T) + \frac{1}{\widetilde{\sigma}_\nu^2}(E_N \otimes J_T)\right]^2$$
$$= \frac{1}{2}\,\text{tr}\left[\frac{T^2}{\widetilde{\sigma}_2^4}(\overline{J}_N \otimes \overline{J}_T) + \frac{T^2}{\widetilde{\sigma}_\nu^4}(E_N \otimes \overline{J}_T)\right]$$

$$= \frac{T^2}{2}\left[\frac{1}{\widetilde{\sigma}_2^4} + \frac{(N-1)}{\widetilde{\sigma}_\nu^4}\right]$$

$$J_{12} = E[-\partial^2 L/\partial\theta_1\partial\theta_2] = \frac{1}{2}\ \text{tr}[\Omega^{-1}(I_N \otimes J_T)\Omega^{-1}(J_N \otimes I_T)]$$

with

$$\widetilde{J}_{12} = \frac{1}{2}\ \text{tr}\left[\frac{1}{\widetilde{\sigma}_2^2}(\bar{J}_N \otimes J_T) + \frac{1}{\widetilde{\sigma}_\nu^2}(E_N \otimes J_T)\right]\left[\frac{1}{\widetilde{\sigma}_2^2}(J_N \otimes I_T)\right]$$

$$= \frac{1}{2}\ \text{tr}\left[\frac{NT}{\widetilde{\sigma}_2^4}(\bar{J}_N \otimes \bar{J}_T)\right] = \frac{NT}{2\widetilde{\sigma}_2^4}$$

$$J_{13} = E[-\partial^2 L/\partial\theta_1\partial\theta_3] = \frac{1}{2}\ \text{tr}[\Omega^{-1}(I_N \otimes J_T)\Omega^{-1}]$$

with

$$\widetilde{J}_{13} = \frac{1}{2}\ \text{tr}\left[\frac{1}{\widetilde{\sigma}_2^4}(\bar{J}_N \otimes J_T) + \frac{1}{\widetilde{\sigma}_\nu^4}(E_N \otimes J_T)\right]$$

$$= \frac{T}{2}\left[\frac{1}{\widetilde{\sigma}_2^4} + \frac{(N-1)}{\widetilde{\sigma}_\nu^4}\right]$$

$$J_{22} = E[-\partial^2 L/\partial\theta_2^2] = \frac{1}{2}\ \text{tr}[\Omega^{-1}(J_N \otimes I_T)]^2$$

with

$$\widetilde{J}_{22} = \frac{1}{2}\ \text{tr}\left[\frac{1}{\widetilde{\sigma}_2^2}(J_N \otimes I_T)\right]^2 = \frac{1}{2}\ \text{tr}\left[\frac{N^2}{\widetilde{\sigma}_2^4}(\bar{J}_N \otimes I_T)\right] = \frac{N^2 T}{2\widetilde{\sigma}_2^4}$$

$$J_{23} = E[-\partial^2 L/\partial\theta_2\partial\theta_3] = \frac{1}{2}\ \text{tr}[\Omega^{-1}(J_N \otimes I_T)\Omega^{-1}]$$

with

$$\widetilde{J}_{23} = \frac{1}{2}\ \text{tr}\left[\frac{N}{\widetilde{\sigma}_2^4}(\bar{J}_N \otimes I_T)\right] = \frac{NT}{2\widetilde{\sigma}_2^4}$$

and

$$J_{33} = E[-\partial^2 L/\partial\theta_3^2] = \frac{1}{2}\ \text{tr}[\Omega^{-1}]^2$$

with

$$\widetilde{J}_{33} = \frac{1}{2}\ \text{tr}\left[\frac{1}{\widetilde{\sigma}_2^4}(\bar{J}_N \otimes I_T) + \frac{1}{2\widetilde{\sigma}_\nu^4}(E_N \otimes I_T)\right]$$

$$= \frac{T}{2}\left[\frac{1}{\widetilde{\sigma}_2^4} + \frac{(N-1)}{\widetilde{\sigma}_\nu^4}\right]$$

We have all the terms of the information matrix. Upon inverting this 3×3 matrix, we get the (1,1)th element of the inverse to obtain the two-sided LM statistic for H_0^d :

$$\mathrm{LM}_\mu = \frac{2\widetilde{\sigma}_1^4\widetilde{\sigma}_\nu^4}{T(T-1)[\widetilde{\sigma}_\nu^4 + (N-1)\widetilde{\sigma}_2^4]}\left(\widetilde{D}_\mu\right)^2$$

The one-sided LM test for H_0^d is its square root which is given in (4.34).

One can easily check that if $\widetilde{\sigma}_\lambda^2 \to 0$, then $\widetilde{\sigma}_2^2 \to \widetilde{\sigma}_\nu^2$ and LM_μ given in (4.34), tends to the one-sided Honda test given in (4.25).

Exercise 4.8 *(Conditional Lagrange multiplier test: random time effects).* Show that the alternative LM test statistic for testing $H_0^e : \sigma_\lambda^2 = 0$ (assuming $\sigma_\mu^2 > 0$) can be obtained as follows:

$$\mathrm{LM}_\lambda = \frac{\sqrt{2}\widetilde{\sigma}_1^2\widetilde{\sigma}_\nu^2}{\sqrt{N(N-1)[\widetilde{\sigma}_\nu^4 + (T-1)\widetilde{\sigma}_1^4]}}\widetilde{D}_\lambda \tag{4.36}$$

where

$$\widetilde{D}_\lambda = \frac{N}{2}\left\{\frac{1}{\widetilde{\sigma}_1^2}\left[\frac{\widetilde{u}'(\bar{J}_N \otimes \bar{J}_T)\widetilde{u}}{\widetilde{\sigma}_1^2} - 1\right] + \frac{(T-1)}{\widetilde{\sigma}_\nu^2}\left[\frac{\widetilde{u}'(\bar{J}_N \otimes E_T)\widetilde{u}}{(T-1)\widetilde{\sigma}_\nu^2} - 1\right]\right\} \tag{4.37}$$

with $\widetilde{\sigma}_1^2 = \widetilde{u}'(I_N \otimes \bar{J}_T)\widetilde{u}/N$, $\widetilde{\sigma}_\nu^2 = \widetilde{u}'(I_N \otimes E_T)\widetilde{u}/N(T-1)$. The estimated disturbances $\widetilde{u}$ denote the one-way GLS residuals using the maximum likelihood estimates $\widetilde{\sigma}_\nu^2$ and $\widetilde{\sigma}_1^2$. The test statistic LM_λ is asymptotically distributed as $N(0,1)$ under H_0^e.

Solution

This follows a similar derivation to that in Exercise 4.7. Under $H_0^e : \sigma_\lambda^2 = 0$ (assuming $\sigma_\mu^2 > 0$), this is the one-way error component model described in (2.9) with

$$\Omega^{-1} = \frac{1}{\sigma_1^2}(I_N \otimes \bar{J}_T) + \frac{1}{\sigma_\nu^2}(I_N \otimes E_T) \tag{4.38}$$

given in (2.11). Here, $\sigma_1^2 = T\sigma_\mu^2 + \sigma_\nu^2$ and the restricted maximum likelihood estimator of σ_ν^2 is $\widetilde{u}'(I_N \otimes E_T)\widetilde{u}/N(T-1)$ and that of σ_1^2 is $\widetilde{\sigma}_1^2 = \widetilde{u}'(I_N \otimes \bar{J}_T)\widetilde{u}/N$. These are the solutions to $D_\nu = \partial L/\partial\sigma_\nu^2 = 0$ and $D_\mu = \partial L/\partial\sigma_\mu^2 = 0$. $\widetilde{u}$ is the one-way GLS residual using the restricted maximum likelihood estimates $\widetilde{\sigma}_\nu^2$ and $\widetilde{\sigma}_1^2$. In fact, from (4.17),

$$D_\lambda = \partial L/\partial\sigma_\lambda^2 = -\frac{1}{2}\,\mathrm{tr}[\Omega^{-1}(J_N \otimes I_T)] + \frac{1}{2}[u'\Omega^{-1}(J_N \otimes I_T)\Omega^{-1}u]$$

Under the null hypothesis H_0^e, this yields

$$\widetilde{D}_\lambda = \frac{N}{2}\left\{\frac{1}{\widetilde{\sigma}_1^2}\left[\frac{\widetilde{u}'(\bar{J}_N \otimes \bar{J}_T)\widetilde{u}}{\widetilde{\sigma}_1^2} - 1\right] + \frac{(T-1)}{\widetilde{\sigma}_\nu^2}\left[\frac{\widetilde{u}'(\bar{J}_N \otimes E_T)\widetilde{u}}{(T-1)\widetilde{\sigma}_\nu^2} - 1\right]\right\}$$

which is the term given in (4.37). Similarly,

$$\widetilde{D}_\mu = -\frac{1}{2\widetilde{\sigma}_1^2}\operatorname{tr}(I_N \otimes J_T) + \frac{1}{2\widetilde{\sigma}_1^4}\widetilde{u}'(I_N \otimes J_T)\widetilde{u}$$

$$\widetilde{D}_\nu = -\frac{1}{2\widetilde{\sigma}_1^2}\operatorname{tr}(I_N \otimes \bar{J}_T) - \frac{1}{2\widetilde{\sigma}_\nu^2}\operatorname{tr}(I_N \otimes E_T) + \frac{1}{2\widetilde{\sigma}_1^4}\widetilde{u}'(I_N \otimes \bar{J}_T)\widetilde{u}$$
$$+\frac{1}{2\widetilde{\sigma}_\nu^4}u'(I_N \otimes E_T)\widetilde{u}$$

The last two score equations when set equal to zero yield estimates of σ_1^2 and σ_ν^2.

Using (4.19), Ω^{-1} under H_0^e and $\partial\Omega/\Omega\theta_r$ for $r = 1, 2, 3$, we get the information matrix. For example,

$$J_{11} = E[-\partial^2 L/\partial\theta_1^2] = \frac{1}{2}\operatorname{tr}[\Omega^{-1}(I_N \otimes J_T)]^2$$

with

$$\widetilde{J}_{11} = \frac{1}{2}\operatorname{tr}\left[\frac{T^2}{\sigma_1^4}(I_N \otimes \bar{J}_T)\right] = \frac{NT^2}{\widetilde{\sigma}_1^4}$$

$$J_{12} = E[-\partial^2 L/\partial\theta_1\partial\theta_2] = \frac{1}{2}\operatorname{tr}[\Omega^{-1}(I_N \otimes J_T)\Omega^{-1}(J_N \otimes I_T)]$$

with

$$\widetilde{J}_{12} = \frac{1}{2}\operatorname{tr}\left[\frac{T}{\widetilde{\sigma}_1^4}(J_N \otimes \bar{J}_T)\right] = \frac{NT}{2\widetilde{\sigma}_1^4}$$

$$J_{13} = E[-\partial^2 L/\partial\theta_1\partial\theta_3] = \frac{1}{2}\operatorname{tr}[\Omega^{-1}(I_N \otimes J_T)\Omega^{-1}]$$

with

$$\widetilde{J}_{13} = \frac{1}{2}\operatorname{tr}\left[\frac{T}{\widetilde{\sigma}_1^4}(I_N \otimes \bar{J}_T)\right] = \frac{NT}{2\widetilde{\sigma}_1^4}$$

$$J_{22} = E[-\partial^2 L/\partial\theta_2^2] = \frac{1}{2}\operatorname{tr}[\Omega^{-1}(J_N \otimes I_T)]^2$$

with

$$\widetilde{J}_{22} = \frac{1}{2}\operatorname{tr}\left[\frac{(J_N \otimes \bar{J}_T)}{\widetilde{\sigma}_1^2} + \frac{(J_N \otimes E_T)}{\widetilde{\sigma}_\nu^2}\right]^2$$
$$= \frac{N^2}{2}\left[\frac{1}{\widetilde{\sigma}_4^2} + \frac{(T-1)}{\widetilde{\sigma}_\nu^4}\right]$$

$$J_{23} = E[-\partial^2 L/\partial\theta_2\partial\theta_3] = \frac{1}{2}tr[\Omega^{-1}(J_N \otimes I_T)\Omega^{-1}]$$

with
$$\widetilde{J}_{23} = \frac{1}{2}\operatorname{tr}\left[\frac{1}{\widetilde{\sigma}_1^4}(J_N \otimes \overline{J}_T) + \frac{1}{\widetilde{\sigma}_\nu^4}(J_N \otimes E_T)\right]$$
$$= \frac{N}{2}\left[\frac{1}{\widetilde{\sigma}_1^4} + \frac{(T-1)}{\widetilde{\sigma}_\nu^4}\right]$$

and
$$J_{33} = E[-\partial^2 L/\partial\theta_3^2] = \frac{1}{2}\operatorname{tr}[\Omega^{-1}]^2$$

with
$$\widetilde{J}_{33} = \frac{1}{2}\operatorname{tr}\left[\frac{1}{\widetilde{\sigma}_1^4}(I_N \otimes \overline{J}_T) + \frac{1}{\widetilde{\sigma}_\nu^4}(I_N \otimes E_T)\right]$$
$$= \frac{N}{2}\left[\frac{1}{\widetilde{\sigma}_1^4} + \frac{(T-1)}{\widetilde{\sigma}_\nu^4}\right]$$

We have all the terms of the information matrix. Upon inverting this 3×3 matrix, we get the (2,2)th element of the inverse to obtain the two-sided LM statistic for H_0^e:
$$\text{LM}_\lambda = \frac{2\widetilde{\sigma}_1^4\widetilde{\sigma}_\nu^4}{N(N-1)[\widetilde{\sigma}_\nu^4 + (T-1)\widetilde{\sigma}_1^4]}\left(\widetilde{D}_\lambda\right)^2$$

The one-sided LM test for H_0^e is its square root which is given in (4.36).

Exercise 4.9 *(Testing for poolability using Grunfeld's data).* This is based on Example 1 in Baltagi (2008, p.61). Grunfeld (1958) considered the investment equation
$$I_{it} = \alpha + \beta_1 F_{it} + \beta_2 C_{it} + u_{it} \tag{4.39}$$

where I_{it} denotes real gross investment for firm i in year t, F_{it} is the real value of the firm (shares outstanding) and C_{it} is the real value of the capital stock. These panel data consist of 10 large US manufacturing firms over 20 years, 1935–54, and are available on the Wiley web site as Grunfeld.fil. This data set, even though dated, is of manageable size for classroom use and has been used by Zellner (1962). We apply the tests considered above to the Grunfeld (1958) investment equation.

(a) Test the null hypothesis $H_0: \delta_i = \delta$ for all $i = 1, 2, \ldots, N$, using the Chow (1960) test described in Exercise 4.1 and equation (4.8).
(b) Test the null hypothesis $H_0: \delta_i = \delta$ for all $i = 1, 2, \ldots, N$, using the Roy (1957) and Zellner (1962) test described in Exercise 4.2 and equation (4.14).

Solution

(a) For the Grunfeld data, Chow's test for poolability across firms as in (4.1) gives an observed F-statistic of 27.75 and is distributed as $F(27, 170)$ under $H_0: \delta_i = \delta$ for

$i = 1, \ldots, N$. The RRSS = 1755850.48 is obtained from pooled OLS, and the URSS = 324728.47 is obtained from summing the RSS from 10 individual firm OLS regressions, each with 17 degrees of freedom. There are 27 restrictions and the test rejects poolability across firms for all coefficients. One can test for poolability of slopes only, allowing for varying intercepts. The restricted model is the within regression with firm dummies. The RRSS = 523478, while the unrestricted regression is the same as above. The observed F-statistic is 5.78 which is distributed as $F(18, 170)$ under $H_0: \beta_i = \beta$ for $i = 1, \ldots, N$. This again is significant at the 5% level and rejects poolability of the slopes across firms.

(b) The Roy–Zellner test for poolability across firms, allowing for one-way error component disturbances, yields an observed F-value of 4.35 which is distributed as $F(27, 170)$ under $H_0: \delta_i = \delta$ for $i = 1, \ldots, N$. This still rejects poolability across firms even after allowing for one-way error component disturbances.

Exercise 4.10 *(Testing for random time and individual effects using Grunfeld's data).* This is based on Problem 4.9 in Baltagi (2008). Using the Grunfeld (1958) investment equation:

(a) Test the null hypotheses $H_0^a: \sigma_\mu^2 = 0$; $H_0^b: \sigma_\lambda^2 = 0$; and $H_0^c: \sigma_\mu^2 = \sigma_\lambda^2 = 0$, using the Breusch and Pagan (1980) two-sided test derived in Exercise 4.3.

(b) Test the null hypotheses $H_0^a: \sigma_\mu^2 = 0$; $H_0^b: \sigma_\lambda^2 = 0$; and $H_0^c: \sigma_\mu^2 = \sigma_\lambda^2 = 0$, using the Honda (1985) one-sided tests given in (4.25), (4.29) and (4.31).

(c) Test the null hypotheses $H_0^c: \sigma_\mu^2 = \sigma_\lambda^2 = 0$, using the King and Wu (1997) LMMP one-sided test given by (4.30) and derived in Exercise 4.4.

(d) Compute the standardized Honda (1985) LM test for $H_0^a: \sigma_\mu^2 = 0$ and $H_0^b: \sigma_\lambda^2 = 0$ using (4.26), (4.27) and (4.28).

(e) Compute the F-statistics for testing that firm dummy variables are jointly significant, the time dummy variables are jointly significant, both firm and time dummy variables are jointly significant, firm dummy variables are jointly significant conditional on the presence of the time dummies, and finally that the time dummy variables are jointly significant conditional on the presence of the firm dummies. These are simple F tests obtained from fixed effects regressions, the first of which was given in (2.8) in Exercise 2.3.

(f) Compute the likelihood ratio test statistics under normality for testing $H_0^a: \sigma_\mu^2 = 0$; $H_0^b: \sigma_\lambda^2 = 0$; $H_0^c: \sigma_\mu^2 = \sigma_\lambda^2 = 0$; $H_0^d: \sigma_\mu^2 = 0$ (assuming $\sigma_\lambda^2 > 0$); and $H_0^e: \sigma_\lambda^2 = 0$ (assuming $\sigma_\mu^2 > 0$).

(g) Compute the conditional Lagrange multiplier test statistics derived in Exercises 4.7 and 4.8 for testing $H_0^d: \sigma_\mu^2 = 0$ (assuming $\sigma_\lambda^2 > 0$) and $H_0^e: \sigma_\lambda^2 = 0$ (assuming $\sigma_\mu^2 > 0$).

(h) Comment on the results.

Solution

Table 4.1 in Baltagi (2008, p.69) gives the observed test statistics. This is reproduced here for convenience. All the tests strongly suggest that there are individual specific effects. However, for testing time-specific effects, except for the two-sided LM Breusch and Pagan (1980) test which rejects $H_0^b: \sigma_\lambda^2 = 0$, all the tests suggest that there are no time-specific effects for this data. The conflict occurs because B takes on a large negative value (−2.540) for this data set. This means that the two-sided LM test is $B^2 = 6.454$, which is larger than the χ_1^2 critical value (3.841). Whereas, the one-sided LM, SLM, LR and F-tests for this

Table 4.1 Test Results for the Grunfeld Example*

Null Hypothesis	H_0^a	H_0^b	H_0^c	H_0^d	H_0^e
Tests	$\sigma_\mu^2 = 0$	$\sigma_\lambda^2 = 0$	$\sigma_\mu^2 = \sigma_\lambda^2 = 0$	$\sigma_\mu^2 = 0/\sigma_\lambda^2 > 0$	$\sigma_\lambda^2 = 0/\sigma_\mu^2 > 0$
Breusch–Pagan	798.162 (3.841)	6.454 (3.841)	804.615 (5.991)	–	–
HO	28.252 (1.645)	−2.540 (1.645)	18.181 (1.645)	–	–
KW	–	–	21.832 (1.645)	–	–
SLM	32.661 (1.645)	−2.433 (1.645)	–	–	–
F	49.177 (1.930)	0.235 (1.645)	17.403 (1.543)	52.362 (1.648)	1.403 (1.935)
LR	193.091 (2.706)	0 (2.706)	193.108 (4.231)	193.108 (2.706)	0.017 (2.706)
LM_μ	–	–	–	28.252 (2.706)	–
LM_λ	–	–	–	–	0.110 (2.706)

*Numbers in parentheses are asymptotic critical values at the 5% level.

Source: Baltagi *et al.* (1992). Reproduced by permission of Elsevier Science Publishers B.V. (North Holland).

hypothesis do not reject H_0^b. In fact, the LM_λ test proposed by Baltagi *et al.* (1992) for testing $H_0^e: \sigma_\lambda^2 = 0$ (assuming $\sigma_\mu^2 > 0$) as well as the LR and F-tests for this hypothesis do not reject H_0^e. These data clearly support the use of the one-sided test in empirical applications.

The SAS programs written in matrix language that reproduce most of the results in this table are given on the Wiley web site. Unfortunately, Stata only replicates the Breusch and Pagan (1980) test for $H_0^a: \sigma_\mu^2 = 0$ with the command xttest0. This is shown in Table 4.2 in Baltagi (2008, p.70). The F-statistics can be replicated with EViews as shown in Table 4.3 in Baltagi (2008, p.71).

4.3 HAUSMAN'S TEST FOR CORRELATED EFFECTS

A critical assumption in the error component regression model is that $E(u_{it}/X_{it}) = 0$. This is important, given that the disturbances contain individual invariant effects (the μ_i) which are unobserved and may be correlated with the X_{it}. For example, in an earnings equation these μ_i may denote unobservable ability of the individual and this may be correlated with the schooling variable included on the right-hand side of this equation. In this case, $E(u_{it}/X_{it}) \neq 0$ and the GLS estimator $\widehat{\beta}_{\text{GLS}}$ becomes biased and inconsistent for β. However, the within transformation wipes out these μ_i and leaves the within estimator $\widetilde{\beta}_{\text{Within}}$ unbiased and consistent for β. Hausman (1978) suggests comparing $\widehat{\beta}_{\text{GLS}}$ and $\widetilde{\beta}_{\text{Within}}$, both of which are consistent under the null hypothesis $H_0: E(u_{it}/X_{it}) = 0$, but which will have different probability limits if H_0 is not true. In fact, $\widetilde{\beta}_{\text{Within}}$ is consistent whether H_0 is true or not, while $\widehat{\beta}_{\text{GLS}}$ is BLUE, consistent and asymptotically efficient under H_0, but is inconsistent when H_0 is false. A natural test statistic would be based on $\widetilde{q}_1 = \widehat{\beta}_{\text{GLS}} - \widetilde{\beta}_{\text{Within}}$.

Exercise 4.11 *(Hausman (1978) test based on a contrast of two estimators)*

(a) Show that under $H_0: E(u_{it}/X_{it}) = 0$, plim $\widehat{q}_1 = 0$ and $\text{cov}(\widehat{q}_1, \widehat{\beta}_{\text{GLS}}) = 0$.
(b) Show that $\text{var}(\widehat{q}_1) = \text{var}(\widetilde{\beta}_{\text{Within}}) - \text{var}(\widehat{\beta}_{\text{GLS}})$.

Solution

(a) Under $H_0: E(u_{it}/X_{it}) = 0$, both $\widetilde{\beta}_{\text{Within}}$ and $\widehat{\beta}_{\text{GLS}}$ are consistent, therefore plim $\widehat{q}_1 = 0$. Using the fact that $\widehat{\beta}_{\text{GLS}} - \beta = (X'\Omega^{-1}X)^{-1}X'\Omega^{-1}u$ and $\widetilde{\beta}_{\text{Within}} - \beta = (X'QX)^{-1}X'Qu$ yields $E(\widehat{q}_1) = 0$ and

$$\begin{aligned}\text{cov}(\widehat{\beta}_{\text{GLS}}, \widehat{q}_1) &= \text{var}(\widehat{\beta}_{\text{GLS}}) - \text{cov}(\widehat{\beta}_{\text{GLS}}, \widetilde{\beta}_{\text{Within}})\\ &= (X'\Omega^{-1}X)^{-1} - (X'\Omega^{-1}X)^{-1}X\Omega^{-1}E(uu')QX(X'QX)^{-1}\\ &= (X'\Omega^{-1}X)^{-1} - (X'\Omega^{-1}X)^{-1} = 0\end{aligned}$$

(b) Using the fact that $\widetilde{\beta}_{\text{Within}} = \widehat{\beta}_{\text{GLS}} - \widehat{q}_1$ leads to

$$\text{var}(\widetilde{\beta}_{\text{Within}}) = \text{var}(\widehat{\beta}_{\text{GLS}}) + \text{var}(\widehat{q}_1)$$

since $\text{cov}(\widehat{\beta}_{\text{GLS}}, \widehat{q}_1) = 0$. Therefore,

$$\text{var}(\widehat{q}_1) = \text{var}(\widetilde{\beta}_{\text{Within}}) - \text{var}(\widehat{\beta}_{\text{GLS}}) = \sigma_\nu^2(X'QX)^{-1} - (X'\Omega^{-1}X)^{-1} \tag{4.40}$$

Hence, the Hausman test statistic is given by

$$m_1 = \hat{q}_1'[\text{var}(\widehat{q}_1)]^{-1}\widehat{q}_1 \tag{4.41}$$

and under $H_0: E(u_{it}/X_{it}) = 0$ is asymptotically distributed as χ^2_K, where K denotes the dimension of slope vector β. In order to make this test operational, Ω is replaced by a consistent estimator $\widehat{\Omega}$, and GLS by its corresponding feasible GLS. Stata substitutes the Swamy and Arora (1972) estimator of Ω.

Exercise 4.12 *(Hausman (1978) test based on an artificial regression).* This is based on Problem 4.12 in Baltagi (2008). Consider the augmented regression

$$y^* = X^*\beta + \widetilde{X}\gamma + w \tag{4.42}$$

where $y^* = \sigma_\nu\Omega^{-1/2}y$, $X^* = \sigma_\nu\Omega^{-1/2}X$, and $\widetilde{X} = QX$. Hausman (1978) suggested an alternative asymptotically equivalent test based on testing whether $\gamma = 0$.

(a) Show that OLS on (4.42) yields

$$\widehat{\gamma} = \widetilde{\beta}_{\text{Within}} - \widehat{\beta}_{\text{Between}}$$

(b) Show that $\text{var}(\widehat{\gamma}) = \text{var}(\widetilde{\beta}_{\text{Within}}) + \text{var}(\widehat{\beta}_{\text{Between}})$.

(c) Show that Hausman's test in part (a) can be alternatively obtained using either of the following artificial regressions:

$$y^* = X^*\beta + \overline{X}\gamma + w_2 \tag{4.43}$$

$$y^* = X^*\beta + X\gamma + w_3 \tag{4.44}$$

where $\overline{X} = PX$. Hausman's test is equivalent to testing whether $\gamma = 0$ from any one of these OLS regressions (see Baltagi and Liu, 2007).

Solution

(a) This is a standard Wald test for the omission of the variables $\widetilde{X}$ from (4.42). In fact, performing OLS on (4.42) yields

$$\begin{pmatrix} \widehat{\beta} \\ \widehat{\gamma} \end{pmatrix} = \begin{bmatrix} X'(Q+\phi^2 P)X & X'QX \\ X'QX & X'QX \end{bmatrix}^{-1} \begin{pmatrix} X'(Q+\phi^2 P)y \\ X'Qy \end{pmatrix}$$

where $\sigma_\nu \Omega^{-1/2} = Q + \phi P$ and $\phi = \sigma_\nu/\sigma_1$ (see (2.12)). Using partitioned inverse formulas, one can show that

$$\begin{pmatrix} \widehat{\beta} \\ \widehat{\gamma} \end{pmatrix} = \begin{bmatrix} G & -G \\ -G & (X'QX)^{-1} + G \end{bmatrix} \begin{pmatrix} X'(Q+\phi^2 P)y \\ X'Qy \end{pmatrix}$$

where $G = (X'PX)^{-1}/\phi^2$. Simple matrix multiplication yields

$$\begin{aligned} \widehat{\beta} &= GX'(Q+\phi^2 P)y - GX'Qy \\ &= G(\phi^2 X'Py) = \phi^2 (X'PX)^{-1}(X'Py)/\phi^2 = (X'PX)^{-1}X'Py \\ &= \widehat{\beta}_{\text{Between}} \end{aligned} \tag{4.45}$$

Also,

$$\begin{aligned} \widehat{\gamma} &= -GX'(Q+\phi^2 P)y + (X'QX)^{-1}X'Qy + GX'Qy \\ &= -\phi^2 (X'PX)^{-1}X'Py/\phi^2 + (X'QX)^{-1}X'Qy \\ &= \widetilde{\beta}_{\text{Within}} - \widehat{\beta}_{\text{Between}} \end{aligned} \tag{4.46}$$

(b) Substituting the within and between estimators of β into (4.46) yields

$$\widehat{\gamma} = (X'QX)^{-1}X'Q\nu - (X'PX)^{-1}X'Pu \tag{4.47}$$

It is easy to show that $E(\widehat{\gamma}) = 0$ and

$$\text{var}(\widehat{\gamma}) = E(\widehat{\gamma}\widehat{\gamma}') = \sigma_\nu^2 (X'QX)^{-1} + \sigma_1^2 (X'PX)^{-1} = \text{var}(\widetilde{\beta}_{\text{Within}}) + \text{var}(\widehat{\beta}_{\text{Between}}) \tag{4.48}$$

since the cross-product terms are zero. Hausman (1978) tests $\gamma = 0$ from (4.42) using an F-statistic. The restricted regression yields OLS of y^* on X^*. This is the Fuller and

Battese (1973) regression yielding GLS as described in Exercise 2.5. The unrestricted regression adds the matrix of within regressors $\widetilde{X}$ as in (4.42). The test for $\gamma = 0$ is based on $\widehat{\gamma} = \widetilde{\beta}_{\text{Within}} - \widehat{\beta}_{\text{Between}} = 0$ and the corresponding test statistic would therefore be $\widehat{\gamma}'(\text{var}(\widehat{\gamma}))^{-1}\widehat{\gamma}$, which looks different from the Hausman m_1 statistic given in (4.41). These tests are numerically exactly identical (see Hausman and Taylor, 1981) and Exercise 4.13.

(c) We show this result for (4.43). The proof for (4.44) is quite similar and is omitted to save space. Performing OLS on (4.43) yields

$$\begin{aligned}
\begin{pmatrix} \hat{\beta} \\ \hat{\gamma} \end{pmatrix} &= \left[\begin{pmatrix} X^{*\prime} \\ \widetilde{X}' \end{pmatrix} \begin{pmatrix} X^* & \widetilde{X} \end{pmatrix} \right]^{-1} \begin{pmatrix} X^{*\prime} \\ \widetilde{X}' \end{pmatrix} y^* \\
&= \begin{bmatrix} \tilde{X}'\tilde{X} + \phi^2 \overline{X}'\overline{X} & \phi \overline{X}'\overline{X} \\ \phi \overline{X}'\overline{X} & \overline{X}'\overline{X} \end{bmatrix}^{-1} \begin{pmatrix} \tilde{X}'\tilde{y} + \phi^2 \overline{X}'\overline{y} \\ \phi \overline{X}'\overline{y} \end{pmatrix} \\
&= \begin{bmatrix} \left(\tilde{X}'\tilde{X}\right)^{-1} & -\phi \left(\tilde{X}'\tilde{X}\right)^{-1} \\ -\phi \left(\tilde{X}'\tilde{X}\right)^{-1} & \phi^2 \left(\tilde{X}'\tilde{X}\right)^{-1} + \left(\overline{X}'\overline{X}\right)^{-1} \end{bmatrix} \begin{pmatrix} \tilde{X}'\tilde{y} + \phi^2 \overline{X}'\overline{y} \\ \phi \overline{X}'\overline{y} \end{pmatrix} \\
&= \begin{pmatrix} \left(\tilde{X}'\tilde{X}\right)^{-1} \tilde{X}'\tilde{y} \\ \phi \left[\left(\overline{X}'\overline{X}\right)^{-1} \overline{X}'\overline{y} - \left(\tilde{X}'\tilde{X}\right)^{-1} \tilde{X}'\tilde{y} \right] \end{pmatrix}
\end{aligned}$$

using partitioned inversion and the fact that $\tilde{X}'\overline{X} = 0$. Hence,

$$\hat{\gamma} = \phi \left(\hat{\beta}_{\text{BE}} - \widetilde{\beta}_{\text{FE}} \right)$$

and under H_0, $E\left(\hat{\gamma}\right) = 0$, and

$$\begin{aligned}
\text{var}\left(\hat{\gamma}\right) &= E\left(\hat{\gamma}\hat{\gamma}'\right) \\
&= \phi^2 E \left[\left(\overline{X}'\overline{X}\right)^{-1} \overline{X}'\overline{u}\overline{u}'\overline{X} \left(\overline{X}'\overline{X}\right)^{-1} + \left(\tilde{X}'\tilde{X}\right)^{-1} \tilde{X}'\tilde{u}\tilde{u}'\tilde{X} \left(\tilde{X}'\tilde{X}\right)^{-1} \right] \\
&= \phi^2 \left[\sigma_1^2 \left(\overline{X}'\overline{X}\right)^{-1} + \sigma_\nu^2 \left(\tilde{X}'\tilde{X}\right)^{-1} \right] \\
&= \phi^2 \left[\text{var}\left(\hat{\beta}_{\text{BE}}\right) + \text{var}\left(\widetilde{\beta}_{\text{FE}}\right) \right]
\end{aligned}$$

since the cross-product terms are zero. Therefore, the Wald test statistic of $\gamma = 0$ is numerically exactly identical to testing that the contrast $\widehat{q}_3 = \widetilde{\beta}_{\text{FE}} - \widehat{\beta}_{\text{BE}}$ is equal to zero.

We remark that methods are equivalent because any two variable combinations using X^*, $\tilde{X}$, $\overline{X}$ and X span the same space as $\left\{\tilde{X}, \overline{X}\right\}$.

Exercise 4.13 *(Three contrasts yield the same Hausman test).* This is based on Problem 4.13 in Baltagi (2008).

(a) Show that Hausman's test can be performed using any of the following three paired differences: $\widehat{q}_1 = \widehat{\beta}_{\text{GLS}} - \widetilde{\beta}_{\text{Within}}$; $\widehat{q}_2 = \widehat{\beta}_{\text{GLS}} - \widehat{\beta}_{\text{Between}}$; or $\widehat{q}_3 = \widetilde{\beta}_{\text{Within}} - \widehat{\beta}_{\text{Between}}$. The corresponding test statistics can be computed as $m_i = \widehat{q}_i' V_i^{-1} \widehat{q}_i$, where $V_i = \text{var}(\widehat{q}_i)$. These are asymptotically distributed as χ_K^2 for $i = 1, 2, 3$ under $H_0 \colon E(u_{it}/X_{it}) = 0$.

(b) Verify that the test statistics derived in part (a) are also exactly numerically identical to $m_4 = \widehat{q}_4' V_4^{-1} \widehat{q}_4$ where $\widehat{q}_4 = \widehat{\beta}_{\text{GLS}} - \widehat{\beta}_{\text{OLS}}$ and $V_4 = \text{var}(\widehat{q}_4)$. This is based on Baltagi (1989a) and Koning (1990).

Solution

(a) Hausman and Taylor (1981) proved that these three test statistics differ from each other by non-singular matrices. This easily follows from the fact that

$$\widehat{\beta}_{\text{GLS}} = W_1 \widetilde{\beta}_{\text{Within}} + (I - W_1) \widehat{\beta}_{\text{Between}}$$

derived in (2.22). So $\widehat{q}_1 = \widehat{\beta}_{\text{GLS}} - \widetilde{\beta}_{\text{Within}} = (I - W_1)(\widehat{\beta}_{\text{Between}} - \widetilde{\beta}_{\text{Within}}) = \Gamma \widehat{q}_3$, where $\Gamma = W_1 - I$. Also, $\text{var}(\widehat{q}_1) = \Gamma \text{var}(\widehat{q}_3) \Gamma'$ and

$$\begin{aligned} m_1 &= \widehat{q}_1' [\text{var}(\widehat{q}_1)]^{-1} \widehat{q}_1 = \widehat{q}_3' \Gamma' [\Gamma \text{var}(\widehat{q}_3) \Gamma']^{-1} \Gamma \widehat{q}_3 \\ &= \widehat{q}_3' [\text{var}(\widehat{q}_3)]^{-1} \widehat{q}_3 = m_3 \end{aligned}$$

This proves that m_1 and m_3 are numerically identical.

Next, we show that m_2 is numerically identical to m_3. We have $m_2 = \widehat{q}_2' V_2^{-1} \widehat{q}_2$, where $\widehat{q}_2 = \widehat{\beta}_{\text{GLS}} - \widehat{\beta}_{\text{Between}}$. Using the fact that $\widehat{\beta}_{\text{GLS}} = W_1 \widetilde{\beta}_{\text{Within}} + (I - W_1) \widehat{\beta}_{\text{Between}}$ from (2.22) yields $\widehat{q}_2 = W_1(\widetilde{\beta}_{\text{Within}} - \widehat{\beta}_{\text{Between}}) = W_1 \widehat{q}_3$. Also, $V_2 = \text{var}(\widehat{q}_2) = W_1 \text{var}(\widehat{q}_3) W_1'$. Substituting $\widehat{q}_2 = W_1 \widehat{q}_3$ and $V_2 = W_1 V_3 W_1'$ in m_2 gives

$$m_2 = \widehat{q}_2' V_2^{-1} \widehat{q}_2 = \widehat{q}_3' W_1' (W_1 V_3 W_1')^{-1} W_1 q_3 = \widehat{q}_3' V_3^{-1} q_3 = m_3$$

This proves that m_2 and m_3 are numerically identical.

(b) $\widehat{q}_4 = \widehat{\beta}_{\text{GLS}} - \widehat{\beta}_{\text{OLS}}$ with $\widehat{\beta}_{\text{GLS}} = W_1 \widetilde{\beta}_{\text{Within}} + (I - W_1) \widehat{\beta}_{\text{Between}}$ from (2.22). But $\widehat{\beta}_{\text{OLS}} = (X'QX + X'PX)^{-1}(X'Qy + X'Py) = \Delta \widetilde{\beta}_{\text{Within}} + (I - \Delta) \widehat{\beta}_{\text{Between}}$ where $\Delta = (X'X)^{-1} X'QX$. Hence, $\widehat{q}_4 = (W_1 - \Delta)(\widetilde{\beta}_{\text{Within}} - \widehat{\beta}_{\text{Between}}) = (W_1 - \Delta) \widehat{q}_3$ with

$$V_4 = \text{var}(\widehat{q}_4) = (W_1 - \Delta) \text{var}(\widehat{q}_3)(W_1 - \Delta)'$$

Therefore,

$$\begin{aligned} m_4 &= \widehat{q}_4' V_4^{-1} q_4 = \widehat{q}_3' (W_1 - \Delta)' [(W_1 - \Delta) V_3 (W_1 - \Delta)']^{-1} (W_1 - \Delta) \widehat{q}_3 \\ &= \widehat{q}_3' V_3^{-1} \widehat{q}_3 = m_3 \end{aligned}$$

More recently, Arellano (1993) provided an alternative variable addition test to the Hausman test which is robust to autocorrelation and heteroskedasticity of arbitrary form. In particular, Arellano (1993) suggests constructing the regression

$$\begin{pmatrix} y_i^+ \\ \overline{y}_i \end{pmatrix} = \begin{bmatrix} X_i^+ & 0 \\ \overline{X}_i' & \overline{X}_i' \end{bmatrix} \begin{pmatrix} \beta \\ \gamma \end{pmatrix} + \begin{pmatrix} u_i^+ \\ \overline{u}_i \end{pmatrix} \tag{4.49}$$

where $y_i^+ = (y_{i1}^+, \ldots, y_{iT}^+)'$ and $X_i^+ = (X_{i1}^+, \ldots, X_{iT}^+)'$ is a $T \times K$ matrix and $u_i^+ = (u_{i1}^+, \ldots, u_{iT}^+)'$. Also

$$y_{it}^+ = \left[\frac{T-t}{T-t+1}\right]^{1/2} \left[y_{it} - \frac{1}{(T-t)}(y_{i,t+1} + \cdots + y_{iT})\right], \quad t = 1, 2, \ldots, T-1$$

defines the forward orthogonal deviations operator, $\overline{y}_i = \Sigma_{t=1}^T y_{it}/T$, X_{it}^+, $\overline{X}_i$, and u_{it}^+ and $\overline{u}_i$ are similarly defined. OLS on this model yields $\widehat{\beta} = \widetilde{\beta}_{\text{Within}}$ and $\widehat{\gamma} = \widehat{\beta}_{\text{Between}} - \widetilde{\beta}_{\text{Within}}$. Therefore, Hausman's test can be obtained from the artificial regression (4.49) by testing for $\gamma = 0$. If the disturbances are heteroskedastic and/or serially correlated, then neither $\widetilde{\beta}_{\text{Within}}$ nor $\widehat{\beta}_{\text{GLS}}$ is optimal under the null or alternative. Also, the standard formulas for the asymptotic variances of these estimators are no longer valid. Moreover, these estimators cannot be ranked in terms of efficiency so that the var(q) is not the difference of the two variances var($\widetilde{\beta}_W$)−var($\widehat{\beta}_{\text{GLS}}$). Arellano (1993) suggests using White's (1984) robust variance–covariance matrix from OLS on (4.49) and applying a standard Wald test for $\gamma = 0$ using these robust standard errors. This can be easily calculated using any standard regression package that computes White robust standard errors. This test is asymptotically distributed as χ_K^2 under the null.

Exercise 4.14 *(Testing for correlated effects in panels).* This is based on Baltagi (1995a) and is also Problem 4.14 in Baltagi (2008). Consider Arellano's (1993) extended regression given by (4.49) but now using an alternative transformation of the data. In particular, let $H = (C', \iota_T/T)'$ where C is the first $(T-1)$ rows of the within transformation $E_T = I_T - \overline{J}_T$, I_T is an identity matrix of dimension T, and $\overline{J}_T = \iota_T \iota_T'/T$ with ι_T a vector of ones of dimension T.

(a) Show that the matrix C satisfies the properties $C\iota_T = 0$, $C'(CC')^{-1}C = I_T - \overline{J}_T$; see Arellano and Bover (1995).

(b) For the transformed model $y_i^+ = Hy_i = (y_i^{*\prime}, \overline{y}_i)'$, where $y_i^* = Cy_i$ and $\overline{y}_i = \Sigma_{t=1}^T y_{it}/T$. The typical element of y_i^* is given by $y_{it}^* = [y_{it} - \overline{y}_i]$ for $t = 1, 2, \ldots, T-1$. Consider the extended regression similar to (4.49),

$$\begin{bmatrix} y_i^* \\ \overline{y}_i \end{bmatrix} = \begin{bmatrix} X_i^{*\prime} & 0 \\ \overline{X}_i' & \overline{X}_i' \end{bmatrix} \begin{bmatrix} \beta \\ \gamma \end{bmatrix} + \begin{bmatrix} u_i^* \\ \overline{u}_i \end{bmatrix} \tag{4.50}$$

and show that GLS on this extended regression yields $\widehat{\beta} = \widetilde{\beta}_{\text{Within}}$ and $\widehat{\gamma} = \widehat{\beta}_{\text{Between}} - \widetilde{\beta}_{\text{Within}}$, where $\widetilde{\beta}_{\text{Within}}$ and $\widehat{\beta}_{\text{Between}}$ are the familiar panel data estimators. Conclude that Hausman's test for $H_0: E(\mu_i/X_i) = 0$ can be based on a test for $\gamma = 0$, as shown by Arellano (1993). See Xiong (1996b).

Solution

(a) Let C be the first $(T-1)$ rows of $(I_T - \overline{J}_T)$. Since $(I_T - \overline{J}_T)\iota_T = 0$, it follows that the first $(T-1)$ rows postmultiplied by ι_T will yield zero. Hence, $C\iota_T = 0$. Actually,

$$E_T = I_T - \overline{J}_T = \begin{bmatrix} (1-\frac{1}{T}) & -\frac{1}{T} & \cdots & -\frac{1}{T} \\ -\frac{1}{T} & (1-\frac{1}{T}) & \cdots & -\frac{1}{T} \\ \vdots & \vdots & \cdots & \vdots \\ -\frac{1}{T} & -\frac{1}{T} & \cdots & (1-\frac{1}{T}) \end{bmatrix}$$

If we let

$$E_T = \begin{pmatrix} C \\ a' \end{pmatrix}$$

where a' is the last row of E_T, then

$$E_T E_T' = E_T = \begin{pmatrix} CC' & Ca \\ a'C' & a'a \end{pmatrix}$$

It is clear from partitioning the above matrix that

$$CC' = I_{T-1} - (J_{T-1}/T) = (E_{T-1} + \overline{J}_{T-1}) - \left(\frac{T-1}{T}\right)\overline{J}_{T-1} = E_{T-1} + (\overline{J}_{T-1}/T)$$

where the second equality holds by applying the Wansbeek and Kapteyn (1982) trick of substituting $E_{T-1} + \overline{J}_{T-1}$ for I_{T-1} and $(T-1)\overline{J}_{T-1}$ for J_{T-1}. Hence, $(C_1C_1')^{-1} = E_{T-1} + T\overline{J}_{T-1}$.

From the above matrix,

$$C = \left[\left(I_{T-1} - \frac{J_{T-1}}{T}\right), -(\iota_{T-1}/T)\right] = [E_{T-1} + (\overline{J}_{T-1}/T), -(\iota_{T-1}/T)] \quad (4.51)$$

Therefore $(CC')^{-1}C = [(E_{T-1} + \overline{J}_{T-1}), -\iota_{T-1}] = [I_{T-1}, -\iota_{T-1}]$ and

$$C'(CC')^{-1}C = \begin{pmatrix} E_{T-1} + \frac{J_{T-1}}{T} \\ -\frac{\iota_{T-1}'}{T} \end{pmatrix}(I_{T-1}, -\iota_{T-1}) = \begin{bmatrix} E_{T-1} + \frac{J_{T-1}}{T} & -\frac{\iota_{T-1}}{T} \\ -\frac{\iota_{T-1}'}{T} & \frac{T-1}{T} \end{bmatrix} \quad (4.52)$$
$$= I_T - \overline{J}_T = E_T$$

(b) Stacking the $y_i^* = Cy_i$ observations on top of the $\overline{y}_i$ observations in Arellano's (1993) extended regression gives

$$\begin{bmatrix} y^* \\ \overline{y} \end{bmatrix} = \begin{bmatrix} X^* & 0 \\ \overline{X} & \overline{X} \end{bmatrix}\begin{bmatrix} \beta \\ \gamma \end{bmatrix} + \begin{bmatrix} u^* \\ \overline{u} \end{bmatrix} \quad (4.53)$$

where $X^* = (I_N \otimes C)X$ and $\overline{X} = (I_N \otimes \iota_T'/T)X$ with X being the $NT \times K$ matrix of regressors. Also, $u^* = (I_N \otimes C)u = (I_N \otimes C)\nu$ since $C\iota_T = 0$, and $\overline{u} = (I_N \otimes \iota_T'/T)u$. The transformed disturbances have zero mean and variance–covariance matrix

$$\Sigma = \begin{bmatrix} \sigma_\nu^2(I_N \otimes CC') & 0 \\ 0 & \sigma_1^2 I_N/T \end{bmatrix}$$

where $\sigma_1^2 = T\sigma_\mu^2 + \sigma_\nu^2$. This follows from the error component Ω given in (2.9) and

$$\begin{aligned} (I_N \otimes C)\Omega(I_N \otimes C') &= \sigma_\nu^2(I_N \otimes CC') \\ (I_N \otimes \iota_T'/T)\Omega(I_N \otimes \iota_T/T) &= \sigma_1^2 I_N/T \\ (I_N \otimes C)\Omega(I_N \otimes \iota_T/T) &= \sigma_\nu^2(I_N \otimes C)(I_N \otimes \iota_T/T) = 0 \end{aligned}$$

Hence,

$$\Sigma^{-1} = \begin{bmatrix} (I_N \otimes (CC')^{-1})/\sigma_\nu^2 & 0 \\ 0 & TI_N/\sigma_1^2 \end{bmatrix}$$

and GLS yields

$$\begin{pmatrix} \hat{\beta} \\ \hat{\gamma} \end{pmatrix} = \begin{bmatrix} X'(I_N \otimes C'(CC')^{-1}C)X/\sigma_\nu^2 + T\overline{X}'\overline{X}/\sigma_1^2 & T\overline{X}'\overline{X}/\sigma_1^2 \\ T\overline{X}'\overline{X}/\sigma_1^2 & T\overline{X}'\overline{X}/\sigma_1^2 \end{bmatrix}^{-1}$$

$$\times \begin{pmatrix} X'(I_N \otimes C'(CC')^{-1}C)y/\sigma_\nu^2 + T\overline{X}'\overline{y}/\sigma_1^2 \\ T\overline{X}'\overline{y}/\sigma_1^2 \end{pmatrix}$$

Using the fact that $C'(CC')^{-1}C = E_T$ and denoting by $\tilde{X} = (I_N \otimes E_T)X$ yields, after partitioned inversion,

$$\begin{pmatrix} \hat{\beta} \\ \hat{\gamma} \end{pmatrix} = \begin{bmatrix} \sigma_\nu^2\left(\tilde{X}'\tilde{X}\right)^{-1} & -\sigma_\nu^2\left(\tilde{X}'\tilde{X}\right)^{-1} \\ -\sigma_\nu^2\left(\tilde{X}'\tilde{X}\right)^{-1} & \sigma_\nu^2\left(\tilde{X}'\tilde{X}\right)^{-1} + \sigma_1^2\left(\overline{X}'\overline{X}\right)^{-1}/T \end{bmatrix} \begin{pmatrix} (\tilde{X}'\tilde{y}/\sigma_\nu^2) + (T\overline{X}'\overline{y}/\sigma_1^2) \\ T\overline{X}'\overline{y}/\sigma_1^2 \end{pmatrix}$$

$$= \begin{pmatrix} \left(\tilde{X}'\tilde{X}\right)^{-1}\tilde{X}'\tilde{y} \\ -\left(\tilde{X}'\tilde{X}\right)^{-1}\tilde{X}'\tilde{y} + \left(\overline{X}'\overline{X}\right)^{-1}\overline{X}'\overline{y} \end{pmatrix} = \begin{pmatrix} \widetilde{\beta}_{\text{Within}} \\ \widehat{\beta}_{\text{Between}} - \widetilde{\beta}_{\text{Within}} \end{pmatrix}$$

Hence, Hausman's test for uncorrelated effects can be based upon testing $H_0: \gamma = 0$ in the above augmented regression model.

Exercise 4.15 *(Hausman's test as a Gauss–Newton regression).* This is based on Baltagi (1997). Ahn and Low (1996) showed that Hausman's test statistic can be obtained from the artificial regression of the GLS residuals $(y_{it}^* - X_{it}^{*\prime}\widehat{\beta}_{\text{GLS}})$ on $\widetilde{X}$ and $\overline{X}$, where $\widetilde{X}$ has typical element $\widetilde{X}_{it,k}$ and $\overline{X}$ is the matrix of regressors averaged over time. The test statistic is NT times the R^2 of this regression.

(a) Using (4.42), derive the Gauss–Newton regression (GNR) to test $H_0: \gamma = 0$. Knowing θ, show that this GNR is simply the regression of the GLS residuals $(y_{it}^* - X_{it}^{*\prime}\widehat{\beta}_{\text{GLS}})$ on X_{it}^* and $\widetilde{X}_{it}$.
(b) Prove that the GNR test derived in part (a) yields exactly the same test statistic as that proposed by Ahn and Low (1996).

Solution

(a) Knowing θ, the restricted estimates under $H_0: \gamma = 0$, yield $\widehat{\beta} = \widehat{\beta}_{\text{GLS}}$ and $\widehat{\gamma} = 0$. Therefore, the GNR on (4.42) regresses the GLS residuals $(y_{it}^* - X_{it}^{*\prime}\widehat{\beta}_{\text{GLS}})$ on the derivatives of the regression function (4.42) with respect to β and γ evaluated at $\widehat{\beta}_{\text{GLS}}$ and $\widehat{\gamma} = 0$. These regressors are X_{it}^* and $\widetilde{X}_{it}$, respectively. Hence, the GNR is simply the regression of the GLS residuals $(y_{it}^* - X_{it}^{*\prime}\widehat{\beta}_{\text{GLS}})$ on X_{it}^* and $\widetilde{X}_{it}$.
(b) Since X_{it}^* and $\widetilde{X}_{it}$ span the same space as $\widetilde{X}_{it}$ and $\overline{X}_{i.}$, the GNR in part (a) yields the same regression sums of squares and, therefore, the same Hausman test statistic (NT times R^2) as that proposed by Ahn and Low (1996). See Davidson and MacKinnon (1993) for an excellent exposition of GNR.

Exercise 4.16 *(Hausman's test using Grunfeld's data).* This is based on Problem 4.15 in Baltagi (2008). Consider the Grunfeld investment equation described in Exercise 4.9 and equation (4.39).

(a) Compute the Hausman test statistic based on the three contrasts described in Exercise 4.13. Use the Swamy and Arora (1972) feasible GLS estimates instead of the true GLS estimates.
(b) Compute the Hausman test statistic based on the artificial regression in Exercise 4.12 and equation (4.42).

Solution

(a) The within estimates are given by $(\widetilde{\beta}_1, \widetilde{\beta}_2) = (0.1101238, 0.310065)$, with variance–covariance matrix

$$\text{var}(\widetilde{\beta}_{\text{Within}}) = \begin{bmatrix} 0.14058 & -0.077468 \\ & 0.3011788 \end{bmatrix} \times 10^{-3}$$

The between estimates are given by $(0.1346461, 0.03203147)$, with variance–covariance matrix

$$\text{var}(\widehat{\beta}_{\text{Between}}) = \begin{bmatrix} 0.82630142 & -3.7002477 \\ & 36.4572431 \end{bmatrix} \times 10^{-3}$$

From Exercise 4.13, the resulting Hausman χ_2^2 test statistic based on $\widehat{q}_3 = \widetilde{\beta}_{\text{Within}} - \widehat{\beta}_{\text{Between}}$ is $m_3 = 2.131$ which is not significant at the 5% level. Hence, we do not reject the null hypothesis $H_0: E(u_{it}/X_{it}) = 0$ of no correlation between the individual effects and the X_{it}. Similarly, based on the Swamy and Arora (1972) feasible GLS estimates, one can compute $m_1 = 2.330$ based on $\widehat{q}_1 = \widehat{\beta}_{\text{GLS}} - \widetilde{\beta}_{\text{Within}}$, and $m_2 = 2.131$ based on $\widehat{q}_2 = \widehat{\beta}_{\text{GLS}} - \widehat{\beta}_{\text{Between}}$. These give the same decision; see the associated Stata output in Tables 4.4 and 4.5 of Baltagi (2008, p.77).

(b) The augmented regression, given in (4.42) based on the Swamy and Arora (1972) feasible GLS estimates of θ, yields the estimates $\widehat{\beta} = (0.135, 0.032)$ and $\widehat{\gamma} = (-0.025, 0.278)$ with an observed F-value for $H_0: \gamma = 0$, equal to 1.066. This is distributed under H_0 as $F(2, 195)$. This is again not significant at the 5% level and leads to non-rejection of H_0.

Exercise 4.17 *(Relative efficiency of the between estimator with respect to the within estimator).* This is based on Baltagi (1999) and is also Problem 4.18 in Baltagi (2008). Consider the simple panel data regression model

$$y_{it} = \alpha + \beta x_{it} + u_{it}, \quad i = 1, 2, \ldots, N, \quad t = 1, 2, \ldots, T \tag{4.54}$$

where α and β are scalars. Subtract the mean equation to get rid of the constant

$$y_{it} - \overline{y}_{..} = \beta(x_{it} - \overline{x}_{..}) + u_{it} - \overline{u}_{..} \tag{4.55}$$

where $\overline{x}_{..} = \sum_{i=1}^{N}\sum_{t=1}^{T} x_{it}/NT$ and $\overline{y}_{..}$ and $\overline{u}_{..}$ are similarly defined. Add and subtract $\overline{x}_{i.}$ from the regressor in parentheses and rearrange

$$y_{it} - \overline{y}_{..} = \beta(x_{it} - \overline{x}_{i.}) + \beta(\overline{x}_{i.} - \overline{x}_{..}) + u_{it} - \overline{u}_{..} \tag{4.56}$$

where $\overline{x}_{i.} = \sum_{t=1}^{T} x_{it}/T$. Now run the unrestricted least squares regression

$$y_{it} - \overline{y}_{..} = \beta_w(x_{it} - \overline{x}_{i.}) + \beta_b(\overline{x}_{i.} - \overline{x}_{..}) + u_{it} - \overline{u}_{..} \tag{4.57}$$

where β_w is not necessarily equal to β_b.

(a) Show that the least squares estimator of β_w from (4.57) is the within estimator and that of β_b is the between estimator.
(b) Show that if $u_{it} = \mu_i + \nu_{it}$ where $\mu_i \sim \text{IID}(0, \sigma_\mu^2)$ and $\nu_{it} \sim \text{IID}(0, \sigma_\nu^2)$ independent of each other and among themselves, then OLS is equivalent to GLS on (4.57).
(c) Show that for the model given in (4.54), the relative efficiency of the between estimator with respect to the within estimator is equal to $(B_{XX}/W_{XX})[(1-\rho)/(T\rho + (1-\rho))]$, where $W_{XX} = \sum_{i=1}^{N}\sum_{t=1}^{T}(x_{it} - \overline{x}_{i.})^2$ denotes the within variation and $B_{XX} = T\sum_{i=1}^{N}(\overline{x}_{i.} - \overline{x}_{..})^2$ denotes the between variation. Also, $\rho = \sigma_\mu^2/(\sigma_\mu^2 + \sigma_\nu^2)$ denotes the equicorrelation coefficient.
(d) Show that the square of the t-statistic used to test $H_0: \beta_w = \beta_b$ in (4.57) yields exactly Hausman's (1978) specification test.

Solution

(a) In matrix form, the model in (4.54) can be written as in (2.3),

$$y = \alpha \iota_{NT} + x\beta + u$$

where $y = (y_{11}, \ldots, y_{1T}, \ldots, y_{N1}, \ldots, y_{NT})'$ is $NT \times 1$, x is $NT \times 1$ and ι_{NT} is a vector of ones of dimension NT. Equation (4.55) can be written as

$$(I_{NT} - \bar{J}_{NT})y = (I_{NT} - \bar{J}_{NT})x\beta + (I_{NT} - \bar{J}_{NT})u$$

where I_{NT} denotes an identity matrix of dimension NT and $\bar{J}_{NT} = J_{NT}/NT$ denotes the averaging matrix with J_{NT} being a matrix of ones of dimension NT. Finally, (4.57) can be written as

$$(I_{NT} - \bar{J}_{NT})y = Qx\beta_W + (P - \bar{J}_{NT})x\beta_b + (I_{NT} - \bar{J}_{NT})u \quad (4.58)$$

where $P = I_N \otimes \bar{J}_N$ is the averaging matrix across time for each individual and $Q = I_{NT} - P$ is the deviations from means for each individual defined in Exercise 2.1. The typical element of Qx is $x_{it} - \bar{x}_{i.}$ and the typical element of $(P - \bar{J}_{NT})x$ is $\bar{x}_{i.} - \bar{x}_{..}$. Equation (4.58) can be rewritten as

$$y^* = Z\delta + u^* \quad (4.59)$$

where $y^* = (I_{NT} - \bar{J}_{NT})y$, $Z = [Qx, (P - \bar{J}_{NT})x]$, $u^* = (I_{NT} - \bar{J}_{NT})u$, and $\delta' = (\beta_W, \beta_b)$. Note that the regressors in (4.58) or (4.59) are orthogonal to each other since Q and $P - \bar{J}_{NT}$ are orthogonal. Hence, it is easily verified that $\widehat{\delta}_{\text{OLS}} = (Z'Z)^{-1}Z'y^*$ yields $\widehat{\beta}_W = (x'Qx)^{-1}x'Qy$ which is the within estimator of β and $\widehat{\beta}_b = [x'(P - \bar{J}_{NT})x]^{-1}x'(P - \bar{J}_{NT})y$ which is the between estimator of β.

(b) From (2.10), $\text{var}(u) = \Omega = \sigma_1^2 P + \sigma_\nu^2 Q$, where $\sigma_1^2 = T\sigma_\mu^2 + \sigma_\nu^2$. Hence,

$$\text{var}(u^*) = \Omega^* = (I_{NT} - \bar{J}_{NT})\Omega(I_{NT} - \bar{J}_{NT})' = \sigma_1^2(P - \bar{J}_{NT}) + \sigma_\nu^2 Q \quad (4.60)$$

since $P\bar{J}_{NT} = \bar{J}_{NT}$ and $Q\bar{J}_{NT} = 0$. Zyskind's (1967) necessary and sufficient condition for OLS to be equivalent to GLS on (4.59) is given by $P_Z\Omega^* = \Omega^* P_Z$, where $P_Z = Z(Z'Z)^{-1}Z'$ denotes the projection matrix on Z. The latter is given by

$$\begin{aligned} P_Z &= P_{Qx} + P_{(P-\bar{J}_{NT})x} \\ &= Qx(x'Qx)^{-1}x'Q + (P - \bar{J}_{NT})x[x'(P - \bar{J}_{NT})x]^{-1}x'(P - \bar{J}_{NT}) \end{aligned}$$

It is easy to verify using (4.60) that $P_Z\Omega^* = \sigma_\nu^2 Qx(x'Qx)^{-1}x'Q + \sigma_1^2(P - \bar{J}_{NT})x[x'(P - \bar{J}_{NT})x]^{-1}x'(P - \bar{J}_{NT}) = \Omega^* P_Z$. Alternatively, one can use the generalized inverse

$$\Omega^{*-} = (P - \bar{J}_{NT})/\sigma_1^2 + Q/\sigma_\nu^2$$

to show that $\widehat{\delta}_{\text{GLS}} = (Z'\Omega^{*-}Z)^{-1}Z'\Omega^{*-}y^* = \widehat{\delta}_{\text{OLS}}$.

(c) If the true model is the restricted model given by (4.54), then $\widehat{\beta}_w = \beta + (x'Qx)^{-1}x'Qu$ with $E(\widehat{\beta}_w) = \beta$ and $\text{var}(\widehat{\beta}_w) = \sigma_\nu^2(x'Qx)^{-1}$. Similarly, $\widehat{\beta}_b = \beta + (x'(P - \overline{J}_{NT})x)^{-1}x'(P - \overline{J}_{NT})u$ with $E(\widehat{\beta}_b) = \beta$ and $\text{var}(\widehat{\beta}_b) = \sigma_1^2(x'(P - \overline{J}_{NT})x)^{-1}$. Therefore, both $\widehat{\beta}_w$ and $\widehat{\beta}_b$ are unbiased for β. The relative efficiency of the between estimator with respect to the within estimator is equal to

$$\begin{aligned}\text{var}(\widehat{\beta}_w)/\text{var}(\widehat{\beta}_b) &= \sigma_\nu^2(x'Qx)^{-1}/\sigma_1^2(x'(P - \overline{J}_{NT})x)^{-1} \\ &= (B_{XX}/W_{XX})[(1-\rho)/(T\rho + (1-\rho))]\end{aligned}$$

where $W_{XX} = x'Qx$ denotes the within variation, $B_{XX} = x'(P - \overline{J}_{NT})x$ denotes the between variation, and $\rho = \sigma_\mu^2/(\sigma_\mu^2 + \sigma_\nu^2)$ denotes the equicorrelation coefficient. If $B_{XX}/W_{XX} = 3$ and $\rho = 0.2, 0.5, 0.8$ then for $T = 10$ this relative efficiency is 0.86, 0.27 and 0.07, respectively. However, if $B_{XX}/W_{XX} = 1$ then these relative efficiencies are 0.29, 0.09 and 0.02, respectively.

(d) The square of the t-statistic used for testing $H_0: \beta_w = \beta_b$ in (4.57) yields

$$t^2 = (\widehat{\beta}_w - \widehat{\beta}_b)^2/\text{var}(\widehat{\beta}_w - \widehat{\beta}_b) = (\widehat{\beta}_w - \widehat{\beta}_b)^2/[\text{var}(\widehat{\beta}_w) + \text{var}(\widehat{\beta}_b)]$$

as desribed in Hausman and Taylor (1981). The last equality follows from the fact that $\text{cov}(\widehat{\beta}_w, \widehat{\beta}_b) = 0$. This can be easily verified from the expressions for $\widehat{\beta}_w$ and $\widehat{\beta}_b$ given in part (c) and the fact that Q and $P - \overline{J}_{NT}$ are orthogonal. See also Gurmu (2000).

Exercise 4.18 *(Hausman's test using Munnell's data).* This is based on Problem 4.17 in Baltagi (2008). Consider the Munnell (1990) data set described in Exercise 3.13 and used to estimate the Cobb–Douglas production function described in (3.38).

(a) Compute the Hausman test statistic for the one-way model based on RE vs FE. Use the Swamy and Arora (1972) feasible GLS estimates instead of the true GLS estimates.
(b) Compute the Hausman test statistic for the one-way model but now with the contrast of the between and RE estimators.
(c) Compute the Hausman test statistic for the mixed two-way model considered in Exercise 3.13, part (d). What do you conclude?

Solution

(a) With EViews, one runs the RE one-way model using the Swamy and Arora (1972) feasible GLS estimates option. This was reported in Exercise 3.13 and is not reproduced here. From this Swamy and Arora run, one asks for the Hausman option which rejects the null hypothesis that the RE estimator is efficient (Table 4.2). The backup FE one-way regression is also given by EViews but this is not reproduced here since it was reported in Exercise 3.13. The Hausman one-way test based on FE vs RE is 9.717 and is significant at the 5% level. Note that Stata gives a slightly different statistic but the same decision.

Table 4.2 Public Capital Productivity Data. Hausman Test FE vs RE

Correlated Random Effects-Hausman Test
Equation : EQ01
Test cross-section random effects

Test Summary	Chi-Sq. Statistic	Chi-Sq.d.f.	Prob.
Cross-section random	9.717662	4	0.0455

Cross-section random effects test comparisons:

Variable	Fixed	Random	Var(Diff.)	Prob.
LNK1	−0.026146	0.004441	0.000297	0.0757
LNK2	0.292008	0.310549	0.000242	0.2328
LNL	0.768156	0.729668	0.000289	0.0235
U	−0.005298	−0.006173	0.000000	0.0289

(b) Using Stata, one stores the between and RE estimates as bbe and bre and issues the command shown in Table 4.3. The null hypothesis is rejected at the 5% level.

Table 4.3 Public Capital Productivity Data. Hausman Test Between vs RE

```
hausman bbe bre
                   ---- Coefficients ----
             |      (b)            (B)              (b-B)        sqrt(diag(V_b-V_B))
             |      bbe            bre            Difference            S.E.
-------------+----------------------------------------------------------------
          k1 |   .1793651       .0044385           .1749265          .0680558
           k |   .3019542       .3105484          -.0085942          .0368349
           l |   .5761274       .7296706          -.1535432          .0505675
       unemp |  -.0038903      -.0061725           .0022822          .0098667
------------------------------------------------------------------------------
                      b = consistent under Ho and Ha; obtained from xtreg
       B = inconsistent underHa, efficient under Ho; obtained from xtreg

    Test: Ho:  difference in coefficients not systematic

                  chi2(4) =(b-B)'[(V_b-V_B)^(-1)](b-B)
                          =        9.74
                Prob>chi2 =      0.0451
```

(c) The Hausman test for the mixed two-way model with fixed time effects and random state effects is shown in Table 4.4. The estimation output was reported in Exercise 3.13, part (d), and is not reproduced here. The Hausman test rejects the null hypothesis that the mixed effects estimator is efficient. The backup FE two-way regression is also given by EViews but this is not reproduced here since it was reported in Exercise 3.13.

Table 4.4 Public Capital Productivity Data. Hausman Test for the Mixed Model

Correlated Random Effects-Hausman Test
Equation: EQ01
Test cross-section random effects

Test Summary	Chi-Sq. Statistic	Chi-Sq. d.f.	Prob.
Cross-section random	35.698560	4	0.0000

Cross-section random effects test comparisons:

Variable	Fixed	Random	Var(Diff.)	Prob.
LNK1	-0.030173	0.031111	0.000170	0.0000
LNK2	0.168832	0.242728	0.000274	0.0000
LNL	0.769303	0.743566	0.000238	0.0953
U	-0.004221	-0.004555	0.000000	0.2457

4.3.1 Empirical Example

Glick and Rose (2002) considered the following gravity type trade equation in order to estimate the effect of currency union membership on international trade based on a data set including 422, 715 observations on annual bilateral trade data among 217 countries over the period 1948–1997:

$$\begin{aligned}\ln \text{Trade}_{ijt} &= \alpha + \beta_1 \ln \text{CU}_{ijt} + \beta_2 \ln \text{DIST}_{ij} + \beta_3 \ln(Y_i Y_j)_t + \beta_4 \ln\left(\frac{Y_i Y_j}{\text{Pop}_i \text{Pop}_j}\right)_t \\ &+\beta_5 \text{Comlang}_{ij} + \beta_6 \text{Border}_{ij} + \beta_7 \text{Regional}_{ij} + \beta_8 \text{Landl}_{ij} + \beta_9 \text{Island}_{ij} \\ &+\beta_{10} \text{lareap}_{ij} + \beta_{11} \text{Comcol}_{ij} + \beta_{12} \text{Curcol}_{ijt} + \beta_{13} \text{Colony}_{ij} + \beta_{14} \text{Comctry}_{ij} + u_{ijt}\end{aligned}$$

where CU_{ijt} is a dummy variable which is unity if i and j use the same currency at time t; DIST_{ij} is the distance between countries i and j; Y_i is real GDP and Pop_i is the population of country i; Comlang_{ij} is a dummy variable which is unity if i and j have a common language; Border_{ij} is a dummy variable which is unity if i and j share a land border; Regional_{ijt} is a dummy variable which is unity if i and j belong to the same regional trade agreement; Landl_{ij} is the number of landlocked countries in the country pair (0, 1, or 2); Island_{ij} is the number of island nations in the pair (0, 1, or 2); lareap_{ij} is the Log of product of land areas; Comcol_{ij} is a dummy variable which is unity for common colonizer post 1945; Curcol_{ijt} is a dummy variable which is unity if i and j are currently in a colonial relationship; Colony_{ij} is a dummy variable which is unity for pairs ever in colonial relationship; and Comctry_{ij} is a dummy for the same nation/perennial colonies. Glick and Rose (2002) find that the coefficient of the currency union dummy is positive, significant and insensitive to a series of perturbation when using different panel data methods to estimate the model. In fact, they find that countries who use the same currency more than double their trade.

Exercise 4.19 *(Currency Union and Trade).* This is based on Problem 4.19, in Baltagi (2008). Using the Glick and Rose (2002) data set, downloadable from Rose's web site at http://haas.berkeley.edu:

(a) Replicate their results (reported in Table 4 of their paper) for the OLS with time dummies and robust standard errors, the FE and RE with country pair effects; compare the effects of joining a curency union versus not on trade.
(b) Perform the Hausman test based on the FE vs RE for country pair effects.

Solution

(a) Rose posts the data set and Stata log files on his web site. Here we replicate the results using EViews. Tables 4.5, 4.6, and 4.7, respectively, report the OLS with time dummies

Table 4.5 Currency Union and Trade. OLS with Time Dummies

Dependent Variable: LTRADE
Method: Panel Least Squares

Sample: 1 508949
Cross-sections included: 11178
Total panel (unbalanced) observations: 219558
White period standard errors & covariance (d.f. corrected)

Variable	Coefficient	Std. Error	t-Statistic	Prob.
CUSTRICT	1.298118	0.127858	10.15281	0.0000
LDIST	−1.105322	0.023375	−47.28628	0.0000
LRGDP	0.927435	0.009971	93.01180	0.0000
LRGDPPC	0.457196	0.015148	30.18242	0.0000
COMLANG	0.324542	0.042270	7.677772	0.0000
BORDER	0.426679	0.119538	3.569406	0.0004
REGIONAL	0.986432	0.130109	7.581602	0.0000
LANDL	−0.143233	0.033992	−4.213681	0.0000
ISLAND	0.053434	0.038154	1.400465	0.1614
LAREAP	−0.092400	0.008201	−11.26735	0.0000
COMCOL	0.450326	0.069852	6.446850	0.0000
CURCOL	0.824015	0.253593	3.249360	0.0012
COLONY	1.308253	0.130023	10.06170	0.0000
COMCTRY	−0.228142	1.050930	−0.217085	0.8281
C	−30.58112	0.376778	−81.16489	0.0000

Effects Specification

Period fixed (dummy variables)

R-squared	0.637669	Mean dependent var	10.04162
Adjusted R-squared	0.637565	S.D. dependent var	3.358780
S.E. of regression	2.022071	Akaike info criterion	4.246413
Sum squared resid	897460.6	Schwarz criterion	4.249415
Log likelihood	−466103.0	F-statistic	6131.586
Durbin-Watson stat	0.427859	Prob.(F-statistic)	0.000000

Table 4.6 Currency Union and Trade. Fixed Effects Results

Dependent Variable: LTRADE
Method: Panel Least Squares

Sample: 1 508949
Cross-sections included: 11178
Total panel (unbalanced) observations: 219558

Variable	Coefficient	Std. Error	t-Statistic	Prob.
CUSTRICT	0.651232	0.050578	12.87579	0.0000
LRGDP	0.047951	0.008775	5.464751	0.0000
LRGDPPC	0.790950	0.014017	56.42613	0.0000
REGIONAL	0.692351	0.045007	15.38309	0.0000
CURCOL	0.358431	0.088131	4.067028	0.0000
C	−4.956947	0.228282	−21.71411	0.0000

Effects Specification

Cross-section fixed (dummy variables)

R-squared	0.852961	Mean dependent var	10.04162
Adjusted R-squared	0.845071	S.D. dependent var	3.358780
S.E. of regression	1.322050	Akaike info criterion	3.445836
Sum squared resid	364201.5	Schwarz criterion	3.970426
Log likelihood	−367097.4	F-statistic	108.0997
Durbin-Watson stat	0.896738	Prob.(F-statistic)	0.000000

Table 4.7 Currency Union and Trade. RE Swamy and Arora Estimator

Dependent Variable: LTRADE
Method: Panel EGLS (Cross-section random effects)

Sample: 1 508949
Cross-sections included: 11178
Total panel (unbalanced) observations: 219558
Swamy and Arora estimator of component variances

Variable	Coefficient	Std. Error	t-Statistic	Prob.
CUSTRICT	0.725479	0.048701	14.89663	0.0000
LDIST	−1.337264	0.023613	−56.63337	0.0000
LRGDP	0.361756	0.006396	56.55954	0.0000
LRGDPPC	0.434098	0.010197	42.57156	0.0000
COMLANG	0.212942	0.046270	4.602172	0.0000
BORDER	0.506668	0.122313	4.142399	0.0000
REGIONAL	0.636351	0.043924	14.48748	0.0000
LANDL	−0.840599	0.032140	−26.15411	0.0000
ISLAND	−0.014011	0.038743	−0.361648	0.7176
LAREAP	0.207270	0.007103	29.17900	0.0000
COMCOL	−0.263460	0.059284	−4.444055	0.0000
CURCOL	0.476816	0.087600	5.443100	0.0000
COLONY	3.060644	0.152385	20.08492	0.0000
COMCTRY	1.166532	1.177886	0.990360	0.3220
C	−9.046332	0.251164	−36.01756	0.0000

Effects Specification

Cross-section random S.D./Rho	1.632183	0.6038
Idiosyncratic random S.D./Rho	1.322050	0.3962

Weighted Statistics

R-squared	0.151375	Mean dependent var	1.499543
Adjusted R-squared	0.151321	S.D. dependent var	1.483607
S.E. of regression	1.366754	Sum squared resid	410110.2
F-statistic	2797.250	Durbin-Watson stat	0.810917
Prob.(F-statistic)	0.000000		

Unweighted Statistics

R-squared	0.426223	Mean dependent var	10.04162
Sum squared resid	1421195	Durbin-Watson stat	0.276168

and robust standard errors, the FE with country pairs dummies, and the RE estimator based on the Swamy and Arora (1972) feasible GLS estimates. Note that we could have also computed the latter with the Wallace and Hussain or Amemiya options, but we do not report those for lack of space. Note that the effect of joining a currency union on trade is $e^{0.65} - 1$ for fixed effects and $e^{0.72} - 1$ for random effects. In either case this leads to more than doubling the trade.

(b) The Hausman test based on FE vs RE for country pair effects is given in Table 4.8. It rejects the null and the efficiency of the RE estimator.

Table 4.8 Currency Union and Trade. Hausman Test FE vs RE

Correlated Random Effects-HausmanTest
Equation: EQTABLE2
Test cross-section random effects

Test Summary	Chi-Sq. Statistic	Chi-Sq.d.f.	Prob.
Cross-section random	7894.053484	5	0.0000

Cross-section random effects test comparisons:

Variable	Fixed	Random	Var(Diff.)	Prob.
CUSTRICT	0.651232	0.725479	0.000186	0.0000
LRGDP	0.047951	0.361756	0.000036	0.0000
LRGDPPC	0.790950	0.434098	0.000093	0.0000
REGIONAL	0.692351	0.636351	0.000096	0.0000
CURCOL	0.358431	0.476816	0.000093	0.0000

5

Heteroskedasticity and Serial Correlation

5.1 HETEROSKEDASTIC ERROR COMPONENT MODEL

The standard error component model given by equations (2.1) and (2.2) assumes that the regression disturbances are homoskedastic with the same variance across time and individuals. This may be a restrictive assumption for panels, where the cross-sectional units may be of varying size and as a result may exhibit different variation. For example, when dealing with gasoline demand across OECD countries, steam electric generation across various size utilities, or estimating cost functions for various US airline firms, one should expect to find heteroskedasticity in the disturbance term. Assuming homoskedastic disturbances when heteroskedasticity is present will still result in consistent estimates of the regression coefficients, but these estimates will not be efficient. Also, the standard errors of these estimates will be biased and one should compute robust standard errors correcting for the possible presence of heteroskedasticity. In this section, we relax the assumption of homoskedasticity of the disturbances and introduce heteroskedasticity into the error component model.

Exercise 5.1 *(Heteroskedastic individual effects).* This is based on Problems 5.1 and 5.2 in Baltagi (2008). Mazodier and Trognon (1978) generalized the homoskedastic error component model to the case where the μ_i are heteroskedastic, i.e., $\mu_i \sim (0, w_i^2)$ for $i = 1, \ldots, N$, but $\nu_{it} \sim \text{IID}(0, \sigma_\nu^2)$. In vector form, $\mu \sim (0, \Sigma_\mu)$ where $\Sigma_\mu = \text{diag}[w_i^2]$ is a diagonal matrix of dimension $N \times N$, and $\nu \sim (0, \sigma_\nu^2 I_{NT})$.

(a) Show that

$$\Omega = \text{diag}[Tw_i^2 + \sigma_\nu^2] \otimes \bar{J}_T + \text{diag}[\sigma_\nu^2] \otimes E_T \tag{5.1}$$

(b) Show that $y^* = \sigma_\nu \Omega^{-1/2} y$ has a typical element $y_{it}^* = y_{it} - \theta_i \bar{y}_{i.}$ where $\theta_i = 1 - (\sigma_\nu/\tau_i)$ and $\tau_i^2 = Tw_i^2 + \sigma_\nu^2$ for $i = 1, \ldots, N$.

Solution

(a) Using the fact that $u = Z_\mu \mu + \nu$, we get

$$\Omega = E(uu') = Z_\mu E(\mu\mu')Z_\mu' + E(\nu\nu') \tag{5.2}$$

where the cross-product terms have zero expectations since μ and ν are independent. The only difference from the standard error component model is that $E(\mu\mu') = \Sigma_\mu =$

$\text{diag}[w_i^2]$ is a diagonal matrix of dimension $(N \times N)$. Hence,

$$\begin{aligned}
\Omega &= (I_N \otimes \iota_T)\text{diag}[w_i^2](I_N \otimes \iota_T') + \sigma_\nu^2 I_{NT} \\
&= \begin{bmatrix} \iota_T & 0 & \cdots & 0 \\ 0 & \iota_T & \cdots & 0 \\ \vdots & \vdots & \ddots & \vdots \\ 0 & 0 & \cdots & \iota_T \end{bmatrix} \begin{bmatrix} w_1^2 & 0 & \cdots & 0 \\ 0 & w_2^2 & \cdots & 0 \\ \vdots & \vdots & \ddots & \vdots \\ 0 & 0 & \cdots & w_N^2 \end{bmatrix} \begin{bmatrix} \iota_T' & 0 & \cdots & 0 \\ 0 & \iota_T' & \cdots & 0 \\ \vdots & \vdots & \ddots & \vdots \\ 0 & 0 & \cdots & \iota_T' \end{bmatrix} + \sigma_\nu^2 I_{NT} \\
&= \begin{bmatrix} w_1^2 J_T & 0 & \cdots & 0 \\ 0 & w_2^2 J_T & \cdots & 0 \\ \vdots & \vdots & \ddots & \vdots \\ 0 & 0 & \cdots & w_N^2 J_T \end{bmatrix} + \sigma_\nu^2 (I_N \otimes I_T) \\
&= \text{diag}[w_i^2] \otimes J_T + \text{diag}[\sigma_\nu^2] \otimes I_T
\end{aligned} \tag{5.3}$$

with $J_T = \iota_T \iota_T'$. Using the Wansbeek and Kapteyn (1982) trick, we replace J_T by $T\bar{J}_T$ and I_T by $E_T + \bar{J}_T$, where E_T is by definition $I_T - \bar{J}_T$. Substituting these in (5.3), we get $\Omega = \text{diag}[Tw_i^2] \otimes \bar{J}_T + \text{diag}[\sigma_\nu^2] \otimes (E_T + \bar{J}_T)$. Collecting like terms in $\bar{J}_T$ leads to $\Omega = \text{diag}[Tw_i^2 + \sigma_\nu^2] \otimes \bar{J}_T + \text{diag}[\sigma_\nu^2] \otimes E_T$.

(b) From (5.1), we get

$$\Omega^r = \text{diag}[(\tau_i^2)^r] \otimes \bar{J}_T + \text{diag}[(\sigma_\nu^2)^r] \otimes E_T \tag{5.4}$$

where $\tau_i^2 = Tw_i^2 + \sigma_\nu^2$, and r is any arbitrary scalar. Therefore,

$$\Omega^{-1/2} = \text{diag}[1/\tau_i] \otimes \bar{J}_T + \text{diag}[1/\sigma_\nu] \otimes E_T$$

The Fuller and Battese (1973) transformation extended to the *heteroskedastic case* premultiplies the model by

$$\sigma_\nu \Omega^{-1/2} = \text{diag}[\sigma_\nu/\tau_i] \otimes \bar{J}_T + (I_N \otimes E_T)$$

Hence, $y^* = \sigma_\nu \Omega^{-1/2} y$ has a typical element $y_{it}^* = y_{it} - \theta_i \bar{y}_{i.}$ where $\theta_i = 1 - (\sigma_\nu/\tau_i)$ for $i = 1, \ldots, N$. GLS can now be performed as OLS of y^* on Z^* where $Z^* = \sigma_\nu \Omega^{-1/2} Z$. This transformation was derived by Baltagi and Griffin (1988).

Exercise 5.2 *(An alternative heteroskedastic error component model).* This is based on Problems 5.4 and 5.5 in Baltagi (2008). Let the μ_i remain homoskedastic with $\mu_i \sim \text{IID}(0, \sigma_\mu^2)$ and impose the heteroskedasticity on the remainder disturbances ν_{it}, i.e., $\nu_{it} \sim (0, w_i^2)$; see Baltagi (1988b) and Wansbeek (1989).

(a) Show that

$$\Omega = \text{diag}[T\sigma_\mu^2 + w_i^2] \otimes \bar{J}_T + \text{diag}[w_i^2] \otimes E_T \tag{5.5}$$

(b) Show that $y^* = \Omega^{-1/2}y$ has a typical element $y^*_{it} = (y_{it} - \theta_i \bar{y}_{i.})/w_i$, where $\theta_i = 1 - (w_i/\tau_i)$ and $\tau_i^2 = T\sigma_\mu^2 + w_i^2$ for $i = 1, \ldots, N$.

Solution

(a) In this case, $E(\mu\mu') = \sigma_\mu^2 I_N$, but ν_{it}, the remainder disturbance, is heteroskedastic across $i = 1, \ldots, N$. In fact, $\nu_{it} \sim (0, w_i^2)$ or, in vector form,

$$E(\nu\nu') = \begin{bmatrix} w_1^2 I_T & 0 & \cdots & 0 \\ 0 & w_2^2 I_T & \cdots & 0 \\ \vdots & \vdots & \ddots & \vdots \\ 0 & 0 & \cdots & w_N^2 I_T \end{bmatrix} = \text{diag}[w_i^2] \otimes I_T$$

where $\text{diag}[w_i^2]$ is of dimension $(N \times N)$. Using (5.2) leads to

$$\begin{aligned} \Omega &= Z_\mu(\sigma_\mu^2 I_N)Z'_\mu + \text{diag}[w_i^2] \otimes I_T \\ &= \sigma_\mu^2(I_N \otimes J_T) + \text{diag}[w_i^2] \otimes I_T \\ &= \text{diag}[\sigma_\mu^2] \otimes J_T + \text{diag}[w_i^2] \otimes I_T \end{aligned} \tag{5.6}$$

Replacing J_T by $T\bar{J}_T$ and I_T by $E_T + \bar{J}_T$ in (5.6) we get

$$\Omega = \text{diag}[T\sigma_\nu^2] \otimes \bar{J}_T + \text{diag}[w_i^2] \otimes (E_T + \bar{J}_T)$$

Collecting like terms in $\bar{J}_T$ yields

$$\Omega = \text{diag}[T\sigma_\mu^2 + w_i^2] \otimes \bar{J}_T + \text{diag}[w_i^2] \otimes E_T$$

which verifies (5.5).

(b) Let $\tau_i^2 = T\sigma_\mu^2 + w_i^2$, from (5.5) we get

$$\Omega = \text{diag}[\tau_i^2] \otimes \bar{J}_T + \text{diag}[w_i^2] \otimes E_T$$

Therefore

$$\Omega^{-1/2} = \text{diag}[1/\tau_i] \otimes \bar{J}_T + \text{diag}[1/w_i] \otimes E_T$$

and $y^* = \Omega^{-1/2}y$ has a typical element

$$y^*_{it} = (\bar{y}_{i.}/\tau_i) + (y_{it} - \bar{y}_{i.})/w_i$$

Upon rearranging terms, we get

$$y^*_{it} = \frac{1}{w_i}(y_{it} - \theta_i \bar{y}_{i.}), \qquad \text{where } \theta_i = 1 - (w_i/\tau_i)$$

Exercise 5.3 *(An LM test for heteroskedasticity in a one-way error component model).* This is based on Problem 5.3 in Baltagi (2008). Holly and Gardiol (2000) derived a score test for heteroskedasticity in a one-way error component model where the μ_i are independent and distributed as $N(0, \sigma_\mu^2 h(z_i'\gamma))$ with σ_μ^2 strictly positive. Here, z_i is a $p \times 1$ vector of explanatory variables such that $z_i'\gamma$ does not contain a constant term and h is a strictly positive and twice differentiable function satisfying $h(0) = 1$ with $h'(0) \neq 0$ and $h''(0) \neq 0$.

(a) Show that in this case

$$\Omega^{-1} = \text{diag}[(\tau_i^2)^{-1}] \otimes \bar{J}_T + \text{diag}[(\sigma_\nu^2)^{-1}] \otimes E_T$$

where $\tau_i^2 = T\sigma_\mu^2 h(z_i'\gamma) + \sigma_\nu^2$.

(b) Show that the score test statistic for $H_0 : \gamma = 0$ is one half the explained sum of squares of the OLS regression of $(\tilde{s}/\bar{s}) - \iota_N$ on the p regressors in Z as in the Breush and Pagan (1979) test for heteroskedasticity. Here, $\tilde{s}_i = \widetilde{u}_i'\bar{J}_T\widetilde{u}_i$ and $\bar{s} = \sum_{i=1}^N \tilde{s}_i/N$, with $\widetilde{u}$ denoting the maximum likelihood residuals from the restricted model under $H_0 : \gamma = 0$. This LM statistic is asymptotically distributed as χ_p^2 under the null.

Solution

(a) Note that the Holly and Gardiol (2000) heteroskedasticity is a special case of the Mazodier and Trognon (1978) heteroskedasticity considered in Exercise 5.1 with $w_i^2 = \sigma_\mu^2 h(z_i'\gamma)$. From (5.2) and (5.3) we get the variance–covariance matrix of the disturbances

$$\Omega = \text{diag}[\sigma_\mu^2 h(z_i'\gamma)] \otimes J_T + \text{diag}[\sigma_\nu^2] \otimes I_T \tag{5.7}$$

Using the Wansbeek and Kapteyn (1982) trick, we replace J_T by $T\bar{J}_T$ and I_T by $E_T + \bar{J}_T$, so that

$$\Omega = \text{diag}[T\sigma_\mu^2 h(z_i'\gamma)] \otimes \bar{J}_T + \text{diag}[\sigma_\nu^2] \otimes (E_T + \bar{J}_T)$$

Collecting like terms in $\bar{J}_T$ leads to

$$\Omega = \text{diag}[T\sigma_\mu^2 h(z_i'\gamma) + \sigma_\nu^2] \otimes \bar{J}_T + \text{diag}[\sigma_\nu^2] \otimes E_T$$

Therefore,

$$\Omega^{-1} = \text{diag}[(\tau_i^2)^{-1}] \otimes \bar{J}_T + \text{diag}[(\sigma_\nu^2)^{-1}] \otimes E_T$$

where $\tau_i^2 = T\sigma_\mu^2 h(z_i'\gamma) + \sigma_\nu^2$ as required.

(b) The log likelihood function under normality of the disturbances is given by (4.15),

$$L(\delta, \theta) = \text{ constant} - \frac{1}{2}\log|\Omega| - \frac{1}{2}u'\Omega^{-1}u$$

where $\theta' = (\sigma_\nu^2, \sigma_\mu^2, \gamma)$. The information matrix is block-diagonal between θ and δ. Since $H_0 : \gamma = 0$ involves only θ, the part of the information matrix due to δ is ignored. To get the score, we use the general formula given in (4.17),

$$\partial L/\partial\theta_r = -\frac{1}{2}\mathrm{tr}[\Omega^{-1}(\partial\Omega/\partial\theta_r)] + \frac{1}{2}[u'\Omega^{-1}(\partial\Omega/\partial\theta_r)\Omega^{-1}u]$$

for $r = 1, 2, 3$. Also, from (5.7), $(\partial\Omega/\partial\theta_r) = (I_N \otimes I_T)$ for $r = 1$, $\mathrm{diag}[h(z_i'\gamma)] \otimes J_T$ for $r = 2$, and $\sigma_\mu^2\ \mathrm{diag}[h'(z_i'\gamma)z_i] \otimes J_T$ for $r = 3$. The restricted maximum likelihood estimator of Ω under H_0 is $\widetilde{\Omega} = \widetilde{\sigma}_\nu^2 I_{NT} + \widetilde{\sigma}_\mu^2(I_N \otimes J_T)$, where $\widetilde{\sigma}_\nu^2 = \widetilde{u}'Q\widetilde{u}/N(T-1)$, $\widetilde{\sigma}_1^2 = \widetilde{u}'P\widetilde{u}/N$, and $\widetilde{\sigma}_\mu^2 = (\widetilde{\sigma}_1^2 - \widetilde{\sigma}_\nu^2)/T$ with $\widetilde{u}$ denoting the restricted maximum likelihood residuals obtained from a homoskedastic one-way error component model. Therefore,

$$\partial L/\partial\sigma_\nu^2 = -\frac{1}{2}\ \mathrm{tr}[\Omega^{-1}] + \frac{1}{2}\mathrm{tr}[u'\Omega^{-1}\Omega^{-1}u]$$

with, under H_0, $\Omega^{-1} = P/\sigma_1^2 + Q/\sigma_\nu^2$. Hence,

$$\partial L/\partial\sigma_\nu^2|_{H_0} = -\frac{1}{2}\left[\frac{N}{\widetilde{\sigma}_1^2} + \frac{N(T-1)}{\widetilde{\sigma}_\nu^2}\right] + \frac{1}{2}\ \mathrm{tr}\left[u'\left(\frac{1}{\widetilde{\sigma}_1^4}P + \frac{1}{\widetilde{\sigma}_\nu^4}Q\right)u\right]$$

Similarly, under H_0, $\partial\Omega/\partial\sigma_\mu^2 = I_N \otimes J_T = TP$. Hence,

$$\partial L/\partial\sigma_\mu^2|_{H_0} = -\frac{1}{2}\left[\frac{NT}{\widetilde{\sigma}_1^2}\right] + \frac{1}{2}\ \mathrm{tr}\left[T\frac{u'Pu}{\widetilde{\sigma}_1^4}\right]$$

and, under H_0, $\partial\Omega/\partial\gamma = \sigma_\mu^2\ \mathrm{diag}[h'(0)z_i] \otimes J_T$. Hence,

$$\begin{aligned}\partial L/\partial\gamma|_{H_0} &= -\frac{1}{2}\mathrm{tr}\left[\frac{T\widetilde{\sigma}_\mu^2}{\widetilde{\sigma}_1^2}\ \mathrm{diag}[h'(0)z_i]\right] + \frac{1}{2}\mathrm{tr}\left\{u'\left[\frac{\widetilde{\sigma}_\mu^2\ \mathrm{diag}[h'(0)z_i] \otimes J_T}{\widetilde{\sigma}_1^4}\right]u\right\} \\ &= \frac{T\widetilde{\sigma}_\mu^2 h'(0)}{2\widetilde{\sigma}_1^4}\left[\sum_{i=1}^N(\widetilde{u}_i'\bar{J}_T\widetilde{u}_i)z_i - \widetilde{\sigma}_1^2\sum_{i=1}^N z_i\right]\end{aligned}$$

The first two scores, when set equal to zero, solve for the restricted maximum likelihood estimates of $\widetilde{\sigma}_\nu^2$ and $\widetilde{\sigma}_\mu^2$. Hence, when we substitute these estimates, the first two scores are equal to zero. For the information matrix, we use the general formula given in (4.19),

$$J_{rs} = E[-\partial^2 L/\partial\theta_r\partial\theta_s] = \frac{1}{2}\mathrm{tr}[\Omega^{-1}(\partial\Omega/\partial\theta_r)\Omega^{-1}(\partial\Omega/\partial\theta_s)]$$

Under H_0,

$$J_{11} = E[-\partial^2 L/\partial\sigma_\nu^4] = \frac{1}{2}\,\mathrm{tr}\left[\frac{1}{\widetilde{\sigma}_1^4}P + \frac{1}{\widetilde{\sigma}_\nu^4}Q\right] = \frac{N}{2\widetilde{\sigma}_1^4} + \frac{N(T-1)}{2\widetilde{\sigma}_\nu^4}$$

$$J_{12} = E[-\partial^2 L/\partial\sigma_\nu^2\partial\sigma_\mu^2] = \frac{1}{2}\,\mathrm{tr}\left[\frac{TP}{\widetilde{\sigma}_1^4}\right] = \frac{NT}{2\widetilde{\sigma}_1^4}$$

$$J_{13} = E[-\partial^2 L/\partial\sigma_\nu^2\partial\gamma'] = \frac{1}{2}\,\mathrm{tr}\left[\frac{T\widetilde{\sigma}_\mu^2\,\mathrm{diag}[h'(0)z_i']}{\widetilde{\sigma}_1^4}\right] = \frac{T\widetilde{\sigma}_\mu^2}{2\widetilde{\sigma}_1^4}h'(0)\sum\nolimits_{i=1}^N z_i'$$

$$J_{22} = E[-\partial^2 L/\partial\sigma_\mu^4] = \frac{1}{2}\,\mathrm{tr}\left[\frac{T^2P}{\widetilde{\sigma}_1^4}\right] = \frac{NT^2}{2\widetilde{\sigma}_1^4}$$

$$J_{23} = E[-\partial^2 L/\partial\sigma_\mu^2\partial\gamma'] = \frac{1}{2}\,\mathrm{tr}\left[\frac{T^2\widetilde{\sigma}_\mu^2\,\mathrm{diag}[h'(0)z_i']}{\widetilde{\sigma}_1^4}\right] = \frac{T^2\widetilde{\sigma}_\mu^2}{2\widetilde{\sigma}_1^4}h'(0)\sum\nolimits_{i=1}^N z_i'$$

$$J_{33} = E[-\partial^2 L/\partial\gamma\partial\gamma'] = \frac{1}{2}\,\mathrm{tr}\left[\frac{T^2\widetilde{\sigma}_\mu^4\,\mathrm{diag}[h'(0)^2 z_i z_i']}{\widetilde{\sigma}_1^4}\right] = \frac{T^2\widetilde{\sigma}_\mu^4}{2\widetilde{\sigma}_1^4}(h'(0))^2 Z'Z$$

where Z is an $n \times p$ matrix of regressors with the ith row being z_i'. Let $\widetilde{s}_i = \widetilde{u}_i'\bar{J}_T\widetilde{u}_i$; then $\bar{s} = \widetilde{\sigma}_1^2$ and

$$\partial L/\partial\gamma|_{H_0} = \frac{T\widetilde{\sigma}_\mu^2 h'(0)}{2\widetilde{\sigma}_1^4}\sum_{i=1}^N \widetilde{s}_i(z_i - \bar{z})$$

where $\bar{z} = \sum_{i=1}^N z_i/N$.

Also, J^{33}, the (3, 3)th element of the inverse of the information matrix, is given by

$$J^{33} = \frac{2\widetilde{\sigma}_1^4}{T^2\widetilde{\sigma}_\mu^4(h'(0))^2}[Z'(I_N - \bar{J}_N)Z]^{-1} = \frac{2\widetilde{\sigma}_1^4}{T^2\widetilde{\sigma}_\mu^4(h'(0))^2}(\underline{Z}'\underline{Z})^{-1}$$

where $\underline{Z} = (I_N - \bar{J}_N)Z$. Hence, the LM statistic is given by

$$LM = \frac{1}{2\widetilde{\sigma}_1^4}\widetilde{s}'\underline{Z}(\underline{Z}'\underline{Z})^{-1}\underline{Z}'\widetilde{s}$$

and, using the fact that $\widetilde{\sigma}_1^2 = \bar{s}_1$, we get

$$LM = \frac{1}{2}\left(\frac{\widetilde{s}}{\bar{s}} - \iota_N\right)'\underline{Z}(\underline{Z}'\underline{Z})^{-1}\underline{Z}'\left(\frac{\widetilde{s}}{\bar{s}} - \iota_N\right)$$

Hence, the LM statistic is one half the explained sum of squares of the OLS regression of $(\widetilde{s}/\bar{s}) - \iota_N$ on $\underline{Z}$.

5.2 SERIAL CORRELATION IN THE ERROR COMPONENT MODEL

The classical error component disturbances given by (2.2) assume that the only correlation over time is due to the presence of the same individual across the panel. In Chapter 2, this equicorrelation coefficient was shown to be correl$(u_{it}, u_{is}) = \sigma_\mu^2/(\sigma_\mu^2 + \sigma_\nu^2)$ for $t \neq s$. Note that it is the same no matter how far t is from s. This may be a restrictive assumption for economic relationships, like investment or consumption, where an unobserved shock this period will affect the behavioral relationship for at least the next few periods. This type of serial correlation is not allowed for in the simple error component model. Ignoring serial correlation when it is present results in consistent but inefficient estimates of the regression coefficients and biased standard errors. This section introduces serial correlation in the ν_{it}, first as a first-order autoregressive process AR(1), next as a second-order autoregressive process AR(2), also as a special fourth-order autoregressive process AR(4) for quarterly data, and finally as a first-order moving average process MA(1). For all these serial correlation specifications, a simple generalization of the Fuller and Battese (1973) transformation is derived and the implications for predictions are given. Testing for individual effects and serial correlation is taken up in the last subsection.

Exercise 5.4 *(AR(1) process).* This is based on Problem 5.6 in Baltagi (2008). Consider the one-way error component model with serially correlated remainder disturbances (the ν_{it}) that follow an AR(1) process. In this case $\mu_i \sim \text{IID}(0, \sigma_\mu^2)$, whereas

$$\nu_{it} = \rho\nu_{i,t-1} + \varepsilon_{it} \tag{5.8}$$

$|\rho| < 1$ and $\varepsilon_{it} \sim \text{IID}(0, \sigma_\varepsilon^2)$. The μ_i are independent of the ν_{it} and $\nu_{i0} \sim (0, \sigma_\varepsilon^2/(1-\rho^2))$. Apply the Prais-Winsten (PW) transformation matrix

$$C = \begin{bmatrix} (1-\rho^2)^{1/2} & 0 & 0 & \cdots & 0 & 0 & 0 \\ -\rho & 1 & 0 & \cdots & 0 & 0 & 0 \\ \cdot & \cdot & \cdot & \cdots & \cdot & \cdot & \cdot \\ \cdot & \cdot & \cdot & \cdots & \cdot & \cdot & \cdot \\ 0 & 0 & 0 & \cdots & -\rho & 1 & 0 \\ 0 & 0 & 0 & \cdots & 0 & -\rho & 1 \end{bmatrix} \tag{5.9}$$

to transform the remainder AR(1) disturbances into serially uncorrelated classical errors. For panel data, this has to be applied for N individuals. The transformed regression disturbances, in vector form, are given by

$$u^* = (I_N \otimes C)u = (I_N \otimes C\iota_T)\mu + (I_N \otimes C)\nu \tag{5.10}$$

(a) Show that

$$\Omega^* = E(u^*u^{*\prime}) = d^2\sigma_\mu^2(1-\rho)^2[I_N \otimes \iota_T^\alpha\iota_T^{\alpha\prime}/d^2] + \sigma_\varepsilon^2(I_N \otimes I_T) \tag{5.11}$$

where $d^2 = \iota_T^{\alpha\prime}\iota_T^\alpha = \alpha^2 + (T-1)$, $\iota_T^{\alpha\prime} = (\alpha, \iota_{T-1}')$, and $\alpha = \sqrt{(1+\rho)/(1-\rho)}$.

(b) Show that

$$\sigma_\varepsilon \Omega^{*-1/2} = I_N \otimes I_T - \theta_\alpha(I_N \otimes \overline{J}_T^\alpha)$$

where $\theta_\alpha = 1 - (\sigma_\varepsilon/\sigma_\alpha)$, $\overline{J}_T^\alpha = J_T^\alpha/d^2$, and $J_T^\alpha = \iota_T^\alpha\iota_T^{\alpha\prime}$. This is the Fuller and Battese (1973) transformation extended to the AR(1) case and was derived by Baltagi and Li (1991a).

(c) What happens to this transformation when $\rho = 0$? or when $\sigma_\mu^2 = 0$?

Solution

(a) Note that

$$C\iota_T = ((1-\rho^2)^{1/2}, (1-\rho), \ldots, (1-\rho))' = (1-\rho)(\alpha, 1, \ldots, 1)'$$

where $\alpha = \sqrt{(1+\rho)/(1-\rho)}$. Defining $\iota_T^\alpha = (\alpha, \iota_{T-1}')'$, we can write

$$u^* = (1-\rho)(I_N \otimes \iota_T^\alpha)\mu + (I_N \otimes C)\nu \qquad (5.12)$$

and the transformed variance–covariance matrix is given by

$$\Omega^* = E(u^*u^{*\prime}) = (1-\rho)^2(I_N \otimes \iota_T^\alpha)E(\mu\mu')(I_N \otimes \iota_T^{\alpha\prime}) + (I_N \otimes C)E(\nu\nu')(I_N \otimes C')$$

Substituting $E(\mu\mu') = \sigma_\mu^2 I_N$ and noting that the last term reduces to $\sigma_\varepsilon^2 I_{NT}$, we get

$$\Omega^* = \sigma_\mu^2(1-\rho)^2(I_N \otimes \iota_T^\alpha\iota_T^{\alpha\prime}) + \sigma_\varepsilon^2(I_N \otimes I_T)$$

Note that ι_T^α is a vector of dimension T and one can define $J_T^\alpha = \iota_T^\alpha\iota_T^{\alpha\prime}$ as for the classical error component model. In order to make this $(T \times T)$ matrix idempotent one has to divide by its length which in this case is $\iota_T^{\alpha\prime}\iota_T^\alpha = \alpha^2 + (T-1)$ and denoted by d^2. Replacing J_T^α by $d^2\overline{J}_T^\alpha$, where by definition $\overline{J}_T^\alpha = J_T^\alpha/d^2$, we get

$$\Omega^* = d^2\sigma_\mu^2(1-\rho)^2(I_N \otimes \overline{J}_T^\alpha) + \sigma_\varepsilon^2(I_N \otimes I_T)$$

which verifies (5.11).

(b) One can extend the Wansbeek and Kapteyn (1982) trick by replacing J_T^α by $(d^2\overline{J}_T^\alpha)$ and I_T by $(E_T^\alpha + \overline{J}_T^\alpha)$, where E_T^α is by definition $(I_T - \overline{J}_T^\alpha)$. This gives

$$\Omega^* = d^2\sigma_\mu^2(1-\rho)^2(I_N \otimes \overline{J}_T^\alpha) + \sigma_\varepsilon^2(I_N \otimes (E_T^\alpha + \overline{J}_T^\alpha))$$

Collecting like terms in $\overline{J}_T^\alpha$ leads to

$$\Omega^* = \sigma_\alpha^2(I_N \otimes \overline{J}_T^\alpha) + \sigma_\varepsilon^2(I_N \otimes E_T^\alpha) \qquad (5.13)$$

where $\sigma_\alpha^2 = d^2\sigma_\mu^2(1-\rho)^2 + \sigma_\varepsilon^2$. Therefore,

$$\sigma_\varepsilon \Omega^{*-1/2} = (\sigma_\varepsilon/\sigma_\alpha)(I_N \otimes \overline{J}_T^\alpha) + (I_N \otimes E_T^\alpha) = I_N \otimes I_T - \theta_\alpha(I_N \otimes \overline{J}_T^\alpha) \tag{5.14}$$

where $\theta_\alpha = 1 - (\sigma_\varepsilon/\sigma_\alpha)$.

Premultiplying the PW transformed observations $y^* = (I_N \otimes C)y$ by $\sigma_\varepsilon \Omega^{*-1/2}$, we get $y^{**} = \sigma_\varepsilon \Omega^{*-1/2} y^*$. The typical elements of $y^{**} = \sigma_\varepsilon \Omega^{*-1/2} y^*$ are given by

$$(y_{i1}^* - \theta_\alpha \alpha b_i, y_{i2}^* - \theta_\alpha b_i, \ldots, y_{iT}^* - \theta_\alpha b_i)' \tag{5.15}$$

where $b_i = [(\alpha y_{i1}^* + \sum_2^T y_{it}^*)/d^2]$ for $i = 1, \ldots, N$. The first observation gets special attention in the AR(1) error component model. First, the PW transformation gives it a special weight $\sqrt{1-\rho^2}$ in y^*. Second, the Fuller and Battese transformation gives it another special weight $\alpha = \sqrt{(1+\rho)/(1-\rho)}$ in computing the weighted average b_i and the pseudo-difference in (5.15).

(c) Note that if $\rho = 0$, then $\alpha = 1$, $d^2 = T$, $\sigma_\alpha^2 = \sigma_1^2$ and $\theta_\alpha = \theta$. Therefore, the typical element of y_{it}^{**} reverts to the familiar $(y_{it} - \theta \overline{y}_{i.})$ transformation for the one-way error component model with no serial correlation. If $\sigma_\mu^2 = 0$, then $\sigma_\alpha^2 = \sigma_\varepsilon^2$ and $\theta_\alpha = 0$. Therefore, the typical element of y_{it}^{**} reverts to the PW transformation y_{it}^*.

The BQU estimators of the variance components arise naturally from the spectral decomposition of Ω^*. In fact, $(I_N \otimes E_T^\alpha)u^* \sim (0, \sigma_\varepsilon^2[I_N \otimes E_T^\alpha])$ and $(I_N \otimes \overline{J}_T^\alpha)u^* \sim (0, \sigma_\alpha^2[I_N \otimes \overline{J}_T^\alpha])$, and

$$\widehat{\sigma}_\varepsilon^2 = u^{*\prime}(I_N \otimes E_T^\alpha)u^*/N(T-1) \quad \text{and} \quad \widehat{\sigma}_\alpha^2 = u^{*\prime}(I_N \otimes \overline{J}_T^\alpha)u^*/N \tag{5.16}$$

provide the BQU estimators of σ_ε^2 and σ_α^2, respectively.

Exercise 5.5 *(Unbiased estimates of the variance components under the AR(1) model).* This is based on Problem 5.8 in Baltagi (2008). Prove that $\widehat{\sigma}_\varepsilon^2$ and $\widehat{\sigma}_\alpha^2$ given by (5.16) are unbiased estimates of σ_ε^2 and σ_α^2, respectively.

Solution

$$\begin{aligned}
E(u^{*\prime}(I_N \otimes E_T^\alpha)u^*) &= E[\mathrm{tr}(u^{*\prime}(I_N \otimes E_T^\alpha)u^*)] \\
&= E[\mathrm{tr}(u^* u^{*\prime}(I_N \otimes E_T^\alpha))] = \mathrm{tr}[E(u^* u^{*\prime})(I_N \otimes E_T^\alpha)] \\
&= \mathrm{tr}[\Omega^*(I_N \otimes E_T^\alpha)] = \mathrm{tr}[\sigma_\varepsilon^2(I_N \otimes E_T^\alpha)] \\
&= \sigma_\varepsilon^2 \mathrm{tr}(I_N \otimes E_T^\alpha) = \sigma_\varepsilon^2 N(T-1)
\end{aligned}$$

where the fifth equality follows from (5.13), noting that $\overline{J}_T^\alpha E_T^\alpha = 0$. The last equality follows from the fact that $\mathrm{tr}(E_T^\alpha) = \mathrm{tr}(I_T^\alpha - \overline{J}_T^\alpha) = T - 1$ since $\mathrm{tr}(\overline{J}_T^\alpha) = 1$. Therefore $E(\widehat{\sigma}_\varepsilon^2) = E[u^{*\prime}(I_N \otimes E_T^\alpha)u^*/N(T-1)] = \sigma_\varepsilon^2$ and $\widehat{\sigma}_\varepsilon^2$ is unbiased for σ_ε^2. Similarly,

$$\begin{aligned}
E(u^{*\prime}(I_N \otimes \overline{J}_T^\alpha)u^*) &= E[\mathrm{tr}(u^* u^{*\prime}(I_N \otimes \overline{J}_T^\alpha))] \\
&= \mathrm{tr}[E(u^* u^{*\prime})(I_N \otimes \overline{J}_T^\alpha)] = \mathrm{tr}[\Omega^*(I_N \otimes \overline{J}_T^\alpha)] \\
&= \mathrm{tr}[\sigma_\alpha^2(I_N \otimes \overline{J}_T^\alpha)] = \sigma_\alpha^2 \mathrm{tr}(I_N \otimes \overline{J}_T^\alpha) = \sigma_\alpha^2 N
\end{aligned}$$

where the fourth equality follows from (5.13), noting that $E\iota_T^{\alpha}\overline{J}_T^{\alpha} = 0$. The last equality follows from the fact that $\text{tr}(\overline{J}_T^{\alpha}) = 1$. Therefore, $E(u^{*\prime}(I_N \otimes \overline{J}_T^{\alpha})u^*/N) = \sigma_\alpha^2$ and $\widehat{\sigma}_\alpha^2$ is unbiased for σ_α^2.

Therefore, the estimation of an AR(1) serially correlated error component model is considerably simplified by (i) applying the PW transformation in the first step, as is usually done in the time-series literature, and (ii) subtracting a pseudo-average from these transformed data as in (5.15) in the second step.

Exercise 5.6 *(AR(2) process).* This is based on Problem 5.9 in Baltagi (2008). Consider the one-way error component model with serially correlated remainder disturbances (the ν_{it}) that follow an AR(2) process. In this case $\mu_i \sim \text{IID}(0, \sigma_\mu^2)$, whereas

$$\nu_{it} = \rho_1 \nu_{i,t-1} + \rho_2 \nu_{i,t-2} + \varepsilon_{it} \tag{5.17}$$

with $\varepsilon_{it} \sim \text{IIN}(0, \sigma_\varepsilon^2)$, $|\rho_2| < 1$ and $|\rho_1| < (1 - \rho_2)$. Let $E(\nu_i \nu_i') = \sigma_\varepsilon^2 V$, where $\nu_i' = (\nu_{i1}, \ldots, \nu_{iT})$ and note that V is invariant to $i = 1, \ldots, N$. The unique $T \times T$ lower triangular matrix C with positive diagonal elements which satisfies $CVC' = I_T$ is given by

$$C = \begin{bmatrix} \gamma_0 & 0 & 0 & 0 & \ldots & 0 & 0 & 0 & 0 \\ -\gamma_2 & \gamma_1 & 0 & 0 & \ldots & 0 & 0 & 0 & 0 \\ -\rho_2 & -\rho_1 & 1 & 0 & \ldots & 0 & 0 & 0 & 0 \\ \cdot & \cdot & \cdot & \cdot & & \cdot & \cdot & \cdot & \cdot \\ \cdot & \cdot & \cdot & \cdot & & \cdot & \cdot & \cdot & \cdot \\ 0 & 0 & 0 & 0 & \ldots & -\rho_2 & -\rho_1 & 1 & 0 \\ 0 & 0 & 0 & 0 & \ldots & 0 & -\rho_2 & -\rho_1 & 1 \end{bmatrix} \tag{5.18}$$

where $\gamma_0 = \sigma_\varepsilon/\sigma_\nu$, $\gamma_1 = \sqrt{1 - \rho_2^2}$, $\gamma_2 = \gamma_1[\rho_1/(1 - \rho_2)]$, and

$$\sigma_\nu^2 = \sigma_\varepsilon^2(1 - \rho_2)/(1 + \rho_2)[(1 - \rho_2)^2 - \rho_1^2]$$

The transformed disturbances are given by $u^* = (I_N \otimes C)u$ as in (5.10) but with the new C for the AR(2) model defined by (5.18).

(a) Show that

$$\Omega^* = E(u^* u^{*\prime}) = \sigma_\mu^2(1 - \rho_1 - \rho_2)^2[I_N \otimes J_T^{\alpha}] + \sigma_\varepsilon^2[I_N \otimes I_T] \tag{5.19}$$

where $\iota_T^{\alpha\prime} = (\alpha_1, \alpha_2, \iota_{T-2}')$ with $\alpha_1 = \sigma_\varepsilon/\sigma_\nu(1 - \rho_1 - \rho_2)$, $\alpha_2 = \sqrt{(1 + \rho_2)/(1 - \rho_2)}$, and $J_T^{\alpha} = \iota_T^{\alpha}\iota_T^{\alpha\prime}$.

(b) Show that $y^{**} = \sigma_\varepsilon \Omega^{*-1/2} y^*$, where $y^* = (I_N \otimes C)y$ has a typical element given by

$$(y_{i1}^* - \theta_\alpha \alpha_1 b_i, y_{i2}^* - \theta_\alpha \alpha_2 b_i, y_{i3}^* - \theta_\alpha b_i, \ldots, y_{iT}^* - \theta_\alpha b_i) \tag{5.20}$$

where $b_i = [(\alpha_1 y_{i1}^* + \alpha_2 y_{i2}^* + \sum_3^T y_{it}^*)/d^2]$, with $d^2 = \alpha_1^2 + \alpha_2^2 + (T - 2)$ and $\theta_\alpha = 1 - (\sigma_\varepsilon/\sigma_\alpha)$.

Solution

(a) This solution is similar to that of Exercise 5.4. In this case, $C\iota_T = (1 - \rho_1 - \rho_2)\times$ (the new ι_T^α) where $\iota_T^{\alpha\prime} = (\alpha_1, \alpha_2, \iota_{T-2}^{\prime})$, with $\alpha_1 = \sigma_\varepsilon/\sigma_\nu(1 - \rho_1 - \rho_2)$ and $\alpha_2 = \sqrt{(1 + \rho_2)/(1 - \rho_2)}$, and the transformed disturbances are given by

$$u^* = (I_N \otimes C)u = (1 - \rho_1 - \rho_2)(I_N \otimes \iota_T^\alpha)\mu + (I_N \otimes C)\nu \qquad (5.21)$$

Hence, the transformed variance–covariance matrix is given by

$$\Omega^* = E(u^*u^{*\prime}) = (1-\rho_1-\rho_2)^2(I_N \otimes \iota_T^\alpha)E(\mu\mu')(I_N \otimes \iota_T^{\alpha\prime}) + (I_N \otimes C)E(\nu\nu')(I_N \otimes C')$$

Substituting $E(\mu\mu') = \sigma_\mu^2 I_N$ and noting that the last term reduces to $\sigma_\varepsilon^2 I_{NT}$, we get

$$\Omega^* = \sigma_\mu^2(1 - \rho_1 - \rho_2)^2[I_N \otimes J_T^\alpha] + \sigma_\varepsilon^2[I_N \otimes I_T]$$

where $J_T^\alpha = \iota_T^\alpha \iota_T^{\alpha\prime}$, and $\overline{J}_T^\alpha = J_T^\alpha/d^2$, with $d^2 = \iota_T^{\alpha\prime}\iota_T^\alpha = \alpha_1^2 + \alpha_2^2 + (T-2)$. The major difference here from Exercise 5.4 is that $(1 - \rho_1 - \rho_2)$ replaces $(1 - \rho)$ and ι_T^α is defined in terms of α_1 and α_2 rather than α.

(b) Similarly, one can extend the Wansbeek and Kapteyn (1982) trick by replacing J_T^α by $(d^2\overline{J}_T^\alpha)$ and I_T by $(E_T^\alpha + \overline{J}_T^\alpha)$, where E_T^α is by definition $(I_T - \overline{J}_T^\alpha)$. This gives

$$\Omega^* = d^2\sigma_\mu^2(1 - \rho_1 - \rho_2)(I_N \otimes \overline{J}_T^\alpha) + \sigma_\varepsilon^2(I_N \otimes (E_T^\alpha + \overline{J}_T^\alpha))$$

Collecting like terms in $\overline{J}_T^\alpha$, we get

$$\Omega^* = \sigma_\alpha^2(I_N \otimes \overline{J}_T^\alpha) + \sigma_\varepsilon^2(I_N \otimes E_T^\alpha)$$

where $\sigma_\alpha^2 = d^2\sigma_\mu^2(1 - \rho_1 - \rho_2)^2 + \sigma_\varepsilon^2$. Therefore, $\sigma_\varepsilon\Omega^{*-1/2}$ is given by (5.15) with $\sigma_\alpha^2 = d^2\sigma_\mu^2(1 - \rho_1 - \rho_2)^2 + \sigma_\varepsilon^2$. The typical elements of $y^{**} = \sigma_\varepsilon\Omega^{*-1/2}y^*$ are given by

$$(y_{i1}^* - \theta_\alpha\alpha_1 b_i, y_{i2}^* - \theta_\alpha\alpha_2 b_i, y_{i3}^* - \theta_\alpha b_i, \ldots, y_{iT}^* - \theta_\alpha b_i)$$

where $y^* = (I_N \otimes C)y$ and $b_i = [(\alpha_1 y_{i1}^* + \alpha_2 y_{i2}^* + \sum_3^T y_{it}^*)/d^2]$ as required in (5.20). The first two observations get special attention in the AR(2) error component model, first in the matrix C defined in (5.18) and second in computing the average b_i and the Fuller and Battese transformation in (5.20). Therefore, we can obtain GLS on this model by (i) transforming the data as in the time-series literature by the C matrix defined in (5.18) and (ii) subtracting a pseudo-average in the second step as in (5.20).

Exercise 5.7 *(AR(4) process for quarterly data).* This is based on Problem 5.10 in Baltagi (2008). Consider the one-way error component model with remainder disturbances ν_{it} following a specialized AR(4) process

$$\nu_{it} = \rho\nu_{i,t-4} + \varepsilon_{it}$$

with $|\rho| < 1$ and $\varepsilon_{it} \sim \text{IIN}(0, \sigma_\varepsilon^2)$. The required C transformation is given by

$$C = \begin{bmatrix} \sqrt{1-\rho^2} & 0 & 0 & 0 & 0 & \cdots & 0 & 0 \\ 0 & \sqrt{1-\rho^2} & 0 & 0 & 0 & \cdots & 0 & 0 \\ 0 & 0 & \sqrt{1-\rho^2} & 0 & 0 & \cdots & 0 & 0 \\ 0 & 0 & 0 & \sqrt{1-\rho^2} & 0 & \cdots & 0 & 0 \\ 0 & 0 & 0 & -\rho & 1 & \cdots & 0 & 0 \\ \vdots & \vdots & \vdots & \vdots & \vdots & \vdots & \vdots & \vdots \\ 0 & 0 & 0 & 0 & 0 & \cdots & -\rho & 1 \end{bmatrix} \tag{5.22}$$

The transformed disturbances $u_i^* = Cu_i$ yield

$$\begin{aligned} u_{it}^* &= \sqrt{1-\rho^2}u_{it} \quad \text{for } t = 1, 2, 3, 4 \\ &= u_{it} - \rho u_{i,t-4} \quad \text{for } t = 5, 6, \ldots, T \end{aligned} \tag{5.23}$$

This means that the μ_i component of u_{it} gets transformed as $\sqrt{1-\rho^2}\mu_i$ for $t = 1, 2, 3, 4$ and as $(1-\rho)\mu_i$ for $t = 5, 6, \ldots, T$. This can be rewritten as $\alpha(1-\rho)\mu_i$ for $t = 1, 2, 3, 4$ where $\alpha = \sqrt{(1+\rho)/(1-\rho)}$, and $(1-\rho)\mu_i$ for $t = 5, \ldots, T$. So $u^* = (I_N \otimes C)u$ is given by (5.10) with a new C defined in (5.22) and the same α.

(a) For this specialized AR(4) process, show that $\Omega^* = E(u^*u^{*\prime})$ is given by (5.12) but with a new definition of ι_T^α and d^2.

(b) Show that the typical elements of $y^{**} = \sigma_\varepsilon \Omega^{*-1/2} y^*$, where $y^* = (I_N \otimes C)y$, are given by

$$(y_{i1}^* - \theta_\alpha \alpha b_i, \ldots, y_{i4}^* - \theta_\alpha \alpha b_i, y_{i5}^* - \theta_\alpha b_i, \ldots, y_{iT}^* - \theta_\alpha b_i) \tag{5.24}$$

where $b_i = \left[\left(\alpha\left(\sum_{t=1}^4 y_{it}^*\right) + \sum_{t=5}^T y_{it}^*\right)/d^2\right]$ and θ_α is as described in Exercise 5.3.

Solution

(a) Note that

$$\begin{aligned} C\iota_T &= (\sqrt{1-\rho^2}, \sqrt{1-\rho^2}, \sqrt{1-\rho^2}, \sqrt{1-\rho^2}, (1-\rho), \ldots, (1-\rho))' \\ &= (1-\rho)(\alpha, \alpha, \alpha, \alpha, 1, \ldots, 1)' = (1-\rho)\iota_T^{\alpha'} \end{aligned}$$

where

$$\iota_T^\alpha = (\alpha, \alpha, \alpha, \alpha, \iota_{T-4}')$$

Also

$$d^2 = \iota_T^{\alpha'}\iota_T^\alpha = 4\alpha^2 + \iota_{T-4}'\iota_{T-4} = 4\alpha^2 + (T-4)$$

Armed with these new definitions of ι_T^α and d^2, the derivations of Ω^* in (5.13) and of $\sigma_\varepsilon \Omega^{*-1/2}$ in (5.14) do not change, nor does the definition of σ_α^2 and θ_α.

(b) For the ith individual, one can compute $\iota_T^{\alpha\prime} y_i^* = (\alpha y_{i1}^* + \alpha y_{i2}^* + \alpha y_{i3}^* + \alpha y_{i4}^* + \sum_{t=5}^T y_{i,t}^*)$. Dividing both sides by d^2 leads to $b_i = [(\alpha(\sum_{t=1}^4 y_{it}^*) + \sum_{t=5}^T y_{it}^*)/d^2]$ as described below (5.24). Hence, $\overline{J}_T^\alpha y_i^* = \iota_T^\alpha \iota_T^{\alpha\prime} y_i^*/d^2$ has for its elements $(\alpha b_i, \alpha b_i, \alpha b_i, \alpha b_i, b_i, \ldots, b_i)'$. Therefore, the typical elements of $y^{**} = \sigma_\varepsilon \Omega^{*-1/2} y^*$ for the ith individual are as described in (5.24), that is, $(y_{i1}^* - \theta_\alpha \alpha b_i, \ldots, y_{i4}^* - \theta_\alpha \alpha b_i, y_{i5}^* - \theta_\alpha b_i, \ldots, y_{iT}^* - \theta_\alpha b_i)'$. Once again, GLS can be easily computed by applying (5.23) to the data in the first step and (5.24) in the second step and doing OLS.

Exercise 5.8 *(MA(1) process)*. This is based on Problem 5.11 in Baltagi (2008). Consider the one-way error component model with remainder disturbances ν_{it} following the MA(1) process given by

$$\nu_{it} = \varepsilon_{it} + \lambda \varepsilon_{i,t-1} \tag{5.25}$$

where $\varepsilon_{it} \sim \text{IIN}(0, \sigma_\varepsilon^2)$ and $|\lambda| < 1$. Balestra (1980) gives the C matrix $C = D^{-1/2}P$, where $D = \text{diag}\{a_t, a_{t-1}\}$ for $t = 1, \ldots, T$,

$$P = \begin{bmatrix} 1 & 0 & 0 & \ldots & 0 \\ \lambda & a_1 & 0 & \ldots & 0 \\ \lambda^2 & a_1\lambda & a_2 & \ldots & 0 \\ \vdots & \vdots & \vdots & & \vdots \\ \lambda^{T-1} & a_1\lambda^{T-2} & a_2\lambda^{T-3} & \ldots & a_{T-1} \end{bmatrix}$$

and $a_t = 1 + \lambda^2 + \cdots + \lambda^{2t}$ with $a_0 = 1$. For this MA(1) process, show that $\Omega^* = E(u^* u^{*\prime})$ is given by (5.13) with a new definition of ι_T^α and d^2.

Solution

For the Balestra (1980) C matrix, define the new $\iota_T^\alpha = C\iota_T = (\alpha_1, \alpha_2, \ldots, \alpha_T)'$. Note that these α_t can be solved for recursively as follows:

$$\begin{aligned} \alpha_1 &= (a_0/a_1)^{1/2} \\ \alpha_t &= \lambda(a_{t-2}/a_{t-1})^{1/2}\alpha_{t-1} + (a_{t-1}/a_t)^{1/2}, \quad t = 2, \ldots, T \end{aligned} \tag{5.26}$$

Therefore, $d^2 = \iota_T^{\alpha\prime}\iota_T^\alpha = \sum_{t=1}^T \alpha_t^2$, $\sigma_\alpha^2 = d^2\sigma_\mu^2 + \sigma_\varepsilon^2$ and the spectral decomposition of Ω^* is the same as that given in (5.13), with the newly defined ι_T^α and σ_α^2. The typical elements of $y^{**} = \sigma_\varepsilon \Omega^{*-1/2} y^*$, where $y^* = (I_N \otimes C)y$, are given by

$$(y_{i1}^* - \theta_\alpha \alpha_1 b_i, \ldots, y_{iT}^* - \theta_\alpha \alpha_T b_i) \tag{5.27}$$

where $b_i = [\sum_{t=1}^{T} \alpha_t y_{it}^*/d^2]$. Therefore, for an MA(1) error component model, one applies the recursive transformation given in (5.26) in the first step and subtracts a pseudo-average described in (5.27) in the second step; see Baltagi and Li (1992b) for more details.

In summary, a simple transformation for the one-way error component model with serial correlation can be easily generalized to any error process generating the remainder disturbances ν_{it} as long as there exists a *simple* $(T \times T)$ matrix C such that the transformation $(I_N \otimes C)\nu$ has zero mean and variance $\sigma^2 I_{NT}$.

Step 1: Perform the C transformation on the observations of each individual $y_i' = (y_{i1}, \ldots, y_{it})$ to obtain $y_i^* = Cy_i$ free of serial correlation.

Step 2: Perform another transformation on the y_{it}^*, obtained in step 1, which subtracts from y_{it}^* a fraction of a weighted average of observations on y_{it}^*, i.e.,

$$y_{it}^{**} = y_{it}^* - \theta_\alpha \alpha_t \left(\sum_{s=1}^{T} \alpha_s y_{is}^* \right) / \left(\sum_{s=1}^{T} \alpha_s^2 \right) \tag{5.28}$$

where the α_t are the elements of $\iota_T^\alpha = C\iota_T \equiv (\alpha_1, \alpha_2, \ldots, \alpha_T)'$ and $\theta_\alpha = 1 - (\sigma/\sigma_\alpha)$ with $\sigma_\alpha^2 = \sigma_\mu^2(\sum_{t=1}^{T} \alpha_t^2) + \sigma^2$.

Exercise 5.9 *(MA(q) process).* Consider the case where the remainder disturbance ν_{it} follows an MA(q) process, i.e.,

$$\nu_{it} = \varepsilon_{it} - \lambda_1 \varepsilon_{i,t-1} - \lambda_2 \varepsilon_{i,t-2} - \ldots, \lambda_q \varepsilon_{i,t-q} \tag{5.29}$$

with $\varepsilon_{it} \sim \text{IIN}(0, \sigma_\varepsilon^2)$. In the time-series literature, Choudhury and St. Louis (1990) proposed an approximation method for estimating the MA(q) process. This method is based on the C matrix

$$C = \begin{bmatrix} 1 & 0 & 0 & \ldots & 0 \\ \lambda_1 & 1 & 0 & \ldots & 0 \\ \lambda_1^2 + \lambda_2 & \lambda_1 & 1 & \ldots & 0 \\ \lambda_1^3 + 2\lambda_1\lambda_2 + \lambda_3 & \lambda_{21}^2 + \lambda_2 & \lambda_1 & \ldots & 0 \\ \vdots & \vdots & \vdots & \ddots & \vdots \end{bmatrix} \tag{5.30}$$

They showed that as long as the moving-average parameters are not near the boundary region of invertibility, this approximation works well (according to relative efficiency with respect to true GLS) and is recommended.

(a) Using this approximation, show how one can transform the error component model with MA(q) disturbances into spherical disturbances.

(b) Show how GLS can be performed using weighted least squares. This is based on Baltagi and Li (1992d).

Solution

(a) Applying this C matrix defined in (5.30) to our panel data model, we get $u_i^* = Cu_i$, which can be obtained using the following recursive procedure:

$$u_{i1}^* = u_{i1}$$

$$u_{it}^* = u_{it} + \sum_{s=1}^{t-1} \lambda_s u_{i,t-s}^* \qquad \text{for } t = 2, 3, \ldots, q$$

$$u_{it}^* = u_{it} + \sum_{s=1}^{q} \lambda_s u_{i,t-s}^* \qquad \text{for } t = q+1, q+2, \ldots, T$$

Other variables such as y_{it}^* and X_{it}^* can be obtained similarly. In this case $\iota_T^\alpha = C\iota_T = (\alpha_1, \alpha_2, \ldots, \alpha_t)'$, where the α_t can be obtained recursively as follows:

$$\alpha_1 = 1$$

$$\alpha_t = 1 + \sum_{s=1}^{t-1} \lambda_s \alpha_{t-s} \qquad \text{for } t = 2, 3, \ldots, q$$

$$\alpha_t = 1 + \sum_{s=1}^{q} \lambda_s \alpha_{t-s} \qquad \text{for } t = q+1, q+2, \ldots, T$$

with $d^2 = \iota_T^{\alpha\prime}\iota_T^\alpha = \sum_{t=1}^T \alpha_T^2$.

(b) The derivations of the Fuller and Battese tranformation and weighted least squares follow the two-step procedure given in (5.28). See Baltagi and Li (1994) for the exact transformation for the MA(q) case, and Galbraith and Zinde-Walsh (1995) for the ARMA(p, q) case.

Exercise 5.10 *(Prediction in the serially correlated error component model).* This is based on Problem 5.12 in Baltagi (2008). Goldberger's (1962) BLUP of $y_{i,T+1}$, the one-period-ahead forecast for the ith individual, is given in (2.28) in Exercise 2.13 as

$$\widehat{y}_{i,T+1} = Z_{i,T+1}'\widehat{\delta}_{\text{GLS}} + w'\Omega^{-1}\widehat{u}_{\text{GLS}} \tag{5.31}$$

where $\widehat{u}_{\text{GLS}} = y - Z\widehat{\delta}_{\text{GLS}}$ and $w = E(u_{i,T+1}u)$. For the AR(1) model with no error components, a standard result is that the last term in (5.31) reduces to $\rho\widehat{u}_{i,T}$, where $\widehat{u}_{i,T}$ is the Tth GLS residual for the ith individual. For the one-way error component model without serial correlation (see Taub, 1979; or Exercise 2.13), the last term of (5.31) reduces to $[T\sigma_\mu^2/(T\sigma_\mu^2 + \sigma_\nu^2)]\overline{\widehat{u}}_{i.}$, where $\overline{\widehat{u}}_{i.} = \sum_{t=1}^T \widehat{u}_{it}/T$ is the average of the ith individual's GLS residuals.

(a) For the one-way error component model with AR(1) remainder disturbances considered in Exercise 5.4, show that

$$w'\Omega^{-1}\widehat{u}_{\text{GLS}} = \rho\widehat{u}_{i,T} + \left(\frac{(1-\rho)^2\sigma_\mu^2}{\sigma_\alpha^2}\right)\left[\alpha\hat{u}_{i1}^* + \sum\nolimits_{t=2}^{T}\hat{u}_{it}^*\right] \tag{5.32}$$

where $u^* = (I_N \otimes C)u$, $\alpha = \sqrt{(1+\rho)/(1-\rho)}$, $\sigma_\alpha^2 = d^2\sigma_\mu^2(1-\rho)^2 + \sigma_\varepsilon^2$, and $d^2 = \alpha^2 + (T-1)$ are all defined in Exercise 5.4.

(b) For the one-way error component model with remainder disturbances following an AR(2) process considered in Exercise 5.4, show that

$$\begin{aligned} w'\Omega^{-1}\widehat{u}_{\text{GLS}} &= \rho_1\widehat{u}_{i,T-1} + \rho_2\widehat{u}_{i,T-2} \\ &+ \left[\frac{(1-\rho_1-\rho_2)^2\sigma_\mu^2}{\sigma_\alpha^2}\right]\left[\alpha_1\hat{u}_{i1}^* + \alpha_2\hat{u}_{i2}^* + \sum\nolimits_{t=3}^{T}\hat{u}_{it}^*\right] \end{aligned} \tag{5.33}$$

where

$$\begin{aligned} \alpha_1 &= \sigma_\varepsilon/\sigma_\nu(1-\rho_1-\rho_2) \\ \alpha_2 &= \sqrt{(1+\rho_2)/(1-\rho_2)} \\ \sigma_\alpha^2 &= d^2\sigma_\mu^2(1-\rho_1-\rho_2)^2 + \sigma_\varepsilon^2 \\ d^2 &= \alpha_1^2 + \alpha_2^2 + (T-2) \end{aligned}$$

and

$$\begin{aligned} \hat{u}_{i1}^* &= (\sigma_\varepsilon/\sigma_\nu)\widehat{u}_{i1} \\ \hat{u}_{i2}^* &= \sqrt{1-\rho_2^2}[\widehat{u}_{i2} - (\rho_1/(1-\rho_2))\widehat{u}_{i1}] \\ \hat{u}_{it}^* &= \widehat{u}_{it} - \rho_1\widehat{u}_{i,t-1} - \rho_2\widehat{u}_{i,t-2} \quad \text{for } t = 3,\ldots,T \end{aligned}$$

(c) For the one-way error component model with remainder disturbances following the specialized AR(4) process for quarterly data considered in Exercise 5.8, show that

$$w'\Omega^{-1}\widehat{u}_{\text{GLS}} = \rho\widehat{u}_{i,T-3} + \left[\frac{(1-\rho)^2\sigma_\mu^2}{\sigma_\alpha^2}\right]\left[\alpha\sum_{t=1}^{4}\hat{u}_{it}^* + \sum\nolimits_{t=5}^{T}\hat{u}_{it}^*\right] \tag{5.34}$$

where $\alpha = \sqrt{(1+\rho)/(1-\rho)}$, $\sigma_\alpha^2 = d^2(1-\rho)^2\sigma_\mu^2 + \sigma_\varepsilon^2$, $d^2 = 4\alpha^2 + (T-4)$, and

$$\begin{aligned} u_{it}^* &= \sqrt{1-\rho^2}u_{it} \quad \text{for } t = 1,2,3,4 \\ &= u_{it} - \rho u_{i,t-4} \quad \text{for } t = 5,6,\ldots,T \end{aligned}$$

(d) For the one-way error component model with remainder disturbances following an MA(1) process considered in Exercise 5.8, show that

$$w'\Omega^{-1}\widehat{u}_{\text{GLS}} = -\lambda\left(\frac{a_{T-1}}{a_T}\right)^{1/2}\hat{u}_{it}^{*} + \left[1+\lambda\left(\frac{a_{T-1}}{a_T}\right)^{1/2}\alpha_T\right]\left(\frac{\sigma_\mu^2}{\sigma_\alpha^2}\right)\left[\sum_{t=1}^{T}\alpha_t\hat{u}_{it}^{*}\right] \tag{5.35}$$

where the $\hat{u}_{it}^{*}$ can be solved for recursively as follows:

$$\begin{aligned} \hat{u}_{i1}^{*} &= (a_0/a_1)^{1/2}\hat{u}_{i1} \\ \hat{u}_{it}^{*} &= \lambda(a_{t-2}/a_{t-1})^{1/2}\hat{u}_{i,t-1}^{*} + (a_{t-1}/a_t)^{1/2}\hat{u}_{i,t} \quad t=2,\ldots,T \end{aligned} \tag{5.36}$$

Solution

This solution is based on Baltagi and Li (1992b), and in order to derive the BLUP predictor for the various models in parts (a)–(d), we follow the general approach given in that paper. Here, in order to save space, we confine ourselves to treating (d) only. Let $\nu \sim (0, \sigma_\nu^2(I_N \otimes V))$ where V could be the matrix I_T for the classical error component model or the $T \times T$ variance–covariance matrix of an AR(1) process given by

$$V = \begin{bmatrix} 1 & \rho & \cdots & \rho^{T-1} \\ \rho & 1 & \cdots & \rho^{T-2} \\ \cdot & \cdot & \cdots & \cdot \\ \cdot & \cdot & \cdots & \cdot \\ \rho^{T-1} & \rho^{T-2} & \cdots & 1 \end{bmatrix}$$

For the one-way component model given in (2.4) with $\mu \sim (0, \sigma_\mu^2 I_N)$ independent of ν, we get $\Omega = E(uu') = \sigma_\mu^2(I_N \otimes J_T) + \sigma_\nu^2(I_N \otimes V)$ or $\Omega = I_N \otimes \Lambda$ where $\Lambda = \sigma_\mu^2 J_T + \sigma_\nu^2 V$. When we transform the regression disturbances to get rid of the serial correlation in the ν_{it} we get $u^* = (I_N \otimes C)u$ with variance–covariance matrix

$$\Omega = E(u^*u^{*\prime}) = (I_N \otimes C)\Omega(I_N \otimes C') = I_N \otimes C\Lambda C' = I_N \otimes \Lambda^*$$

where

$$\Lambda^* = C\Lambda C' = \sigma_\mu^2 C J_T C' + \sigma_\nu^2 C V C'$$

For the Prais-Winsten C transformation for the AR(1) model, C has the properties that $CVC' = (1-\rho^2)I_T$ and $C\iota_T = (1-\rho)\iota_T^{\alpha}$ where $\iota_T^{\alpha\prime} = (\alpha, \iota_{T-1}')$ and $\alpha = \sqrt{(1+\rho)/(1-\rho)}$. Therefore, for the AR(1) case,

$$\Lambda^* = \sigma_\mu^2(1-\rho)^2 J_T^{\alpha} + \sigma_\varepsilon^2 I_T$$

where $J_T^\alpha = \iota_T^\alpha \iota_T^{\alpha\prime}$. The Wansbeek and Kapteyn (1982) trick can be used to get $\Lambda^* = \sigma_\alpha^2 \overline{J}_T^\alpha + \sigma_\varepsilon^2 E_T^\alpha$ where $\sigma_\alpha^2 = d^2\sigma_\mu^2(1-\rho)^2 + \sigma_\varepsilon^2$, $\overline{J}_T^\alpha = J_T^\alpha/d^2$, $E_T^\alpha = I_T - \overline{J}_T^\alpha$ and $d^2 = \iota_T^{\alpha\prime}\iota_T^\alpha = \alpha^2 + (T-1)$. Therefore,

$$\Lambda^{*-1} = \frac{1}{\sigma_\alpha^2}\overline{J}_T^\alpha + \frac{1}{\sigma_\varepsilon^2}E_T^\alpha$$

Now, we return to prediction. From (5.31) we need to compute $w'\Omega^{-1}\widehat{u}_{\text{GLS}}$. In general, this is going to be

$$w'\Omega^{-1}\widehat{u}_{\text{GLS}} = E[u_{i,T+1}(u_1', u_2', \ldots, u_N')]\begin{bmatrix} \Lambda^{-1} & 0 & 0 & \cdots & 0 \\ 0 & \Lambda^{-1} & 0 & \cdots & 0 \\ \cdot & \cdot & \cdot & & \cdot \\ \cdot & \cdot & \cdot & \cdot & \cdot \\ \cdot & \cdot & \cdot & \cdot & \cdot \\ 0 & 0 & & & \Lambda^{-1} \end{bmatrix}\begin{bmatrix} \widehat{u}_1 \\ \widehat{u}_2 \\ \cdot \\ \cdot \\ \cdot \\ \widehat{u}_N \end{bmatrix}$$

$$= \sum_{j=1}^{N} E[u_{i,T+1}u_j']\Lambda^{-1}\widehat{u}_j = E[u_{i,T+1}u_i']\Lambda^{-1}\widehat{u}_i \tag{5.37}$$

where $u_i' = (u_{i1}, u_{i2}, \ldots, u_{it})$ and the $\widehat{u}_i$ denote the GLS residuals. The last equality uses the fact that errors of different individuals are independent of each other. Using the fact that $u_{i,T+1} = \mu_i + \nu_{i,T+1}$, this can be written as the sum of two terms:

$$E(u_{i,T+1}u_i')\Lambda^{-1}\widehat{u}_i = E(\mu_i u_i')^{-1}\Lambda^{-1}\widehat{u}_i + E(\nu_{i,T+1}u_i')\Lambda^{-1}\widehat{u}_i \tag{5.38}$$

Recall that $\Lambda^* = C\Lambda C'$, hence $\Lambda^{-1} = C'\Lambda^{*-1}C$. Also, for the AR(1) case,

$$Cu_i = (1-\rho)\iota_T^\alpha \mu_i + C\nu_i$$

where $\nu_i' = (\nu_{i1}, \nu_{i2}, \ldots, \nu_{it})$. Therefore, the first term of (5.38) can be written as

$$E[\mu_i(Cu_i)']\Lambda^{*-1}C\widehat{u}_i = \sigma_\mu^2(1-\rho)\iota_T^{\alpha\prime}\Lambda^{*-1}C\widehat{u}_i = \sigma_\mu^2(1-\rho)(\iota_T^{\alpha\prime}/\sigma_\alpha^2)\widehat{u}_i^* \tag{5.39}$$

$$= \frac{(1-\rho)\sigma_\mu^2}{\sigma_\alpha^2}\left[\alpha u_{i1}^* + \sum_{t=2}^{T} u_{it}^*\right]$$

where the first equality follows from the independence of ν_i and μ_i and the second equality follows from the fact that $\iota_T^{\alpha\prime}\Lambda^{*-1} = \iota_T^{\alpha\prime}/\sigma_\alpha^2$ and $C\widehat{u}_i = \widehat{u}_i^*$, the PW-transformed GLS residuals. The second term of (5.38) can be written as:

$$E(\nu_{i,T+1}u_i')(C'\Lambda^{*-1}C)\widehat{u}_i = E(\nu_{i,T+1}u_i')C'\left[\frac{I_T}{\sigma_\varepsilon^2} + \left(\frac{1}{\sigma_\alpha^2} - \frac{1}{\sigma_\varepsilon^2}\right)\overline{J}_T^\alpha\right]C\widehat{u}_i$$

$$= \sigma_\nu^2\rho(\rho^{T-1}, \rho^{T-2}, \ldots, \rho, 1)\left[\left(\frac{C'C}{\sigma_\varepsilon^2}\right)\widehat{u}_i - \frac{(1-\rho)^2\sigma_\mu^2}{\sigma_\alpha^2\sigma_\varepsilon^2}C'\left(\frac{C\iota_T}{1-\rho}\right)(\iota_T^{\alpha\prime}\widehat{u}_i^*)\right]$$

$$= \sigma_v^2 \rho(\rho^{T-1}, \rho^{T-2}, \ldots, \rho, 1)\left(\frac{C'C}{\sigma_\varepsilon^2}\right)\left[\widehat{u}_i - \frac{(1-\rho)\sigma_\mu^2}{\sigma_\alpha^2}\iota_T(\iota_T^{\alpha\prime}\widehat{u}_i^*)\right]$$

$$= \rho(0, 0, \ldots, 0, 1)\left[\widehat{u}_i - \frac{(1-\rho)\sigma_\mu^2}{\sigma_\alpha^2}\iota_T(\iota_T^{\alpha\prime}\widehat{u}_i^*)\right]$$

$$= \rho\widehat{u}_i - \frac{\sigma_\mu^2}{\sigma_\alpha^2}\rho(1-\rho)\left[\alpha\widehat{u}_{i1}^* + \sum_{t=2}^{T}\widehat{u}_{it}^*\right] \tag{5.40}$$

where the second equality uses the definition of $\iota_T^\alpha = C\iota_T/(1-\rho)$ and the fourth equality uses the standard result in the AR(1) model, i.e., $\sigma_v^2(\rho^{T-1}, \rho^{T-2}, \ldots, \rho, 1)$ is the last row of $[C'C/\sigma_\varepsilon^2]^{-1}$. Combining these two terms yields (5.32).

If $\sigma_\mu^2 = 0$, so that only serial correlation is present, $w'\Omega^{-1}\widehat{u}_{\text{GLS}}$ reduces to $\rho\widehat{u}_{i,T}$. Similarly, if $\rho = 0$, so that only error components are present, $w'\Omega^{-1}\widehat{u}_{\text{GLS}}$ reduces to $[T\sigma_\mu^2/(T\sigma_\mu^2 + \sigma_v^2]\bar{\widehat{u}}_{i.}$. Using an analogous derivation to the AR(1) case, one can derive (5.33) for the AR(2) case, (5.34) for the specialized AR(4) case and (5.35) for the MA(1) case. We will demonstrate this for the MA(1) case. In this case, (5.37) and (5.38) are the same, while (5.39) reduces to

$$\left(\sigma_\mu^2/\sigma_\alpha^2\right)\iota_T^{\alpha\prime}\widehat{u}_i^* = \left(\sigma_\mu^2/\sigma_\alpha^2\right)\left[\sum_{t=1}^{T}\alpha_t\widehat{u}_{it}^*\right] \tag{5.41}$$

where $\widehat{u}_i^* = C\widehat{u}_i$ and the $\widehat{u}_{it}^*$ can be solved for recursively as in (5.36). The second equality in (5.40) becomes

$$\sigma_\varepsilon^2(0, 0, \ldots, -\lambda)\left[\frac{C'\widehat{u}_i^*}{\sigma_\varepsilon^2} - \frac{\sigma_\mu^2 C'}{\sigma_\alpha^2\sigma_\varepsilon^2}\iota_T^\alpha(\iota_T^{\alpha\prime}\widehat{u}_i^*)\right] \tag{5.42}$$

This follows from the fact that the v_{it} more than one period apart are uncorrelated, and $E(v_{i,T+1}v_{i,T}) = -\lambda\sigma_\varepsilon^2$. Now, C' is an upper-triangular matrix with $(C')_{TT} = (a_{T-1}/a_T)^{1/2}$. Therefore, (5.42) reduces to

$$\left(0, 0, \ldots, -\lambda\left(\frac{a_{t-1}}{a_T}\right)^{1/2}\right)\left[\widehat{u}_i^* - \left(\frac{\sigma_\mu^2}{\sigma_\alpha^2}\right)\iota_T^\alpha(\iota_T^{\alpha\prime}\widehat{u}_i^*)\right]$$

$$= -\lambda\left(\frac{a_{t-1}}{a_T}\right)^{1/2}\widehat{u}_{it}^* + \lambda\left(\frac{a_{t-1}}{a_T}\right)^{1/2}\left(\frac{\sigma_\mu^2}{\sigma_\alpha^2}\right)\alpha_T\left[\sum_{t=1}^{T}\alpha_t\widehat{u}_{it}^*\right] \tag{5.43}$$

Combining equations (5.41) and (5.43) leads to (5.35). If $\lambda = 0$, then $\alpha_t = 1$ for all t, and (5.35) reduces to the predictor for the error component model with no serial correlation. If $\sigma_\mu^2 = 0$, the second term in (5.35) is zero and the predictor reduces to that of the MA(1) process.

Exercise 5.11 *(A joint LM test for serial correlation and random individual effects).* This is based on Problems 5.13 and 5.14 in Baltagi (2008). Consider the panel data regression with one-way error component disturbances $u_{it} = \mu_i + \nu_{it}$ where $\mu_i \sim \text{IIN}(0, \sigma_\mu^2)$ and the remainder disturbance follow a stationary AR(1) process, $\nu_{it} = \rho\nu_{i,t-1} + \varepsilon_{it}$ with $|\rho| < 1$, or an MA(1) process, $\nu_{it} = \varepsilon_{it} + \lambda\varepsilon_{i,t-1}$ with $|\lambda| < 1$, and $\varepsilon_{it} \sim \text{IIN}(0, \sigma_\varepsilon^2)$. Show that the *joint* LM test statistic $H_1^a : \sigma_\mu^2 = 0,\ \lambda = 0$ is the same as that for $H_1^b : \sigma_\mu^2 = 0,\ \rho = 0$.

Solution

Let us consider first the joint LM test for the error component model where the remainder disturbances follow an MA(1) process. In this case, the variance–covariance matrix of the disturbances is given by

$$\Omega = E(uu') = \sigma_\mu^2 I_N \otimes J_T + \sigma_\varepsilon^2 I_N \otimes V_\lambda \tag{5.44}$$

where

$$V_\lambda = \begin{pmatrix} 1+\lambda^2 & \lambda & 0 & \dots & 0 \\ \lambda & 1+\lambda^2 & \lambda & \dots & 0 \\ \vdots & \vdots & \vdots & \ddots & \vdots \\ 0 & 0 & 0 & \dots & 1+\lambda^2 \end{pmatrix} \tag{5.45}$$

and the loglikelihood function is given by $L(\delta, \theta)$ in (4.15) with $\theta = (\lambda, \sigma_\mu^2, \sigma_\varepsilon^2)'$. In order to construct the LM test statistic for $H_1^a : \sigma_\mu^2 = 0,\ \lambda = 0$, one needs $D(\theta) = \partial L(\theta)/\partial\theta$ and the information matrix $J(\theta) = E[-\partial^2 L(\theta)/\partial\theta\partial\theta']$ evaluated at the restricted maximum likelihood estimator $\widehat{\theta}$. Note that under the null hypothesis $\Omega^{-1} = (1/\sigma_\varepsilon^2)I_{NT}$. Using the general Hemmerle and Hartley (1973) formula given in (4.17), we get the scores

$$\partial L(\theta)/\partial\lambda = NT \sum_{i=1}^{N}\sum_{t=2}^{T} \widehat{u}_{it}\widehat{u}_{i,t-1} \Big/ \sum_{i=1}^{N}\sum_{t=2}^{T} \widehat{u}_{it}^2 \equiv NT(\widehat{u}'\widehat{u}_{-1}/\widehat{u}'\widehat{u}) \tag{5.46}$$

$$\partial L(\theta)/\partial\sigma_\mu^2 = -(NT/2\widehat{\sigma}_\varepsilon^2)[1 - \widehat{u}'(I_N \otimes J_T)\widehat{u}/(\widehat{u}'\widehat{u})] \tag{5.47}$$

where $\widehat{u}$ denotes the OLS residuals and $\widehat{\sigma}_\varepsilon^2 = \widehat{u}'\widehat{u}/NT$. Using (4.19) (see Harville, 1977), we get the information matrix

$$\widehat{J} = (NT/2\widehat{\sigma}_\varepsilon^4) \begin{pmatrix} T & 2(T-1)\widehat{\sigma}_\varepsilon^2/T & 1 \\ 2(T-1)\widehat{\sigma}_\varepsilon^2/T & 2\widehat{\sigma}_\varepsilon^4(T-1)/T & 0 \\ 1 & 0 & 1 \end{pmatrix} \tag{5.48}$$

Hence, the LM statistic for the null hypothesis $H_1^a : \sigma_\mu^2 = 0,\ \lambda = 0$ is given by

$$\text{LM}_1 = \widehat{D}'\widehat{J}^{-1}\widehat{D} = \frac{NT^2}{2(T-1)(T-2)}[A^2 - 4AB + 2TB^2] \tag{5.49}$$

where $A = [\widehat{u}'(I_N \otimes J_T)\widehat{u}/(\widehat{u}'\widehat{u})] - 1$ and $B = (\widehat{u}'\widehat{u}_{-1}/\widehat{u}'\widehat{u})$. This is asymptotically distributed (for large N) as χ_2^2 under H_1^a.

It remains to show that LM_1 is exactly the same as the joint test statistic for $H_1^b : \sigma_\mu^2 = 0,\ \rho = 0$, where the remainder disturbances follow an AR(1) process (see Baltagi and Li,

1991b). In fact, if we repeat the derivation given in (5.46)–(5.49), the only difference is to replace the V_λ matrix by its AR(1) counterpart,

$$V_\rho = \begin{pmatrix} 1 & \rho & \dots & \rho^{T-1} \\ \rho & 1 & \dots & \rho^{T-2} \\ \vdots & \vdots & \ddots & \vdots \\ \rho^{T-1} & \rho^{T-2} & \dots & 1 \end{pmatrix} \tag{5.50}$$

Note that under the null hypothesis, we have $(V_\rho)_\rho = 0 = I_T = (V_\lambda)_{\lambda=0}$ and

$$(\partial V_\rho/\partial\rho)_{\rho=0} = G = (\partial V_\lambda/\partial\lambda)_{\lambda=0} \tag{5.51}$$

where G is the bidiagonal matrix with bidiagonal elements all equal to one. Using these results, the resulting joint LM test statistic is the same whether the residual disturbances follow an AR(1) or an MA(1) process. Hence, the joint LM test statistic for random individual effects and first-order serial correlation is independent of the form of serial correlation, whether it is AR(1) or MA(1). This extends the Breusch and Godfrey (1981) result from time-series regression to a panel data regression using an error component model.

Exercise 5.12 *(Conditional LM test for serial correlation assuming random individual effects).* This is based on Problem 5.15 in Baltagi (2008). Derive the LM test for first-order serial correlation given the existence of random individual effects. Show that this LM test is the same whether the remainder error is AR(1) or MA(1).

Solution

In case of an AR(1) model, the null hypothesis is $H_2^b : \rho = 0$ (given $\sigma_\mu^2 > 0$). The variance–covariance matrix under the alternative $H_2^{b'} : \rho \neq 0$ (given $\sigma_\mu^2 > 0$) is

$$\Omega_1 = \sigma_\mu^2(I_N \otimes J_T) + \sigma_\nu^2(I_N \otimes V_\rho)$$

Under the null hypothesis H_2^b, we have

$$\begin{aligned}
(\Omega_1^{-1})_{\rho=0} &= (1/\sigma_\varepsilon^2)I_N \otimes E_T + (1/\sigma_1^2)I_N \otimes \bar{J}_T \\
(\partial\Omega_1/\partial\rho)\,|_{\rho=0} &= \sigma_\varepsilon^2(I_N \otimes G) \\
(\partial\Omega_1/\partial\sigma_\mu^2)\,|_{\rho=0} &= (I_N \otimes J_T) \\
(\partial\Omega_1/\partial\sigma_\varepsilon^2)\,|_{\rho=0} &= (I_N \otimes I_T)
\end{aligned}$$

where $\bar{J}_T = \iota_T\iota_T'/T$, $E_T = I_T - \bar{J}_T$, G is a bidiagonal matrix with bidiagonal elements all equal to one, and $\sigma_1^2 = T\sigma_\mu^2 + \sigma_\varepsilon^2$. Substituting these into (4.17) yields the score

$$\begin{aligned}
D_\rho = (\partial L/\partial\rho)\,|_{\rho=0} &= [N(T-1)/T]\frac{\sigma_1^2 - \sigma_\varepsilon^2}{\sigma_1^2} \\
&+ (\sigma_\varepsilon^2/2)u'\{I_N \otimes [(\bar{J}_T/\sigma_1^2 + E_T/\sigma_\varepsilon^2)G(\bar{J}_T/\sigma_1^2 + E_T/\sigma_\varepsilon^2)]\}u
\end{aligned}$$

Using (4.19) and the results for $(\partial\Omega_1/\partial\theta_r)\mid_{\rho=0}$ for $r = 1, 2, 3$ and $\theta = (\rho, \sigma_\mu^2, \sigma^2)'$, we get the information matrix

$$\widehat{J} = \begin{pmatrix} \widehat{J}_{\rho\rho} & N(T-1)\widehat{\sigma}_\varepsilon^2/\widehat{\sigma}_1^4 & \frac{N(T-1)}{T}\widehat{\sigma}_\varepsilon^2[1/\widehat{\sigma}_1^4 - 1/\widehat{\sigma}_\varepsilon^4] \\ & (NT^2/2\widehat{\sigma}_1^4) & NT/2\widehat{\sigma}_1^4 \\ & & \frac{N}{2}\left[\frac{1}{\widehat{\sigma}_1^4} + \frac{T-1}{\widehat{\sigma}_\varepsilon^4}\right] \end{pmatrix}$$

where $\widehat{J}_{\rho\rho} = N[2a^2(T-1)^2 + 2a(2T-3) + (T-1)]$ and $a = [(\widehat{\sigma}_\varepsilon^2 - \widehat{\sigma}_1^2)/T\widehat{\sigma}_1^2]$. Thus the LM test statistic is

$$\mathrm{LM} = \widehat{D}'\widehat{J}^{-1}\widehat{D} = (\widehat{D}_\rho)^2\hat{J}^{11} \tag{5.52}$$

where $\hat{J}^{11} = N^2T^2(T-1)/\det(\widehat{J})4\widehat{\sigma}_1^4\widehat{\sigma}_\varepsilon^4$. Under the null hypothesis H_4^b, LM is asymptotically distributed (for large N) as χ_1^2. $\widehat{\sigma}_\varepsilon^2 = \widehat{u}'(I_N \otimes E_T)\widehat{u}/N(T-1)$ and $\widehat{\sigma}_1^2 = \widehat{u}'(I_N \otimes \overline{J}_T)\widehat{u}/N$, where $\widehat{u}$ are the maximum likelihood residuals under the null hypothesis.

When the first-order serial correlation is of MA(1) type, the null hypothesis becomes $H_2^a : \lambda = 0$ (given that $\sigma_\mu^2 > 0$) vs $H_2^{a'} : \lambda \neq 0$ (given that $\sigma_\mu^2 > 0$). In this case, the variance–covariance matrix is

$$\Omega_2 = \sigma_\mu^2(I_N \otimes J_T) + \sigma_\varepsilon^2(I_N \otimes V_\lambda)$$

and under the null hypothesis H_2^a,

$$(\Omega_2^{-1})_{\lambda=0} = (1/\sigma_\varepsilon^2)(I_N \otimes E_T) + (1/\sigma_1^2)(I_N \otimes \overline{J}_T) = (\Omega_1^{-1})_{\rho=0}$$

$$(\partial\Omega_2/\partial\lambda)_{\lambda=0} = \sigma_\varepsilon^2(I_N \otimes G) = (\partial\Omega_1/\partial\rho)\mid_{\rho=0}$$

$$(\partial\Omega_2/\partial\sigma_\mu^2)\mid_{\lambda=0} = (I_N \otimes J_T) = (\partial\Omega_1/\partial\sigma_\mu^2)\mid_{\rho=0}$$

$$(\partial\Omega_2/\partial\sigma_\varepsilon^2)\mid_{\lambda=0} = (I_N \otimes I_T) = (\partial\Omega_1/\partial\sigma_\varepsilon^2)\mid_{\rho=0}$$

Using these results, the reader can verify that the test statistic for H_2^a is the same as (5.52).

To summarize, the LM test statistics for testing first-order serial correlation, assuming random individual effects, are invariant to the form of serial correlation (i.e., whether it is AR(1) or MA(1)). Also, we see that the LM test in this case is no longer simple. This is due to the fact that under the null hypothesis, the model is a one-way error component model with individual effects, and GLS rather than OLS residuals are involved.

Exercise 5.13 *(An LM test for first-order serial correlation in a fixed effects model).* This is based on Problem 5.16 in Baltagi (2008). Consider a panel data regression with fixed effects and remainder disturbances that exhibit first-order serial correlation. Derive the LM test for the null hypothesis $H_3^b : \rho = 0$, and show that it is the same whether the remainder error process is AR(1) or MA(1).

Solution

Writing each individual's variables in a $T \times 1$ vector form, we have

$$y_i = Z_i\delta + \mu_i\iota_T + \nu_i \tag{5.53}$$

where $y_i = (y_{i1}, y_{i2}, \ldots, y_{it})'$, Z_i is $T \times (K+1)$ and ν_i is $T \times 1$, $\nu_i \sim N(0, \Omega_\rho)$, where $\Omega_\rho = \sigma_\varepsilon^2 V_\rho$ for the AR(1) disturbances. The loglikelihood function is

$$L(\delta, \rho, \mu, \sigma_\varepsilon^2) = \text{constant} - \frac{1}{2}\log|\Omega|$$
$$-\frac{1}{2\sigma_\varepsilon^2}\sum_{i=1}^{N}[(y_i - Z_i\delta - \mu_i\iota_T)'V_\rho^{-1}(y_i - Z_i\delta - \mu_i\iota_T)] \tag{5.54}$$

where $\Omega = I_N \otimes \Omega_\rho$ is the variance–covariance matrix of $\nu' = (\nu_1', \ldots, \nu_N')$. One can easily check that the maximum likelihood estimator of μ_i is given by $\widehat{\mu}_i = \{(\iota_T' V_\rho^{-1}\iota_T)^{-1}[\iota_T' V_\rho^{-1}(y_i - Z_i\widehat{\delta})]\}_{\rho=0} = \overline{y}_{i.} - \overline{Z}_{i.}'\widehat{\delta}$, where $\widehat{\delta}$ is the maximum likelihood estimator of δ, $\overline{y}_{i.} = \sum_{t=1}^{T} y_{it}/T$, and $\overline{Z}_{i.}$ is a $(K+1) \times 1$ vector of averages of Z_{it} across time.

Write the loglikelihood function in vector form of ν as

$$L(\delta, \mu, \theta) = \text{constant} - \frac{1}{2}\log|\Omega| - \frac{1}{2}\nu'\Omega^{-1}\nu \tag{5.55}$$

where $\theta' = (\rho, \sigma_\varepsilon^2)$. By following a similar derivation to that given earlier, one can easily verify that the LM test statistic for testing H_3^b is

$$\text{LM} = [NT^2/(T-1)](\widehat{\nu}'\widehat{\nu}_{-1}/\widehat{\nu}'\widehat{\nu})^2 \tag{5.56}$$

which is asymptotically distributed (for large T) as χ_1^2 under the null hypothesis H_3^b. Note that

$$\widehat{\nu}_{it} = y_{it} - Z_{it}'\widehat{\delta} - \widehat{\mu}_i = (\widetilde{y}_{it} - \widetilde{Z}_{it}'\widehat{\delta}) + (\overline{y}_{i.} - \overline{Z}_{i.}'\widehat{\delta} - \widehat{\mu}_i)$$

where $\widetilde{y}_{it} = y_{it} - \overline{y}_{i.}$ is the usual within transformation. Under the null of $\rho = 0$, the last term in parentheses is zero since $\{\widehat{\mu}_i\}_{\rho=0} = \overline{y}_{i.} - \overline{Z}_{i.}'\widehat{\delta}$ and $\{\widehat{\nu}_{it}\}_{\rho=0} = \widetilde{y}_{it} - \widetilde{Z}_{it}\widehat{\delta} = \widetilde{\nu}_{it}$.

By a similar argument, one can show that the LM test statistic for $H_3^a : \lambda = 0$, in a fixed effects model with MA(1) residual disturbances, is identical to the LM statistic given in (5.56).

Exercise 5.14 *(Gasoline demand example with first-order serial correlation).* This is based on Problem 5.20 in Baltagi (2008). Consider the Baltagi and Griffin (1983) data set described in Exercise 2.8.

(a) Estimate the gasoline demand equation with state fixed effects but now allowing for an AR(1) remainder disturbance as described in Exercise 5.4.
(b) Repeat part (a) allowing for state random effects and an AR(1) remainder disturbance. What do you conclude?

Solution

(a) The Stata output for the FE one-way model allowing for an AR(1) remainder disturbance is reported in Table 5.1. The estimates show that price and income elasticities are even lower in absolute value than the FE estimates reported in Exercise 2.8 when you allow for serial correlated disturbances of the AR(1) type. Note that the Bhargava *et al.* (1982) Durbin–Watson statistic is 0.31, and the Baltagi and Wu (1999) test statistic is 0.53. Both test statistics reject the null hypothesis of no first-order serial correlation; see Baltagi (2008) for more discussion on these tests.

Table 5.1 Gasoline Demand Data. FE and AR(1) Remainder Disturbances

```
. xtregar  gas inc pmg car,fe lbi

FE (within) regression withAR(1) disturbances    Number of obs        =        324
Group variable: co                               Number of groups     =         18

R-sq:  within  = 0.4155                          Obs per group: min   =         18
       between = 0.5672                                         avg   =       18.0
       overall = 0.6033                                         max   =         18

                                                 F(3,303)             =      71.80
corr(u_i,Xb)   = -0.3400                         Prob > F             =     0.0000

------------------------------------------------------------------------------
         gas |      Coef.   Std. Err.      t    P>|t|     [95% Conf. Interval]
-------------+----------------------------------------------------------------
         inc |   .3484888   .0773058     4.51   0.000     .1963647     .500613
         pmg |  -.2411952   .0312932    -7.71   0.000    -.3027747   -.1796156
         car |  -.6175493    .049328   -12.52   0.000    -.7146182   -.5204805
       _cons |   .8113155   .0635549    12.77   0.000     .6862506    .9363804
-------------+----------------------------------------------------------------
      rho_ar |  .85890468
     sigma_u |  .36422345
     sigma_e |  .04568374
     rho_fov |  .98451154   (fraction of variancebecause of u_i)
-------------+----------------------------------------------------------------
F test that all u_i=0:     F(17,303) =     15.41              Prob > F = 0.0000
modified Bhargava et al. Durbin-Watson =  .31034479
Baltagi-Wu LBI = .53052393
```

(b) The RE-AR(1) Stata output is shown in Table 5.2. Note that price and income elasticities are again lower in absolute value than the RE estimates reported in Exercise 2.8 when you allow for serial correlated disturbances of the AR(1) type.

Table 5.2 Gasoline Demand Data. RE and AR(1) Remainder Disturbances

```
. xtregar gas inc pmg car, re lbi

RE GLS regression with AR(1) disturbances       Number of obs        =        342
Group variable: co                              Number of groups     =         18

R-sq:  within  = 0.8322                         Obs per group : min =         19
       between = 0.6480                                         avg =       19.0
       overall = 0.6786                                         max =         19

                                                Wald chi2(4)         =     593.40
corr(u_i, Xb)        = 0 (assumed)              Prob> chi2           =     0.0000

------------------------------------------------------------------------------
         gas |      Coef.   Std. Err.      z    P>|z|     [95% Conf. Interval]
-------------+----------------------------------------------------------------
         inc |   .3881747   .0631455     6.15   0.000     .2644119    .5119375
         pmg |  -.3014495   .0324786    -9.28   0.000    -.3651065   -.2377925
         car |  -.5367399   .0283423   -18.94   0.000    -.5922898     -.48119
       _cons |      1.667   .2449245     6.81   0.000     1.186957    2.147043
-------------+----------------------------------------------------------------
      rho_ar |  .85890468   (estimated autocorrelation coefficient)
     sigma_u |  .22475556
     sigma_e |  .05508736
     rho_fov |   .9433308   (fraction of variance due to u_i)
       theta |   .7029263
------------------------------------------------------------------------------
modified Bhargava et al. Durbin-Watson = .31034479
Baltagi-Wu LBI =.53052393
```

Exercise 5.15 *(Public capital example with first-order serial correlation).* This is based on Problem 5.21 in Baltagi (2008). Consider the Munnell (1990) data set described in Exercise 3.13.

(a) Estimate the Cobb–Douglas production function described in (3.38) with state fixed effects but now allowing for an AR(1) remainder disturbance as described in Exercise 5.4.

(b) (b) Repeat part (a) allowing for state random effects and an AR(1) remainder disturbance. What do you conclude?

Solution

(a) The Stata output for the FE one-way model allowing for an AR(1) remainder disturbance is reported in Table 5.3. The estimates show that public capital is not significant. Note that the Bhargava *et al.* (1982) Durbin–Watson statistic is 0.39, and the Baltagi and Wu (1999) test statistic is 0.65. Both test statistics reject the null hypothesis of no first-order serial correlation; see Baltagi (2008) for more discussion on these tests.

(b) The RE-AR(1) Stata output is shown in Table 5.4. Note that public capital is now significant at the 5% significance level.

Table 5.3 Public Capital Productivity Data. FE and AR(1) Remainder Disturbances

```
. xtregar y kl k l unemp, fe lbi

FE (within) regression with AR(1) disturbances  Number of obs      =       768
Group variable: state                           Number of groups   =        48

R-sq:  within  = 0.7312                         Obs per group: min =        16
       between = 0.9786                                        avg =      16.0
       overall = 0.9775                                        max =        16

                                                F(4,716)           =    486.83
corr(u_i, Xb) = -0.0441                         Prob > F           =    0.0000

------------------------------------------------------------------------------
           y |      Coef.   Std. Err.       t    P>|t|     [95% Conf. Interval]
-------------+----------------------------------------------------------------
          kl |  -.0354469   .0541613    -0.65   0.513     -.141781    .0708871
           k |   .0087117   .0230899     0.38   0.706    -.0366203    .0540436
           l |   1.023762   .0401443    25.50   0.000     .9449473    1.102576
       unemp |  -.0034528     .00082    -4.21   0.000    -.0050628   -.0018429
       _cons |   3.668508   .0763277    48.06   0.000     3.518655    3.818361
-------------+----------------------------------------------------------------
      rho_ar |  .85369326
     sigma_u |  .14911549
     sigma_e |  .02047485
     rho_fov |  .98149521   (fraction of variance because of u_i)
------------------------------------------------------------------------------
F test that all u_i=0:     F(47,716) =     5.66             Prob > F = 0.0000
modified Bhargava et al. Durbin-Watson = .38971069
Baltagi-Wu LBI = .65075706
```

Table 5.4 Public Capital Productivity Data. RE and AR(1) Remainder Disturbances

```
. xtregar y kl k l unemp, re lbi

RE GLS regression with AR(1) disturbances       Number of obs      =       816
Group variable: state                           Number of groups   =        48

R-sq:  within  = 0.9387                         Obs per group: min =        17
       between = 0.9903                                        avg =      17.0
       overall = 0.9891                                        max =        17

                                                Wald chi2(5)       =  11937.52
corr(u_i, Xb)       = 0 (assumed)               Prob > chi2        =    0.0000

------------------------------------------------------------------------------
           y |      Coef.   Std. Err.       z    P>|z|     [95% Conf. Interval]
-------------+----------------------------------------------------------------
          kl |   .0707818   .0310185     2.28   0.022     .0099867    .1315769
           k |   .1713853   .0198521     8.63   0.000     .1324759    .2102946
           l |   .8078356   .0277709    29.09   0.000     .7534056    .8622656
       unemp |  -.0062959   .0007473    -8.42   0.000    -.0077605   -.0048312
       _cons |   2.423142   .1455901    16.64   0.000      2.13779    2.708493
-------------+----------------------------------------------------------------
      rho_ar |  .85369326   (estimated autocorrelation coefficient)
     sigma_u |  .07550899
     sigma_e |  .02361255
     rho_fov |  .91092216   (fraction of variance due to u_i)
```

6

Seemingly Unrelated Regressions with Error Components

In economics, one often needs to estimate a set of equations. This could be a set of demand equations, across different sectors, industries or regions. Other examples include the estimation of a translog cost function along with the corresponding cost share equations. In these cases, Zellner's (1962) seemingly unrelated regressions (SUR) approach is popular since it captures the efficiency due to the correlation of the disturbances across equations. Applications of the SUR procedure with time-series or cross-section data are too numerous to cite. In this chapter, we focus on the estimation of a set of SUR equations with panel data.

Exercise 6.1 *(Seemingly unrelated regressions with one-way error component disturbances).* This is based on Problems 6.1 and 6.2 in Baltagi (2008). Consider a set of M equations,

$$y_j = Z_j\delta_j + u_j \quad (j = 1, \ldots, M) \tag{6.1}$$

where y_j is $NT \times 1$, Z_j is $NT \times k'_j$, $\delta'_j = (\alpha_j, \beta'_j)$, β_j is $k_j \times 1$ and $k'_j = k_j + 1$. Each equation has a one-way error component disturbance given by

$$u_j = Z_\mu \mu_j + \nu_j \quad (j = 1, \ldots, M) \tag{6.2}$$

where $Z_\mu = (I_N \otimes \iota_T)$, and $\mu'_j = (\mu_{1j}, \mu_{2j}, \ldots, \mu_{Nj})$ and $\nu'_j = (\nu_{11j}, \ldots, \nu_{1Tj}, \ldots, \nu_{N1j}, \ldots, \nu_{NTj})$ are random vectors with zero means and covariance matrix

$$E\begin{pmatrix}\mu_j \\ \nu_j\end{pmatrix}(\mu'_l, \nu'_l) = \begin{bmatrix} \sigma^2_{\mu_{jl}} I_N & 0 \\ 0 & \sigma^2_{\nu_{jl}} I_{NT} \end{bmatrix} \tag{6.3}$$

for $j, l = 1, 2, \ldots, M$. This can be justified as follows: $\mu \sim (0, \Sigma_\mu \otimes I_N)$ and $\nu \sim (0, \Sigma_\nu \otimes I_{NT})$ where $\mu' = (\mu'_1, \mu'_2, \ldots, \mu'_M)$, $\nu' = (\nu'_1, \nu'_2, \ldots, \nu'_M)$, $\Sigma_\mu = [\sigma^2_{\mu_{jl}}]$ and $\Sigma_\nu = [\sigma^2_{\nu_{jl}}]$ for $j, l = 1, 2, \ldots, M$. In other words, *each* error component follows the same standard Zellner (1962) SUR assumptions imposed on classical disturbances.

(a) Show that $\Omega = E(uu')$ can be written as

$$\Omega = \Sigma_1 \otimes P + \Sigma_\nu \otimes Q \tag{6.4}$$

where $\Sigma_1 = T\Sigma_\mu + \Sigma_\nu$, $P = I_N \otimes \bar{J}_T$ and $Q = I_{NT} - P$.

(b) Find Ω^r, where r is an arbitrary scalar. In particular, find Ω^{-1}, $\Omega^{-1/2}$ and verify that $\Omega\Omega^{-1} = I$ and $\Omega^{-1/2}\Omega^{-1/2} = \Omega^{-1}$.

Solution

(a) The variance–covariance matrix between the disturbances of the jth and ℓth equation can be obtained from (6.2) as follows:

$$\Omega_{j\ell} = E(u_j u'_\ell) = Z_\mu E(\mu_j \mu'_\ell) Z'_\mu + E(\nu_j \nu'_\ell)$$

The cross-product terms have zero expectations since the μs and the νs are uncorrelated as described in (6.3). Using the fact that $E(\mu_j \mu'_\ell) = \sigma^2_{\mu_{j\ell}} I_N$ and $E(\nu_j \nu'_\ell) = \sigma^2_{\nu_{j\ell}} I_{NT}$ from (6.3), we get

$$\Omega_{j\ell} = \sigma^2_{\mu_{j\ell}} Z_\mu Z'_\mu + \sigma^2_{\nu_{j\ell}} I_{NT} = \sigma^2_{\mu_{j\ell}} (I_N \otimes J_T) + \sigma^2_{\nu_{j\ell}} I_{NT} \tag{6.5}$$

In this case, the covariance matrix between the disturbances of different equations has the same one-way error component form. Except now, there are additional *cross-equation* variance components to be estimated. The variance–covariance matrix for the set of M equations is given by

$$\Omega = E(uu') = \Sigma_\mu \otimes (I_N \otimes J_T) + \Sigma_\nu \otimes (I_N \otimes I_T) \tag{6.6}$$

where $u' = (u'_1, u'_2, \ldots, u'_M)$ is a $1 \times MNT$ vector of disturbances with u_j defined in (6.2) for $j = 1, 2, \ldots, M$. $\Sigma_\mu = [\sigma^2_{\mu_{jl}}]$ and $\Sigma_\nu = [\sigma^2_{\nu_{jl}}]$ are both $M \times M$ matrices. Replacing J_T by $T\bar{J}_T$ and I_T by $E_T + \bar{J}_T$, and collecting terms leads to

$$\begin{aligned} \Omega &= (T\Sigma_\mu + \Sigma_\nu) \otimes (I_N \otimes \bar{J}_T) + \Sigma_\nu \otimes (I_N \otimes E_T) \\ &= \Sigma_1 \otimes P + \Sigma_\nu \otimes Q \end{aligned} \tag{6.7}$$

where $\Sigma_1 = T\Sigma_\mu + \Sigma_\nu$ as described in (6.4).

(b) The spectral decomposition of Ω given by (6.4) was derived by Baltagi (1980). In fact,

$$\Omega^r = \Sigma_1^r \otimes P + \Sigma_\nu^r \otimes Q \tag{6.8}$$

where r is an arbitrary scalar (see also Magnus, 1982). For $r = -1$ we get the inverse Ω^{-1}, and for $r = -\frac{1}{2}$ we get

$$\Omega^{-1/2} = \Sigma_1^{-1/2} \otimes P + \Sigma_\nu^{-1/2} \otimes Q \tag{6.9}$$

It is clear that

$$\begin{aligned} \Omega\Omega^{-1} &= (\Sigma_1 \otimes P + \Sigma_\nu \otimes Q)(\Sigma_1^{-1} \otimes P + \Sigma_\nu^{-1} \otimes Q) \\ &= (\Sigma_1 \Sigma_1^{-1} \otimes P) + (\Sigma_\nu \Sigma_\nu^{-1} \otimes Q) = I_M \otimes (P + Q) \\ &= I_M \otimes I_{NT} \end{aligned}$$

as required. Also,

$$\begin{aligned} \Omega^{-1/2}\Omega^{-1/2} &= (\Sigma_1^{-1/2} \otimes P + \Sigma_\nu^{-1/2} \otimes Q)(\Sigma_1^{-1/2} \otimes P + \Sigma_\nu^{-1/2} \otimes Q) \\ &= \Sigma_1^{-1} \otimes P + \Sigma_\nu^{-1} \otimes Q = \Omega^{-1} \end{aligned}$$

as required.

Exercise 6.2 *(Unbiased estimates of the variance components of the one-way SUR model).* This is based on Problem 6.7, part (a), in Baltagi (2008). Knowing the true disturbances, one can estimate Σ_ν and Σ_1 by

$$\widehat{\Sigma}_\nu = U'QU/N(T-1) \quad \text{and} \quad \widehat{\Sigma}_1 = U'PU/N \tag{6.10}$$

where $U = [u_1, \ldots, u_M]$ is the $NT \times M$ matrix of disturbances for all M equations. Show that $\widehat{\Sigma}_\nu$ and $\widehat{\Sigma}_1$ yield unbiased estimates of Σ_ν and Σ_1, respectively.

Solution

Note that $E(U'QU)$ has a typical element

$$E(u'_\ell Qu_j) = E\{\text{tr}(u_j u'_\ell Q)\} = \text{tr}(\Omega_{j\ell}Q) = \sigma^2_{\nu_{j\ell}}\text{tr}(Q) = \sigma^2_{\nu_{j\ell}}N(T-1)$$

Hence, $E(\widehat{\Sigma}_\nu) = \Sigma_\nu$. Similarly, $E(U'PU)$ has a typical element

$$E(u'_\ell Pu_j) = E\{tr(u_j u'_\ell P)\} = \text{tr}(\Omega_{j\ell}P) = \sigma^2_{1_{j\ell}}\text{tr}(P) = N\sigma^2_{1_{j\ell}}$$

Hence, $E(\widehat{\Sigma}_1) = \Sigma_1$.

For this model, a block-diagonal Ω makes GLS on the whole system equivalent to GLS on each equation separately. However, when the same X appear in each equation, GLS on the whole system is not equivalent to GLS on each equation separately (see Avery, 1977; Baltagi, 1980). Let us demonstrate this with a two-equation system.

Exercise 6.3 *(Special cases of the SUR model with one-way error component disturbances).* This is based on Problem 6.3, parts (a) and (b), in Baltagi (2008). Consider a set of two SUR equations as in (6.1) with $M = 2$, so that

$$\begin{pmatrix} y_1 \\ y_2 \end{pmatrix} = \begin{pmatrix} Z_1 & 0 \\ 0 & Z_2 \end{pmatrix}\begin{pmatrix} \delta_1 \\ \delta_2 \end{pmatrix} + \begin{pmatrix} u_1 \\ u_2 \end{pmatrix}$$

with one-way error components disturbances given by (6.2).

(a) Show that if the variance–covariance matrix between the two equations is block-diagonal, then GLS on the system is *equivalent* to GLS on each equation separately.
(b) Show that if the explanatory variables are the *same* across the two equations, GLS on the system does *not* necessarily revert to GLS on each equation separately.

Solution

(a) For Ω block-diagonal, $\Omega_{12} = 0$, so that $\sigma^2_{\mu_{12}} = \sigma^2_{\nu_{12}} = 0$ using (6.5) for $j = 1$ and $\ell = 2$. Hence, both Σ_μ and Σ_ν are diagonal. In this case

$$\Omega = E\begin{pmatrix} u_1 \\ u_2 \end{pmatrix}(u'_1, u'_2) = \begin{bmatrix} \Omega_{11} & 0 \\ 0 & \Omega_{22} \end{bmatrix}$$

and

$$\Omega^{-1} = \begin{bmatrix} \Omega_{11}^{-1} & 0 \\ 0 & \Omega_{22}^{-1} \end{bmatrix}$$

so that the GLS estimator of the system of two equations is given by

$$\begin{pmatrix} \widehat{\delta}_1 \\ \widehat{\delta}_2 \end{pmatrix} = \left[\begin{pmatrix} Z_1' & 0 \\ 0 & Z_2' \end{pmatrix} \begin{pmatrix} \Omega_{11}^{-1} & 0 \\ 0 & \Omega_{22}^{-1} \end{pmatrix} \begin{pmatrix} Z_1 & 0 \\ 0 & Z_2 \end{pmatrix} \right]^{-1}$$

$$\left[\begin{pmatrix} Z_1' & 0 \\ 0 & Z_2' \end{pmatrix} \begin{pmatrix} \Omega_{11}^{-1} & 0 \\ 0 & \Omega_{22}^{-1} \end{pmatrix} \begin{pmatrix} y_1 \\ y_2 \end{pmatrix} \right]$$

$$= \begin{pmatrix} Z_1'\Omega_{11}^{-1}Z_1 & 0 \\ 0 & Z_2'\Omega_{22}^{-1}Z_2 \end{pmatrix}^{-1} \begin{pmatrix} Z_1'\Omega_{11}^{-1}y_1 \\ Z_2'\Omega_{22}^{-1}y_2 \end{pmatrix}$$

$$= \begin{pmatrix} (Z_1'\Omega_{11}^{-1}Z_1)^{-1}Z_1'\Omega_{11}^{-1}y_1 \\ (Z_2'\Omega_{22}^{-1}Z_2)^{-1}Z_2'\Omega_{22}^{-1}y_2 \end{pmatrix}$$

which are exactly the GLS estimates of δ_1 and δ_2 on each equation separately.

(b) If $Z_1 = Z_2 = Z$ and $\Omega_{12} \neq 0$, then Σ_μ and Σ_ν are not diagonal and $\Omega = \Sigma_1 \otimes P + \Sigma_\nu \otimes Q$ as described in (6.4). Then GLS on the system is

$$\begin{pmatrix} \widehat{\delta}_1 \\ \widehat{\delta}_2 \end{pmatrix}_{\text{GLS}} = [(I_2 \otimes Z')[\Sigma_1^{-1} \otimes P + \Sigma_\nu^{-1} \otimes Q](I_2 \otimes Z)]^{-1}$$

$$(I_2 \otimes Z')(\Sigma_1^{-1} \otimes P + \Sigma_\nu^{-1} \otimes Q)y$$

$$= [(\Sigma_1^{-1} \otimes Z'PZ) + (\Sigma_\nu^{-1} \otimes Z'QZ)]^{-1}[(\Sigma_1^{-1} \otimes Z'P)y + (\Sigma_\nu^{-1} \otimes Z'Q)y]$$

where $y' = (y_1', y_2')$. This is different, in general, from GLS on each equation separately.

Exercise 6.4 *(Seemingly unrelated regressions with two-way error component disturbances).* This is based on Problems 6.4 and 6.5 in Baltagi (2008). Consider the set of M equations defined in (6.1). However, now each equation has two-way error component disturbances given by

$$u_j = Z_\mu \mu_j + Z_\lambda \lambda_j + \nu_j \quad (j = 1, \ldots, M) \tag{6.11}$$

where $\lambda_j' = (\lambda_{1j}, \ldots, \lambda_{Tj})$ is a random vector with zero mean and covariance matrix given by

$$E\begin{pmatrix} \mu_j \\ \lambda_j \\ \nu_j \end{pmatrix}(\mu_l', \lambda_l', \nu_l') = \begin{bmatrix} \sigma_{\mu_{jl}}^2 I_N & 0 & 0 \\ 0 & \sigma_{\lambda_{jl}}^2 I_T & 0 \\ 0 & 0 & \sigma_{\nu_{jl}}^2 I_{NT} \end{bmatrix}$$

for $j, l = 1, 2, \ldots, M$. In this case, $\lambda \sim (0, \Sigma_\lambda \otimes I_T)$ where $\lambda' = (\lambda_1, \lambda_2, \ldots, \lambda_T)$ and $\Sigma_\lambda = [\sigma_{\lambda_{jl}}^2]$ is $M \times M$. Like μ and v, the λ follows a standard Zellner SUR-type assumption.

(a) Show that $\Omega = E(uu')$ can be written as

$$\Omega = \sum_{i=1}^{4} \Lambda_i \otimes Q_i \tag{6.12}$$

where $\Lambda_1 = \Sigma_\nu$, $\Lambda_2 = T\Sigma_\mu + \Sigma_\nu$, $\Lambda_3 = N\Sigma_\lambda + \Sigma_\nu$, and $\Lambda_4 = T\Sigma_\mu + N\Sigma_\lambda + \Sigma_\nu$, with Q_i defined in Excercise 3.2 below (3.17).

(b) Find Ω^r where r is an arbitrary scalar. In particular, find Ω^{-1} and $\Omega^{-1/2}$, and verify that $\Omega\Omega^{-1} = I$ and $\Omega^{-1/2}\Omega^{-1/2} = \Omega^{-1}$.

Solution

(a) The variance–covariance matrix between the disturbances of the jth and ℓth equation can be obtained from (6.11) as follows:

$$\Omega_{j\ell} = E(u_j u'_\ell) = Z_\mu E(\mu_j \mu'_\ell) Z'_\mu + Z_\lambda E(\lambda_j \lambda'_\ell) Z'_\lambda + E(\nu_j \nu'_\ell)$$

The cross-product terms have zero expectations since the μs, λs and the νs are uncorrelated. Using the fact that $E(\mu_j \mu'_\ell) = \sigma^2_{\mu_{j\ell}} I_N$, $E(\lambda_j \lambda'_\ell) = \sigma^2_{\lambda_{j\ell}} I_T$, and $E(\nu_j \nu'_\ell) = \sigma^2_{\nu_{j\ell}} I_{NT}$, we get

$$\begin{aligned} \Omega_{jl} = E(u_j u'_l) &= \sigma^2_{\mu_{j\ell}} Z_\mu Z'_\mu + \sigma^2_{\lambda_{jl}} Z_\lambda Z'_\lambda + \sigma^2_{\nu_{jl}} I_{NT} \\ &= \sigma^2_{\mu_{jl}} (I_N \otimes J_T) + \sigma^2_{\lambda_{jl}} (J_N \otimes I_T) + \sigma^2_{\nu_{jl}} (I_N \otimes I_T) \qquad (6.13) \end{aligned}$$

As in the one-way SUR model, the covariance between the disturbances of different equations has the same two-way error component form. Except now, there are additional cross-equations variance components to be estimated. The variance–covariance matrix of the system of M equations is given by

$$\Omega = E(uu') = \Sigma_\mu \otimes (I_N \otimes J_T) + \Sigma_\lambda \otimes (J_N \otimes I_T) + \Sigma_\nu \otimes (I_N \otimes I_T)$$

where $u' = (u'_1, u'_2, \ldots, u'_M)$ with u_j defined below (6.10). Replacing J_T by $T\bar{J}_T$, J_N by $N\bar{J}_N$, I_N by $E_N + \bar{J}_N$ and I_T by $E_T + \bar{J}_T$, we get

$$\begin{aligned} \Omega = &\, T\Sigma_\mu \otimes (E_N + \bar{J}_N) \otimes \bar{J}_T + N\Sigma_\lambda \otimes \bar{J}_N \otimes (E_T + \bar{J}_T) \\ &+ \Sigma_\nu \otimes (E_N + \bar{J}_N) \otimes (E_T + \bar{J}_T) \end{aligned}$$

Multiplying out and collecting like terms leads to

$$\begin{aligned} \Omega &= (T\Sigma_\mu + \Sigma_\nu) \otimes E_N \otimes \bar{J}_T + (N\Sigma_\lambda + \Sigma_\nu) \otimes \bar{J}_N \otimes E_T \\ &\quad + (T\Sigma_\mu + N\Sigma_\lambda + \Sigma_\nu) \otimes \bar{J}_N \otimes \bar{J}_T + \Sigma_\nu \otimes E_N \otimes E_T \\ &= \sum_{i=1}^{4} \Lambda_i \otimes Q_i \end{aligned}$$

as described in (6.12).

(b) The spectral decomposition of Ω given by (6.12) was derived by Baltagi (1980). In fact,

$$\Omega^r = \sum_{i=1}^{4} \Lambda_i^r \otimes Q_i \qquad (6.14)$$

for r an arbitrary scalar. When $r = -1$ we get the inverse Ω^{-1}, and when $r = -\frac{1}{2}$ we get

$$\Omega^{-1/2} = \sum_{i=1}^{4} \Lambda_i^{-1/2} \otimes Q_i \tag{6.15}$$

It is clear that

$$\Omega\Omega^{-1} = \left(\sum_{i=1}^{4} \Lambda_i \otimes Q_i\right)\left(\sum_{i=1}^{4} \Lambda_i^{-1} \otimes Q_i\right) = \sum_{i=1}^{4}(\Lambda_i\Lambda_i^{-1} \otimes Q_i)$$
$$= \sum_{i=1}^{4}(I_M \otimes Q_i) = I_M \otimes \sum_{i=1}^{4} Q_i = I_M \otimes I_{NT}$$

Also,

$$\Omega^{-1/2}\Omega^{-1/2} = \left(\sum_{i=1}^{4} \Lambda_i^{-1/2} \otimes Q_i\right)\left(\sum_{i=1}^{4} \Lambda_i^{-1/2} \otimes Q_i\right) = \sum_{i=1}^{4} \Lambda_i^{-1} \otimes Q_i = \Omega^{-1}$$

as required.

Exercise 6.5 *(Unbiased estimates of the variance components of the two-way SUR model).* This is based on Problem 6.7, part (b), in Baltagi (2008). Knowing the true disturbances U, quadratic unbiased estimates of the variance components are obtained from

$$\widehat{\Lambda}_1 = \frac{U'Q_1U}{(N-1)(T-1)}, \widehat{\Lambda}_2 = \frac{U'Q_2U}{(N-1)}, \widehat{\Lambda}_3 = \frac{U'Q_3U}{(T-1)} \tag{6.16}$$

Show that $\widehat{\Lambda}_1$, $\widehat{\Lambda}_2$ and $\widehat{\Lambda}_3$ yield unbiased estimates of Λ_1, Λ_2 and Λ_3, respectively.

Solution

Note that $E(U'Q_iU)$ has typical element

$$E(u_\ell' Q_i u_j) = E\{\text{tr}(u_j u_\ell' Q_i)\} = \text{tr}(\Omega_{j\ell} Q_i) = \lambda_{i_{j\ell}} \text{tr}(Q_i) = \sigma^2_{\nu_{j\ell}}(N-1)(T-1) \text{ for } i = 1$$
$$= \lambda_{2_{j\ell}}(N-1) \text{ for } i = 2$$
$$= \lambda_{3_{j\ell}}(T-1) \text{ for } i = 3$$

Hence, $E(\widehat{\Lambda}_i) = \Lambda_i$ for $i = 1, 2, 3$.

Exercise 6.6 *(Special cases of the SUR model with two-way error component disturbances).* This is based on Problem 6.3, part (c), in Baltagi (2008). Does your answer to parts (a) and (b) of Exercise 6.3 change if the disturbances follow a two-way error component model as in (6.11)?

Solution

(a) For the two-way error component model, the proof of part (a) is still the same as that for the one-way error component model. Only Ω changes, but $\Omega_{12} = 0$, and this is all that is needed for the proof.

(b) The proof of part (b) has to be modified to account for the Ω matrix given in (6.12). In this case,

$$\begin{pmatrix} \widehat{\delta}_1 \\ \widehat{\delta}_2 \end{pmatrix}_{\text{GLS}} = \left[(I_2 \otimes Z')\left(\sum_{i=1}^{4} \Lambda_1^{-1} \otimes Q_i\right)(I_2 \otimes Z)\right]^{-1}$$

$$\left[(I_2 \otimes Z')\left(\sum_{i=1}^{4} \Lambda_i^{-1} \otimes Q_i\right) y\right]$$

$$= \left[\sum_{i=1}^{4} \Lambda_i^{-1} \otimes Z'Q_iZ\right]^{-1} \left[\sum_{i=1}^{4} \Lambda_i^{-1} \otimes Z'Q_i\right] y$$

This obviously differs from GLS on each equation alone.

7

Simultaneous Equations with Error Components

7.1 SINGLE EQUATION ESTIMATION

Endogeneity of the right-hand regressors is a serious problem in econometrics. By endogeneity we mean the correlation of the right-hand-side regressors and the disturbances. Endogeneity causes inconsistency of the usual OLS estimates and requires instrumental variable methods such as two-stage least squares (2SLS) to obtain consistent parameter estimates. The applied literature is full of examples of endogeneity: demand and supply equations for labor, money, goods and commodities, to mention a few. We assume that the reader is familiar with the identification and estimation of a single equation and a system of simultaneous equations. In this chapter we focus on the estimation of simultaneous equations using panel data.

Consider the following first structural equation of a simultaneous equation model:

$$y_1 = Z_1\delta_1 + u_1 \tag{7.1}$$

where $Z_1 = [Y_1, X_1]$ and $\delta_1' = (\gamma_1', \beta_1')$. As in the standard simultaneous equation literature, Y_1 is the set of g_1 right-hand-side endogenous variables, and X_1 is the set of k_1 included exogenous variables. Let $X = [X_1, X_2]$ be the set of all exogenous variables in the system. This equation is identified with k_2 the number of excluded exogenous variables from the first equation (X_2) being larger than or equal to g_1.

Exercise 7.1 *(2SLS as a GLS estimator).* Assuming that $u_1 \sim (0, \sigma_{11}^2 I_{NT})$, show that 2SLS on (7.1) with instruments X is equivalent to premultiplying (7.1) by X' and performing GLS.

Solution

Premultiplying (7.1) by X', we get

$$X'y_1 = X'Z_1\delta_1 + X'u_1 \tag{7.2}$$

with variance–covariance matrix of the disturbances $X'u_1$ given by

$$E(X'u_1u_1'X) = X'E(u_1u_1')X = \sigma_{11}^2(X'X)$$

Therefore, GLS on (7.2) yields

$$\begin{aligned}\widehat{\delta}_1 &= (Z_1'X[\sigma_{11}^2(X'X)]^{-1}X'Z_1)^{-1}Z_1'X[\sigma_{11}^2(X'X)]^{-1}X'y_1\\ &= (Z_1'P_XZ_1)^{-1}Z_1'P_Xy_1 = \widehat{\delta}_{1,2SLS}\end{aligned}$$

with $P_X = X(X'X)^{-1}X'$, and $\text{var}(\widehat{\delta}_{1,2SLS}) = \sigma_{11}^2(Z_1'P_XZ_1)^{-1}$.

Now, consider the one-way error component model

$$u_1 = Z_\mu \mu_1 + \nu_1 \tag{7.3}$$

where $Z_\mu = (I_N \otimes \iota_T)$, and $\mu_1' = (\mu_{11}, \ldots, \mu_{N1})$ and $\nu_1' = (\nu_{111}, \ldots, \nu_{NT1})$ are random vectors with zero means and covariance matrix

$$E\begin{pmatrix}\mu_1\\ \nu_1\end{pmatrix}(\mu_1', \nu_1') = \begin{bmatrix}\sigma_{\mu_{11}}^2 I_N & 0\\ 0 & \sigma_{\nu_{11}}^2 I_{NT}\end{bmatrix} \tag{7.4}$$

This differs from the SUR setup in Chapter 6 only in the fact that there are right-hand-side endogenous variables in Z_1. In this case,

$$E(u_1 u_1') = \Omega_{11} = \sigma_{\nu_{11}}^2 I_{NT} + \sigma_{\mu_{11}}^2 (I_N \otimes J_T) \tag{7.5}$$

In other words, the first structural equation has the typical variance–covariance matrix of a one-way error component model. The only difference is that now a double subscript (1,1) is attached to the variance components to specify that this is the first equation of a simultaneous equation model.

Exercise 7.2 *(Within 2SLS and between 2SLS)*

(a) Show that within 2SLS on (7.1) can be obtained by premultiplying (7.1) by $Q = I_{NT} - P$, with $P = I_N \otimes \overline{J}_T$, and performing 2SLS with instruments $\widetilde{X} = QX$.
(b) Show that between 2SLS on (7.1) can be obtained by premultiplying (7.1) by P, and performing 2SLS with instruments $\overline{X} = PX$.

Solution

(a) Transforming (7.1) by Q yields

$$Qy_1 = QZ_1\delta_1 + Qu_1 \tag{7.6}$$

Let $\widetilde{y}_1 = Qy_1$ and $\widetilde{Z}_1 = QZ_1$. Performing 2SLS on (7.6) with $\widetilde{X} = QX$ as the set of instruments, yields the within 2SLS estimator of δ_1,

$$\widetilde{\delta}_{1,\text{W2SLS}} = (\widetilde{Z}_1' P_{\widetilde{X}} \widetilde{Z}_1)^{-1} \widetilde{Z}_1' P_{\widetilde{X}} \widetilde{y}_1 \tag{7.7}$$

with $P_{\widetilde{X}} = \widetilde{X}(\widetilde{X}'\widetilde{X})^{-1}\widetilde{X}'$ and $\text{var}(\widehat{\delta}_{1,\text{W2SLS}}) = \sigma_{\nu_{11}}^2 (\widetilde{Z}_1' P_{\widetilde{X}} \widetilde{Z}_1)^{-1}$.

(b) Similarly, transforming (7.1) by P yields

$$Py_1 = PZ_1\delta_1 + Pu_1 \tag{7.8}$$

Let $\overline{y}_1 = Py_1$ and $\overline{Z}_1 = PZ_1$. Performing 2SLS on (7.8) with $\overline{X} = PX$ as the set of instruments yields the between 2SLS estimator of δ_1,

$$\widehat{\delta}_{1,\text{B2SLS}} = (\overline{Z}_1' P_{\overline{X}} \overline{Z}_1)^{-1} \overline{Z}_1' P_{\overline{X}} \overline{y}_1 \tag{7.9}$$

with $P_{\overline{X}} = \overline{X}(\overline{X}'\overline{X})^{-1}\overline{X}'$ and $\text{var}(\widehat{\delta}_{1,\text{B2SLS}}) = \sigma_{1_{11}}^2 (\overline{Z}_1' P_{\overline{X}} \overline{Z}_1)^{-1}$, where $\sigma_{1_{11}}^2 = T\sigma_{\mu_{11}}^2$ $+\sigma_{\nu_{11}}^2$.

Exercise 7.3 *(Within 2SLS and between 2SLS as GLS estimators).* This is based on Problem 7.1 in Baltagi (2008).

(a) Show that within 2SLS can be obtained as GLS on (7.6) after premutiplying it by the matrix of instruments $\widetilde{X}'$.
(b) Show that between 2SLS can be obtained as GLS on (7.8) after premutiplying it by the matrix of instruments $\overline{X}'$.

Solution

(a) Premutiplying (7.6) by the matrix of instruments $\widetilde{X}'$, we get

$$\widetilde{X}'\widetilde{y}_1 = \widetilde{X}'\widetilde{Z}_1\delta_1 + \widetilde{X}'\widetilde{u}_1 \tag{7.10}$$

with variance–covariance matrix of the disturbances in (7.10) given by

$$E(\widetilde{X}'\widetilde{u}_1\widetilde{u}_1'\widetilde{X}) = \widetilde{X}'E(\widetilde{u}_1\widetilde{u}_1')\widetilde{X} = \widetilde{X}'QE(u_1u_1')Q\widetilde{X} = \widetilde{X}'Q\Omega_{11}Q\widetilde{X} = \sigma^2_{\nu_{11}}(\widetilde{X}'\widetilde{X})$$

where $Q\Omega_{11}Q = \sigma^2_{\nu_{11}}Q$ and $Q\widetilde{X} = QQX = \widetilde{X}$. Therefore, GLS on (7.10) yields

$$\begin{aligned}\widehat{\delta}_1 &= (\widetilde{Z}_1'\widetilde{X}[\sigma^2_{\nu_{11}}\widetilde{X}'\widetilde{X}]^{-1}\widetilde{X}'\widetilde{Z}_1)^{-1}\widetilde{Z}_1'\widetilde{X}[\sigma^2_{\nu_{11}}\widetilde{X}'\widetilde{X}]^{-1}\widetilde{X}'\widetilde{y}_1\\ &= (\widetilde{Z}_1'P_{\widetilde{X}}\widetilde{Z}_1)^{-1}\widetilde{Z}_1'P_{\widetilde{X}}\widetilde{y}_1 = \widetilde{\delta}_{1,\text{W2SLS}}\end{aligned}$$

which is the within 2SLS described in (7.7).

(b) Similarly, premutiplying (7.8) by the matrix of instruments $\overline{X}'$ we get

$$\overline{X}'\overline{y}_1 = \overline{X}'\overline{Z}_1\delta_1 + \overline{X}'\overline{u}_1 \tag{7.11}$$

with variance–covariance matrix of the disturbances in (7.11) given by

$$\begin{aligned}E(\overline{X}'\overline{u}_1\overline{u}_1'\overline{X}) &= \overline{X}'E(\overline{u}_1\overline{u}_1')\overline{X} = \overline{X}'PE(\overline{u}_1\overline{u}_1')P\overline{X}\\ &= \overline{X}'P\Omega_{11}P\overline{X} = \sigma^2_{1_{11}}\overline{X}'\overline{X}\end{aligned}$$

where $\sigma^2_{1_{11}} = T\sigma^2_{\mu_{11}} + \sigma^2_{\nu_{11}}$, $P\Omega_{11}P = \sigma^2_{1_{11}}P$ and $P\overline{X} = PPX = \overline{X}$. Therefore, GLS on (7.11) yields

$$\begin{aligned}\widehat{\delta}_1 &= (\overline{Z}_1'\overline{X}[\sigma^2_{1_{11}}\overline{X}'\overline{X}]^{-1}\overline{X}'\overline{Z}_1)^{-1}\overline{Z}_1'\overline{X}[\sigma^2_{1_{11}}\overline{X}'\overline{X}]^{-1}\overline{X}'\overline{y}_1\\ &= (\overline{Z}_1'P_{\overline{X}}\overline{Z}_1)^{-1}\overline{Z}_1'P_{\overline{X}}\overline{y}_1 = \widehat{\delta}_{1,\text{B2SLS}}\end{aligned}$$

which is the between 2SLS described in (7.9).

Exercise 7.4 *(Error component two-stage least squares).* This is based on Problem 7.2 in Baltagi (2008). Stack the two transformed equations in (7.10) and (7.11) as a system and note that δ_1 is the same for these two transformed equations

$$\begin{pmatrix}\widetilde{X}'\widetilde{y}_1\\ \overline{X}'\overline{y}_1\end{pmatrix} = \begin{pmatrix}\widetilde{X}'\widetilde{Z}_1\\ \overline{X}'\overline{Z}_1\end{pmatrix}\delta_1 + \begin{pmatrix}\widetilde{X}'\widetilde{u}_1\\ \overline{X}'\overline{u}_1\end{pmatrix} \tag{7.12}$$

(a) Derive the GLS estimator of δ_1 in (7.12).
(b) Show that this GLS estimator of δ_1 can be written as a matrix-weighted average of $\widetilde{\delta}_{1,\mathrm{W2SLS}}$ and $\widehat{\delta}_{1,\mathrm{B2SLS}}$ derived in Exercise 7.2 with weights depending on their respective variance–covariance matrices.
(c) Show that this GLS estimator of δ_1 can also be obtained as a 2SLS estimator of equation (7.1) after premultiplying it by $\Omega_{11}^{-1/2}$, where Ω_{11} is given in (7.5), using the set of instruments $[\widetilde{X}, \overline{X}]$.

Solution

(a) The variance–covariance matrix of the disturbances in (7.12) is given by

$$\mathrm{var}\begin{pmatrix}\widetilde{X}'\widetilde{u}_1\\ \overline{X}'\overline{u}_1\end{pmatrix} = \begin{bmatrix}\sigma^2_{\nu_{11}}\widetilde{X}'\widetilde{X} & 0\\ 0 & \sigma^2_{1_{11}}\overline{X}'\overline{X}\end{bmatrix}$$

GLS on (7.12) yields

$$\widehat{\delta}_1 = \left([\widetilde{Z}_1'\widetilde{X}, \overline{Z}_1'\overline{X}]\begin{bmatrix}(\widetilde{X}'\widetilde{X})^{-1}/\sigma^2_{\nu_{11}} & 0\\ 0 & (\overline{X}'\overline{X})^{-1}/\sigma^2_{1_{11}}\end{bmatrix}\begin{pmatrix}\widetilde{X}'\widetilde{Z}_1\\ \overline{X}'\overline{Z}_1\end{pmatrix}\right)^{-1}$$
$$\left([\widetilde{Z}_1'\widetilde{X}, \overline{Z}_1'\overline{X}]\begin{bmatrix}(\widetilde{X}'\widetilde{X})^{-1}/\sigma^2_{\nu_{11}} & 0\\ 0 & (\overline{X}'\overline{X})^{-1}/\sigma^2_{1_{11}}\end{bmatrix}\begin{pmatrix}\widetilde{X}'\widetilde{y}_1\\ \overline{X}'\overline{y}_1\end{pmatrix}\right)$$

Straightforward matrix multiplication gives

$$\widehat{\delta}_1 = \left[\frac{\widetilde{Z}_1'P_{\widetilde{X}}\widetilde{Z}_1}{\sigma^2_{\nu_{11}}} + \frac{\overline{Z}_1'P_{\overline{X}}\overline{Z}_1}{\sigma^2_{1_{11}}}\right]^{-1}\left[\frac{\widetilde{Z}_1'P_{\widetilde{X}}\widetilde{y}_1}{\sigma^2_{\nu_{11}}} + \frac{\overline{Z}_1'P_{\overline{X}}\overline{y}_1}{\sigma^2_{1_{11}}}\right] = \widehat{\delta}_{1,\mathrm{EC2SLS}} \tag{7.13}$$

which yields the error component two-stage least squares (EC2SLS) estimator of δ_1 derived by Baltagi (1981) and denoted by $\widehat{\delta}_{1,\mathrm{EC2SLS}}$. The $\mathrm{var}(\widehat{\delta}_{1,\mathrm{EC2SLS}})$ is given by the first inverted bracket in (7.13).

(b) From (7.13), $\widehat{\delta}_{1,\mathrm{EC2SLS}}$ can also be written as a matrix-weighted average of $\widetilde{\delta}_{1,\mathrm{W2SLS}}$ and $\widehat{\delta}_{1,\mathrm{B2SLS}}$ given in (7.7) and (7.9) with weights depending on their respective variance–covariance matrices:

$$\widehat{\delta}_{1,\mathrm{EC2SLS}} = W_1\widehat{\delta}_{1,\mathrm{W2SLS}} + W_2\widehat{\delta}_{1,\mathrm{B2SLS}} \tag{7.14}$$

with

$$W_1 = \left[\frac{\widetilde{Z}_1'P_{\widetilde{X}}\widetilde{Z}_1}{\sigma^2_{\nu_{11}}} + \frac{\overline{Z}_1'P_{\overline{X}}\overline{Z}_1}{\sigma^2_{1_{11}}}\right]^{-1}\left[\frac{\widetilde{Z}_1'P_{\widetilde{X}}\widetilde{Z}_1}{\sigma^2_{\nu_{11}}}\right]$$

and

$$W_2 = \left[\frac{\widetilde{Z}_1'P_{\widetilde{X}}\widetilde{Z}_1}{\sigma^2_{\nu_{11}}} + \frac{\overline{Z}_1'P_{\overline{X}}\overline{Z}_1}{\sigma^2_{1_{11}}}\right]^{-1}\left[\frac{\overline{Z}_1'P_{\overline{X}}\overline{Z}_1}{\sigma^2_{1_{11}}}\right]$$

(c) Premultiplying (7.1) by $\Omega_{11}^{-1/2}$, where Ω_{11} is given in (7.5), we get

$$y_1^* = Z_1^*\delta_1 + u_1^* \tag{7.15}$$

with $y_1^* = \Omega_{11}^{-1/2}y_1$, $Z_1^* = \Omega_{11}^{-1/2}Z_1$, and $u_1^* = \Omega_{11}^{-1/2}u_1$. In this case, $\Omega_{11}^{-1/2}$ is given by

$$\Omega_{11}^{-1/2} = (P/\sigma_{1_{11}}) + Q/\sigma_{\nu_{11}}) \tag{7.16}$$

Therefore, the typical element of y_1^* is $y_{1_{it}}^* = (y_{1_{it}} - \theta_1\overline{y}_{1_{i.}})/\sigma_{\nu_{11}}$ where $\theta_1 = 1 - (\sigma_{\nu_{11}}/\sigma_{1_{11}})$ and $\overline{y}_{1_{i.}} = \sum_{t=1}^{T} y_{1_{it}}/T$. See Exercise 2.5.

Given a set of instruments A, the 2SLS estimator of δ_1 in (7.15) using the set of instruments A is in general given by

$$\widehat{\delta}_{1,2SLS} = (Z_1^{*\prime}P_AZ_1^*)^{-1}Z_1^{*\prime}P_Ay_1^* \tag{7.17}$$

where $P_A = A(A'A)^{-1}A'$. Let $A = [\widetilde{X}, \overline{X}] = [QX, PX]$. Since QX is orthogonal to PX, we get that $P_A = P_{\widetilde{X}} + P_{\overline{X}}$. This also means that

$$\begin{aligned} P_AZ_1^* &= (P_{\widetilde{X}} + P_{\overline{X}})[\Omega_{11}^{-1/2}Z_1] \\ &= (P_{\widetilde{X}} + P_{\overline{X}})\left[\frac{Q}{\sigma_{\nu_{11}}} + \frac{P}{\sigma_{1_{11}}}\right]Z_1 = \frac{P_{\widetilde{X}}\widetilde{Z}_1}{\sigma_{\nu_{11}}} + \frac{P_{\overline{X}}\overline{Z}_1}{\sigma_{1_{11}}} \end{aligned}$$

with

$$Z_1^{*\prime}P_AZ_1^* = \left(\frac{\widetilde{Z}_1'P_{\widetilde{X}}\widetilde{Z}_1}{\sigma_{\nu_{11}}^2} + \frac{\overline{Z}_1'P_{\overline{X}}\overline{Z}_1}{\sigma_{1_{11}}^2}\right)$$

and

$$Z_1^{*\prime}P_Ay_1^* = \left(\frac{\widetilde{Z}_1'P_{\widetilde{X}}\widetilde{y}_1}{\sigma_{\nu_{11}}^2} + \frac{\overline{Z}_1'P_{\overline{X}}\overline{y}_1}{\sigma_{1_{11}}^2}\right)$$

Therefore, $\widehat{\delta}_{1,EC2SLS}$ given by (7.13) is the same as (7.17) with $A = [\widetilde{X}, \overline{X}]$. This solution is based on Cornwell *et al.* (1992).

Using the results in White (1986), the optimal set of instrumental variables in (7.15) is

$$X^* = \Omega_{11}^{-1/2}X = \frac{QX}{\sigma_{\nu_{11}}} + \frac{PX}{\sigma_{1_{11}}} = \frac{\widetilde{X}}{\sigma_{\nu_{11}}} + \frac{\overline{X}}{\sigma_{1_{11}}} \tag{7.18}$$

Using $A = X^*$, one gets the Balestra and Varadharajan-Krishnakumar (1987) generalized two-stage least squares (G2SLS) estimator of δ_1:

$$\widehat{\delta}_{1,G2SLS} = (Z_1^{*\prime}P_{X^*}Z_1^*)^{-1}Z_1^{*\prime}P_{X^*}y_1^* \tag{7.19}$$

Exercise 7.5 *(Equivalence of several EC2SLS estimators).* This is based on Problem 7.3 in Baltagi (2008).

(a) Show that $A = [\widetilde{X}, \overline{X}]$, $B = [X^*, \widetilde{X}]$, and $C = [X^*, \overline{X}]$ yield the same EC2SLS estimator given by (7.13).

(b) Show that $P_A P_{X^*} = P_{X^*}$, and that $P_A - P_{X^*}$ is idempotent. Use this result to prove that the var $(\sqrt{n}\widehat{\beta}_{\text{G2SLS}})$ − var $(\sqrt{n}\widehat{\beta}_{\text{EC2SLS}})$ is positive semi-definite, where var denotes asymptotic variance and $n = NT$.

Solution

(a) Since X^* is a linear combination of $\widetilde{X}$ and $\overline{X}$, this implies that the set of instruments used by Baltagi (1981), i.e., $A = [\widetilde{X}, \overline{X}]$, spans the set of instruments used by Balestra and Varadharajan-Krishnakumar (1987), i.e., $X^* = [\widetilde{X}/\sigma_{\nu_{11}} + \overline{X}/\sigma_{1_{11}}]$. This also means that $A = [\widetilde{X}, \overline{X}]$, $B = [X^*, \widetilde{X}]$, and $C = [X^*, \overline{X}]$ yield the same projection matrices P_A, P_B and P_C. Substituting these in (7.17) proves that these instruments all yield the same 2SLS estimator of δ_1 given by EC2SLS.

Without going into proofs, we note that Baltagi and Li (1992c) showed that $\widehat{\delta}_{1,\text{G2SLS}}$ and $\widehat{\delta}_{1,\text{EC2SLS}}$ yield the same asymptotic variance–covariance matrix. Therefore, $\widetilde{X}$ in B and $\overline{X}$ in C are 'redundant' with respect to the optimal set of instruments X^*. Redundant instruments can be interpreted loosely as additional sets of instruments that do not yield extra gains in asymptotic efficiency; see White (1986) for the strict definition and Baltagi and Li (1992c) for the proof in this context.

(b) Note that

$$
\begin{aligned}
P_{\tilde{X}} P_{X^*} &= \tilde{X}\left(\tilde{X}'\tilde{X}\right)^{-1}\tilde{X}'X^*\left(X^{*\prime}X^*\right)^{-1}X^{*\prime} \\
&= \tilde{X}\left(\tilde{X}'\tilde{X}\right)^{-1}\tilde{X}'\left(\frac{\tilde{X}}{\sigma_\nu}+\frac{\overline{X}}{\sigma_1}\right)\left(X^{*\prime}X^*\right)^{-1}X^{*\prime} \\
&= \frac{1}{\sigma_\nu}\tilde{X}\left(\tilde{X}'\tilde{X}\right)^{-1}\tilde{X}'\tilde{X}\left(X^{*\prime}X^*\right)^{-1}X^{*\prime} \\
&= \frac{1}{\sigma_\nu}\tilde{X}\left(X^{*\prime}X^*\right)^{-1}X^{*\prime}
\end{aligned}
$$

using the fact that $\tilde{X}'\overline{X} = 0$, and $QP = 0$. Also,

$$
\begin{aligned}
P_{\overline{X}} P_{X^*} &= \overline{X}\left(\overline{X}'\overline{X}\right)^{-1}\overline{X}'X^*\left(X^{*\prime}X^*\right)^{-1}X^{*\prime} \\
&= \overline{X}\left(\overline{X}'\overline{X}\right)^{-1}\overline{X}'\left(\frac{\tilde{X}}{\sigma_\nu}+\frac{\overline{X}}{\sigma_1}\right)\left(X^{*\prime}X^*\right)^{-1}X^{*\prime} \\
&= \frac{1}{\sigma_1}\overline{X}\left(\overline{X}'\overline{X}\right)^{-1}\overline{X}'\overline{X}\left(X^{*\prime}X^*\right)^{-1}X^{*\prime} \\
&= \frac{1}{\sigma_1}\overline{X}\left(X^{*\prime}X^*\right)^{-1}X^{*\prime}
\end{aligned}
$$

Summing these two equations gives

$$\left(P_{\tilde{X}} + P_{\overline{X}}\right) P_{X^*} = \frac{1}{\sigma_\nu}\tilde{X}\left(X^{*\prime}X^*\right)^{-1} X^{*\prime} + \frac{1}{\sigma_1}\overline{X}\left(X^{*\prime}X^*\right)^{-1} X^{*\prime}$$

$$= X^*\left(X^{*\prime}X^*\right)^{-1} X^{*\prime} = P_{X^*}$$

Using the result that $P_A = P_{\tilde{X}} + P_{\overline{X}}$, we get the required result that $P_A P_{X^*} = P_{X^*}$. Also

$$(P_A - P_{X^*})^2 = P_A + P_{X^*} - P_A P_{X^*} - P_{X^*} P_A = P_A - P_{X^*}$$

Hence, $P_A - P_{X^*}$ is idempotent.

It is well known that the asymptotic variance of $\sqrt{n}\widehat{\beta}_{\text{G2SLS}}$ is given by $\text{var}\left(\sqrt{n}\widehat{\beta}_{\text{G2SLS}}\right) = \text{plim}(Z^{*\prime}P_{X^*}Z^*/n)^{-1}$, and that of $\sqrt{n}\widehat{\beta}_{\text{EC2SLS}}$ is given by $\text{var}\left(\sqrt{n}\widehat{\beta}_{\text{EC2SLS}}\right) = \text{plim}(Z^{*\prime}P_A Z^*/n)^{-1}$. Therefore, $\text{var}\left(\sqrt{n}\widehat{\beta}_{\text{G2SLS}}\right) - \text{var}\left(\sqrt{n}\widehat{\beta}_{\text{EC2SLS}}\right)$ is positive semi-definite if $(Z^{*\prime} P_A Z^*/n) - (Z^{*\prime}P_{X^*}Z^*/n)$ is positive semi-definite, or equivalently, if $(Z^{*\prime}(P_A - P_{X^*}) Z^*/n)$ is positive semi-definite. The latter holds since $P_A - P_{X^*}$ was shown to be idempotent. While this result may not be of consequence asymptotically since both estimators are asymptotically efficient, it may lead to smaller standard errors in finite samples. This intuition comes from the fact that extra instruments will in general lead to more efficient estimators and, in small samples, to lower standard errors.

Exercise 7.6 *(Hausman test based on FE2SLS vs EC2SLS).* This is based on Baltagi (2004), and is also Problem 7.13 in Baltagi (2008). Consider the first structural equation of a simultaneous equation panel data model given in (7.1). Hausman (1978) suggests comparing the FE and RE estimators in the classic panel data regression; see Exercise 4.11. With endogenous right-hand-side regressors like Y_1, this test can be generalized to test $H_0: E(u_1 \mid Z_1) = 0$ based on $\widehat{q}_1 = \widetilde{\delta}_{1,\text{FE2SLS}} - \widehat{\delta}_{1,\text{EC2SLS}}$, where $\widetilde{\delta}_{1,\text{FE2SLS}}$ is defined in (7.7) and $\widehat{\delta}_{1,\text{EC2SLS}}$ is defined in (7.13). (Note that we are using FE2SLS and within 2SLS interchangeably.)

(a) Show that under $H_0: E(u_1 \mid Z_1) = 0$, $\text{plim}\,\widehat{q}_1 = 0$ and the asymptotic $\text{cov}(\widehat{q}_1, \widehat{\delta}_{1,\text{EC2SLS}}) = 0$.
(b) Conclude that $\text{var}(\widehat{q}_1) = \text{var}(\widetilde{\delta}_{1,\text{FE2SLS}}) - \text{var}(\widehat{\delta}_{1,\text{EC2SLS}})$, where var denotes the asymptotic variance. This is used in computing the Hausman test statistic for H_0 given by $m_1 = \hat{q}_1'[\text{var}(\widehat{q}_1)]^{-1}\widehat{q}_1$. Under H_0, m_1 is asymptotically distributed as χ^2_r, where r denotes the dimension of the slope vector of the time varying variables in Z_1.
(c) Show that Hausman's test based on the contrast between FE2SLS and EC2SLS can alternatively be obtained from any one of the following artificial 2SLS regressions with instruments $A = \left[\tilde{X}, \overline{X}\right]$:

$$y_1^* = Z_1^*\delta_1 + \tilde{Z}_1\gamma_1 + \omega_1$$

$$y_1^* = Z_1^*\delta_1 + \overline{Z}_1\gamma_1 + \omega_2$$

$$y_1^* = Z_1^*\delta_1 + Z_1\gamma_1 + \omega_3$$

Here $Z_1^* = \sigma_{\nu_{11}}\Omega_{11}^{-1/2}Z_1 = (Q+\phi P)Z_1 = \tilde{Z}_1 + \phi\overline{Z}_1$, where $\phi = \sigma_{\nu_{11}}/\sigma_{1_{11}}$, $\widetilde{Z}_1 = QZ_1$, and $\overline{Z}_1 = PZ_1$, where $\Omega_{11}^{-1/2}$ is defined in (7.16). $\tilde{X}$, $\overline{X}$ and y^* are similarly defined. Show that Hausman's test is equivalent to testing whether $\gamma_1 = 0$ in any one of these three 2SLS regressions (see Baltagi and Liu, 2007).

Solution

(a) From (7.7) we have

$$\widetilde{\delta}_{1,\mathrm{FE2SLS}} = (\widetilde{Z}_1' P_{\widetilde{X}} \widetilde{Z}_1)^{-1} \widetilde{Z}_1' P_{\widetilde{X}} \widetilde{y}_1 = \delta_1 + (\widetilde{Z}_1' P_{\widetilde{X}} \widetilde{Z}_1)^{-1} \widetilde{Z}_1' P_{\widetilde{X}} u_1$$

Under H_0, $\mathrm{plim}(\widetilde{\delta}_{1,\mathrm{FE2SLS}}) = \delta_1$ and the asymptotic variance of $\widetilde{\delta}_{1,\mathrm{FE2SLS}}$ is given by $\mathrm{var}(\widetilde{\delta}_{1,\mathrm{FE2SLS}}) = \sigma_{\nu_{11}}^2 (\widetilde{Z}_1' P_{\widetilde{X}} \widetilde{Z}_1)^{-1}$. Also, from (7.13),

$$\widehat{\delta}_{1,\mathrm{EC2SLS}} = \delta_1 + \left[\frac{\widetilde{Z}_1' P_{\widetilde{X}} \widetilde{Z}_1}{\sigma_{\nu_{11}}^2} + \frac{\overline{Z}_1' P_{\overline{X}} \overline{Z}_1}{\sigma_{1_{11}}^2}\right]^{-1} \left[\frac{\widetilde{Z}_1' P_{\widetilde{X}} u_1}{\sigma_{\nu_{11}}^2} + \frac{\overline{Z}_1' P_{\overline{X}} u_1}{\sigma_{1_{11}}^2}\right]$$

Under H_0, $\mathrm{plim}(\widehat{\delta}_{1,\mathrm{EC2SLS}}) = \delta_1$ and the asymptotic variance of $\widehat{\delta}_{1,\mathrm{EC2SLS}}$ is given by

$$\mathrm{var}(\widehat{\delta}_{1,\mathrm{EC2SLS}}) = \left[\frac{\widetilde{Z}_1' P_{\widetilde{X}} \widetilde{Z}_1}{\sigma_{\nu_{11}}^2} + \frac{\overline{Z}_1' P_{\overline{X}} \overline{Z}_1}{\sigma_{1_{11}}^2}\right]^{-1}$$

Under H_0, both $\widetilde{\delta}_{1,\mathrm{FE2SLS}}$ and $\widehat{\delta}_{1,\mathrm{EC2SLS}}$ are consistent, with plim $\widehat{q}_1 = 0$. Using the expressions for $\widehat{\delta}_{1,\mathrm{EC2SLS}} - \delta_1$ and $\widetilde{\delta}_{1,\mathrm{FE2SLS}} - \delta_1$, one gets the asymptotic covariance

$$\begin{aligned}
&\mathrm{cov}(\widetilde{\delta}_{1,\mathrm{FE2SLS}}, \widehat{\delta}_{1,\mathrm{EC2SLS}}) \\
&= \mathrm{plim}(\widetilde{Z}_1' P_{\widetilde{X}} \widetilde{Z}_1)^{-1} \widetilde{Z}_1' P_{\widetilde{X}} u_1 \left[\frac{u_1' P_{\widetilde{X}} \widetilde{Z}_1}{\sigma_{\nu_{11}}^2} + \frac{u_1' P_{\overline{X}} \overline{Z}_1}{\sigma_{1_{11}}^2}\right] \left[\frac{\widetilde{Z}_1' P_{\widetilde{X}} \widetilde{Z}_1}{\sigma_{\nu_{11}}^2} + \frac{\overline{Z}_1' P_{\overline{X}} \overline{Z}_1}{\sigma_{1_{11}}^2}\right]^{-1} \\
&= \left[\mathrm{plim}(\widetilde{Z}_1' P_{\widetilde{X}} \widetilde{Z}_1)^{-1} \frac{\widetilde{Z}_1' P_{\widetilde{X}} u_1 u_1' P_{\widetilde{X}} \widetilde{Z}_1}{\sigma_{\nu_{11}}^2} + \mathrm{plim}(\widetilde{Z}_1' P_{\widetilde{X}} \widetilde{Z}_1)^{-1} \frac{\widetilde{Z}_1' P_{\widetilde{X}} u_1 u_1' P_{\overline{X}} \overline{Z}_1}{\sigma_{1_{11}}^2}\right] \\
&\quad \times \left[\frac{\widetilde{Z}_1' P_{\widetilde{X}} \widetilde{Z}_1}{\sigma_{\nu_{11}}^2} + \frac{\overline{Z}_1' P_{\overline{X}} \overline{Z}_1}{\sigma_{1_{11}}^2}\right]^{-1} \\
&= \left[\mathrm{plim}(\widetilde{Z}_1' P_{\widetilde{X}} \widetilde{Z}_1)^{-1} \frac{\sigma_{\nu_{11}}^2 [\widetilde{Z}_1' P_{\widetilde{X}} \widetilde{Z}_1]}{\sigma_{\nu_{11}}^2}\right] \left[\frac{\widetilde{Z}_1' P_{\widetilde{X}} \widetilde{Z}_1}{\sigma_{\nu_{11}}^2} + \frac{\overline{Z}_1' P_{\overline{X}} \overline{Z}_1}{\sigma_{1_{11}}^2}\right]^{-1} \\
&= \left[\frac{\widetilde{Z}_1' P_{\widetilde{X}} \widetilde{Z}_1}{\sigma_{\nu_{11}}^2} + \frac{\overline{Z}_1' P_{\overline{X}} \overline{Z}_1}{\sigma_{1_{11}}^2}\right]^{-1} = \mathrm{var}(\widehat{\delta}_{1,\mathrm{EC2SLS}})
\end{aligned}$$

This makes use of the following:

$$\mathrm{plim}(\widetilde{X}' u_1 u_1' \widetilde{X}/n) = \widetilde{X}' \mathrm{plim}(u_1 u_1'/n) \widetilde{X} = \widetilde{X}' Q \Omega_{11} Q \widetilde{X} = \sigma_{\nu_{11}}^2 (\widetilde{X}' \widetilde{X})$$

where $n = NT$. Also,

$$\text{plim}(\widetilde{X}'u_1u_1'\overline{X}/n) = \widetilde{X}'\text{plim}(u_1u_1'/n)\overline{X} = \widetilde{X}'Q\Omega_{11}P\overline{X} = 0$$

since $PQ = 0$. Hence $\text{cov}(\widehat{q}_1, \widehat{\delta}_{1,\text{EC2SLS}}) = \text{cov}(\widetilde{\delta}_{1,\text{FE2SLS}}, \widehat{\delta}_{1,\text{EC2SLS}}) - \text{var}(\widehat{\delta}_{1,\text{EC2SLS}}) = 0$.

(b) Using the fact that $\widetilde{\delta}_{1,\text{FE2SLS}} = \widehat{\delta}_{1,\text{EC2SLS}} + \widehat{q}_1$, one gets

$$\text{var}(\widetilde{\delta}_{1,\text{FE2SLS}}) = \text{var}(\widehat{\delta}_{1,\text{EC2SLS}}) + \text{var}(\widehat{q}_1)$$

since $\text{cov}(\widehat{q}_1, \widehat{\delta}_{1,\text{EC2SLS}}) = 0$. Therefore,

$$\text{var}(\widehat{q}_1) = \text{var}(\widetilde{\delta}_{1,\text{FE2SLS}}) - \text{var}(\widehat{\delta}_{1,\text{EC2SLS}})$$

This is used in computing the Hausman test statistic given by $m_1 = \hat{q}_1'[\text{var}(\widehat{q}_1)]^{-1}\widehat{q}_1$. Under H_0, m_1 is asymptotically distributed as χ^2_r, where r denotes the dimension of the slope vector of the time-varying variables in Z_1.

(c) We show this result for one artificial 2SLS regression,

$$y_1^* = Z_1^*\delta_1 + \tilde{Z}_1\gamma_1 + \omega_1$$

with instruments $A = \left[\tilde{X}, \overline{X}\right]$. The remaining proofs are quite similar and are omitted to save space. Premultiplying this equation by $P_A = P_{\tilde{X}} + P_{\overline{X}}$, we get

$$P_A y_1^* = P_A Z_1^*\delta_1 + P_A\tilde{Z}_1\gamma_1 + P_A\omega_1$$

Performing OLS on this obtains 2SLS. To do this, we need partitioned inversion:

$$\begin{aligned}
&\begin{bmatrix} Z_1^{*\prime}P_AZ_1^* & Z_1^{*\prime}P_A\tilde{Z}_1 \\ \tilde{Z}_1'P_AZ_1^* & \tilde{Z}_1'P_A\tilde{Z}_1 \end{bmatrix}^{-1} \\
&= \begin{bmatrix} \left(\tilde{Z}_1 + \phi\overline{Z}_1\right)'(P_{\tilde{X}} + P_{\overline{X}})\left(\tilde{Z}_1 + \phi\overline{Z}_1\right) & \left(\tilde{Z}_1 + \phi\overline{Z}_1\right)'(P_{\tilde{X}} + P_{\overline{X}})\tilde{Z}_1 \\ \tilde{Z}_1'(P_{\tilde{X}} + P_{\overline{X}})\left(\tilde{Z}_1 + \phi\overline{Z}_1\right) & \tilde{Z}_1'(P_{\tilde{X}} + P_{\overline{X}})\tilde{Z}_1 \end{bmatrix}^{-1} \\
&= \begin{bmatrix} \tilde{Z}_1'P_{\tilde{X}}\tilde{Z}_1 + \phi^2\overline{Z}_1'P_{\overline{X}}\overline{Z}_1 & \tilde{Z}_1'P_{\tilde{X}}\tilde{Z}_1 \\ \tilde{Z}_1'P_{\tilde{X}}\tilde{Z}_1 & \tilde{Z}_1'P_{\tilde{X}}\tilde{Z}_1 \end{bmatrix}^{-1} \\
&= \begin{bmatrix} \phi^{-2}\left(\overline{Z}_1'P_{\overline{X}}\overline{Z}_1\right)^{-1} & -\phi^{-2}\left(\overline{Z}_1'P_{\overline{X}}\overline{Z}_1\right)^{-1} \\ -\phi^{-2}\left(\overline{Z}_1'P_{\overline{X}}\overline{Z}_1\right)^{-1} & \left(\tilde{Z}_1'P_{\tilde{X}}\tilde{Z}_1\right)^{-1} + \phi^{-2}\left(\overline{Z}_1'P_{\overline{X}}\overline{Z}_1\right)^{-1} \end{bmatrix}
\end{aligned}$$

and

$$\begin{aligned}
\begin{bmatrix} Z_1^{*\prime}P_Ay_1^* \\ \tilde{Z}_1'P_Ay_1^* \end{bmatrix} &= \begin{bmatrix} \left(\tilde{Z}_1 + \phi\overline{Z}_1\right)'(P_{\tilde{X}} + P_{\overline{X}})(\widetilde{y}_1 + \phi\overline{y}_1) \\ \tilde{Z}_1'(P_{\tilde{X}} + P_{\overline{X}})(\widetilde{y}_1 + \phi\overline{y}_1) \end{bmatrix} \\
&= \begin{bmatrix} \tilde{Z}_1'P_{\tilde{X}}\widetilde{y}_1 + \phi^2\overline{Z}_1'P_{\overline{X}}\overline{y}_1 \\ \tilde{Z}_1'P_{\tilde{X}}\widetilde{y}_1 \end{bmatrix}
\end{aligned}$$

Hence, the 2SLS estimator is given by the product

$$\begin{pmatrix}\widehat{\delta}_1\\ \hat{\gamma}_1\end{pmatrix}=\begin{bmatrix}\phi^{-2}\left(\overline{Z}_1'P_{\overline{X}}\overline{Z}_1\right)^{-1} & -\phi^{-2}\left(\overline{Z}_1'P_{\overline{X}}\overline{Z}_1\right)^{-1}\\ -\phi^{-2}\left(\overline{Z}_1'P_{\overline{X}}\overline{Z}_1\right)^{-1} & \left(\tilde{Z}_1'P_{\tilde{X}}\tilde{Z}_1\right)^{-1}+\phi^{-2}\left(\overline{Z}_1'P_{\overline{X}}\overline{Z}_1\right)^{-1}\end{bmatrix}$$

$$\times\begin{bmatrix}\tilde{Z}_1'P_{\tilde{X}}\widetilde{y}_1+\phi^2\overline{Z}_1'P_{\overline{X}}\overline{y}_1\\ \tilde{Z}_1'P_{\tilde{X}}\widetilde{y}_1\end{bmatrix}$$

$$=\begin{bmatrix}\phi^{-2}\left(\overline{Z}_1'P_{\overline{X}}\overline{Z}_1\right)^{-1}\left(\tilde{Z}_1'P_{\tilde{X}}\widetilde{y}_1+\phi^2\overline{Z}_1'P_{\overline{X}}\overline{y}_1\right)\\ -\phi^{-2}\left(\overline{Z}_1'P_{\overline{X}}\overline{Z}_1\right)^{-1}\left(\tilde{Z}_1'P_{\tilde{X}}\widetilde{y}_1\right)\\ \\ -\phi^{-2}\left(\overline{Z}_1'P_{\overline{X}}\overline{Z}_1\right)^{-1}\left(\tilde{Z}_1'P_{\tilde{X}}\widetilde{y}_1+\phi^2\overline{Z}_1'P_{\overline{X}}\overline{y}_1\right)\\ +\left[\left(\tilde{Z}_1'P_{\tilde{X}}\tilde{Z}_1\right)^{-1}+\phi^{-2}\left(\overline{Z}_1'P_{\overline{X}}\overline{Z}_1\right)^{-1}\right]\tilde{Z}_1'P_{\tilde{X}}\widetilde{y}_1\end{bmatrix}$$

$$=\begin{bmatrix}\left(\overline{Z}_1'P_{\overline{X}}\overline{Z}_1\right)^{-1}\overline{Z}_1'P_{\overline{X}}\overline{y}_1\\ \left(\tilde{Z}_1'P_{\tilde{X}}\tilde{Z}_1\right)^{-1}\tilde{Z}_1'P_{\tilde{X}}\widetilde{y}_1-\left(\overline{Z}_1'P_{\overline{X}}\overline{Z}_1\right)^{-1}\overline{Z}_1'P_{\overline{X}}\overline{y}_1\end{bmatrix}$$

$$=\begin{bmatrix}\widehat{\delta}_{1,\mathrm{BE2SLS}}\\ \widetilde{\delta}_{1,\mathrm{FE2SLS}}-\widehat{\delta}_{1,\mathrm{BE2SLS}}\end{bmatrix}$$

So, $\hat{\gamma}_1=\widetilde{\delta}_{1,\mathrm{FE2SLS}}-\widehat{\delta}_{1,\mathrm{BE2SLS}}$, with

$$\mathrm{var}\begin{pmatrix}\widehat{\delta}_1\\ \hat{\gamma}_1\end{pmatrix}=\sigma_{\nu_{11}}^2\begin{bmatrix}\phi^{-2}\left(\overline{Z}_1'P_{\overline{X}}\overline{Z}_1\right)^{-1} & -\phi^{-2}\left(\overline{Z}_1'P_{\overline{X}}\overline{Z}_1\right)^{-1}\\ -\phi^{-2}\left(\overline{Z}_1'P_{\overline{X}}\overline{Z}_1\right)^{-1} & \left(\tilde{Z}_1'P_{\tilde{X}}\tilde{Z}_1\right)^{-1}+\phi^{-2}\left(\overline{Z}_1'P_{\overline{X}}\overline{Z}_1\right)^{-1}\end{bmatrix}$$

hence,

$$\mathrm{var}\left(\hat{\gamma}_1\right)=\sigma_{\nu_{11}}^2\left[\left(\tilde{Z}_1'P_{\tilde{X}}\tilde{Z}_1\right)^{-1}+\phi^{-2}\left(\overline{Z}_1'P_{\overline{X}}\overline{Z}_1\right)^{-1}\right]=\mathrm{var}(\widetilde{\delta}_{1,\mathrm{FE2SLS}})+\mathrm{var}\left(\widehat{\delta}_{1,\mathrm{BE2SLS}}\right)$$

Let $\widehat{q}_{1,2\mathrm{SLS}}=\widetilde{\delta}_{1,\mathrm{FE2SLS}}-\widehat{\delta}_{1,\mathrm{EC2SLS}}$, $\hat{q}_{2,2\mathrm{SLS}}=\widehat{\delta}_{1,\mathrm{BE2SLS}}-\widehat{\delta}_{1,\mathrm{EC2SLS}}$, and $\hat{q}_{3,2\mathrm{SLS}}=\widetilde{\delta}_{1,\mathrm{FE2SLS}}-\widehat{\delta}_{1,\mathrm{BE2SLS}}$. Then $\hat{m}_i=\hat{q}_i'\left[\mathrm{var}\left(\hat{q}_i\right)\right]^{-1}\hat{q}_i$ for $i=1,2,3$. As shown in (7.14), $\widehat{\delta}_{1,\mathrm{EC2SLS}}=W_1\widetilde{\delta}_{1,\mathrm{FE2SLS}}+W_2\widehat{\delta}_{1,\mathrm{B2SLS}}$ where W_1 and W_2 are matrix weights depending on the variance–covariance matrices of $\widetilde{\delta}_{1,\mathrm{FE2SLS}}$ and $\widehat{\delta}_{1,\mathrm{B2SLS}}$. In this case, one can show, as in the Hausman and Taylor (1981) case (see Exercise 4.13), that

$$\begin{aligned}\hat{q}_{1,2\mathrm{SLS}}&=\widetilde{\delta}_{1,\mathrm{FE2SLS}}-\widehat{\delta}_{1,\mathrm{EC2SLS}}\\ &=\widetilde{\delta}_{1,\mathrm{FE2SLS}}-\left(W_1\widetilde{\delta}_{1,\mathrm{FE2SLS}}+W_2\widehat{\delta}_{1,\mathrm{B2SLS}}\right)\\ &=W_2\left(\widetilde{\delta}_{1,\mathrm{FE2SLS}}-\widehat{\delta}_{1,\mathrm{BE2SLS}}\right)\\ &=W_2\hat{q}_{3,2\mathrm{SLS}}\end{aligned}$$

since $W_1 + W_2 = I$. So,

$$\begin{aligned}\hat{m}_{1,2SLS} &= \hat{q}'_{1,2SLS}\left[\operatorname{var}\left(\hat{q}_{1,2SLS}\right)\right]^{-1}\hat{q}_{1,2SLS}\\ &= \left(W_2\hat{q}_{3,2SLS}\right)'\left[\operatorname{var}\left(W_2\hat{q}_{3,2SLS}\right)\right]^{-1}\left(W_2\hat{q}_{3,2SLS}\right)\\ &= \hat{q}'_{3,2SLS}\left[\operatorname{var}\left(\hat{q}_{3,2SLS}\right)\right]^{-1}\hat{q}_{3,2SLS} = \hat{m}_{3,2SLS}\end{aligned}$$

This proves that $\hat{m}_{1,2SLS}$ and $\hat{m}_{3,2SLS}$ are numerically identical. Notice that the contrast based on $\hat{q}_{3,2SLS}$ generates the Hausman test statistic suggested in Baltagi (2004). Here we have shown that it can be generated with a Wald test statistic of $\hat{\gamma} = 0$ from an artificial 2SLS regression.

7.2 SYSTEM ESTIMATION

Consider the system of identified equations

$$y = Z\delta + u \tag{7.20}$$

where $y' = (y'_1, \ldots, y'_M)$, $Z = \operatorname{diag}[Z_j]$, $\delta' = (\delta'_1, \ldots, \delta'_M)$, and $u' = (u'_1, \ldots, u'_M)$, with $Z_j = [Y_j, X_j]$ of dimension $NT \times (g_j + k_j)$, for $j = 1, \ldots, M$. In this case, there are g_j included right-hand-side Y_j and k_j included right-hand-side X_j. This differs from the SUR model only in the fact that there are right-hand-side endogenous variables in the system of equations.

Exercise 7.7 *(3SLS as a GLS estimator).* Assume that $u \sim (0, \Sigma \otimes I_{NT})$, where $\Sigma = [\sigma_{jl}]$ for $j, l = 1, \ldots, M$. Show that 3SLS on (7.20) with instruments X is equivalent to premultiplying (7.20) by $I_M \otimes X'$ and performing GLS.

Solution

Premultiplying (7.20) by $I_M \otimes X'$, we get

$$(I_M \otimes X')y = (I_M \otimes X')Z\delta + (I_M \otimes X')u \tag{7.21}$$

with variance–covariance matrix of the disturbances $(I_M \otimes X')u$ given by

$$E[(I_M \otimes X')uu'(I_M \otimes X)] = (I_M \otimes X')(\Sigma \otimes I_{NT})(I_M \otimes X) = (\Sigma \otimes X'X)$$

GLS on the transformed system (7.21) yields

$$\begin{aligned}\widehat{\delta} &= [Z'(I_M \otimes X)(\Sigma^{-1} \otimes (X'X)^{-1})(I_M \otimes X')Z]^{-1}\\ &\quad [Z'(I_M \otimes X)(\Sigma^{-1} \otimes (X'X)^{-1})(I_M \otimes X')y]\\ &= [Z'(\Sigma^{-1} \otimes P_X)Z]^{-1}[Z'(\Sigma^{-1} \otimes P_X)y] = \widehat{\delta}_{3SLS}\end{aligned}$$

with $P_X = X(X'X)^{-1}X'$, and $\operatorname{var}(\widehat{\delta}_{3SLS}) = [Z'(\Sigma^{-1} \otimes P_X)Z]^{-1}$.

For the one-way error component model, the disturbance of the jth equation u_j is given by (6.2) and $\Omega_{jl} = E(u_j u'_l)$ is given by (6.5) as in the SUR case. Once again, the covariance matrix between the disturbances of different equations has the same error component form, except now there are additional cross-equation variance components to be estimated. The variance–covariance matrix of the set of M structural equations $\Omega = E(uu')$ is given by (6.4) and $\Omega^{-1/2}$ is given by (6.8).

Exercise 7.8 *(Within 3SLS and between 3SLS)*

(a) Show that within 3SLS on (7.20) can be obtained by premultiplying (7.20) by $(I_M \otimes Q)$ and performing 3SLS with instruments $(I_M \otimes \widetilde{X})$ where $\widetilde{X} = QX$.
(b) Show that between 3SLS on (7.20) can be obtained by premultiplying (7.20) by $(I_M \otimes P)$ and performing 3SLS with instruments $(I_M \otimes \overline{X})$ where $\overline{X} = PX$.

Solution

(a) Premultiplying (7.20) by $(I_M \otimes Q)$ yields

$$\widetilde{y} = \widetilde{Z}\delta + \widetilde{u} \tag{7.22}$$

where $\widetilde{y} = (I_M \otimes Q)y$, $\widetilde{Z} = (I_M \otimes Q)Z$, and $\widetilde{u} = (I_M \otimes Q)u$. Performing 3SLS on (7.22) with $(I_M \otimes \widetilde{X})$ as the set of instruments, one gets the within 3SLS estimator

$$\widetilde{\delta}_{\text{W3SLS}} = [\widetilde{Z}'(\Sigma_\nu^{-1} \otimes P_{\widetilde{X}})\widetilde{Z}]^{-1}[\widetilde{Z}'(\Sigma_\nu^{-1} \otimes P_{\widetilde{X}})\widetilde{y}] \tag{7.23}$$

with $P_{\widetilde{X}} = \widetilde{X}(\widetilde{X}'\widetilde{X})^{-1}\widetilde{X}'$ and $\text{var}(\widetilde{\delta}_{\text{W3SLS}}) = [\widetilde{Z}'(\Sigma_\nu^{-1} \otimes P_{\widetilde{X}})\widetilde{Z}]^{-1}$.

(b) Similarly, transforming (7.20) by$(I_M \otimes P)$ yields

$$\overline{y} = \overline{Z}\delta + \overline{u} \tag{7.24}$$

where $\overline{y} = (I_M \otimes P)y$, $\overline{Z} = (I_M \otimes P)Z$, and $\overline{u} = (I_M \otimes P)u$. Performing 3SLS on the transformed system (7.24) using $(I_M \otimes \overline{X})$ as the set of instruments, one gets the between 3SLS estimator

$$\widehat{\delta}_{\text{B3SLS}} = [\overline{Z}'(\Sigma_1^{-1} \otimes P_{\overline{X}})\overline{Z}]^{-1}[\overline{Z}'(\Sigma_1^{-1} \otimes P_{\overline{X}})\overline{y}] \tag{7.25}$$

with $P_{\overline{X}} = \overline{X}(\overline{X}'\overline{X})^{-1}\overline{X}'$ and $\text{var}(\widehat{\delta}_{1,\text{B3SLS}}) = [\overline{Z}'(\Sigma_1^{-1} \otimes P_{\overline{X}})\overline{Z}]^{-1}$, where $\Sigma_1 = T\Sigma_\mu + \Sigma_\nu$.

Exercise 7.9 *(Within 3SLS and between 3SLS as GLS estimators).* This is based on Problem 7.4 in Baltagi (2008).

(a) Show that within 3SLS can be obtained as GLS on (7.22) after premutiplying it by the matrix of instruments $(I_M \otimes \widetilde{X}')$.
(b) Show that between 2SLS can be obtained as GLS on (7.24) after premutiplying it by the matrix of instruments $(I_M \otimes \overline{X}')$.

Solution

(a) Premultiplying (7.22) by $(I_M \otimes \widetilde{X}')$, we get

$$(I_M \otimes \widetilde{X}')\widetilde{y} = (I_M \otimes \widetilde{X}')\widetilde{Z}\delta + (I_M \otimes \widetilde{X}')\widetilde{u} \tag{7.26}$$

The variance–covariance matrix of the transformed disturbances in (7.26) is given by

$$\begin{aligned} E[(I_M \otimes \widetilde{X}')\widetilde{u}\widetilde{u}'(I_M \otimes \widetilde{X})] &= (I_M \otimes \widetilde{X}')E(\widetilde{u}\widetilde{u}')(I_M \otimes \widetilde{X}) \\ &= (I_M \otimes \widetilde{X}')(\Sigma_\nu \otimes Q)(I_M \otimes \widetilde{X}) \\ &= \Sigma_\nu \otimes \widetilde{X}'\widetilde{X} \end{aligned}$$

This makes use of the fact that

$$\begin{aligned} E(\widetilde{u}\widetilde{u}') &= E[(I_M \otimes Q)uu'(I_M \otimes Q)] \\ &= (I_M \otimes Q)(\Sigma_1 \otimes P + \Sigma_\nu \otimes Q)(I_M \otimes Q) \\ &= (\Sigma_\nu \otimes Q) \end{aligned}$$

where $E(uu') = \Omega$ and is given in (6.6) and $QP = 0$. Also $Q\widetilde{X} = QQX = \widetilde{X}$. GLS on the above transformed system yields

$$\begin{aligned} \widehat{\delta} &= [\widetilde{Z}'(I_M \otimes \widetilde{X})(\Sigma_\nu^{-1} \otimes (\widetilde{X}'\widetilde{X})^{-1})(I_M \otimes \widetilde{X}')\widetilde{Z}]^{-1} \\ &\quad [\widetilde{Z}'(I_M \otimes \widetilde{X})(\Sigma_\nu^{-1} \otimes (\widetilde{X}'\widetilde{X})^{-1})(I_M \otimes \widetilde{X}')\widetilde{y}] \\ &= [\widetilde{Z}'(\Sigma_\nu^{-1} \otimes P_{\widetilde{X}})\widetilde{Z}]^{-1}[\widetilde{Z}'(\Sigma_\nu \otimes P_{\widetilde{X}})\widetilde{y}] = \widetilde{\delta}_{\text{W3SLS}} \end{aligned}$$

which is the within 3SLS estimator $\widetilde{\delta}_{\text{W3SLS}}$ given in (7.23).

(b) Similarly, premultiplying (7.24) by $(I_M \otimes \overline{X}')$ yields

$$(I_M \otimes \overline{X}')\overline{y} = (I_M \otimes \overline{X}')\overline{Z}\delta + (I_M \otimes \overline{X}')\overline{u} \tag{7.27}$$

The variance–covariance matrix of the transformed disturbances in (7.27) is given by

$$\begin{aligned} E[(I_M \otimes \overline{X}')\overline{u}\overline{u}'(I_M \otimes \overline{X})] &= (I_M \otimes \overline{X}')E(\overline{u}\overline{u}')(I_M \otimes \overline{X}) \\ &= (I_M \otimes \overline{X}')(\Sigma_1 \otimes P)(I_M \otimes \overline{X}) \\ &= \Sigma_1 \otimes \overline{X}'\overline{X} \end{aligned}$$

This makes use of the fact that

$$\begin{aligned} E(\overline{u}\overline{u}') &= E[(I_M \otimes P)uu'(I_M \otimes P)] \\ &= (I_M \otimes P)(\Sigma_1 \otimes P + \Sigma_\nu \otimes Q)(I_M \otimes P) \\ &= \Sigma_1 \otimes P \end{aligned}$$

where $E(uu') = \Omega$ is given in (6.6) and $PQ = 0$. Also $P\overline{X} = PPX = \overline{X}$. GLS on the above transformed system yields

$$\begin{aligned} \widehat{\delta} &= [\overline{Z}'(I_M \otimes \overline{X})[\Sigma_1^{-1} \otimes (\overline{X}'\overline{X})^{-1}](I_M \otimes \overline{X}')\overline{Z}]^{-1} \\ &\quad [\overline{Z}'(I_M \otimes \overline{X})[\Sigma_1^{-1} \otimes (\overline{X}'\overline{X})^{-1}](I_M \otimes \overline{X}')\overline{y}] \\ &= [\overline{Z}'(\Sigma_1^{-1} \otimes P_{\overline{X}})\overline{Z}]^{-1}[\overline{Z}'(\Sigma_1^{-1} \otimes P_{\overline{X}})\overline{y}] = \widehat{\delta}_{\text{B3SLS}} \end{aligned}$$

which is the between 3SLS estimator $\widehat{\delta}_{\text{B3SLS}}$ given in (7.25).

Exercise 7.10 *(Error component three-stage least squares).* This is based on Problem 7.5 in Baltagi (2008). Stacking the two transformed systems of equations given in (7.26) and (7.27) on top of each other and noting that δ is the same for these two transformed systems, one gets

$$\begin{pmatrix}(I_M \otimes \widetilde{X}')\widetilde{y}\\(I_M \otimes \overline{X}')\overline{y}\end{pmatrix} = \begin{pmatrix}(I_M \otimes \widetilde{X}')\widetilde{Z}\\(I_M \otimes \overline{X}')\overline{Z}\end{pmatrix}\delta + \begin{pmatrix}(I_M \otimes \widetilde{X}')\widetilde{u}\\(I_M \otimes \overline{X}')\overline{u}\end{pmatrix} \tag{7.28}$$

(a) Derive the GLS estimator of δ in (7.28).
(b) Show that this GLS estimator of δ can be written as a matrix-weighted average of $\widetilde{\delta}_{\text{W3SLS}}$ and $\widehat{\delta}_{\text{B3SLS}}$ (both of which were derived in Exercise 7.8) with weights depending on their respective variance–covariance matrices.
(c) Show that this GLS estimator of δ can also be obtained as a 3SLS estimator of equation (7.20) after premultiplying it by $\Omega^{-1/2}$, where Ω is given in (6.4), using the set of instruments $[I_M \otimes \widetilde{X}, I_M \otimes \overline{X}]$.

Solution

(a) The variance–covariance matrix of the disturbances in (7.28) is given by

$$\text{var}\begin{pmatrix}(I_M \otimes \widetilde{X}')\widetilde{u}\\(I_M \otimes \overline{X}')\overline{u}\end{pmatrix} = \begin{bmatrix}\Sigma_\nu \otimes \widetilde{X}'\widetilde{X} & 0\\ 0 & \Sigma_1 \otimes \overline{X}'\overline{X}\end{bmatrix}$$

where use is made of the fact that

$$\begin{aligned}E(\widetilde{u}\overline{u}') &= E[(I_M \otimes Q)uu'(I_M \otimes P)]\\ &= (I_M \otimes Q)(\Sigma_1 \otimes P + \Sigma_\nu \otimes Q)(I_M \otimes P) = 0\end{aligned}$$

since $QP = 0$. Performing GLS on (7.28) yields

$$\begin{aligned}\widehat{\delta} &= \left([\widetilde{Z}'(I_M \otimes \widetilde{X}), \overline{Z}'(I_M \otimes \overline{X})]\begin{bmatrix}\Sigma_\nu^{-1} \otimes (\widetilde{X}'\widetilde{X})^{-1} & 0\\ 0 & \Sigma_1^{-1} \otimes (\overline{X}'\overline{X})^{-1}\end{bmatrix}\right.\\ &\quad \times \left.\begin{pmatrix}(I_M \otimes \widetilde{X}')\widetilde{Z}\\(I_M \otimes \overline{X}')\overline{Z}\end{pmatrix}\right)^{-1}\left([\widetilde{Z}'(I_M \otimes \widetilde{X}), \overline{Z}'(I_M \otimes \overline{X})]\right.\\ &\quad \times \left.\begin{bmatrix}\Sigma_\nu^{-1} \otimes (\widetilde{X}'\widetilde{X})^{-1} & 0\\ 0 & \Sigma_1^{-1} \otimes (\overline{X}'\overline{X})^{-1}\end{bmatrix}\begin{pmatrix}(I_M \otimes \widetilde{X}')\widetilde{y}\\(I_M \otimes \overline{X}')\overline{y}\end{pmatrix}\right)\\ &= [\widetilde{Z}'(\Sigma_\nu^{-1} \otimes P_{\widetilde{X}})\widetilde{Z} + \overline{Z}'(\Sigma_1^{-1} \otimes P_{\overline{X}})\overline{Z}]^{-1}[\widetilde{Z}'(\Sigma_\nu^{-1} \otimes P_{\widetilde{X}})\widetilde{y} + \overline{Z}'(\Sigma_1^{-1} \otimes P_{\overline{X}})\overline{y}]\\ &= \widehat{\delta}_{\text{EC3SLS}}\end{aligned}$$

which is the error component three-stage least squares (EC3SLS) estimator of δ derived by Baltagi (1981); $\text{var}(\widehat{\delta}_{\text{EC3SLS}})$ is given by the first inverted bracket in the expression for $\widehat{\delta}_{\text{EC3SLS}}$ given above.

(b) Note that $\widehat{\delta}_{\mathrm{EC3SLS}}$ can also be written as a matrix-weighted average of $\widehat{\delta}_{\mathrm{W3SLS}}$ and $\widehat{\delta}_{\mathrm{B3SLS}}$, both of which were derived in Exercise 7.8 and given by (7.23) and (7.25) with weights depending on their respective variance–covariance matrices:

$$\widehat{\delta}_{\mathrm{EC3SLS}} = W_1\widehat{\delta}_{\mathrm{W3SLS}} + W_2\widehat{\delta}_{\mathrm{B3SLS}} \tag{7.29}$$

with

$$W_1 = [\widetilde{Z}'(\Sigma_\nu^{-1} \otimes P_{\widetilde{X}})\widetilde{Z} + \overline{Z}'(\Sigma_1^{-1} \otimes P_{\overline{X}})\overline{Z}]^{-1}[\widetilde{Z}'(\Sigma_\nu^{-1} \otimes P_{\widetilde{X}})\widetilde{Z}]$$

and

$$W_2 = [\widetilde{Z}'(\Sigma_\nu^{-1} \otimes P_{\widetilde{X}})\widetilde{Z} + \overline{Z}'(\Sigma_1^{-1} \otimes P_{\overline{X}})\overline{Z}]^{-1}[\overline{Z}'(\Sigma_1^{-1} \otimes P_{\overline{X}})\overline{Z}]$$

(c) Using $\Omega^{-1/2}$ from (6.8), one can transform (7.20) to get

$$y^* = Z^*\delta + u^* \tag{7.30}$$

with $y^* = \Omega^{-1/2}y$, $Z^* = \Omega^{-1/2}Z$, and $u^* = \Omega^{-1/2}u$. For an arbitrary set of instruments A, the 3SLS estimator of (7.30) becomes

$$\widehat{\delta}_{\mathrm{3SLS}} = (Z^{*\prime}P_A Z^*)^{-1}Z^{*\prime}P_A y^* \tag{7.31}$$

Since $\widetilde{X}$ is orthogonal to $\overline{X}$, we get that $P_A = P_{I_M \otimes \widetilde{X}} + P_{I_M \otimes \overline{X}} = I_M \otimes P_{\widetilde{X}} + I_M \otimes P_{\overline{X}}$. This also means that

$$\begin{aligned}
P_A Z^* &= (I_M \otimes P_{\widetilde{X}} + I_M \otimes P_{\overline{X}})[\Omega^{-1/2}Z] \\
&= (I_M \otimes P_{\widetilde{X}} + I_M \otimes P_{\overline{X}})\left[\Sigma_\nu^{-1/2} \otimes Q + \Sigma_1^{-1/2} \otimes P\right]Z \\
&= \left(\Sigma_\nu^{-1/2} \otimes P_{\widetilde{X}}\right)\widetilde{Z} + \left(\Sigma_1^{-1/2} \otimes P_{\overline{X}}\right)\overline{Z}
\end{aligned}$$

with

$$Z^{*\prime}P_A Z^* = \widetilde{Z}'\left(\Sigma_\nu^{-1} \otimes P_{\widetilde{X}}\right)\widetilde{Z} + \overline{Z}'\left(\Sigma_1^{-1} \otimes P_{\overline{X}}\right)\overline{Z}$$

and

$$Z^{*\prime}P_A y^* = \widetilde{Z}'\left(\Sigma_\nu^{-1} \otimes P_{\widetilde{X}}\right)\widetilde{y} + \overline{Z}'\left(\Sigma_1^{-1} \otimes P_{\overline{X}}\right)\overline{y}$$

Therefore, $\widehat{\delta}_{\mathrm{EC3SLS}}$ given in (7.29) is the same as the expression in (7.31) with $A = [I_M \otimes \widetilde{X}, I_M \otimes \overline{X}]$.

Using the results of White (1986), the optimal set of instruments is

$$X^* = \Omega^{-1/2}(I_M \otimes X) = (\Sigma_\nu^{-1/2} \otimes QX) + (\Sigma_1^{-1/2} \otimes PX) \tag{7.32}$$

Substituting $A = X^*$ in (7.31), one gets the efficient three-stage least squares (E3SLS) estimator of δ:

$$\widehat{\delta}_{\text{E3SLS}} = (Z^{*\prime} P_{X^*} Z^*)^{-1} Z^{*\prime} P_{X^*} y^* \tag{7.33}$$

Exercise 7.11 *(Equivalence of several EC3SLS estimators).* This is based on Problem 7.6 in Baltagi (2008).

(a) Prove that $A = (I_M \otimes \widetilde{X}, I_M \otimes \overline{X})$ yields the same projection as $B = (H \otimes \widetilde{X}, G \otimes \overline{X})$ or $C = [(H \otimes \widetilde{X} + G \otimes \overline{X}), H \otimes \widetilde{X}]$ or $D = [H \otimes \widetilde{X} + G \otimes \overline{X}), G \otimes \overline{X}]$, where H and G are non-singular $M \times M$ matrices (see Baltagi and Li, 1992c). Conclude that these sets of instruments yield the same EC3SLS estimator of δ.

(b) For $A = (I_M \otimes \widetilde{X}, I_M \otimes \overline{X})$, show that $P_A = P_{I_M \otimes \widetilde{X}} + P_{I_M \otimes \overline{X}}$. For $B = (\Sigma_\nu^{-1/2} \otimes \widetilde{X}, \Sigma_1^{-1/2} \otimes \overline{X})$, show that $P_A P_B = P_B$, and that $P_A - P_B$ is idempotent. Use these results to prove that the var $\left(\sqrt{n}\hat{\delta}_{\text{E3SLS}}\right)$ − var $\left(\sqrt{n}\hat{\delta}_{\text{EC3SLS}}\right)$ is positive semi-definite.

Solution

(a) Note that

$$B'B = \begin{bmatrix} H'H \otimes \tilde{X}'\tilde{X} & 0 \\ 0 & G'G \otimes \overline{X}'\overline{X} \end{bmatrix}$$

since $\widetilde{X}$ and $\overline{X}$ are orthogonal. Hence, $P_B = B(B'B)^{-1}B' = P_H \otimes P_{\widetilde{X}} + P_G \otimes P_{\overline{X}}$. But H and G are non-singular, hence $P_G = P_H = I_M$, which proves that $P_B = P_A = I_M \otimes P_{\widetilde{X}} + I_M \otimes P_{\overline{X}}$. Note that $H \otimes \widetilde{X} + G \otimes \overline{X}$ is spanned by A, which in turn means that $P_C = P_D = P_B = P_A$. Substituting these in (7.31) proves that these instruments all yield the same 3SLS estimator of δ given by EC3SLS.

The set of instruments $[I_M \otimes \widetilde{X}, I_M \otimes \overline{X}]$ used by Baltagi (1981) spans the set of instruments $[\Sigma_\nu^{-1/2} \otimes \widetilde{X} + \Sigma_1^{-1/2} \otimes \overline{X}]$ needed for E3SLS. In addition, we note without proof that Baltagi and Li (1992c) showed that $\widehat{\delta}_{\text{EC3SLS}}$ and $\widehat{\delta}_{\text{E3SLS}}$ yield the same asymptotic variance–covariance matrix. Let $H = \Sigma_\nu^{-1/2}$ and $G = \Sigma_1^{-1/2}$, and note that A is the set of instruments proposed by Baltagi (1981), while B is the optimal set of instruments X^* defined in (7.32). Hence, we conclude that $H \otimes \widetilde{X}$ is redundant in C and $G \otimes \overline{X}$ is redundant in D with respect to the optimal set of instruments X^*. Therefore, using White's (1984) terminology, the extra instruments used by Baltagi (1981) do not yield extra gains in asymptotic efficiency.

(b) Letting $A = (I_M \otimes \widetilde{X}, I_M \otimes \overline{X})$, then

$$P_A = I_M \otimes (P_{\widetilde{X}} + P_{\overline{X}}) = P_{I_M \otimes \widetilde{X}} + P_{I_M \otimes \overline{X}}$$

since $\widetilde{X}'\overline{X} = 0$ (see Exercise 7.5). Letting $B = (\Sigma_\nu^{-1/2} \otimes \widetilde{X}, \Sigma_1^{-1/2} \otimes \overline{X})$, then

$$\begin{aligned} P_{I_M \otimes \widetilde{X}} P_B &= \left(I_M \otimes P_{\widetilde{X}}\right)\left(\Sigma_\nu^{-1/2} \otimes \tilde{X} + \Sigma_1^{-1/2} \otimes \overline{X}\right)\left(B'B\right)^{-1} B' \\ &= \left(\Sigma_\nu^{-1/2} \otimes \tilde{X}\right)\left(B'B\right)^{-1} B' \end{aligned}$$

using the fact that $P_{\widetilde{X}}\overline{X} = 0$, since $QP = 0$. Also,

$$P_{I_M \otimes \overline{X}} P_B = (I_M \otimes P_{\overline{X}}) \left(\Sigma_\nu^{-1/2} \otimes \tilde{X} + \Sigma_1^{-1/2} \otimes \overline{X}\right) (B'B)^{-1} B'$$
$$= \left(\Sigma_1^{-1/2} \otimes \overline{X}\right) (B'B)^{-1} B'$$

Summing these two equations gives

$$\left(P_{I_M \otimes \tilde{X}} + P_{I_M \otimes \overline{X}}\right) P_B = \left(\Sigma_\nu^{-1/2} \otimes \tilde{X}\right) (B'B)^{-1} B' + \left(\Sigma_1^{-1/2} \otimes \overline{X}\right) (B'B)^{-1} B' = P_B$$

Using the result that $P_A = P_{I_M \otimes \tilde{X}} + P_{I_M \otimes \overline{X}}$, we get $P_A P_B = P_B$. Finally, $P_A - P_B$ is idempotent because $(P_A - P_B)^2 = P_A + P_B - P_A P_B - P_B P_A = P_A - P_B$.

It is well known that the asymptotic variance of $\sqrt{n}\hat{\delta}_{\text{E3SLS}}$ is given by var $(\sqrt{n}\hat{\delta}_{\text{E3SLS}}) = \text{plim}(Z^{*\prime} P_B Z^*/n)^{-1}$, and that of $\sqrt{n}\hat{\delta}_{\text{EC3SLS}}$ is given by var$(\sqrt{n}$ $\hat{\delta}_{\text{EC3SLS}}) = \text{plim}(Z^{*\prime} P_A Z^*/n)^{-1}$. Therefore, $\text{var}(\sqrt{n}\hat{\delta}_{\text{E3SLS}}) - \text{var}(\sqrt{n}\hat{\delta}_{\text{EC3SLS}})$ is positive semi-definite if $(Z^{*\prime} P_A Z^*/n) - (Z^{*\prime} P_B Z^*/n)$ is positive semi-definite, or equivalently, if $(Z^{*\prime}(P_A - P_B)Z^*/n)$ is positive semi-definite. The latter holds since $P_A - P_B$ is idempotent.

Exercise 7.12 *(Special cases of the simultaneous equations model with one-way error component disturbances).* This is based on Problem 7.7 in Baltagi (2008). Consider a set of two simultaneous equations as in (7.20) with $M = 2$, so that

$$\begin{pmatrix} y_1 \\ y_2 \end{pmatrix} = \begin{pmatrix} Z_1 & 0 \\ 0 & Z_2 \end{pmatrix} \begin{pmatrix} \delta_1 \\ \delta_2 \end{pmatrix} + \begin{pmatrix} u_1 \\ u_2 \end{pmatrix} \tag{7.34}$$

with one-way error component disturbances given by (6.2) and Ω given by (6.5).

(a) Show that if the variance–covariance matrix between the two equations is block-diagonal, then EC3SLS is equivalent to EC2SLS (see Baltagi, 1981).
(b) Show that if this system of two equations with one-way error component disturbances is just identified, then EC3SLS does not necessarily reduce to EC2SLS (see Baltagi, 1981).

Solution

(a) For Ω block-diagonal, $\Omega_{12} = 0$, with $\sigma^2_{\mu_{12}} = \sigma^2_{\nu_{12}} = 0$; see (6.5). Hence, both Σ_μ and Σ_ν are diagonal. In this case, both

$$\Omega = E\begin{pmatrix} u_1 \\ u_2 \end{pmatrix}(u_1', u_2') = \begin{bmatrix} \Omega_{11} & 0 \\ 0 & \Omega_{22} \end{bmatrix}$$

and

$$\Omega^{-1} = \begin{bmatrix} \Omega_{11}^{-1} & 0 \\ 0 & \Omega_{22}^{-1} \end{bmatrix}$$

are block-diagonal, with Ω_{11} and Ω_{22} taking the form of the usual one-way error component variance–covariance matrix described in (6.5) for $j = 1$ and $\ell = 2$. In Exercise 7.10, we showed that EC3SLS can be derived as a GLS estimator on the system of transformed equations given in (7.28). In fact, both Σ_ν and Σ_1 are diagonal and

$$\widetilde{Z}'(\Sigma_\nu^{-1} \otimes P_{\widetilde{X}})\widetilde{Z} = \begin{bmatrix} \frac{\widetilde{Z}_1' P_{\widetilde{X}} \widetilde{Z}_1}{\sigma_{\nu_{11}}^2} & 0 \\ 0 & \frac{\widetilde{Z}_2' P_{\widetilde{X}} \widetilde{Z}_2}{\sigma_{\nu_{22}}^2} \end{bmatrix}$$

and

$$\overline{Z}'(\Sigma_1^{-1} \otimes P_{\overline{X}})\overline{Z} = \begin{bmatrix} \frac{\overline{Z}_1' P_{\overline{X}} \overline{Z}_1}{\sigma_{1_{22}}^2} & 0 \\ 0 & \frac{\overline{Z}_2' P_{\overline{X}} \overline{Z}_2}{\sigma_{1_{22}}^2} \end{bmatrix}$$

are block-diagonal. Similarly,

$$\widetilde{Z}'(\Sigma_\nu^{-1} \otimes P_{\widetilde{X}})\widetilde{y} = \begin{bmatrix} \frac{\widetilde{Z}_1' P_{\widetilde{X}} \widetilde{y}_1}{\sigma_{\nu_{11}}^2} \\ \frac{\widetilde{Z}_2' P_{\widetilde{X}} \widetilde{y}_2}{\sigma_{\nu_{22}}^2} \end{bmatrix}$$

and

$$\overline{Z}'(\Sigma_1^{-1} \otimes P_{\overline{X}})\overline{y} = \begin{bmatrix} \frac{\overline{Z}_1' P_{\overline{X}} \overline{y}_1}{\sigma_{1_{11}}^2} \\ \frac{\overline{Z}_2' P_{\overline{X}} \overline{y}_2}{\sigma_{1_{22}}^2} \end{bmatrix}$$

Hence, $\widehat{\delta}_{\text{EC3SLS}}$ given in (7.29) reduces to

$$\begin{pmatrix} \widehat{\delta}_1 \\ \widehat{\delta}_2 \end{pmatrix}_{\text{EC3SLS}} = \begin{pmatrix} \left[\frac{\widetilde{Z}_1' P_{\widetilde{X}} \widetilde{Z}_1}{\sigma_{\nu_{11}}^2} + \frac{\overline{Z}_1' P_{\overline{X}} \overline{Z}_1}{\sigma_{1_{11}}^2} \right]^{-1} \left[\frac{\widetilde{Z}_1' P_{\widetilde{X}} \widetilde{y}_1}{\sigma_{\nu_{11}}^2} + \frac{\overline{Z}_1' P_{\overline{X}} \overline{y}_1}{\sigma_{1_{11}}^2} \right] \\ \left[\frac{\widetilde{Z}_2' P_{\widetilde{X}} \widetilde{Z}_2}{\sigma_{\nu_{22}}^2} + \frac{\overline{Z}_2' P_{\overline{X}} \overline{Z}_2}{\sigma_{1_{22}}^2} \right]^{-1} \left[\frac{\widetilde{Z}_2' P_{\widetilde{X}} \widetilde{y}_2}{\sigma_{\nu_{22}}^2} + \frac{\overline{Z}_2' P_{\overline{X}} \overline{y}_2}{\sigma_{1_{22}}^2} \right] \end{pmatrix}$$

which are exactly the EC2SLS estimates of δ_1 and δ_2 on each equation separately; see (7.13). This is analogous to the equivalence between 2SLS and 3SLS in the classical simultaneous equations model when the variance–covariance matrix across equations is diagonal.

(b) If each equation is just identified, then $X'Z_1$ and $X'Z_2$ are square and generally non-singular. Hence, $\widetilde{X}'Z_1$ and $\overline{X}'Z_1$ are square and generally non-singular. From Exercises 7.1 and 7.2, we get

$$\widehat{\delta}_{1,\text{2SLS}} = (Z_1' P_X Z_1)^{-1} Z_1' P_X y_1 = (X'Z_1)^{-1} X' y_1$$
$$\widetilde{\delta}_{1,\text{W2SLS}} = (\widetilde{Z}_1' P_{\widetilde{X}} \widetilde{Z}_1)^{-1} \widetilde{Z}_1' P_{\widetilde{X}} \widetilde{y}_1 = (\widetilde{X}'Z_1)^{-1} \widetilde{X}' y_1$$
$$\widehat{\delta}_{1,\text{B2SLS}} = (\overline{Z}_1' P_{\overline{X}} \overline{Z}_1)^{-1} \overline{Z}_1' P_{\overline{X}} \overline{y}_1 = (\overline{X}'Z_1)^{-1} \overline{X}' y_1$$

Note that $\widehat{\delta}_{1,\mathrm{EC2SLS}}$ is given in (7.14) as a matrix-weighted average of $\widetilde{\delta}_{1,\mathrm{W2SLS}}$ and $\widehat{\delta}_{1,\mathrm{B2SLS}}$.

Also, from Exercises 7.7 and 7.8, we get

$$\begin{aligned}\widehat{\delta}_{3\mathrm{SLS}} &= [\mathrm{diag}[Z_i'X](\Sigma^{-1}\otimes(X'X)^{-1})\mathrm{diag}[X'Z_i]]^{-1}\\&\quad[\mathrm{diag}[Z_i'X](\Sigma^{-1}\otimes(X'X)^{-1})(I_M\otimes X')y\\&= [\mathrm{diag}[X'Z_i]^{-1}(I_M\otimes X')y\end{aligned}$$

which reduces to $\widehat{\delta}_{1,2\mathrm{SLS}}$ and $\widehat{\delta}_{2,2\mathrm{SLS}}$ on each equation separately. Also,

$$\begin{aligned}\widetilde{\delta}_{\mathrm{W3SLS}} &= [\mathrm{diag}[\widetilde{Z}_i'\widetilde{X}](\Sigma_\nu^{-1}\otimes(\widetilde{X}'\widetilde{X})^{-1})\mathrm{diag}[\widetilde{X}'\widetilde{Z}_i]]^{-1}\\&\quad[\mathrm{diag}[\widetilde{Z}_i'\widetilde{X}](\Sigma_\nu^{-1}\otimes(\widetilde{X}'\widetilde{X})^{-1})(I_M\otimes\widetilde{X}')\widetilde{y}\\&= \mathrm{diag}[\widetilde{X}'\widetilde{Z}_i]^{-1}(I_M\otimes\widetilde{X}')\widetilde{y}\end{aligned}$$

which reduces to $\widetilde{\delta}_{1,\mathrm{W2SLS}}$ and $\widetilde{\delta}_{2,\mathrm{W2SLS}}$ on each equation separately. And

$$\begin{aligned}\widehat{\delta}_{\mathrm{B3SLS}} &= [\mathrm{diag}[\overline{Z}_i'\overline{X}](\Sigma_1^{-1}\otimes(\overline{X}'\overline{X})^{-1})\mathrm{diag}[\overline{X}'\overline{Z}_i]]^{-1}\\&\quad[\mathrm{diag}[\overline{Z}_i'\overline{X}](\Sigma_1^{-1}\otimes(\overline{X}'\overline{X})^{-1})(I_M\otimes\overline{X}')\overline{y}\\&= \mathrm{diag}[\overline{X}'\overline{Z}_i]^{-1}(I_M\otimes\overline{X}')\overline{y}\end{aligned}$$

which reduces to $\widehat{\delta}_{1,\mathrm{B2SLS}}$ and $\widehat{\delta}_{2,\mathrm{B2SLS}}$ on each equation separately. Note that $\widehat{\delta}_{\mathrm{EC3SLS}}$ is given in (7.29) as a matrix-weighted average of $\widehat{\delta}_{\mathrm{W3SLS}}$ and $\widehat{\delta}_{\mathrm{B3SLS}}$. It is clear that $\widehat{\delta}_{\mathrm{EC3SLS}}$ does not simplify any further and does not yield EC2SLS on each equation separately. This is different from the analogous conditions between 2SLS and 3SLS in the classical simultaneous equations model.

7.3 ENDOGENOUS EFFECTS

Let us reconsider the single equation estimation case but now focus on endogeneity occurring through the unobserved individual effects. Examples where μ_i and the explanatory variables may be correlated include an earnings equation, where the unobserved individual ability may be correlated with schooling and experience; and a production function, where managerial ability may be correlated with the inputs.

Exercise 7.13 *(Mundlak's (1978) augmented regression).* This is based on Problem 7.8 in Baltagi (2008). Mundlak (1978) considered the one-way error component regression model in (2.5) but with the additional auxiliary regression

$$\mu_i = \overline{X}_{i.}'\pi + \varepsilon_i \tag{7.35}$$

where $\varepsilon_i \sim \mathrm{IIN}(0, \sigma_\varepsilon^2)$ and $\overline{X}_{i.}'$ is $1\times K$ vector of observations on the explanatory variables averaged over time. In other words, Mundlak assumed that the individual effects are a linear function of the averages of *all* the explanatory variables across time. These effects are uncorrelated with the explanatory variables if and only if $\pi = 0$. Mundlak (1978) assumed, without loss of generality, that the X are deviations from their sample mean. In vector form, one can write (7.35) as

$$\mu = Z'_{\mu} X\pi/T + \varepsilon \tag{7.36}$$

where $\mu' = (\mu_1, \ldots, \mu_N)$, $Z_\mu = I_N \otimes \iota_T$, and $\varepsilon' = (\varepsilon_1, \ldots, \varepsilon_N)$. Substituting (7.36) in (2.5), with no constant, one gets

$$y = X\beta + PX\pi + (Z_\mu \varepsilon + \nu) \tag{7.37}$$

where $P = I_N \otimes \overline{J}_T$.

(a) Using the partitioned inverse, show that GLS on (7.37) yields

$$\widehat{\beta}_{\text{GLS}} = \widetilde{\beta}_{\text{Within}} = (X'QX)^{-1}X'Qy \tag{7.38}$$

and

$$\widehat{\pi}_{\text{GLS}} = \widehat{\beta}_{\text{Between}} - \widetilde{\beta}_{\text{Within}} = (X'PX)^{-1}X'Py - (X'QX)^{-1}X'Qy \tag{7.39}$$

(b) Show that

$$\begin{aligned} \text{var}(\widehat{\pi}_{\text{GLS}}) &= \text{var}(\widehat{\beta}_{\text{Between}}) + \text{var}(\widetilde{\beta}_{\text{Within}}) \\ &= (T\sigma_\varepsilon^2 + \sigma_\nu^2)(X'PX)^{-1} + \sigma_\nu^2(X'QX)^{-1} \end{aligned} \tag{7.40}$$

(c) Show that the test for $H_0\colon \pi = 0$ in (7.37) is basically a Hausman test based on the contrast using the between and within estimators.

Solution

(a) Using the fact that the ε and the ν are uncorrelated, the new error in (7.37) has zero mean and variance–covariance matrix

$$V = E(Z_\mu \varepsilon + \nu)(Z_\mu \varepsilon + \nu)' = \sigma_\varepsilon^2 (I_N \otimes J_T) + \sigma_\nu^2 I_{NT} \tag{7.41}$$

This variance–covariance matrix can be written in the familiar error component form as

$$V = (T\sigma_\varepsilon^2 + \sigma_\nu^2)P + \sigma_\nu^2 Q$$

where $P = I_N \otimes \overline{J}_T$ and $Q = I_{NT} - P$. Also,

$$V^{-1} = (T\sigma_\varepsilon^2 + \sigma_\nu^2)^{-1}P + (\sigma_\nu^2)^{-1}Q$$

Hence, GLS on (7.37) yields

$$\begin{pmatrix}\widehat{\beta}\\ \widehat{\pi}\end{pmatrix} = \left(\begin{bmatrix}X'\\ X'P\end{bmatrix} V^{-1}[X \quad PX]\right)^{-1}\begin{bmatrix}X'\\ X'P\end{bmatrix} V^{-1}y$$

$$= \begin{bmatrix}X'V^{-1}X & X'PX/c\\ X'PX/c & X'PX/c\end{bmatrix}^{-1}\begin{bmatrix}X'V^{-1}y\\ X'Py/c\end{bmatrix}$$

where $c = T\sigma_\varepsilon^2 + \sigma_\nu^2$ and $PV^{-1} = P(P/c + Q/\sigma_\nu^2) = P/c$ since $PQ = 0$. Using the partitioned inverse formulas, it turns out that the inverse is a matrix B with

$$B_{11} = \left[X'V^{-1}X - \frac{X'PX}{c}\left(\frac{X'PX}{c}\right)^{-1}\frac{X'PX}{c}\right]^{-1} = \left[X'V^{-1}X - \frac{X'PX}{c}\right]^{-1}$$

$$= \left(\frac{X'QX}{\sigma_\nu^2}\right)^{-1}$$

using the expression for V^{-1} described above. Also,

$$B_{12} = -\left(\frac{X'QX}{\sigma_\nu^2}\right)^{-1}\left(\frac{X'PX}{c}\right)\left(\frac{X'PX}{c}\right)^{-1} = -\left(\frac{X'QX}{\sigma_\nu^2}\right)^{-1}$$

$$B_{21} = -\left(\frac{X'PX}{c}\right)^{-1}\left(\frac{X'PX}{c}\right)\left(\frac{X'QX}{\sigma_\nu^2}\right)^{-1} = -\left(\frac{X'QX}{\sigma_\nu^2}\right)^{-1}$$

$$B_{22} = \left(\frac{X'PX}{c}\right)^{-1} + \left(\frac{X'PX}{c}\right)^{-1}\left(\frac{X'PX}{c}\right)\left(\frac{X'QX}{\sigma_\nu^2}\right)^{-1}\left(\frac{X'PX}{c}\right)\left(\frac{X'PX}{c}\right)^{-1}$$

$$= \left(\frac{X'PX}{c}\right)^{-1} + \left(\frac{X'QX}{\sigma_\nu^2}\right)^{-1}$$

Substituting these expressions for the inverse and multiplying out, we get

$$\widehat{\beta} = \left(\frac{X'QX}{\sigma_\nu^2}\right)^{-1}(X'V^{-1}y) - \left(\frac{X'QX}{\sigma_\nu^2}\right)^{-1}\left(\frac{X'Py}{c}\right) = \left(\frac{X'QX}{\sigma_\nu^2}\right)^{-1} X'(V^{-1} - P/c)y$$

$$= (X'QX)^{-1}(X'Qy) = \widetilde{\beta}_{\text{Within}}$$

since $V^{-1} = P/c + Q/\sigma_\nu^2$. Also,

$$\widehat{\pi} = -\left(\frac{X'QX}{\sigma_\nu^2}\right)^{-1} X'V^{-1}y + \left(\frac{X'PX}{c}\right)^{-1}\frac{X'Py}{c} + \left(\frac{X'QX}{\sigma_\nu^2}\right)^{-1}\frac{X'Py}{c}$$

Substituting $V^{-1} = P/c + Q/\sigma_\nu^2$ gives

$$\widehat{\pi} = -\left(\frac{X'QX}{\sigma_\nu^2}\right)^{-1}\left(\frac{X'Qy}{\sigma_\nu^2}\right) + \left(\frac{X'PX}{c}\right)^{-1}\frac{X'Py}{c} = \widehat{\beta}_{\text{Between}} - \widetilde{\beta}_{\text{Within}}$$

as described in (7.39).

(b) The variance–covariance matrix of $(\widehat{\beta}, \widehat{\pi})'$ is given by the inverted matrix whose inverse was obtained in part (a). In fact, $\text{var}(\widehat{\beta}) = B_{11} = \sigma_\nu^2(X'QX)^{-1}$ which is $\text{var}(\widetilde{\beta}_{\text{Within}})$ and

$$\text{var}(\widehat{\pi}) = B_{22} = c(X'PX)^{-1} + \sigma_\nu^2(X'QX)^{-1} = \text{var}(\widehat{\beta}_{\text{Between}}) + \text{var}(\widetilde{\beta}_{\text{Within}})$$

as described in (7.40).

(c) Therefore, Mundlak (1978) showed that the best linear unbiased estimator of (2.5) becomes the fixed effects (within) estimator once these individual effects are modeled as a linear function of the averages of *all* the X_{it} as in (7.35). The random effects estimator, on the other hand, is biased because it ignores (7.35). The Wald test for $H_0: \pi = 0$ is based upon

$$\widehat{\pi}'_{\text{GLS}}(\text{var}(\widehat{\pi}'_{\text{GLS}}))^{-1}\widehat{\pi}_{\text{GLS}} \overset{H_0}{\rightarrow} \chi_K^2 \tag{7.42}$$

But $\widehat{\pi} = \widehat{\beta}_{\text{Between}} - \widetilde{\beta}_{\text{Within}}$ and $\text{var}(\widehat{\pi}) = \text{var}(\widehat{\beta}_{\text{Between}}) + \text{var}(\widetilde{\beta}_{\text{Within}})$. Hence, (7.42) is a Hausman test based on the contrast using the between and within estimators.

Mundlak's (1978) formulation in (7.37) assumes that *all* the explanatory variables are related to the individual effects. The random effects model, on the other hand, assumes *no* correlation between the explanatory variables and the individual effects. The random effects model generates the GLS estimator, whereas Mundlak's formulation produces the within estimator. Instead of this 'all or nothing' correlation among the X and the μ_i, we now consider a model where *some* of the explanatory variables are related to the μ_i.

Exercise 7.14 *(Hausman and Taylor (1981) estimator).* Hausman and Taylor (1981), henceforth referred to as HT, consider the model

$$y_{it} = X_{it}\beta + Z_i\gamma + \mu_i + \nu_{it} \tag{7.43}$$

where the Z_i are cross-sectional time-invariant variables. HT split X and Z into two sets of variables, $X = [X_1; X_2]$ and $Z = [Z_1; Z_2]$, where X_1 is $n \times k_1$, X_2 is $n \times k_2$, Z_1 is $n \times g_1$, Z_2 is $n \times g_2$, and $n = NT$. X_1 and Z_1 are assumed exogenous in that they are not correlated with the μ_i and the ν_{it}, while X_2 and Z_2 are endogenous because they are correlated with the μ_i but not the ν_{it}. The within transformation would sweep the μ_i and remove the bias, but in the process it would also remove the Z_i, and hence the within estimator will not give an estimate of γ. Let $u_{it} = \mu_i + \nu_{it}$, and let $\Omega = E(uu')$ given by (2.10). Assuming there are no extra instruments as in (7.1), HT's efficient estimator premultiplies the model by $\Omega^{-1/2}$, given by (2.12), and uses the set of instruments $A = [Q, X_1, Z_1]$, where $Q = I_{NT} - P$ and $P = (I_N \otimes \bar{J}_T)$. Show that this set of instruments, which is not feasible, is equivalent to the feasible set of instruments, $B = [QX_1, QX_2, X_1, Z_1]$ and $C = [QX_1, QX_2, PX_1, Z_1]$, suggested by Breusch, Mizon and Schmidt (1989), henceforth referred to as BMS.

Solution

The HT efficient estimator premultiplies (7.43) by $\Omega^{-1/2}$,

$$\Omega^{-1/2}y_{it} = \Omega^{-1/2}X_{it}\beta + \Omega^{-1/2}Z_i\gamma + \Omega^{-1/2}u_{it} \tag{7.44}$$

and uses $A = [Q, X_1, Z_1]$ as the set of instruments. Note that Q is of dimension $NT \times NT$, so this set of instruments is not feasible. Let $H = [X_1, Z_1]$; then $A = [Q, H]$. Also

$$P_A = Q + P_{PH} = Q + PH(H'PH)^{-1}H'P \tag{7.45}$$

The column space of B is the same as the column space of C, since $[QX_1, PX_1]$ span the same column space as $[QX_1, X_1]$. Hence $P_B = P_C$, and both B and C lead to the same instrumental variable estimator. Note that $P_C \neq P_A$. In fact, P_C is strictly contained in P_A. However, for the transformed regressors in (7.44), the projections onto A and C are the same, resulting in the same instrumental variables estimator. To show this, write

$$P_A\Omega^{-1/2}X_1 = P_A\left[\frac{QX_1}{\sigma_\nu} + \frac{PX_1}{\sigma_1}\right] = \left[\frac{QX_1}{\sigma_\nu} + \frac{PX_1}{\sigma_1}\right] = \Omega^{-1/2}X_1$$

since $P_AQ = Q$ and $P_APX_1 = P_{PH}PX_1 = PX_1$. This uses the fact that $PQ = 0$ and $PH = P_{PH}PH = P_{PH}[PX_1, PZ_1]$. Similarly,

$$P_C\Omega^{-1/2}X_1 = P_C\left[\frac{QX_1}{\sigma_\nu} + \frac{PX_1}{\sigma_1}\right] = \left[\frac{QX_1}{\sigma_\nu} + \frac{PX_1}{\sigma_1}\right] = \Omega^{-1/2}X_1$$

since $P_CQX_1 = QX_1$ and $P_CPX_1 = PX_1$, which follows from $P_CC = C$. Also

$$P_A\Omega^{-1/2}Z_1 = P_A\left[\frac{QZ_1}{\sigma_\nu} + \frac{PZ_1}{\sigma_1}\right] = P_A\left[\frac{Z_1}{\sigma_1}\right] = \frac{Z_1}{\sigma_1}$$

since $QZ_1 = 0$, $PZ_1 = Z_1$ and $P_AZ_1 = Z_1$. Similarly,

$$P_C\Omega^{-1/2}Z_1 = P_C\left[\frac{QZ_1}{\sigma_\nu} + \frac{PZ_1}{\sigma_1}\right] = P_C\left[\frac{Z_1}{\sigma_1}\right] = \frac{Z_1}{\sigma_1}$$

since $QZ_1 = 0$, $PZ_1 = Z_1$ and $P_CZ_1 = Z_1$. Now

$$P_A\Omega^{-1/2}Z_2 = P_A\left[\frac{QZ_2}{\sigma_\nu} + \frac{PZ_2}{\sigma_1}\right] = P_A\left[\frac{Z_2}{\sigma_1}\right] = P_{PH}\left[\frac{Z_2}{\sigma_1}\right]$$

since $QZ_2 = 0$, $PZ_2 = Z_2$ and $P_AZ_2 = (Q + P_{PH})Z_2 = P_{PH}Z_2$. And

$$P_C\Omega^{-1/2}Z_2 = P_C\left[\frac{QZ_2}{\sigma_\nu} + \frac{PZ_2}{\sigma_1}\right] = P_C\left[\frac{Z_2}{\sigma_1}\right]$$

since $QZ_2 = 0$, $PZ_2 = Z_2$. Hence, $P_A\Omega^{-1/2}Z_2 = P_C\Omega^{-1/2}Z_2$, since $P_{PH}Z_2 = P_CZ_2$. Similarly,

$$P_C\Omega^{-1/2}X_2 = P_C\left[\frac{QX_2}{\sigma_\nu} + \frac{PX_2}{\sigma_1}\right] = \left[\frac{QX_2}{\sigma_\nu} + \frac{P_CPX_2}{\sigma_1}\right]$$

$$P_A\Omega^{-1/2}X_2 = P_A\left[\frac{QX_2}{\sigma_\nu} + \frac{PX_2}{\sigma_1}\right] = \left[\frac{QX_2}{\sigma_\nu} + \frac{P_{PH}PX_2}{\sigma_1}\right]$$

Hence, $P_A\Omega^{-1/2}X_2 = P_C\Omega^{-1/2}X_2$, since $P_{PH}PX_2 = P_CPX_2$.

It is worth emphasizing that the set of instruments B and C are feasible, while A is not. Note also that $\widetilde{X}_1 = QX_1$, $\widetilde{X}_2 = QX_2$, $\overline{X}_1 = PX_1$, and Z_1 are used as instruments for $[X_1, X_2, Z_2, Z_1]$. Therefore, X_1 is used twice, once as averages and another time as deviations from these averages. This is an advantage of panel data allowing instruments from *within* the model. The order condition for identification comes out naturally, giving the result that k_1, the number of variables in X_1, must be at least as large as g_2, the number of variables in Z_2. Note also that the HT efficient estimator is related to the EC2SLS estimator derived by Baltagi (1981) in Exercise 7.4. Both estimation methods mutiply by $\Omega^{-1/2}$ and use $[QX, PX]$ as the set of instruments for a valid instrument set X. The basic difference is that HT does not necessarily use outside instruments and relies on the between and within variation of the exogenous regressors as instruments. In particular, HT excludes Z_2 and PX_2 from this set of instruments because Z_2 and X_2 are correlated with μ_i. This leaves PX_1 as extra instruments to be used for Z_2.

Exercise 7.15 *(Cornwell and Rupert (1988): Hausman and Taylor application).* This is based on Problem 7.12 in Baltagi (2008). In Exercise 2.14, we considered an earnings equation for 595 individuals observed over the period 1976–82 and drawn from the Panel Study of Income Dynamics. This data was obtained from Cornwell and Rupert (1988) and is available as a Stata data set named cornrup.dta.

(a) Perform the Hausman (1978) test based on the difference between the fixed effects (within) and random effects (GLS) estimators.
(b) Estimate the model with the HT estimator using $X_1 =$ (OCC, SOUTH, SMSA, IND), $X_2 =$ (EXP, EXP^2, WKS, MS, UNION), $Z_1 =$ (FEM, BLK) and $Z_2 =$ (ED) in the notation of Exercise 7.14.
(c) Perform the Hausman (1978) test based on the difference between the fixed effects and HT estimates.

Table 7.1 Hausman's Test Based on FE vs RE

```
. hausman fixef glsre

                 ---- Coefficients ----
             |      (b)          (B)            (b-B)     sqrt(diag(V_b-V_B))
             |     fixef        glsre        Difference          S.E.
-------------+----------------------------------------------------------------
         wks |   .0008359     .0010347       -.0001987              .
       south |  -.0018612    -.0166176        .0147564         .0217436
        smsa |  -.0424691    -.0138231       -.0286461              .
          ms |  -.0297259    -.0746283        .0449025              .
         exp |   .1132083     .0820544        .0311539              .
        exp2 |  -.0004184    -.0008084        .0003901              .
         occ |  -.0214765    -.0500664        .0285899              .
         ind |   .0192101     .0037441         .015466              .
       union |   .0327849     .0632232       -.0304384              .
------------------------------------------------------------------------------
                           b = consistent under Ho and Ha; obtained from xtreg
            B = inconsistent under Ha, efficient under Ho; obtained from xtreg

    Test:  Ho:  difference in coefficients not systematic

                  chi2(9) = (b-B)'[(V_b-V_B)^(-1)](b-B)
                          =     5075.25
                Prob>chi2 =      0.0000
```

Solution

(a) As reported in Exercise 2.14, the within estimates were quite different from those of GLS, and the Hausman test based on the contrast of these two estimates yields $\chi_9^2 = 5075$ which is significant. This is reported in Table 7.1 using Stata. This rejects the null hypothesis of no correlation between the individual effects and the explanatory variables and rejects the GLS estimator as inconsistent.

(b) Stata has simple commands to perform the HT estimator. This was demonstrated in Table 7.5 in Baltagi (2008, p.138) and is reproduced here as Table 7.2 for convenience. This HT estimator is based on X_1 = (OCC, SOUTH, SMSA, IND), X_2 = (EXP, EXP^2,

Table 7.2 Hausman and Taylor Estimates of a Mincer Wage Equation

```
. xthtaylor lwage occ south smsa ind exp exp2 wks ms union fem blk ed, endog
(exp exp2 wks ms union ed)

Hausman-Taylor estimation                      Number of obs      =      4165
Group variable (i): id                         Number of groups   =       595

                                               Obs per group: min =         7
                                                              avg =         7
                                                              max =         7

Random effects u_i ~ i.i.d.                    Wald chi2(12)      =   6891.87
                                               Prob > chi2        =    0.0000

------------------------------------------------------------------------------
       lwage |      Coef.   Std. Err.      z    P>|z|     [95% Conf. Interval]
-------------+----------------------------------------------------------------
TVexogenous  |
         occ |  -.0207047   .0137809    -1.50   0.133    -.0477149    .0063055
       south |   .0074398    .031955     0.23   0.816    -.0551908    .0700705
        smsa |  -.0418334   .0189581    -2.21   0.027    -.0789906   -.0046761
         ind |   .0136039   .0152374     0.89   0.372    -.0162608    .0434686
TVendogenous |
         exp |   .1131328    .002471    45.79   0.000     .1082898    .1179758
        exp2 |  -.0004189   .0000546    -7.67   0.000    -.0005259   -.0003119
         wks |   .0008374   .0005997     1.40   0.163    -.0003381    .0020129
          ms |  -.0298508     .01898    -1.57   0.116    -.0670508    .0073493
       union |   .0327714   .0149084     2.20   0.028     .0035514    .0619914
TIexogenous  |
         fem |  -.1309236    .126659    -1.03   0.301    -.3791707    .1173234
         blk |  -.2857479   .1557019    -1.84   0.066    -.5909179    .0194221
TIendogenous |
          ed |    .137944   .0212485     6.49   0.000     .0962977    .1795902
             |
       _cons |   2.912726   .2836522    10.27   0.000     2.356778    3.468674
-------------+----------------------------------------------------------------
     sigma_u |  .94180304
     sigma_e |  .15180273
         rho |  .97467788   (fraction of variance due to u_i)
------------------------------------------------------------------------------
note:   TV refers to time-varying; TI refers to time-invariant.
```

Table 7.3 Hausman's Test Based on FE vs HT

```
. hausman fixef haust

                 ---- Coefficients ----
             |      (b)          (B)            (b-B)     sqrt(diag(V_b-V_B))
             |     fixef        haust         Difference          S.E.
-------------+----------------------------------------------------------------
         wks |    .0008359     .0008374       -1.46e-06               .
       south |   -.0018612     .0074398        -.009301        .0124627
        smsa |   -.0424691    -.0418334       -.0006358        .0042486
          ms |   -.0297259    -.0298508        .0001249        .0003699
         exp |    .1132083     .1131328        .0000755        .0000201
        exp2 |   -.0004184    -.0004189        5.13e-07               .
         occ |   -.0214765    -.0207047       -.0007718        .0002742
         ind |    .0192101     .0136039        .0056062         .002532
       union |    .0327849     .0327714        .0000134        .0006561
------------------------------------------------------------------------------
              b = consistent under Ho and Ha; obtained from xthtaylor
   B = inconsistent under Ha, efficient under Ho; obtained from xtreg

   Test:  Ho:  difference in coefficients not systematic

                 chi2(8) = (b-B)'[(V_b-V_B)^(-1)](b-B)
                         =        5.26
               Prob>chi2 =      0.7295
```

WKS, MS, UNION), $Z_1 = $ (FEM, BLK) and $Z_2 = $ (ED). The coefficient of ED, which is the returns to schooling, is estimated as 0.13, higher than the estimate obtained using GLS (0.10).

(c) A Hausman test based on the difference between HT and the within estimator is reported in Table 7.3 using Stata. This yields $\chi_3^2 = 5.26$, which is not significant at the 5% level. There are three degrees of freedom since there are three overidentifying conditions (the number of X_1 variables minus the number of Z_2 variables). Therefore, we cannot reject the hypothesis that the set of instruments X_1 and Z_1 chosen is legitimate. This is based on the replication by Baltagi and Khanti-Akom (1990). Note that Stata incorrectly gives 8 degrees of freedom for this test statistic; the observed test statistic (5.26) is correct, but the corresponding degrees of freedom and p-value are not.

Exercise 7.16 *(Serlenga and Shin (2007): gravity models of intra-EU trade).* Serlenga and Shin (2007) applied the Hausman–Taylor estimation methodology to a gravity equation of bilateral trade flows among 15 European countries over the period 1960–2001. Among their findings is that the impact of country specific variables, like distance, common language and common border can be recovered using this approach in addition to allowing such variables to be endogenous. In particular, they argue that common language is a proxy for cultural, historical and linguistic proximity, and this in turn is highly correlated with country-specific effects. This exercise asks the reader to replicate the HT results in Table II of this paper. The Serlenga and Shin (2007) data set can be downloaded from the *Journal of Applied Econometrics* web site. The general model regresses bilateral trade (Trade) on GDP, similarity in relative size (Sim), differences in relative factor endowments between trading partners (Rlf), real exchange rate (Rer), a dummy variable which is 1 when both countries belong to the European community (Cee), a dummy variable which is 1 when both countries adopt a common cuurency (Emu); distance between capital cities (Dist); common border (Bor); and common language (Lan). (a) Replicate the FE results in Table II for the full model. (b) Replicate the HT estimation results in Table II; (c) Perform the Hausman test for overidentification when GDP, RLF and RER are used as instruments for Lan in the HT estimation.

Solution

(a) We first replicate the FE results in Table II of Serlenga and Shin (2007, p.373); see Table 7.4. Since distance, common border, and common language are time invariant, they are dropped from the FE regression by Stata.

Table 7.4 Gravity Models of Intra-EU Trade. Fixed Effects Results

```
. xtreg Trade Gdp Sim Rlf Rer Cee Emu Dist Bor Lan, fe

Fixed-effects (within) regression               Number of obs      =      3822
Group variable: id                              Number of groups   =        91

R-sq:  within  = 0.8977                         Obs per group: min =        42
       between = 0.7884                                        avg =      42.0
       overall = 0.8132                                        max =        42

                                                F(6,3725)          =   5448.32
corr(u_i, Xb)  = -0.0109                        Prob > F           =    0.0000

------------------------------------------------------------------------------
       Trade |      Coef.   Std. Err.      t    P>|t|     [95% Conf. Interval]
-------------+----------------------------------------------------------------
         Gdp |   1.812493   .0198184    91.46   0.000     1.773637    1.851349
         Sim |   1.172255   .0555686    21.10   0.000     1.063307    1.281203
         Rlf |   .0325083   .0078883     4.12   0.000     .0170424    .0479741
         Rer |   .0609803   .0086324     7.06   0.000     .0440556     .077905
         Cee |   .3093359   .0160267    19.30   0.000      .277914    .3407579
         Emu |   .0852087   .0267894     3.18   0.001     .0326854     .137732
        Dist |  (dropped)
         Bor |  (dropped)
         Lan |  (dropped)
       _cons |  -18.20631    .287792   -63.26   0.000    -18.77056   -17.64207
-------------+----------------------------------------------------------------
     sigma_u |  .77246591
     sigma_e |  .29291817
         rho |  .87428502   (fraction of variance due to u_i)
------------------------------------------------------------------------------
F test that all u_i=0:     F(90, 3725) =   128.46            Prob > F = 0.0000
```

Table 7.5 Gravity Models of Intra-EU Trade. Second Stage OLS on Time Invariant Regressors

```
. reg dfe Dist Bor Lan

      Source |       SS       df       MS              Number of obs =    3822
-------------+------------------------------           F(  3,  3818) = 1097.91
       Model |  1044.63098     3  348.210328           Prob > F      =  0.0000
    Residual |  1210.90855  3818  .317157817           R-squared     =  0.4631
-------------+------------------------------           Adj R-squared =  0.4627
       Total |  2255.53953  3821  .590300845           Root MSE      =  .56317
             |
------------------------------------------------------------------------------
         dfe |      Coef.   Std. Err.      t    P>|t|     [95% Conf. Interval]
-------------+----------------------------------------------------------------
        Dist |   -.595308   .0194304   -30.64   0.000     -.633403   -.557213
         Bor |   .4287645   .0317724    13.49   0.000      .366472    .4910569
         Lan |   .4498106   .0305997    14.70   0.000     .3898173     .509804
       _cons |    4.11265   .1423603    28.89   0.000      3.83354    4.391759
------------------------------------------------------------------------------
```

(b) Assuming that the time-invariant variables distance, common border, and common language are all uncorrelated with the country pair effects, one can recapture their effects on trade by running OLS of FE residuals (saved as dfe) on these variables; see Table 7.5. This replicates the column labeled OLS under HT estimation in Table II of Serlenga

Table 7.6 Gravity Models of Intra-EU Trade. Second Stage 2SLS on Time Invariant Regressors

```
ivreg dfe Dist Bor (Lan = Rer)

Instrumental variables (2SLS) regression

      Source |       SS       df       MS              Number of obs =    3822
-------------+------------------------------           F(  3,  3818) =  835.50
       Model |  628.14787      3  209.382623           Prob > F      =  0.0000
    Residual | 1627.39166   3818  .426241923           R-squared     =  0.2785
-------------+------------------------------           Adj R-squared =  0.2779
       Total | 2255.53953   3821  .590300845           Root MSE      =  .65287

------------------------------------------------------------------------------
         dfe |      Coef.   Std. Err.      t    P>|t|     [95% Conf. Interval]
-------------+----------------------------------------------------------------
         Lan |   1.558674    .105935    14.71   0.000     1.350979    1.766369
        Dist |  -.3815958   .0296227   -12.88   0.000    -.4396736   -.3235181
         Bor |   .6013204   .0399747    15.04   0.000     .5229467    .6796942
       _cons |   2.446406   .2230137    10.97   0.000     2.009169    2.883644
------------------------------------------------------------------------------
Instrumented:  Lan
Instruments:   Dist Bor Rer
------------------------------------------------------------------------------
```

Table 7.7 Gravity Models of Intra-EU Trade. Hausman and Taylor Estimates, One Time Varying Instrument

```
. xthtaylor Trade Gdp Sim Rlf Rer Cee Emu Dist Bor Lan, endog( Gdp Rlf Sim Cee
  Emu Lan)

Hausman-Taylor estimation                       Number of obs      =      3822
Group variable: id                              Number of groups   =        91

                                                Obs per group: min =        42
                                                               avg =        42
                                                               max =        42

Random effects u_i ~ i.i.d.                     Wald chi2(9)       =  32924.65
                                                Prob > chi2        =    0.0000

------------------------------------------------------------------------------
       Trade |      Coef.   Std. Err.      z    P>|z|     [95% Conf. Interval]
-------------+----------------------------------------------------------------
TVexogenous  |
         Rer |   .0609803   .0086367     7.06   0.000     .0440526     .077908
TVendogenous |
         Gdp |   1.812493   .0198284    91.41   0.000      1.77363    1.851356
         Rlf |   .0325083   .0078923     4.12   0.000     .0170397    .0479769
         Sim |   1.172255   .0555967    21.08   0.000     1.063288    1.281223
         Cee |   .3093359   .0160348    19.29   0.000     .2779083    .3407636
         Emu |   .0852087   .0268029     3.18   0.001      .032676    .1377415
TIexogenous  |
        Dist |  -.3815958   .1917947    -1.99   0.047    -.7575065   -.0056851
         Bor |   .6013204   .2586476     2.32   0.020     .0943805     1.10826
TIendogenous |
         Lan |   1.558674   .7070635     2.20   0.027     .1728551    2.944493
             |
       _cons |  -15.75991   1.502941   -10.49   0.000    -18.70562   -12.81419
-------------+----------------------------------------------------------------
     sigma_u |  .65096562
     sigma_e |  .29268254
         rho |  .83184173   (fraction of variance due to u_i)
------------------------------------------------------------------------------
Note: TV refers to time varying; TI refers to time invariant.
```

and Shin (2007, p.373). If Lan is correlated with the country pair effects, and is instrumented by real exchange rate (Rer), we get a higher effect of common language on Trade; see Table 7.6. Note that this is a just identified equation and the HT estimation will yield the same estimates as FE for the time-varying variables if we assume RER is the only exogenous time-varying variable and Lan is the only endogenous time-invariant variable; see Table 7.7.

If we assume Sim, Cee, Emu, and Lan are endogenous, we get an overidentified equation and the HT estimation yields the results given in Table 7.8. Note that this is not the same estimate as Lan in Table II of Serlenga and Shin (2007, p.373), and the HT estimates are not necessarily the same as FE for the time-varying variables.

(c) The Hausman test for overidentification when GDP, RLF and RER are used as instruments for Lan is based on the contrast between FE (bfe) and HT (bht2) and is shown in Table 7.9. This yields $\chi_2^2 = 2.24$ which is not significant at the 5% level. Note that Stata incorrectly gives 6 degrees of freedom for this test statistic; the observed test statistic (2.24) is correct but the corresponding degrees of freedom and p-value are not. This is not significant and does not reject the efficiency of the HT estimator.

Table 7.8 Gravity Models of Intra-EU Trade. Hausman and Taylor Estimates, Three Time Varying Instrument

```
xthtaylor Trade Gdp Sim Rlf Rer Cee Emu Dist Bor Lan, endog(Sim Cee Emu Lan)

Hausman-Taylor estimation                    Number of obs      =      3822
Group variable: id                           Number of groups   =        91

                                             Obs per group: min =        42
                                                            avg =        42
                                                            max =        42

Random effects u_i ~ i.i.d.                  Wald chi2(9)       =  33167.80
                                             Prob > chi2        =    0.0000

------------------------------------------------------------------------------
       Trade |      Coef.   Std. Err.      z    P>|z|     [95% Conf. Interval]
-------------+----------------------------------------------------------------
TVexogenous  |
         Gdp |   1.805507   .0192419    93.83   0.000     1.767794    1.843221
         Rlf |   .0325371   .0078427     4.15   0.000     .0171656    .0479086
         Rer |   .0625332   .0085438     7.32   0.000     .0457877    .0792786
TVendogenous |
         Sim |   1.197439   .0528833    22.64   0.000     1.093789    1.301088
         Cee |   .3109107   .0159875    19.45   0.000     .2795758    .3422455
         Emu |   .0855045   .0267842     3.19   0.001     .0330084    .1380005
TIexogenous  |
        Dist |  -.3775983   .1913561    -1.97   0.048    -.7526495   -.0025472
         Bor |   .6101144   .2636025     2.31   0.021     .0934629    1.126766
TIendogenous |
         Lan |   1.559897   .6754906     2.31   0.021     .2359596    2.883834
             |
       _cons |  -15.66188   1.496354   -10.47   0.000    -18.59468   -12.72908
-------------+----------------------------------------------------------------
     sigma_u |  .67259975
     sigma_e |  .29268254
         rho |  .84079079   (fraction of variance due to u_i)
------------------------------------------------------------------------------
Note: TV refers to time varying; TI refers to time invariant.
```

Table 7.9 Gravity Models of Intra-EU Trade. Hausman Test FE vs HT

```
.hausman bfe bht2

                 ---- Coefficients ----
             |      (b)          (B)            (b-B)     sqrt(diag(V_b-V_B))
             |      bfe          bht2         Difference          S.E.
-------------+----------------------------------------------------------------
         Gdp |    1.812493     1.805507         .006986         .0047453
         Sim |    1.172255     1.197439       -.0251831         .0170653
         Rlf |    .0325083     .0325371       -.0000288         .0008468
         Rer |    .0609803     .0625332       -.0015529         .0012338
         Cee |    .3093359     .3109107       -.0015748         .0011208
         Emu |    .0852087     .0855045       -.0002957         .0005279
------------------------------------------------------------------------------
                          b = consistent under Ho and Ha; obtained from xtreg
           B = inconsistent under Ha, efficient under Ho; obtained from xthtaylor

    Test:  Ho:  difference in coefficients not systematic

                  chi2(6) = (b-B)'[(V_b-V_B)^(-1)](b-B)
                          =        2.24
                Prob>chi2 =      0.8963
```

Exercise 7.17 *(Cornwell and Trumbull (1994): crime in North Carolina).* This is based on Problem 7.11 in Baltagi (2008). Cornwell and Trumbull (1994) estimated an economic model of crime using panel data on 90 counties in North Carolina over the period 1981–87. The empirical model relates the crime rate (which is an FBI index measuring the number of crimes divided by the county population) to a set of explanatory variables which include deterrent variables as well as variables measuring returns to legal opportunities. All variables are in logs except for the regional and time dummies. The explanatory variables consist of the probability of arrest (which is measured by the ratio of arrests to offenses), probability of conviction given arrest (which is measured by the ratio of convictions to arrests), probability of a prison sentence given a conviction (measured by the proportion of total convictions resulting in prison sentences). Average prison sentence in days is a proxy for sanction severity. The number of police per capita is a measure of the county's ability to detect crime. The population density is the county population divided by county land area. A dummy variable indicates whether the county is in the SMSA with population larger than 50 000. Percent minority is the proportion of the county's population that is minority or non-white. Percent young male is the proportion of the county's population that is male and between the ages of 15 and 24. There are regional dummies for western and central counties. Opportunities in the legal sector are captured by the average weekly wage in the county by industry. These industries are: construction; transportation, utilities and communication; wholesale and retail trade; finance, insurance and real estate; services; manufacturing; and federal, state and local government.

(a) Perform the FE estimator including the county and time dummies and comment on the results. These results should match those in Table 3 of Cornwell and Trumbull (1994).
(b) Cornwell and Trumbull worried about the endogeneity of police per capita and the probability of arrest. They used as instruments two additional variables. The first of these was offense mix, which is the ratio of crimes involving face-to-face contact (such as robbery, assault and rape) to those that do not. The rationale for using this variable is that arrest is facilitated by positive identification of the offender. The second instrument was per capita tax revenue. This is justified on the basis that counties with preferences

for law enforcement will vote for higher taxes to fund a larger police force. Compute the FE2SLS estimates using these two instruments and comment on the results. These results should match the results in Baltagi (2006a).

(c) Perform the EC2SLS estimator described in Exercise 7.4 and the G2SLS estimator described in (7.19) using the two instruments described in part (b).

(d) Using the results in Exercise 7.6 perform the Hausman test based on FE2SLS and EC2SLS. What do you conclude?

Solution

(a) Table 7.10 reports the FE results including both county and time dummies using Stata. They show that the probability of arrest, the probability of conviction given arrest, and

Table 7.10 FE Estimates of the Crime Equation for North Carolina

```
. xtreg  lcrmrte lprbarr lprbconv lprbpris lavgsen lpolpc ldensity lwcon lwtuc
lwtrd lwfir lwser lwmfg lwfed lwsta lwloc lpctymle d82 d83 d84 d85 d86 d87, fe

Fixed-effects (within) regression               Number of obs      =       630
Group variable (i): county                      Number of groups   =        90

R-sq:  within  = 0.4634                         Obs per group: min =         7
       between = 0.5537                                        avg =       7.0
       overall = 0.5445                                        max =         7

                                                F(22,518)          =     20.33
corr(u_i, Xb)  = -0.2394                        Prob > F           =    0.0000

------------------------------------------------------------------------------
     lcrmrte |      Coef.   Std. Err.      t    P>|t|     [95% Conf. Interval]
-------------+----------------------------------------------------------------
     lprbarr |  -.3548297   .0322049   -11.02   0.000    -.4180979   -.2915615
    lprbconv |  -.2815691   .0211376   -13.32   0.000    -.3230951   -.2400431
    lprbpris |  -.1731041   .0323027    -5.36   0.000    -.2365645   -.1096437
     lavgsen |   -.002453    .026119    -0.09   0.925    -.0537652    .0488592
      lpolpc |    .413162   .0266232    15.52   0.000     .3608593    .4654646
    ldensity |   .4143897   .2825413     1.47   0.143     -.140678    .9694573
       lwcon |  -.0377918   .0390756    -0.97   0.334    -.1145579    .0389743
       lwtuc |   .0455253   .0190115     2.39   0.017     .0081761    .0828745
       lwtrd |  -.0205017   .0404789    -0.51   0.613    -.1000247    .0590214
       lwfir |  -.0038992   .0282572    -0.14   0.890    -.0594119    .0516136
       lwser |   .0088771   .0191314     0.46   0.643    -.0287075    .0464618
       lwmfg |  -.3598524   .1118352    -3.22   0.001    -.5795587   -.1401461
       lwfed |  -.3093168   .1761642    -1.76   0.080     -.655401    .0367673
       lwsta |   .0528856   .1135305     0.47   0.642    -.1701513    .2759224
       lwloc |   .1816065   .1176542     1.54   0.123    -.0495315    .4127445
    lpctymle |   .6267536   .3636058     1.72   0.085    -.0875696    1.341077
         d82 |   .0226837    .025931     0.87   0.382    -.0282591    .0736265
         d83 |  -.0405141   .0357204    -1.13   0.257    -.1106887    .0296605
         d84 |  -.0434463   .0464791    -0.93   0.350     -.134757    .0478645
         d85 |   -.016551   .0634444    -0.26   0.794    -.1411909     .108089
         d86 |   .0347737   .0781032     0.45   0.656    -.1186643    .1882117
         d87 |   .0997564   .0930562     1.07   0.284    -.0830576    .2825704
       _cons |    2.39326   1.677812     1.43   0.154    -.9028932    5.689413
-------------+----------------------------------------------------------------
     sigma_u |  .37897131
     sigma_e |  .13652117
         rho |  .88513286   (fraction of variance due to u_i)
------------------------------------------------------------------------------
F test that all u_i=0:     F(89, 518) =     36.38            Prob > F = 0.0000
```

the probability of imprisonment given conviction all have a negative and significant effect on the crime rate, with estimated elasticities of −0.355, −0.282 and −0.173, respectively. The sentence severity has a negative but insignificant effect on the crime rate. The greater the number of police per capita, the greater the number of reported crimes per capita. The estimated elasticity is 0.413 and is significant. This could be explained by the fact that the larger the police force, the larger the reported crime. Alternatively, this could be an endogeneity problem with more crime resulting in the hiring of more police. The higher the density of the population the higher the crime rate, but this is non-significant. Returns to legal activity are non-significant except for wages in the manufacturing sector and wages in the transportation, utilities and communication sector. The manufacturing wage has a negative and significant effect on crime with an estimated elasticity of −0.36, while the transportation, utilities and communication sector wage has a positive and significant effect on crime with an estimated elasticity of 0.046. Percent young male is non-significant at the 5% level.

(b) Table 7.11 reports the FE2SLS results based on the replication by Baltagi (2006a). All deterrent variables had non-significant t-statistics. These include the probability of arrest, the probability of conviction given arrest, as well as the probability of imprisonment given conviction. Also non-significant were sentence severity, police per capita, and manufacturing wage.

(c) An alternative to dealing with the endogeneity problem is to run a random effects 2SLS estimator that allows for the endogeneity of police per capita and the probability of arrest. This estimator is a matrix-weighted average of between 2SLS and fixed effects 2SLS and was denoted by EC2SLS in Exercise 7.4. This was demonstrated using the (xtivreg, EC2SLS) command in Stata in Table 7.2 of Baltagi (2008, p.128). This is reproduced here as Table 7.12 for convenience. All the deterrent variables are significant, with slightly higher elasticities than fixed effects. The sentence severity variable is still non-significant and police per capita is still positive and significant. Manufacturing wage is negative and significant, and percent minority is positive and significant. Obtaining an estimate of the last coefficient is an advantage of EC2SLS over the fixed effects estimators, because it allows us to recapture estimates of variables that were invariant across time and wiped out by the fixed effects transformation. Table 7.13 gives the random effects (G2SLS) estimator described in (7.19) using the Stata command (xtivreg, re). This reproduces Table 7.3 of Baltagi (2008, p.129). G2SLS gives basically the same results as EC2SLS but the standard errors are higher. Remember that EC2SLS uses more instruments than G2SLS.

(d) Exercise 7.6 suggests a Hausman test based on FE2SLS and EC2SLS. For the crime data, this yields a Hausman statistic of 19.50 which is distributed as $\chi^2(22)$ and is non-significant with a p-value of 0.614. This does not reject the null hypothesis that EC2SLS yields a consistent estimator. This can be computed using the Hausman command after storing the EC2SLS and FE2SLS estimates (see Table 7.14). Recall that the random effects estimator was rejected by Cornwell and Trumbull (1994) based on the standard Hausman (1978) test. The latter was based on the contrast between fixed effects and random effects assuming that the endogeneity comes entirely from the correlation

Table 7.11 FE-2SLS Estimates of the Crime Equation

```
. xtivreg  lcrmrte lprbconv lprbpris lavgsen ldensity lwcon lwtuc lwtrd lwfir
lwser lwmfg lwfed lwsta lwloc lpctymle d82 d83 d84 d85 d86 d87 (lprbarr lpolpc=
lmix ltaxpc), fe

Fixed-effects (within) IV regression          Number of obs      =        630
Group variable: county                        Number of groups   =         90

R-sq:  within  = 0.3587                       Obs per group: min =          7
       between = 0.4442                                      avg =        7.0
       overall = 0.4431                                      max =          7

                                              Wald chi2(22)      = 368611.90
corr(u_i, Xb)  = -0.1867                      Prob > chi2        =    0.0000

------------------------------------------------------------------------------
     lcrmrte |      Coef.   Std. Err.      z    P>|z|     [95% Conf. Interval]
-------------+----------------------------------------------------------------
     lprbarr |  -.5755058    .8021842    -0.72   0.473    -2.147758    .9967464
      lpolpc |    .657527    .8468673     0.78   0.437    -1.002303    2.317356
    lprbconv |  -.4231446    .5019375    -0.84   0.399    -1.406924    .5606348
    lprbpris |   -.250255    .2794602    -0.90   0.371     -.797987    .2974769
     lavgsen |   .0090987    .0489879     0.19   0.853    -.0869157    .1051132
    ldensity |    .139412    1.021239     0.14   0.891     -1.86218    2.141004
       lwcon |  -.0287308    .0535145    -0.54   0.591    -.1336174    .0761558
       lwtuc |   .0391292    .0308568     1.27   0.205    -.0213491    .0996074
       lwtrd |  -.0177536    .0453142    -0.39   0.695    -.1065677    .0710605
       lwfir |  -.0093443    .0365519    -0.26   0.798    -.0809846     .062296
       lwser |   .0185854    .0388155     0.48   0.632    -.0574916    .0946623
       lwmfg |  -.2431684    .4195485    -0.58   0.562    -1.065468    .5791315
       lwfed |  -.4513372    .5271232    -0.86   0.392     -1.48448    .5818053
       lwsta |  -.0187458    .2808182    -0.07   0.947    -.5691393    .5316477
       lwloc |   .2632585    .3123945     0.84   0.399    -.3490235    .8755405
    lpctymle |   .3511166    1.011033     0.35   0.728    -1.630473    2.332706
         d82 |   .0378562     .061704     0.61   0.540    -.0830814    .1587939
         d83 |  -.0443801    .0423891    -1.05   0.295    -.1274613     .038701
         d84 |  -.0451868    .0549023    -0.82   0.410    -.1527933    .0624198
         d85 |  -.0209411    .0738508    -0.28   0.777    -.1656861    .1238039
         d86 |   .0063234    .1280571     0.05   0.961    -.2446639    .2573106
         d87 |   .0435055    .2158287     0.20   0.840     -.379511    .4665221
       _cons |   2.942906     2.69405     1.09   0.275    -2.337335    8.223148
-------------+----------------------------------------------------------------
     sigma_u |  .41829323
     sigma_e |  .14923892
         rho |  .88708128   (fraction of variance due to u_i)
------------------------------------------------------------------------------
F  test that all u_i=0:     F(89,518) =    29.66         Prob > F    = 0.0000
------------------------------------------------------------------------------
Instrumented:   lprbarr lpolpc
Instruments:    lprbconv lprbpris lavgsen ldensity lwcon lwtuc lwtrd lwfir
lwser lwmfg lwfed lwsta lwloc lpctymle d82 d83 d84 d85 d86 d87 lmix
ltaxpc
```

between the county effects and the explanatory variables. This does not account for the endogeneity of the conventional simultaneous equation type between police per capita and the probability of arrest and the crime rate. This alternative Hausman test based on the contrast between FE2SLS and EC2SLS failed to reject the null hypothesis. Accounting for this endogeneity, the random effects 2SLS becomes a viable estimator whose

Table 7.12 EC2SLS Estimates for the Crime Data

```
. xtivreg lcrmrte lprbconv lprbpris lavgsen ldensity lwcon lwtuc lwtrd lwfir
lwser lwmfg lwfed lwsta lwloc lpctymle lpctmin west central urban d82 d83 d84
d85 d86 d87 (lprbarr lpolpc= ltaxpc lmix), ec2sls

EC2SLS Random-effects regression               Number of obs      =       630
Group variable: county                         Number of groups   =        90

R-sq:  within  = 0.4521                        Obs per group: min =         7
       between = 0.8158                                       avg =       7.0
       overall = 0.7840                                       max =         7

                                               Wald chi2(26)      =    575.74
corr(u_i, X)       = 0 (assumed)               Prob > chi2        =    0.0000

------------------------------------------------------------------------------
     lcrmrte |      Coef.   Std. Err.      z    P>|z|     [95% Conf. Interval]
-------------+----------------------------------------------------------------
     lprbarr |  -.4129261    .097402    -4.24   0.000    -.6038305   -.2220218
      lpolpc |   .4347492    .089695     4.85   0.000     .2589502    .6105482
    lprbconv |  -.3228872   .0535517    -6.03   0.000    -.4278465   -.2179279
    lprbpris |  -.1863195   .0419382    -4.44   0.000    -.2685169   -.1041222
     lavgsen |  -.0101765   .0270231    -0.38   0.706    -.0631408    .0427877
    ldensity |   .4290282   .0548483     7.82   0.000     .3215275     .536529
       lwcon |  -.0074751   .0395775    -0.19   0.850    -.0850455    .0700954
       lwtuc |    .045445   .0197926     2.30   0.022     .0066522    .0842379
       lwtrd |  -.0081412   .0413828    -0.20   0.844    -.0892499    .0729676
       lwfir |  -.0036395   .0289238    -0.13   0.900    -.0603292    .0530502
       lwser |   .0056098   .0201259     0.28   0.780    -.0338361    .0450557
       lwmfg |  -.2041398   .0804393    -2.54   0.011     -.361798   -.0464816
       lwfed |  -.1635108   .1594496    -1.03   0.305    -.4760263    .1490047
       lwsta |  -.0540503   .1056769    -0.51   0.609    -.2611732    .1530727
       lwloc |   .1630523    .119638     1.36   0.173    -.0714339    .3975384
    lpctymle |  -.1081057   .1396949    -0.77   0.439    -.3819026    .1656912
     lpctmin |    .189037   .0414988     4.56   0.000     .1077009    .2703731
        west |  -.2268433   .0995913    -2.28   0.023    -.4220387   -.0316479
     central |  -.1940428   .0598241    -3.24   0.001    -.3112958   -.0767898
       urban |  -.2251539   .1156302    -1.95   0.052    -.4517851    .0014772
         d82 |   .0107452   .0257969     0.42   0.677    -.0398158    .0613062
         d83 |  -.0837944   .0307088    -2.73   0.006    -.1439825   -.0236063
         d84 |  -.1034997   .0370885    -2.79   0.005    -.1761918   -.0308076
         d85 |  -.0957017   .0494502    -1.94   0.053    -.1926223    .0012189
         d86 |  -.0688982   .0595956    -1.16   0.248    -.1857036    .0479071
         d87 |  -.0314071   .0705197    -0.45   0.656    -.1696232    .1068091
       _cons |  -.9538032   1.283966    -0.74   0.458    -3.470331    1.562725
-------------+----------------------------------------------------------------
     sigma_u |  .21455964
     sigma_e |  .14923892
         rho |  .67394413   (fraction of variance due to u_i)
------------------------------------------------------------------------------
Instrumented:  lprbarr lpolpc
Instruments:   lprbconv lprbpris lavgsen ldensity lwcon lwtuc lwtrd lwfir lwser
               lwmfg lwfed lwsta lwloc lpctymle lpctmin west central urban d82
               d83 d84 d85 d86 d87 ltaxpc lmix
```

Table 7.13 Random Effects 2SLS Estimates for the Crime Data (G2SLS)

```
. xtivreg lcrmrte lprbconv lprbpris lavgsen ldensity lwcon lwtuc lwtrd lwfir
lwser lwmfg lwfed lwsta lwloc lpctymle lpctmin west central urban d82 d83 d84
d85 d86 d87 (lprbarr lpolpc= ltaxpc lmix), re

G2SLS Random-effects regression                 Number of obs      =       630
Group variable: county                          Number of groups   =        90

R-sq:  within  = 0.4521                         Obs per group: min =         7
       between = 0.8036                                        avg =       7.0
       overall = 0.7725                                        max =         7

                                                Wald chi2(26)      =    542.48
corr(u_i, X)       = 0 (assumed)                Prob > chi2        =    0.0000

------------------------------------------------------------------------------
     lcrmrte |      Coef.   Std. Err.      z    P>|z|     [95% Conf. Interval]
-------------+----------------------------------------------------------------
     lprbarr |  -.4141383   .2210496    -1.87   0.061    -.8473875    .0191109
      lpolpc |   .5049461   .2277778     2.22   0.027     .0585098    .9513824
    lprbconv |  -.3432506   .1324648    -2.59   0.010    -.6028768   -.0836244
    lprbpris |  -.1900467   .0733392    -2.59   0.010     -.333789   -.0463045
     lavgsen |  -.0064389   .0289407    -0.22   0.824    -.0631617    .0502838
    ldensity |   .4343449   .0711496     6.10   0.000     .2948943    .5737956
       lwcon |  -.0042958   .0414226    -0.10   0.917    -.0854826    .0768911
       lwtuc |   .0444589   .0215448     2.06   0.039     .0022318    .0866859
       lwtrd |  -.0085579   .0419829    -0.20   0.838    -.0908428     .073727
       lwfir |  -.0040305   .0294569    -0.14   0.891    -.0617649    .0537038
       lwser |   .0105602   .0215823     0.49   0.625    -.0317403    .0528608
       lwmfg |   -.201802   .0839373    -2.40   0.016    -.3663161   -.0372878
       lwfed |  -.2134579   .2151046    -0.99   0.321    -.6350551    .2081393
       lwsta |  -.0601232   .1203149    -0.50   0.617     -.295936    .1756896
       lwloc |   .1835363   .1396775     1.31   0.189    -.0902265    .4572992
    lpctymle |  -.1458703   .2268086    -0.64   0.520    -.5904071    .2986664
     lpctmin |   .1948763   .0459385     4.24   0.000     .1048384    .2849141
        west |  -.2281821    .101026    -2.26   0.024    -.4261894   -.0301747
     central |  -.1987703   .0607475    -3.27   0.001    -.3178332   -.0797075
       urban |  -.2595451   .1499718    -1.73   0.084    -.5534844    .0343942
         d82 |   .0132147   .0299924     0.44   0.660    -.0455692    .0719987
         d83 |  -.0847693    .032001    -2.65   0.008    -.1474901   -.0220485
         d84 |  -.1062027   .0387893    -2.74   0.006    -.1822284   -.0301769
         d85 |  -.0977457   .0511681    -1.91   0.056    -.1980334     .002542
         d86 |  -.0719451   .0605819    -1.19   0.235    -.1906835    .0467933
         d87 |  -.0396595   .0758531    -0.52   0.601    -.1883289    .1090099
       _cons |  -.4538501   1.702983    -0.27   0.790    -3.791636    2.883935
-------------+----------------------------------------------------------------
     sigma_u |  .21455964
     sigma_e |  .14923892
         rho |  .67394413   (fraction of variance due to u_i)
------------------------------------------------------------------------------
Instrumented:  lprbarr lpolpc
Instruments:   lprbconv lprbpris lavgsen ldensity lwcon lwtuc lwtrd lwfir lwser
               lwmfg lwfed lwsta lwloc lpctymle lpctmin west central urban d82
               d83 d84 d85 d86 d87 ltaxpc lmix
```

Table 7.14 Hausman's Test Based on FE2SLS and EC2SLS

```
hausman fe2sls ec2sls

                 ---- Coefficients ----
             |      (b)          (B)            (b-B)     sqrt(diag(V_b-V_B))
             |    fe2sls       ec2sls        Difference          S.E.
-------------+----------------------------------------------------------------
     lprbarr |   -.5755058    -.4129261       -.1625797        .7962489
      lpolpc |     .657527     .4347492        .2227778         .842104
    lprbconv |   -.4231446    -.3228872       -.1002574        .4990726
    lprbpris |    -.250255    -.1863195       -.0639355        .2762955
     lavgsen |    .0090987    -.0101765        .0192753        .0408603
    ldensity |     .139412     .4290282       -.2896163        1.019765
       lwcon |   -.0287308    -.0074751       -.0212557        .0360198
       lwtuc |    .0391292      .045445       -.0063159        .0236727
       lwtrd |   -.0177536    -.0081412       -.0096124        .0184619
       lwfir |   -.0093443    -.0036395       -.0057048        .0223484
       lwser |    .0185854     .0056098        .0129756        .0331902
       lwmfg |   -.2431684    -.2041398       -.0390286         .411765
       lwfed |   -.4513372    -.1635108       -.2878264        .5024288
       lwsta |   -.0187458    -.0540503        .0353045        .2601754
       lwloc |    .2632585     .1630523        .1002063        .2885777
    lpctymle |    .3511166    -.1081057        .4592223        1.001336
         d82 |    .0378562     .0107452        .0271111        .0560527
         d83 |   -.0443801    -.0837944        .0394143          .02922
         d84 |   -.0451868    -.1034997        .0583129         .040481
         d85 |   -.0209411    -.0957017        .0747606         .054851
         d86 |    .0063234    -.0688982        .0752216        .1133445
         d87 |    .0435055    -.0314071        .0749126        .2039829
------------------------------------------------------------------------------
                    b = consistent under Ho and Ha; obtained from xtivreg
       B = inconsistent under Ha, efficient under Ho; obtained from xtivreg

    Test:  Ho:  difference in coefficients not systematic

                  chi2(22) = (b-B)'[(V_b-V_B)^(-1)](b-B)
                           =        19.50
                Prob>chi2 =       0.6140
```

consistency cannot be rejected. This example confirms Cornwell and Trumbull's (1994) conclusion that county effects cannot be ignored in estimating an economic model of crime using panel data in North Carolina. It also shows that the usual Hausman test based on the difference between fixed effects and random effects may lead to misleading inference if there are endogenous regressors of the conventional simultaneous equation type. An alternative Hausman test based on the difference between fixed effects 2SLS and random effects 2SLS did not reject the consistency of random effects 2SLS, an estimator which yields plausible estimates of the crime equation.

8

Dynamic Panels

Many economic relationships are dynamic in nature, and one of the advantages of panel data is that they allow the researcher to better understand the dynamics of adjustment. See, for example, Arellano and Bond (1991) on a dynamic model of employment. These dynamic relationships are characterized by the presence of a lagged dependent variable among the regressors, i.e.,

$$y_{it} = \delta y_{i,t-1} + x'_{it}\beta + u_{it}, \quad i = 1, \ldots, N, \quad t = 1, \ldots, T \tag{8.1}$$

where δ is a scalar, x'_{it} is $1 \times K$ and β is $K \times 1$. We will assume that the u_{it} follow a one-way error component model

$$u_{it} = \mu_i + \nu_{it} \tag{8.2}$$

where $\mu_i \sim \text{IID}(0, \sigma_\mu^2)$ and $\nu_{it} \sim \text{IID}(0, \sigma_\nu^2)$ independent of each other and among themselves. The dynamic panel data regression described in (8.1) and (8.2) is characterized by two sources of persistence over time: Autocorrelation due to the presence of a lagged dependent variable among the regressors; and individual effects characterizing the heterogeneity among the individuals.

Exercise 8.1 *(Bias of OLS, FE and RE estimators in a dynamic panel data model).* Show that OLS, fixed effects and random effects estimators of (8.1) are biased and inconsistent for fixed T as N gets large.

Solution

Since y_{it} is a function of μ_i, it immediately follows that $y_{i,t-1}$ is also a function of μ_i. Therefore, $y_{i,t-1}$, a right-hand-side regressor in (8.1), is correlated with the error term. This renders the OLS estimator biased and inconsistent even if the ν_{it} are not serially correlated.

For the FE estimator, the within transformation wipes out the μ_i, but the right-hand-side regressor $\widetilde{y}_{i,t-1} = (y_{i,t-1} - \overline{y}_{i.-1})$, where $\overline{y}_{i.-1} = \sum_{t=2}^{T} y_{i,t-1}/(T-1)$, will still be correlated with $(\nu_{it} - \overline{\nu}_{i.})$ even if the ν_{it} are not serially correlated. This is because $y_{i,t-1}$ is correlated with $\overline{\nu}_{i.}$ by construction, since the latter term contains $\nu_{i,t-1}$. In fact, the within estimator will have $O(1/T)$ bias and be inconsistent for T fixed; see Nickell (1981). More recently, Kiviet (1995) derived an approximation for the bias of the within estimator in a dynamic panel data model with serially uncorrelated disturbances and strongly exogenous regressors.

The random effects GLS estimator is also biased in a dynamic panel data model. In order to apply GLS, quasi-demeaning is performed, and the right-hand-side regressor $y^*_{i,t-1} = (y_{i,t-1} - \theta\overline{y}_{i.,-1})$ will be correlated with $u^*_{i,t} = (u_{i,t} - \theta\overline{u}_{i.,-1})$, again because $y_{i,t-1}$ is correlated with $\overline{u}_{i.,-1}$ by construction since the latter term contains $\nu_{i,t-1}$.

Exercise 8.2 *(Anderson and Hsiao (1981) estimator).* Show that if we first-difference (FD) the model in (8.1) and apply an instrumental variable (IV) estimator using $y_{i,t-2}$ or $\Delta y_{i,t-2}$ as an instrument for $\Delta y_{i,t-1} = (y_{i,t-1} - y_{i,t-2})$, we get a consistent estimator suggested by Anderson and Hsiao (1981).

Solution

Note that the FD transformation is an alternative transformation that wipes out the individual effects. In fact, $\Delta u_{it} = \Delta \nu_{it} = \nu_{i,t} - \nu_{i,t-1}$, and μ_i drops out. The FD estimator is biased and inconsistent since $y_{i,t-1}$ is correlated with $\nu_{i,t-1}$. However, in this case, it is easier to deal with the correlation between the right-hand-side differenced predetermined explanatory variables, i.e., $\Delta y_{i,t-1} = (y_{i,t-1} - y_{i,t-2})$, and the remainder error term, $\Delta \nu_{it} = \nu_{i,t} - \nu_{i,t-1}$. Note that $y_{i,t-2}$, unlike $y_{i,t-1}$, is not correlated with $\nu_{i,t-1}$, as long as there is no serial correlation in the ν_{it}. Anderson and Hsiao (1981) suggested using $y_{i,t-2}$ or $\Delta y_{i,t-2} = (y_{i,t-2} - y_{i,t-3})$ as an instrument for $\Delta y_{i,t-1} = (y_{i,t-1} - y_{i,t-2})$. These instruments will be correlated with the right-hand-side regressor $\Delta y_{i,t-1} = (y_{i,t-1} - y_{i,t-2})$, but not correlated with the remainder error $\Delta \nu_{it} = \nu_{i,t} - \nu_{i,t-1}$. This IV estimation method leads to consistent but not necessarily efficient estimates of the parameters in the model because it does not make use of all the available moment conditions, as we will see in the next problem, and because it does not take into account the differenced structure on the residual disturbances ($\Delta \nu_{it}$).

Exercise 8.3 *(Arellano and Bond (1991) estimator).* This is based on Problem 8.1 in Baltagi (2008). Consider the simple autoregressive model given by (8.1) but with no regressors:

$$y_{it} = \delta y_{i,t-1} + u_{it}, \quad i = 1, \ldots, N, \quad t = 1, \ldots, T \tag{8.3}$$

where u_{it} is given by (8.2). Difference (8.3) to eliminate the individual effects

$$y_{it} - y_{i,t-1} = \delta(y_{i,t-1} - y_{i,t-2}) + (\nu_{it} - \nu_{i,t-1}) \tag{8.4}$$

and note that $(\nu_{it} - \nu_{i,t-1})$ is MA(1) with unit root.

(a) Show that for $t = 3$, y_{i1} is a valid instrument for the right-hand-side regressor in (8.4). For $t = 4$, show that (y_{i1}, y_{i2}) are valid instruments for the right-hand-side regressor in (8.4). Deduce that for period T, $(y_{i1}, y_{i2}, \ldots, y_{i,T-2})$ are valid instruments for the right-hand-side regressor in (8.4).
(b) Stack the differenced equations for $t = 3, 4, \ldots, T$ on top of each other for each individual and derive the variance–covariance matrix of the disturbances of this system. Now stack these differenced errors on top of each other for each individual $i = 1, 2, \ldots, N$. Derive the variance–covariance matrix of the disturbances of this system.
(c) Premultiply this system of equations by the matrix of valid instruments described in part (a) and perform GLS on the transformed model using the variance–covariance matrix derived in (b). The resulting estimator is the one-step generalized method of moments (GMM) estimator of δ_1 suggested by Arellano and Bond (1991).

Solution

(a) For $t = 3$, the first period we observe this relationship, we have

$$y_{i3} - y_{i2} = \delta(y_{i2} - y_{i1}) + (v_{i3} - v_{i2})$$

In this case, y_{i1} is a valid instrument, since it is highly correlated with $(y_{i2} - y_{i1})$ and not correlated with $(v_{i3} - v_{i2})$ as long as the v_{it} are not serially correlated. This utilizes the moment condition $E(y_{i1}\Delta v_{i3}) = 0$. But note what happens for $t = 4$, the second period we observe (8.4):

$$y_{i4} - y_{i3} = \delta(y_{i3} - y_{i2}) + (v_{i4} - v_{i3})$$

In this case, y_{i2} as well as y_{i1} are valid instruments for $(y_{i3} - y_{i2})$, since both y_{i2} and y_{i1} are not correlated with $(v_{i4} - v_{i3})$. This utilizes the moment conditions

$$E(y_{i1}\Delta v_{i4}) = E(y_{i2}\Delta v_{i4}) = 0$$

One can continue in this fashion, adding an extra valid instrument with each forward period, so that for period T, the set of valid instruments becomes $(y_{i1}, y_{i2}, \ldots, y_{i,T-2})$.

(b) $\Delta v_i' = (v_{i3} - v_{i2}, \ldots, v_{iT} - v_{i,T-1})$, with $v_{it} \sim \text{IID}(0, \sigma_v^2)$. Therefore,

$$(\Delta v_i \Delta v_i') = E\begin{pmatrix} v_{i3} - v_{i2} \\ v_{i4} - v_{i3} \\ \vdots \\ v_{iT} - v_{i,T-1} \end{pmatrix}(v_{i3} - v_{i2}, \ldots, v_{iT} - v_{i,T-1})$$

$$= \sigma_v^2 \begin{bmatrix} 2 & -1 & 0 & \cdots & 0 & 0 \\ -1 & 2 & -1 & \cdots & 0 & 0 \\ \vdots & \vdots & \vdots & \ddots & \vdots & \vdots \\ 0 & 0 & 0 & \cdots & 2 & -1 \\ 0 & 0 & 0 & \cdots & -1 & 2 \end{bmatrix} = \sigma_v^2 G \qquad (8.5)$$

This follows because $\Delta v_{it} = v_{it} - v_{i,t-1}$ is MA(1) with unit root, so that the variance is always equal to $\text{var}(v_{it}) + \text{var}(v_{i,t-1}) = 2\sigma_v^2$ and the covariance is $-\sigma_v^2$ for one-period-apart first differences and zero otherwise. G is a $(T-2) \times (T-2)$ matrix with 2 on the diagonal and -1 on the two adjacent parallel diagonals. The system differenced error term stacking Δv_i on top of each other for $i = 1, 2, \ldots, N$ yields the variance–covariance matrix $E(\Delta v \Delta v') = \sigma_v^2(I_N \otimes G)$.

(c) Define W_i to be the matrix of instruments for individual i described in part (a):

$$W_i = \begin{bmatrix} [y_{i1}] & & & 0 \\ & [y_{i1}, y_{i2}] & & \\ & & \ddots & \\ 0 & & & [y_{i1}, \ldots, y_{i,T-2}] \end{bmatrix} \qquad (8.6)$$

Stack the matrices of instruments for each individual $i = 1, 2, \ldots, N$ on top of each other to get $W = [W_1', \ldots, W_N']'$. The moment restrictions resulting from these instruments are given by $E(W_i'\Delta\nu_i) = 0$. Premultiplying the differenced equation (8.4) in vector form by W' gives

$$W'\Delta y = W'(\Delta y_{-1})\delta + W'\Delta\nu \tag{8.7}$$

Performing GLS on (8.7) leads to the Arellano and Bond (1991) one-step GMM consistent estimator of δ_1 given by

$$\begin{aligned}\widehat{\delta_1} &= [(\Delta y_{-1})'W(W'(I_N \otimes G)W)^{-1}W'(\Delta y_{-1})]^{-1} \\ &\times[(\Delta y_{-1})'W(W'(I_N \otimes G)W)^{-1}W'(\Delta y)]\end{aligned} \tag{8.8}$$

with asymptotic variance var($\widehat{\delta_1}$) given by the first term in (8.8).

The optimal GMM estimator of δ_1 for $N \to \infty$ and T fixed using only the above moment restrictions yields the same expression as in (8.8), except that

$$W'(I_N \otimes G)W = \sum_{i=1}^{N} W_i'GW_i$$

is replaced by

$$V_N = \sum_{i=1}^{N} W_i'(\Delta\nu_i)(\Delta\nu_i)'W_i$$

To operationalize this estimator, $\Delta\nu$ is replaced by differenced residuals obtained from the one-step consistent estimator $\widehat{\delta_1}$. The resulting estimator is the two-step Arellano and Bond (1991) GMM estimator:

$$\widehat{\delta_2} = [(\Delta y_{-1})'W\widehat{V}_N^{-1}W'(\Delta y_{-1})]^{-1}[(\Delta y_{-1})'W\widehat{V}_N^{-1}W'(\Delta y)] \tag{8.9}$$

A consistent estimate of the asymptotic variance var($\widehat{\delta_2}$) is given by the first term in (8.9). Arellano and Bond (1991) suggest Sargan's (1958) test of overidentifying restrictions given by

$$m = \Delta\widehat{\nu}'W\left[\sum_{i=1}^{N} W_i'(\Delta\widehat{\nu}_i)(\Delta\widehat{\nu}_i)'W_i\right]^{-1} W'(\Delta\widehat{\nu}) \sim \chi^2_{p-K-1} \tag{8.10}$$

where p refers to the number of columns of W and $\Delta\widehat{\nu}$ denote the residuals from a two-step estimation given in (8.9).

Exercise 8.4 *(Sargan's (1958) test of overidentifying restrictions).* This is based on Problem 8.3 in Baltagi (2008). Consider the simple autoregressive model with no regressors given in (8.3).

(a) For $T = 3$, show that for the Arellano and Bond (1991) estimator, there is only one restriction identifying δ. Hence, the model is just identified.

(b) For $T = 5$, show that for the Arellano and Bond (1991) estimator, there are six restrictions identifying δ. Hence, the model is overidentified, and Sargan's (1958) test of overidentifying restrictions tests five restrictions.

Solution

(a) For $T = 3$, there is only one orthogonal restriction identifying one parameter δ, given by

$$E[(y_{i,1}(\nu_{i,3} - \nu_{i,2})] = 0$$

The first restriction can be used to identify δ even if there are individual effects in (8.3). Hence, the model is just identified.

(b) For $T = 5$, there are six restrictions identifying δ, given by

$$E[y_{i1}(\nu_{it} - \nu_{i,t-1})] = 0 \quad \text{for } t = 3, 4, 5$$

$$E[y_{i2}(\nu_{it} - \nu_{i,t-1})] = 0 \quad \text{for } t = 4, 5$$

$$E[y_{i3}(\nu_{i5} - \nu_{i,4})] = 0 \quad \text{for } t = 5$$

Hence, the model is overidentified, and Sargan's (1958) test for overidentifying restrictions tests five restrictions.

Ahn and Schmidt (1995) show that under the standard assumptions used in a dynamic panel data model, there are additional moment conditions that are ignored by Arellano and Bond (1991). Consider the simple dynamic model with no regressors given in (8.3) and assume that $y_{i0}, \ldots, y_{iT}$ are observable. In vector form, this is given by

$$y_i = \delta y_{i-1} + u_i \tag{8.11}$$

where $y_i' = (y_{i1}, \ldots, y_{iT})$, $y_{i-1}' = (y_{i0}, \ldots, y_{i,T-1})$, and $u_i' = (u_{i1}, \ldots, u_{iT})$. The standard assumptions on the dynamic model are as follows:

(A.1) For all i, ν_{it} is uncorrelated with y_{i0} for all t.
(A.2) For all i, ν_{it} is uncorrelated with μ_i for all t.
(A.3) For all i, the ν_{it} are mutually uncorrelated.

Ahn and Schmidt (1995) argue that these assumptions on the initial value y_{i0} are weaker than those often made in the literature (see Hsiao, 2003). Under these assumptions, one obtains the following $T(T-1)/2$ moment conditions:

$$E(y_{is}\Delta u_{it}) = 0, \quad t = 2, \ldots, T, \quad s = 0, \ldots, t-2 \tag{8.12}$$

These are the same moment restrictions given after (8.6) and exploited by Arellano and Bond (1991). However, Ahn and Schmidt (1995) find $T - 2$ additional moment conditions not implied by (8.12). These are given by

$$E(u_{iT}\Delta u_{it}) = 0, \quad t = 2, \ldots, T-1 \tag{8.13}$$

Therefore, (8.12) and (8.13) imply a set of $T(T-1)/2 + (T-2)$ moment conditions which represent all of the moment conditions implied by the assumptions that the ν_{it} are mutually uncorrelated among themselves and with μ_i and y_{i0}.

Exercise 8.5 *(Ahn and Schmidt (1995) moment conditions).* Set up the variance–covariance matrix for ν_{it}, μ_i and y_{i0}. Show that these imply $T(T-1)/2+(T-2)$ restrictions on the variance–covariance matrix for the observable disturbances u_{it} and y_{i0}.

Solution

The variance–covariance matrix for ν_{it}, μ_i and y_{i0} is given by

$$\Sigma = \mathrm{cov}\begin{bmatrix} \nu_{i1} \\ \nu_{i2} \\ \vdots \\ \nu_{iT} \\ y_{i0} \\ \mu_i \end{bmatrix} = \begin{bmatrix} \sigma_{11} & \sigma_{12} & \cdots & \sigma_{1T} & \sigma_{10} & \sigma_{1\mu} \\ \sigma_{21} & \sigma_{22} & \cdots & \sigma_{2T} & \sigma_{20} & \sigma_{2\mu} \\ \vdots & \vdots & & \vdots & \vdots & \vdots \\ \sigma_{T1} & \sigma_{T2} & \cdots & \sigma_{TT} & \sigma_{T0} & \sigma_{T\mu} \\ \sigma_{01} & \sigma_{02} & \cdots & \sigma_{0T} & \sigma_{00} & \sigma_{0\mu} \\ \sigma_{\mu 1} & \sigma_{\mu 2} & \cdots & \sigma_{\mu T} & \sigma_{\mu 0} & \sigma_{\mu\mu} \end{bmatrix} \tag{8.14}$$

But, we do not observe μ_i and ν_{it}, only their sum $u_{it}=\mu_i+\nu_{it}$ which can be written in terms of the data and δ. Hence, to get observable moment restrictions, we have to look at the following covariance matrix:

$$\Lambda = \mathrm{cov}\begin{bmatrix} \mu_i+\nu_{i1} \\ \mu_i+\nu_{i2} \\ \vdots \\ \mu_i+\nu_{iT} \\ y_{i0} \end{bmatrix} = \begin{bmatrix} \lambda_{11} & \lambda_{12} & \cdots & \lambda_{1T} & \lambda_{10} \\ \lambda_{21} & \lambda_{22} & \cdots & \lambda_{2T} & \lambda_{20} \\ \vdots & \vdots & & \vdots & \vdots \\ \lambda_{T1} & \lambda_{T2} & \cdots & \lambda_{TT} & \lambda_{T0} \\ \lambda_{01} & \lambda_{02} & \cdots & \lambda_{0T} & \lambda_{00} \end{bmatrix}$$

$$= \begin{bmatrix} \sigma_{\mu\mu}+\sigma_{11}+2\sigma_{\mu 1} & \sigma_{\mu\mu}+\sigma_{12}+\sigma_{\mu 1}+\sigma_{\mu 2} & \cdots & \sigma_{\mu\mu}+\sigma_{1T}+\sigma_{\mu 1}+\sigma_{\mu T} & \sigma_{0\mu}+\sigma_{01} \\ \sigma_{\mu\mu}+\sigma_{12}+\sigma_{\mu 1}+\sigma_{\mu 2} & \sigma_{\mu\mu}+\sigma_{22}+2\sigma_{\mu 2} & \cdots & \sigma_{\mu\mu}+\sigma_{2T}+\sigma_{\mu 2}+\sigma_{\mu T} & \sigma_{0\mu}+\sigma_{02} \\ \vdots & \vdots & \cdots & \vdots & \vdots \\ \sigma_{\mu\mu}+\sigma_{1T}+\sigma_{\mu 1}+\sigma_{\mu T} & \sigma_{\mu\mu}+\sigma_{2T}+\sigma_{\mu 2}+\sigma_{\mu T} & \cdots & \sigma_{\mu\mu}+\sigma_{TT}+2\sigma_{\mu T} & \sigma_{0\mu}+\sigma_{0T} \\ \sigma_{0\mu}+\sigma_{01} & \sigma_{0\mu}+\mu_{02} & \cdots & \sigma_{0\mu}+\sigma_{0T} & \sigma_{00} \end{bmatrix} \tag{8.15}$$

Under the standard assumptions (A.1)–(A.3), we have $\sigma_{ts}=0$ for all $t\neq s$, and $\sigma_{\mu t}=\sigma_{0t}=0$ for all t. Then Λ simplifies as follows:

$$\Lambda = \begin{bmatrix} (\sigma_{\mu\mu}+\sigma_{11}) & \sigma_{\mu\mu} & \cdots & \sigma_{\mu\mu} & \sigma_{0\mu} \\ \sigma_{\mu\mu} & (\sigma_{\mu\mu}+\sigma_{22}) & \cdots & \sigma_{\mu\mu} & \sigma_{0\mu} \\ \vdots & \vdots & & \vdots & \vdots \\ \sigma_{\mu\mu} & \sigma_{\mu\mu} & \cdots & (\sigma_{\mu\mu}+\sigma_{TT}) & \sigma_{0\mu} \\ \sigma_{0\mu} & \sigma_{0\mu} & \cdots & \sigma_{0\mu} & \sigma_{00} \end{bmatrix} \tag{8.16}$$

Therefore, the standard assumptions given by (A.1)–(A.3), impose $T-1$ restrictions, that $\lambda_{0t}=E(y_{i0}u_{it})$ is the same for $t=1,\ldots,T$, and $T(T-1)/2-1$ restrictions, that $\lambda_{ts}=E(u_{is}u_{it})$ is the same for $t,s=1,\ldots,T$, $t\neq s$. Summing the number of restrictions, we get $T(T-1)/2+(T-2)$.

In order to see how these additional moment restrictions are utilized, consider our simple dynamic model in differenced form, along with the last period's observation in levels:

$$\Delta y_{it} = \delta \Delta y_{i,t-1} + \Delta u_{it}, \quad t = 2, 3, \ldots, T \tag{8.17}$$

$$y_{iT} = \delta y_{i,T-1} + u_{iT} \tag{8.18}$$

The usual IV estimator, utilizing the restrictions in (8.12), amounts to estimating the FD equations (8.17) by three-stage least squares, imposing the restriction that δ is the same in every equation, where the instrument set is y_{i0} for $t = 2, (y_{i0}, y_{i1})$ for $t = 3, \ldots, (y_{i0}, \ldots, y_{i,T-2})$ for $t = T$. Even though there are no legitimate observable instruments for the levels equation (8.18), Ahn and Schmidt argue that (8.18) is still useful in estimation because of the additional covariance restrictions implied by (8.13), i.e., that the u_{iT} are uncorrelated with Δu_{it} for $t = 2, \ldots, T-1$. Ahn and Schmidt show that any additional covariance restrictions besides (8.13) are redundant and implied by the basic moment conditions given by (8.12).

Exercise 8.6 *(Ahn and Schmidt (1995) additional moment conditions).* This is based on Problem 8.6 in Baltagi (2008). For $T = 4$ and the simple autoregressive model considered in (8.3):

(a) What are the moment restrictions given by (8.12)? Compare with Exercise 8.4.
(b) What are the additional moment restrictions given by (8.13)?
(c) Write down the system of equations to be estimated by 3SLS using these additional restrictions and list the matrix of instruments for each equation.

Solution

(a) For the simple autoregressive model considered in (8.3), the moment restrictions described in (8.12) yield

$$E(y_{is}\Delta u_{it}) = 0, \quad t = 2, 3, 4, \quad s = 0, \ldots, t-2$$

which can be rewritten as

$$\begin{array}{ll} t = 2 & E[y_{io}(u_{i2} - u_{i1})] = 0 \\ t = 3 & E[y_{io}(u_{i3} - u_{i2})] = 0 \text{ and } E[y_{i1}(u_{i3} - u_{i2})] = 0 \\ t = 4 & E[y_{io}(u_{i4} - u_{i3})] = 0, \ [y_{i1}(u_{i4} - u_{i3})] = 0, \text{ and } E[y_{i2}(u_{i4} - u_{i3})] = 0 \end{array}$$

Since the initial period is zero, not one, this compares with Exercise 8.4 (for $T = 5$ with the initial period one). In fact, these are the same $6 = T(T-1)/2$ restrictions given in that problem.

(b) The additional $2 = T - 2$ moment restrictions given by (8.13) are

$$E(u_{i4}\Delta u_{it}) = 0 \quad \text{for } t = 2, 3$$

or simply

$$E[u_{i4}(u_{i2} - u_{i1})] = 0 \quad \text{and} \quad E[u_{i4}(u_{i3} - u_{i2})] = 0$$

Note that $u_{i4} = \mu_i + \nu_{i4}$ and $u_{i2} - u_{i1} = \nu_{i2} - \nu_{i1}$. $E[u_{i4}(u_{i2} - u_{i1})] = 0$ follows from the fact that μ_i is not correlated with ν_{it}, and ν_{i4} is not correlated with $(\nu_{i2} - \nu_{i1})$.

(c) The system of equations to be estimated by 3SLS using these conditional restrictions is given in (8.17) and (8.18). For $T = 4$, these reduce to the four equations

$$\begin{aligned} y_{i2} - y_{i1} &= \delta(y_{i1} - y_{io}) + (u_{i2} - u_{i1}) \\ y_{i3} - y_{i2} &= \delta(y_{i2} - y_{i1}) + (u_{i3} - u_{i2}) \\ y_{i4} - y_{i3} &= \delta(y_{i3} - y_{i2}) + (u_{i4} - u_{i3}) \\ y_{i4} &= \delta y_{i3} + u_{i4} \end{aligned}$$

The set of instruments is given by

$$W_i = \begin{pmatrix} y_{i0} & 0 & 0 \\ 0 & [y_{i0}, y_{i1}] & 0 \\ 0 & 0 & [y_{i0}, y_{i1}, y_{i2}] \end{pmatrix}$$

There are no legitimate observable instruments for the last equation. However, it is included in the system estimation because of the additional covariance restrictions implied by the orthogonality conditions given in part (b).

Exercise 8.7 *(Arellano and Bond (1991) weak instruments).* Consider the simple autoregressive panel data model with no exogenous regressors given in (8.3). Focus on the case where $T = 3$, i.e., where there is only one orthogonality condition given by $E(y_{i1}\Delta u_{i3}) = 0$, so that δ is just identified (see Exercise 8.4). In this case, the first-stage IV regression is obtained by running Δy_{i2} on y_{i1}. Show that in the typical case where $E(y_{i1}\mu_i)>0$, as in the earnings equation with y denoting earnings and μ_i denoting ability, this first-stage regression yields a biased estimator of δ.

Solution

Note that the first-stage IV regression can be obtained from (8.3) by evaluating it at $t = 2$ and subtracting y_{i1} from both sides of this equation, i.e.,

$$\Delta y_{i2} = (\delta - 1)y_{i,1} + \mu_i + \nu_{i2} \tag{8.19}$$

In this case, we did not difference the equation and μ_i is not differenced out. Since we expect $E(y_{i1}\mu_i) > 0$, $(\delta - 1)$ will be biased upwards with

$$\text{plim}(\widehat{\delta} - 1) = (\delta - 1)\frac{c}{c + (\sigma_\mu^2/\sigma_u^2)} \tag{8.20}$$

where $c = (1 - \delta)/(1 + \delta)$; see Blundell and Bond (1998). The bias term effectively scales the estimated coefficient on the instrumental variable y_{i1} towards zero. In fact, Blundell and Bond also find that the F-statistic of the first-stage IV regression converges to χ_1^2 with non-centrality parameter

$$\tau = \frac{(\sigma_u^2 c)^2}{\sigma_\mu^2 + \sigma_u^2 c} \to 0 \quad \text{as} \quad \delta \to 1 \tag{8.21}$$

As $\tau \to 0$, the instrumental variable estimator performs poorly. Hence, Blundell and Bond attribute the bias and the poor precision of the FD GMM estimator to the problem of weak instruments and characterize this weak IV by its concentration parameter τ.

Arellano and Bover (1995) develop a unifying GMM framework for looking at efficient IV estimators for dynamic panel data models. They do that in the context of the Hausman and Taylor (1981) model (see Exercise 7.14), which in static form is reproduced here for convenience:

$$y_{it} = x_{it}'\beta + Z_i'\gamma + u_{it} \tag{8.22}$$

where β is $K \times 1$ and γ is $g \times 1$. The Z_i are time-invariant variables, whereas the x_{it} vary over individuals and time. In vector form, (8.22) can be written as

$$y_i = W_i\eta + u_i \tag{8.23}$$

with the disturbances following a one-way error component model

$$u_i = \mu_i \iota_T + \nu_i \tag{8.24}$$

where $y_i = (y_{i1}, \ldots, y_{iT})'$, $u_i = (u_{i1}, \ldots, u_{iT})'$, $\eta' = (\beta', \gamma')$, $W_i = [X_i, \iota_T Z_i']$, $X_i = (x_{i1}, \ldots, x_{iT})'$, and ι_T is a vector of ones of dimension T. In general, $E(u_i u_i'/w_i)$ will be unrestricted depending on $w_i = (x_i', Z_i')'$ where $x_i = (x_{i1}', \ldots, x_{iT}')'$. However, the literature emphasizes two cases with cross-sectional homoskedasticity.

Case 1: $E(u_i u_i') = \Omega$ independent of w_i, but general to allow for arbitrary Ω as long as it is the same across individuals, i.e., Ω is the same for $i = 1, \ldots, N$.
Case 2: the traditional error component model where $\Omega = \sigma_\nu^2 I_T + \sigma_\mu^2 \iota_T \iota_T'$.

Arellano and Bover transform the system of T equations in (8.15) using the non-singular transformation

$$H = \begin{bmatrix} C \\ \iota_T'/T \end{bmatrix} \tag{8.25}$$

where C is any $(T-1) \times T$ matrix of rank $(T-1)$ such that $C\iota_T = 0$. For example, C could be the first $T-1$ rows of the within-group operator or the FD operator. Arellano and Bover (1995) also discuss a forward orthogonal deviations operator as another example of C which is useful in the context of models with predetermined variables. This transformation essentially subtracts the mean of future observations available in the sample from the first $T-1$ observations.

Exercise 8.8 *(Alternative transformations that wipe out the individual effects).* This is based on Problem 8.4 in Baltagi (2008). Consider three $(T-1) \times T$ matrices defined in (8.25) as follows: C_1 consists of the first $T-1$ rows of $(I_T - \overline{J}_T)$, C_2 is the FD operator, and

C_3 is the forward orthogonal deviations operator which subtracts the mean of future observations from the first $T-1$ observations. This last matrix is given by Arellano and Bover (1995) as

$$C_3 = \text{diag}\left[\frac{T-1}{T}, \ldots, \frac{1}{2}\right]^{1/2} \begin{bmatrix} 1 & -\frac{1}{(T-1)} & -\frac{1}{(T-1)} & \cdots & -\frac{1}{(T-1)} & -\frac{1}{(T-1)} & -\frac{1}{(T-1)} \\ 0 & 1 & -\frac{1}{(T-2)} & \cdots & -\frac{1}{(T-2)} & -\frac{1}{(T-2)} & -\frac{1}{(T-2)} \\ \vdots & \vdots & \vdots & & \vdots & \vdots & \vdots \\ 0 & 0 & 0 & \cdots & 1 & -\frac{1}{2} & -\frac{1}{2} \\ 0 & 0 & 0 & \cdots & 0 & 1 & -1 \end{bmatrix}$$

Verify that each one of these C matrices satisfies:

(a) $C_j \iota_T = 0$ for $j = 1, 2, 3$.
(b) $C_j'(C_j C_j')^{-1} C_j = I_T - \bar{J}_T$, the within transformation, for $j = 1, 2, 3$.
(c) For C_3, show that $C_3 C_3' = I_{T-1}$ and $C_3' C_3 = I_T - \bar{J}_T$. Hence, $C_3 = (C'C)^{-1/2} C$ for any upper triangular C such that $C\iota_T = 0$.

Solution

Let C_1 be the first $T-1$ rows of $(I_T - \bar{J}_T)$. Since $(I_T - \bar{J}_T)\iota_T = 0$, it follows that the first $T-1$ rows postmultiplied by ι_T will yield zero. Hence, $C_1 \iota_T = 0$. Actually

$$E_T = I_T - \bar{J}_T = \begin{bmatrix} (1-\frac{1}{T}) & -\frac{1}{T} & \cdots & -\frac{1}{T} \\ -\frac{1}{T} & (1-\frac{1}{T}) & \cdots & -\frac{1}{T} \\ \vdots & \vdots & \cdots & \vdots \\ -\frac{1}{T} & -\frac{1}{T} & \cdots & (1-\frac{1}{T}) \end{bmatrix}$$

If we let $E_T = (C_1, a')'$, where a' is the last row of E_T, then

$$E_T E_T' = E_T = \begin{pmatrix} C_1 C_1' & C_1 a \\ a' C_1' & a'a \end{pmatrix}$$

It is clear from partitioning the above matrix that

$$C_1 C_1' = I_{T-1} - (J_{T-1}/T) = (E_{T-1} + \bar{J}_{T-1}) - \left(\frac{T-1}{T}\right)\bar{J}_{T-1} = E_{T-1} + (\bar{J}_{T-1}/T)$$

where the second equality holds by applying the Wansbeek and Kapteyn (1982) trick of substituting $E_{T-1} + \bar{J}_{T-1}$ for I_{T-1} and $(T-1)\bar{J}_{T-1}$ for J_{T-1}. Hence, $(C_1 C_1')^{-1} = E_{T-1} + T\bar{J}_{T-1}$.

From the above matrix,

$$C_1 = [(I_{T-1} - \frac{J_{T-1}}{T}), -(\iota_{T-1}/T)] = [E_{T-1} + (\bar{J}_{T-1}/T), -(\iota_{T-1}/T)]$$

Therefore, $(C_1C_1')^{-1}C_1 = [(E_{T-1} + \overline{J}_{T-1}), -\iota_{T-1}] = [I_{T-1}, -\iota_{T-1}]$ and

$$C_1'(C_1C_1')^{-1}C_1 = \begin{pmatrix} E_{T-1} + \frac{\overline{J}_{T-1}}{T} \\ \\ -\frac{\iota_{T-1}'}{T} \end{pmatrix} (I_{T-1}, -\iota_{T-1}) = \begin{bmatrix} E_{T-1} + \frac{\overline{J}_{T-1}}{T} & -\frac{\iota_{T-1}}{T} \\ -\frac{\iota_{T-1}'}{T} & \frac{T-1}{T} \end{bmatrix}$$

$$= I_T - \overline{J}_T = E_T$$

This proves parts (a) and (b) for matrix C_1.

Note that the transformed disturbances

$$u_i^+ = Hu_i = \begin{bmatrix} Cu_i \\ \overline{u}_i \end{bmatrix} \tag{8.26}$$

have the first $T-1$ transformed errors free of μ_i. Hence, all exogenous variables are valid instruments for these first $T-1$ equations. Let m_i denote the subset of variables of w_i assumed to be uncorrelated in levels with μ_i and such that the dimension of m_i is greater than or equal to the dimension of η. In the Hausman and Taylor study, $X = [X_1, X_2]$ and $Z = [Z_1, Z_2]$, where X_1 and Z_1 are exogenous of dimension $NT \times k_1$ and $N \times g_1$. X_2 and Z_2 are correlated with the individual effects and are of dimension $NT \times k_2$ and $N \times g_2$. In this case, m_i includes the set of X_1 and Z_1 variables and m_i would be based on $(Z_{1,i}', \overline{x}_{1,i}')'$. Therefore, a valid IV matrix for the complete transformed system is

$$M_i = \begin{bmatrix} w_i' & & & 0 \\ & \ddots & & \\ & & w_i' & \\ 0 & & & m_i' \end{bmatrix} \tag{8.27}$$

and the moment conditions are given by

$$E(M_i'Hu_i) = 0 \tag{8.28}$$

Defining $W = (W_1', \ldots, W_N')'$, $y = (y_1', \ldots, y_N')'$, $M = (M_1', \ldots, M_N')'$, $\overline{H} = I_N \otimes H$, and $\overline{\Omega} = I_N \otimes \Omega$, and premultiplying (8.23) in vector form by $M'\overline{H}$, we get

$$M'\overline{H}y = M'\overline{H}W\eta + M'\overline{H}u \tag{8.29}$$

Performing GLS on (8.29) gives the Arellano and Bover (1995) estimator

$$\widehat{\eta} = [W'\overline{H}'M(M'\overline{H}\,\overline{\Omega}\,\overline{H}'M)^{-1}M'\overline{H}W]^{-1}W'\overline{H}'M(M'\overline{H}\,\overline{\Omega}\,\overline{H}'M)^{-1}M'\overline{H}y \tag{8.30}$$

In practice, the covariance matrix of the transformed system $\Omega^+ = H\Omega H'$ is replaced by a consistent estimator, usually

$$\widehat{\Omega}^+ = \sum_{i=1}^{N} \widehat{u}_i^+ \widehat{u}_i^{+\prime}/N \tag{8.31}$$

where $\widehat{u}_i^+$ are residuals based on consistent preliminary estimates. The resulting $\widehat{\eta}$ is the optimal GMM estimator of η with constant Ω based on the above moment restrictions. Further efficiency can be achieved using Hansen's (1982) GMM-type estimator which replaces $\sum_i M_i'\Omega^+ M_i$ in (8.31) by $\sum_i M_i'\widehat{u}_i^+\widehat{u}_i^{+\prime}M_i$. For the error component model, $\widetilde{\Omega}^+ = H\widetilde{\Omega}H'$ with $\widetilde{\Omega} = \widetilde{\sigma}_\nu^2 I_T + \widetilde{\sigma}_\mu^2\iota_T\iota_T'$, where $\widetilde{\sigma}_\nu^2$ and $\widetilde{\sigma}_\mu^2$ denote consistent estimates σ_ν^2 and σ_μ^2.

The Hausman and Taylor (1981) estimator, given in Exercise 7.14, is $\widehat{\eta}$ with $\widetilde{\Omega}^+$ and $m_i = (Z_{1,i}', \overline{x}_{1,i}')'$ where $\overline{x}_i' = \iota_T' X_i/T = (\overline{x}_{1,i}', \overline{x}_{2,i}')$. The Amemiya and MaCurdy (1986) (AM) estimator is $\widehat{\eta}$ with $\widetilde{\Omega}^+$ and $m_i = (Z_{1i}', x_{1,i1}', \ldots, x_{1,iT}')'$. The Breusch, Mizon and Schmidt (1989) estimator exploits the additional moment restrictions that the correlation between $x_{2,it}$, and μ_i is constant over time. In this case, $\widetilde{x}_{2,it} = x_{2,it} - \overline{x}_{2,i}$ are valid instruments for the last equation of the transformed system. Hence, BMS is $\widehat{\eta}$ with $\widetilde{\Omega}^+$ and $m_i = (Z_{1,i}', x_{1,i1}', \ldots, x_{1,iT}', \widetilde{x}_{2,i1}', \ldots, \widetilde{x}_{2,iT}')'$.

Because the set of instruments M_i is block-diagonal, Arellano and Bover show that $\widehat{\eta}$ is invariant to the choice of C. Another advantage of their representation is that the form of $\Omega^{-1/2}$ need not be known. Hence, this approach generalizes the HT-, AM-, and BMS-type estimators to a more general form of Ω than that of error components, and it easily extends to the dynamic panel data case.

Exercise 8.9 *(Arellano and Bover (1995) estimator).* This is based on Problem 8.5 in Baltagi (2008). For the error component model with $\widetilde{\Omega} = \widetilde{\sigma}_\nu^2 I_T + \widetilde{\sigma}_\mu^2 J_T$ and $\widetilde{\sigma}_\nu^2$ and $\widetilde{\sigma}_\mu^2$ denoting consistent estimates of σ_ν^2 and σ_μ^2, respectively, show that the Arellano and Bover (1995) estimator $\widehat{\eta}$ in (8.30) can be written as

$$\widehat{\eta} = \left[\sum_{i=1}^N W_i'(I_T - \bar{J}_T)W_i + \widetilde{\theta}^2 T\sum_{i=1}^N \overline{w}_i m_i' \left(\sum_{i=1}^N m_i m_i'\right)^{-1}\sum_{i=1}^N m_i\overline{w}_i'\right]^{-1}$$

$$\times\left[\sum_{i=1}^N W_i'(I_T - \bar{J}_T)y_i + \widetilde{\theta}^2 T\sum_{i=1}^N \overline{w}_i m_i' \left(\sum_{i=1}^N m_i m_i'\right)^{-1}\sum_{i=1}^N m_i\overline{y}_i\right]$$

where $\overline{w}_i = W_i'\iota_T/T$ and $\widetilde{\theta}^2 = \widetilde{\sigma}_\nu^2/(T\widetilde{\sigma}_\mu^2 + \widetilde{\sigma}_\nu^2)$. These are the familiar expressions for the HT, AM, and BMS estimators for the corresponding choices of m_i.

Solution

This proof is based on the Appendix of Arellano and Bover (1995). Let

$$W_i^+ = HW_i = \begin{bmatrix} CW_i \\ \overline{w}_i' \end{bmatrix} \quad \text{and} \quad M_i = \begin{pmatrix} I_{T-1}\otimes w_i' & 0 \\ 0 & m_i' \end{pmatrix} \tag{8.32}$$

so that

$$W_i^{+\prime}M_i = \left[W_i'C'(I_{T-1}\otimes w_i'), \overline{w}_i m_i'\right]$$

Using the fact that $C\iota_T = 0$, as demonstrated in Exercise 8.8, we get that $CW_i = [CX_i, 0]$. Also, for $\Omega = \sigma_\nu^2 I_T + \sigma_\mu^2 \iota_T \iota_T'$, we get that

$$\Omega^+ = H\Omega H' = \begin{bmatrix} C \\ \iota_T'/T \end{bmatrix} (\sigma_\nu^2 I_T + \sigma_\mu^2 \iota_T \iota_T') [C', \iota_T/T] = \sigma_\nu^2 \begin{pmatrix} CC' & 0 \\ 0 & \frac{1}{\theta^2 T} \end{pmatrix}$$

Therefore,

$$M_i'\Omega^+ M_i = \sigma_\nu^2 \begin{pmatrix} (I_{T-1} \otimes w_i)CC'(I_{T-1} \otimes w_i') & 0 \\ 0 & \frac{1}{\theta^2 T} m_i m_i' \end{pmatrix}$$

and the inverted term in (8.30) becomes

$$[W'\overline{H}'M(M'\overline{H}\,\overline{\Omega}\,\overline{H}'M)^{-1}M'\overline{H}W] = \sum_{i=1}^{N} W_i^{+\prime} M_i \left(\sum_{i=1}^{N} M_i'\Omega^+ M_i\right)^{-1} \sum_{i=1}^{N} M_i' W_i^+$$

$$= \frac{1}{\sigma_\nu^2}\begin{pmatrix} M_d & 0 \\ 0 & 0 \end{pmatrix} + \theta^2 T \sum_{i=1}^{N} \overline{w}_i m_i' \left(\sum_{i=1}^{N} m_i m_i'\right)^{-1} \sum_{i=1}^{N} m_i \overline{w}_i'$$

where

$$M_d = \left[\sum_{i=1}^{N} X_i'C'(I_{T-1} \otimes w_i') \left(\sum_{i=1}^{N} (I_{T-1} \otimes w_i)CC'(I_{T-1} \otimes w_i')\right)^{-1} \sum_{i=1}^{N} (I_{T-1} \otimes w_i)CX_i\right]$$

$$= \left[\sum_{i=1}^{N} X_i'(I_{T-1} \otimes w_i') \left(C'(CC')^{-1}C \otimes \left[\sum_{i=1}^{N} w_i w_i'\right]^{-1}\right) \sum_{i=1}^{N} (I_{T-1} \otimes w_i)X_i\right]$$

But $C'(CC')^{-1}C = I_T - \overline{J}_T = C_3'C_3$, as shown in Exercise 8.8. C_3 is the forward orthogonal deviations operator, and the columns of $C_3 X_i$ are linear combinations of the columns of $(I_{T-1} \otimes w_i')$, and M_d becomes

$$M_d = \left[\sum_{i=1}^{N} X_i'C_3'(I_{T-1} \otimes w_i') \left(\sum_{i=1}^{N} (I_{T-1} \otimes w_i w_i')\right)^{-1} \sum_{i=1}^{N} (I_{T-1} \otimes w_i)C_3 X_i\right]$$

$$= \left[\sum_{i=1}^{N} X_i'C_3'C_3 X_i\right] = \left[\sum_{i=1}^{N} X_i'(I_T - \overline{J}_T)X_i\right]$$

so that the inverted term in (8.30) becomes

$$\frac{1}{\sigma_\nu^2}\left(\sum_{i=1}^{N} W_i'(I_T - \overline{J}_T)W_i + \theta^2 T \sum_{i=1}^{N} \overline{w}_i m_i' \left(\sum_{i=1}^{N} m_i m_i'\right)^{-1} \sum_{i=1}^{N} m_i \overline{w}_i'\right)$$

The derivation of the second term in (8.30) is similar and is left to the reader.

Let us now introduce a lagged dependent variable into the right-hand side of (8.22):

$$y_{it} = \delta y_{i,t-1} + x_{it}'\beta + Z_i'\gamma + u_{it} \tag{8.33}$$

Assuming that $t = 0$ is observed, we redefine $\eta' = (\delta, \beta', \gamma')$ and $W_i = [y_{i(-1)}, X_i, \iota_T Z_i']$ with $y_{i(-1)} = (y_{i,0}, \ldots, y_{i,T-1})'$. Provided there are enough valid instruments to ensure identification, the GMM estimator defined in (8.30) remains consistent for this model. The matrix of instruments M_i is the same as before, adjusting for the fact that $t = 0$ is now the first period observed, so that $w_i = [x_{i0}', \ldots, x_{iT}', Z_i']'$. In this case $y_{i(-1)}$ is excluded despite its presence in W_i. The same range of choices for m_i are available, for example $m_i = (Z_{1i}', x_{1i}', \widetilde{x}_{2,i1}', \ldots \widetilde{x}_{2,iT}')$ is the BMS-type estimator. However, for this choice of m_i the rows of CX_i are linear combinations of m_i. This means that the same instrument set is valid for all equations and we can use $M_i = I_T \otimes m_i'$ without altering the estimator. The consequence is that the transformation is unnecessary and the estimator can be obtained by applying 3SLS to the original system of equations using m_i as the vector of instruments for all equations:

$$\begin{aligned}\widehat{\eta} = &\left[\sum_i (W_i \otimes m_i)' \left(\widehat{\Omega} \otimes \sum_i m_i m_i'\right)^{-1} \sum_i (W_i \otimes m_i)\right]^{-1} \sum_i (W_i \otimes m_i)' \\ &\times \left(\widehat{\Omega} \otimes \sum_i m_i m_i'\right)^{-1} \sum_i (y_i \otimes m_i)\end{aligned} \tag{8.34}$$

Arellano and Bover (1995) prove that this 3SLS estimator is asymptotically equivalent to the limited information maximum likelihood procedure with Ω unrestricted developed by Bhargava and Sargan (1983).

Exercise 8.10 *(Baltagi and Levin (1986): dynamic demand for cigarettes).* This is based on Problem 8.8 in Baltagi (2008). Baltagi and Levin (1986) estimate a dynamic demand model for cigarettes based on panel data from 46 American states. This data, covering the period 1963–92, are available on the Wiley web site as cigar.txt. The estimated equation is

$$\ln C_{it} = \alpha + \beta_1 \ln C_{i,t-1} + \beta_2 \ln P_{it} + \beta_3 \ln Y_{it} + \beta_4 \ln Pn_{it} + u_{it} \tag{8.35}$$

where the subscript i denotes the ith state ($i = 1, \ldots, 46$), and the subscript t denotes the tth year ($t = 1, \ldots, 30$). C_{it} is real per capita sales of cigarettes by persons of smoking age (14 years and older). This is measured in packs of cigarettes per head. P_{it} is the average retail price of a pack of cigarettes measured in real terms. Y_{it} is real per capita disposable income. Pn_{it} denotes the minimum real price of cigarettes in any neighboring state. This last variable is a proxy for the casual smuggling effect across state borders. The disturbance term is specified as a two-way error component model:

$$u_{it} = \mu_i + \lambda_t + \nu_{it}, \quad i = 1, \ldots, 46, \quad t = 1, \ldots, 30 \tag{8.36}$$

where μ_i denotes a state-specific effect and λ_t denotes a year-specific effect. The time-period effects (the λ_t) are assumed fixed parameters to be estimated as coefficients of time dummies for each year in the sample.

(a) Estimate equation (8.36) using 2SLS, FE and FE2SLS. (Assume only $\ln C_{i,t-1}$ is endogenous and use one lag of the exogenous variables as instruments.)
(b) Perform the two-step robust Arellano and Bond (1991) GMM estimator.
(c) Perform the two-step robust Arellano and Bover (1995) system GMM estimator.

Solution

(a) Table 8.1 gives the Stata output for the 2SLS estimates with one lag of the exogenous variables as instruments. The coefficient estimate of lagged consumption is 0.85 and is highly significant. The short-run price elasticity is −0.21 and is significant. This 2SLS estimate ignores the state and time period effects.

Table 8.1 2SLS Estimates of the Cigarette Demand Equation

```
. ivreg lnc  lnrp lnrpn lnrdi (lnc1=lnrp1 lnrpn1 lnrdi1)

Instrumental variables (2SLS) regression

      Source |       SS       df       MS              Number of obs =    1334
-------------+------------------------------           F(4,1329)     = 2398.66
       Model |  63.7233966     4  15.9308492           Prob > F      =  0.0000
    Residual |  3.02301324  1329  .002274653           R-squared     =  0.9547
-------------+------------------------------           Adj R-squared =  0.9546
       Total |  66.7464099  1333  .050072325           Root MSE      =  .04769
             |
-------------+----------------------------------------------------------------
         lnc |      Coef.   Std. Err.      t    P>|t|     [95% Conf. Interval]
-------------+----------------------------------------------------------------
        lnc1 |   .8499651   .0335508    25.33   0.000     .7841469    .9157834
        lnrp |  -.2050104   .0356031    -5.76   0.000    -.2748547   -.1351661
       lnrpn |   .0523477   .0168147     3.11   0.002     .0193614    .0853339
       lnrdi |  -.0169926   .0077967    -2.18   0.029    -.0322878   -.0016975
       _cons |   1.601765   .2547925     6.29   0.000     1.101925    2.101604
------------------------------------------------------------------------------
Instrumented:  lnc1
Instruments:   lnrp lnrpn lnrdi lnrp1 lnrpn1 lnrdi1
------------------------------------------------------------------------------
```

The FE estimator is reported in Table 8.2 with both state and time effects. This yields a short-run price elasticity of −0.30, and a lagged consumption coefficient estimate of 0.83, both of which are significant. Both state and time dummies were jointly significant with an observed F-statistic of 7.39 and a p-value of 0.0001. The observed F-statistic for the significance of state dummies (given the existence of time dummies) is 4.16 with a p-value of 0.0001. The observed F-statistic for the significance of time dummies (given the existence of state dummies) is 16.05 with a p-value of 0.0001. These results emphasize the importance of including state and time effects in the cigarette demand equation.

This is a dynamic equation and the FE estimator does not take into account the endogeneity of lagged consumption. Hence, we report FE2SLS in Table 8.3 using as instruments the lagged exogenous regressors. These results give a lower estimate of lagged consumption 0.60 and a higher estimate of the short-run price elasticity −0.50, both of which are highly significant.

(b) Table 8.4 gives the Stata output for the Arellano and Bond (1991) GMM two-step estimator using (xtabond2, twostep). This is also Table 8.2 in Baltagi (2008, p.174) and is reproduced here for convenience. This estimator yields a lagged consumption

Table 8.2 Fixed Effects Estimates of the Cigarette Demand Equation

```
. xtreg lnc lncl lnrp lnrpn lnrdi dum3-dum30,fe

Fixed-effects (within) regression               Number of obs      =      1334
Group variable (i) : state                      Number of groups   =        46

R-sq:  within  = 0.9381                         Obs per group: min =        29
       between = 0.9850                                        avg =      29.0
       overall = 0.9648                                        max =        29

                                                F(32,1256)         =    594.64
corr(u_i, Xb)  = 0.4009                         Prob > F           =    0.0000

------------------------------------------------------------------------------
         lnc |      Coef.   Std. Err.      t    P>|t|     [95% Conf. Interval]
-------------+----------------------------------------------------------------
        lncl |   .8333827   .0125616    66.34   0.000     .8087387    .8580267
        lnrp |  -.2985979    .023601   -12.65   0.000    -.3448996   -.2522962
       lnrpn |   .0340452   .0274653     1.24   0.215    -.0198377    .0879281
       lnrdi |   .1002794   .0238499     4.20   0.000     .0534894    .1470694
             |
-------------+----------------------------------------------------------------
     sigma_u |  .02532726
     sigma_e |  .03621218
         rho |  .32848861   (fraction of variance due to u_i)
------------------------------------------------------------------------------
F test that all u_i=0:     F(45, 1256) =  4.15             Prob > F = 0.0000
Time dummies are not shown to save space.
```

Table 8.3 Fixed Effects 2SLS Estimates of the Cigarette Demand Equation

```
. xtivreg lnc  lnrp lnrpn lnrdi dum3-dum30 (lncl=lnrpl lnrpnl lnrdil),fe

Fixed-effects (within) IV regression         Number of obs      =        1334
Group variable: state                        Number of groups   =          46

R-sq:  within  = 0.9213                      Obs per group: min =          29
       between = 0.9369                                     avg =        29.0
       overall = 0.9230                                     max =          29

                                             Wald chi2(32)      = 20834118.30
corr(u_i, Xb)  = 0.4579                      Prob > chi2        =     0.0000
------------------------------------------------------------------------------
         lnc |      Coef.   Std. Err.      z    P>|z|     [95% Conf. Interval]
-------------+----------------------------------------------------------------
        lncl |   .6016292    .035302    17.04   0.000     .5324387    .6708198
        lnrp |  -.4956815   .0382645   -12.95   0.000    -.5706786   -.4206845
       lnrpn |  -.0159481   .0317401    -0.50   0.615    -.0781575    .0462613
       lnrdi |    .189382   .0296233     6.39   0.000     .1313215    .2474426
             |
-------------+----------------------------------------------------------------
     sigma_u |  .05744479
     sigma_e |  .04082517
         rho |  .66441929   (fraction of variance due to u_i)
------------------------------------------------------------------------------
F  test that all u_i=0:     F(45,1256) = 3.74           Prob > F    = 0.0000
------------------------------------------------------------------------------
Instrumented:   lncl
Instruments:    lnrp lnrpn lnrdi dum3 dum4 dum5 dum6 dum7 dum8 dum9 dum10 dum11
                dum12 dum13 dum14 dum15 dum16 dum17 dum18 dum19 dum20 dum21
                dum22 dum23 dum24 dum25 dum26 dum27 dum28 dum29 dum30 lnrpl
                lnrpnl lnrdil
Time dummies are not shown to save space.
```

Table 8.4 Robust Arellano and Bond GMM Estimates of the Cigarette Demand Equation

```
. xtabond2 lnc L.(lnc) lnrp lnrpn lnrdi dum3 dum8 dum10-dum29, gmm(L.(lnc ),
collapse) iv(lnrp lnrpn lnrdi dum3 dum8 dum10-dum29) noleveleq robust nomata
twostep
Dynamic panel-data estimation, two-step difference GMM
------------------------------------------------------------------------------
Group variable: state                           Number of obs      =      1288
Time variable : yr                              Number of groups   =        46
Number of instruments = 53                      Obs per group: min =        28
Wald chi2(26) =   5492.89                                      avg =     28.00
Prob > chi2   =     0.000                                      max =        28
------------------------------------------------------------------------------
             |              Corrected
             |      Coef.   Std. Err.      z    P>|z|     [95% Conf. Interval]
-------------+----------------------------------------------------------------
         lnc |
         L1. |   .6993342   .0688738    10.15   0.000     .5643441    .8343242
        lnrp |  -.3956542   .0659587    -6.00   0.000    -.5249309   -.2663775
       lnrpn |  -.1054687   .0846056    -1.25   0.213    -.2712926    .0603552
       lnrdi |   .1258248   .0359738     3.50   0.000     .0553173    .1963322

------------------------------------------------------------------------------
Arellano-Bond test for AR(1) in first differences: z =  -4.74  Pr > z =  0.000
Arellano-Bond test for AR(2) in first differences: z =   1.82  Pr > z =  0.069

Hansen test of overid. restrictions: chi2(27)    =  32.25  Prob > chi2 =  0.223
Warning: Sargan/Hansen tests are weak when instruments are many.
------------------------------------------------------------------------------
Time dummies are not shown here to save space.
```

Table 8.5 System GMM Estimates of Cigarette Demand

```
. xtabond2 lnc L.(lnc) lnrp lnrpn lnrdi dum3 dum8 dum10-dum29, gmm(L.(lnc ),
collapse) iv(lnrp lnrpn lnrdi dum3 dum8 dum10-dum29) robust nomata twostep
Dynamic panel-data estimation, two-step system GMM
------------------------------------------------------------------------------
Group variable: state                           Number of obs      =      1334
Time variable : yr                              Number of groups   =        46
Number of instruments = 55                      Obs per group: min =        29
Wald chi2(26) =   6937.61                                      avg =     29.00
Prob > chi2   =     0.000                                      max =        29
------------------------------------------------------------------------------
             |              Corrected
             |      Coef.   Std. Err.      z    P>|z|     [95% Conf. Interval]
-------------+----------------------------------------------------------------
         lnc |
         L1. |   .6961172    .078724     8.84   0.000     .5418211    .8504133
        lnrp |  -.4152584   .0962569    -4.31   0.000    -.6039185   -.2265982
       lnrpn |  -.0034555   .0500122    -0.07   0.945    -.1014777    .0945667
       lnrdi |   .0925415   .0276142     3.35   0.001     .0384187    .1466644

------------------------------------------------------------------------------
Arellano-Bond test for AR(1) in first differences: z =  -4.63  Pr > z =  0.000
Arellano-Bond test for AR(2) in first differences: z =   1.92  Pr > z =  0.055

Hansen test of overid. restrictions: chi2(28)    =  26.79  Prob > chi2 =  0.530
Warning: Sargan/Hansen tests are weak when instruments are many.
------------------------------------------------------------------------------
Time dummies are not shown here to save space.
```

coefficient estimate of 0.70 and an own price elasticity of −0.40, both highly significant. This output gives the robust standard errors proposed by Windmeijer (2005). Note that the two-step Sargan test for overidentification does not reject the null, but this could be due to the bad power of this test for $N = 46$ and $T = 28$. Not all the moment conditions are used and in fact the collapse option was invoked to reduce these moment conditions. The test for first-order serial correlation rejects the null of no first-order serial correlation, but it does not reject the null that there is no second-order serial correlation. This is what one expects in a first-differenced equation with the original untransformed disturbances assumed to be not serially correlated.

(c) The two-step robust Arellano and Bover (1995) system GMM estimator is performed using Stata xtabond2. This is demonstrated in Table 8.3 in Baltagi (2008, p.175), reproduced here for convenience as Table 8.5. This estimator uses the moment conditions on equations in levels in addition to the moment conditions on the first-differenced equation (see Exercise 8.9).

The Sargan test for overidentification does not reject the null, and the tests for first-order and second-order serial correlation yield the expected diagnostics. System GMM yields a lagged consumption coefficient estimate of 0.70 and an own price elasticity of −0.42, both highly significant, but with higher standard errors than the corresponding Arellano and Bond estimates reported in Table 8.4.

9

Unbalanced Panels

9.1 THE UNBALANCED ONE-WAY ERROR COMPONENT MODEL

So far we have dealt only with 'complete panels' or 'balanced panels' – cases where the individuals are observed over the entire sample period. Incomplete panels are more likely to be the norm in typical economic empirical settings. For example, in collecting data on US airlines over time, a researcher may find that some firms have dropped out of the market while new entrants emerged over the sample period observed. Similarly, while using labor or consumer panels on households, one may find that some households moved and can no longer be included in the panel. Additionally, if collecting data on a set of countries over time, a researcher may find some countries can be traced back longer than others. These typical scenarios lead to 'unbalanced' or 'incomplete' panels. To simplify the presentation, we analyze the case of two cross-sections with an unequal number of time-series observations and then generalize the analysis to the case of N cross-sections. Let n_1 be the shorter time series observed for the first cross-section ($i = 1$), and n_2 be the extra time-series observations available for the second cross-section ($i = 2$). Stacking the n_1 observations for the first individual on top of the $(n_1 + n_2)$ observations on the second individual, we get

$$\begin{pmatrix} y_1 \\ y_2 \end{pmatrix} = \begin{pmatrix} X_1 \\ X_2 \end{pmatrix} \beta + \begin{pmatrix} u_1 \\ u_2 \end{pmatrix} \tag{9.1}$$

where y_1 and y_2 are vectors of dimensions n_1 and $n_1 + n_2$, respectively. X_1 and X_2 are matrices of dimensions $n_1 \times K$ and $(n_1 + n_2) \times K$, respectively. In this case, $u_1' = (u_{11}, \ldots, u_{1,n_1})$ and $u_2' = (u_{21}, \ldots, u_{2,n_1}, \ldots, u_{2,n_1+n_2})$.

Exercise 9.1 *(Variance–covariance matrix of unbalanced panels).* This is based on Baltagi (1985) and is also Problem 9.1 in Baltagi (2008).

(a) Show that the variance–covariance matrix of the disturbances in (9.1) is given by

$$\Omega = \begin{bmatrix} \sigma_\nu^2 I_{n_1} + \sigma_\mu^2 J_{n_1 n_1} & 0 & 0 \\ 0 & \sigma_\nu^2 I_{n_1} + \sigma_\mu^2 J_{n_1 n_1} & \sigma_\mu^2 J_{n_1 n_2} \\ 0 & \sigma_\mu^2 J_{n_2 n_1} & \sigma_\nu^2 I_{n_2} + \sigma_\mu^2 J_{n_2 n_2} \end{bmatrix} \tag{9.2}$$

where $u' = (u_1', u_2')$, I_{n_i} denotes an identity matrix of order n_i and $J_{n_i n_j}$ denotes a matrix of ones of dimension $n_i \times n_j$.

(b) Show that two non-zero block matrices in (9.2) can be written as

$$\Omega_j = (T_j \sigma_\mu^2 + \sigma_\nu^2) \bar{J}_{T_j} + \sigma_\nu^2 E_{T_j} \tag{9.3}$$

where $\bar{J}_{T_j} = J_{T_j}/T_j$, $E_{T_j} = I_{T_j} - \bar{J}_{T_j}$, and $T_j = \sum_{i=1}^{j} n_i$, for $j = 1, 2$.

(c) Show that $\sigma_\nu \Omega_j^{-1/2} y_j$ has a typical element $(y_{jt} - \theta_j \bar{y}_{j.})$, where $\theta_j = 1 - \sigma_\nu/\omega_j$ and $\omega_j^2 = T_j \sigma_\mu^2 + \sigma_\nu^2$.

(d) Show that the above results can be extended no matter how the observations for the two firms overlap, and also to the case of several cross-sections.

Solution

(a) For the case of two cross-sections, the variance–covariance matrix of the disturbances in (9.1) is

$$\Omega = E\begin{pmatrix} u_1 \\ u_2 \end{pmatrix}(u_1', u_2') = \begin{bmatrix} \Omega_{11} & \Omega_{12} \\ \Omega_{21} & \Omega_{22} \end{bmatrix}$$

where $\Omega_{ij} = E(u_i u_j')$. Since the error component disturbances are not correlated for different cross-sections, it immediately follows that $\Omega_{12} = \Omega_{21} = 0$. The variance–covariance matrix of each u_i alone is of the typical error component type described in Exercise 2.4. The only difference here is that the number of time-series observations available for each cross-section is different. Hence, $\Omega_{11} = \sigma_\mu^2 J_{n_1 n_1} + \sigma_\nu^2 I_{n_1}$, while $\Omega_{22} = \sigma_\mu^2 J_{n_1+n_2} + \sigma_\nu^2 I_{n_1+n_2}$. This verifies (9.2). Note that all the non-zero off-diagonal elements of Ω are equal to σ_μ^2.

(b) Defining $T_1 = n_1$ and $T_2 = n_1 + n_2$, we get $\Omega_{11} = \sigma_\mu^2 J_{T_1} + \sigma_\nu^2 I_{T_1}$ and $\Omega_{22} = \sigma_\mu^2 J_{T_2} + \sigma_\nu^2 I_{T_2}$. Although Ω is unbalanced, each of the non-zero sub-block matrices, Ω_{11} and Ω_{22}, is balanced. Replacing J_{T_i} by $T_i \bar{J}_{T_i}$ and I_{T_i} by $E_{T_i} + \bar{J}_{T_i}$ and collecting like terms, the Wansbeek and Kapteyn (1982) trick yields

$$\Omega_{ii} = (T_i \sigma_\mu^2 + \sigma_\nu^2)\bar{J}_{T_i} + \sigma_\nu^2 E_{T_i}$$

which verifies (9.3).

(c) For each Ω_{jj}, its spectral decomposition is given by (9.3) with the double subscript reverting back to a single subscript since Ω is now block-diagonal. Hence,

$$\Omega_j^r = (T_j \sigma_\mu^2 + \sigma_\nu^2)^r \bar{J}_{T_j} + (\sigma_\nu^2)^r E_{T_j} \tag{9.4}$$

where r is any scalar. For $r = -1/2$, we get

$$\Omega_j^{-1/2} = (T_j \sigma_\mu^2 + \sigma_\nu^2)^{-1/2} \bar{J}_{T_j} + (\sigma_\nu^2)^{-1/2} E_{T_j}$$

Let $w_j^2 = T_j \sigma_\mu^2 + \sigma_\nu^2$. Then the Fuller and Battese (1973) transformation for the unbalanced case is

$$\sigma_\nu \Omega_j^{-1/2} = (\sigma_\nu/w_j)\bar{J}_{T_j} + E_{T_j} = I_{T_j} - \theta_j \bar{J}_{T_j} \tag{9.5}$$

where $\theta_j = 1 - \sigma_\nu/w_j$, and $\sigma_\nu \Omega_j^{-1/2} y_j$ has a typical element $(y_{jt} - \theta_j \bar{y}_{j.})$ with $\bar{y}_{j.} = \sum_{t=1}^{T_j} y_{jt}/T_j$. Note that θ_j varies for each cross-sectional unit j depending on T_j. Hence, GLS can be obtained as a simple weighted least squares as in the complete panel data case (see Exercise 2.5). The basic difference, however, is that in the incomplete panel data case the weights are crucially dependent on the lengths of the time series available for each cross-section.

(d) The above results generalize in two directions: (i) the same analysis applies no matter how the observations for the two firms overlap; (ii) the results extend from the two cross-sections to the N cross-sections case. The proof is simple. Since the off-diagonal elements of the covariance matrix are zero for observations belonging to different firms, Ω remains block-diagonal as long as the observations are ordered by firms. Also, the non-zero off-diagonal elements are all equal to σ_μ^2. Hence $\Omega_j^{-1/2}$ can be derived along the same lines shown above.

In general, the regression model with unbalanced one-way error component disturbances is given by

$$y_{it} = \alpha + X'_{it}\beta + u_{it}, \quad i = 1, \ldots, N, \quad t = 1, \ldots, T_i \tag{9.6}$$

$$u_{it} = \mu_i + \nu_{it}$$

where X_{it} is a $K \times 1$ vector of regressors, $\mu_i \sim \text{IIN}(0, \sigma_\mu^2)$ and independent of $\nu_{it} \sim \text{IIN}(0, \sigma_\nu^2)$. This model is unbalanced in the sense that there are N individuals observed over varying time-period length (T_i for $i = 1, \ldots, N$). Writing this equation in vector form, we have

$$y = \alpha\iota_n + X\beta + u = Z\delta + u \tag{9.7}$$

$$u = Z_\mu\mu + \nu$$

where y and Z are of dimensions $n \times 1$ and $n \times (K+1)$, respectively, $Z = (\iota_n, X)$, $\delta' = (\alpha', \beta')$, $n = \sum T_i$, $Z_\mu = \text{diag}(\iota_{T_i})$, and ι_{T_i} is a vector of ones of dimension T_i. $\mu = (\mu_1, \mu_2, \ldots, \mu_N)'$ and $\nu = (\nu_{11}, \ldots, \nu_{1T_1}, \ldots, \nu_{N1}, \ldots, \nu_{NT_N})'$.

Exercise 9.2 *(Fixed effects for the one-way unbalanced panel data model)*

(a) Show that the projection matrix on Z_μ is the averaging matrix over time for each individual, but with each individual averaging across different numbers of observations T_i; call this matrix P.

(b) Let $Q = I_n - P$, show that P and Q are symmetric and idempotent matrices that are orthogonal to each other and sum to the identity matrix.

(c) Using the Frisch–Waugh–Lovell theorem, show that the least squares dummy variables estimator from (9.6) can be obtained as an unbalanced 'within regression' by premultiplying the model by Q and performing OLS on the resulting transformed model:

$$Qy = QX\beta + Q\nu \tag{9.8}$$

Solution

(a) Note that $Z'_\mu Z_\mu = \text{diag}(\iota'_{T_i}\iota_{T_i}) = \text{diag}(T_i)$ and $Z_\mu Z'_\mu = \text{diag}(\iota_{T_i}\iota'_{T_i}) = \text{diag}(J_{T_i})$, where J_{T_i} is a matrix of ones of dimension T_i. Hence, $P = Z_\mu(Z'_\mu Z_\mu)^{-1}Z'_\mu$, the projection matrix on Z_μ, reduces to $P = \text{diag}[\bar{J}_{T_i}]$, where $\bar{J}_{T_i} = J_{T_i}/T_i$. P is a matrix which averages the observations across time for each individual, but now over different numbers of observations for each individual (see also Exercise 2.1). The typical element of Py is $\bar{y}_{i.} = \sum_{t=1}^{T_i} y_{it}/T_i$ repeated T_i times for each individual.

(b) Let $Q = I_n - P = \text{diag}(I_{T_i} - \bar{J}_{T_i}) = \text{diag}(E_{T_i})$, where $E_{T_i} = (I_{T_i} - \bar{J}_{T_i})$. This is the orthogonal projection matrix on Z_μ which yields the residuals from the regression of any variable on Z_μ. The typical element of Qy is $(y_{it} - \bar{y}_{i.})$, which obtains the deviations from individual means. Because P and Q are projection matrices, they are (i) symmetric and idempotent, i.e., $P' = P$ and $P^2 = P$. This means that the rank$(P) = \text{tr}(P) = N$ and rank$(Q) = \text{tr}(Q) = n - N$. Also, (ii) P and Q are orthogonal, i.e., $PQ = 0$, since $PQ = P(I_n - P) = P - P^2 = P - P = 0$, and (iii) they sum to the identity matrix $P + Q = I_n$ (see Exercise 2.1 for similar results in the balanced panel case).

(c) Using the FWL theorem, LSDV on (9.6) yields the same estimates of β and the same residuals as OLS on (9.8). This uses the fact that P is the projection matrix on Z_μ and $Q = I_n - P$, and the fact that $QZ_\mu = Q\iota_n = 0$, since $PZ_\mu = Z_\mu$. Note that the Q matrix wipes out the individual effects. Also, $QZ = [0, QX]$ since $Q\iota_n = 0$. This is a regression of $\widetilde{y} = Qy$ with typical element $(y_{it} - \bar{y}_{i.})$ on $\widetilde{X} = QX$ with typical element $(X_{it,k} - \bar{X}_{i.,k})$ for the kth regressor, $k = 1, 2, \ldots, K$. The resulting OLS estimator is

$$\widetilde{\beta} = (\widetilde{X}'\widetilde{X})^{-1}\widetilde{X}'\widetilde{y} = \left(X'QX\right)^{-1} X'Qy \tag{9.9}$$

with $\text{var}(\widetilde{\beta}) = \sigma_\nu^2(\widetilde{X}'\widetilde{X})^{-1} = \sigma_\nu^2(X'QX)^{-1}$, since $E(Q\nu) = 0$ and $\text{var}(Q\nu) = Q\text{var}(\nu)Q' = \sigma_\nu^2 Q$, using the fact that $\nu \sim (0, \sigma_\nu^2 I_n)$. The estimate of the intercept can be retrieved as follows: $\widetilde{\alpha} = (\bar{y}_{..} - \bar{X}_{..}\widetilde{\beta})$ where the dot indicates summation and the bar indicates averaging, for example $\bar{y}_{..} = \sum\sum y_{it}/n$. Following Amemiya (1971), the within residuals $\widetilde{u}$ for the unbalanced panel are given by

$$\widetilde{u} = y - \widetilde{\alpha}\iota_n - X\widetilde{\beta} \tag{9.10}$$

The ANOVA estimators are method of moments-type estimators, which equate quadratic sums of squares to their expectations and solve the resulting linear system of equations. For the balanced model, ANOVA estimators are best quadratic unbiased estimators of the variance components (see Searle, 1971). Under normality of the disturbances, these ANOVA estimators are minimum variance unbiased. For the unbalanced one-way model, BQU estimators of the variance components are a function of the variance components themselves. Still, unbalanced ANOVA methods are available (see Searle, 1987), but optimal properties beyond unbiasedness are lost. In what follows, we generalize some of the ANOVA methods described in Chapter 2 to the unbalanced case. In particular, we consider the two quadratic forms defining the within and between sums of squares:

$$q_1 = u'Qu \quad \text{and} \quad q_2 = u'Pu \tag{9.11}$$

where $Q = \text{diag}[E_{T_i}]$ and $P = \text{diag}[\bar{J}_{T_i}]$. Since the true disturbances are not known, we follow the Wallace and Hussain (1969) suggestion of substituting OLS residuals $\widehat{u}_{\text{OLS}}$ for u in (9.11).

Exercise 9.3 *(Wallace and Hussain (1969)-type estimators for the variance components of a one-way unbalanced panel data model).* This is based on Problem 9.2 in Baltagi (2008). Show that

$$E(\widehat{q}_1) = E(\hat{u}'_{\text{OLS}} Q \hat{u}_{\text{OLS}}) = \delta_{11}\sigma_\mu^2 + \delta_{12}\sigma_\nu^2$$
$$E(\widehat{q}_2) = E(\hat{u}'_{\text{OLS}} P \hat{u}_{\text{OLS}}) = \delta_{21}\sigma_\mu^2 + \delta_{22}\sigma_\nu^2 \tag{9.12}$$

where $\widehat{u}_{\text{OLS}} = y - Z\widehat{\delta}_{\text{OLS}}$, and $\delta_{11}, \delta_{12}, \delta_{21}, \delta_{22}$ are given by

$$\delta_{11} = \text{tr}((Z'Z)^{-1}Z'Z_\mu Z'_\mu Z) - \text{tr}((Z'Z)^{-1}Z'PZ(Z'Z)^{-1}Z'Z_\mu Z'_\mu Z)$$
$$\delta_{12} = n - N - K - 1 + \text{tr}((Z'Z)^{-1}Z'PZ)$$
$$\delta_{21} = n - 2\text{tr}((Z'Z)^{-1}Z'Z_\mu Z'_\mu Z) + \text{tr}((Z'Z)^{-1}Z'PZ(Z'Z)^{-1}Z'Z_\mu Z'_\mu Z)$$
$$\delta_{22} = N - \text{tr}((Z'Z)^{-1}Z'PZ).$$

Solution

Let $\widehat{q}_1 = \widehat{u}'_{\text{OLS}} Q \widehat{u}_{\text{OLS}}$, with $\widehat{u}_{\text{OLS}} = y - Z\widehat{\delta}_{\text{OLS}} = \overline{P}_Z u$, where $\overline{P}_Z = I - P_Z$ and $P_Z = Z(Z'Z)^{-1}Z'$. Using $Q = \text{diag}[E_{T_i}]$, we get

$$E(\widehat{q}_1) = E(\widehat{u}'_{\text{OLS}} Q \widehat{u}_{\text{OLS}}) = E(u'\overline{P}_Z Q \overline{P}_Z u)$$
$$= \text{tr}E(uu'\overline{P}_Z Q \overline{P}_Z) = \text{tr}(\Omega \overline{P}_Z Q \overline{P}_Z)$$

where $\Omega = E(uu') = \sigma_\nu^2 I_n + \sigma_\mu^2 Z_\mu Z'_\mu$, with $Z_\mu = \text{diag}(\iota_{T_i})$. Hence,

$$E(\widehat{q}_1) = \sigma_\nu^2 \text{tr}(\overline{P}_Z Q \overline{P}_Z) + \sigma_\mu^2 \text{tr}(Z_\mu Z'_\mu \overline{P}_Z Q \overline{P}_Z)$$

It remains to show that $\delta_{11} = \text{tr}(Z_\mu Z'_\mu \overline{P}_Z Q \overline{P}_Z)$ and $\delta_{12} = \text{tr}(\overline{P}_Z Q \overline{P}_Z)$. Using the fact that $Q = I_n - P$ and $P = \text{diag}[\overline{J}_{T_i}]$,

$$\delta_{11} = \text{tr}(Z_\mu Z'_\mu \overline{P}_Z \overline{P}_Z) - \text{tr}(Z_\mu Z'_\mu \overline{P}_Z P \overline{P}_Z)$$
$$= \text{tr}(Z_\mu Z'_\mu) - \text{tr}(Z_\mu Z'_\mu P_Z) - \text{tr}(Z_\mu Z'_\mu P) - \text{tr}(Z_\mu Z'_\mu P_Z P P_Z) + \text{tr}(Z_\mu Z'_\mu P_Z P)$$
$$+ \text{tr}(Z_\mu Z'_\mu P P_Z)$$

But $Z'_\mu P = \text{diag}[\iota'_{T_i}]\ \text{diag}[\overline{J}_{T_i}] = \text{diag}[\iota'_{T_i}] = Z'_\mu$. Therefore,

$$\delta_{11} = \text{tr}(Z_\mu Z'_\mu) - \text{tr}(Z_\mu Z'_\mu P_Z) - \text{tr}(Z_\mu Z'_\mu) - \text{tr}(Z_\mu Z'_\mu P_Z P P_Z)$$
$$+ \text{tr}(Z_\mu Z'_\mu P_Z) + \text{tr}(Z_\mu Z'_\mu P_Z)$$
$$= \text{tr}(Z_\mu Z'_\mu P_Z) - \text{tr}(Z_\mu Z'_\mu P_Z P P_Z)$$

which is the required expression. Similarly,

$$\delta_{12} = \text{tr}(\overline{P}_Z) - \text{tr}(\overline{P}_Z P \overline{P}_Z) = n - \text{tr}(P_Z) - \text{tr}(P) - \text{tr}(P_Z P P_z)$$
$$+\text{tr}(P P_Z) + \text{tr}(P_Z P)$$

Using the fact that $\text{tr}(P_Z) = K + 1$, $\text{tr}(P) = N$, and $\text{tr}(P_Z P P_Z) = \text{tr}(P_Z P_Z P) = \text{tr}(P_Z P)$, we get $\delta_{12} = n - K - 1 - N - \text{tr}(P P_Z)$, which is the required expression.

Also, $\widehat{q}_2 = \widehat{u}'_{\text{OLS}} P \widehat{u}_{\text{OLS}}$, with $E(\widehat{q}_2) = E(u'\overline{P}_Z P \overline{P}_Z u) = \text{tr}(\Omega \overline{P}_Z P \overline{P}_Z)$. Substituting the expression for Ω given above leads to

$$E(\widehat{q}_2) = \sigma_\nu^2 \text{tr}(\overline{P}_Z P \overline{P}_Z) + \sigma_\mu^2 \text{tr}(Z_\mu Z'_\mu \overline{P}_Z P \overline{P}_Z)$$

It remains to show that

$$\delta_{21} = \text{tr}(Z_\mu Z'_\mu \overline{P}_Z P \overline{P}_Z)$$

But $\delta_{21} = \text{tr}(Z_\mu Z'_\mu P) - \text{tr}(Z_\mu Z'_\mu P_Z P) - \text{tr}(Z_\mu Z'_\mu P P_Z) + \text{tr}(Z_\mu Z'_\mu P_Z P P_Z)$. Using the fact that $P Z_\mu = Z_\mu$,

$$\delta_{21} = \text{tr}(Z_\mu Z'_\mu) - \text{tr}(Z_\mu Z'_\mu P_Z) - \text{tr}(Z_\mu Z'_\mu P_Z) + \text{tr}(Z_\mu Z'_\mu P_Z P P_Z)$$
$$= n - 2\text{tr}(Z_\mu Z'_\mu P_Z) + \text{tr}(Z_\mu Z'_\mu P_Z P P_Z)$$

which is the required expression. Also,

$$\delta_{22} = \text{tr}(\overline{P}_Z P) = \text{tr}(P) - \text{tr}(P_Z P) = N - \text{tr}(P_Z P)$$

which is the required expression.

Equating $\widehat{q}_i$ to its expected value $E(\widehat{q}_i)$ in (9.12) and solving the system of equations, we get the Wallace and Hussain-type estimators of the variance components.

Exercise 9.4 *(Comparison of variance component estimators using balanced vs unbalanced data).* This exercise is based on Baltagi and Li (1990a) and Koning (1991). It is also Problem 9.5 in Baltagi (2008). Consider the following unbalanced one-way analysis of variance model:

$$y_{it} = \mu_i + \nu_{it}, \quad i = 1, \ldots, N, \quad t = 1, 2, \ldots, T_i$$

where for simplicity's sake no explanatory variables are included. y_{it} could be the output of firm i at time period t and μ_i could be the managerial ability of firm i, while ν_{it} is a remainder disturbance term. Assume that $\mu_i \sim \text{IIN}(0, \sigma_\mu^2)$ and $\nu_{it} \sim \text{IIN}(0, \sigma_\nu^2)$ independent of each other. Let T be the maximum overlapping period over which a complete panel could be established ($T \leqslant T_i$ for all i). In this case the corresponding vector of balanced observations on y_{it} is denoted by y_b and is of dimension NT. One could estimate the variance components using this complete panel as follows:

$$\widehat{\sigma}_\nu^2 = y'_b(I_N \otimes E_T) y_b / N(T - 1)$$
$$\sigma_\mu^2 = [y'_b(I_N \otimes \overline{J}_T) y_b / NT] - (\widehat{\sigma}_\nu^2 / T)$$

where $E_T = I_T - \overline{J}_T, \overline{J}_T = J_T/T$, and J_T is a matrix of ones of dimension T. $\widehat{\sigma}_\nu^2$ and $\widehat{\sigma}_\mu^2$ are the BQU estimators of the variance components based on the complete panel (see Balestra, 1973). Alternatively, one could estimate the variance components from the entire unbalanced panel as follows:

$$\widetilde{\sigma}_\nu^2 = y'\text{diag}(E_{T_i})y/(n-N)$$

where $n = \sum_{i=1}^N T_i$ and $E_{T_i} = I_{T_i} - \overline{J}_{T_i}$. Also, $\sigma_i^2 = (T_i\sigma_\mu^2 + \sigma_\nu^2)$ can be estimated by $\widetilde{\sigma}_i^2 = y_i'\overline{J}_{T_i}y_i$, where y_i denotes the vector of T_i observations on the ith individual. Therefore, there are N estimators of σ_μ^2 obtained from $(\widetilde{\sigma}_i^2 - \widetilde{\sigma}_\nu^2)/T_i$ for $i = 1, \ldots, N$. One simple way of combining them is to take the average

$$\widetilde{\sigma}_\mu^2 = \sum_{i=1}^N [(\widetilde{\sigma}_i^2 - \widetilde{\sigma}_\nu^2)/T_i]/N = \left\{y'\text{diag}[\overline{J}_{T_i}/T_i]y - \sum_{i=1}^N \widetilde{\sigma}_\nu^2/T_i\right\}/N$$

(a) Show that $\widetilde{\sigma}_\nu^2$ and $\widetilde{\sigma}_\mu^2$ are unbiased estimators σ_ν^2 and σ_μ^2.
(b) Show that $\text{var}(\widetilde{\sigma}_\nu^2) \leqslant \text{var}(\widehat{\sigma}_\nu^2)$ and $\text{var}(\widetilde{\sigma}_\mu^2) \leqslant \text{var}(\widehat{\sigma}_\mu^2)$.

Solution

(a) Using Lemma 1 of Balestra (1973), which states that $E(u'Qu) = \text{tr}Q\Omega$, if $u \sim N(0, \Omega)$, we get

$$E(y_iy_i') = \sigma_\mu^2 J_{T_i} + \sigma_\nu^2 I_{T_i} \equiv \Sigma_i$$

We define $\Sigma = \text{diag}(\Sigma_i)$, which is $E(yy')$. Now we have

$$E(\widetilde{\sigma}_i^2) = \frac{1}{n-N}\text{tr diag}(E_{T_i})\text{ diag}(\Sigma_i) = \frac{1}{n-N}\text{tr diag}(E_{T_i}\Sigma_i)$$
$$= \frac{1}{n-N}\sigma_\nu^2\sum_{i=1}^N \text{tr}E_{T_i} = \sigma_\nu^2$$

Similarly,

$$E(\widetilde{\sigma}_i^2) = \text{tr}(\overline{J}_{T_i}\Sigma_i) = T_i\sigma_\mu^2 + \sigma_\nu^2 = \sigma_i^2$$

and

$$E(\widetilde{\sigma}_\mu^2) = \frac{1}{N}E\left(\sum_{i=1}^N \frac{\widetilde{\sigma}_i^2 - \widetilde{\sigma}_\nu^2}{T_i}\right) = \frac{1}{N}\sum_{i=1}^N \frac{\sigma_i^2 - \sigma_\nu^2}{T_i} = \sigma_\mu^2$$

(b) Variances of these estimators can be found using Lemma 6 of Balestra: $\text{var}(u'Qu) = 2\text{tr}(Q\Omega Q\Omega)$, if $u \sim N(0, \Omega)$. We have

$$\text{var}(\widetilde{\sigma}_\nu^2) = \frac{2}{(n-N)^2}\text{tr}A\Sigma A\Sigma = \sum_{i=1}^N \text{tr}E_{T_i}\Sigma_i E_{T_i}\Sigma_i = \frac{2\sigma_\nu^4}{n-N}$$

where $A = \text{diag}(E_{T_i})$. The corresponding formula for $\widehat{\sigma}_\nu^2$ (the estimate of σ_ν^2 based on the balanced sample) is given by

$$\text{var}(\widehat{\sigma}_\nu^2) = 2\text{tr}(A_\mu \Omega_b A_\mu \Omega_b)$$

where $A_\mu = I_N \otimes E_T/N(T-1)$ and $\Omega_b = E(y_b y_b') = \sigma_1^2(I_N \otimes \overline{J}_T) + \sigma_\nu^2(I_N \otimes E_T)$. Therefore,

$$\text{var}(\widehat{\sigma}_\nu^2) = \frac{2\sigma_\nu^4}{N(T-1)} \geqslant \frac{2\sigma_\nu^4}{n-N}$$

as $n - N \geqslant N(T-1)$. To evaluate $\text{var}(\widetilde{\sigma}_\mu^2)$ is more tedious:

$$\text{var}(\widetilde{\sigma}_\mu^2) = \frac{2}{N^2}\text{tr}(B-C)\Sigma(B-C)\Sigma$$

where $B = \text{diag}(\overline{J}_{T_i}/T_i)$ and $C = \text{diag}(E_{T_i})$ where

$$c \equiv \frac{1}{n-N}\sum_{i=1}^{N}\frac{1}{T_i}$$

The ith block of $(B-C)\Sigma$ is

$$[(B-C)\Sigma]_i = B_i\Sigma_i - C_i\Sigma_i = \frac{1}{T_i}\overline{J}_{T_i}\Sigma_i - cE_{T_i}\Sigma_i = \frac{\sigma_\mu^2}{T_i}J_{T_i} + \frac{\sigma_\nu^2}{T_i}\overline{J}_{T_i} - c\sigma_\nu^2 E_{T_i}$$

Its square is

$$[(B-C)\Sigma]_i^2 = \sigma_\mu^4\overline{J}_{T_i} + \frac{2}{T_i}\sigma_\mu^2\sigma_\nu^2\overline{J}_{T_i} + \frac{\sigma_\mu^4}{T_i^2}\overline{J}_{T_i} + c^2\sigma_\nu^4 E_{T_i}$$

The trace of the ith block of $[(B-C)\Sigma]^2$ is seen to be

$$\text{tr}[(B-C)\Sigma]_i^2 = \sigma_\mu^4 + \frac{2\sigma_\mu^2\sigma_\nu^2}{T_i} + \frac{\sigma_\nu^4}{T_i^2} + c^2\sigma_\nu^2(T_i - 1)$$

Therefore,

$$\text{var}(\widetilde{\sigma}_\mu^2) = \frac{2N\sigma_\mu^4 + 4(n-N)c\sigma_\mu^2\sigma_\nu^2 + 2d\sigma_\nu^4 + 2c^2\sigma_\nu^4(n-N)}{N^2}$$

where $d \equiv \sum_{i=1}^{N}(1/T_i^2)$. The corresponding formula for the balanced panel data case is

$$\text{var}(\widehat{\sigma}_\mu^2) = 2\text{tr}(A_\nu\Omega_b A_\nu\Omega_b)$$

where

$$A_\nu = \frac{1}{NT}\left[I_N \otimes \bar{J}_T - \frac{(I_N \otimes E_T)}{T-1}\right]$$

Hence,

$$\mathrm{var}(\widehat{\sigma}_\mu^2) = \frac{1}{N^2}\left\{2N\sigma_\mu^4 + \frac{4N\sigma_\mu^2\sigma_\nu^2}{T} + \frac{2N}{T^2}\sigma_\nu^4 + 2\frac{N}{T^2(T-1)}\sigma_\nu^4\right\}$$

As $(n-N)c \leqslant N/T$, $d \leqslant N/T^2$ and $c^2(n-N) \leqslant N/[T^2(T-1)]$, we see that $\mathrm{var}(\widetilde{\sigma}_\mu^2) \leqslant \mathrm{var}(\widehat{\sigma}_\mu^2)$.

9.2 THE UNBALANCED TWO-WAY ERROR COMPONENT MODEL

Wansbeek and Kapteyn (1989) consider the regression model with unbalanced two-way error component disturbances

$$y_{it} = X'_{it}\beta + u_{it}, \quad i = 1, \ldots, N_t, \quad t = 1, \ldots, T \tag{9.13}$$
$$u_{it} = \mu_i + \lambda_t + \nu_{it}$$

where $N_t(N_t \leqslant N)$ denotes the number of individuals observed in year t, with $n = \sum_t N_t$. Let D_t be the $(N_t \times N)$ matrix obtained from I_N by omitting the rows corresponding to individuals not observed in year t. Define

$$\Delta = (\Delta_1, \Delta_2) \equiv \begin{bmatrix} D_1 & D_1\iota_N & & \\ \vdots & & \ddots & \\ D_T & & & D_T\iota_N \end{bmatrix} \tag{9.14}$$

where $\Delta_1 = (D'_1, \ldots, D'_T)'$ is $n \times N$ and $\Delta_2 = \mathrm{diag}[D_t\iota_N] = \mathrm{diag}[\iota_{N_t}]$ is $n \times T$. The matrix Δ gives the dummy variable structure for the incomplete data model. Note that Wansbeek and Kapteyn (1989) order the data on the N individuals in T consecutive sets, so that t runs slowly and i runs fast. This is exactly the opposite ordering to that used so far in the text. For complete panels, $\Delta_1 = (\iota_T \otimes I_N)$ and $\Delta_2 = I_T \otimes \iota_N$.

If the μ_i and λ_t are fixed and $\nu_{it} \sim \mathrm{IIN}(0, \sigma_\nu^2)$, one has to run the regression given in (9.13) with the matrix of dummies given in (9.14). Most likely, this will be infeasible for large panels with many households or individuals and we need the familiar within transformation. This was easy for the balanced case and extended easily to the unbalanced one-way case. However, for the unbalanced two-way case, Wansbeek and Kapteyn (1989) showed that this transformation is a little complicated but nevertheless manageable. To see this, we need some more matrix results.

Exercise 9.5 *(Fixed effects for the two-way unbalanced panel data model).* This is based on Problem 9.6 in Baltagi (2008).

(a) Show that $\Delta_N \equiv \Delta_1'\Delta_1 = \text{diag}[T_i]$, where T_i is the number of years individual i is observed in the panel. Also, $\Delta_T \equiv \Delta_2'\Delta_2 = \text{diag}[N_t]$, where N_t is the number of individuals observed in year t and $\Delta_{TN} \equiv \Delta_2'\Delta_1$ is the $(T \times N)$ matrix of zeros and ones indicating the absence or presence of a household in a certain year. Show that for the complete panel data case $\Delta_N = TI_N$, $\Delta_T = NI_T$, and $\Delta_{TN} = J_{TN}$ which is a matrix of ones of dimension $(T \times N)$.

(b) Define $P_{[\Delta]} = \Delta(\Delta'\Delta)^{-}\Delta'$; then the within transformation is given by $Q_{[\Delta]} = I_n - P_{[\Delta]}$. For $X = (X_1, X_2)$, use the result that the generalized inverse of $(X'X)$ is

$$(X'X)^{-} = \begin{bmatrix} (X_1'X_1)^{-} & 0 \\ 0 & 0 \end{bmatrix} + \begin{bmatrix} -(X_1'X_1)^{-}X_1'X_2 \\ I \end{bmatrix} (X_2'Q_{[X_1]}X_2)^{-}[-X_2'X_1(X_1'X_1)^{-} I]$$

to show that $P_{[X]} = P_{[X_1]} + P_{[Q_{[X_1]}X_2]}$. See the Appendix in Davis (2002).

(c) Apply this result to the two-way unbalanced model with $\Delta = (\Delta_1, \Delta_2)$ given by (9.14), and show that

$$P_{[\Delta]} = P_{\Delta_1} + P_{[Q_{[\Delta_1]}\Delta_2]}$$

and

$$Q_{[\Delta]} = Q_{[\Delta_1]} - Q_{[\Delta_1]}\Delta_2(\Delta_2'Q_{[\Delta_1]}\Delta_2)^{-}\Delta_2'Q_{[\Delta_1]} \tag{9.15}$$

which is the result obtained by Wansbeek and Kapteyn (1989). Show that for the complete panel data case, $Q = E_T \otimes E_N$, as described in equation (3.3) and Exercise 3.1.

Solution

(a) From (9.14), $\Delta_1 = (D_1', \ldots, D_T')'$ where D_t is the $(N_t \times N)$ matrix obtained from I_N by omitting the rows corresponding to individuals not observed in year t. Therefore,

$$\Delta_N \equiv \Delta_1'\Delta_1 = \sum_{t=1}^{T} D_t'D_t = \text{diag}[T_i]$$

$D_t'D_t$ is an $N \times N$ diagonal matrix that has ones on the diagonal only for individuals observed in period t. Summing these matrices across t yields a diagonal matrix with each element of the diagonal representing the number of periods that particular individual is observed over the entire sample, i.e., T_i. Hence, $\Delta_N = \text{diag}[T_i]$ where T_i is the number of years individual i is observed in the panel. Now $\Delta_T \equiv \Delta_2'\Delta_2$, where $\Delta_2 = \text{diag}[D_t\iota_N] = \text{diag}[\iota_{N_t}]$ since $D_t\iota_N$ yields a vector of N_t ones. Hence,

$$\Delta_T = \text{diag}[\iota_{N_t}']\text{diag}[\iota_{N_t}] = \text{diag}[\iota_{N_t}'\iota_{N_t}] = \text{diag}[N_t]$$

where N_t is the number of individuals observed in year t. For complete panels, all individuals are observed in every period. Therefore, $N_t = N$ and $D_t = I_N$ for every t. Hence, $\Delta_1 = (I_N, \ldots, I_N)' = \iota_T \otimes I_N$. In this case

$$\Delta_N = \Delta_1'\Delta_1 = (\iota_T' \otimes I_N)(\iota_T \otimes I_N) = TI_N$$

Similarly, $\Delta_2 = \text{diag}[\iota_N] = (I_T \otimes \iota_N)$ and

$$\Delta_T = \Delta_2'\Delta_2 = I_T \otimes \iota_N'\iota_N = NI_T$$

$\Delta_{TN} \equiv \Delta_2'\Delta_1$ is the $(T \times N)$ matrix of zeros and ones indicating the absence or presence of a household in a certain year. For complete panels, $\Delta_2 = I_T \otimes \iota_N$ and $\Delta_1 = \iota_T \otimes I_N$, therefore $\Delta_{TN} = (I_T \otimes \iota_N')(\iota_T \otimes I_N) = \iota_T \otimes \iota_N' = J_{TN}$ as required, since we observe every household in any specific year.

(b) Premultiplying $(X'X)^-$ by $X = (X_1, X_2)$, we get

$$\begin{aligned} X(X'X)^- &= [X_1(X_1'X_1)^- \quad 0] + [X_2 - X_1(X_1'X_1)^- X_1'X_2] \\ &\quad (X_2'Q_{[X_1]}X_2)^-[-X_2'X_1(X_1'X_1)^- \quad I] \end{aligned}$$

Postmultiplying by X' we get

$$\begin{aligned} P_{[X]} &= P_{[X_1]} + \left[X_2 - X_1(X_1'X_1)^- X_1'X_2\right](X_2'Q_{[X_1]}X_2)^-[X_2' - X_2'P_{[X_1]}] \\ &= P_{[X_1]} + (X_2'Q_{[X_1]}X_2)(X_2'Q_{[X_1]}X_2)^-(X_2'Q_{[X_1]}X_2) \\ &= P_{[X_1]} + P_{[Q_{[X_1]}X_2]} \end{aligned}$$

(c) Applying the result in part (b) to the two-way unbalanced model with $\Delta = (\Delta_1, \Delta_2)$ given by (9.14), we get

$$P_{[\Delta]} = P_{\Delta_1} + P_{[Q_{[\Delta_1]}\Delta_2]}$$

and hence the within transformation is given by $Q_{[\Delta]} = I_n - P_{[\Delta]}$, which upon substitution gives

$$Q_{[\Delta]} = Q_{[\Delta_1]} - Q_{[\Delta_1]}\Delta_2(\Delta_2'Q_{[\Delta_1]}\Delta_2)^-\Delta_2'Q_{[\Delta_1]}$$

as required. For complete panels, $\Delta_1 = \iota_T \otimes I_N$, with

$$P_{\Delta_1} = \Delta_1(\Delta_1'\Delta_1)^{-1}\Delta_1' = (\iota_T \otimes I_N)(TI_N)^{-1}(\iota_T' \otimes I_N) = \bar{J}_T \otimes I_N$$

Hence,

$$\begin{aligned} Q_{[\Delta_1]} &= I_n - P_{\Delta_1} = (I_T - \bar{J}_T) \otimes I_N = E_T \otimes I_N \\ Q_{[\Delta_1]}\Delta_2 &= (E_T \otimes I_N)(I_T \otimes \iota_N) = E_T \otimes \iota_N \\ \Delta_2'Q_{[\Delta_1]}\Delta_2 &= (I_T \otimes \iota_N')(E_T \otimes \iota_N) = NE_T \end{aligned}$$

with

$$(\Delta_2'Q_{[\Delta_1]}\Delta_2)^- = \frac{1}{N}E_T$$

Hence,

$$Q_{[\Delta_1]}\Delta_2(\Delta_2'Q_{[\Delta_1]}\Delta_2)^-\Delta_2'Q_{[\Delta_1]} = (E_T \otimes \iota_N)(\frac{1}{N}E_T)(E_T \otimes \iota_N') = E_T \otimes \bar{J}_N$$

and

$$Q_{[\Delta]} = (E_T \otimes I_N) - (E_T \otimes \bar{J}_N) = E_T \otimes (I_N - \bar{J}_N) = E_T \otimes E_N$$

as required.

Davis (2002) generalizes the Wansbeek and Kapteyn (1989) results to the three-way, four-way and higher-order error component models. Davis shows that the within transformation can be applied in stages to the variables in the regression, just as in (9.15). This reduces the computational burden considerably.

Exercise 9.6 *(Fixed effects for the three-way unbalanced panel data model).* This is based on Problem 9.7 in Baltagi (2008).

(a) Consider the three-way error component model described in Exercise 3.11, reproduced here for convenience:

$$u_{itq} = \mu_i + \lambda_t + \eta_q + \nu_{itq}$$

The panel data can be unbalanced and the matrices of dummy variables are $\Delta = [\Delta_1, \Delta_2, \Delta_3]$ with

$$u = \Delta_1\mu + \Delta_2\lambda + \Delta_3\eta + \nu \tag{9.16}$$

If the μ_i and λ_t are fixed and $\nu_{it} \sim \text{IIN}(0, \sigma_\nu^2)$, one has to run the regression given in (9.13) with the matrix of dummies given in (9.16). Most likely, this will be infeasible and the familiar within transformation can be applied in stages. Show that $P_{[\Delta]} = P_{[A]} + P_{[B]} + P_{[C]}$ where $A = \Delta_1$, $B = Q_{[A]}\Delta_2$ and $C = Q_{[B]}Q_{[A]}\Delta_3$. This is Corollary 1 of Davis (2002, p.70).

(b) Deduce that the within transformation can be obtained as $Q_{[\Delta]} = Q_{[A]} - P_{[B]} - P_{[C]}$.

(c) Show that $Q_{[A]}Q_{[B]} = Q_{[B]}Q_{[A]}$ and $P_{[B]}Q_{[A]} = P_{[B]}$, and deduce that $Q_{[A]}Q_{[B]}Q_{[A]} = Q_{[A]}Q_{[B]}$.

Solution

(a) Apply (9.15) twice. Let $X_1 = \Delta_1 = A$ and $X_2 = (\Delta_2, \Delta_3)$. Using Exercise 9.7, we get $P_{[X]} = P_{[\Delta_1]} + P_{[Q_{[\Delta_1]}X_2]} = P_{[A]} + P_{[Q_{[\Delta_1]}X_2]}$. Now, $Q_{[\Delta_1]}X_2 = Q_{[\Delta_1]}(\Delta_2, \Delta_3) = [B, Q_{[A]}\Delta_3]$. Applying (9.15) again, we get $P_{[B, Q_{[A]}\Delta_3]} = P_{[B]} + P_{[Q_{[B]}Q_{[A]}\Delta_3]} = P_{[B]} + P_{[C]}$. Hence, $P_{[\Delta]} = P_{[A]} + P_{[B]} + P_{[C]}$ as required.

(b) $Q_{[\Delta]} = I_n - P_{[\Delta]} = Q_{[A]} - P_{[B]} - P_{[C]}$ where $A = \Delta_1$, $B = Q_{[A]}\Delta_2$, and $C = Q_{[B]}Q_{[A]}\Delta_3$. This idea generalizes readily to higher-order FE error components models.

(c) $Q_{[A]}Q_{[B]} = Q_{[A]}(I_n - P_{[B]}) = Q_{[A]} - P_{[B]}$, since $Q_{[A]}$ is idempotent with $Q_{[A]}B = Q_{[A]}^2\Delta_2 = Q_{[A]}\Delta_2 = B$. This immediately implies that $Q_{[A]}P_{[B]} = P_{[B]}$. Similarly, $Q_{[B]}Q_{[A]} = (I_n - P_{[B]})Q_{[A]} = Q_{[A]} - P_{[B]}$, since $P_{[B]}$ is symmetric with $P_{[B]} = P_{[B]}Q_{[A]}$. Alternatively, we can use the fact that $B'Q_{[A]} = \Delta_2'Q_{[A]}^2 = \Delta_2'Q_{[A]} = B'$, and hence that $P_{[B]}Q_{[A]} = P_{[B]}$. Therefore, $Q_{[A]}Q_{[B]} = Q_{[B]}Q_{[A]}$. Premultiplying this last equality by $Q_{[A]}$, we get $Q_{[A]}Q_{[B]} = Q_{[A]}Q_{[B]}Q_{[A]}$ as required.

For the random two-way error component model with unbalanced data, we can write the disturbances as

$$u = \Delta_1\mu + \Delta_2\lambda + \nu \tag{9.17}$$

where $\mu' = (\mu_1, \ldots, \mu_N)$, $\lambda' = (\lambda_1, \ldots, \lambda_T)$, and ν are random variables described in Chapter 3. μ, λ and ν are independent of each other and among themselves with zero means and variances σ_μ^2, σ_λ^2 and σ_ν^2, respectively. In this case,

$$\begin{aligned}\Omega = E(uu') &= \sigma_\nu^2 I_n + \sigma_\mu^2 \Delta_1\Delta_1' + \sigma_\lambda^2 \Delta_2\Delta_2' \\ &= \sigma_\nu^2(I_n + \phi_1\Delta_1\Delta_1' + \phi_2\Delta_2\Delta_2') = \sigma_\nu^2\Sigma \end{aligned} \tag{9.18}$$

with $\phi_1 = \sigma_\mu^2/\sigma_\nu^2$ and $\phi_2 = \sigma_\lambda^2/\sigma_\nu^2$.

Exercise 9.7 *(Random effects for the unbalanced two-way panel data model)*

(a) Let $X = (X_1, X_2)$ with $|I + XX'| \neq 0$. Using the result that

$$[I_n + XX']^{-1} = I_n - X(I + X'X)^{-1}X'$$

apply the partitioned inverse formula to show that

$$(I_n + XX')^{-1} = \widetilde{Q}_{[X_2]} - \widetilde{Q}_{[X_2]}X_1S^{-1}X_1'\widetilde{Q}_{[X_2]}$$

where

$$\widetilde{Q}_{[X_2]} = I - X_2(I + X_2'X_2)^{-1}X_2' = (I + X_2X_2')^{-1}$$

and $S = I + X_1'\widetilde{Q}_{[X_2]}X_1$. This is Lemma 2 of Davis (2002).

(b) Apply the results in part (a) using $X = (\frac{\sigma_\mu}{\sigma_\nu}\Delta_1, \frac{\sigma_\lambda}{\sigma_\nu}\Delta_2)$ to obtain Σ^{-1}, where Σ is given in (9.18).

Solution

(a) Applying the partitioned inverse formula, we get

$$[I + X'X]^{-1} = \begin{bmatrix} I + X_1'X_1 & X_1'X_2 \\ X_2'X_1 & I + X_2'X_2 \end{bmatrix}^{-1}$$

$$\times \begin{bmatrix} S^{-1} & -S^{-1}X_1'X_2 \\ & (I + X_2'X_2)^{-1} \\ -(I + X_2'X_2)^{-1}X_2' & (I + X_2'X_2)^{-1} \\ X_1S^{-1} & [I + X_2'X_1S^{-1}X_1'X_2(I + X_2'X_2)^{-1}] \end{bmatrix}$$

where

$$S = I + X_1'X_1 - X_1'X_2(I + X_2'X_2)^{-1}X_2'X_1 = I + X_1'\widetilde{Q}_{[X_2]}X_1$$

Postmultiplying by X' gives

$$\begin{bmatrix} S^{-1}X_1' - S^{-1}X_1'\widetilde{P}_{[X_2]} \\ -(I + X_2'X_2)^{-1}X_2'X_1S^{-1}X_1' + (I + X_2'X_2)^{-1}\left[I + X_2'X_1S^{-1}X_1'X_2(I + X_2'X_2)^{-1}\right]X_2' \end{bmatrix}$$

where $\widetilde{P}_{[X_2]} = X_2(I + X_2'X_2)^{-1}X_2'$. Premultiplying by X, we get

$$\begin{aligned} X[I + X'X]^{-1}X' &= X_1S^{-1}X_1'\widetilde{Q}_{[X_2]} - \widetilde{P}_{[X_2]}X_1S^{-1}X_1' + \widetilde{P}_{[X_2]} + \widetilde{P}_{[X_2]}X_1S^{-1}X_1'\widetilde{P}_{[X_2]} \\ &= \widetilde{P}_{[X_2]} + \widetilde{Q}_{[X_2]}X_1S^{-1}X_1'\widetilde{Q}_{[X_2]} \end{aligned}$$

Therefore,

$$(I_n + XX')^{-1} = I_n - X(I + X'X)^{-1}X' = \widetilde{Q}_{[X_2]} - \widetilde{Q}_{[X_2]}X_1S^{-1}X_1'\widetilde{Q}_{[X_2]}$$

as required.

(b) Let $X = (\frac{\sigma_\mu}{\sigma_\nu}\Delta_1, \frac{\sigma_\lambda}{\sigma_\nu}\Delta_2)$. Then $XX' = \phi_1\Delta_1\Delta_1' + \phi_2\Delta_2\Delta_2'$ and Σ in (9.18) is now of the form $(I_n + XX')$. Hence, Σ^{-1} can be obtained by applying the results in part (a). In fact, Wansbeek and Kapteyn (1989) chose $X_2 = \frac{\sigma_\mu}{\sigma_\nu}\Delta_1$ and $X_1 = \frac{\sigma_\lambda}{\sigma_\nu}\Delta_2$ to obtain

$$\Sigma^{-1} = \widetilde{Q}_{[\Delta_1]} - \widetilde{Q}_{[\Delta_1]}\Delta_2S^{-1}\Delta_2'\widetilde{Q}_{[\Delta_1]} \tag{9.19}$$

where

$$\widetilde{Q}_{[\Delta_1]} = I - \phi_1\Delta_1(I + \phi_1\Delta_1'\Delta_1)^{-1}\Delta_1' = (I + \phi_1\Delta_1\Delta_1')^{-1}$$

Note that we can no longer obtain the simple Fuller and Battese (1973) transformation for the unbalanced two-way model. The expression for Σ^{-1} is messy and asymmetric in individuals and time, but it reduces computational time considerably relative to inverting Σ numerically. Davis (2002) shows that the Wansbeek and Kapteyn results can be generalized to an arbitrary number of random error components.

Exercise 9.8 *(Random effects for the unbalanced three-way panel data model).* This is based on Problem 9.8 in Baltagi (2008). Consider the three-way error component model described in (9.16) in Exercise 9.6. In this case, μ, λ, η and ν are independent of each other and among themselves with zero means and variances σ_μ^2, σ_λ^2, σ_η^2 and σ_ν^2, respectively. In this case

$$\begin{aligned} \Omega = E(uu') &= \sigma_\nu^2 I_n + \sigma_\mu^2\Delta_1\Delta_1' + \sigma_\lambda^2\Delta_2\Delta_2' + \sigma_\eta^2\Delta_3\Delta_3' \\ &= \sigma_\nu^2(I_n + \phi_1\Delta_1\Delta_1' + \phi_2\Delta_2\Delta_2' + \phi_3\Delta_3\Delta_3') = \sigma_\nu^2\Sigma \end{aligned} \tag{9.20}$$

with $\phi_1 = \sigma_\mu^2/\sigma_\nu^2$, $\phi_2 = \sigma_\lambda^2/\sigma_\nu^2$, and $\phi_3 = \sigma_\eta^2/\sigma_\nu^2$. Apply the results in Exercise 9.7 using $X = (\frac{\sigma_\mu}{\sigma_\nu}\Delta_1, \frac{\sigma_\lambda}{\sigma_\nu}\Delta_2, \frac{\sigma_\eta}{\sigma_\nu}\Delta_3)$ to obtain Σ^{-1}.

Solution

The added random error component η adds an extra $\sigma_\eta^2\Delta_3\Delta_3'$ term to the variance–covariance matrix for the two-way unbalanced model given in (9.18) to yield the Σ given in (9.20). Therefore, Σ remains of $(I_n + XX')$ form and its inverse $(I_n + XX')^{-1}$ can be obtained by repeated application of the inversion formula described in Exercise 9.7. This idea generalizes readily to higher-order unbalanced random error component models. Let $Y_1 = \frac{\sigma_\mu}{\sigma_\nu}\Delta_1$, $Y_2 = \frac{\sigma_\lambda}{\sigma_\nu}\Delta_2$, and $Y_3 = \frac{\sigma_\eta}{\sigma_\nu}\Delta_3$. Then $X = (Y_1, Y_2, Y_3)$ with $X_1 = Y_1$ and $X_2 = (Y_2, Y_3)$. Since

$$\widetilde{Q}_{[X_2]} = I - X_2(I + X_2'X_2)^{-1}X_2' = (I + X_2X_2')^{-1}$$

the above results can be applied a *second time* to provide an analytic expression for $\widetilde{Q}_{[X_2]} = \widetilde{Q}_{[Y_2,Y_3]}$. In fact,

$$(I_n + XX')^{-1} = \widetilde{Q}_{[Y_2,Y_3]} - \widetilde{Q}_{[Y_2,Y_3]}Y_1S_1^{-1}Y_1'\widetilde{Q}_{[Y_2,Y_3]}$$

with

$$\begin{aligned}
\widetilde{Q}_{[Y_2,Y_3]} &= \widetilde{Q}_{[Y_3]} - \widetilde{Q}_{[Y_3]}Y_2S_2^{-1}Y_2'\widetilde{Q}_{[Y_3]} \\
\widetilde{Q}_{[Y_3]} &= I - Y_3(I + Y_3'Y_3)^{-1}Y_3' \\
S_1 &= I + Y_1'\widetilde{Q}_{[Y_2,Y_3]}Y_1 \quad \text{and} \quad S_2 = I + Y_2'\widetilde{Q}_{[Y_3]}Y_2
\end{aligned}$$

One computes the inverse of three matrices, S_1, S_2, and $(I + Y_3'Y_3)$. These matrices have dimensions equal to the number of columns of Y_1, Y_2, and Y_3, respectively. Davis (2002, p.301) suggests judicious choice of Y_3 to minimize the dimension of the numerical inversion.

Exercise 9.9 *(Wansbeek and Kapteyn (1989)-type estimators for the variance components of a two-way unbalanced panel data model).* This is based on Problem 9.8, part (e), in Baltagi (2008). For the two-way unbalanced random effects model considered in Exercise 9.7, Wansbeek and Kapteyn suggest an ANOVA-type quadratic unbiased estimator of the variance components based on the within residuals. Let $\widetilde{\beta} = (X'Q_{[\Delta]}X)^{-1}X'Q_{[\Delta]}y$ denote the within estimates, where $Q_{[\Delta]}$ was derived in Exercise 9.5 and is given by (9.15). Let $e = y - X\widetilde{\beta}$ denote the corresponding residuals. Define

$$q_W = e'Q_{[\Delta]}e \tag{9.21}$$

$$q_i = e'P_{[\Delta_i]}e \quad \text{for } i = 1, 2 \tag{9.22}$$

By equating q_W and q_i for $i = 1, 2$ to their expected values and solving these three equations, one gets quadratic unbiased estimators of σ_ν^2, σ_μ^2 and σ_λ^2. Derive $E(q_W)$ and $E(q_i)$ for $i = 1, 2$.

Solution

Letting

$$M = I_n - X\left(X'Q_{[\Delta]}X\right)^{-1}X'Q_{[\Delta]}$$

then $e = My = Mu$. Then

$$E(q_W) = E(e'Q_{[\Delta]}e) = E(u'M'Q_{[\Delta]}Mu) = E(\text{tr}\{uu'M'Q_{[\Delta]}M\})$$
$$= \text{tr}\{\Omega M'Q_{[\Delta]}M\} = \text{tr}\{M\Omega M'Q_{[\Delta]}\}$$

with

$$M\Omega = \Omega - X\left(X'Q_{[\Delta]}X\right)^{-1}X'Q_{[\Delta]}\Omega$$

But

$$Q_{[\Delta]}\Omega = \sigma_\nu^2 Q_{[\Delta]}, \quad \text{since } Q_{[\Delta]}\Delta_i = 0 \text{ for } i = 1, 2$$

Hence,

$$M\Omega = \Omega - \sigma_\nu^2 X\left(X'Q_{[\Delta]}X\right)^{-1}X'Q_{[\Delta]}$$
$$M\Omega M' = \Omega - \sigma_\nu^2 X\left(X'Q_{[\Delta]}X\right)^{-1}X'Q_{[\Delta]} - \sigma_\nu^2 Q_{[\Delta]}X\left(X'Q_{[\Delta]}X\right)^{-1}X'$$
$$+\sigma_\nu^2 X\left(X'Q_{[\Delta]}X\right)^{-1}X'$$
$$\text{tr}\{M\Omega M'Q_{[\Delta]}\} = \sigma_\nu^2\text{tr}\{Q_{[\Delta]}\} - \sigma_\nu^2\text{tr}\{X'Q_{[\Delta]}X\left(X'Q_{[\Delta]}X\right)^{-1}\}$$

with

$$\text{tr}\{Q_{[\Delta]}\} = n - \text{tr}\{P_{[\Delta_1]}\} - \text{tr}\{(\Delta_2'Q_{[\Delta_1]}\Delta_2)(\Delta_2'Q_{[\Delta_1]}\Delta_2)^{-}\}$$
$$= n - \text{tr}\{P_{[\Delta_1]}\} - \text{tr}\{P_{[Q_{[\Delta_1]}\Delta_2]}\} = n - t_1 - t_2$$

where $t_1 = tr\{P_{[\Delta_1]}\} = \text{rank}(\Delta_1)$, $t_2 = \text{tr}\{P_{[Q_{[\Delta_1]}\Delta_2]}\} = \text{rank}(Q_{[\Delta_1]}\Delta_2)$. Hence,

$$E(q_W) = \text{tr}\{M\Omega M'Q_{[\Delta]}\} = \sigma_\nu^2(n - t_1 - t_2 - k_w)$$

where $k_w = \text{tr}\{X'Q_{[\Delta]}X(X'Q_{[\Delta]}X)^{-1}\}$. Similarly,

$$E(q_i) = E(e'P_{[\Delta_i]}e) = E(u'M'P_{[\Delta_i]}Mu) = E(\text{tr}\{uu'M'P_{[\Delta_i]}M\})$$
$$= \text{tr}\{\Omega M'P_{[\Delta_i]}M\} = \text{tr}\{M\Omega M'P_{[\Delta_i]}\}$$

Using $P_{[\Delta_i]}Q_{[\Delta]} = 0$, we get

$$\text{tr}\{M\Omega M'P_{[\Delta_i]}\} = \text{tr}\{P_{[\Delta_i]}\Omega\} + \sigma_\nu^2\text{tr}\{X'P_{[\Delta_i]}X\left(X'Q_{[\Delta]}X\right)^{-1}\}$$
$$= \text{tr}\{P_{[\Delta_i]}\Omega\} + \sigma_\nu^2 k_i \quad \text{for } i = 1, 2$$

where $k_i = \text{tr}\{X'P_{[\Delta_i]}X(X'Q_{[\Delta]}X)^{-1}\}$ for $i = 1, 2$. But

$$\text{tr}\{P_{[\Delta_i]}\Delta_i\Delta_i'\} = tr\{\Delta_i\Delta_i'\} = n, \qquad \text{tr}\{P_{[\Delta_1]}\} = N, \qquad \text{tr}\{P_{[\Delta_2]}\} = T$$

Hence,

$$E(q_1) = n\sigma_\mu^2 + \sigma_\nu^2(N + k_1) + \sigma_\lambda^2 k_{12}$$
$$E(q_2) = k_{21}\sigma_\mu^2 + \sigma_\nu^2(T + k_2) + n\sigma_\lambda^2$$

where $k_{ij} = \text{tr}\{P_{[\Delta_i]}\Delta_j\Delta_j'\}$ for $i, j = 1, 2$. Solving these three equations for three unknowns, we get the unbiased estimates of the variance components.

9.3 TESTING FOR INDIVIDUAL AND TIME EFFECTS USING UNBALANCED PANEL DATA

In Chapter 4, we derived the Breusch and Pagan (1980) LM test for $H_0: \sigma_\mu^2 = \sigma_\lambda^2 = 0$ in a complete panel data model with two-way error component disturbances. Baltagi and Li (1990b) derived the corresponding LM test for the unbalanced two-way error component model. This model is given by (9.13) and the variance–covariance matrix of the disturbances is given by (9.18).

Exercise 9.10 *(Breusch and Pagan (1980) LM test for unbalanced panel data).* This is based on Problem 9.10 in Baltagi (2008).

(a) Show that under normality of the disturbances,

$$\partial\Omega/\partial\sigma_\mu^2 = \Delta_1\Delta_1', \qquad \partial\Omega/\partial\sigma_\lambda^2 = \Delta_2\Delta_2', \qquad \partial\Omega/\partial\sigma_\nu^2 = I_n \tag{9.23}$$

(b) Show that the score evaluated under H_0 is given by

$$\widetilde{D} = (\partial L/\partial\theta)\mid_{\theta=\widetilde{\theta}} = (n/2\widetilde{\sigma}_\nu^2)\begin{bmatrix} A_1 \\ A_2 \\ 0 \end{bmatrix} \tag{9.24}$$

where $\theta' = (\sigma_\mu^2, \sigma_\lambda^2, \sigma_\nu^2)$, $\widetilde{\theta}$ denotes the restricted maximum likelihood estimate of θ under H_0, $\widetilde{\sigma}_\nu^2 = \widetilde{u}'\widetilde{u}/NT$, and $A_r = [(\widetilde{u}'\Delta_r\Delta_r'\widetilde{u}/\widetilde{u}'\widetilde{u}) - 1]$ for $r = 1, 2$, with $\widetilde{u}$ denoting the OLS residuals. Show that the information matrix under H_0 given by

$$\widetilde{J} = n/2\widetilde{\sigma}_\nu^4 \begin{bmatrix} M_{11}/n & 1 & 1 \\ 1 & M_{22}/n & 1 \\ 1 & 1 & 1 \end{bmatrix} \tag{9.25}$$

where $M_{11} = \sum_{i=1}^N T_i^2$ and $M_{22} = \sum_{t=1}^T N_t^2$.

Solution

(a) Under normality of the disturbances, the loglikelihood function is given by

$$L(\beta, \theta) = \text{constant} - \frac{1}{2}\log\mid\Omega\mid - \frac{1}{2}u'\Omega^{-1}u \tag{9.26}$$

where $\theta' = (\sigma_\mu^2, \sigma_\lambda^2, \sigma_\nu^2)$ and Ω is given by (9.18). It immediately follows from (9.18) that

$$\partial\Omega/\partial\sigma_\mu^2 = \Delta_1\Delta_1', \qquad \partial\Omega/\partial\sigma_\lambda^2 = \Delta_2\Delta_2', \qquad \partial\Omega/\partial\sigma_\nu^2 = I_n$$

(b) The information matrix is block-diagonal between θ and β. Since H_0 involves only θ, the part of the information matrix due to β is ignored. Recall the Hartley and Rao (1967) or Hemmerle and Hartley (1973) general formula to obtain $D(\theta)$ given in (4.17) and reproduced here for convenience:

$$\partial L/\partial\theta_r = -\frac{1}{2}\text{tr}[\Omega^{-1}(\partial\Omega/\partial\theta_r)] + \frac{1}{2}[u'\Omega^{-1}(\partial\Omega/\partial\theta_r)\Omega^{-1}u]$$

for $r = 1, 2, 3$. The restricted maximum likelihood estimator of Ω under H_0 is $\widetilde{\Omega} = \widetilde{\sigma}_\nu^2 I_{NT}$, where $\widetilde{\sigma}_\nu^2 = \widetilde{u}'\widetilde{u}/NT$ and $\widetilde{u}$ are the OLS residuals. Using the results

$$\text{tr}(\Delta_2\Delta_2') = \text{tr}(\Delta_2'\Delta_2) = \text{tr}(\text{diag}[N_t]) = \sum_{t=1}^{T} N_t = n \tag{9.27}$$

$$\text{tr}(\Delta_1'\Delta_1) = \text{tr}(\text{diag}[T_i]) = \sum_{i=1}^{N} T_i = n \tag{9.28}$$

$$\text{tr}(\Delta_2\Delta_2')^2 = \sum_{t=1}^{T} N_t^2, \ \ \text{tr}(\Delta_1\Delta_1')^2 = \sum_{i=1}^{N} T_i^2 \tag{9.29}$$

$$\text{tr}[(\Delta_1\Delta_1')(\Delta_2\Delta_2')] = \sum_{t=1}^{T} \text{tr}[(D_t D_t')J_{N_t}] = \sum_{t=1}^{T} \text{tr}(J_{N_t}) = \sum_{t=1}^{T} N_t = n$$

one gets the LM statistic

$$\text{LM} = \widetilde{D}'\widetilde{J}^{-1}\widetilde{D} = 1/2n^2[A_1^2/(M_{11} - n) + A_2^2/(M_{22} - n)] \tag{9.30}$$

which is asymptotically distributed as χ_2^2 under the null hypothesis. For computational purposes, one need not form the Δ_r matrices to compute $A_r (r = 1, 2)$. In fact,

$$\widetilde{u}\Delta_1\Delta_1'\widetilde{u} = \sum_{i=1}^{N} \widetilde{u}_{i.}^2 \quad \text{where } \widetilde{u}_{i.} = \sum_{t=1}^{T_i} \widetilde{u}_{it} \tag{9.31}$$

and

$$\widetilde{u}'\Delta_2\Delta_2'\widetilde{u} = \sum_{t=1}^{T} \widetilde{u}_{.t}^2 \quad \text{where } \widetilde{u}_{.t} = \sum_{i=1}^{N_t} \widetilde{u}_{it} \tag{9.32}$$

Equation (9.32) is obvious, since $\Delta_2 = \text{diag}[\iota_{N_t}]$, and (9.31) can be similarly obtained, by restacking the residuals such that the faster index is t. The LM statistic given in

(9.30) is easily computed using least squares residuals, and retains a similar form to that for the complete panel data case. In fact, when $N_t = N$, (9.30) reverts back to the LM statistic derived in Breusch and Pagan (1980). Also, (9.30) retains the additive property exhibited in the complete panel data case, i.e., if $H_0: \sigma_\mu^2 = 0$, the LM test reduces to the first term of (9.30), whereas if $H_0: \sigma_\lambda^2 = 0$, the LM test reduces to the second term of (9.30). Both test statistics are asymptotically distributed as χ_1^2 under the respective null hypotheses.

These variance components cannot be negative and therefore $H_0: \sigma_\mu^2 = 0$ has to be against a one-sided alternative $H_1: \sigma_\mu^2 > 0$. Moulton and Randolph (1989) derived the one-sided LM_1 statistic

$$\text{LM}_1 = n[2(M_{11} - n)]^{-1/2} A_1 \tag{9.33}$$

which is the square root of the first term in (9.30). Under weak conditions as $n \to \infty$ and $N \to \infty$ the LM_1 statistic has an asymptotic standard normal distribution under H_0. However, Moulton and Randolph (1989) showed that this asymptotic $N(0, 1)$ approximation can be poor even in large samples. This occurs when the number of regressors is large or the intra-class correlation of some of the regressors is high. They suggest an alternative standardized Lagrange multiplier given by

$$\text{SLM} = \frac{\text{LM}_1 - E(\text{LM}_1)}{\sqrt{\text{var}(\text{LM}_1)}} = \frac{d - E(d)}{\sqrt{\text{var}(d)}} \tag{9.34}$$

where $d = (\tilde{u}'D\tilde{u})/\tilde{u}'\tilde{u}$ and $D = \Delta_1\Delta_1'$. Using the results on moments of quadratic forms in regression residuals (see Evans and King, 1985), we get

$$E(d) = \text{tr}(D\overline{P}_Z)/p$$

where $p = [n - (K + 1)]$, and

$$\text{var}(d) = 2\{p\text{tr}(D\overline{P}_Z)^2 - [\text{tr}(D\overline{P}_Z)]^2\}/p^2(p + 2)$$

Under H_0, this SLM has the same asymptotic $N(0, 1)$ distribution as the LM_1 statistic. However, the asymptotic critical values for the SLM are generally closer to the exact critical values than those of the LM_1 statistic. Similarly, for $H_0: \sigma_\lambda^2 = 0$, the one-sided LM test statistic is the square root of the second term in (9.30), i.e.

$$\text{LM}_2 = n[2(M_{22} - n)]^{-1/2} A_2 \tag{9.35}$$

Honda's (1985) 'handy' one-sided test for the two-way model with unbalanced data is simply

$$\text{HO} = (\text{LM}_1 + \text{LM}_2)/\sqrt{2}$$

Exercise 9.11 *(Locally mean most powerful one-sided test for unbalanced panel data).* This is based on Problem 9.11 in Baltagi (2008). Show that the LMMP one-sided test suggested by King and Wu (1997) for the unbalanced two-way error component model is given by

$$\mathrm{KW} = \frac{\sqrt{M_{11} - n}}{\sqrt{M_{11} + M_{22} - 2n}}\mathrm{LM}_1 + \frac{\sqrt{M_{22} - n}}{\sqrt{M_{11} + M_{22} - 2n}}\mathrm{LM}_2 \tag{9.36}$$

where LM_1 and LM_2 are given by (9.33) and (9.35), respectively.

Solution

The King and Wu (1997) LMMP test for $H_0^c : \sigma_\mu^2 = \sigma_\lambda^2 = 0$ in the unbalanced case is given as

$$\mathrm{KW} = \widetilde{S}^+ / (\iota_2'(g^{11})^{-1}\iota_2)^{1/2}$$

where ι_2 is a vector of ones of dimension 2. The numerator of this test statistic is obtained from the scores

$$\widetilde{S}^+ = \sum_{i=1}^{2} (\partial L/\partial \theta_i)_{\widetilde{\theta}' = (0,0,\widetilde{\sigma}_\nu^2)}$$

where $(\partial L/\partial \theta_i)_{\widetilde{\theta}' = (0,0,\widetilde{\sigma}_\nu^2)}$ is given by (9.24) and $\widetilde{\sigma}_\nu^2 = \widetilde{u}'\widetilde{u}/NT$ with $\widetilde{u}$ denoting the OLS residuals. Substituting (9.24) into $\widetilde{S}^+$ gives

$$\widetilde{S}^+ = \frac{n}{2\widetilde{\sigma}_\nu^2}[A_1 + A_2]$$

where $A_r = [(\widetilde{u}'\Delta_r\Delta_r'\widetilde{u}/\widetilde{u}'\widetilde{u}) - 1]$ for $r = 1, 2$ and Δ_1 and Δ_2 are defined below (9.14).

The information matrix for the unbalanced two-way error component model evaluated at the restricted maximum likelihood estimate estimator $\widetilde{\theta}$ is given in (9.25) as

$$\widetilde{J} = \frac{n}{2\widetilde{\sigma}_\nu^4}\begin{bmatrix} M_{11}/n & 1 & 1 \\ 1 & M_{22}/n & 1 \\ 1 & 1 & 1 \end{bmatrix}$$

where $M_{11} = \sum_{i=1}^N T_i^2$ and $M_{22} = \sum_{t=1}^T N_t^2$. Taking the inverse of the above information matrix and concentrating on the upper 2×2 sub-matrix, we get

$$g^{11} = \frac{2\widetilde{\sigma}_\nu^4}{n\left(\frac{M_{22}}{n} - 1\right)\left(\frac{M_{11}}{n} - 1\right)}\begin{bmatrix} \frac{M_{22}}{n} - 1 & 0 \\ 0 & \frac{M_{11}}{n} - 1 \end{bmatrix} = \frac{2\widetilde{\sigma}_\nu^4}{n}\begin{bmatrix} \frac{1}{\frac{M_{11}}{n} - 1} & 0 \\ 0 & \frac{1}{\frac{M_{22}}{n} - 1} \end{bmatrix}$$

The denominator of KW is obtained as follows:

$$\begin{aligned}(\iota_2'(g^{11})^{-1}\iota_2) &= \frac{n}{2\widetilde{\sigma}_\nu^2}(1, 1)\begin{bmatrix} \frac{M_{11}}{n} - 1 & 0 \\ 0 & \frac{M_{22}}{n} - 1 \end{bmatrix}\begin{pmatrix} 1 \\ 1 \end{pmatrix} \\ &= \frac{n}{2\widetilde{\sigma}_\nu^2}\left[\frac{M_{11}}{n} + \frac{M_{22}}{n} - 2\right] = \frac{M_{11} + M_{22} - 2n}{2\widetilde{\sigma}_\nu^2}\end{aligned}$$

Dividing $\widetilde{S}^+$ by $(\iota_2'(g^{11})^{-1}\iota_2)^{1/2}$ leads to

$$\mathrm{KW} = \frac{n}{\sqrt{2}\sqrt{M_{11}+M_{22}-2n}}[A_1 + A_2]$$

But $\mathrm{LM}_1 = n[2(M_{11}-n)]^{-1/2}A_1$ and $\mathrm{LM}_2 = n[2(M_{22}-n)]^{-1/2}A_2$ as described in (9.33) and (9.35), respectively. Therefore, KW can be expressed in terms of LM_1 and LM_2 as follows:

$$\begin{aligned}\mathrm{KW} &= \frac{n}{\sqrt{2}\sqrt{M_{11}+M_{22}-2n}}\left[\frac{\sqrt{2}\sqrt{M_{11}-n}}{n}\mathrm{LM}_1 + \frac{\sqrt{2}\sqrt{M_{22}-n}}{n}\mathrm{LM}_2\right]\\ &= \frac{\sqrt{M_{11}-n}}{\sqrt{M_{11}+M_{22}-2n}}\mathrm{LM}_1 + \frac{\sqrt{M_{22}-n}}{\sqrt{M_{11}+M_{22}-2n}}\mathrm{LM}_2\end{aligned}$$

as described in (9.36). Both HO and KW are asymptotically distributed as $N(0,1)$ under H_0.

Exercise 9.12 *(Standardized Honda (1985) and King and Wu (1997) tests for unbalanced panel data).* This is based on Problem 9.12 in Baltagi (2008). Show that the HO and KW test statistics can be standardized and the resulting SLM given by $\{d - E(d)\}/\sqrt{\mathrm{var}(d)}$ where $d = \tilde{u}'D\tilde{u}/\tilde{u}'\tilde{u}$ with

$$D = \frac{1}{2}\frac{n}{\sqrt{M_{11}-n}}(\Delta_1\Delta_1') + \frac{1}{2}\frac{n}{\sqrt{M_{22}-n}}(\Delta_2\Delta_2') \tag{9.37}$$

for Honda's (1985) version, and

$$D = \frac{n}{\sqrt{2}\sqrt{M_{11}+M_{22}-2n}}[(\Delta_1\Delta_1') + (\Delta_2\Delta_2')] \tag{9.38}$$

for the King and Wu (1997) version of this test. $E(d)$ and $\mathrm{var}(d)$ are obtained from the same formulas shown below (9.34) using the appropriate D matrices.

Solution

For $H_0^c: \sigma_\mu^2 = \sigma_\lambda^2 = 0$, Honda's (1985) 'handy' one-sided test applied to the unbalanced two-way error component model is given by $\mathrm{HO} = (\mathrm{LM}_1 + \mathrm{LM}_2)/\sqrt{2}$, where LM_1 is defined in (9.33) and LM_2 in (9.35). Honda's standardized test statistic can be based upon

$$\frac{n}{\sqrt{2}\sqrt{M_{11}-n}}\left[\frac{\widetilde{u}'\Delta_1\Delta_1'\widetilde{u}}{\widetilde{u}'\widetilde{u}}\right] + \frac{n}{\sqrt{2}\sqrt{M_{22}-n}}\left[\frac{\widetilde{u}'\Delta_2\Delta_2'\widetilde{u}}{\widetilde{u}'\widetilde{u}}\right]$$

since the (-1) terms in both LM_1 and LM_2 cancel out when we subtract the expectations of the HO statistic. This can be rewritten as $d = \widetilde{u}'D\widetilde{u}/\widetilde{u}'\widetilde{u}$ with D defined in (9.37).

Similarly, the King and Wu (1997) test for H_0^c derived in the solution to Exercise 9.11 can be written as

$$\mathrm{KW} = \frac{n}{\sqrt{2}\sqrt{M_{11}+M_{22}-2n}}[A_1 + A_2]$$

where A_1 and A_2 are defined below (9.24). King and Wu's standardized test statistic for the unbalanced case can be based upon

$$\frac{n}{\sqrt{2}\sqrt{M_{11}+M_{22}-2n}}\left[\frac{\widetilde{u}'\Delta_1\Delta_1'\widetilde{u}}{\widetilde{u}'\widetilde{u}}+\frac{\widetilde{u}'\Delta_2\Delta_2'\widetilde{u}}{\widetilde{u}'\widetilde{u}}\right]$$

since the (-1) terms in both A_1 and A_2 cancel out when we subtract the expectations of the KW statistic. This can be rewritten as $d = \widetilde{u}'D\widetilde{u}/\widetilde{u}'\widetilde{u}$ with D defined in (9.38).

9.3.1 Empirical Example

Baltagi and Chang (1994) apply the various unbalanced variance component methods to the data set collected by Harrison and Rubinfeld (1978) for a study of hedonic housing prices and the willingness to pay for clean air. These data are available on the Wiley web site as Hedonic.xls. The total number of observations is 506 census tracts in the Boston area in 1970, and the number of variables is 14. One can identify 92 towns, consisting of 15 within Boston and 77 in its surrounding area. Thus, it is possible to group these data and analyze them as an unbalanced one-way model with random group effects. The group sizes range from 1 to 30 observations. The dependent variable is the median value (MV) of owner-occupied homes. The regressors include two structural variables: RM, the average number of rooms; and AGE, representing the proportion of owner units built prior to 1940. In addition, there are eight neighborhood variables: B, the proportion of blacks in the population; LST, the proportion of population that is lower status; CRIM, the crime rate; ZN, the proportion of 25 000 square feet residential lots; INDUS, the proportion of non-retail business acres; TAX, the full value property tax rate (\$/\$10 000); PTRATIO, the pupil–teacher ratio; and CHAS, a dummy variable taking the value 1 if a tract bounds the Charles River. There are also two accessibility variables: DIS, the weighted distances to five employment centers in the Boston region; and RAD, the index of accessibility to radial highways. One more regressor is an air pollution variable NOX, the annual average nitrogen oxide concentration in parts per hundred million.

Exercise 9.13 *(Harrison and Rubinfeld (1978): hedonic housing)*

(a) Replicate the FE, Wallace and Hussain (1969) and the Swamy and Arora (1972) estimates of the RE model reported in Table 9.1 of Baltagi (2008, p.188).
(b) Perform the Hausman test based on RE vs FE for this unbalanced data.
(c) Perform the Breusch and Pagan (1980) LM test for no random town effects for this unbalanced data.

Solution

(a) The FE estimates with town effects for this unbalanced data set are given in Table 9.1. Note that the town effects are significant as indicated by the $F(91, 406) = 6.15$ statistic.

Table 9.1 Hedonic Housing. Fixed Effects Results

```
.xtreg mv crim zn indus chas nox rm age dis rad tax pt b lst ,fe

Fixed-effects (within) regression               Number of obs      =       506
Group variable (i) :town                        Number of groups   =        92

R-sq:  within  = 0.6792                         Obs per group: min =         1
       between = 0.6038                                        avg =       5.5
       overall = 0.6524                                        max =        30

                                                F(8,406)           =    107.45
corr(u_i,Xb)   = -0.1946                        Prob > F           =    0.0000

------------------------------------------------------------------------------
          mv |      Coef.   Std. Err.      t    P>|t|     [95% Conf. Interval]
-------------+----------------------------------------------------------------
        crim |   -.006254   .0010401    -6.01   0.000    -.0082987   -.0042093
          zn |  (dropped)
       indus |  (dropped)
        chas |  -.0452414   .0298531    -1.52   0.130    -.1039273    .0134446
         nox |  -.0055894   .0013501    -4.14   0.000    -.0082435   -.0029353
          rm |    .009272   .0012247     7.57   0.000     .0068645    .0116796
         age |   -.001407    .000486    -2.89   0.004    -.0023624   -.0004515
         dis |   .0801436   .0711727     1.13   0.261    -.0597694    .2200566
         rad |  (dropped)
         tax |  (dropped)
          pt |  (dropped)
           b |   .6634046   .1032222     6.43   0.000      .460488    .8663213
         lst |  -.2453027   .0255633    -9.60   0.000    -.2955557   -.1950498
       _cons |   8.993272   .1347381    66.75   0.000       8.7284    9.258143
-------------+----------------------------------------------------------------
     sigma_u |   .2216403
     sigma_e |  .13024876
         rho |  .74330529   (fraction of variance due to u_i)
------------------------------------------------------------------------------
F test that all u_i=0:     F(91, 406) =     6.15           Prob > F = 0.0000
```

The FE regression drops town invariant variables like zn, indus, rad, tax and pt. The Stata run replicates the column entitled within estimator in Table 9.1 of Baltagi (2008, p.188). The EViews run for the Wallace Hussain estimator is given in Table 9.2. The EViews run for the Swamy and Arora estimator is shown in Table 9.3. This is slightly different from the Stata output for Swamy and Arora given in Table 9.3 in Baltagi (2008, p.190).

(b) The Hausman test based on RE vs FE for this unbalanced data using EViews is given in Table 9.4.

(c) The Breusch and Pagan (1980) LM test for no random town effects for this unbalanced data can be obtained using Stata as shown in Table 9.5. This rejects the null of no random town effects.

Table 9.2 Hedonic Housing. Wallace and Hussain Estimator

Dependent Variable: MV
Method: Panel EGLS (Cross-section random effects)

Sample: 1 506
Periods included: 30
Cross-sections included: 92
Total panel (unbalanced) observations: 506
Wallace and Hussain estimator of component variances

	Coefficient	Std. Error	t-Statistic	Prob.
C	9.684427	0.207691	46.62904	0.0000
CRIM	−0.007376	0.001090	−6.769233	0.0000
ZN	7.22E-05	0.000685	0.105443	0.9161
INDUS	0.001649	0.004264	0.386860	0.6990
CHAS	−0.005646	0.030403	−0.185703	0.8528
NOX	−0.005847	0.001298	−4.503496	0.0000
RM	0.009081	0.001237	7.339410	0.0000
AGE	−0.000871	0.000487	−1.788760	0.0743
DIS	−0.142361	0.046276	−3.076343	0.0022
RAD	0.096136	0.028065	3.425493	0.0007
TAX	−0.000377	0.000187	−2.018658	0.0441
PTRATIO	−0.029514	0.009584	−3.079674	0.0022
B	0.565195	0.106121	5.325958	0.0000
LSTAT	−0.289908	0.024930	−11.62891	0.0000

Effects Specification

	S.D.	Rho
Cross-section random	0.126983	0.4496
Idiosyncratic random	0.140499	0.5504

Weighted Statistics

R-squared	0.990793	Mean dependent var	3.786443
Adjusted R-squared	0.990549	S.D. dependent var	1.386297
S.E. of regression	0.134769	Sum squared resid	8.935982
F-statistic	4072.547	Durbin-Watson stat	1.616416
Prob.(F-statistic)	0.000000		

Unweighted Statistics

R-squared	0.783589	Mean dependent var	9.942268

Table 9.3 Hedonic Housing. Swamy and Arora Estimator

Dependent Variable: MV
Method: Panel EGLS (Cross-section random effects)

Sample: 1 506
Periods included: 30
Cross-sections included: 92
Total panel (unbalanced) observations: 506
Swamy and Arora estimator of component variances

	Coefficient	Std. Error	t-Statistic	Prob.
C	9.685867	0.190219	50.91965	0.0000
CRIM	−0.007412	0.001009	−7.344914	0.0000
ZN	7.89E-05	0.000626	0.125998	0.8998
INDUS	0.001556	0.003886	0.400504	0.6890
CHAS	−0.004425	0.028133	−0.157277	0.8751
NOX	−0.005843	0.001199	−4.871949	0.0000
RM	0.009055	0.001145	7.910184	0.0000
AGE	−0.000858	0.000451	−1.903602	0.0575
DIS	−0.144418	0.042466	−3.400809	0.0007
RAD	0.095984	0.025629	3.745199	0.0002
TAX	−0.000377	0.000170	−2.214836	0.0272
PTRATIO	−0.029476	0.008735	−3.374443	0.0008
B	0.562775	0.098209	5.730377	0.0000
LSTAT	−0.291075	0.023044	−12.63129	0.0000

Effects Specification

	S.D.	Rho
Cross-section random	0.115052	0.4383
Idiosyncratic random	0.130249	0.5617

Weighted Statistics

R-squared	0.990891	Mean dependent var	3.856094
Adjusted R-squared	0.990651	S.D. dependent var	1.398686
S.E. of regression	0.135242	Sum squared resid	8.998817
F-statistic	4117.125	Durbin-Watson stat	1.607931
Prob.(F-statistic)	0.000000		

Unweighted Statistics

R-squared	0.784142	Mean dependent var	9.942268
Sum squared resid	18.21347	Durbin-Watson stat	0.794438

Table 9.4 Hedonic Housing. Hausman Test FE vs RE

Correlated Random Effects-Hausman Test
Equation: Untitled
Test cross-section random effects

Test Summary	Chi-Sq. Statistic	Chi-Sq.d.f.	Prob.
Cross-section random	54.189329	8	0.0000

Cross-section random effects test comparisons:

Variable	Fixed	Random	Var(Diff.)	Prob.
CRIM	−0.006254	−0.007412	0.000000	0.0000
CHAS	−0.045241	−0.004425	0.000100	0.0000
NOX	−0.005589	−0.005843	0.000000	0.6832
RM	0.009272	0.009055	0.000000	0.6183
AGE	−0.001407	−0.000858	0.000000	0.0026
DIS	0.080144	−0.144418	0.003262	0.0001
B	0.663405	0.562775	0.001010	0.0015
LSTAT	−0.245303	−0.291075	0.000122	0.0000

Table 9.5 Hedonic Housing. Breusch and Pagan LM Test

```
xttest0

Breusch and Pagan Lagrangian multiplier test for random effects:

        mv[town,t] = Xb + u[town] + e[town,t]

        Estimated results:
                                |       Var      sd = sqrt(Var)
                        --------+-------------------------------
                             mv |    .1670831         .408758
                              e |    .0169647        .1302488
                              u |     .016832         .129738

        Test:   Var(u) = 0
                                   chi2(1) =    240.80
                               Prob > chi2 =    0.0000
```

10

Special Topics

10.1 MEASUREMENT ERROR AND PANEL DATA

Micro panel data on households, individuals and firms are highly likely to exhibit measurement error. Duncan and Hill (1985) found serious measurement error in average hourly earnings in the Panel Study of Income Dynamics. This got worse for a two-year recall as compared to a one-year recall. Bound *et al.* (1990) use two validation data sets to study the extent of measurement error in labor market variables. The first data set is the Panel Study of Income Dynamics Validation Study, which uses a two-wave panel survey taken in 1983 and 1987 from a single large manufacturing company. The second data set matches panel data on earnings from the 1977 and 1978 waves of the US Current Population Survey (CPS) to Social Security earnings records for those same individuals. They find that biases from measurement errors could be very serious for hourly wages and unemployment spells, but not severe for annual earnings. Griliches and Hausman (1986) showed that one can identify and estimate a variety of errors in variables models *without* the use of external instruments. The following exercise illustrates their approach with a simple regression with random individual effects.

Exercise 10.1 *(Measurement error and panel data).* This is based on Problem 10.1 in Baltagi (2008). Consider the simple regression

$$y_{it} = \alpha + \beta x_{it}^* + u_{it}, \quad i = 1, \ldots, N, \quad t = 1, \ldots, T \tag{10.1}$$

where the error follows a one-way error component model

$$u_{it} = \mu_i + \nu_{it} \tag{10.2}$$

and the x_{it}^* are observed only with error

$$x_{it} = x_{it}^* + \eta_{it} \tag{10.3}$$

In this case, $\mu_i \sim \text{IID}(0, \sigma_\mu^2)$, $\nu_{it} \sim \text{IID}(0, \sigma_\nu^2)$, and $\eta_{it} \sim \text{IID}(0, \sigma_\eta^2)$ are all independent of each other. Additionally, x_{it}^* is independent of u_{it} and η_{it}. In terms of observable variables, the model becomes

$$y_{it} = \alpha + \beta x_{it} + \varepsilon_{it} \tag{10.4}$$

where

$$\varepsilon_{it} = \mu_i + \nu_{it} - \beta\eta_{it} \tag{10.5}$$

It is clear that OLS on (10.4) is inconsistent, since x_{it} is correlated with η_{it} and therefore ε_{it}.

(a) Show that the first-difference estimator of β, denoted by $\widehat{\beta}_{\text{FD}}$, has probability limit

$$\text{plim } \widehat{\beta}_{\text{FD}} = \beta\left(1 - \frac{2\sigma_\eta^2}{\text{var}(\Delta x)}\right) \tag{10.6}$$

where $\Delta x_{it} = x_{it} - x_{i,t-1}$.

(b) Show that the FE estimator of β, denoted by $\widetilde{\beta}_{\text{FE}}$, has probability limit

$$\text{plim } \widetilde{\beta}_{\text{FE}} = \beta\left(1 - \frac{T-1}{T}\frac{\sigma_\eta^2}{\text{var}(\widetilde{x})}\right) \tag{10.7}$$

where $\widetilde{x}_{it} = x_{it} - \overline{x}_{i\cdot}$.

(c) For most economic series, the x_{it}^* are positively serially correlated exhibiting a declining correlogram, with

$$\text{var}(\Delta x) < \frac{2T}{T-1}\text{var}(\widetilde{x}) \quad \text{for } T > 2 \tag{10.8}$$

Using this result, conclude that

$$|\text{bias}\widehat{\beta}_{\text{FD}}| > |\text{bias}\widetilde{\beta}_{\text{FE}}|$$

(d) Solve the expressions in parts (a) and (b) for β and σ_η^2 and verify that

$$\widehat{\beta} = \frac{[2\widetilde{\beta}_{\text{FE}}/\text{var}(\Delta x) - (T-1)\widehat{\beta}_{\text{FD}}/T\ \text{var}(\widetilde{x})]}{[2/\text{var}(\Delta x) - (T-1)/T\ \text{var}(\widetilde{x})]}$$

$$\sigma_\eta^2 = (\widehat{\beta} - \widehat{\beta}_{\text{FD}})\ \text{var}(\Delta x)/2\widehat{\beta}$$

(e) For $T = 2$, the FE estimator is the same as the FD estimator since $\frac{1}{2}\Delta x_{it} = \widetilde{x}_{it}$. Verify that the expressions in part (a) and (b) are also the same.

Solution

(a) The FD form of (10.4) leads to

$$y_{it} - y_{i,t-1} = \beta(x_{it} - x_{i,t-1}) + (\varepsilon_{it} - \varepsilon_{i,t-1})$$

and the FD estimator is

$$\widehat{\beta}_{\text{FD}} = \frac{\sum\sum(y_{it} - y_{i,t-1})(x_{it} - x_{i,t-1})}{\sum\sum(x_{it} - x_{i,t-1})^2} = \beta + \frac{\sum\sum(x_{it} - x_{i,t-1})(\varepsilon_{it} - \varepsilon_{i,t-1})}{\sum\sum(x_{it} - x_{i,t-1})^2}$$

Taking probability limits, we get

$$\text{plim } \widehat{\beta}_{\text{FD}} = \beta + \frac{\text{cov}(x_{it} - x_{i,t-1}, \varepsilon_{it} - \varepsilon_{i,t-1})}{\text{var}(x_{it} - x_{i,t-1})}$$

But from (10.5),

$$\varepsilon_{it} - \varepsilon_{i,t-1} = (\nu_{it} - \nu_{i,t-1}) - \beta(\eta_{it} - \eta_{i,t-1})$$

and the x_{it} are not correlated with the ν_{it}. Therefore,

$$\text{plim } \widehat{\beta}_{\text{FD}} = \beta - \beta \frac{\text{cov}(x_{it} - x_{i,t-1}, \eta_{it} - \eta_{i,t-1})}{\text{var}(\Delta x)}$$

where $\Delta x_{it} = x_{it} - x_{i,t-1}$. Using the fact that $\text{cov}(x_{it} - x_{i,t-1}, \eta_{it} - \eta_{i,t-1}) = \text{var}(\eta_{it} - \eta_{i,t-1}) = 2\sigma_\eta^2$ since the η_{it} are $\text{IID}(0, \sigma_\eta^2)$, we get the required result

$$\text{plim } \widehat{\beta}_{\text{FD}} = \beta \left(1 - \frac{2\sigma_\eta^2}{\text{var}(\Delta x)}\right)$$

(b) The FE estimator is based upon the regression of

$$\widetilde{y}_{it} = \beta \widetilde{x}_{it} + \widetilde{\varepsilon}_{it}$$

where $\widetilde{y}_{it} = y_{it} - \overline{y}_{i.}$. In fact

$$\widetilde{\beta}_{\text{FE}} = \frac{\sum\sum \widetilde{x}_{it}\widetilde{y}_{it}}{\sum\sum \widetilde{x}_{it}^2} = \beta + \frac{\sum\sum \widetilde{x}_{it}\widetilde{\varepsilon}_{it}}{\sum\sum \widetilde{x}_{it}^2}$$

Taking probability limits, we get

$$\text{plim } \widetilde{\beta}_{\text{FE}} = \beta + \frac{\text{cov}(\widetilde{x}_{it}, \widetilde{\varepsilon}_{it})}{\text{var}(\widetilde{x}_{it})}$$

But from (10.5),

$$\widetilde{\varepsilon}_{it} = \widetilde{\nu}_{it} - \beta \widetilde{\eta}_{it}$$

and the x_{it} are not correlated with the ν_{it}. Therefore,

$$\text{plim } \widetilde{\beta}_{\text{FE}} = \beta - \beta \frac{\text{cov}(\widetilde{x}_{it}, \widetilde{\eta}_{it})}{\text{var}(\widetilde{x}_{it})}$$

Using the fact that

$$\begin{aligned}\text{cov}(\widetilde{x}_{it}, \widetilde{\eta}_{it}) &= \text{var}(\widetilde{\eta}_{it}) = \text{var}(\eta_{it} - \overline{\eta}_{i.}) = \text{var}(\eta_{it}) + \text{var}(\overline{\eta}_{i.}) - 2\text{cov}(\eta_{it}, \overline{\eta}_{i.}) \\ &= \sigma_\eta^2 + \frac{\sigma_\eta^2}{T} - 2\frac{\sigma_\eta^2}{T} = \sigma_\eta^2\left(1 - \frac{1}{T}\right)\end{aligned}$$

Hence,

$$\text{plim } \widetilde{\beta}_{\text{FE}} = \beta \left[1 - \frac{T-1}{T} \cdot \frac{\sigma_\eta^2}{\text{var}(\widetilde{x}_{it})}\right]$$

as required.

(c) For most economic series, the x_{it}^* are positively serially correlated with a declining correlogram with

$$\text{var}(\Delta x) < \frac{2T}{T-1}\text{ var }(\widetilde{x}) \quad \text{for } T > 2$$

Equivalently, this can be rewritten as

$$\frac{1}{\text{var}(\Delta x)} > \frac{T-1}{2T} \cdot \frac{1}{\text{var}(\widetilde{x})} \text{ for } T > 2$$

But $|\text{bias }\widehat{\beta}_{\text{FD}}| = |\text{plim }\widehat{\beta}_{\text{FD}} - \beta| = 2\sigma_\eta^2/\text{var}(\Delta x)$ and

$$|\text{bias}\widetilde{\beta}_{\text{FE}}| = |\text{plim }\widetilde{\beta}_{\text{FE}} - \beta| = \frac{T-1}{T} \cdot \frac{\sigma_\eta^2}{\text{var}(\widetilde{x})}$$

Therefore, for $T > 2$,

$$|\text{bias }\widehat{\beta}_{\text{FD}}| > \frac{2\sigma_\eta^2}{\text{var}(\widetilde{x})} \cdot \frac{T-1}{2T} = |\text{bias }\widetilde{\beta}_{\text{FE}}|$$

(d) Equating plim $\widehat{\beta}_{\text{FD}}$ to $\widehat{\beta}_{\text{FD}}$ in part (a) and plim $\widetilde{\beta}_{\text{FE}}$ to $\widetilde{\beta}_{\text{FE}}$ in part (b) leads to two equations in β and σ_η^2 in terms of $\widehat{\beta}_{\text{FD}}$ and $\widetilde{\beta}_{\text{FE}}$. In other words,

$$\widehat{\beta}_{\text{FD}}\text{var}(\Delta x) = \beta\text{var}(\Delta x) - 2\beta\sigma_\eta^2$$
$$T\widetilde{\beta}_{\text{FE}}\text{var}(\widetilde{x}) = T\beta\text{var}(\widetilde{x}) - (T-1)\beta\sigma_\eta^2$$

To eliminate σ_η^2, one can multiply the first equation by $(T-1)$ and the second equation by (-2) and sum:

$$(T-1)\widehat{\beta}_{\text{FD}}\text{var}(\Delta x) - 2T\widetilde{\beta}_{\text{FE}}\text{var}(\widetilde{x}) = \beta[(T-1)\text{var}(\Delta x) - 2T\text{var}(\widetilde{x})]$$

which yields

$$\widehat{\beta} = \frac{(T-1)\widehat{\beta}_{\text{FD}}\text{var}(\Delta x) - 2T\widetilde{\beta}_{\text{FE}}\text{var}(\widetilde{x})}{(T-1)\text{var}(\Delta x) - 2T\text{var}(\widetilde{x})}$$

which is the required expression. One can also deduce σ_η^2 from the first equation as $2\widehat{\beta}\sigma_\eta^2 = (\widehat{\beta} - \widehat{\beta}_{\text{FD}})\text{var}(\Delta x)$ or, equivalently, as

$$\sigma_\eta^2 = (\widehat{\beta} - \widehat{\beta}_{\text{FD}})\text{var}(\Delta x)/2\widehat{\beta}$$

(e) For $T = 2$, the FE estimator is the same as the FD estimator since $\frac{1}{2}\Delta x_{it} = \widetilde{x}_{it}$. In this case $\frac{1}{4}\text{ var}(\Delta x_{it}) = \text{var}(\widetilde{x}_{it})$. In part (b), for $T = 2$,

$$\text{plim }\widetilde{\beta}_{\text{FE}} = \beta\left[1 - \frac{1}{2} \cdot \frac{\sigma_\eta^2}{\text{var}(\widetilde{x})}\right] = \beta\left[1 - \frac{1}{2} \cdot \frac{4\sigma_\eta^2}{\text{var}(\Delta x)}\right] = \text{plim }\widehat{\beta}_{\text{FD}}$$

10.2 ROTATING PANELS

Biorn (1981) considers the case of rotating panels, where in order to keep the *same* number of households in the survey, the fraction of households that drops from the sample in the second period is replaced by an equal number of new households that are freshly surveyed. This is a necessity in survey panels where the same household may not want to be interviewed again and again. In the study by Biorn and Jansen (1983) based on data from the Norwegian household budget surveys, half the sample is rotated in each period. In other words, half the households surveyed drop from the sample each period and are replaced by new households. The following exercises illustrate the basics of rotating panels.

Exercise 10.2 *(Rotating panel with two waves).* Assume that $T = 2$ and that half the sample is rotated each period. In this case, without loss of generality, households $1, 2, \ldots, N/2$ are replaced by households $N+1, N+2, \ldots, N+N/2$ in period 2. It is clear that only households $N/2+1, N/2+2, \ldots, N$ are observed over two periods.

(a) For the one-way error component model, derive the variance–covariance matrix of the disturbances Ω.
(b) Derive $\Omega^{-1/2}$ and describe the transformation needed to make GLS a weighted least squares regression.
(c) How would you consistently estimate the variance components σ_μ^2 and σ_ν^2?

Solution

(a) In general, for any T, as long as the fraction of the sample being rotated is greater than or equal to half, then no individual will be observed more than twice. In this case there are $3N/2$ distinct households, only $N/2$ of which are observed for two periods. In our case, the first and last $N/2$ households surveyed are only observed for one period. Now consider the one-way error component model

$$u_{it} = \mu_i + \nu_{it}$$

with $\mu_i \sim \text{IID}(0, \sigma_\mu^2)$ and $\nu_{it} \sim \text{IID}(0, \sigma_\nu^2)$ independent of each other and the x_{it}. Order the observations such that the faster index is that of households and the slower index is that of time. In this case, $u' = (u_{11}, u_{21}, \ldots, u_{N1}, u_{N/2+1,2}, \ldots, u_{3N/2,2})$ and

$$E(uu') = \Omega = \begin{bmatrix} \sigma^2 I_{N/2} & 0 & 0 & 0 \\ 0 & \sigma^2 I_{N/2} & \sigma_\mu^2 I_{N/2} & 0 \\ 0 & \sigma_\mu^2 I_{N/2} & \sigma^2 I_{N/2} & 0 \\ 0 & 0 & 0 & \sigma^2 I_{N/2} \end{bmatrix} \tag{10.9}$$

where $\sigma^2 = \sigma_\mu^2 + \sigma_\nu^2$.

(b) It is easy to see that Ω is block-diagonal and that the middle block has the usual error component model form $\sigma_\mu^2(J_2 \otimes I_{N/2}) + \sigma_\nu^2(I_2 \otimes I_{N/2})$. Therefore,

$$\Omega^{-1/2} = \begin{bmatrix} \frac{1}{\sigma} I_{N/2} & 0 & 0 \\ 0 & \left(\frac{1}{\sigma_1^*}\overline{J}_2 + \frac{1}{\sigma_\nu} E_2\right) \otimes I_{N/2} & 0 \\ 0 & 0 & \frac{1}{\sigma} I_{N/2} \end{bmatrix} \tag{10.10}$$

where $E_2 = I_2 - \overline{J}_2$, $\overline{J}_2 = J_2/2$, and $\sigma_1^{*2} = 2\sigma_\mu^2 + \sigma_\nu^2$. Premultiplying the regression model by $\Omega^{-1/2}$ and performing OLS gives the GLS estimator of the rotating panel. In this case, one divides the first and last $N/2$ observations by σ. For the middle N observations, with $i = N/2 + 1, \ldots, N$ and $t = 1, 2$, quasi-demeaning similar to the usual error component transformation is performed, i.e., $(y_{it} - \theta^* \overline{y}_{i.})/\sigma_\nu$ with $\theta^* = 1 - (\sigma_\nu/\sigma_1^*)$ and $\overline{y}_{i.} = (y_{i1} + y_{i2})/2$. A similar transformation is also performed on the regressors.

(c) In order to make this GLS estimator feasible, we need estimates of σ_μ^2 and σ_ν^2. One consistent estimator of σ_ν^2 can be obtained from the middle N observations or simply the households that are observed over two periods. For these observations, σ_ν^2 is estimated consistently from the FE residuals,

$$\widetilde{\sigma}_\nu^2 = \sum_{t=1}^{2} \sum_{i=\frac{N}{2}+1}^{N} [(y_{it} - \overline{y}_{i.}) - (x_{it} - \overline{x}_{i.})'\widetilde{\beta}_{\text{FE}}]^2/N \tag{10.11}$$

whereas the total variance can be estimated consistently from the least squares mean square error over the entire sample,

$$\widetilde{\sigma}^2 = \widetilde{\sigma}_\nu^2 + \widetilde{\sigma}_\mu^2 = \sum_{t=1}^{2} \sum_{i=1}^{3N/2} (y_{it} - x_{it}'\widehat{\beta}_{\text{OLS}})^2/(3N/2) \tag{10.12}$$

Note that we could have reordered the data such that households observed over one period are stacked on top of households observed over two time periods. This way the rotating panel problem becomes an unbalanced panel problem with N households observed over one period and $N/2$ households observed for two periods. In fact, except for this different way of ordering the observations, one can handle the estimation as in Chapter 9. This feasible GLS estimation can easily be derived for other rotating schemes.

Exercise 10.3 *(Rotating panel with three waves).* This is based on Problem 10.2 in Baltagi (2008). Assume that $T = 3$ and that the number of households being replaced each period is equal to $N/2$.

(a) For the one-way error component model, derive the variance–covariance matrix of the disturbances Ω.
(b) Derive $\Omega^{-1/2}$ and describe the transformation needed to make GLS a weighted least squares regression.
(c) How would you consistently estimate the variance components σ_μ^2 and σ_ν^2?
(d) Repeat this exercise for the case where the number of households being replaced each period is $N/3$. How about $2N/3$?

Solution

(a) In this case, $T = 3$ and half the sample is being rotated in each period. Without loss of generality, we can choose households $1, 2, \ldots, N/2$ to be replaced by households $N+1, N+2, \ldots, N+N/2$ in period 2. Then households $N/2+1, \ldots, N$ are replaced by households $N+N/2+1, \ldots, 2N$ in period 3. The first $N/2$ and last $N/2$ households surveyed are only observed for one period and the middle N households are observed over two periods. In this case, there are $2N$ distinct households. Ordering the data such that the N households observed over one period are stacked on top of the other N households observed over two time periods, this rotating panel becomes an unbalanced panel and can be treated using the methods described in Chapter 9. Ordering the observations with the faster index being that of households and the slower index being time, we get

$$u' = (u_{11}, u_{21}, \ldots, u_{N1}, u_{N/2+1,2}, \ldots, u_{N,2}, u_{N+1,2}, \ldots, u_{3N/2}, 2,$$
$$u_{N+1,3}, \ldots, u_{3N/2,3}, u_{3N/2+1,3}, \ldots, u_{2N,3})$$

and

$$E(uu') = \Omega = \begin{bmatrix} \sigma^2 I_{N/2} & 0 & 0 & 0 & 0 & 0 \\ 0 & \sigma^2 I_{N/2} & \sigma_\mu^2 I_{N/2} & 0 & 0 & 0 \\ 0 & \sigma_\mu^2 I_{N/2} & \sigma^2 I_{N/2} & 0 & 0 & 0 \\ 0 & 0 & 0 & \sigma^2 I_{N/2} & \sigma_\mu^2 I_{N/2} & 0 \\ 0 & 0 & 0 & \sigma_\mu^2 I_{N/2} & \sigma^2 I_{N/2} & 0 \\ 0 & 0 & 0 & 0 & 0 & \sigma^2 I_{N/2} \end{bmatrix}$$

where $\sigma^2 = \sigma_\mu^2 + \sigma_\nu^2$.

(b) The two middle blocks have the usual error component structure

$$\sigma_\mu^2(J_2 \otimes I_{N/2}) + \sigma_\nu^2(I_2 \otimes I_{N/2})$$

Therefore,

$$\Omega = \begin{bmatrix} \sigma^2 I_{N/2} & 0 & 0 & 0 \\ 0 & (\sigma_1^* \overline{J}_2 + \sigma_\nu^2 E_2) \otimes I_{N/2} & 0 & 0 \\ 0 & 0 & (\sigma_1^* \overline{J}_2 + \sigma_\nu^2 E_2) \otimes I_{N/2} & 0 \\ 0 & 0 & 0 & \sigma^2 I_{N/2} \end{bmatrix}$$

and

$$\Omega^{-1/2} = \begin{bmatrix} \frac{1}{\sigma} I_{N/2} & 0 & 0 & 0 \\ 0 & \left(\frac{1}{\sigma_1^*}\overline{J}_2 + \frac{1}{\sigma_\nu}E_2\right) \otimes I_{N/2} & 0 & 0 \\ 0 & 0 & \left(\frac{1}{\sigma_1^*}\overline{J}_2 + \frac{1}{\sigma_\nu}E_2\right) \otimes I_{N/2} & 0 \\ 0 & 0 & 0 & \frac{1}{\sigma} I_{N/2} \end{bmatrix}$$

where $E_2 = I_2 - \overline{J}_2$, $\overline{J}_2 = J_2/2$ and $\sigma_1^{*2} = 2\sigma_\mu^2 + \sigma_\nu^2$. Premultiplying the regression model by $\Omega^{-1/2}$ and performing OLS gives the GLS estimator of the rotating panel. In this case, one divides the first and last $N/2$ observations by σ. For the first middle N observations, with $i = N/2+1, \ldots, N$ and $t = 1, 2$, quasi-demeaning similar to the usual error component transformation is performed, i.e., $\frac{1}{\sigma_\nu}(y_{it} - \theta^* \overline{y}_{i.})$ with $\theta^* = 1 - \sigma_\nu/\sigma_1^*$ and $\overline{y}_{i.} = (y_{i1} + y_{i2})/2$. For the second middle N observations, with $i = N+1, \ldots, 3N/2$ and $t = 2, 3$, quasi-demeaning similar to that given above is performed, i.e., $\frac{1}{\sigma_\nu}(y_{it} - \theta^* \overline{y}_{i.})$ with $\theta^* = 1 - \sigma_\nu/\sigma_1^*$ and $\overline{y}_{i.} = (y_{i2} + y_{i3})/2$.

(c) One consistent estimator of σ_ν^2 can be obtained from the middle $2N$ observations or simply the households that are observed over two time periods. For these observations, σ_ν^2 can be estimated consistently from the FE residuals as in (10.11):

$$\widetilde{\sigma}_\nu^2 = \sum_{t=1}^{2} \sum_{i=\frac{N}{2}+1}^{N} [\widetilde{y}_{it} - \widetilde{x}_{it}\widetilde{\beta}_w]^2/N + \sum_{t=2}^{3} \sum_{i=N+1}^{3N/2} [\widetilde{y}_{it} - \widetilde{x}_{it}\widetilde{\beta}_w]^2/N$$

where $\widetilde{y}_{it} = y_{it} - \overline{y}_{i.}$ and $\widetilde{x}_{it} = x_{it} - \overline{x}_{i.}$ with $\overline{y}_{i.} = y_{i1} + y_{i2}/2$ for the first sum and $(y_{i2} + y_{i3})/2$ for the second sum. The same is true for $\overline{x}_{i.}$ since the individuals in each summation are only observed over the indicated periods in that summation. Similarly, the total variance σ^2 can be estimated consistently from the least squares mean square error over the entire sample as in (10.12), i.e.,

$$\widetilde{\sigma}^2 = \widetilde{\sigma}_\nu^2 + \widetilde{\sigma}_\mu^2 = \sum_{t=1}^{3}\sum_{i=1}^{2N}(y_{it} - x_{it}\widehat{\beta}_{\text{OLS}})^2/2N$$

(d) This part considers the case of $T = 3$ with $N/3$ households rotating each period. Without loss of generality, we can choose households $1, 2, \ldots, N/3$ to be replaced by households $N+1, \ldots, N+N/3$ in period 2. Then households $N/3+1, \ldots, 2N/3$ are replaced by households $N+N/3+1, \ldots, N+2N/3$ in period 3. The first $N/3$ and last $N/3$ households surveyed are only observed for one period. Households $N/3+1, \ldots, 2N/3$ and households $N+1, \ldots, N+N/3$ are observed for two periods, while households $2N/3+1, \ldots, N$ are observed in all three periods. In this case, there are $N+2N/3$ distinct households. Ordering the data such that the $2N/3$ households observed over one period are stacked on top of the $2N/3$ households observed for two time periods and the $N/3$ households observed over three time periods, this rotating panel becomes an unbalanced panel and can be treated using the methods described in Chapter 9. Ordering the observations as

$$u' = (u_{11}, \ldots, u_{N/3,1}, u_{N/3+1,1}, \ldots, u_{2N/3,1}, u_{N/3+1,2}, \ldots, u_{2N/3,2}, u_{2N/3+1,1}, \ldots,$$
$$u_{N,1}, u_{2N/3+1,2}, \ldots, u_{N,2}, u_{2N/3+1,3}, \ldots, u_{N,3}, u_{N+1,2}, \ldots, u_{N+N/3,2}, u_{N+1,3}, \ldots,$$
$$u_{N+N/3,3}, u_{4N/3+1,3}, \ldots, u_{5N/3,3})$$

we get

$$E(uu') = \begin{bmatrix} \sigma^2 I_{N/3} & 0 & 0 & 0 & 0 \\ 0 & (\sigma_\mu^2 J_2 + \sigma_\nu^2 I_2) \otimes I_{N/3} & 0 & 0 & 0 \\ 0 & 0 & (\sigma_\mu^2 J_3 + \sigma_\nu^2 I_3) \otimes I_{N/3} & 0 & 0 \\ 0 & 0 & 0 & (\sigma_\mu^2 J_2 + \sigma_\nu^2 I_2) \otimes I_{N/3} & 0 \\ 0 & 0 & 0 & 0 & \sigma^2 I_{N/3} \end{bmatrix}$$

and

$$\Omega^{-1/2} = \begin{bmatrix} \frac{1}{\sigma} I_{N/3} & 0 & 0 & 0 & 0 \\ 0 & \left(\frac{1}{\sigma_1^*}\overline{J}_2 + \frac{1}{\sigma_\nu} E_2\right) \otimes I_{N/3} & 0 & 0 & 0 \\ 0 & 0 & \left(\frac{1}{\sigma_2^*}\overline{J}_3 + \frac{1}{\sigma_\nu} E_3\right) \otimes I_{N/3} & 0 & 0 \\ 0 & 0 & 0 & \left(\frac{1}{\sigma_1^*}\overline{J}_2 + \frac{1}{\sigma_\nu} E_2\right) \otimes I_{N/3} & 0 \\ 0 & 0 & 0 & 0 & \frac{1}{\sigma} I_{N/3} \end{bmatrix}$$

with $\sigma_1^{*2} = 2\sigma_\mu^2 + \sigma_\nu^2$ and $\sigma_2^{*2} = 3\sigma_\mu^2 + \sigma_\nu^2$.

For the case of $T = 3$, and $2N/3$ households rotating in each period, only the last $N/3$ households are observed over two periods. Ordering the observations as

$$u' = (u_{11}, \ldots, u_{2N/3,1}, \ldots, u_{\frac{2N}{3}+1,1}, \ldots, u_{N,1}, u_{2N/3+1,2}, \ldots, u_{N,2}, u_{N+1,2}, \ldots,$$
$$u_{N+N/3,2}, \ldots, u_{N+2N/3,2}, u_{4N/3+1,3}, \ldots, u_{5N/3,3}, u_{5N/3+1,3}, \ldots, u_{7N/3,3})$$

we get

$$E(uu') = \begin{bmatrix} \sigma^2 I_{2N/3} & 0 & 0 & 0 & 0 \\ 0 & (\sigma_\mu^2 J_2 + \sigma_\nu^2 I_2) \otimes I_{N/3} & 0 & 0 & 0 \\ 0 & 0 & \sigma^2 I_{N/3} & 0 & 0 \\ 0 & 0 & 0 & (\sigma_\mu^2 J_2 + \sigma_\nu^2 I_2) \otimes I_{N/3} & 0 \\ 0 & 0 & 0 & 0 & \sigma^2 I_{2N/3} \end{bmatrix}$$

and

$$\Omega^{-1/2} = \begin{bmatrix} \frac{1}{\sigma} I_{2N/3} & 0 & 0 & 0 & 0 \\ 0 & (\frac{1}{\sigma_1^*}\overline{J}_2 + \frac{1}{\sigma_\nu} E_2) \otimes I_{N/3} & 0 & 0 & 0 \\ 0 & 0 & \frac{1}{\sigma} I_{N/3} & 0 & 0 \\ 0 & 0 & 0 & (\frac{1}{\sigma_1^*}\overline{J}_2 + \frac{1}{\sigma_\nu} E_2) \otimes I_{N/3} & 0 \\ 0 & 0 & 0 & 0 & \frac{1}{\sigma} I_{2N/3} \end{bmatrix}$$

with $\sigma_1^{*2} = 2\sigma_\mu^2 + \sigma_\nu^2$.

10.3 SPATIAL PANELS

In randomly drawn samples at the individual level, one does not usually worry about cross-section correlation. However, when one starts looking at a cross-section of countries, regions, states, counties, etc., these aggregate units are likely to exhibit cross-sectional correlation that has to be dealt with. There is an extensive literature using spatial statistics that deals with this type of correlation. These spatial dependence models are popular in regional science and urban economics. More specifically, these models deal with spatial interaction (spatial autocorrelation) and spatial structure (spatial heterogeneity) primarily in cross-section data; see Anselin (1988, 2001) for a nice introduction to this literature. With the increasing availability of micro– as well as macro-level panel data, spatial panel data models are becoming increasingly attractive in empirical economic research. The following exercises open a little window onto spatial panels.

Exercise 10.4 *(Spatially autocorrelated error component model).* Consider the panel data regression model

$$y_{ti} = X'_{ti}\beta + u_{ti}, \quad i = 1, \ldots, N, \quad t = 1, \ldots, T \tag{10.13}$$

where y_{ti} is the observation on the ith country for the tth time period, X_{ti} denotes the $k \times 1$ vector of observations on the non-stochastic regressors and u_{ti} is the regression disturbance. In vector form, the disturbance vector is assumed to have random country effects as well as spatially autocorrelated remainder disturbances (see Anselin, 1988):

$$u_t = \mu + \varepsilon_t \tag{10.14}$$

with spatial AR(1) disturbances

$$\varepsilon_t = \lambda W \varepsilon_t + \nu_t \tag{10.15}$$

where $\mu' = (\mu_1, \ldots, \mu_N)$ denote the vector of random country effects which are assumed to be IIN$(0, \sigma_\mu^2)$. λ is the scalar spatial autoregressive coefficient with $|\lambda| < 1$. W is a known $N \times N$ spatial weight matrix whose diagonal elements are zero. W also satisfies the condition that $I_N - \lambda W$ is non-singular. $\nu'_t = (\nu_{t1}, \ldots, \nu_{tN})$, where ν_{ti} is assumed to be IIN$(0, \sigma_\nu^2)$ and also independent of μ_i.

(a) Derive the variance–covariance matrix of the disturbances Ω and its inverse Ω^{-1}.
(b) Using the Goldberger (1962) best linear unbiased prediction results discussed in Exercise 2.13, equation (2.28), derive the BLUP of $y_{i,T+S}$ for the ith country at period $T + S$ for this spatial panel model. This is based on Baltagi and Li (1999) and Song and Jung (2000). This is also Problem 10.6 in Baltagi (2008).

Solution

(a) One can rewrite (10.15) as

$$\varepsilon_t = (I_N - \lambda W)^{-1}\nu_t = B^{-1}\nu_t$$

where $B = I_N - \lambda W$ and I_N is an identity matrix of dimension N. Model (10.13) can be rewritten in matrix notation as

$$y = X\beta + u \tag{10.16}$$

where y is now of dimension $NT \times 1$, X is $NT \times k$, β is $k \times 1$, and u is $NT \times 1$. X is assumed to be of full column rank and its elements are assumed to be bounded in absolute value. Equation (10.14) can be written in vector form as

$$u = (\iota_T \otimes I_N)\mu + (I_T \otimes B^{-1})\nu \tag{10.17}$$

where $\nu' = (\nu_1', \ldots, \nu_T')$. Under these assumptions, the variance–covariance matrix for u is given by

$$\Omega = \sigma_\mu^2(J_T \otimes I_N) + \sigma_\nu^2(I_T \otimes (B'B)^{-1}) \tag{10.18}$$

This matrix can be rewritten as

$$\Omega = \sigma_\nu^2\left[\overline{J}_T \otimes (T\phi I_N + (B'B)^{-1}) + E_T \otimes (B'B)^{-1}\right] = \sigma_\nu^2 \Sigma \tag{10.19}$$

where $\phi = \sigma_\mu^2/\sigma_\nu^2$, $\overline{J}_T = J_T/T$, and $E_T = I_T - \overline{J}_T$. Using results in Wansbeek and Kapteyn (1982), Σ^{-1} is given by

$$\Sigma^{-1} = \overline{J}_T \otimes (T\phi I_N + (B'B)^{-1})^{-1} + E_T \otimes B'B \tag{10.20}$$

(b) Note that for period $T + S$,

$$u_{T+S,i} = \mu_i + \varepsilon_{T+S,i} \tag{10.21}$$

with $E(u_{T+S,i}u_{tj}) = \sigma_\mu^2$ for $i = j$ and zero otherwise, since the εs are not correlated over time. In this case

$$w = E(u_{T+S,i}u) = E\left[\left(\mu_i + \varepsilon_{T+S,i}\right)u\right] = \sigma_\mu^2(\iota_T \otimes l_i) \tag{10.22}$$

where l_i is the ith column of I_N. Using $\Omega^{-1} = \Sigma^{-1}/\sigma_\nu^2$ as defined in (10.20), we get

$$w'\Omega^{-1} = \frac{\sigma_\mu^2}{\sigma_\nu^2}\left(\iota_T' \otimes l_i'\right)\left[\left(\overline{J}_T \otimes V^{-1}\right) + \left(E_T \otimes (B'B)\right)\right] = \phi\left(\iota_T' \otimes l_i'V^{-1}\right)$$

where $V = T\phi I_N + (B'B)^{-1}$. The second equality follows from the fact that $\iota_T'E_T = 0$. Therefore,

$$w'\Omega^{-1}\widehat{u}_{\mathrm{GLS}} = \phi\left(\iota_T' \otimes l_i'V^{-1}\right)\widehat{u}_{\mathrm{GLS}} = \phi l_i'V^{-1}\sum_{t=1}^{T}\widehat{u}_{tj,\mathrm{GLS}} \tag{10.23}$$
$$= T\phi\sum_{j=1}^{N}\delta_j\overline{\widehat{u}}_{.j,\mathrm{GLS}}$$

where δ_j is the jth element of the ith row of V^{-1} and $\overline{\widehat{u}}_{.j,\mathrm{GLS}} = \sum_{t=1}^{T}\widehat{u}_{tj,\mathrm{GLS}}/T$.

The BLUP of $y_{T+S,i}$ adds to $x'_{T+S,i}\widehat{\beta}_{\text{GLS}}$ a weighted average of the GLS residuals for the N countries averaged over time. The weights depend upon the spatial matrix W and the spatial autocorrelation coefficient λ.

Exercise 10.5 *(Random effects and spatial autocorrelation with equal weights).* This is based on Baltagi (2006b) and is also Problem 10.8 in Baltagi (2008). Consider the panel data regression model described in (10.13) with random individual effects and spatially autocorrelated remainder disturbances described by (10.14) and (10.15). In this special case, W is an $N \times N$ weighting matrix with zero elements across the diagonal, and *equal elements* $(1/(N-1))$ off the diagonal. In other words, the disturbance for each unit is related to an average of the $(N-1)$ disturbances of the remaining units. Such a weighting matrix would naturally arise if all units are neighbors to each other and there is no other reasonable or observable measure of distance between them.

(a) Show that GLS on this model can be obtained using an OLS regression of $y^*_{ti} = (y_{ti} - \theta_1\overline{y}_{t.} - \theta_2\overline{y}_{.i} + \theta_3\overline{y}_{..})$ on X^* similarly defined. Here $\overline{y}_{t.}$ denotes the sample average over individuals, $\overline{y}_{.i}$ denotes the sample average over time, and $\overline{y}_{..}$ denotes the average over the entire sample. The θs are scalars which depend on N, λ and the variance components σ^2_μ and σ^2_ν.
(b) Show that if there is no spatial autocorrelation, i.e., $\lambda = 0$, then y^*_{ti} reduces to $(y_{ti} - \theta_2\overline{y}_{.i})$. This is the familiar Fuller and Battese (1973) random effects transformation that was obtained in Chapter 2 (see Exercise 2.5). Show that if there are no random effects, i.e., $\sigma^2_\mu = 0$, and $N \to \infty$, then $y^*_{ti} = (y_{ti} - \lambda\overline{y}_{t.})$.
(c) Show that in the *cross-section* spatial regression model with $T = 1$ and equal weight matrix, OLS is equivalent to GLS as long as there is a constant in the regression.
(d) For the spatial *panel* regression with equal weights, show that two special cases where OLS is equivalent to GLS are the following: (i) the trivial case where $\sigma^2_\mu = 0$ and $\lambda = 0$; and (ii) when the matrix of regressors X is invariant across time.

Solution

(a) Kelejian and Prucha (2002) showed that W_N can be written as

$$W_N = \frac{J_N}{N-1} - \frac{I_N}{N-1}$$

where J_N is a matrix of ones, and I_N is an identity matrix, both of dimension N. Defining $\overline{J}_N = J_N/N$ and $E_N = I_N - \overline{J}_N$, and replacing J_N and I_N by their equivalent terms $N\overline{J}_N$ and $(E_N + \overline{J}_N)$ and collecting like terms (see Wansbeek and Kapteyn, 1982), we get

$$W_N = \overline{J}_N - \frac{E_N}{N-1}$$

with

$$B_N = I_N - \lambda W_N = \frac{N-1+\lambda}{N-1}E_N + (1-\lambda)\overline{J}_N$$

Therefore,

$$B_N^{-1} = (I_N - \lambda W_N)^{-1} = \frac{N-1}{N-1+\lambda}E_N + \frac{1}{(1-\lambda)}\overline{J}_N$$

Note that W_N is symmetric and

$$(B_N' B_N)^{-1} = \frac{(N-1)^2}{(N-1+\lambda)^2}E_N + \frac{1}{(1-\lambda)^2}\overline{J}_N = c_1 E_N + c_2 \overline{J}_N$$

where

$$c_1 = \frac{(N-1)^2}{(N-1+\lambda)^2}, \qquad c_2 = \frac{1}{(1-\lambda)^2}$$

Replacing J_T and I_T by their equivalent terms $T\overline{J}_T$ and $E_T + \overline{J}_T$, we get

$$\Omega = T\sigma_\mu^2(\overline{J}_T \otimes (E_N + \overline{J}_N)) + \sigma_\nu^2((E_T + \overline{J}_T) \otimes (c_1 E_N + c_2 \overline{J}_N))$$

Collecting like terms, we obtain the spectral decomposition of Ω,

$$\begin{aligned}\Omega = &(T\sigma_\mu^2 + c_1\sigma_\nu^2)(\overline{J}_T \otimes E_N) + (T\sigma_\mu^2 + c_2\sigma_\nu^2)(\overline{J}_T \otimes \overline{J}_N) \\ &+ c_1\sigma_\nu^2(E_T \otimes E_N) + c_2\sigma_\nu^2(E_T \otimes \overline{J}_N)\end{aligned}$$

Hence,

$$\begin{aligned}\Omega^{-1} = &\frac{1}{T\sigma_\mu^2 + c_1\sigma_\nu^2}(\overline{J}_T \otimes E_N) + \frac{1}{T\sigma_\mu^2 + c_2\sigma_\nu^2}(\overline{J}_T \otimes \overline{J}_N) \\ &+ \frac{1}{c_1\sigma_\nu^2}(E_T \otimes E_N) + \frac{1}{c_2\sigma_\nu^2}(E_T \otimes \overline{J}_N)\end{aligned}$$

and

$$\begin{aligned}\Omega^{-1/2} = &\frac{1}{\sqrt{T\sigma_\mu^2 + c_1\sigma_\nu^2}}(\overline{J}_T \otimes E_N) + \frac{1}{\sqrt{T\sigma_\mu^2 + c_2\sigma_\nu^2}}(\overline{J}_T \otimes \overline{J}_N) \\ &+ \frac{1}{\sqrt{c_1\sigma_\nu^2}}(E_T \otimes E_N) + \frac{1}{\sqrt{c_2\sigma_\nu^2}}(E_T \otimes \overline{J}_N)\end{aligned}$$

Premultiplying the regression by $\sigma_\nu\sqrt{c_1}\Omega^{-1/2}$, we get a similar transformation to that suggested by Fuller and Battese (1973) for the random effects panel data model. In fact $y^* = \sigma_\nu\sqrt{c_1}\Omega^{-1/2}y$ will have typical elements $y_{ti}^* = y_{ti} - \theta_1\overline{y}_{t.} - \theta_2\overline{y}_{.i} + \theta_3\overline{y}_{..}$ where $\overline{y}_{t.}$ denotes the sample average over regions, $\overline{y}_{.i}$ denotes the sample average over time, and $\overline{y}_{..}$ denotes the average over the entire sample. The θs can be easily obtained from the corresponding $(c_1, c_2, \sigma_\mu^2, \sigma_\nu^2)$ parameters. For example, θ_1 is the coefficient corresponding to $(I_T \otimes \overline{J}_N)$ which can be verified to be $\left(1 - \sqrt{\frac{c_1}{c_2}}\right)$; θ_2 is the coefficient corresponding to $(\overline{J}_T \otimes I_N)$ which can be verified to be $\left(1-\sqrt{c_1\sigma_\nu^2/(T\sigma_\mu^2+c_1\sigma_\nu^2)}\right)$; and θ_3 is the coefficient corresponding to $(\overline{J}_T \otimes \overline{J}_N)$ which can be verified to be $\left(1-\sqrt{c_1/c_2}-\sqrt{c_1\sigma_\nu^2/(T\sigma_\mu^2+c_1\sigma_\nu^2)}+\sqrt{c_1\sigma_\nu^2/(T\sigma_\mu^2+c_2\sigma_\nu^2)}\right)$.

(b) Note that if $\lambda = 0$, so that there is no spatial autocorrelation, then $c_1 = c_2 = 1$ and Ω reduces to the familiar variance–covariance matrix of the random effects panel data model given by

$$\Omega = (T\sigma_\mu^2 + \sigma_\nu^2)(\overline{J}_T \otimes I_N) + \sigma_\nu^2(E_T \otimes I_N)$$

In this case, $\theta_1 = \theta_3 = 0$ and $\theta_2 = 1 - \sigma_\nu/\sqrt{T\sigma_\mu^2 + \sigma_\nu^2}$, which reduces y_{ti}^* to $(y_{ti} - \theta_2 \overline{y}_{.i})$. This is the familiar Fuller and Battese (1973) random effects transformation that allows us to obtain GLS as weighted least squares.

If $\sigma_\mu^2 = 0$ (the case of no random effects), the variance–covariance matrix reduces to

$$\Omega = \sigma_\nu^2(I_T \otimes (B_N' B_N)^{-1})$$

which can be rewritten as

$$\Omega = \sigma_\nu^2(I_T \otimes (c_1 E_N + c_2 \overline{J}_N))$$

Hence,

$$\Omega^{-1} = \frac{1}{c_1\sigma_\nu^2}(I_T \otimes E_N) + \frac{1}{c_2\sigma_\nu^2}(I_T \otimes \overline{J}_N)$$

and

$$\Omega^{-1/2} = \frac{1}{\sigma_\nu\sqrt{c_1}}(I_T \otimes E_N) + \frac{1}{\sigma_\nu\sqrt{c_2}}(I_T \otimes \overline{J}_N)$$

so that the typical element of $y^* = \sigma_\nu\sqrt{c_1}\Omega^{-1/2} y$ is $y_{ti}^* = (y_{ti} - \theta_1 \overline{y}_{t.})$ where $\theta_1 = 1 - \sqrt{c_1/c_2}$. Note that as $N \to \infty$, $\sqrt{c_1/c_2} \to 1 - \lambda$, and $\theta_1 \to \lambda$.

(c) A special case of this model is the *cross-section* spatial regression model with $T = 1$ and equal weight matrix. In this case, one can show that OLS is equivalent to GLS as long as there is a constant in the regression. To prove this, note that the model becomes

$$y_N = \alpha\iota_N + X_N\beta + u_N = Z_N\gamma + u_N$$

where $Z_N = (\iota_N, X_N)$ and $\gamma = (\alpha, \beta)'$. Here y_N is a vector of observations on the dependent variable and ι_N is a vector of ones, both of dimension N. X_N is an $N \times K$ matrix of observations on the K explanatory variables. The disturbance vector is assumed to follow a spatial autoregressive process

$$u_N = \lambda W_N u_N + \nu_N$$

where W_N is an $N \times N$ equal weighting matrix. In fact, one can prove that the Zyskind (1967) necessary and sufficient condition for OLS to be equivalent to GLS is satisfied.

This calls for $P_Z\Sigma = \Sigma P_Z$, where $Z = Z_N = (\iota_N, X_N)$ is the matrix of regressors and $\Sigma = E(u_N u_N') = \sigma_v^2\Omega$ is the variance–covariance matrix of the disturbances. It is straightforward to show that $\Omega = c_1 E_N + c_2 \overline{J}_N$ and

$$P_Z\Omega = \frac{(N-1)^2}{(N-1+\lambda)^2}(P_Z - \overline{J}_N) + \frac{1}{(1-\lambda)^2}\overline{J}_N$$

since $P_Z\iota_N = \iota_N$, $P_Z\overline{J}_N = \overline{J}_N$, and $P_Z E_N = P_Z - \overline{J}_N$. Similarly,

$$\Omega P_Z = \frac{(N-1)^2}{(N-1+\lambda)^2}(P_Z - \overline{J}_N) + \frac{1}{(1-\lambda)^2}\overline{J}_N$$

Hence, $P_Z\Omega = \Omega P_Z$.

In fact, another necessary and sufficient condition for OLS to be equivalent to GLS, which relies on Ω^{-1}, is given by Milliken and Albohali (1984), and this condition calls for $Z'\Omega^{-1}(I_N - P_Z) = 0$. Here, from

$$\Omega^{-1} = \frac{(N-1+\lambda)^2}{(N-1)^2}E_N + (1-\lambda)^2\overline{J}_N$$

and the fact that $\overline{J}_N(I_N - P_Z) = 0$, we get

$$\Omega^{-1}(I_N - P_Z) = \frac{(N-1+\lambda)^2}{(N-1)^2}E_N(I_N - P_Z) + (1-\lambda)^2\overline{J}_N(I_N - P_Z)$$
$$= \frac{(N-1+\lambda)^2}{(N-1)^2}(I_N - P_Z)$$

Hence,

$$Z'\Omega^{-1}(I_N - P_Z) = \frac{(N-1+\lambda)^2}{(N-1)^2}Z'(I_N - P_Z) = 0$$

since $Z'P_Z = Z'$.

Note that

$$\operatorname{var}(\widehat{\gamma}_{\text{OLS}}) = \operatorname{var}(\widehat{\gamma}_{\text{GLS}}) = \sigma_v^2(Z'\Omega^{-1}Z)^{-1}$$
$$= \sigma_v^2\left[(1-\lambda)^2(Z'\overline{J}_N Z) + \frac{(N-1+\lambda)^2}{(N-1)^2}(Z'E_N Z)\right]^{-1}$$

and this, in general, is *not* equal to the usual formula for $\operatorname{var}(\widehat{\gamma}_{\text{OLS}})$ computed by regression packages, i.e., $\sigma_v^2(Z'Z)^{-1}$, unless $\lambda = 0$, which is the case of no spatial correlation.

(d) For the spatial *panel* regression with equal weights, this result is not necessarily true as long as $\sigma_\mu^2 > 0$. Two special cases where OLS is the same as GLS, i.e., $\widehat{\gamma}_{\text{OLS}} = (Z'Z)^{-1}Z'y = \widehat{\gamma}_{\text{GLS}} = (Z'\Omega^{-1}Z)^{-1}Z'\Omega^{-1}y$ are the following: (i) the trivial case where $\sigma_\mu^2 = 0$ and $\lambda = 0$, in fact, when $\lambda = 0$, $c_1 = c_2 = 1$, $\theta_1 = 0$ and $y_{ti}^* = y_{ti}$, and GLS reduces to OLS; (ii) when the matrix of regressors X is invariant across time, i.e., when $X = \iota_T \otimes X_N$, with X_N being the $N \times k$ matrix of exogenous regressors that is invariant across time. To show this, we prove that the Zyskind (1967) necessary and sufficient condition for OLS to be equivalent to GLS is satisfied. This calls for $P_Z\Omega = \Omega P_Z$, where $Z = \iota_T \otimes Z_N = \iota_T \otimes (\iota_N, X_N)$ is the matrix of regressors and Ω is the variance–covariance matrix of the disturbances. It is straightforward to show that $P_Z = \overline{J}_T \otimes P_{Z_N}$ and that $P_{Z_N}\iota_N = \iota_N$, $P_{Z_N}\overline{J}_N = \overline{J}_N$ and $P_{Z_N}E_N = P_{Z_N} - \overline{J}_N$. Hence,

$$\begin{aligned} P_Z\Omega &= \sigma_\nu^2(\overline{J}_T \otimes P_{Z_N})(I_T \otimes (c_1E_N + c_2\overline{J}_N)) \\ &= \sigma_\nu^2(\overline{J}_T \otimes (c_1(P_{Z_N} - \overline{J}_N) + c_2\overline{J}_N)) \end{aligned}$$

Similarly,

$$\begin{aligned} \Omega P_Z &= \sigma_\nu^2(I_T \otimes (c_1E_N + c_2\overline{J}_N))(\overline{J}_T \otimes P_{Z_N}) \\ &= \sigma_\nu^2(\overline{J}_T \otimes (c_1(P_{Z_N} - \overline{J}_N) + c_2\overline{J}_N)) \end{aligned}$$

Hence, $P_Z\Omega = \Omega P_Z$.

In fact, another necessary and sufficient condition for OLS to be equivalent to GLS, which relies on Ω^{-1}, is given by Milliken and Albohali (1984), and this condition calls for $Z'\Omega^{-1}(I_{TN} - P_Z) = 0$. Using the fact that $\overline{J}_N(I_N - P_{Z_N}) = 0$, we get

$$\begin{aligned} \Omega^{-1}(I_{TN} - P_Z) &= \left(\frac{1}{c_1\sigma_\nu^2}(I_T \otimes E_N) + \frac{1}{c_2\sigma_\nu^2}(I_T \otimes \overline{J}_N)\right)(I_{TN} - P_Z) \\ &= \left(\frac{1}{c_1\sigma_\nu^2}(I_T \otimes E_N) + \frac{1}{c_2\sigma_\nu^2}(I_T \otimes \overline{J}_N)\right) \\ &\quad - \left(\frac{1}{c_1\sigma_\nu^2}(\overline{J}_T \otimes (P_{Z_N} - \overline{J}_N)) + \frac{1}{c_2\sigma_\nu^2}(\overline{J}_T \otimes \overline{J}_N)\right) \\ &= \frac{1}{c_1\sigma_\nu^2}((I_T \otimes E_N) - (\overline{J}_T \otimes (P_{Z_N} - \overline{J}_N))) \\ &\quad + \frac{1}{c_2\sigma_\nu^2}(E_T \otimes \overline{J}_N) \end{aligned}$$

Hence,

$$\begin{aligned} Z'\Omega^{-1}(I_{TN} - P_Z) &= \frac{1}{c_1\sigma_\nu^2}\{(\iota_T' \otimes Z_N')((I_T \otimes E_N) - (\overline{J}_T \otimes (P_{Z_N} - \overline{J}_N)))\} \\ &= \frac{1}{c_1\sigma_\nu^2}\{(\iota_T' \otimes Z_N'E_N) - (\iota_T' \otimes (Z_N' - Z_N'\overline{J}_N))\} = 0 \end{aligned}$$

since $\iota_T'\overline{J}_T = \iota_T'$ and $Z_N'P_{Z_N} = Z_N'$.

10.4 COUNT PANEL DATA

Examples of panel data where the dependent variable is a count include the number of bids on an offshore oil lease by a firm, or the number of visits to a doctor by an individual, or the number of cigarettes smoked per day, or the number of patents filed by a research and development (R&D) firm, all of which are observed over time. Though one can still treat such count data with a panel regression, the occurrence of zeros and the discrete non-negative nature of the dependent variable suggest that perhaps a Poisson panel regression model should be used. See Cameron and Trivedi (1998) and Winkelmann (2000) for excellent books on this subject and Hausman *et al.* (1984) for popularizing this approach using panel data.

Exercise 10.6 *(Poisson panel regression model).* Consider the Poisson panel regression given by

$$\Pr(Y_{it} = y_{it}/x_{it}) = \frac{e^{-\lambda_{it}}\lambda_{it}^{y_{it}}}{y_{it}!}$$
$$\text{where } y_{it} = 0, 1, 2, \ldots, i = 1, \ldots, N, t = 1, \ldots, T$$

with i denoting households, individuals, firms, countries, etc., and t denoting time. The most common specification is the loglinear model $\ln \lambda_{it} = \mu_i + x'_{it}\beta$, where μ_i denotes the *unobservable* individual specific effect.

(a) For the *fixed effects* specification, show that the conditional Poisson likelihood which maximizes the joint probability of $(y_{i1}, y_{i2}, \ldots, y_{iT})$ conditioning on their sum $\sum_{t=1}^{T} y_{it}$ yields a likelihood that is free of μ_i.
(b) For the *random effects* Poisson panel data model, assuming that e^{μ_i} is distributed as *gamma* with mean 1 and variance θ, show that the resulting distribution is a *negative binomial*.

Solution

(a) For the *fixed effects* specification,

$$E(y_{it}/x_{it}) = \text{var}(y_{it}/x_{it}) = \lambda_{it} = e^{\mu_i + x'_{it}\beta}$$

The marginal effect of a continuous variable x_k is given by $\partial E(y_{it}/x_{it})/\partial x_k = \lambda_{it}\beta_k$. In this case, one can write the likelihood function as the product of the marginals

$$L(\beta, \lambda_{it}) = \sum_{i=1}^{N}\sum_{t=1}^{T}\left[-\lambda_{it} + y_{it}(\mu_i + x'_{it}\beta) - \ln y_{it}!\right]$$

The first-order conditions of this loglikelihood are given by

$$\partial L(\beta, \lambda_{it})/\partial\beta = \sum_{i=1}^{N}\sum_{t=1}^{T}(y_{it} - \lambda_{it})x_{it} = 0$$

and

$$\partial L(\beta, \lambda_{it})/\partial \mu_i = \sum_{t=1}^{T}(y_{it} - \lambda_{it}) = \sum_{t=1}^{T}(y_{it} - e^{\mu_i} e^{x'_{it}\beta}) = 0$$

for $i = 1, \ldots, N$. Solving for μ_i in terms of β in this model gives

$$\widehat{\mu}_i = \ln\left[\frac{\sum_{t=1}^{T} y_{it}}{\sum_{t=1}^{T} e^{x'_{it}\widehat{\beta}}}\right]$$

The conditional Poisson likelihood which maximizes the joint probability of $(y_{i1}, y_{i2}, \ldots, y_{iT})$ conditioning on their sum yields a likelihood that is free of μ_i. This is similar to the conditional logit approach in panel data, see Chamberlain (1984) and Chapter 11. In fact, the sum of T independent Poissons each with parameter λ_{it} is a Poisson with parameter $\sum_{t=1}^{T} \lambda_{it}$, i.e.,

$$\Pr\left[\sum_{t=1}^{T} y_{it}\right] = \frac{\exp\left(-\sum_{t=1}^{T} \lambda_{it}\right)\left(\sum_{t=1}^{T} \lambda_{it}\right)^{\sum_{t=1}^{T} y_{it}}}{\left(\sum_{t=1}^{T} y_{it}\right)!}$$

Since μ_i is a fixed parameter, the joint probability is the product of the marginals

$$\Pr\left[y_{i1}, y_{i2}, \ldots, y_{iT}\right] = \frac{\exp\left(-\sum_{t=1}^{T} \lambda_{it}\right)\prod_{t=1}^{T} \lambda_{it}^{y_{it}}}{\prod_{t=1}^{T} y_{it}!}$$

Hence, the conditional likelihood is

$$\Pr\left[y_{i1}, y_{i2}, \ldots, y_{iT} \mid \sum_{t=1}^{T} y_{it}\right] = \frac{\exp\left(-\sum_{t=1}^{T} \lambda_{it}\right)\prod_{t=1}^{T} \lambda_{it}^{y_{it}} / \prod_{t=1}^{T} y_{it}!}{\exp\left(-\sum_{t=1}^{T} \lambda_{it}\right)\left(\sum_{t=1}^{T} \lambda_{it}\right)^{\sum_{t=1}^{T} y_{it}} / \left(\sum_{t=1}^{T} y_{it}\right)!}$$

$$= \frac{\left(\sum_{t=1}^{T} y_{it}\right)!}{\prod_{t=1}^{T} y_{it}!}\prod_{t=1}^{T} p_{it}^{y_{it}}$$

where

$$p_{it} = \frac{\lambda_{it}}{\sum_{t=1}^{T} \lambda_{it}} = \frac{e^{\mu_i + x'_{it}\beta}}{\sum_{t=1}^{T}(e^{\mu_i + x'_{it}\beta})} = \frac{e^{x'_{it}\beta}}{\sum_{t=1}^{T} e^{x'_{it}\beta}}$$

As is clear from this conditional likelihood, it is free of μ_i. Also, zero counts in every period do not contribute to this conditional loglikelihood.

(b) For the *random effects* Poisson panel data model, the μ_i are correlated across periods for the same individual. We will encounter this phenomenon when studying random effects probits in Chapter 11. The same idea applies here for the estimation of the maximum likelihood. First, one conditions on the random effects and writes the joint probability

$$\Pr(y_{i1}, y_{i2}, \ldots, y_{iT}|\mu_i) = \prod_{t=1}^{T} \Pr(y_{it}/\mu_i)$$

then one integrates out the effect of μ_i, i.e.,

$$\begin{aligned}\Pr(y_{i1}, y_{i2}, \ldots, y_{iT}) &= \int \Pr(y_{i1}, y_{i2}, \ldots, y_{iT}, \mu_i)d\mu_i \\ &= \int \Pr(y_{i1}, y_{i2}, \ldots, y_{iT}|\mu_i)g(\mu_i)d\mu_i\end{aligned}$$

Assuming $\Pr(y_{it}|\mu_i)$ is distributed as Poisson$(\lambda_{it} = e^{\mu_i + x'_{it}\beta})$, we get

$$\begin{aligned}\Pr(y_{i1}, y_{i2}, \ldots, y_{iT}|\mu_i) &= \frac{\exp\left(-\sum_{t=1}^{T}\lambda_{it}\right)\prod_{t=1}^{T}\lambda_{it}^{y_{it}}}{\prod_{t=1}^{T} y_{it}!} \\ &= \frac{\exp\left(-e^{\mu_i}\sum_{t=1}^{T}\gamma_{it}\right)\left(\prod_{t=1}^{T}\gamma_{it}^{y_{it}}\right)(e^{\mu_i})^{\sum_{t=1}^{T} y_{it}}}{\prod_{t=1}^{T} y_{it}!}\end{aligned}$$

where $\gamma_{it} = e^{x'_{it}\beta}$. Let $\varepsilon_i = e^{\mu_i}$ be distributed as *gamma* with mean 1 and variance θ. Then

$$g(\varepsilon_i) = \frac{\theta^\theta}{\Gamma(\theta)}\varepsilon_i^{\theta-1}\exp(-\theta\varepsilon_i)$$

for $\varepsilon_i > 0$, so that

$$\begin{aligned}\Pr(y_{i1}, y_{i2}, \ldots, y_{iT}) &= \frac{\theta^\theta}{\Gamma(\theta)}\frac{\prod_{t=1}^{T}\gamma_{it}^{y_{it}}}{\prod_{t=1}^{T} y_{it}!}\int_0^\infty \exp\left(-\varepsilon_i(\theta + \sum_{t=1}^{T}\gamma_{it})\right)\varepsilon_i^{\left(\theta+\sum_{t=1}^{T} y_{it}\right)-1} d\varepsilon_i \\ &= \frac{\theta^\theta}{\Gamma(\theta)}\frac{\prod_{t=1}^{T}\gamma_{it}^{y_{it}}}{\prod_{t=1}^{T} y_{it}!}\frac{\Gamma\left(\theta + \sum_{t=1}^{T} y_{it}\right)}{\left(\theta + \sum_{t=1}^{T}\gamma_{it}\right)^{\left(\theta+\sum_{t=1}^{T} y_{it}\right)}}\end{aligned}$$

Let $q_i = \theta/\left(\theta + \sum_{t=1}^{T}\gamma_{it}\right)$. Then

$$\Pr(y_{i1}, y_{i2}, \ldots, y_{iT}) = \frac{\prod_{t=1}^{T}\gamma_{it}^{y_{it}}}{\prod_{t=1}^{T} y_{it}!}\frac{\Gamma\left(\theta + \sum_{t=1}^{T} y_{it}\right)}{\Gamma(\theta)\left(\sum_{t=1}^{T}\gamma_{it}\right)^{\sum_{t=1}^{T} y_{it}}} q_i^\theta (1 - q_i)^{\sum_{t=1}^{T} y_{it}}$$

which is a *negative binomial*.

Exercise 10.7 *(Patents and R&D expenditures).* This is based on Problem 10.9 in Baltagi (2008). Hall *et al.* (1986) studied the relationship between patents and R&D expenditures using panel data. Their data covered 346 US firms observed over the period 1975–79. The count dependent variable is the number of patents applied for by the firm during the year (that were eventually granted). Some of the explanatory variables included are (i) real R&D spending (in 1972 dollars) and its lagged values; (ii) the logarithm of the book value of capital in 1972 as a measure of size of the firm (LOGK); (iii) a dummy for whether the firm is in the scientific sector (SCISECT); (iii) a two-digit code for the applied R&D industrial classification; (iv) the sum of patents applied for in 1972–79. See the empirical example in Section 10.8 of Baltagi (2008).

(a) Run the fixed effects specification using the Poisson distribution.
(b) Run the random effects specification (including variables that are time invariant like LOGK and SCISECT) using the Poisson distribution.

Solution

Tables 10.1 and 10.2 show the Stata output for the fixed and random effects specification using the Poisson distributions. These are also Tables 10.1 and 10.3 in Baltagi (2008,

Table 10.1 Poisson Fixed Effects for the R&D Data

```
. xtpois PAT LOGR LOGR1 LOGR2 LOGR3 LOGR4 LOGR5 dyear2 dyear3 dyear4 dyear5,fe
note: 22 groups (110 obs) dropped due to all zero outcomes


Conditional fixed-effects Poisson regression    Number of obs      =      1620
Group variable (i): id                          Number of groups   =       324

                                                Obs per group: min =         5
                                                               avg =       5.0
                                                               max =         5

                                                Wald chi2(10)      =    245.39
Log likelihood  = -3536.3086                    Prob > chi2        =    0.0000

------------------------------------------------------------------------------
         PAT |      Coef.   Std. Err.      z    P>|z|     [95% Conf. Interval]
-------------+----------------------------------------------------------------
        LOGR |   .3222105   .0459412     7.01   0.000     .2321674    .4122535
       LOGR1 |  -.0871295   .0486887    -1.79   0.074    -.1825576    .0082986
       LOGR2 |   .0785816    .044784     1.75   0.079    -.0091934    .1663567
       LOGR3 |     .00106   .0414151     0.03   0.980    -.0801122    .0822322
       LOGR4 |  -.0046414   .0378489    -0.12   0.902    -.0788238    .0695411
       LOGR5 |   .0026068   .0322596     0.08   0.936    -.0606209    .0658346
      dyear2 |  -.0426076    .013132    -3.24   0.001    -.0683458   -.0168695
      dyear3 |  -.0400462   .0134677    -2.97   0.003    -.0664423     -.01365
      dyear4 |  -.1571185   .0142281   -11.04   0.000    -.1850051   -.1292319
      dyear5 |  -.1980306   .0152946   -12.95   0.000    -.2280074   -.1680538
------------------------------------------------------------------------------
```

Table 10.2 Poisson Random Effects for the R&D Data

```
. xtpois PAT LOGR LOGR1 LOGR2 LOGR3 LOGR4 LOGR5 dyear2 dyear3 dyear4 dyear5
  LOGK  SCISECT, re

Fitting Poisson model:

Random-effects Poisson regression               Number of obs      =      1730
Group variable (i): id                          Number of groups   =       346

Random effects u_i ~ Gamma                      Obs per group: min =         5
                                                               avg =       5.0
                                                               max =         5

                                                Wald chi2(12)      =   1272.14
Log likelihood  = -5234.9265                    Prob > chi2        =    0.0000
```

PAT	Coef.	Std. Err.	z	P>|z|	[95% Conf.	Interval]
LOGR	.4034537	.0435022	9.27	0.000	.318191	.4887165
LOGR1	−.0461765	.0482224	−0.96	0.338	−.1406906	.0483376
LOGR2	.1079235	.0447115	2.41	0.016	.0202905	.1955565
LOGR3	.0297733	.0413235	0.72	0.471	−.0512193	.110766
LOGR4	.0106957	.0377074	0.28	0.777	−.0632094	.0846008
LOGR5	.0406111	.0315738	1.29	0.198	−.0212724	.1024946
dyear2	−.0449624	.0131291	−3.42	0.001	−.070695	−.0192298
dyear3	−.0483864	.0134018	−3.61	0.000	−.0746534	−.0221193
dyear4	−.1741619	.0139702	−12.47	0.000	−.201543	−.1467809
dyear5	−.2258977	.0146645	−15.40	0.000	−.2546396	−.1971557
LOGK	.2916932	.0393368	7.42	0.000	.2145945	.368792
SCISECT	.2570001	.1122716	2.29	0.022	.0369517	.4770484
_cons	.4107881	.1467443	2.80	0.005	.1231746	.6984016
/lnalpha	−.156739	.0809735			−.3154441	.0019661
alpha	.8549271	.0692264			.7294648	1.001968

```
Likelihood-ratio test of alpha=0: chibar2(01) =  2.5e+04 Prob>=chibar2 = 0.000
```

pp.229–231). The fixed effects estimates show that only the current R&D spending is significant, while the random effects specification shows that LOGK and SCISECT are significant. The current R&D spending has a larger effect on patents for the Poisson random effects than for the Poisson fixed effects (0.40 as compared to 0.32).

11

Limited Dependent Variables

In many economic studies, the dependent variable is discrete, indicating, for example, that a household purchased a car or that an individual is unemployed or that he or she joined a union. This dependent variable is usually represented by a binary choice variable y_{it} taking the value 1 if the event happens and 0 if it does not for individual i at time t. In fact, if p_{it} is the probability that household i purchases a car at time t, then $E(y_{it}) = 1 \cdot p_{it} + 0 \cdot (1 - p_{it}) = p_{it}$, and this is usually modeled as a function of some explanatory variables

$$p_{it} = \Pr[y_{it} = 1] = E(y_{it} \mid x_{it}) = F(x'_{it}\beta) \tag{11.1}$$

For the linear probability model, $F(x'_{it}\beta) = x'_{it}\beta$ and the usual panel data methods apply except that $\widehat{y}_{it}$ is not guaranteed to lie in the unit interval. The standard solution has been to use the logistic or normal cumulative distribution functions that constrain $F(x'_{it}\beta)$ to be between zero and one. These probability functions are known in the literature as logit and probit, corresponding to the logistic and normal distributions, respectively. For example, a worker participates in the labor force if his offered wage exceeds his unobserved reservation wage. This threshold can be described as

$$y_{it} = \begin{cases} 1 & \text{if } y^*_{it} > 0 \\ 0 & \text{if } y^*_{it} \leq 0 \end{cases} \tag{11.2}$$

where $y^*_{it} = x'_{it}\beta + u_{it}$, so that

$$\Pr[y_{it} = 1] = \Pr[y^*_{it} > 0] = \Pr[u_{it} > -x'_{it}\beta] = F(x'_{it}\beta) \tag{11.3}$$

where the last equality holds as long as the density function describing F is symmetric around zero. This is true for the logistic and normal density functions. For panel data, the presence of individual effects complicates matters significantly. The following exercises give the reader a sample of these complications.

Exercise 11.1 *(Fixed effects logit model).* This is based on Problem 11.1 in Baltagi (2008). Consider the fixed effects panel data model

$$y^*_{it} = x'_{it}\beta + \mu_i + \nu_{it} \tag{11.4}$$

with

$$\Pr[y_{it} = 1] = \Pr[y^*_{it} > 0] = \Pr[\nu_{it} > -x'_{it}\beta - \mu_i] = F(x'_{it}\beta + \mu_i) \tag{11.5}$$

where the last equality holds as long as the density function describing F is symmetric around zero. In this case, μ_i and β are unknown parameters and as $N \to \infty$, for a fixed T, the number of parameters μ_i increases with N. This means that μ_i cannot be consistently estimated for a fixed T. This is known as the incidental parameters problem in statistics, and it is discussed by Neyman and Scott (1948) and reviewed more recently by Lancaster (2000). The usual solution to this incidental parameters (μ_i) problem is to find a minimal sufficient statistic for μ_i. For the logit model, Chamberlain (1980) finds that $\sum_{t=1}^{T} y_{it}$ is a minimum sufficient statistic for μ_i. Therefore, Chamberlain suggests maximizing the *conditional* likelihood function

$$L_c = \prod_{i=1}^{N} \Pr\left(y_{i1}, \ldots, y_{iT} \mid \sum_{t=1}^{T} y_{it}\right) \tag{11.6}$$

to obtain the conditional logit estimates for β. By definition of a sufficient statistic, the distribution of the data given this sufficient statistic will not depend on μ_i.

(a) For $T = 2$, show that the conditional logistic likelihood which maximizes the joint probability of (y_{i1}, y_{i2}), conditioning on their sum $(y_{i1} + y_{i2})$, yields a likelihood that is free of μ_i. Also, show that this conditional logit maximization can be done using a standard logit package restricting the observations to *switchers* from $y_{i1} = 1$ to $y_{i2} = 0$, and from $y_{i1} = 0$ to $y_{i2} = 1$.
(b) Extend this result to the case where $T = 3$, i.e., show that the conditional logistic likelihood which maximizes the joint probability of (y_{i1}, y_{i2}, y_{i3}), conditioning on their sum $(y_{i1} + y_{i2} + y_{i3})$, yields a likelihood that is free of μ_i.
(c) Convince yourself that this can be extended to $T = 10$.

Solution

(a) For the fixed effects logit model with $T = 2$, the observations over the two periods and for all individuals are independent and the *unconditional* likelihood is given by

$$L = \prod_{i=1}^{N} \Pr(y_{i1})\Pr(y_{i2}) \tag{11.7}$$

The sum $(y_{i1} + y_{i2})$ can be 0, 1 or 2. If it is 0, both y_{i1} and y_{i2} are 0 and

$$\Pr[y_{i1} = 0, y_{i2} = 0 \mid y_{i1} + y_{i2} = 0] = 1 \tag{11.8}$$

Similarly, if the sum is 2, both y_{i1} and y_{i2} are 1 and

$$\Pr[y_{i1} = 1, y_{i2} = 1 \mid y_{i1} + y_{i2} = 2] = 1 \tag{11.9}$$

These terms add nothing to the conditional loglikelihood since log $1 = 0$. Only the observations for which $y_{i1} + y_{i2} = 1$ matter in log L_c and these are given by

$$\Pr[y_{i1} = 0, y_{i2} = 1 \mid y_{i1} + y_{i2} = 1] \quad \text{and} \quad \Pr[y_{i1} = 1, y_{i2} = 0 \mid y_{i1} + y_{i2} = 1]$$

The latter can be calculated as $\Pr[y_{i1} = 1, y_{i2} = 0]/\Pr[y_{i1} + y_{i2} = 1]$ with

$$\Pr[y_{i1} + y_{i2} = 1] = \Pr[y_{i1} = 0, y_{i2} = 1] + \Pr[y_{i1} = 1, y_{i2} = 0]$$

since the latter two events are mutually exclusive. For the logit model, the functional form is given by

$$\Pr[y_{it} = 1] = \frac{e^{\mu_i + x'_{it}\beta}}{1 + e^{\mu_i + x'_{it}\beta}} \tag{11.10}$$

and

$$\Pr[y_{it} = 0] = 1 - \frac{e^{\mu_i + x'_{it}\beta}}{1 + e^{\mu_i + x'_{it}\beta}} = \frac{1}{1 + e^{\mu_i + x'_{it}\beta}}$$

Therefore,

$$\Pr[y_{i1} = 1, y_{i2} = 0] = \frac{e^{\mu_i + x'_{i1}\beta}}{1 + e^{\mu_i + x'_{i1}\beta}} \frac{1}{1 + e^{\mu_i + x'_{i2}\beta}}$$

and

$$\Pr[y_{i1} = 0, y_{i2} = 1] = \frac{1}{1 + e^{\mu_i + x'_{i1}\beta}} \frac{e^{\mu_i + x'_{i2}\beta}}{1 + e^{\mu_i + x'_{i2}\beta}}$$

with

$$\begin{aligned}\Pr[y_{i1} + y_{i2} = 1] &= \Pr[y_{i1} = 1, y_{i2} = 0] + \Pr[y_{i1} = 0, y_{i2} = 1] \\ &= \frac{e^{\mu_i + x'_{i1}\beta} + e^{\mu_i + x'_{i2}\beta}}{(1 + e^{\mu_i + x'_{i1}\beta})(1 + e^{\mu_i + x'_{i2}\beta})}\end{aligned}$$

Therefore,

$$\Pr[y_{i1} = 1, y_{i2} = 0 \mid y_{i1} + y_{i2} = 1] = \frac{\Pr[y_{i1} = 1, y_{i2} = 0]}{\Pr[y_{i1} + y_{i2} = 1]} \tag{11.11}$$

$$= \frac{e^{\mu_i + x'_{i1}\beta}}{e^{\mu_i + x'_{i1}\beta} + e^{\mu_i + x'_{i2}\beta}} = \frac{e^{x'_{i1}\beta}}{e^{x'_{i1}\beta} + e^{x'_{i2}\beta}} = \frac{1}{1 + e^{(x_{i2} - x_{i1})'\beta}}$$

Similarly,

$$\Pr[y_{i1} = 0, y_{i2} = 1 \mid y_{i1} + y_{i2} = 1] = \frac{e^{x'_{i2}\beta}}{e^{x'_{i1}\beta} + e^{x'_{i2}\beta}} = \frac{e^{(x_{i2} - x_{i1})'\beta}}{1 + e^{(x_{i2} - x_{i1})'\beta}} \tag{11.12}$$

and neither probability involves the μ_i. Therefore, by conditioning on $y_{i1} + y_{i2}$, we have swept away the μ_i. The product of terms such as these with $y_{i1} + y_{i2} = 1$ gives the conditional likelihood function which can be maximized with respect to β using conventional maximum likelihood logit programs. In this case, only the observations for individuals who *switched* status are used in the estimation. A standard logit package can be used with $x'_{i2} - x'_{i1}$ as explanatory variables and the dependent variable taking the value one if y_{it} switches from 0 to 1, and zero if y_{it} switches from 1 to 0.

(b) For $T = 3$, the observations over the three periods and for all individuals are independent and the unconditional likelihood is given by

$$L = \prod_{i=1}^{N} \Pr(y_{i1})\Pr(y_{i2})\Pr(y_{i3})$$

The sum $(y_{i1} + y_{i2} + y_{i3})$ can be 0, 1, 2, or 3. If this sum is 0, then $y_{i1} = y_{i2} = y_{i3} = 0$ and

$$\Pr[y_{i1} = 0, y_{i2} = 0, y_{i3} = 0 \mid y_{i1} + y_{i2} + y_{i3} = 0] = 1$$

Similarly, if this sum is 3, then $y_{i1} = y_{i2} = y_{i3} = 1$ and

$$\Pr[y_{i1} = 1, y_{i2} = 1, y_{i3} = 1 \mid y_{i1} + y_{i2} + y_{i3} = 3] = 1$$

These terms add nothing to the conditional loglikelihood since $\log 1 = 0$. Only the observations for which $y_{i1} + y_{i2} + y_{i3} = 1$ or 2 matter in the conditional loglikelihood and these are given by

$$\Pr[y_{i1} = 1, y_{i2} = 0, y_{i3} = 0 \mid y_{i1} + y_{i2} + y_{i3} = 1]$$
$$\Pr[y_{i1} = 0, y_{i2} = 1, y_{i3} = 0 \mid y_{i1} + y_{i2} + y_{i3} = 1]$$
$$\Pr[y_{i1} = 0, y_{i2} = 0, y_{i3} = 1 \mid y_{i1} + y_{i2} + y_{i3} = 1]$$
$$\Pr[y_{i1} = 1, y_{i2} = 1, y_{i3} = 0 \mid y_{i1} + y_{i2} + y_{i3} = 2]$$
$$\Pr[y_{i1} = 1, y_{i2} = 0, y_{i3} = 1 \mid y_{i1} + y_{i2} + y_{i3} = 2]$$
$$\Pr[y_{i1} = 0, y_{i2} = 1, y_{i3} = 1 \mid y_{i1} + y_{i2} + y_{i3} = 2]$$

These probabilities can be computed as

$$\Pr[y_{i1} = 1, y_{i2} = 0, y_{i3} = 0] \mid \Pr[y_{i1} + y_{i2} + y_{i3} = 1]$$

with the latter probability computed from

$$\begin{aligned}\Pr[y_{i1} + y_{i2} + y_{i3} = 1] = \Pr[y_{i1} = 1, y_{i2} = 0, y_{i3} = 0]\\ + \Pr[y_{i1} = 0, y_{i2} = 1, y_{i3} = 0]\\ + \Pr[y_{i1} = 0, y_{i2} = 0, y_{i3} = 1]\end{aligned}$$

since the latter three events are mutually exclusive. For the logit model,

$$\Pr[y_{it} = 1] = \frac{e^{\mu_i + X'_{it}\beta}}{1 + e^{\mu_i + X'_{it}\beta}}$$

we get

$$\Pr[y_{i1}=1]=\frac{e^{\mu_i+X'_{i1}\beta}}{1+e^{\mu_i+X'_{i1}\beta}},\ \Pr[y_{i2}=0]=\frac{1}{1+e^{\mu_i+X'_{i2}\beta}},\ \Pr[y_{i3}=0]=\frac{1}{1+e^{\mu_i+X'_{i3}\beta}}$$

and

$$\Pr[y_{i1}=1,\ y_{i2}=0,\ y_{i3}=0]=\frac{e^{\mu_i+X'_{i1}\beta}}{(1+e^{\mu_i+X'_{i1}\beta})(1+e^{\mu_i+X'_{i2}\beta})(1+e^{\mu_i+X'_{i3}\beta})}$$

Similarly, one can compute $\Pr[y_{i1}=0,\ y_{i2}=1,\ y_{i3}=0]$ and $\Pr[y_{i1}=0,\ y_{i2}=0,\ y_{i3}=1]$. From these, one gets their sum

$$\Pr[y_{i1}+y_{i2}+y_{i3}=1]=\frac{e^{\mu_i+X'_{i1}\beta}+e^{\mu_i+X'_{i2}\beta}+e^{\mu_i+X'_{i3}\beta}}{(1+e^{\mu_i+X'_{i1}\beta})(1+e^{\mu_i+X'_{i2}\beta})(1+e^{\mu_i+X'_{i3}\beta})}$$

Hence,

$$\Pr[y_{i1}=1,\ y_{i2}=0,\ y_{i3}=0\mid y_{i1}+y_{i2}+y_{i3}=1]$$
$$=\frac{e^{\mu_i+X'_{i1}\beta}}{e^{\mu_i+X'_{i1}\beta}+e^{\mu_i+X'_{i2}\beta}+e^{\mu_i+X'_{i3}\beta}}=\frac{e^{X'_{i1}\beta}}{e^{X'_{i1}\beta}+e^{X'_{i2}\beta}+e^{X'_{i3}\beta}}$$

and this probability does not involve the μ_i. The same can be shown for each of the other five conditional probabilities given above. Therefore, conditioning on $y_{i1}+y_{i2}+y_{i3}$, we have swept away the μ_i.

(c) For $T=10$, the sum $(y_{i1}+y_{i2}+\ldots+y_{i,10})$ can be $0, 1, 2, \ldots, 10$. If the sum is zero, all the y_{it} are zero and

$$\Pr\left[y_{i1}=0,\ldots,y_{i,10}=0\mid \sum\nolimits_{t=1}^{10} y_{it}=0\right]=1$$

Similarly, if the sum is 10, all the y_{it} are 1 and $\Pr[y_{i1}=1,\ldots,y_{i,10}=1\mid \sum_{t=1}^{10} y_{it}=10]=1$. These terms do not contribute to the conditional loglikelihood since $\log 1=0$. Hence, one can focus on conditional probabilities for the sum being $1, 2, \ldots, 9$. The number of probability computations are increasing as can be seen from conditioning on the sum being 1. These terms are

$$\Pr\left[y_{i1}=1,\ y_{i2}=0,\ldots,y_{i,10}=0\mid \sum_{t=1}^{10} y_{it}=1\right]$$

$$\Pr\left[y_{i1}=0,\ y_{i2}=1,\ldots,y_{i,10}=0\mid \sum_{t=1}^{10} y_{it}=1\right]$$

$$\vdots$$

$$\Pr\left[y_{i1}=0,\ y_{i2}=0,\ldots,y_{i,10}=1\mid \sum_{t=1}^{10} y_{it}=1\right]$$

The other terms can be listed for each conditional sum and the computations follow the approach given in parts (a) and (b). This is laborious but will show that conditioning on $\sum_{t=1}^{10} y_{it}$ gets rid of the μ_i.

Exercise 11.2 *(Equivalence of two estimators of the fixed effects logit model).* This is based on Abrevaya (1997) and is also Problem 11.4 in Baltagi (2008). Consider the fixed effects logit model given in (11.4) with $T = 2$. In (11.11) and (11.12) we showed the conditional maximum likelihood of β, call it $\widehat{\beta}_{\text{CML}}$, can be obtained by running a logit estimator of the dependent variable $1(\Delta y = 1)$ on the independent variables Δx for the subsample of observations satisfying $y_{i1} + y_{i2} = 1$. Here $1(\Delta y = 1)$ is an indicator function taking the value one if $\Delta y = 1$. Therefore, $\widehat{\beta}_{\text{CML}}$ maximizes the loglikelihood

$$\ln L_c(\beta) = \sum_{i\in\vartheta}[1(\Delta y = 1)\ln F(\Delta x'\beta) + 1(\Delta y = -1)\ln(1 - F(\Delta x'\beta))]$$

where $\vartheta = \{i : y_{i1} + y_{i2} = 1\}$. This follows from the fact that $\Pr[y_{i2} = 1 \mid y_{i1} + y_{i2} = 1] = \Pr[\Delta y_{it} = 1] = F(\Delta x'_{it}\beta)$ as described in (11.12). Also, $\Pr[y_{i1} = 1 \mid y_{i1} + y_{i2} = 1] = \Pr[\Delta y_{it} = -1] = 1 - F(\Delta x'_{it}\beta)$ as described in (11.11).

(a) Maximize the unconditional loglikelihood for (11.5) given by

$$\ln L(\beta, \mu_i) = \sum_{i=1}^{N}\sum_{t=1}^{2}[y_{it}\ln F(x'_{it}\beta + \mu_i) + (1 - y_{it})\ln(1 - F(x'_{it}\beta + \mu_i))]$$

with respect to μ_i and show that

$$\widehat{\mu}_i = \begin{cases} -\infty & \text{if } y_{i1} + y_{i2} = 0 \\ -(x_{i1} + x_{i2})'\beta/2 & \text{if } y_{i1} + y_{i2} = 1 \\ +\infty & \text{if } y_{i1} + y_{i2} = 2 \end{cases}$$

(b) Concentrate the likelihood by plugging $\widehat{\mu}_i$ in the unconditional likelihood and show that

$$\ln L(\beta, \widehat{\mu}_i) = \sum_{i\in\vartheta} 2[1(\Delta y = 1)\ln F(\Delta x'\beta/2) + 1(\Delta y = -1)\ln(1 - F(\Delta x'\beta/2))]$$

Hint: Use the symmetry of F and the fact that

$$1(\Delta y = 1) = y_{i2} = 1 - y_{i1} \quad \text{and} \quad 1(\Delta y = -1) = y_{i1} = 1 - y_{i2} \qquad \text{for } i \in \vartheta$$

(c) Conclude that $\ln L(\beta, \widehat{\mu}_i) = 2\ln L_c(\beta/2)$. This shows that a scale-adjusted maximum likelihood estimator is equivalent to the conditional maximum likelihood estimator, i.e., $\widehat{\beta}_{\text{ML}} = 2\widehat{\beta}_{\text{CML}}$. Whether a similar result hold for $T > 2$ remains an open question.

Solution

(a) Maximizing the unconditional loglikelihood given by $\ln L(\beta, \mu_i)$ with respect to μ_i yields the first-order conditions

$$\frac{\partial \ln L(\beta, \mu_i)}{\partial \mu_i} = \sum_{t=1}^{2}\frac{y_{it}}{F}f + \sum_{t=1}^{2}(1 - y_{it})\frac{1}{1 - F}(-f)$$

$$= \sum_{t=1}^{2}\frac{f[y_{it} - F]}{F(1 - F)} = 0$$

where F stands for $F(x'_{it}\beta + \mu_i)$ and f is the probability density function which is the derivative of F evaluated at $x'_{it}\beta + \mu_i$. Using the fact that $f = F(1 - F)$ for the logistic distribution, we get

$$\frac{\ln L(\beta, \mu_i)}{\partial \mu_i} = \sum_{t=1}^{2}[y_{it} - F(x'_{it}\beta + \mu_i)] = 0$$

This can be rewritten as

$$\begin{aligned} y_{i1} + y_{i2} &= F(x'_{i1}\beta + \mu_i) + F(x'_{i2}\beta + \mu_i) \\ &= \frac{e^{x'_{i1}\beta+\mu_i}}{1 + e^{x'_{i1}\beta+\mu_i}} + \frac{e^{x'_{i2}\beta+\mu_i}}{1 + e^{x'_{i2}\beta+\mu_i}} \end{aligned}$$

Solving for μ_i yields

$$\widehat{\mu}_i = \begin{cases} -\infty & \text{if } y_{i1} + y_{i2} = 0 \\ -(x_{i1} + x_{i2})'\beta/2 & \text{if } y_{i1} + y_{i2} = 1 \\ +\infty & \text{if } y_{i1} + y_{i2} = 2 \end{cases}$$

(b) Concentrating the likelihood by substituting $\widehat{\mu}_i$ into the unconditional likelihood, we eliminate terms for which $i \notin \vartheta$. For $y_{i1} + y_{i2} = 0$, $\widehat{\mu}_i = -\infty$ and the terms in the unconditional likelihood corresponding to this set of y_{it} have to have $y_{i1} = y_{i2} = 0$. This means that $\sum_{i=1}^{N}\sum_{t=1}^{2} y_{it} \ln F(x'_{it}\beta + \widehat{\mu}_i)$ is zero and the second term reduces to $\sum_{i=1}^{N}\sum_{t=1}^{2} y_{it} \ln(1 - F(x'_{it}\beta - \infty))$, which is also zero since $F(-\infty) = 0$.

For $y_{i1} + y_{i2} = 2$, $\widehat{\mu}_i = +\infty$ and the terms in the unconditional likelihood corresponding to this set of y_{it} have to have $y_{i1} = y_{i2} = 1$. This means that

$$\sum_{i=1}^{N}\sum_{t=1}^{2}(1 - y_{it}) \ln(1 - F(x'_{it}\beta + \widehat{\mu}_i)) = 0$$

and the first term reduces to $\sum_{i=1}^{N}\sum_{t=1}^{2} \ln F(x'_{it}\beta + \infty)$ which is also zero since $F(+\infty) = 1$. The concentrated likelihood is therefore based on $i \in \vartheta$ where $y_{i1} + y_{i2} = 1$ and $\widehat{\mu}_i = -(x_{i1} + x_{i2})'\beta/2$. This is given by

$$\begin{aligned} \ln L(\beta, \widehat{\mu}_i) = \sum\nolimits_{i\in\vartheta} &[y_{i1} \ln F(-\Delta x'_i\beta/2) + (1 - y_{i1}) \ln(1 - F(-\Delta x'_i\beta/2)) \\ &+ y_{i2} \ln F(\Delta x'_i\beta/2) \\ &+ (1 - y_{i2}) \ln(1 - F(\Delta x'_i\beta/2))] \end{aligned}$$

Using $1(\Delta y = 1) = y_{i2} = 1 - y_{i1}$ and $1(\Delta y = -1) = y_{i1} = 1 - y_{i2}$ for $i \in \vartheta$, the concentrated likelihood simplifies to

$$\begin{aligned} \ln L(\beta, \widehat{\mu}_i) = \sum\nolimits_{i\in\vartheta} &[1(\Delta y = -1) \ln(1 - F(\Delta x'_i\beta/2)) + 1(\Delta y = 1) \ln F(\Delta x'_i\beta/2) \\ &+ 1(\Delta y = 1) \ln F(\Delta x'_i\beta/2) + 1(\Delta y - 1) \ln(1 - F(\Delta x'_i\beta/2))] \end{aligned}$$

using the symmetry of F for the logistic distribution. Hence,

$$\ln L(\beta, \widehat{\mu}_i) = \sum_{i \in \vartheta} 2[1(\Delta y = 1) \ln F(\Delta x_i'\beta/2) + 1(\Delta y = -1) \ln(1 - F(\Delta x_i'\beta/2))]$$

(c) The concentrated likelihood $\ln(\beta, \widehat{\mu}_i)$ obtained in part (b) is related to the conditional likelihood $\ln L_c(\beta)$ as follows: $\ln L(\beta, \widehat{\mu}_i) = 2 \ln L_c(\beta/2)$. Hence, $\widehat{\beta}_{\text{CML}}$ which maximizes the conditional maximum likelihood L_c is half of the $\widehat{\beta}_{\text{ML}}$ which maximizes the concentrated $\ln L(\beta, \widehat{\mu}_i)$.

Exercise 11.3 *(Dynamic fixed effects logit model with no regressors).* This is based on Problem 11.2 in Baltagi (2008). The fixed effects conditional logit approach can be generalized to include lags of the dependent variable, provided there are *no* explanatory variables and $T \geq 4$ (see Chamberlain, 1985). Assuming that the initial period y_{i0} is observed but its probability is unspecified, the model is given by

$$\Pr[y_{i0} = 1 \mid \mu_i] = p_0(\mu_i)$$

$$\Pr[y_{it} = 1 \mid \mu_i, y_{i0}, y_{i1}, \ldots, y_{i,t-1}] = \frac{e^{\gamma y_{i,t-1} + \mu_i}}{1 + e^{\gamma y_{i,t-1} + \mu_i}} \qquad t = 1, \ldots, T \qquad (11.13)$$

where $p_0(\mu_i)$ is unknown but the logit specification is imposed from period 1 to T. Consider the two events

$$A = \{y_{i0} = d_0, y_{i1} = 0, y_{i2} = 1, y_{i3} = d_3\} \qquad (11.14)$$

$$B = \{y_{i0} = d_0, y_{i1} = 1, y_{i2} = 0, y_{i3} = d_3\} \qquad (11.15)$$

where d_0 and d_3 are either 0 or 1. Show that for $T = 3$, $\Pr[A \mid y_{i1} + y_{i2} = 1, \mu_i]$ and therefore $\Pr[B \mid y_{i1} + y_{i2} = 1, \mu_i]$ do not depend on μ_i.

Solution

From (11.13), we have

$$\Pr[y_{i0} = 1 \mid \mu_i] = p_0(\mu_i)$$

which means that

$$\Pr[y_{i0} = d_0 \mid \mu_i] = p_0(\mu_i)^{d_0}[1 - p_0(\mu_i)]^{1-d_0} \quad \text{for } d_0 = 0, 1$$

Also, from (11.13)

$$\Pr[y_{i1} = 1 \mid \mu_i, y_{i0}] = \frac{e^{\gamma y_{i0} + \mu_i}}{1 + e^{\gamma y_{i0} + \mu_i}}$$

and

$$\Pr[y_{i1} = 0 \mid \mu_i, y_{i0}] = \frac{1}{1 + e^{\gamma y_{i0} + \mu_i}}$$

Similarly,

$$\Pr[y_{i2} = 1 \mid \mu_i, y_{i0}, y_{i1}] = \frac{e^{\gamma y_{i1} + \mu_i}}{1 + e^{\gamma y_{i1} + \mu_i}}$$

and

$$\Pr[y_{i2} = 0 \mid \mu_i, y_{i0}, y_{i1}] = \frac{1}{1 + e^{\gamma y_{i1} + \mu_i}}$$

and so on. Substituting 0 and 1 values for y_{i1} and y_{i2}, we get

$$\Pr[y_{i3} = 1 \mid \mu_i, y_{i0} = d_0, y_{i1} = 0, y_{i2} = 1] = \frac{e^{\gamma + \mu_i}}{1 + e^{\gamma + \mu_i}}$$

and

$$\Pr[y_{i3} = 0 \mid \mu_i, y_{i0} = d_0, y_{i1} = 0, y_{i2} = 1] = \frac{1}{1 + e^{\gamma + \mu_i}}$$

which can be rewritten as

$$\Pr[y_{i3} = d_3 \mid \mu_i, y_{i0} = d_0, y_{i1} = 0, y_{i2} = 1] = \frac{e^{d_3 \gamma + d_3 \mu_i}}{1 + e^{\gamma + \mu_i}}$$

Also,

$$\Pr[y_{i3} = 1 \mid \mu_i, y_{i0} = d_0, y_{i1} = 1, y_{i2} = 0] = \frac{e^{\mu_i}}{1 + e^{\mu_i}}$$

and

$$\Pr[y_{i3} = 0 \mid \mu_i, y_{i0} = d_0, y_{i1} = 1, y_{i2} = 0] = \frac{1}{1 + e^{\mu_i}}$$

which can be rewritten as

$$\Pr[y_{i3} = d_3 \mid \mu_i, y_{i0} = d_0, y_{i1} = 1, y_{i2} = 0] = \frac{e^{d_3 \mu_i}}{1 + e^{\mu_i}}$$

Putting all these ingredients together, we get

$$\begin{aligned}\Pr(A/\mu_i) = {} & \Pr[y_{i0} = d_0 \mid \mu_i] \Pr[y_{i1} = 0 \mid \mu_i, \ y_{i0} = d_0] \\ & \Pr[y_{i2} = 1 \mid \mu_i, \ y_{i0} = d_0, \ y_{i1} = 0] \Pr[y_{i3} = d_3 \mid \mu_i, \ y_{i0} = d_0, \ y_{i1} = 0, \ y_{i2} = 1]\end{aligned}$$

Therefore,

$$\Pr(A \mid \mu_i) = p_0(\mu_i)^{d_0}[1 - p_0(\mu_i)]^{1-d_0} \frac{1}{1 + e^{\gamma d_0 + \mu_i}} \frac{e^{\mu_i}}{1 + e^{\mu_i}} \frac{e^{d_3 \gamma + d_3 \mu_i}}{1 + e^{\gamma + \mu_i}}$$

Similarly,

$$\begin{aligned}\Pr(B \mid \mu_i) = {} & \Pr[y_{i0} = d_0 \mid \mu_i] \Pr[y_{i1} = 1 \mid \mu_i, y_{i0}] \\ & \Pr[y_{i2} = 0 \mid \mu_i, \ y_{i0}, \ y_{i1} = 1] \Pr[y_{i3} = d_3 \mid \mu_i, \ y_{i0} = d_0, \ y_{i1} = 1, \ y_{i2} = 0]\end{aligned}$$

Therefore,

$$\Pr(B \mid \mu_i) = p_0(\mu_i)^{d_0}[1 - p_0(\mu_i)]^{1-d_0} \frac{e^{\gamma d_0 + \mu_i}}{1 + e^{\gamma d_0 + \mu_i}} \frac{1}{1 + e^{\gamma + \mu_i}} \frac{e^{d_3 \mu_i}}{1 + e^{\mu_i}}$$

Hence,

$$\Pr[A \mid \mu_i, y_{i1}+y_{i2}=1] = \frac{\Pr[A \mid \mu_i]}{\Pr[A \mid \mu_i]+\Pr[B \mid \mu_i]} = \frac{e^{d_3\gamma+d_3\mu_i}}{e^{d_3\gamma+d_3\mu_i}+e^{d_3\mu_i+\gamma d_0}}$$

$$= \frac{1}{1+e^{\gamma(d_0-d_3)}}, \text{ independent of } \mu_i$$

and

$$\Pr[B \mid \mu_i, y_{i1}+y_{i2}=1] = \frac{\Pr[B \mid \mu_i]}{\Pr[A \mid \mu_i]+\Pr[B \mid \mu_i]} = \frac{e^{d_3\mu_i+\gamma d_0}}{e^{d_3\mu_i+\gamma d_0}+e^{d_3\gamma+d_3\mu_i}}$$

$$= \frac{1}{1+e^{\gamma(d_3-d_0)}}, \text{ independent of } \mu_i$$

Exercise 11.4 *(Dynamic fixed effects logit model with regressors).* This is based on Problem 11.3 in Baltagi (2008). Honoré and Kyriazidou (2000) consider the identification and estimation of panel data discrete choice models with lags of the dependent variable and strictly exogenous variables that allow for unobservable heterogeneity. In particular, they extend Chamberlain's (1985) fixed effects logit model in (11.13) to include strictly exogenous variables $x_i' = (x_{i1}, \ldots, x_{it})$, i.e.,

$$\Pr[y_{i0}=1 \mid x_i', \mu_i] = p_0(x_i', \mu_i)$$

$$\Pr[y_{it}=1 \mid x_i', \mu_i, y_{i0}, \ldots, y_{i,t-1}] = \frac{e^{x_{it}'\beta+\gamma y_{i,t-1}+\mu_i}}{1+e^{x_{it}'\beta+\gamma y_{i,t-1}+\mu_i}}, \quad t=1,\ldots,T \quad (11.16)$$

The crucial assumption is that the errors in the threshold-crossing model leading to (11.16) are IID over time with logistic distributions and independent of (x_i', μ_i, y_{i0}) at all time periods.

(a) Show that for $T=3$, $\Pr[A \mid x_i', \mu_i, A\cup B]$ and $\Pr[B \mid x_i', \mu_i, A\cup B]$ both depend on μ_i. This means that the conditional likelihood approach will *not* eliminate the fixed effect μ_i.
(b) Show that if $x_{i2}'=x_{i3}'$, then $\Pr[A \mid x_i', \mu_i, A\cup B, x_{i2}'=x_{i3}']$ and $\Pr[B \mid x_i', \mu_i, A\cup B, x_{i2}'=x_{i3}']$ do *not* depend on μ_i.

Solution

(a) Using (11.16) and similar tricks used in the solution to Exercise 11.3, we get

$$\Pr[A \mid x_i', \mu_i] = \Pr[y_{i0}=d_0 \mid x_i', \mu_i]\Pr[y_{i1}=0 \mid x_i', \mu_i, y_{i0}=d_0]$$
$$\times \Pr[y_{i2}=1 \mid x_i', \mu_i, y_{i0}=d_0, y_{i1}=0]\Pr[y_{i3}$$
$$= d_3 \mid x_i', \mu_i, y_{i0}=d_0, y_{i1}=0, y_{i2}=1]$$

Therefore,

$$\Pr[A \mid x_i', \mu_i] = p_0(x_i', \mu_i)^{d_0}[1 - p_0(x_i', \mu_i)]^{1-d_0} \frac{1}{1 + e^{x_{i1}'\beta + \gamma d_0 + \mu_i}}$$
$$\times \frac{e^{x_{i2}'\beta + \mu_i}}{1 + e^{x_{i2}'\beta + \mu_i}} \frac{e^{d_3 x_{i3}'\beta + d_3\gamma + d_3\mu_i}}{1 + e^{x_{i3}'\beta + \gamma + \mu_i}}$$

Also

$$\Pr[B \mid x_i', \mu_i] = \Pr\,[y_{i0} = d_0 \mid x_i', \mu_i]\Pr\,[y_{i1} = 1 \mid x_i', \mu_i, y_{i0} = d_0]$$
$$\times \Pr\,[y_{i2} = 0 \mid x_i', \mu_i, y_{i0} = d_0, y_{i1} = 1]\Pr[y_{i3}$$
$$= d_3 \mid x_i', \mu_i, y_{i0} = d_0, y_{i1} = 1, y_{i2} = 0]$$

with

$$\Pr[B \mid x_i', \mu_i] = p_0(x_i', \mu_i)^{d_0}[1 - p_0(x_i', \mu_i)]^{1-d_0} \frac{e^{x_{i1}'\beta + \gamma d_0 + \mu_i}}{1 + e^{x_{i1}'\beta + \gamma d_0 + \mu_i}}$$
$$\times \frac{1}{1 + e^{x_{i2}'\beta + \mu_i + \gamma}} \frac{e^{d_3 x_{i3}'\beta + d_3\mu_i}}{1 + e^{x_{i3}'\beta + \mu_i}}$$

Therefore, conditional on the event that $y_{i1} + y_{i2} = 1$, we get

$$\Pr[A \mid x_i', \mu_i, A \cup B] = \frac{\Pr[A \mid x_i', \mu_i]}{\Pr[A \mid x_i', \mu_i] + \Pr[B \mid x_i', \mu_i]}$$

which depends upon μ_i. Similarly, $\Pr[B \mid x_i', \mu_i, A \cup B] = 1 - \Pr[A \mid x_i', \mu_i, A \cup B]$ also depends upon μ_i.

(b) If $x_{i2}' = x_{i3}'$, then from part (a)

$$\Pr[A \mid x_i', \mu_i, A \cup B, x_{i2}' = x_{i3}'] = \left[1 + \frac{\Pr(B \mid x_i', \mu_i, A \cup B, x_{i2}' = x_{i3}')}{\Pr(A \mid x_i', \mu_i, A \cup B, x_{i2}' = x_{i3}')}\right]^{-1}$$
$$= \left[1 + \frac{e^{x_{i1}'\beta + \gamma d_0 + \mu_i}\, e^{d_3 x_{i3}'\beta + d_3\mu_i}}{e^{x_{i2}'\beta + \mu_i}\, e^{d_3 x_{i3}'\beta + d_3\gamma + d_3\mu_i}}\right]^{-1} \tag{11.17}$$

Therefore,

$$\Pr(A \mid x_i', \mu_i, A \cup B, x_{i2}' = x_{i3}') = \frac{1}{1 + e^{(x_{i1}' - x_{i2}')\beta + \gamma(d_0 - d_3)}}$$

and

$$\Pr(B \mid x_i', \mu_i, A \cup B, x_{i2}' = x_{i3}') = 1 - \Pr[A \mid x_i', \mu_i, A \cup B, x_{i2}' = x_{i3}']$$
$$= \frac{e^{(x_{i1}' - x_{i2}')\beta + \gamma(d_0 - d_3)}}{1 + e^{(x_{i1}' - x_{i2}')\beta + \gamma(d_0 - d_3)}} = \frac{1}{1 + e^{(x_{i2}' - x_{i1}')\beta + \gamma(d_3 - d_0)}}$$

both of which do *not* depend on μ_i.

Exercise 11.5 *(Binary response model regression).* This is based on Baltagi (1995b), and is also Problem 11.5 in Baltagi (2008). Davidson and MacKinnon (1993) derive an artificial regression for testing hypotheses in a binary response model. For the fixed effects binary response panel data model described in (11.5), the reader is asked to derive the *binary response model regression* (BRMR) to test $H_0: \mu_i = 0$, for $i = 1, 2, \ldots, N$. Show that if $F(.)$ is the logistic (or normal) cumulative distribution function, this BRMR is simply a weighted least squares regression of logit (or probit) residuals, ignoring the fixed effects, on the matrix of regressors X and the matrix of individual dummies. The test statistic in this case is the explained sum of squares from this BRMR. See Gurmu (1996).

Solution

Davidson and MacKinnon (1993) suggested a binary response model regression which for the fixed effects binary response panel data model described in (11.5) reduces to

$$V_{it}^{-1/2}[y_{it} - F(x_{it}'\beta + \mu_i)] = V_{it}^{-1/2} f(x_{it}'\beta + \mu_i)x_{it}'b + V_{it}^{-1/2} f(x_{it}'\beta + \mu_i)z_{it}'c + \text{residuals}$$

where

$$V_{it} = [F(x_{it}'\beta + \mu_i)][1 - F(x_{it}'\beta + \mu_i)]$$

and $f(.)$ denotes the probability density function (p.d.f.) of ν_{it}. Also, z_{it}' is the itth row of the $NT \times N$ matrix of individual dummies $Z_\mu = I_N \otimes \iota_T$, where I_N is an identity matrix of dimension N and ι_T is a vector of ones of dimension T. If we denote by $\widetilde{\beta}$ the vector of maximum likelihood estimates subject to the restriction $H_0: \mu_i = 0$, for $i = 1, 2, \ldots, N$, then we can test H_0 by running the BRMR

$$\widetilde{V}_{it}^{-1/2}[y_{it} - F(x_{it}'\widetilde{\beta})] = \widetilde{V}_{it}^{-1/2} f(x_{it}'\widetilde{\beta})x_{it}'b + \widetilde{V}_{it}^{-1/2} f(x_{it}'\widetilde{\beta})z_{it}'c + \text{residuals}$$

where

$$\widetilde{V}_{it} = [F(x_{it}'\widetilde{\beta})][1 - F(x_{it}'\widetilde{\beta})]$$

The test statistic in this case is the explained sum of squares from this BRMR. It will be asymptotically distributed as χ_N^2 under the null hypothesis. Note that it will not be nR^2 since the total sum of squares is not equal to NT.

For the logistic model, where $F(.)$ is $\Lambda(.)$, this BRMR simplifies to

$$\widetilde{\lambda}_{it}^{1/2}[y_{it} - \Lambda(x_{it}'\widetilde{\beta})] = \widetilde{\lambda}_{it}^{1/2} x_{it}'b + \widetilde{\lambda}_{it}^{-1/2} z_{it}'c + \text{residuals}$$

where we have made use of the fact that for the logistic distribution, its p.d.f. which is denoted by $\lambda(.)$ satisfies the following relationship with its c.d.f. $\Lambda(.)$:

$$\widetilde{\lambda}_{it} = \lambda(x_{it}'\widetilde{\beta}) = [\Lambda(x_{it}'\widetilde{\beta})][1 - \Lambda(x_{it}'\widetilde{\beta})]$$

In this case, the restricted maximum likelihood estimates of β are simply the logit estimates ignoring the fixed estimates. Therefore, this BRMR is simply a weighted least squares regression of logit residuals, ignoring the fixed effects, on the matrix of regressors X and the matrix of individual dummies Z_μ. The weights are easily computable from the logistic p.d.f. $\widetilde{\lambda}_{it}$. The regressand gets a $\widetilde{\lambda}_{it}^{-1/2}$ weight, whereas the regressors get a $\widetilde{\lambda}_{it}^{1/2}$ weight.

Similarly, for the probit model where $F(.)$ is $\Phi(.)$, this BRMR simplifies to

$$\widetilde{\Phi}_{it}^{-1/2}(1-\widetilde{\Phi}_{it})^{-1/2}[y_{it}-\widetilde{\Phi}_{it}] = \widetilde{\Phi}_{it}^{-1/2}(1-\widetilde{\Phi}_{it})^{-1/2}\widetilde{\phi}_{it}x_{it}'b$$
$$+\widetilde{\Phi}_{it}^{-1/2}(1-\widetilde{\Phi}_{it})^{-1/2}\widetilde{\phi}_{it}z_{it}'c + \text{residuals}$$

where

$$\widetilde{\Phi}_{it} = \Phi(x_{it}'\widetilde{\beta}),\ \widetilde{\phi}_{it} = \phi(x_{it}'\widetilde{\beta})$$

and $\phi(.)$ is the normal p.d.f. In this case, the restricted maximum likelihood estimates of β are simply the probit estimates ignoring the fixed effects. Therefore, this BRMR is simply a weighted least squares regression of probit residuals, ignoring the fixed effects, on the matrix of regressors X and the matrix of individual dummies Z_μ. The weights are easily computable from the normal c.d.f. Φ and its p.d.f. ϕ.

In contrast to the fixed effects logit model, the conditional likelihood approach does not yield computational simplifications for the fixed effects probit model. But the probit specification has been popular for the random effects model.

Exercise 11.6 *(Random effects probit model).* In this case, the model given in (11.5) has $\mu_i \sim \text{IIN}(0, \sigma_\mu^2)$ and $\nu_{it} \sim \text{IIN}(0, \sigma_\nu^2)$ independent of each other and the x_{it}. Since $E(u_{it}u_{is}) = \sigma_\mu^2$ for $t \neq s$, the joint likelihood of $(y_{1t}, \ldots, y_{Nt})$ can no longer be written as the product of the marginal likelihoods of the y_{it}. This complicates the derivation of maximum likelihood which will now involve T-dimensional integrals. Show that by conditioning on the μ_i this T-dimensional integral problem reduces to a single integral. This is based on the results of Butler and Moffitt (1982).

Solution

For the random effects probit model, the likelihood function is a multiple integral

$$L_i = \Pr[y_{i1}, y_{i2}, \ldots, y_{iT} \mid X] = \int \ldots \int f(u_{i1}, u_{i2}, \ldots, u_{iT}) du_{i1} du_{i2} \ldots du_{iT} \quad (11.18)$$

which is maximized with respect to β and σ_μ. This gets to be infeasible if T is large. The trick is to write the joint density function as a product of the conditional density and the marginal density of μ_i. In fact,

$$f(u_{i1}, u_{i2}, \ldots, u_{iT}, \mu_i) = f_1(u_{i1}, u_{i2}, \ldots, u_{iT} \mid \mu_i) f_2(\mu_i)$$

so that

$$f(u_{i1}, u_{i2}, \ldots, u_{iT}) = \int f_1(u_{i1}, u_{i2}, \ldots, u_{iT} \mid \mu_i) f_2(\mu_i) d\mu_i$$

By conditioning on the individual effects, this T-dimensional integral problem reduces to a single integral. To see this, note that the u_i conditional on μ_i are independent, so

$$f(u_{i1}, u_{i2}, \ldots, u_{it}) = \int \prod_{t=1}^{T} f_1(u_{it} \mid \mu_i) f_2(\mu_i) d\mu_i$$

Inserting this in the likelihood, we get

$$L_i = \Pr[y_{i1}, y_{i2}, \ldots, y_{iT} \mid X] = \int \cdots \int\int \prod_{t=1}^{T} f_1(u_{it} \mid \mu_i) f_2(\mu_i) d\mu_i du_{i1} du_{i2} \ldots du_{iT}$$

The ranges of integration are independent, so we interchange the order of integration

$$L_i = \Pr[y_{i1}, y_{i2}, \ldots, y_{iT} \mid X] = \int \left[\int \cdots \int \prod_{t=1}^{T} f_1(u_{it} \mid \mu_i) du_{i1} du_{i2} \ldots du_{iT} \right] f_2(\mu_i) d\mu_i$$

The terms in square brackets are the product of individual probabilities

$$L_i = \Pr[y_{i1}, y_{i2}, \ldots, y_{iT} \mid X] = \int \left[\prod_{t=1}^{T} \int f_1(u_{it} \mid \mu_i) du_{iT} \right] f_2(\mu_i) d\mu_i \qquad (11.19)$$

For the probit, the individual probabilities inside the product are given by $\Phi(q_{it}(x'_{it}\beta + \mu_i))$, where $q_{it} = 2y_{it} - 1$. The payoff is that this likelihood involves only one integral. The inner integrals are standard normal c.d.f. This can be evaluated using the Gauss–Hermite quadrature procedure suggested by Butler and Moffitt (1982):

$$\ln L_h = \sum_{i=1}^{N} \left[\ln \left\{ \frac{1}{\sqrt{\pi}} \sum_{h=1}^{H} \prod_{t=1}^{T} w_h \Phi(q_{it}(x'_{it}\beta + \theta z_h)) \right\} \right]$$

where H is the number of points for the quadrature, and w_h and z_h are the weights and nodes of the quadrature. Here $\theta = \sigma_\mu \sqrt{2}$, so an estimate of σ_μ can be obtained by dividing the estimate of θ by $\sqrt{2}$. This approach has the advantage of being computationally feasible even for fairly large T. The accuracy of this quadrature procedure increases with the number of evaluation points.

Exercise 11.7 *(Identification in a dynamic binary choice panel data model).* This is based on Honoré and Tamer (2006, pp.627–628) and is also Problem 11.9 in Baltagi (2008). Suppose that (y_{i1}, y_{i2}, y_{i3}) is a random vector such that

$$P(y_{i1} = 1 \mid \mu_i) = p_1(\mu_i)$$
$$P(y_{it} = 1 \mid \mu_i, y_{i1}, .., y_{it-1}) = F(\mu_i + \gamma y_{it-1}), \text{ for } t = 2, 3 \qquad (11.20)$$

where $p_1(\mu_i)$ is an unknown strictly increasing distribution function taking values between 0 and 1. Show that the sign of γ is identified.

Solution

Consider the probabilities

$$P[(y_{i1}, y_{i2}, y_{i3}) = (0, 1, 0) \mid \mu_i] = (1 - p_1(\mu_i)) \cdot F(\mu_i) \cdot (1 - F(\mu_i + \gamma))$$

and

$$P[(y_{i1}, y_{i2}, y_{i3}) = (0, 0, 1) \mid \mu_i] = (1 - p_1(\mu_i)) \cdot (1 - F(\mu_i)) \cdot F(\mu_i)$$

Then

$$\begin{aligned} P[(y_{i1}, y_{i2}, y_{i3}) = (0, 1, 0) \mid \mu_i] - P[(y_{i1}, y_{i2}, y_{i3}) = (0, 0, 1) \mid \mu_i] \\ = (1 - p_1(\mu_i)) \cdot F(\mu_i) \cdot [F(\mu_i) - F(\mu_i + \gamma)] \end{aligned}$$

This has the same sign as $[F(\mu_i) - F(\mu_i + \gamma)]$, which clearly depends on the sign of γ. This shows that the sign of γ is identified.

Exercise 11.8 *(Union membership).* This is based on Wooldridge (2005) and is also Problem 11.7 in Baltagi (2008). Wooldridge (2005) examines the persistence of union membership using the dynamic probit equation, where for each random individual $i = 1, 2 \ldots, N$,

$$\Pr[y_{it} = 1 \mid x_i', \mu_i, y_{i0}, \ldots, y_{i,t-1}] = \Phi(x_{it}'\beta + \lambda y_{i,t-1} + \mu_i) \quad \text{for } t = 1, 2, \ldots, T$$

with y_{iT} denoting union membership, and $x_i' = (x_{i1}', \ldots, x_{it}')$ including marital status and time dummies. Assuming that

$$(\mu_i \mid x_i', y_{i0}) \sim N((x_i'\delta + \gamma y_{i,0} + \gamma_0), \sigma_\varepsilon^2)$$

Wooldridge (2005) argues that the estimation of this dynamic probit model can be carried out with a standard random effects probit procedure. In fact, if we write

$$\mu_i = x_i'\delta + \gamma y_{i,0} + \gamma_0 + \varepsilon_i$$

with $(\varepsilon_i \mid x_i', y_{i0}) \sim N(0, \sigma_\varepsilon^2)$, then y_{it} given $(x_i', \varepsilon_i, y_{i0}, \ldots, y_{i,t-1})$ follows a probit model with response probability

$$\Phi(x_{it}'\beta + \lambda y_{i,t-1} + x_i'\delta + \gamma y_{i,0} + \gamma_0 + \varepsilon_i)$$

This means that we can estimate this model with (xtprobit, re) in Stata using as regressors $(1, x_{it}', y_{i,t-1}, x_i', y_{i,0})$. In essence, one is adding $x_i', y_{i,0}$ as extra regressors. Using the Wooldridge (2005) study considered in Baltagi (2008, p.250), download the data set posted on the *Journal of Applied Econometrics* web site and:

(a) Replicate the results on union membership given in column 1 of Table I in that article using (xtprobit, re) in Stata.
(b) Replicate the results given in column 2 of Table I adding education and black to the list of variables.

Solution

(a) Table 11.1 replicates the results of column 1 of Table I in Wooldridge (2005, p.52). In the xtprobit, union_l is union lagged ($y_{i,t-1}$) and union80 is $y_{i,0}$.

Table 11.1 Union Membership. Random Effects Probit

```
. xtprobit union married union_1 union80 marr81 marr82 marr83 marr84 marr85
marr86 marr87 d81 d82 d83 d84 d85 d86 d87, re

Random-effects probit regression                Number of obs      =      3815
Group variable (i): nr                          Number of groups   =       545

Random effects u_i ~ Gaussian                   Obs per group: min =         7
                                                               avg =       7.0
                                                               max =         7

                                                Wald chi2(16)      =    403.30
Log likelihood  = -1291.2555                    Prob > chi2        =    0.0000
```

union	Coef.	Std. Err.	z	P>|z|	[95% Conf.	Interval]
married	.1645174	.1086856	1.51	0.130	-.0485024	.3775373
union_1	.9778509	.0845496	11.57	0.000	.8121366	1.143565
union80	1.342638	.1370911	9.79	0.000	1.073944	1.611331
marr81	.0557457	.1927517	0.29	0.772	-.3220408	.4335321
marr82	-.1061208	.2278688	-0.47	0.641	-.5527355	.3404939
marr83	-.0740984	.2307409	-0.32	0.748	-.5263423	.3781455
marr84	.0019333	.248823	0.01	0.994	-.4857507	.4896174
marr85	.3572686	.2346558	1.52	0.128	-.1026483	.8171854
marr86	.1000752	.235037	0.43	0.670	-.3605888	.5607392
marr87	-.3870529	.1835973	-2.11	0.035	-.7468971	-.0272087
d81	-.0765441	.1166593	-0.66	0.512	-.3051922	.1521039
d82	-.0489836	.1149461	-0.43	0.670	-.2742738	.1763065
d83	-.1634238	.1154857	-1.42	0.157	-.3897717	.0629241
d84	-.1246027	.1147137	-1.09	0.277	-.3494374	.1002319
d85	-.3350622	.1172977	-2.86	0.004	-.5649614	-.105163
d86	-.3777447	.1173934	-3.22	0.001	-.6078316	-.1476579
_cons	-1.644473	.1275296	-12.89	0.000	-1.894426	-1.394519
/lnsig2u	-.0889939	.1235904			-.3312267	.1532389
sigma_u	.9564785	.0591058			.8473738	1.079631
rho	.4777662	.0308365			.4179422	.5382349

```
Likelihood-ratio test of rho=0: chibar2(01) =   149.59 Prob >= chibar2 = 0.000
```

(b) Table 11.2 replicates the results of column 2 of Table I in Wooldridge (2005, p.52) which add the educ and black variables.

The lagged union effect is statistically significant and so is the initial union membership effect. When we add the two time-invariant variables: years of education and a dummy variable for whether the individual is black, we find that only the latter is significant.

Table 11.2 Union Membership. Random Effects Probit, including Black and Education

```
xtprobit union married union_1 union80 marr81 marr82 marr83 marr84 marr85
marr86 marr87 educ black d81 d82 d83 d84 d85 d86 d87, re

Random-effects probit regression                Number of obs      =      3815
Group variable (i): nr                          Number of groups   =       545

Random effects u_i ~ Gaussian                   Obs per group: min =         7
                                                               avg =       7.0
                                                               max =         7

                                                Wald chi2(18)      =    413.52
Log likelihood  = -1286.5635                    Prob > chi2        =    0.0000
```

union	Coef.	Std. Err.	z	P>|z|	[95% Conf.	Interval]
married	.1666075	.1089353	1.53	0.126	-.0469017	.3801168
union_1	.976652	.0849498	11.50	0.000	.8101534	1.143151
union80	1.310118	.1370362	9.56	0.000	1.041532	1.578704
marr81	.038103	.1932175	0.20	0.844	-.3405963	.4168022
marr82	-.0688345	.2275028	-0.30	0.762	-.5147318	.3770627
marr83	-.0880275	.2300634	-0.38	0.702	-.5389434	.3628884
marr84	.0258623	.2491106	0.10	0.917	-.4623855	.5141102
marr85	.3708715	.2350619	1.58	0.115	-.0898414	.8315844
marr86	.1068035	.2348234	0.45	0.649	-.3534419	.5670489
marr87	-.359518	.1836126	-1.96	0.050	-.719392	.0003561
educ	-.0156374	.0326283	-0.48	0.632	-.0795877	.0483128
black	.4961749	.1641641	3.02	0.003	.1744193	.8179305
d81	-.075501	.1168569	-0.65	0.518	-.3045363	.1535344
d82	-.0476582	.1150923	-0.41	0.679	-.2732349	.1779185
d83	-.1630849	.1156522	-1.41	0.159	-.3897591	.0635893
d84	-.1242375	.1148798	-1.08	0.279	-.3493978	.1009229
d85	-.3350009	.1174665	-2.85	0.004	-.565231	-.1047709
d86	-.3778186	.1175724	-3.21	0.001	-.6082563	-.1473808
_cons	-1.558261	.400001	-3.90	0.000	-2.342249	-.7742735
/lnsig2u	-.1033883	.1258873			-.3501229	.1433462
sigma_u	.9496192	.0597725			.8394054	1.074304
rho	.4741759	.0313879			.4133526	.5357753

Likelihood-ratio test of rho=0: chibar2(01) = 143.81 Prob >= chibar2 = 0.000

Exercise 11.9 *(Beer taxes and motor vehicle fatality rates).* This is based on Ruhm (1996) and is also Problem 11.8 in Baltagi (2008). Ruhm (1996) used grouped logit analysis with fixed time and state effects to study the impact of beer taxes and a variety of alcohol-control policies on motor vehicle fatality rates. Ruhm collected panel data for 48 states (excluding

Alaska, Hawaii and the District of Columbia) over the period 1982–88. Here, the dependent variable is a proportion, p, denoting the total vehicle fatality rate per capita for state i at time t. One can perform the inverse logit transformation, $\log[p/(1-p)]$, provided p is not 0 or 1, and run the usual fixed effects regression. Denote this dependent variable by (LFVR). The explanatory variables included the real beer tax rate on twenty-four 12 oz. containers of beer (BEERTAX), the minimum legal drinking age (MLDA) in years, the percentage of the population living in dry counties (DRY), the average number of vehicle miles per person aged 16 and over (VMILES), and the percentage of young drivers (15–24 years old) (YNGDRV). There were also dummy variables indicating the presence of alcohol regulations. These included BREATH test laws which is a dummy variable that takes the value 1 if the state authorized the police to administer a pre-arrest breath test to establish probable cause for driving under the influence (DUI), and JAILD which takes the value of 1 if the state passed legislation mandating jail or community service (COMSERD) for the first DUI conviction. Other variables included are the unemployment rate, real per capita income, and state and time dummy variables. Details on these variables are given in Table 1 of Ruhm (1996). Some of the variables in this data set can be downloaded from the Stock and Watson (2003) web site at www.aw.com/stock_watson.

Table 11.3 Beer Taxes and Motor Vehicle Fatality Rates. OLS with Time Dummies

Dependent Variable: LVFR
Method: Panel Least Squares

Sample: 1982 1988
Cross-sections included: 48
Total panel (balanced) observations: 336
White cross-section standard errors & covariance (d.f. corrected)

Variable	Coefficient	Std. Error	t-Statistic	Prob.
C	−9.055212	0.298995	−30.28546	0.0000
BEERTAX	0.117725	0.029004	4.058978	0.0001
MLDA	−0.029707	0.005629	−5.277340	0.0000
DRY	0.004234	0.000807	5.244790	0.0000
VMILES	7.35E-05	3.79E-05	1.938560	0.0534
YNGDRV	2.525457	0.469029	5.384433	0.0000

Effects Specification

Period fixed (dummy variables)

R-squared	0.324035	Mean dependent var	−8.534862
Adjusted R-squared	0.301086	S.D. dependent var	0.276063
S.E. of regression	0.230792	Akaike info criterion	−0.059539
Sum squared resid	17.25784	Schwarz criterion	0.076786
Log likelihood	22.00254	F-statistic	14.11955
Durbin-Watson stat	0.351357	Prob.(F-statistic)	0.000000

(a) Using this data set, replicate to the extent posible the results in Table 2 of Ruhm (1996, p.444), and verify that beer tax is effective in reducing motor vehicle fatality rates, whereas the breath test law is not. How are the standard errors affected by robustifying these regressions?
(b) Test the significance of the state and time dummies.

Solution

(a) We replicate some of the results in Table 2 of Ruhm (1996, p.444). Note that some of the variables used in Ruhm's article were missing from the Stock and Watson data set posted on their web site. Table 11.3 replicates column (a) of Table 2 of Ruhm (1996) with time effects but no state effects. This differs from the results in that table perhaps because we did not use weighted least squares as Ruhm suggests, but rather the robust White cross-section option in EViews.

Table 11.4 replicates column (b) of Table 2 of Ruhm (1996) with both time effects and state effects. This again differs from the results in that table perhaps because we did not use weighted least squares as Ruhm suggests, but rather the robust White cross-section option in EViews. Note how the results change by including the state

Table 11.4 Beer Taxes and Motor Vehicle Fatality Rates. Two-way FE Results

Dependent Variable: LVFR
Method: Panel Least Squares

Sample: 1982 1988
Cross-sections included: 48
Total panel (balanced) observations: 336
White cross-section standard errors & covariance (d.f. corrected)

Variable	Coefficient	Std Error	t-Statistic	Prob.
C	−8.789914	0.127161	−69.12403	0.0000
BEERTAX	−0.203998	0.084805	−2.405499	0.0168
MLDA	0.002290	0.005860	0.390778	0.6963
DRY	0.008846	0.002181	4.055527	0.0001
VMILES	8.64E-06	4.96E-06	1.742469	0.0825
YNGDRV	1.113314	0.517540	2.151167	0.0323

Effects Specification

Cross-section fixed (dummy variables)
Period fixed (dummy variables)

R-squared	0.922077	Mean dependent var	−8.534862
Adjusted R-squared	0.905762	S.D. dependent var	0.276063
S.E. of regression	0.084747	Akaike info criterion	−1.940203
Sum squared resid	1.989416	Schwarz criterion	−1.269936
Log likelihood	384.9540	F-statistic	56.51402
Durbin-Watson stat	1.304337	Prob.(F-statistic)	0.000000

Table 11.5 Beer Taxes and Motor Vehicle Fatality Rates. Two-way FE Results with More Regulation Variables

Dependent Variable: LVFR
Method: Panel Least Squares

Sample: 1982 1988
Cross-sections included: 48
Total panel (unbalanced) observations: 335
White cross-section standard errors & covariance (d.f. corrected)

Variable	Coefficient	Std Error	t-Statistic	Prob.
C	−9.361589	0.132383	−70.71570	0.0000
BEERTAX	−0.183533	0.077658	−2.363344	0.0188
MLDA	−0.004465	0.007814	−0.571427	0.5682
DRY	0.008677	0.002611	3.323523	0.0010
YNGDRV	0.493472	0.450802	1.094651	0.2746
VMILES	6.91E-06	4.23E-06	1.632849	0.1037
BREATH	−0.015930	0.027952	−0.569893	0.5692
JAILD	−0.012623	0.038973	−0.323888	0.7463
COMSERD	0.020238	0.024505	0.825867	0.4096
PERINC	0.060305	0.010275	5.868945	0.0000

Effects Specification

Cross-section fixed (dummy variables)
Period fixed (dummy variables)

R-squared	0.931852	Mean dependent var	−8.534768
Adjusted R-squared	0.916318	S.D. dependent var	0.276471
S.E. of regression	0.079977	Akaike info criterion	−2.046359
Sum squared resid	1.739808	Schwarz criterion	−1.329075
Log likelihood	405.7652	F-statistic	59.98854
Durbin-Watson stat	1.433777	Prob.(F-statistic)	0.000000

Table 11.6 Beer Taxes and Motor Vehicle Fatality Rates. Redundant Fixed Effects

Redundant Fixed Effects Tests
Equation: EQ01
Test cross-section and period fixed effects

Effects Test	Statistic	d.f.	Prob.
Cross-section F	34.901652	(47,272)	0.0000
Cross-section Chi-square	653.350674	47	0.0000
Period F	2.967741	(6,272)	0.0080
Period Chi-square	21.242751	6	0.0017
Cross-Section/Period F	31.866945	(53,272)	0.0000
Cross-Section/Period Chi-square	661.752731	53	0.0000

dummies, making beer tax negative and significant rather than positive and significant. Also, minimum legal drinking age changes from negative and significant to positive and insignificant.

Table 11.5 replicates column (d) of Table 2 of Ruhm (1996) with both time effects and state effects. This does not include test law, dram shop law, administrative, per se law, and implied consent law since these variables were not in the data set. Also, here we have a separate dummy variable for jail and community service. We again did not use weighted least squares as Ruhm suggests, but rather the robust White cross-section option in EViews. The results on beer tax and breath and minimum drinking age are robust as far as their significance is concerned. Most of the regulation variables had little or no impact on traffic mortality. By contrast, higher beer taxes were associated with reductions in crash deaths.

(b) Table 11.6 reports the F-tests for the significance of state and year dummies. We conclude that state and time dummies are jointly significant and that ignoring either set of dummies would bias the results.

12 Nonstationary Panels

12.1 PANEL UNIT ROOT TESTS

Panel unit root tests, such as the one derived by Levin, Lin and Chu (2002) (LLC), are a generalization of the augmented Dickey–Fuller (ADF) individual country unit root tests to a common panel unit root test. The idea is that this panel unit root test will be more powerful than performing individual unit root tests for each cross-section. The null hypothesis is that each individual time series contains a unit root against the alternative that each time series is stationary. Computationally, one may elect to include no exogenous regressors, or to include individual constant terms (fixed effects), or to employ constants and trends.

This panel unit root test has its limitations. First, the test crucially depends upon the *independence assumption* across cross-sections and is not applicable if cross-sectional correlation is present. Second, the assumption that all cross-sections have or do not have a unit root is restrictive. As Maddala (1999) pointed out, the null may be fine for testing convergence in growth among countries, but the alternative restricts every country to converge at the same rate.

Im, Pesaran and Shin (2003) (IPS) propose an alternative testing procedure based on averaging individual unit root ADF test statistics. The null hypothesis is that each series in the panel contains a unit root, and the alternative hypothesis allows for some (but not all) of the individual series to have unit roots. Formally, it requires the fraction of the individual time series that are stationary to be non-zero as $N \to \infty$. This condition is necessary for the consistency of the panel unit root test. The LLC and IPS tests require $N \to \infty$ such that $N/T \to 0$, i.e., N should be small enough relative to T. This means that both tests may not keep nominal size well when either N is small or N is large relative to T. In fact, the simulation results of Im *et al.* (2003) show that both IPS and LLC have size distortions as N grows large relative to T.

Breitung (2000) studied the local power of LLC and IPS tests statistics against a sequence of local alternatives and found that the LLC and IPS tests suffer from a dramatic loss of power if individual specific trends are included. This is due to the bias correction that also removes the mean under the sequence of local alternatives. Breitung suggested a test statistic that does not employ a bias adjustment whose power is substantially higher than that of LLC or the IPS tests using Monte Carlo experiments. Simulation results indicated that the power of LLC and IPS tests is very sensitive to the specification of the deterministic terms.

Maddala and Wu (1999) and Choi (2001) proposed a Fisher-type test which combines the p-values from unit root tests for each cross-section i to test for unit roots in panel data. The advantages of combining p-values tests in this way are that: (i) the cross-sectional dimension, N, can be either finite or infinite; (ii) each group can have different types of non-stochastic and stochastic components; (iii) the time-series dimension, T, can be different for each I; (iv) the alternative hypothesis would allow some groups to have unit roots while others may not. Simulation results for $N = 5$, 10, 25, 50, and 100, and $T = 50$ and 100 show that the combined p-values tests have superior size-adjusted power to the IPS test. In fact, in some cases, this is more than three times that of the IPS test.

Hadri (2000) derives a residual-based Lagrange multiplier test where the null hypothesis is that there is no unit root in any of the series in the panel against the alternative of a unit root in the panel. This is a generalization of the Kwiatkowski *et al.* (1992) test from time series to panel data.

EViews performs the Levin *et al.* (2002), Im *et al.* (2003), and Breitung (2000) tests, the Fisher-type test which combines the p-values from individual unit root tests proposed by Maddala and Wu (1999) and Choi (2001), and the Hadri (2000) residual-based LM test which reverses the null and alternative of the previous tests.

Exercise 12.1 *(Panel unit root tests: GDP of G7 countries).* This is Problem 12.4 in Baltagi (2008). Using the EViews G7 countries work file (Poolg7) containing the GDP of Canada, France, Germany, Italy, Japan, UK and US:

(a) Perform the panel unit root tests using individual effects in the deterministic variables. Check the sensitivity of the results when both individual effects and individual linear trends are included.

Table 12.1 Panel Unit Root Tests: GDP of G7 Countries Allowing for Individual Effects

Group unit root test: Summary
Sample: 1950 1992
Series: GDP_CAN, GDP_FRA, GDP_GER, GDP_ITA, GDP_JPN, GDP_UK, GDP_US
Exogenous variables: Individual effects
Automatic selection of maximum lags
Automatic selection of lags based on SIC: 0 to 1
Newey-West bandwidth selection using Bartlett kernel

Method	Statistic	Prob.**	Cross-sections	Obs
Null: Unit root (assumes common unit root process)				
Levin, Lin & Chu t	1.36042	0.9132	7	292
Breitung t-stat	1.28607	0.9008	7	285
Null: Unit root (assumes individual unit root process)				
Im, Pesaran and Shin W-stat	4.83525	1.0000	7	292
ADF - Fisher Chi-square	0.80568	1.0000	7	292
PP - Fisher Chi-square	0.66842	1.0000	7	294
Null: No unit root (assumes common unit root process)				
Hadri Z-stat	11.5443	0.0000	7	301

** Probabilities for Fisher tests are computed using an asymptotic chi-square distribution. All other tests assume asymptotic normality.

(b) Check the sensitivity of the results in part (a) to a user-specified lag of 1, 2, 3, and 4. Show that all tests are in agreement about the possibility of a common unit root for all series.

Solution

(a) EViews produces a summary table of all panel unit root tests described above. Allowing for individual effects, all the tests in Table 12.1 show that the null of panel unit roots is not rejected for the GDP of G7 countries. In fact, reversing the null and testing for stationarity of all countries using the Hadri test yields rejection of this null. Note that EViews can carry out a Fisher-type test which combines the p-values of individual unit root tests based on ADF as well as Phillips and Perron (1988). Allowing for both individual effects and individual linear trends, we get the output in Table 12.2.

(b) Fixing the lag at 1 (see Table 12.3), we get the same decision. The reader can continue this exercise with EViews, allowing for the lag to be fixed at 2, 3, or 4 and allowing for both individual effects and individual linear trends.

Table 12.2 Panel Unit Root Tests: GDP of G7 Countries Allowing for Both Individual Effects and Individual Linear Trends

Group unit root test: Summary

Sample: 1950 1992
Series: GDP_CAN, GDP_FRA, GDP_GER, GDP_ITA, GDP_JPN, GDP_UK, GDP_US
Exogenous variables: Individual effects, individual linear trends
Automatic selection of maximum lags
Automatic selection of lags based on SIC: 0 to 1
Newey-West bandwidth selection using Bartlett kernel

Method	Statistic	Prob.**	Cross-sections	Obs
Null: Unit root (assumes common unit root process)				
Levin, Lin & Chu t	−0.92186	0.1783	7	289
Breitung t-stat	−1.61499	0.0532	7	282
Null: Unit root (assumes individual unit root process)				
Im, Pesaran and Shin W-stat	−1.56421	0.0589	7	289
ADF - Fisher Chi-square	21.5070	0.0893	7	289
PP - Fisher Chi-square	12.3071	0.5817	7	294
Null: No unit root (assumes common unit root process)				
Hadri Z-stat	3.96309	0.0000	7	301

** Probabilities for Fisher tests are computed using an asymptotic chi-square distribution. All other tests assume asymptotic normality.

Table 12.3 Panel Unit Root Tests: GDP of G7 Countries, Fixing the Lag at 1

Pool unit root test: Summary
GDP of 7 countries, lag specified at 1
Sample: 1950 1992
Series: GDP_CAN, GDP_FRA, GDP_GER, GDP_ITA, GDP_JPN, GDP_UK, GDP_US
Exogenous variables: Individual effects
User specified lags at: 1
Newey-West bandwidth selection using Bartlett kernel
Balanced observations for each test

Method	Statistic	Prob.**	Cross-sections	Obs
Null: Unit root (assumes common unit root process)				
Levin, Lin & Chu t	1.04498	0.8520	7	287
Breitung t-stat	1.12018	0.8687	7	280
Null: Unit root (assumes individual unit root process)				
Im, Pesaran and Shin W-stat	4.49059	1.0000	7	287
ADF - Fisher Chi-square	0.99039	1.0000	7	287
PP - Fisher Chi-square	0.66842	1.0000	7	294
Null: No unit root (assumes common unit root process)				
Hadri Z-stat	11.5443	0.0000	7	301

** Probabilities for Fisher tests are computed using an asymptotic chi-square distribution. All other tests assume asymptotic normality.

12.2 PANEL COINTEGRATION TESTS

Like the panel unit root tests, panel cointegration tests can be motivated by the search for more powerful tests than those obtained by applying individual time-series cointegration tests. The latter tests are known to have low power especially for short T and short span of the data which is often limited to postwar annual data. In the case of purchasing power parity and convergence in growth, economists pool data on similar countries (e.g. G7, OECD or EU countries) in the hopes of adding cross-sectional variation to the data that will increase the power of unit root tests or panel cointegration tests.

Kao (1999) proposed an extension of the Engle and Granger (1987) cointegration test from individual time series to a panel. The basic idea is to examine two $I(1)$ series and see if the residuals of the spurious regression involving these $I(1)$ series are $I(0)$. If this is so, then the series are cointegrated. If the residuals are $I(1)$ then the variables are not cointegrated. Hence, a test for the null hypothesis of no cointegration can be based on an ADF-type unit root test based on these residuals.

Pedroni (2000, 2004) also proposed several tests for the null hypothesis of no cointegration in a panel data model that allows for considerable heterogeneity. His tests can be classified into two categories. The first set is similar to the tests discussed above, involving averaging test statistics for no cointegration in the time series across cross-sections. For the second set, the averaging is done in pieces so that the limiting distributions are based on limits of piecewise numerator and denominator terms.

Larsson *et al.* (2001) presented a likelihood-based (LR) panel test of cointegrating rank in heterogeneous panel models based on the average of the individual rank trace statistics developed by Johansen (1995). The proposed $\overline{\text{LR}}$ statistic is very similar to the IPS $\bar{t}$ statistic. In Monte Carlo simulation, Larsson *et al.* investigated the small-sample properties of the standardized $\overline{\text{LR}}$ statistic. They found that the proposed test requires a large time-series dimension. Even if the panel has a large cross-sectional dimension, the size of the test will be severely distorted.

EViews computes the cointegration tests of Kao (1999) and Pedroni (2000, 2004), as well as a Maddala and Wu (1999) Fisher-type cointegration test combining p-values based on the Johansen cointegration trace test and maximum eigenvalue test. These are applied to two time series on manufacturing shipments and inventories observed over the period 1968M01 to 1995M12. The panel is made up of $N = 8$ sectors: automotive, business supplies, construction, consumer staples, defense products, home goods and apparel, machinery and equipment, and other material and supplies. First-generation panel unit root tests do not reject the hypothesis of a common panel unit root for both series. Kao's (1999) panel cointegration test does not reject the null of no cointegration. This is also the case for 8 out of 11 Pedroni tests. The Fisher-type Johansen test rejects the hypothesis that there are no cointegrating relationships and does not reject the hypothesis of at most one cointegrating relationship. In Exercise 12.2 the reader can replicate these results and check their sensitivity to user-specified lags and to the inclusion of linear trends.

Exercise 12.2 *(Panel cointegration tests: manufacturing shipment and inventories).* This is Problem 12.5 in Baltagi (2008). Obtain the EViews 6 Pool1 work file containing two time series, manufacturing shipment (MM) and inventories (IVM), over the period 1968M01 to 1995M12. These two time series are observed for $N = 8$ sectors as specified in the previous paragraph.

(a) Perform the panel unit root tests using individual effects in the deterministic variables. Check the sensitivity of the results when both individual effects and individual linear trends are included.
(b) Perform the panel cointegration tests of Kao (1999) and Pedroni (2000, 2004) using individual effects in the deterministic variables.
(c) Perform the Fisher panel Johansen cointegration trace test and maximum eigenvalue test using individual effects in the deterministic variables.
(d) Check the sensitivity of these results to a user-specified lag of 1, 2, 3 and 4.
(e) Check the sensitivity of the Pedroni and the Fisher panel Johansen cointegration test results when both individual effects and individual linear trends are included.

Solution

(a) Tables 12.4–12.7 give panel unit roots for inventories (IVM) allowing for individual sector effects; for IVM allowing for individual sector effects and individual linear trends; for shipments (MM) allowing for individual sector effects; and for MM allowing for individual sector effects and individual linear trends, respectively. All results (except for the LLC test for inventories) do not reject the null of a common panel unit root for

Table 12.4 Panel Unit Root Tests: Inventories Allowing for Individual Effects

Panel unit root test: Summary
Series: IVM

Sample: 1968M01 1995M12
Exogenous variables: Individual effects
Automatic selection of maximum lags
Automatic selection of lags based on SIC: 0 to 7
Newey-West bandwidth selection using Bartlett kernel

Method	Statistic	Prob.**	Cross-sections	Obs
Null: Unit root (assumes common unit root process)				
Levin, Lin & Chu t	−2.20538	0.0137	8	2551
Null: Unit root (assumes individual unit root process)				
Im, Pesaran and Shin W-stat	1.49452	0.9325	8	2551
ADF - Fisher Chi-square	6.28297	0.9847	8	2551
PP - Fisher Chi-square	5.08532	0.9953	8	2568

** Probabilities for Fisher tests are computed using an asymptotic chi-square distribution. All other tests assume asymptotic normality.

Table 12.5 Panel Unit Root Tests: Inventories Allowing for Both Individual Effects and Individual Linear Trends

Panel unit root test: Summary
Series: IVM

Sample: 1968M01 1995M12
Exogenous variables: Individual effects, individual linear trends
Automatic selection of maximum lags
Automatic selection of lags based on SIC: 0 to 7
Newey-West bandwidth selection using Bartlett kernel

Method	Statistic	Prob.**	Cross-sections	Obs
Null: Unit root (assumes common unit root process)				
Levin, Lin & Chu t	1.05537	0.8544	8	2551
Breitung t-stat	0.70433	0.7594	8	2543
Null: Unit root (assumes individual unit root process)				
Im, Pesaran and Shin W-stat	2.66094	0.9961	8	2551
ADF - Fisher Chi-square	8.95375	0.9153	8	2551
PP - Fisher Chi-square	4.40319	0.9980	8	2568

** Probabilities for Fisher tests are computed using an asymptotic chi-square distribution. All other tests assume asymptotic normality.

Table 12.6 Panel Unit Root Tests: Manufacturing Shipment Allowing for Individual Effects

Panel unit root test: Summary
Series: MM

Sample: 1968M01 1995M12
Exogenous variables: Individual effects
Automatic selection of maximum lags
Automatic selection of lags based on SIC: 1 to 6
Newey-West bandwidth selection using Bartlett kernel

Method	Statistic	Prob.**	Cross-sections	Obs
Null: Unit root (assumes common unit root process)				
Levin, Lin & Chu t	3.02873	0.9988	8	2548
Null: Unit root (assumes individual unit root process)				
Im, Pesaran and Shin W-stat	6.66735	1.0000	8	2548
ADF - Fisher Chi-square	0.57400	1.0000	8	2548
PP - Fisher Chi-square	0.56812	1.0000	8	2568

** Probabilities for Fisher tests are computed using an asymptotic chi-square distribution. All other tests assume asymptotic normality.

Table 12.7 Panel Unit Root Tests: Manufacturing Shipment Allowing for Both Individual Effects and Individual Linear Trends

Panel unit root test: Summary
Series: MM

Sample: 1968M01 1995M12
Exogenous variables: Individual effects, individual linear trends
Automatic selection of maximum lags
Automatic selection of lags based on SIC: 0 to 6
Newey-West bandwidth selection using Bartlett kernel

Method	Statistic	Prob.**	Cross-sections	Obs
Null: Unit root (assumes common unit root process)				
Levin, Lin & Chu t	0.58341	0.7202	8	2545
Breitung t-stat	1.58036	0.9430	8	2537
Null: Unit root (assumes individual unit root process)				
Im, Pesaran and Shin W-stat	0.31767	0.6246	8	2545
ADF - Fisher Chi-square	14.2524	0.5799	8	2545
PP - Fisher Chi-square	23.9473	0.0907	8	2568

** Probabilities for Fisher tests are computed using an asymptotic chi-square distribution. All other tests assume asymptotic normality.

both MM and IVM. Of course these are all first-generation panel unit roots not allowing for cross-section dependence among the sectors.

(b) Table 12.8 gives the Kao residual cointegration test and Table 12.9 the Pedroni residual cointegration tests, both allowing for individual sector effects. The former does not reject

Table 12.8 Kao Residual Cointegration Test: Manufacturing Shipment and Inventories

Kao Residual Cointegration Test
Series: IVM? MM?

Sample: 1968M01 1995M12
Included observations: 336
Null Hypothesis: No cointegration
Trend assumption: No deterministic trend
Lag selection: Automatic 3 lags by SIC with a max lag of 16
Newey-West bandwidth selection using Bartlett kernel

	t-Statistic	Prob.
ADF	−1.388782	0.0824
Residual variance	257852.7	
HAC variance	730764.3	

Augmented Dickey-Fuller Test Equation
Dependent Variable: D(RESID?)
Method: Panel Least Squares

Sample (adjusted): 1968M05 1994M10
Included observations: 318 after adjustments
Cross-sections included: 8
Total pool (balanced) observations: 2544

	Coefficient	Std. Error	t-Statistic	Prob.
RESID?(−1)	−0.010083	0.002894	−3.484199	0.0005
D(RESID?(−1))	−0.145755	0.019585	−7.442085	0.0000
D(RESID?(−2))	0.084274	0.019744	4.268423	0.0000
D(RESID?(−3))	0.193649	0.019885	9.738481	0.0000

R-squared	0.062195	Mean dependent var	−16.46197
Adjusted R-squared	0.061087	S.D. dependent var	905.6992
S.E. of regression	877.6001	Akaike info criterion	16.39383
Sum squared resid	1.96E+09	Schwarz criterion	16.40301
Log likelihood	−20848.95	Hannan-Quinn criter.	16.39716
Durbin-Watson stat	2.009245		

Table 12.9 Pedroni Residual Cointegration Test: Manufacturing Shipment and Inventories

Pedroni Residual Cointegration Test
Series: IVM MM

Sample: 1968M01 1995M12
Included observations: 2688
Cross-sections included: 8
Null Hypothesis: No cointegration
Trend assumption: No deterministic trend
Lag selection: Automatic SIC with a max lag of 16
Newey-West bandwidth selection with Bartlett kernel

Alternative hypothesis: common AR coefs. (within-dimension)

	Statistic	Prob.	Weighted Statistic	Prob.
Panel v-Statistic	4.219500	0.0001	4.119485	0.0001
Panel rho-Statistic	−0.400152	0.3682	−2.543473	0.0157
Panel PP-Statistic	0.671083	0.3185	−1.254923	0.1815
Panel ADF-Statistic	−0.216806	0.3897	0.172158	0.3931

Alternative hypothesis: individual AR coefs. (between-dimension)

	Statistic	Prob.
Group rho-Statistic	−1.776207	0.0824
Group PP-Statistic	−0.824320	0.2840
Group ADF-Statistic	0.538943	0.3450

Cross-section specific results

Phillips-Peron results (non-parametric)

Cross ID	AR(1)	Variance	HAC	Bandwidth	Obs
AUT	0.959	54057.16	46699.67	23.00	321
BUS	0.959	98387.47	98024.05	7.00	321
CON	0.966	144092.9	125609.0	4.00	321
CST	0.933	579515.0	468780.9	6.00	321
DEP	0.908	896700.4	572964.8	7.00	321
HOA	0.941	146702.7	165065.5	6.00	321
MAE	0.975	2996615.	2018633.	3.00	321
MIS	0.991	2775962.	3950850.	7.00	321

Augmented Dickey-Fuller results (parametric)

Cross ID	AR(1)	Variance	Lag	Max lag	Obs
AUT	0.983	48285.07	5	16	316
BUS	0.971	95843.74	1	16	320
CON	0.966	144092.9	0	16	321
CST	0.949	556149.1	1	16	320
DEP	0.974	647340.5	2	16	319
HOA	0.941	146702.7	0	16	321
MAE	0.976	2459970.	6	16	315
MIS	0.977	2605046.	3	16	318

the null of no cointegration, while the latter do not reject the null of no cointegration in 8 out of 11 tests.

(c) The Johansen Fisher panel cointegration test allowing for individual sector effects is given in Table 12.10. This rejects the hypothesis that there are zero cointegrating relationships and does not reject the hypothesis of at most one cointegrating relationship.

(d) Tables 12.11 and 12.12 check the sensitivity of the Kao residual cointegration test and the Pedroni residual cointegration test to fixing the lag at 1. The results lead by and large to the same decisions. Similar results are obtained when we fix the lag at 2, 3, and 4.

Table 12.10 Johansen Fisher Panel Cointegration Test: Manufacturing Shipment and Inventories

Johansen Fisher Panel Cointegration Test
Series: IVM MM

Sample: 1968M01 1995M12
Included observations: 2688
Trend assumption: No deterministic trend (restricted constant)
Lags interval (in first differences): 1 1

Unrestricted Cointegration Rank Test (Trace and Maximum Eigenvalue)

Hypothesized No. of CE(s)	Fisher Stat.* (from trace test)	Prob.	Fisher Stat.* (from max-eigen test)	Prob.
None	204.7	0.0000	211.0	0.0000
At most 1	12.07	0.7390	12.07	0.7390

* Probabilities are computed using asymptotic chi-square distribution.

Individual cross section results

Cross Section	Trace Test Statistics	Prob.**	Max-Eign Test Statistics	Prob.**
Hypothesis of no cointegration				
AUT	22.1873	0.0268	19.8088	0.0115
BUS	43.1638	0.0000	39.8985	0.0000
CON	56.9099	0.0000	53.2483	0.0000
CST	48.6846	0.0000	42.9905	0.0000
DEP	15.5639	0.1958	12.4301	0.1624
HOA	76.6530	0.0000	70.5817	0.0000
MAE	54.7226	0.0000	52.5119	0.0000
MIS	60.8672	0.0000	59.1997	0.0000
Hypothesis of at most 1 cointegration relationship				
AUT	2.3785	0.7018	2.3785	0.7018
BUS	3.2653	0.5323	3.2653	0.5323
CON	3.6616	0.4648	3.6616	0.4648
CST	5.6942	0.2157	5.6942	0.2157
DEP	3.1338	0.5560	3.1338	0.5560
HOA	6.0714	0.1853	6.0714	0.1853
MAE	2.2107	0.7355	2.2107	0.7355
MIS	1.6675	0.8425	1.6675	0.8425

**MacKinnon-Haug-Michelis (1999) p-values

Table 12.11 Kao Residual Cointegration Test: Fixing the Lag at 1

Kao Residual Cointegration Test
Series: IVM? MM?

Sample: 1968M01 1995M12
Included observations: 336
Null Hypothesis: No cointegration
Trend assumption: No deterministic trend
Lag selection: fixed at 1
Newey-West bandwidth selection using Bartlett kernel

	t-Statistic	Prob.
ADF	−0.603443	0.2731
Residual variance	257852.7	
HAC variance	730764.3	

Augmented Dickey-Fuller Test Equation
Dependent Variable: D(RESID?)
Method: Panel Least Squares

Sample (adjusted): 1968M03 1994M10
Included observations: 320 after adjustments
Cross-sections included: 8
Total pool (balanced) observations: 2560

	Coefficient	Std. Error	t-Statistic	Prob.
RESID?(-1)	−0.007315	0.002909	−2.515054	0.0120
D(RESID?(-1))	−0.144238	0.019629	−7.348100	0.0000

R-squared	0.024125	Mean dependent var	−16.11315
Adjusted R-squared	0.023744	S.D. dependent var	902.9312
S.E. of regression	892.1474	Akaike info criterion	16.42592
Sum squared resid	2.04E+09	Schwarz criterion	16.43049
Log likelihood	−21023.18	Hannan-Quinn criter.	16.42758
Durbin-Watson stat	1.986464		

(e) Tables 12.13 and 12.14 check the sensitivity of the Pedroni residual cointegration test and Johansen Fisher panel cointegration test to the inclusion of linear trends. The Pedroni tests are affected, but still 8 out of 11 do not reject the null of no cointegration. The Fisher-type Johansen test yields the same decision as before, rejecting the hypothesis that there are zero cointegrating relationships and not rejecting the hypothesis of at most one cointegrating relationship.

Table 12.12 Pedroni Residual Cointegration Test: Fixing the Lag at 1

Pedroni Residual Cointegration Test
Series: IVM MM

Sample: 1968M01 1995M12
Included observations: 2688
Cross-sections included: 8
Null Hypothesis: No cointegration
Trend assumption: No deterministic trend
Lag selection: fixed at 1
Newey-West bandwidth selection with Bartlett kernel

Alternative hypothesis: common AR coefs. (within-dimension)

	Statistic	Prob.	Weighted Statistic	Prob.
Panel v-Statistic	4.219500	0.0001	4.119485	0.0001
Panel rho-Statistic	−0.400152	0.3682	−2.543473	0.0157
Panel PP-Statistic	0.671083	0.3185	−1.254923	0.1815
Panel ADF-Statistic	2.177869	0.0372	0.153330	0.3943

Alternative hypothesis: individual AR coefs. (between-dimension)

	Statistic	Prob.
Group rho-Statistic	−1.776207	0.0824
Group PP-Statistic	−0.824320	0.2840
Group ADF-Statistic	0.987833	0.2449

Cross-section specific results

Phillips-Peron results (non-parametric)

Cross ID	AR(1)	Variance	HAC	Bandwidth	Obs
AUT	0.959	54057.16	46699.67	23.00	321
BUS	0.959	98387.47	98024.05	7.00	321
CON	0.966	144092.9	125609.0	4.00	321
CST	0.933	579515.0	468780.9	6.00	321
DEP	0.908	896700.4	572964.8	7.00	321
HOA	0.941	146702.7	165065.5	6.00	321
MAE	0.975	2996615.	2018633.	3.00	321
MIS	0.991	2775962.	3950850.	7.00	321

Augmented Dickey-Fuller results (parametric)

Cross ID	AR(1)	Variance	Lag	Max lag	Obs
AUT	0.971	51730.31	1	--	320
BUS	0.971	95843.74	1	--	320
CON	0.971	142612.1	1	--	320
CST	0.949	556149.1	1	--	320
DEP	0.952	732640.9	1	--	320
HOA	0.946	146673.5	1	--	320
MAE	0.989	2737915.	1	--	320
MIS	0.991	2784387.	1	--	320

Table 12.13 Pedroni Residual Cointegration Test: Deterministic Intercept and Trend

Pedroni Residual Cointegration Test
Series: IVM MM

Sample: 1968M01 1995M12
Included observations: 2688
Cross-sections included: 8
Null Hypothesis: No cointegration
Trend assumption: Deterministic intercept and trend
Lag selection: Automatic SIC with a max lag of 16
Newey-West bandwidth selection with Bartlett kernel

Alternative hypothesis: common AR coefs. (within-dimension)

	Statistic	Prob.	Weighted Statistic	Prob.
Panel v-Statistic	1.165075	0.2024	2.309719	0.0277
Panel rho-Statistic	1.618195	0.1077	0.133578	0.3954
Panel PP-Statistic	2.515132	0.0169	0.637212	0.3256
Panel ADF-Statistic	2.058160	0.0480	1.734333	0.0887

Alternative hypothesis: individual AR coefs. (between-dimension)

	Statistic	Prob.
Group rho-Statistic	0.093508	0.3972
Group PP-Statistic	0.829095	0.2829
Group ADF-Statistic	1.721656	0.0906

Cross-section specific results

Phillips-Peron results (non-parametric)

Cross ID	AR(1)	Variance	HAC	Bandwidth	Obs
AUT	0.989	8423.300	13323.32	9.00	321
BUS	0.939	120754.3	120199.0	7.00	321
CON	0.988	52006.85	55901.93	7.00	321
CST	0.925	628659.8	505527.4	6.00	321
DEP	0.882	1051048.	768151.5	8.00	321
HOA	0.967	53736.13	94599.15	9.00	321
MAE	0.996	571075.3	1637287.	12.00	321
MIS	0.994	2275925.	3332654.	7.00	321

Augmented Dickey-Fuller results (parametric)

Cross ID	AR(1)	Variance	Lag	Max lag	Obs
AUT	0.984	7919.828	3	16	318
BUS	0.955	116950.2	1	16	320
CON	0.988	52006.85	0	16	321
CST	0.943	600470.3	1	16	320
DEP	0.960	752106.3	2	16	319
HOA	0.947	50410.74	3	16	318
MAE	0.986	491973.2	4	16	317
MIS	0.982	2142136.	3	16	318

Table 12.14 Johansen Fisher Panel Cointegration Test: Linear Deterministic Trend (Restricted)

Johansen Fisher Panel Cointegration Test
Series: IVM MM

Sample: 1968M01 1995M12
Included observations: 2688
Trend assumption: Linear deterministic trend (restricted)
Lags interval (in first differences): 1 1

Unrestricted Cointegration Rank Test (Trace and Maximum Eigenvalue)

Hypothesized No. of CE(s)	Fisher Stat.* (from trace test)	Prob.	Fisher Stat.* (from max-eigen test)	Prob.
None	106.3	0.0000	104.1	0.0000
At most 1	17.70	0.3420	17.70	0.3420

* Probabilities are computed using asymptotic chi-square distribution.

Individual cross section results

Cross-section	Trace Test Statistics	Prob.**	Max-Eign Test Statistics	Prob.**
Hypothesis of no cointegration				
AUT	36.6831	0.0015	32.7276	0.0003
BUS	23.3549	0.0997	19.2855	0.0517
CON	29.4446	0.0172	25.1968	0.0064
CST	26.3215	0.0440	20.2897	0.0369
DEP	24.8826	0.0660	24.3029	0.0089
HOA	45.5352	0.0001	36.2994	0.0001
MAE	37.4411	0.0012	25.5592	0.0056
MIS	58.0008	0.0000	46.6195	0.0000
Hypothesis of at most 1 cointegration relationship				
AUT	3.9555	0.7486	3.9555	0.7486
BUS	4.0694	0.7320	4.0694	0.7320
CON	4.2479	0.7060	4.2479	0.7060
CST	6.0317	0.4563	6.0317	0.4563
DEP	0.5797	1.0000	0.5797	1.0000
HOA	9.2359	0.1663	9.2359	0.1663
MAE	11.8819	0.0637	11.8819	0.0637
MIS	11.3813	0.0768	11.3813	0.0768

**MacKinnon-Haug-Michelis (1999) p-values

Exercise 12.3 *(International R&D spillover).* This is based on Problem 12.2 in Baltagi (2008). Coe and Helpman (1995) studied the international R&D spillover phenomenon using a sample of 21 OECD countries and Israel, observed over the period 1971–90. Kao *et al.* (1999) re-examine the effects of domestic and foreign R&D capital stocks (denoted by RD and FRD) on total factor productivity (TFP) of these countries using panel cointegration estimation methods. Download the International R&D spillovers panel data set used by Kao *et al.* (1999) from http://web.syr.edu/~cdkao. Using EViews, replicate the following results:

(a) Perform the panel unit root tests using individual effects in the deterministic variables on log(TFP), log(RD) and log(FRD).
(b) Check the sensitivity of these results when both individual effects and individual linear trends are included.
(c) Perform the panel cointegration tests of Kao (1999) using individual effects in the deterministic variables. Check the sensitivity of this test result to a user specified lag of 1.
(d) Perform the Pedroni and the Fisher panel Johansen cointegration trace test and maximum eigen value test using individual effects in the deterministic variables. Check the sensitivity of the Pedroni and the Fisher panel Johansen cointegration test results when both individual effects and individual linear trends are included.

Solution

(a) Tables 12.15, 12.16 and 12.17 give the panel unit root tests with individual effects for log(TFP), log(RD) and log(FRD), respectively. All the tests do not reject the panel unit roots hypothesis for all three series considered.
(b) The results are sensitive to the inclusion of both individual effects and individual linear trends, as shown in Tables 12.18, 12.19 and 12.20. In fact, for log(TFP), we reject the panel unit root hypothesis except when using the Phillips–Perron Fisher chi-square test. For log(RD), we reject the panel unit root hypothesis except when using the Breitung test and the Phillips–Perron Fisher chi-square test. For log(FRD), we reject the panel unit root hypothesis except when using the Breitung test.
(c) The panel cointegration test of Kao (1999) does not reject the null hypothesis of no cointegration unless we fix the lag at 1; see Table 12.21.
(d) When individual effects are included, the Pedroni tests for the null of no cointegration reject the null in only 3 out of 11 tests at the 5% significance level; see Table 12.22.

Table 12.15 Panel Unit Root Tests: Total Factor Productivity Allowing for Individual Effects

Panel unit root test: Summary
Series: LTFP

Sample: 1971 1990
Exogenous variables: Individual effects
Automatic selection of maximum lags
Automatic selection of lags based on SIC: 0 to 4
Newey-West bandwidth selection using Bartlett kernel

Method	Statistic	Prob.**	Cross-sections	Obs
Null: Unit root (assumes common unit root process)				
Levin, Lin & Chu t	−1.23367	0.1087	22	406
Null: Unit root (assumes individual unit root process)				
Im, Pesaran and Shin W-stat	2.01095	0.9778	22	406
ADF - Fisher Chi-square	37.0662	0.7611	22	406
PP - Fisher Chi-square	29.5427	0.9534	22	418

** Probabilities for Fisher tests are computed using an asymptotic chi-square distribution. All other tests assume asymptotic normality.

Table 12.16 Panel Unit Root Tests: Domestic R&D Allowing for Individual Effects

Panel unit root test: Summary
Series: LRD

Sample: 1971 1990
Exogenous variables: Individual effects
Automatic selection of maximum lags
Automatic selection of lags based on SIC: 0 to 4
Newey-West bandwidth selection using Bartlett kernel

Method	Statistic	Prob.**	Cross-sections	Obs
Null: Unit root (assumes common unit root process)				
Levin, Lin & Chu t	2.98542	0.9986	22	383
Null: Unit root (assumes individual unit root process)				
Im, Pesaran and Shin W-stat	9.45718	1.0000	22	383
ADF - Fisher Chi-square	30.9637	0.9311	22	383
PP - Fisher Chi-square	57.5662	0.0824	22	418

** Probabilities for Fisher tests are computed using an asymptotic chi-square distribution. All other tests assume asymptotic normality.

Table 12.17 Panel Unit Root Tests: Foreign R&D Allowing for Individual Effects

Panel unit root test: Summary
Series: LFRD

Sample: 1971 1990
Exogenous variables: Individual effects
Automatic selection of maximum lags
Automatic selection of lags based on SIC: 0 to 4
Newey-West bandwidth selection using Bartlett kernel

Method	Statistic	Prob.**	Cross-sections	Obs
Null: Unit root (assumes common unit root process)				
Levin, Lin & Chu t	3.30253	0.9995	22	401
Null: Unit root (assumes individual unit root process)				
Im, Pesaran and Shin W-stat	7.61544	1.0000	22	401
ADF - Fisher Chi-square	8.33978	1.0000	22	401
PP - Fisher Chi-square	8.34613	1.0000	22	418

** Probabilities for Fisher tests are computed using an asymptotic chi-square distribution. All other tests assume asymptotic normality.

Table 12.18 Panel Unit Root Tests: Total Factor Productivity Allowing for Both Individual Effects and Individual Linear Trends

Panel unit root test: Summary
Series: LTFP

Sample: 1971 1990
Exogenous variables: Individual effects, individual linear trends
Automatic selection of maximum lags
Automatic selection of lags based on SIC: 0 to 4
Newey-West bandwidth selection using Bartlett kernel

Method	Statistic	Prob.**	Cross-sections	Obs
Null: Unit root (assumes common unit root process)				
Levin, Lin & Chu t	−3.11547	0.0009	22	385
Breitung t-stat	−2.96810	0.0015	22	363
Null: Unit root (assumes individual unit root process)				
Im, Pesaran and Shin W-stat	−3.22005	0.0006	22	385
ADF - Fisher Chi-square	74.0961	0.0030	22	385
PP - Fisher Chi-square	44.1267	0.4663	22	418

** Probabilities for Fisher tests are computed using an asymptotic chi-square distribution. All other tests assume asymptotic normality.

Table 12.19 Panel Unit Root Tests: Domestic R&D Allowing for Both Individual Effects and Individual Linear Trends

Panel unit root test: Summary
Series: LRD

Sample: 1971 1990
Exogenous variables: Individual effects, individual linear trends
Automatic selection of maximum lags
Automatic selection of lags based on SIC: 0 to 4
Newey-West bandwidth selection using Bartlett kernel

Method	Statistic	Prob.**	Cross-sections	Obs
Null: Unit root (assumes common unit root process)				
Levin, Lin & Chu t	−3.96300	0.0000	22	384
Breitung t-stat	−0.42430	0.3357	22	362
Null: Unit root (assumes individual unit root process)				
Im, Pesaran and Shin W-stat	−2.71815	0.0033	22	384
ADF - Fisher Chi-square	77.3428	0.0014	22	384
PP - Fisher Chi-square	18.7207	0.9997	22	418

** Probabilities for Fisher tests are computed using an asymptotic chi-square distribution. All other tests assume asymptotic normality.

Table 12.20 Panel Unit Root Tests: Foreign R&D Allowing for Both Individual Effects and Individual Linear Trends

Panel unit root test: Summary
Series: LFRD

Sample: 1971 1990
Exogenous variables: Individual effects, individual linear trends
Automatic selection of maximum lags
Automatic selection of lags based on SIC: 0 to 4
Newey-West bandwidth selection using Bartlett kernel

Method	Statistic	Prob.**	Cross-sections	Obs
Null: Unit root (assumes common unit root process)				
Levin, Lin & Chu t	−1.62928	0.0516	22	401
Breitung t-stat	0.62162	0.7329	22	379
Null: Unit root (assumes individual unit root process)				
Im, Pesaran and Shin W-stat	−3.22103	0.0006	22	401
ADF - Fisher Chi-square	76.4761	0.0017	22	401
PP - Fisher Chi-square	73.5843	0.0034	22	418

** Probabilities for Fisher tests are computed using an asymptotic chi-square distribution. All other tests assume asymptotic normality.

Table 12.21 Kao Residual Cointegration Test: LTFP LRD LFRD

Kao Residual Cointegration Test
Series: LTFP LRD LFRD

Sample: 1971 1990
Included observations: 440
Null Hypothesis: No cointegration
Trend assumption: No deterministic trend
Lag selection: Automatic 4 lags by SIC with a max lag of 4
Newey-West bandwidth selection using Bartlett kernel

	t-Statistic	Prob.
ADF	−1.069867	0.1423
Residual variance	0.000543	
HAC variance	0.000662	

Kao Residual Cointegration Test
Series: LTFP LRD LFRD

Sample: 1971 1990
Included observations: 440
Null Hypothesis: No cointegration
Trend assumption: No deterministic trend
Lag selection: fixed at 1
Newey-West bandwidth selection using Bartlett kernel

	t-Statistic	Prob.
ADF	−2.305756	0.0106
Residual variance	0.000543	
HAC variance	0.000662	

Table 12.22 Pedroni Residual Cointegration Test: LTFP LRD LFRD

Pedroni Residual Cointegration Test
Series: LTFP LRD LFRD

Sample: 1971 1990
Included observations: 440
Cross-sections included: 22
Null Hypothesis: No cointegration
Trend assumption: No deterministic trend
Lag selection: Automatic SIC with a max lag of 3
Newey-West bandwidth selection with Bartlett kernel

Alternative hypothesis: common AR coefs. (within-dimension)

	Statistic	Prob.	Weighted Statistic	Prob.
Panel v-Statistic	0.429844	0.3637	−0.588507	0.3355
Panel rho-Statistic	−0.587120	0.3358	−0.679037	0.3168
Panel PP-Statistic	−2.011444	0.0528	−2.208595	0.0348
Panel ADF-Statistic	−4.878134	0.0000	−4.717842	0.0000

Alternative hypothesis: individual AR coefs. (between-dimension)

	Statistic	Prob.
Group rho-Statistic	1.710431	0.0924
Group PP-Statistic	−0.709493	0.3102
Group ADF-Statistic	−5.068813	0.0000

Table 12.23 Johansen Fisher Panel Cointegration Test: LTFP LRD LFRD

Johansen Fisher Panel Cointegration Test

Series: LTFP LRD LFRD

Sample: 1971 1990
Included observations: 440
Trend assumption: Linear deterministic trend
Lags interval (in first differences): 1 1

Unrestricted Cointegration Rank Test (Trace and Maximum Eigenvalue)

Hypothesized No. of CE(s)	Fisher Stat.* (from trace test)	Prob.	Fisher Stat.* (from max-eigen test)	Prob.
None	220.0	0.0000	156.6	0.0000
At most 1	108.4	0.0000	83.83	0.0003
At most 2	96.41	0.0000	96.41	0.0000

Table 12.24 Pedroni Residual Cointegration Test Deterministic Intercept and Trend: LTFP LRD LFRD

Pedroni Residual Cointegration Test
Series: LTFP LRD LFRD

Sample: 1971 1990
Included observations: 440
Cross-sections included: 22
Null Hypothesis: No cointegration
Trend assumption: Deterministic intercept and trend
Lag selection: Automatic SIC with a max lag of 3
Newey-West bandwidth selection with Bartlett kernel

Alternative hypothesis: common AR coefs. (within-dimension)

	Statistic	Prob.	Weighted Statistic	Prob.
Panel v-Statistic	−1.895763	0.0661	−3.274764	0.0019
Panel rho-Statistic	1.943748	0.0603	1.539660	0.1219
Panel PP-Statistic	−1.280299	0.1758	−1.706008	0.0931
Panel ADF-Statistic	−5.691515	0.0000	−5.291139	0.0000

Alternative hypothesis: individual AR coefs. (between-dimension)

	Statistic	Prob.
Group rho-Statistic	3.403843	0.0012
Group PP-Statistic	−0.523089	0.3479
Group ADF-Statistic	−4.985305	0.0000

The Fisher panel Johansen cointegration trace test and maximum eigenvalue test using individual effects reject the null of no cointegration as well as the nulls of at most one or two cointegrating relationships; see Table 12.23. Allowing for both individual effects and individual linear trends, the Pedroni tests reject the null of no cointegration in 5 out of 11 tests at the 5% significance level; see Table 12.24.

References

Abadir, K. M. and J. R. Magnus, 2005, *Matrix Algebra* (Cambridge University Press, Cambridge).

Abrevaya, J., 1997, The equivalence of two estimators of the fixed-effects logit model, *Economics Letters* **55**, 41–43.

Ahn, S. C. and S. Low, 1996, A reformulation of the Hausman test for regression models with pooled cross-section time-series data, *Journal of Econometrics* **71**, 309–319.

Ahn, S. C. and P. Schmidt, 1995, Efficient estimation of models for dynamic panel data, *Journal of Econometrics* **68**, 5–27.

Amemiya, T., 1971, The estimation of the variances in a variance–components model, *International Economic Review* **12**, 1–13.

Amemiya, T. and T. E. MaCurdy, 1986, Instrumental-variable estimation of an error components model, *Econometrica* **54**, 869–881.

Anderson, T. W. and C. Hsiao, 1981, Estimation of dynamic models with error components, *Journal of the American Statistical Association* **76**, 598–606.

Anselin, L., 1988, *Spatial Econometrics: Methods and Models* (Kluwer Academic Publishers, Dordrecht).

Anselin, L., 2001, Spatial econometrics, Chapter 14 in B. Baltagi, ed., *A Companion to Theoretical Econometrics* (Blackwell, Malden, MA), 310–330.

Arellano, M., 1993, On the testing of correlated effects with panel data, *Journal of Econometrics* **59**, 87–97.

Arellano, M., 2003, *Panel Data Econometrics* (Oxford University Press, Oxford).

Arellano, M. and S. Bond, 1991, Some tests of specification for panel data: Monte Carlo evidence and an application to employment equations, *Review of Economic Studies* **58**, 277–297.

Arellano, M. and O. Bover, 1995, Another look at the instrumental variables estimation of error-component models, *Journal of Econometrics* **68**, 29–51.

Avery, R. B., 1977, Error components and seemingly unrelated regressions, *Econometrica* **45**, 199–209.

Balestra, P., 1973, Best quadratic unbiased estimators of the variance–covariance matrix in normal regression, *Journal of Econometrics* **2**, 17–28.

Balestra, P., 1980, A note on the exact transformation associated with the first-order moving average process, *Journal of Econometrics* **14**, 381–394.

Balestra, P. and J. Varadharajan-Krishnakumar, 1987, Full information estimations of a system of simultaneous equations with error components structure, *Econometric Theory* **3**, 223–246.

Baltagi, B. H., 1980, On seemingly unrelated regressions with error components, *Econometrica* **48**, 1547–1551.

Baltagi, B. H., 1981, Simultaneous equations with error components, *Journal of Econometrics* **17**, 189–200.

Baltagi, B. H., 1985, Pooling cross-sections with unequal time-series lengths, *Economics Letters* **18**, 133–136.

Baltagi, B. H., 1987, On estimating from a more general time-series cum cross-section data structure, *American Economist* **31**, 69–71.

Baltagi, B. H., 1988a, Prediction with a two-way error component regression model – Problem 88.1.1, *Econometric Theory* **4**, 171.

Baltagi, B. H., 1988b, An alternative heteroscedastic error components model – Problem 88.2.2, *Econometric Theory* **4**, 349–350.

Baltagi, B. H., 1989a, The equivalence of the Boothe–MacKinnon and the Hausman specification tests in the context of panel data – Problem 89.3.3, *Econometric Theory* **5**, 454.

Baltagi, B. H., 1989b, Applications of a necessary and sufficient condition for OLS to be BLUE, *Statistics and Probability Letters* **8**, 457–461.

Baltagi, B. H., 1993, Nested effects – Problem 93.4.2, *Econometric Theory* **9**, 687–688.

Baltagi, B. H., 1995a, Testing for correlated effects in panels – Problem 95.2.5, *Econometric Theory* **11**, 401–402.

Baltagi, B. H., 1995b, Testing for fixed effects in logit and probit models using an artificial regression – Problem 95.5.4, *Econometric Theory* **11**, 1179.

Baltagi, B. H., 1996, Heteroskedastic fixed effects models – Problem 96.5.1, *Econometric Theory* **12**, 867.

Baltagi, B. H., 1997, Hausman's specification test as a Gauss–Newton regression – Problem 97.4.1, *Econometric Theory* **13**, 757.

Baltagi, B. H., 1998, Within two way is equivalent to two withins one way – Problem 98.5.2, *Econometric Theory* **14**, 687.

Baltagi, B. H., 1999, The relative efficiency of the between estimator with respect to the within estimator – Problem 99.4.3, *Econometric Theory* **15**, 630–631.

Baltagi, B. H., 2004, A Hausman test based on the difference between fixed effects two-stage least squares and error components two-stage least squares – Problem 04.1.1, *Econometric Theory* **20**, 223–224.

Baltagi, B. H., 2006a, Estimating an economic model of crime using panel data from North Carolina, *Journal of Applied Econometrics* **21**, 543–547.

Baltagi, B. H., 2006b, Random effects and spatial autocorrelation with equal weights, *Econometric Theory* **22**, 973–984.

Baltagi, B. H., 2008, *Econometric Analysis of Panel Data* (John Wiley, Chichester).

Baltagi, B. H. and Y. J. Chang, 1994, Incomplete panels: a comparative study of alternative estimators for the unbalanced one-way error component regression model, *Journal of Econometrics* **62**, 67–89.

Baltagi, B. H. and J. M. Griffin, 1983, Gasoline demand in the OECD: an application of pooling and testing procedures, *European Economic Review* **22**, 117–137.

Baltagi, B. H. and J. M. Griffin, 1988, A generalized error component model with heteroscedastic disturbances, *International Economic Review* **29**, 745–753.

Baltagi, B. H. and S. Khanti-Akom, 1990, On efficient estimation with panel data: an empirical comparison of instrumental variables estimators, *Journal of Applied Econometrics* **5**, 401–406.

Baltagi, B. H. and W. Krämer, 1994, Consistency, asymptotic unbiasedness and bounds on the bias of s^2 in the linear regression model with error component disturbances, *Statistical Papers* **35**, 323–328.

Baltagi, B. H. and W. Krämer, 1995, A mixed error component model – Problem 95.1.4, *Econometric Theory* **11**, 192–193.

Baltagi, B. H. and D. Levin, 1986, Estimating dynamic demand for cigarettes using panel data: the effects of bootlegging, taxation, and advertising reconsidered, *Review of Economics and Statistics* **68**, 148–155.

Baltagi, B. H. and Q. Li, 1990a, A comparison of variance components estimators using balanced versus unbalanced data – Problem 90.2.3, *Econometric Theory* **6**, 283–285.

Baltagi, B. H. and Q. Li, 1990b, A Lagrange multiplier test for the error components model with incomplete panels, *Econometric Reviews* **9**, 103–107.

Baltagi, B. H. and Q. Li, 1991a, A transformation that will circumvent the problem of autocorrelation in an error component model, *Journal of Econometrics* **48**, 385–393.

Baltagi, B. H. and Q. Li, 1991b, A joint test for serial correlation and random individual effects, *Statistics and Probability Letters* **11**, 277–280.

Baltagi, B. H. and Q. Li, 1991c, Variance component estimation under misspecification – Problem 91.3.3, *Econometric Theory* **7**, 418–419.

Baltagi, B. H. and Q. Li, 1992a, Variance component estimation under misspecification – Solution 91.3.3, *Econometric Theory* **8**, 430–433.

Baltagi, B. H. and Q. Li, 1992b, Prediction in the one-way error component model with serial correlation, *Journal of Forecasting* **11**, 561–567.

Baltagi, B. H. and Q. Li, 1992c, A note on the estimation of simultaneous equations with error components, *Econometric Theory* **8**, 113–119.

Baltagi, B. H. and Q. Li, 1992d, An approximate transformation for the error component model with MA(q) disturbances – Problem 92.4.3, *Econometric Theory* **8**, 582–583.

Baltagi, B. H. and Q. Li, 1994, Estimating error component models with general MA(q) disturbances, *Econometric Theory* **10**, 396–408.

Baltagi, B. H. and D. Li, 1999, Prediction in the spatially autocorrelated error component model – Problem 99.2.4, *Econometric Theory* **15**, 259.

Baltagi, B. H. and L. Liu, 2007, Alternative ways of obtaining Hausman's test using artificial regressions, *Statistics and Probability Letters* **77**, 1413–1417.

Baltagi, B. H. and P. X. Wu, 1999, Unequally spaced panel data regressions with AR (1) disturbances, *Econometric Theory* **15**, 814–823.

Baltagi, B. H., Y. J. Chang and Q. Li, 1992, Monte Carlo results on several new and existing tests for the error component model, *Journal of Econometrics* **54**, 95–120.

Bhargava, A. and J. D. Sargan, 1983, Estimating dynamic random effects models from panel data covering short time periods, *Econometrica* **51**, 1635–1659.

Bhargava, A., L. Franzini and W. Narendranathan, 1982, Serial correlation and fixed effects model, *Review of Economic Studies* **49**, 533–549.

Biorn, E., 1981, Estimating economic relations from incomplete cross-section/time-series data, *Journal of Econometrics* **16**, 221–236.

Biorn, E. and E. S. Jansen, 1983, Individual effects in a system of demand functions, *Scandinavian Journal of Economics* **85**, 461–483.

Blundell, R. and S. Bond, 1998, Initial conditions and moment restrictions in dynamic panel data models, *Journal of Econometrics* **87**, 115–143.

Bound, L., C. Brown, G. J. Duncan and W. L. Rodgers, 1990, Measurement error in cross-sectional and longitudinal labor market surveys: validation study evidence, in J. Hartog, G. Ridder and T. Theeuwes, eds., *Panel Data and Labor Market Studies* (North-Holland, Amsterdam), 1–19.

Breitung, J., 2000, The local power of some unit root tests for panel data, *Advances in Econometrics* **15**, 161–177.

Breusch, T. S., 1987, Maximum likelihood estimation of random effects models, *Journal of Econometrics* **36**, 383–389.

Breusch, T. S. and L. G. Godfrey, 1981, A review of recent work on testing for autocorrelation in dynamic simultaneous models, in D. A. Currie, R. Nobay and D. Peel, eds., *Macroeconomic Analysis, Essays in Macroeconomics and Economics* (Croom Helm, London), 63–100.

Breusch, T. S. and A. R. Pagan, 1979, A simple test for heteroskedasticity and random coefficient variation, *Econometrica* **47**, 1287–1294.

Breusch, T. S. and A. R. Pagan, 1980, The Lagrange multiplier test and its applications to model specification in econometrics, *Review of Economic Studies* **47**, 239–253.

Breusch, T. S., G. E. Mizon and P. Schmidt, 1989, Efficient estimation using panel data, *Econometrica* **57**, 695–700.

Butler, J. S. and R. Moffitt, 1982, A computationally efficient quadrature procedure for the one factor multinominal probit model, *Econometrica* **50**, 761–764.

Cameron, C. and P. Trivedi, 1998, *Regression Analysis of Count Data* (Cambridge University Press, New York).

Chamberlain, G., 1980, Analysis of covariance with qualitative data, *Review of Economic Studies* **47**, 225–238.

Chamberlain, G., 1984, Panel data, Chapter 22 in Z. Griliches and M. Intrilligator, eds., *Handbook of Econometrics* (North-Holland, Amsterdam), 1247–1318.

Chamberlain, G., 1985, Heterogeneity, omitted variable bias and duration dependence, Chapter 1 in J. J. Heckman and B. Singer, eds., *Longitudinal Analysis of Labor Market Data* (Cambridge University Press, Cambridge), 3–38.

Choi, I., 2001, Unit root tests for panel data, *Journal of International Money and Finance* **20**, 249–272.

Choudhury, A. H. and R. D. St. Louis, 1990, A note on Park and Heike's (1983) modified approximate estimator for the first-order moving-average process, *Journal of Econometrics* **46**, 399–406.

Chow, G. C., 1960, Tests of equality between sets of coefficients in two linear regressions, *Econometrica* **28**, 591–605.

Coe, D. and E. Helpman, 1995, International R&D spillovers, *European Economic Review* **39**, 859–887.

Cornwell, C. and P. Rupert, 1988, Efficient estimation with panel data: an empirical comparison of instrumental variables estimators, *Journal of Applied Econometrics* **3**, 149–155.

Cornwell, C. and W. N. Trumbull, 1994, Estimating the economic model of crime with panel data, *Review of Economics and Statistics* **76**, 360–366.

Cornwell, C., P. Schmidt and D. Wyhowski, 1992, Simultaneous equations and panel data, *Journal of Econometrics* **51**, 151–181.

Davidson, R. and J. G. MacKinnon, 1993, *Estimation and Inference in Econometrics* (Oxford University Press, New York).

Davis, P., 2002, Estimating multi-way error components models with unbalanced data structures using instrumental variables, *Journal of Econometrics* **106**, 67–95.

Duncan, G. J. and D. H. Hill, 1985, An investigation of the extent and consequences of measurement error in labor economic survey data, *Journal of Labor Economics* **3**, 508–532.

Engle, R. F. and C. W. J. Granger, 1987, Co-integration and error correction: representation, estimation and testing, *Econometrica* **55**, 251–276.

Evans, M. A. and M. L. King, 1985, Critical value approximations for tests of linear regression disturbances, *Australian Journal of Statistics* **27**, 68–83.

Fiebig, D., R. Bartels and W. Krämer, 1996, The Frisch–Waugh theorem and generalized least squares, *Econometric Reviews* **15**, 431–443.

Fisher, F. M., 1970, Tests of equality between sets of coefficients in two linear regressions: an expository note, *Econometrica* **38**, 361–366.

Frisch, R., and F. V. Waugh, 1933, Partial time regression as compared with individual trends, *Econometrica* **1**, 387–401.

Fuller, W. A. and G. E. Battese, 1973, Transformations for estimation of linear models with nested error structure, *Journal of the American Statistical Association* **68**, 626–632.

Galbraith, J. W. and V. Zinde-Walsh, 1995, Transforming the error-component model for estimation with general ARMA disturbances, *Journal of Econometrics* **66**, 349–355.

Ghosh, S. K., 1976, Estimating from a more general time-series cum cross-section data structure, *American Economist* **20**, 15–21.

Glick, R. and A. K. Rose, 2002, Does a currency union affect trade? The time series evidence, *European Economic Review* **46**, 1125–1151.

Goldberger, A. S., 1962, Best linear unbiased prediction in the generalized linear regression model, *Journal of the American Statistical Association* **57**, 369–375.

Graybill, F. A., 1961, *An Introduction to Linear Statistical Models* (McGraw-Hill, New York).

Griliches, Z. and J. A. Hausman, 1986, Errors in variables in panel data, *Journal of Econometrics* **31**, 93–118.

Grunfeld, Y., 1958, The determinants of corporate investment, unpublished Ph.D. dissertation (University of Chicago, Chicago).

Gurmu, S., 1996, Testing for fixed effects in logit and probit models using an artificial regression – Solution 95.5.4, *Econometric Theory* **12**, 872–874.

Gurmu, S., 2000, The relative efficiency of the between-estimator with respect to the within-estimator – Solution 99.4.3, *Econometric Theory* **16**, 454–456.

Hadri, K., 2000, Testing for stationarity in heterogeneous panel data, *Econometrics Journal* **3**, 148–161.

Hall, B., Z. Griliches and J. A. Hausman, 1986, Patents and R&D: is there a lag?, *International Economic Review* **27**, 265–283.

Hansen, L. P., 1982, Large sample properties of generalized method of moments estimators, *Econometrica* **50**, 1029–1054.

Harrison, D. and D. L. Rubinfeld, 1978, Hedonic housing prices and the demand for clean air, *Journal of Environmental Economics and Management* **5**, 81–102.

Hartley, H. O. and J. N. K. Rao, 1967, Maximum likelihood estimation for the mixed analysis of variance model, *Biometrika* **54**, 93–108.

Harville, D. A., 1977, Maximum likelihood approaches to variance component estimation and to related problems, *Journal of the American Statistical Association* **72**, 320–340.

Hausman, J. A., 1978, Specification tests in econometrics, *Econometrica* **46**, 1251–1271.

Hausman, J. A. and W. E. Taylor, 1981, Panel data and unobservable individual effects, *Econometrica* **49**, 1377–1398.

Hausman, J. A., B. H. Hall and Z. Griliches, 1984, Econometric models for count data with an application to the patents–R&D relationship, *Econometrica* **52**, 909–938.

Hemmerle, W. J. and H. O. Hartley, 1973, Computing maximum likelihood estimates for the mixed A.O.V. model using the W-transformation, *Technometrics* **15**, 819–831.

Holly, A. and L. Gardiol, 2000, A score test for individual heteroscedasticity in a one-way error components model, Chapter 10 in J. Krishnakumar and E. Ronchetti, eds., *Panel Data Econometrics: Future Directions* (North-Holland, Amsterdam), 199–211.

Honda, Y., 1985, Testing the error components model with non-normal disturbances, *Review of Economic Studies* **52**, 681–690.

Honda, Y., 1991, A standardized test for the error components model with the two-way layout, *Economics Letters* **37**, 125–128.

Honoré, B. E. and E. Kyriazidou, 2000, Panel data discrete choice models with lagged dependent variables, *Econometrica* **68**, 839–874.

Honoré, B. E. and E. Tamer, 2006, Bounds on parameters in panel dynamic discrete choice models, *Econometrica* **74**, 611–629.

Hsiao, C., 2003, *Analysis of Panel Data* (Cambridge University Press, Cambridge).

Im, K. S., M. H. Pesaran and Y. Shin, 2003, Testing for unit roots in heterogeneous panels, *Journal of Econometrics* **115**, 53–74.

Johansen, S., 1995, *Likelihood-Based Inference in Cointegrated Vector Autoregressive Models* (Oxford University Press, Oxford).

Kao, C., 1999, Spurious regression and residual-based tests for cointegration in panel data, *Journal of Econometrics* **90**, 1–44.

Kao, C., M. H. Chiang and B. Chen, 1999, International R&D spillovers: an application of estimation and inference in panel cointegration, *Oxford Bulletin of Economics and Statistics* **61**, 691–709.

Kelejian, H. H. and I. R. Prucha, 2002, 2SLS and OLS in a spatial autoregressive model with equal spatial weights, *Regional Science and Urban Economics* **32**, 691–707.

King, M. L. and P. X. Wu, 1997, Locally optimal one-sided tests for multiparameter hypotheses, *Econometric Reviews* **16**, 131–156.

Kiviet, J. F., 1995, On bias, inconsistency and efficiency of various estimators in dynamic panel data models, *Journal of Econometrics* **68**, 53–78.

Kiviet, J. F. and W. Krämer, 1992, Bias of s^2 in the linear regression model with correlated errors, *Empirical Economics* **16**, 375–377.

Kleiber, C., 1997, Heteroskedastic fixed effects models – Solution 96.5.1, *Econometric Theory* **13**, 891–893.

Koning, R. H., 1989, Prediction with a two-way error component regression model – Solution 88.1.1, *Econometric Theory* **5**, 175.

Koning, R. H., 1990, The equivalence of the Boothe–MacKinnon and the Hausman specification tests in the context of panel data – Solution 89.3.3, *Econometric Theory* **6**, 409.

Koning, R. H., 1991, A comparison of variance components estimators using balanced versus unbalanced data – Solution 90.2.3, *Econometric Theory* **6**, 425–427.

Koop, G., D. J. Poirier and J. L. Tobias, 2007, *Bayesian Econometric Methods* (Cambridge University Press, Cambridge).

Kwiatkowski, D., P. C. B. Phillips, P. Schmidt and Y. Shin, 1992, Testing the null hypothesis of stationarity against the alternative of a unit root, *Journal of Econometrics* **54**, 159–178.

Lancaster, T., 2000, The incidental parameter problem since 1948, *Journal of Econometrics* **95**, 391–413.

Larsson, R., J. Lyhagen and M. Löthgren, 2001, Likelihood-based cointegration tests in heterogeneous panels, *Econometrics Journal* **4**, 109–142.

Levin, A., C. F. Lin and C. Chu, 2002, Unit root test in panel data: asymptotic and finite sample properties, *Journal of Econometrics* **108**, 1–24.

Li, D., 1999, Within two way is equivalent to two withins one way – Solution 98.5.2, *Econometric Theory* **15**, 781–783.

Lovell, M. C., 1963, Seasonal adjustment of economic time series, *Journal of the American Statistical Association* **58**, 993–1010.

MacKinnon, J. G., A. A. Haug and L. Michellis, 1999, Numerical distribution functions of likelihood ratio tests for cointegration, *Journal of Applied Econometrics* **14**, 563–577.

Maddala, G. S., 1971, The use of variance components models in pooling cross section and time series data, *Econometrica* **39**, 341–358.

Maddala, G. S., 1999, On the use of panel data methods with cross country data, *Annales d'Économie et de Statistique* **55–56**, 429–448.

Maddala, G. S. and S. Wu, 1999, A comparative study of unit root tests with panel data and a new simple test, *Oxford Bulletin of Economics and Statistics* **61**, 631–652.

Magnus, J. R., 1982, Multivariate error components analysis of linear and nonlinear regression models by maximum likelihood, *Journal of Econometrics* **19**, 239–285.

Mazodier, P. and A. Trognon, 1978, Heteroskedasticity and stratification in error components models, *Annales de l'INSEE* **30–31**, 451–482.

Milliken, G. A. and M. Albohali, 1984, On necessary and sufficient conditions for ordinary least squares estimators to be best linear unbiased estimators, *American Statistician* **38**, 298–299.

Moulton, B. R. and W. C. Randolph, 1989, Alternative tests of the error components model, *Econometrica* **57**, 685–693.

Mundlak, Y., 1978, On the pooling of time series and cross-section data, *Econometrica* **46**, 69–85.

Munnell, A., 1990, Why has productivity growth declined? Productivity and public investment, *New England Economic Review,* 3–22.

Nerlove, M., 1971, A note on error components models, *Econometrica* **39**, 383–396.

Neyman, J. and E. L. Scott, 1948, Consistent estimation from partially consistent observations, *Econometrica* **16**, 1–32.

Nickell, S., 1981, Biases in dynamic models with fixed effects, *Econometrica* **49**, 1417–1426.

Pedroni, P., 2000, Fully modified OLS for heterogeneous cointegrated panels, *Advances in Econometrics* **15**, 93–130.

Pedroni, P., 2004, Panel cointegration: asymptotic and finite sample properties of pooled time series tests with an application to the PPP hypothesis, *Econometric Theory* **20**, 597–625.

Phillips, P. C. B. and P. Perron, 1988, Testing for a unit root in a time series regression, *Biometrika* **75**, 335–346.

Roy, S. N., 1957, *Some Aspects of Multivariate Analysis* (John Wiley, New York).

Ruhm, C. J., 1996, Alcohol policies and highway vehicle fatalities, *Journal of Health Economics* **15**, 435–454.

Salkever, D., 1976, The use of dummy variables to compute predictions, prediction errors, and confidence intervals, *Journal of Econometrics* **4**, 393–397.

Sargan, J. D., 1958, The estimation of economic relationships using instrumental variables, *Econometrica* **26**, 393–415.

Searle, S. R., 1971, *Linear Models* (John Wiley, New York).

Searle, S. R., 1987, *Linear Models for Unbalanced Data* (John Wiley, New York).

Serlenga, L. and Y. Shin, 2007, Gravity models of intra-EU trade: application of the CCEP-HT estimation in heterogeneous panels with unobserved common time-specific factors, *Journal of Applied Econometrics* **22**, 361–381.

Song, S. H. and B. C. Jung, 2000, Prediction in the spatially autocorrelated error component model – Solution 99.2.4, *Econometric Theory* **16**, 149–150.

Stock, J. H. and M. W. Watson, 2003, *Introduction to Econometrics* (Addison Wesley, Boston).

Swamy, P. A. V. B. and S. S. Arora, 1972, The exact finite sample properties of the estimators of coefficients in the error components regression models, *Econometrica* **40**, 261–275.

Taub, A. J., 1979, Prediction in the context of the variance–components model, *Journal of Econometrics* **10**, 103–108.

Wallace, T. D. and A. Hussain, 1969, The use of error components models in combining cross-section and time-series data, *Econometrica* **37**, 55–72.

Wansbeek, T. J., 1989, An alternative heteroscedastic error components model – Solution 88.2.2, *Econometric Theory* **5**, 326.

Wansbeek, T. J. and A. Kapteyn, 1982, A simple way to obtain the spectral decomposition of variance components models for balanced data, *Communications in Statistics* **A11**, 2105–2112.

Wansbeek, T. J. and A. Kapteyn, 1989, Estimation of the error components model with incomplete panels, *Journal of Econometrics* **41**, 341–361.

White, H., 1984, *Asymptotic Theory for Econometricians* (Academic Press, New York).

White, H., 1986, Instrumental variables analogs of generalized least squares estimators, in R. S. Mariano, ed., *Advances in Statistical Analysis and Statistical Computing*, Vol. **1** (JAI Press, New York), 173–277.

Windmeijer, F., 2005, A finite sample correction for the variance of linear efficient two-step GMM estimators, *Journal of Econometrics* **126**, 25–51.

Winkelmann, R., 2000, *Econometric Analysis of Count Data* (Springer, Berlin).

Wooldridge, J. M., 2002, *Econometric Analysis of Cross-Section and Panel Data* (MIT Press, Cambridge, MA).

Wooldridge, J. M., 2005, Simple solutions to the initial conditions problem in dynamic, nonlinear panel data models with unobserved heterogeneity, *Journal of Applied Econometrics* **20**, 39–54.

Xiong, W., 1995, Nested effects – Solution 93.4.2, *Econometric Theory* **11**, 658–659.

Xiong, W., 1996a, A mixed-error component model – Solution 95.1.4, *Econometric Theory* **12**, 401–402.

Xiong, W., 1996b, Testing for correlated effects in panels – Solution 95.2.5, *Econometric Theory* **12**, 405–406.

Zellner, A., 1962, An efficient method of estimating seemingly unrelated regression and tests for aggregation bias, *Journal of the American Statistical Association* **57**, 348–368.

Zyskind, G., 1967, On canonical forms, non-negative covariance matrices and best and simple least squares linear estimators in linear models. *Annals of Mathematical Statistics* **36**, 1092–1109.

Index

Lightning Source UK Ltd.
Milton Keynes UK
01 March 2011

168464UK00001B/31/P

9 780470 744031